Preface to the Third Edition

Since the first revision of this book there has been continued ferment in the reading field. Developments that were scarcely heard of in 1964 have since become the focus of widespread discussion and debate. The report by Jeanne Chall, *The Great Debate,* has once again challenged prevailing assumptions about the role of the alphabet and of phonics in beginning reading instruction. Perhaps most of all, the problems of the inner city school and the so-called disadvantaged child have added urgency to the discovery of new strategies for reading instruction. For the writing of the last two chapters of the book, "Teaching Reading to Children from Culturally Disadvantaged and from Non-English–Speaking Homes" and "Current Approaches to the Teaching of Reading: A Review," the writers secured the services of Dr. Walter J. Moore of the University of Illinois.

Bibliographies and lists of instructional materials have been brought up to date. Sections that seem less pertinent today have been omitted. Especially chapters on readiness for reading and on word recognition have been sharply modified in the light of the more recent literature. Materials that seem as valid today as when they were first presented have been retained. The discussion on reading in the content fields has been enlarged, with a separate chapter devoted to that subject.

It is hoped that the combination of practical suggestion and scholarly discussion in this book will help to serve the needs of both the prospective teacher and the experienced practitioner.

J. J. DeB.
M.D.

Preface to the Revised Edition

Public and professional interest in the teaching of reading has not abated since the appearance of the first edition of this book. Newspapers and general magazines continue to report the activities of schools and school systems in their efforts to improve the quality of instruction in reading. Interesting accounts of research in reading have appeared in the professional magazines. Several new books, addressed to teachers, have been published.

Although the first edition of *The Teaching of Reading* appeared only four years ago, there appears to be ample need of a new edition that takes account of the rapid developments which have occurred. Perhaps no field in education is receiving more attention than reading in the decade of the sixties. The authors of this book hope that the current revision will be of material assistance in keeping the reader informed of significant new emphases and innovations in the teaching of reading.

The basic structure and much of the text material in the book remain the same. Attention has been given, however, to the growing interest in the implications of the science of linguistics for the teaching of reading, the spread of programs of individualized reading, the significance of programed learning and teaching machines, the special reading problems of the gifted child, and new reports on the role of phonics in reading instruction. The discussions of reading in the content fields, so vital to the entire reading program, have been expanded in various parts of the book. Bibliographies and sources for teaching aids have been brought up to date. More space has been given to suggestions for classroom activities, particularly in the descriptions of reading

games. New material on children's interests and children's literature
has been included.

The changes will go on, and there will be no end to the need
for constant revision of such books as these. We must work with what
we know, or think we know, today, and keep alive the hope that some
day most of our present problems in reading will be solved. We may be
sure, however, that when that day comes there will be new problems
and new books about reading!

In addition to the individuals and organizations mentioned in
the preface to the first edition, the following authors and publishers are
due our thanks for their courtesy in permitting us to quote from their
materials: Luella Cole, Mrs. E. W. Dolch, the Educational Testing
Service, and Scott, Foresman & Co.

February 1964   J. J. DeB.
                                                    M.D.

Preface to the First Edition

This book is designed to introduce the student to the problems of reading instruction in the elementary school and to provide him with facts and ideas that he can use in dealing with these problems. It strives to bring together the many viewpoints and techniques that have been described in recent books and articles on the teaching of reading. When viewpoints are in conflict, as in the case of phonic instruction in the initial stages of reading, the authors have not hesitated to take a position and to support it with evidence and arguments. New emphases, such as the current enthusiasm for individual instruction and the use of visual aids, are given due recognition. (For example, as this book goes to press, experiments in individualized reading instruction are being conducted in all parts of the country. Controversy as to the nature and extent of the individualization desirable is being reflected in books and magazine articles. The most recent of these are included in the bibliographies at the end of the appropriate chapters in this book.) These emphases are considered in the light of the fact that sound principles may find varying applications in the years ahead. It is hoped that this volume encourages teachers to experiment with the new ideas as they at the same time keep informed about prevailing practices. The discussion has been geared, however, to the needs of students who are making their first acquaintance with the field.

Part I, intended as a general introduction to the teaching of reading, stresses the relation between reading and society, and between reading and the general development of the child. It considers the place of reading in the school program, the nature of the reading process, and the elements essential to growth in reading.

Part II discusses the specific reading abilities that need to be cultivated in school. This section is unique in the fact that it is divided into "A" and "B" chapters—the former discussing the skills in general terms, and the latter providing specific teaching aids for the development of these skills. This separation between general principles and specific teaching practices is designed to facilitate the use of this book both in teacher education courses and among teachers in service. The teacher of classes in reading will find this organization especially useful when classroom instruction is accompanied by various types of direct experience with children. Experienced teachers, familiar with the general principles, will find numerous ideas in the "B" chapters for ways of developing the various reading skills.

Part III, "The Reading Program in Action," draws together the specific elements in reading instruction and shows how they function in the program as a whole. Chapter 15, which deals with the school-wide program in reading, is intended primarily for the administrator, supervisor, and reading coordinator.

For the many centuries since the invention of movable type, reading has been the major instrument of mass communication. Today, as we see the beginnings of an "exploding" world population and the return of oral-aural communication through electronics, we may, as an editorialist in the *Saturday Review* recently suggested, witness the decline of reading and books as the chief means of transmitting the cultural heritage. At present, reading is keeping pace with its rival media; but if this decline should occur in the future, the loss will be great. Books like this one are designed to help the oncoming generations to share in the unique heritage that only the printed word can bequeath.

We acknowledge our debt to the many individuals whose works are named in this volume, and to many others whom it was not possible to mention. Special thanks are extended to the following writers, editors, and publishers who have permitted us to quote longer passages: Walter B. Barbe; Emmett A. Betts; the Children's Book Council of New York City; E. W. Dolch; Harper & Brothers; J. N. Hook; Thomas D. Horn; the International Reading Association and the *Reading Teacher* (Russell G. Stauffer, Editor); May Lazar; Helen Rand Miller; the National Council of Teachers of English, chiefly for quotations from its magazine, *Elementary English;* the Board of Education of the City of New York and its Bureau of Educational Research; Mary O'Rourke; the Superintendent of Public Instruction, Springfield, Illinois; the University of Chicago Press; Lester Wheeler; and Edwin H. Smith. Appreciation is expressed also to those schools and school systems that made photographs available to us. Individual credits appear with each picture. We are especially grateful to Professor Ruth Strickland of Indiana University for her careful reading of the manuscript and her thoughtful commentary on it. Her suggestions have improved the book, but she should not be held responsible for its point of view or for any errors that may appear in it.

Champaign, Illinois   J. J. DeB.
Delaware, Ohio   M.D.
January 1960

Contents

x   *Contents*

PART ONE

READING
AND
CHILD DEVELOPMENT

CHAPTER 1

---

*The Challenge
of Reading*

In this age of communication, our attention is constantly being drawn to the new technological means of almost instantaneous transmission of sight and sound over long distances. We are aware of the rapid development of telephone, telegraph, radio, television, teletype, and satellite as instruments of communication. Our astronauts quote Genesis from more than 200,000 miles in space to a fascinated world. Indeed, some voices suggest that the new media will soon replace the book.

THE VALUES OF READING

Yet technology has not replaced reading. The printed page reaches millions still untouched by electronics, and for those who can take advantage of the newer devices, reading still serves unique purposes. It is many things to many people. It is a telescope, because through it we can look at the distant stars and speculate about life upon them. It is a microscope, because through it we can not only examine the chromosomes and the atoms but also infer those minute particles that even the finest lenses cannot reveal. It is a never-ending wide-screen film on which the human pageant passes in review. It is still the only known time machine that can recreate the events of the past and open up the vistas of the future. Primitive man calls reading magic, and he is right.

Reading meets needs that the newer media can not fully satisfy. Gray and Rogers have expressed this thought well:

> It is an indispensable factor in modern life, interwoven with work, recreation, and other activities of young people and adults. Its great value lies in two facts: printed materials provide the most illuminating and varied records of human experience that are now available; and they can be examined and restudied time and again at the reader's convenience in acquiring clear understandings, in developing rational attitudes, and in reaching sound conclusions. Some of these values cannot be attained so effectively through other media because the individual is not free to pause and deliberate at will.[1]

Reading is essential to the existence of our complex system of social arrangements. But it is more than that. It is the means by which every age is linked to every other. It makes possible man's capacity for "time binding," the ability to perceive himself in the historic process and the fluid universe around him. If all the inventions of a hundred years were destroyed and only books were left, man could still be man, in the sense intended by the idealists, the poets, the great creators. Teaching reading is a humanizing process.

PUBLIC INTEREST IN READING ABILITY

In view of these values, it is not surprising that there has always been much concern over the question whether Johnny is learning to read. In our own country, from the days of the *New England Primer* to the present, adults have eagerly watched their young take their first faltering steps in the world of print. Each year they spend hundreds of millions of dollars to make reading instruction possible. Each year more than 10 percent of all new books published are for children. Today, the public concern with reading ability is reflected in many popular books, magazine articles, pamphlets, newspaper columns, and editorials devoted to the subject. Surely the teacher of reading is engaged in work of vital importance to the public.

EFFORTS AT THE IMPROVEMENT OF READING

The teaching profession has responded to the public interest by constant intensive efforts to discover ways of improving reading instruction. For example, the National Society for the Study of Edu-

[1] William S. Gray and Bernice Rogers, *Maturity in Reading*, p. 8. Chicago: The University of Chicago Press, 1956.

cation has devoted many of its scholarly yearbooks to the subject. These include *The Report of the Committee on Silent Reading* (edited by Horn, 1921); *The Report of the National Committee on Reading* (edited by Gray, 1925); *The Teaching of Reading* (edited by Gray, 1937); *Reading in High School and College* (edited by Gray, 1948); *Reading in the Elementary School* (edited by Gates, 1949); *Adult Reading* (edited by Clift, 1956); *Development in and through Reading* (edited by Witty, 1961); and *Innovation and Change in Reading Instruction* (edited by Helen M. Robinson, 1968, Part II of the 67th Yearbook of the society).

Conferences devoted to reading and the language arts are annually sponsored by colleges and universities. Many of these schools, for example, the University of Chicago, the University of Pittsburgh, Temple University, and Claremont College, have published or still publish regular volumes of proceedings. Numerous organizations, notably the National Council of Teachers of English, the National Conference on Research in English, the American Educational Research Association, and the International Reading Association, devote much or all of their attention to problems in the teaching of reading.

The International Reading Association (IRA) publishes the monthly *Reading Teacher*, the *Reading Research Quarterly*, and the *Journal of Reading* (for the secondary school). It publishes the proceedings of its annual convention and of its pre- and postconvention conferences and institutes as well as of its world congresses. Reports of convention highlights and bibliographies on specific aspects of reading are part of the IRA program of publications.[2]

The National Council of Teachers of English, founded in 1911, has always concerned itself with the problems of reading. Two of its excellent magazines, *Elementary English* and the *English Journal*, frequently carry articles related to reading.

Agencies other than professional teachers' organizations contribute to our knowledge of the teaching of reading. Independent periodicals such as the *Journal of Educational Research*, the *Elementary School Journal*, and *Education* are but a few examples.

We are at present on the verge of a great expansion of reading research because of the use of computers and improved means of

[2] Addresses of the organizations referred to are: National Council of Teachers of English, 506 South Sixth Street, Champaign, Ill. 61820; National Conference on Research in English, Secretary-Treasurer, Professor William Eller, Foster Hall, State University of New York, Buffalo, N.Y. 14214; American Educational Research Association, 1201 Sixteenth Street, N.W., Washington, D.C. 20036; International Reading Association, Tyre Avenue at Main Street, Newark, Del. 19711.

communication. The number of individual research studies has increased phenomenally in recent years. In the revised edition of this book it was reported that 4,000 research studies in reading had been published in England and America since 1880. Today there are each year so many studies in reading that the annual summaries cannot mention them all, much less evaluate them. Moreover, methods of information retrieval and dissemination are constantly being developed. Thus in 1966 the U.S. Office of Education established the Educational Resources Information Center (ERIC-CRIER), a nationwide information system with headquarters in Washington, D.C., and eighteen special clearinghouses in universities and other institutions throughout the country. The reading clearinghouse is at Indiana University, Bloomington, Indiana. Documents are in addition to the various magazines dealing with libraries and children's literature. Here is a source of much information which persons interested in the field of reading can utilize. From Bloomington can be obtained tapes, microfiche cards, abstracts, and so on, on reading.

All of these discussions, investigations, and reports have not led to complete agreement about methods of teaching reading. Indeed, the differences of opinion are often sharp and the debates sometimes acrimonious. Nevertheless, there is a substantial body of agreement on many important issues. For example, it seems clear from the research that no one method is best for all children under all circumstances, that children differ widely in the kinds of instruction they need. It seems clear also that a wide variety of approaches must be used in order to get best results with most children. Moreover, we have learned much about the psychology of reading, about the role of emotion, motivation, home background, and other factors in reading retardation. We have learned most of all, perhaps, about the nature and extent of individual differences in reading.

INDIVIDUAL DIFFERENCES IN READING

Individual differences among children provide, possibly, the greatest challenge to the teacher of reading. Although all teachers know there are differences among their pupils, many are not fully aware of the vast range of those differences. What they need to learn is the fact that these differences are normal, that they exist at birth and increase as the children grow older. Children differ in every identifiable characteristic—in height, weight, color of hair and eyes, intelligence, home background, emotional adjustment, and educational achievement, to name but a few.

The more complex a skill is, the greater the differences in ability are likely to be. Since reading is a highly complex skill, children differ greatly in their reading needs and achievement. They show variation in the extent to which they are prepared to begin reading when they first enter school. The range in reading ability among pupils in any grade is very wide. Indeed, the better the instruction, the greater the probable range in a classroom. Even among pupils who make equal scores on reading tests, the differences in the *nature* of reading problems and of the reading abilities that produced the scores are significant and numerous.

THE COMPLEXITY OF READING

Reading is a challenge to the teacher also because it is such a complex process. Reading is not a general ability but a composite of many specific abilities. It is therefore necessary to break down general comprehension into the specific skills that constitute it. It is necessary to inquire how well the child is able to grasp the general meaning of a passage; how well he can differentiate between fact and opinion; how well he can follow directions; how well he can interpret maps, graphs, and tables; how well he can organize what he reads and classify ideas; how well he can visualize what he reads; and how well he can locate information.

A single reading skill, although a very important one, well illustrates the complexity of reading. Any teacher who undertakes to cultivate, for example, children's critical discrimination in reading finds that she is dealing with a whole cluster of abilities. Among these are classifying ideas, distinguishing between fact and fancy and between fact and opinion, establishing cause and effect, making generalizations, interpreting idiomatic and figurative language, making inferences, recognizing emotional reactions and motives, judging relevancy, and drawing general conclusions. These abilities must be taught, either with the aid of basal readers or the child's general experiences with research-type or recreatory reading, or both.[3]

READING AND KNOWLEDGE

Reading is an important means of introducing the child to the surrounding world. In this fact we find our opportunity as well as

[3] Gertrude Williams, "Provisions for Critical Reading in Basic Readers," *Elementary English, 36*, pp. 323–331 (May 1959). Reprinted in *Teaching Critical Reading* by Elona Sochor, a bulletin of the National Conference on Research in English. Champaign, Ill.: National Council of Teachers of English, 1959.

our challenge. Through reading the child can view ever-widening horizons and explore ever-new areas in the world of things, people, and events. School need never be dull as long as there are books to tell about the earth, the sea, the sky, faraway places, events past and present, or the plants and animals and physical phenomena around us.

It must require some ingenuity to turn the study of our wonderful world into a dreary chore, but somehow we often succeed in doing so. Consider, for example, the plight of the fifth-grade child filling in the blanks of a workbook that demands in what part of West Virginia hay is raised or what the present population of New Jersey is. Very few elementary school children want to know these facts or have any idea of what to do with them when they find them. Such busywork is necessary only when the school has no books other than textbooks or when the teacher does not know how to teach the use of an atlas, an almanac, or an encyclopedia.

Contrast this picture of an elementary school child with that of one who has discovered a special issue of the *National Geographic Magazine* dealing with our eastern states or become absorbed in a book about our national parks or the life of a great hero. The difference is that in the one case the pupil is engaging in an essentially purposeless activity; in the other he is actively reaching out for information to satisfy his curiosity and to find answers to his own questions.

The pupil's knowledge is, in fact, the distillation of his impressions gained from abundant reading. The residue left by these impressions keeps growing and changing as his contact with the world of reality through experiences with books expands. For this reason, many teachers encourage their pupils to read whole books about important topics rather than merely a few pages in a textbook. The availability of reliable, interesting books for children in nearly all areas of study has fundamentally altered the pattern of instruction in many elementary school subjects. The key to learning, therefore, is the cultivation not only of the ability to read but also of the love of reading. Young children must be helped to think of reading as an activity with an inherent appeal. The child who loves to read is father to the man who keeps informed through reading.

READING AND PERSONALITY

Reading involves skill, it involves thinking, but considered in its broader sense it affects the entire personality. The world of people and events encountered on the printed page may shape a reader's attitude toward his fellows, toward school, toward parents, and toward life in general. It may heighten his appreciation of the physical world about him or give him a sense of excitement about the future. On the other hand, it may cause perplexity, fear, or anxiety. The teacher bears a great responsibility for the judicious selection of reading matter to which the learner is exposed and for providing expert guidance in the interpretation of what is read.

Especially to the young child in school, successful and happy experiences with reading will determine in great measure his feelings about himself and his social environment. He knows, often before he starts school, that success in reading is essential to success in school. He may be afraid of the reading task or frustrated when he has difficulty or rebellious to all adult authority. It is incumbent upon the teacher to make the child feel comfortable and at ease and to give him many opportunities for success experiences that build self-confidence.

READING AND CITIZENSHIP

Our age is one that constantly demands great decisions, decisions that affect the future—even the survival—of the human race. Never before in history has so much depended upon the knowledge and wisdom of both the rulers and the ruled. We need, of course, an informed electorate if government by the consent of the governed is to have real meaning. But perhaps even more, we need an informed leadership. The greatest of our statesmen have been well-informed men—men with a wide reading background, knowledge, and the ability to use the knowledge of others in specific areas. The future leaders of local, state, and national governments, of industry, finance, and the military are at this moment passing through the most critical stage of their apprenticeship in our elementary school classes. If their early experiences in school help them to read critically when critical reading is required, to lay the right foundations, we may look to wise and knowledgeable leadership later. The teacher of reading in the elementary school has, indeed, a heavy responsibility.

FOR FURTHER STUDY

Barbe, Walter B., *Teaching Reading.* New York: Oxford University Press, 1965. Chapter 4, "What Have We Accomplished in Reading?", pp. 37–46; Chapter 5, "The Nature and Types of Reading," pp. 46–56.

Gans, Roma, *Common Sense in Reading.* Indianapolis, Ind.: The Bobbs-Merrill Company, 1963. Chapter 1, "The Quest for Literacy," pp. 11–18.

Harris, Albert J., *Readings on Reading Instruction.* New York: David McKay

Company, Inc., 1963. Chapter 1, "Current Reading Problems: A World View," pp. 1–5.

Mazurkiewicz, Albert J., *New Perspectives in Reading Instruction*. New York: Pitman Publishing Corporation, 1964. Part I, "The State of Reading Instruction," pp. 3–46; Chapter 8, "In Praise of Reading," pp. 76–85; Chapter 9, "The Well-Read Man," pp. 86–93.

Smith, Nila B., *American Reading Instruction*. Newark, Del.: International Reading Association, 1965.

CHAPTER 2

The Nature of Reading

The definition of reading will determine in large measure the objectives and procedures employed in instruction. One can think of reading as a relatively mechanical skill. Such a conception prevailed for hundreds of years in American schools and probably accounted for the dominance of oral reading in the classrooms of this country. Indeed, to many people "reading" has generally meant reading aloud.

This idea, particularly for the initial stages of learning to read, is enjoying support in respectable and influential quarters. Today the favorite expression is "decoding" the printed page—that is, recognizing the oral equivalent of the written symbol. The principle on which the decoding concept rests is that language is, at base, spoken communication and that writing or print is merely a graphic representation of speech. The process is therefore one of discovering the correspondence between the *grapheme* (the written or printed symbol) and the *phoneme* (the speech sound). Young children have always found such correspondence, and the only question is whether this approach is the most efficient and natural one for the teaching of reading, especially in the initial stages.

Another view is that reading, from the beginning, should be a process of the communication of meaning. One writer, C. De Witt Boney, has said that a child should learn to read as he learns to talk. The infant usually talks early if he is surrounded by a world of speech. Other factors, of course, have their effect. He must have stimulus and motive to speak, he must have approval and reinforcement when he speaks, and he must hear others, child and adult, speak to him in situations in which he is involved. Similarly the child who lives in a reading environment, is read to, pages through picture books, plays with alphabet blocks, observes other members of the family reading, and asks questions about words, both spoken and printed, moves with ease into the world of reading.

WHAT HAPPENS IN READING?

The reader is looking at an object in the form of a book or magazine or a billboard or a road sign. Most commonly the object consists of paper, usually white. On the paper appear certain marks, made, as a rule, by the application of dark-colored ink. That is all—just ink marks on white paper. And yet looking at those marks may cause the reader to turn pale, as in the case of a letter containing bad news, or to laugh, smile, cry, or hold his breath in suspense. A laboratory test would reveal that a reader's pulse rate may at times rise sharply when he looks at those curious marks on paper. How can the seeing of those marks bring about such mental and physical experiences?

There is no *meaning* on the page, only ink. The meaning is in the reader's mind. Each mark is a signal that arouses some image or concept that is already in the mind of the reader. The order in which these images and concepts are evoked, the context in which they are called forth, and the relations among these concepts and images as revealed by the arrangement of these marks make it possible for the reader to gain new meanings. But the process depends upon what the reader brings to the printed page and on the questions he asks.

It has often been said that reading is an *active* process. Good reading is a searching out, a reaching for meaning. The child must go to the printed page with anticipation, with questions, with specific intent. A person turns to a newspaper with the purpose of finding out what has happened recently. He searches the headlines and chooses a story that arouses his curiosity. He reads the story in order to find out what the headline means. He gets real meaning from what he reads because he has asked questions as he has gone along.

READING AS SYMBOLIC BEHAVIOR

Man communicates through symbols. A symbol may be a physical act, such as a grimace, a smile, a nodding of the head, or an upraised hand in a discussion. Traffic lights and highway signs are symbols. Spoken language is a complex set of symbols consisting of various combinations of speech sounds. Any representation perceptible to the senses may serve as a symbol.

In reading we employ visual symbols to represent auditory symbols. The basic task in reading is therefore to establish in the mind of the reader automatic connections between specific sights and the sounds they represent. Since the sounds themselves are symbols of meanings, the process of reading involves a hierarchy of skills ranging from auditory and visual discrimination to such higher-order mental activities as organizing ideas, making generalizations, and drawing inferences.

By the time most children first enter school, they have learned to use the symbols of the spoken language to the extent of their needs and their level of development. Some evidence indicates that they have already mastered all the basic sentence patterns of their native tongue. Some children, in fact, have made a beginning in the substitution of visual for auditory symbols. They have started on the road to reading. In any case, the teacher of primary reading has a strong foundation on which to build.

EYE MOVEMENTS IN READING

The visual symbol of the written or printed word is the means by which the appropriate sounds and images are evoked in the mind of the reader. Contrary to common belief, reading does not take place while the eyes move across the line. If a letter, a word, or a phrase is to be perceived, the eyes must pause long enough to take it in. Since in fluent reading the pauses or "fixations" may be as brief as one-fourth of a second, the reader has the illusion that he is reading as the eyes move from left to right on the page. Actually, the movement of the eyes from one stopping point to the next takes a fraction of a second, so that in effect the view of the words in a line seems continuous. The interruptions between the pauses may be likened to the breaks between the individual photographs that make up a motion picture. When we look at a movie, we are not conscious of the fact that we are really seeing an extremely rapid succession of still pictures. So, too, it is when we read a line of type. We cannot "see" while our eyes are in motion.

The important point in the reading act, then, is the instant when the eyes fix upon a specific spot in the line. All else depends on what the reader sees and perceives in this instant. If he sees and perceives only individual letters or small groups of letters, he will not be reading, because meaning is constructed not from letters but from whole words. This is not to say that individual letters will not often help in the perception of the word as a whole. It means only that the reader must perceive the whole word or group of words while the eyes pause. Unless he does so, he is not really reading.

Various methods have been employed in reading laboratories and clinics to study the eye-movement behavior of readers. One of the most common methods has been the photographic method. One instrument, the ophthalmograph, makes motion picture records of eye movements in the process of silent reading. The subject is asked to read a passage on a card. As he reads, a ray of light is directed toward his eyes. As the light reaches the eyes, the corneas reflect it upon a moving film. The film thus records the movements of the eyes as the latter pass from left to right on the line and as they return to the beginning of the next line. It records the number of fixations on each line, the order in which the reader fixes upon each word or phrase, the duration of each fixation, the number of *regressive movements* (return to previous points on the line), *periods of confusion* (points of difficulty revealed by numerous regressive movements), and the accuracy of the *return sweep* (the movement of the eyes to the beginning of the next line).

In the initial stages of reading, the child's eyes may wander over the page in search of familiar words. As competence grows, under the skilled guidance of the teacher, he learns to confine his observation to one line at a time and to move in a habitual progression from left to right. At first, duration of each fixation will tend to be relatively long— perhaps as much as nine-tenths of a second. There will be many fixations per line. There will be many regressive movements in which the reader will make return movements to words that were not recognized or comprehended the first time. When a word gives special difficulty, there may be many regressions, and the ophthalmograph film would show a period of confusion. After much experience, and especially when interest is high, the duration of each fixation will decrease and the number of fixations per line will become steadily smaller. Eventually, as the child masters the basic skills and increases his stock of words recognized at sight, he becomes able to read each line in a fairly regular, rhythmical series of fixations, with a minimum number of regressive movements. By the fourth grade, the frequency of fixations and the number of regressions commonly tend to level off somewhat (always provided that the material is within the reader's comprehension, and the basic eye-movement habits have become reasonably well established). Some studies seem to show an additional spurt at the beginning of the high school period and indicate that the normal growth in rate of reading may continue until grade ten. Individual differences and training will, of course, affect each child's rate of growth, and it must be emphasized that improvement in both rate and comprehension may be brought about at any age.

Regular eye movements, however, are a symptom rather than a cause of good reading. The efforts that have been made in some instances to pace a child's eye movements or to change his reading habits by means of mechanical devices appear to be of questionable value. No doubt many boys and girls improve in their ability to recognize words at sight as a result of exercises with such devices, for any method that will enable a child to recognize a word quickly and accurately will contribute effectively to his reading ability, provided it is accompanied by procedures that sustain and stimulate his genuine interest in the content. But the basic efforts in instruction should be to focus on meaning and to provide abundant opportunity for contact with the printed word in normal, well-motivated reading situations.

VISUAL SHAPES, SOUNDS, AND MEANINGS

In approaching written or printed material, the child typically converts the visual shapes of letters and words into their corresponding sounds. At the beginning he probably utters the sounds aloud or to himself. The sounds then evoke in his mind the images and meanings they represent. As he gains proficiency, he depends less and less on the sound "bridge" between visual stimulus and meaning, although a faint awareness of speech sounds is probably always present in reading. If the sound images continue to be prominent in the child's reading, he will develop habits of vocalization and possibly lip movement. Both speed and comprehension will then suffer. The connection between visual stimulus and meaning must become as direct as possible as soon as possible.

In order to establish habits of meaningful reading, many teachers begin reading instruction with the whole word, the morpheme, which is the smallest meaning-bearing unit, as contrasted with the phoneme, the smallest sound-bearing unit, which by itself ordinarily carries no meaning. The child can identify many short words as quickly and easily as he can individual letters. As we have seen, the mature reader does not read letter by letter but rather in a series of relatively few, brief fixations of the eye per line. Effective reading, then, involves instantaneous recognition of whole words or even phrases. For this reason, in many classrooms, the beginning reader is introduced to whole words that appear again and again in ordinary printed discourse.

Reading must become as soon as possible a process of thought-getting.

It is clear, however, that it would be impossible for a child to learn to recognize at sight all the words he is likely to encounter. He must master certain skills that will enable him to recognize new words independently. The nature of these skills and the methods of teaching them will be discussed in Chapters 5A and 5B.

The term *phonics,* which is based on the Greek word meaning *sound,* is used to designate the practice of sounding out a word in order to identify it. Naturally, if the sounding out is to help in getting meaning, the word must already be a part of the child's vocabulary. In contrast to the alphabet method, phonics deals with *phonograms,* or visual symbols for speech sounds. Since the individual letters of the alphabet may have more than one sound, and since some sounds are made by combinations of letters, the phonics method must be distinguished from the alphabet method. Thus *a* in *cat* is a different phonogram from *a* in *late.* Thus also the letters *ph* and *gh* constitute individual phonograms.

Some linguists and some educators look upon phonics as the natural method of teaching reading. They reason that since words are made up of sounds in various combinations, a child will be able to read if he knows all the symbols that stand for the various sounds of the English language. For example, the late Leonard Bloomfield recommended that the child be introduced first to the letters of the alphabet, one phonetic value at a time. He urged that the child be taught to read by means of a sequence of four stages, in which the aim would be to develop the habit of connecting letters with sounds.

A contrary view is expressed by James E. McDade, who opposes "sounding" in beginning reading. He explains his position in the following way:

> Students of reading now generally agree that word-by-word reading is an evil, because it is the grouping and the relations of words, rather than single words, that express meanings. If the child is kept continually in the active attitude of seeking for meanings in his reading, his eyes sweep forward to search out the sense of phrases and sentences. He unconsciously forms from the beginning perceptual habits that never have to be unlearned. To give the beginning reader the contrary habit of lingering on the single word as a word, or, still worse, on the separate parts of the single word, is to thwart the formation of effective perceptual habits, and build up a complex of frustrations which will become clinical materials for later years of "remedial work." Phonetics in beginning reading move continually, not forward to the mean-

ingful phrase and sentence, but backward in the direction of the meaningless phonogram and the meaningless alphabet. It is not an adequate defense to say that this work prepares the child to get meaning at some future time. Phonetic procedure as a part of beginning method is disastrous in turning away from meaning at the most significant time, when habits are being formed. Thus it shatters the child's earliest reading perceptions into a chaos of meaningless fragments, so numerous as to exceed many times over the twenty-six of the old alphabet method.

Phonetics may well be useful to older children as a means of dealing with an occasional puzzling word, if their habit of reading for meaning is already well established, but at the beginning the effect on the child's reading can be only harmful. . . . If it is desirable that children should love to read, and that libraries should be used more freely and intelligently, every reader's first experiences in reading should be made meaningful, and consequently pleasurable.[1]

Good teachers do not generally follow dogmatic theories in planning their reading programs. They want children to learn to read and to grow as rapidly as possible in their reading ability. They know that young children can learn to recognize some whole words as readily, as quickly, and with as much satisfaction as individual letters. They know also that these children need soon to master skills of word recognition involving the analysis of unfamiliar words into their component parts. For these teachers the questions related to phonics instruction are simply when, how, and how much for which child.

KINDS OF READING

It will be emphasized in this book that reading is not a general ability. The term *reading* embraces a wide variety of tasks, activities, skills, and mental processes. For many of these, special kinds of instructional assistance are needed.

The kind of reading a person does will usually depend upon his purpose. He may read for pure recreation and enjoyment or he may read to study. Ideally he will find pleasure in study-type reading, too, but his approach, attitude, and technique will be different. He may read to find the answer to a question or the solution of a problem, to learn the main idea of a selection or some specific items of information, to discover the outcome of a series of events or to follow directions in

[1] James E. McDade, *Next Steps in Non-Oral Reading*, p. 9. West Palm Beach, Fla.: Palm Beach Press, 1946.

making a model airplane or baking a cake. For all of these purposes he employs different methods in his reading.

Sometimes the reader weighs, tests, and challenges what he reads. At other times he gives himself over to "the willing suspension of disbelief" as he follows an imaginary narrative or he lets the mood of a poet take possession of him. He reads to be enlightened or comforted or inspired. Life is varied, and reading is as varied as life.

Reading occurs at different levels. A child may read easy materials fluently and without help. This is the independent reading level. He may read harder materials, calling for concentration and special effort. This is the level of challenge. He may read materials that require outside help. This is the instructional level.

The diversity of reading tasks, skills, and challenges appears in almost all the areas of the school curriculum. How the school may best deal with them is the essential theme of this book.

FOR FURTHER STUDY

Barbe, Walter B., *Teaching Reading*. New York: Oxford University Press, 1965. Chapter 2, "History and Philosophy of Reading Instruction," pp. 37–70.

Harris, Albert J., *Readings on Reading Instruction*. New York: David McKay Company, Inc., 1963. Chapter 2, "What Have We Accomplished in Reading?", pp. 5–16.

Jennings, Frank G., *This Is Reading*. New York: Teachers College Press, 1965. Chapter 1, "What Is Reading?", pp. 3–22; Chapter 5, "The Value of the Book in the Changing World," pp. 65–77; Chapter 6, "The Use of the Book in Changing the World," pp. 78–89.

Monroe, Marion, and Bernice Rogers, *Foundations of Reading: Informal Pre-Reading Procedures*. Glenview, Ill.: Scott, Foresman and Company, 1964. Chapter 6, "Reading Is Interpreting," pp. 112–141.

Morrison, Ida E., *Teaching Reading in the Elementary School*. New York: The Ronald Press Company, 1968. Chapter 2, "The Reading Process," pp. 22–50.

Spache, George D. and Evelyn B., *Reading in the Elementary School*. Boston: Allyn and Bacon, Inc., 1969. Chapter 1, "Ways of Defining the Reading Process," p. 3–40.

Strang, Ruth, Constance McCullough, and Arthur Traxler. *The Improvement of Reading*. New York: McGraw-Hill Book Company, Inc., 1967. Chapter 1, "Perspective in Reading," pp. 3–39.

CHAPTER 3

Elements Essential
to Growth in Reading

Teaching may be defined as the process of supplying the conditions favorable to learning. The teaching of reading is no exception. This chapter describes some of the conditions needed by children to make maximum progress in learning to read. These conditions include:

1. Physical health
2. Mental health
3. Sight and hearing
4. Intelligence
5. Background of experience
6. Knowledge of language
7. Desire to read
8. Purposes for reading
9. Interest in reading
10. Reading skills

Fortunately, nearly all children come to school already possessing most of these elements in some degree. A minority of children learn to read in spite of the lack of some of these elements. Blind children, deaf children, and sick children can learn to read. But to the extent that children are lacking in the elements named, they will be handicapped in the process of learning to read.

The teacher and the school do not bear exclusive responsibility for providing all the necessary conditions. Other agencies, especially the family, bear major responsibility for some of them. The school, however, is inevitably involved, in one degree or another, in helping to create all of the conditions that contribute to growth in reading.

When we specify those factors in child development that are basic to success in reading, we are not suggesting a hierarchy of educational values. Physical and mental health, for example, are ends in themselves. They do not become important merely because they contribute to good reading, as though reading were the supreme purpose of the school. But since this book is concerned with methods of teaching reading, it must necessarily take the broad developmental context into account.

PHYSICAL HEALTH

We know that a reasonable measure of physical health is essential to all school learning. Physical discomfort, languor, a low energy level, and similar symptoms of health problems may often interfere with normal progress in reading. Nervous tension and even ordinary physical fatigue can reduce enjoyment and interest in reading, with consequent decline in efficiency. Vitamin deficiencies and endocrine disturbances have been associated with poor reading. Smith and Dechant mention adenoids, infected tonsils, poor teeth, rickets, asthma, allergies, tuberculosis, rheumatic fever, and other prolonged illnesses as possible factors in reading retardation.[1] Frequent absence from school resulting from illness necessarily retards progress in reading and may produce attitudes of aversion or indifference toward reading.

We must let the clinician determine whether a case of extreme reading retardation may be attributed to physical causes. For our part as teachers we must do all we can in the classroom to promote the physical well-being of our pupils. Free and inexpensive school lunches help to provide needed nutrition. (In one school, a pupil who was considered just lazy proved to be just hungry.) We can help to provide a healthful physical environment in school—good light, proper humidity and temperature, appropriate seating. We can arrange for periods of rest and of exercise.

MENTAL HEALTH

Among the basic developmental needs of children that affect growth in reading is a feeling of security, of being accepted and loved, and of being adequate to the tasks they are expected to carry out. Everyone performs better in any activity if he has self-confidence, a feeling of successful performance, and a strong desire to achieve. One cannot learn well, in reading or in anything else, if he is distracted by

[1] Henry P. Smith and Emerald V. Dechant, *Psychology in Teaching Reading,* pp. 154–155. Englewood Cliffs, N.J.: Prentice-Hall, Inc., 1961.

anxieties, frustrations, and the sense of failure. For this and other reasons, every effort is made in modern schools to build wholesome attitudes in children, to give them a sense of belonging and a feeling of being accepted and respected, and to provide many success experiences. Good reading is best carried on in a classroom atmosphere that is warm, friendly, and relaxed.

A success experience need not be in reading activity in order to result in growth in reading. Any experience that builds the child's feeling of general adequacy will help to increase his zest in attacking difficult reading situations and to remove the distractions and anxieties that result from the fear of failure in school. The following anecdote illustrates the value of developing the latent interests and abilities of children:

> One little girl who had not succeeded at all in any other classroom activity suddenly began to read with her group after dancing had been introduced in her classroom. Up to that time she had been timid and shy; but when the children danced, she joined them. She was so graceful that her ability was recognized by other children.[2]

Increasingly, teachers are realizing the significance of the relation between social and emotional factors and beginning reading. They recognize that the child accustomed to the give-and-take of a social group, especially of his peers, will be likely to adjust more quickly to the school situation and consequently will be more likely to be ready to read sooner than the child who has lacked contacts with other boys and girls. Also, since reading is taught primarily in group situations, the child who does not feel at ease with others is less likely to be able to attend to the reading. Teachers also realize that such a child is less likely to enjoy what he reads when reading in a group than the child who feels comfortable with his agemates.

Maladjusted homes or poor family relationships have been shown to be contributing causes in many cases of reading disability. As one writer has put it, "Children bring their families to school." They come with all the attitudes and predispositions that were formed in the home and neighborhood during those influential first years of life. Children who are overprotected or the victims of parents who are over-ambitious for their children or boys and girls who are unwanted or neglected or insecure because of conflict between parents or because

[2] From *Fostering Mental Health in Our Schools.* Yearbook of the Association for Supervision and Curriculum Development. Washington, D.C.: National Education Association, 1950.

of the loss of one or both of them are often handicapped in their efforts to learn. On the other hand, children who come from stable homes, who are accepted and loved by their parents, clearly approach the reading task with a great advantage.

When home conditions are unfavorable to the child, it is the responsibility of the school to take these conditions into account and to compensate for them as much as possible. Some children of normal or superior intelligence fail to learn to read because of emotional difficulty, severe anxiety, or insecurity that develops at the time they are first faced with the reading task. The cause may be the arrival of a new baby, parental hostility, or a feeling of anxiety on the part of the parents concerning the child's reading progress—an anxiety that is easily communicated to the child. Worries of this kind interfere with the concentration so necessary in making the fine discriminations involved in reading. Moreover, children who face serious emotional problems frequently have difficulties with such other aspects of language communication as articulation or listening comprehension. Such shortcomings, in turn, contribute to retardation in reading.

The cause-and-effect relation between emotional and social immaturity and poor reading is sometimes reversed. Often, to be sure, lack of various characteristics of the maturing emotional and social life can have a detrimental effect upon reading, but the fact must not be overlooked that frequently inability to read well is a cause of personality defects. The child who cannot read, no matter how normal he was in his emotional reactions when he entered school, is likely to develop undesirable personality traits if he cannot enter into the reading activities that form a large part of the typical elementary school day. Aggression, withdrawal, irritability, and other forms of unsocial or antisocial behavior are often the visible manifestations of a personality thwarted because it cannot engage in activities satisfying to others in the classroom.

SIGHT AND HEARING

Both sight and hearing of a child about to learn to read should be checked.

Sight

It has been estimated that about one-fourth to one-half of elementary school children are in need of visual correction. One of the first questions the reading clinician asks about the nonreader is, "Does this child have satisfactory eyesight?" The child who must strain his eyes to read is not likely to enjoy the process and will usually try to avoid reading. If his vision is so poor that even with considerable effort it is difficult or impossible for him to differentiate between the forms of letters, success in reading will be delayed until he is given reading materials printed in type that he can read comfortably. All teachers should be alerted to signs of visual difficulties among their pupils.

It must not be assumed, however, that poor vision is generally the chief cause of poor reading. Cases of nearsightedness, farsightedness, astigmatism, muscular imbalance, and lack of fusion are found among both good and poor readers. Nevertheless, in good readers as well as in poor readers such conditions tend to result in fatigue and consequent loss in reading ability. Quite probably nearly all readers—slow, normal, and superior—who have visual defects would improve in reading ability if their defects were corrected.

Visual handicaps among children may be of many kinds. While the classroom teacher should not undertake to make a diagnosis of the difficulty in any individual case, she should be aware of the common types of visual deficiencies in order that she may know when a child should be referred to a specialist. In addition to the more usual phenomena of nearsightedness, farsightedness, and astigmatism, the eye specialist often encounters cases of monocular vision. In normal vision, both eyes receive the image of an object, and the two images are fused in the process of perception. This kind of seeing is called binocular vision. Some individuals, however, ignore or suppress the image received by one eye and consequently "see" with only one eye. In some cases the individual alternates between one eye and the other; in other cases he alternates between monocular and binocular vision.

Since most reading involves near-point vision, it is important for the teacher to recognize the difference between far-point and near-point vision. A child whose vision tests normal when looking at a distant object but who has great difficulty in seeing an object singly and clearly at a distance of fourteen inches or less is in need of attention. Preschool children tend to be farsighted. For this reason, teachers in the first and second grades should place heavy reliance upon the chalkboard and on large charts. Children who have visual difficulties should be seated near the chalkboard. Long periods of near-point reading should be avoided.

The Snellen Chart, while useful in the hands of an oculist, has definite limitations as a screening device for primary reading. Teachers should be alert to outward signs of visual difficulties, such as facial contortions, thrusting and tilting of the head, and holding a book too close to the face. When they observe such behavior, they should recommend consultation with a specialist.

Hearing

A child who suffers from hearing loss is at a distinct disadvantage. He will, for example, have difficulty in benefiting from the teacher's oral explanations. Especially if the child is taught by predominantly oral-phonetic methods, auditory acuity is important in the process of learning to read. The child with hearing loss will have inadequate or inaccurate auditory images of the words he reads and consequently may encounter difficulty in word recognition.

As in the case of visual defects, hearing loss may be no more common among poor readers than among good readers. Nevertheless, all readers who have deficient hearing ability would probably be aided in reading performance if they received appropriate attention from parents, teachers, and physicians.

Estimates vary as to the number of children who have significant hearing defects. One of the most conservative estimates places the percentage of children with considerable hearing loss at 1½ to 3½ percent of all children. Other findings suggest as much as 30 percent for girls and 50 percent for boys. Whatever the precise figures may be, we are safe in concluding that careful attention should be given to the hearing ability of all pupils.

INTELLIGENCE

It is known that a fairly close relation exists between intelligence and the ability to read. This relation may be ascribed, in part, to the fact that intelligence tests and reading tests set many tasks that are similar. The fact that the correlation between performance in intelligence tests and reading tests usually tends to be very high may mean merely that a large part of an intelligence test calls for abilities closely related to the ability to read. Moreover, it must be remembered that cultural background and present environment are likely to affect performance in both reading and intelligence tests. Then, too, our general notion of intelligence places a high value on reading ability. Nevertheless, whatever the reasons may be, it has been demonstrated that in our culture, and under present conditions in American schools, a child has a better chance of success in reading if he has average or above average intelligence. Furthermore, if we define a child's intelligence as the rate at which he is able to learn, we may assume that the rate of his growth in reading is affected by and limited by his intelligence.

If intelligence is thought of as an inherited ability, the school and the teacher cannot significantly affect this factor. But there is reason to believe that in the early years of a child's life, environment may have an effect upon what is commonly considered as intelligence. Certainly a rich environment, one that offers many opportunities for learning, can help a child with limited intellectual endowment to make much greater use of his native ability than he could if he were deprived of intellectually stimulating surroundings.

BACKGROUND OF EXPERIENCE

If it is true that success in reading depends on what the reader brings to the printed page, much significance must be attached to the body of direct and indirect experiences he has accumulated in advance of the reading. The child's prior stock of impressions will determine in large measure how much meaning he will derive from the visual symbols before him. These impressions will include both the things that have happened to him directly and the symbolic experiences he has had with reading, listening, viewing motion pictures and television, and the like.

A simple example illustrating the point that written symbols acquire meaning for the reader because of his previous experiences is that of a reader who encounters what to him is a new word, the word *hogan*. The writer states that a hogan is a circular house used by the Navaho Indians as a dwelling. He may go on to give further details—the materials of which these houses are built, the presence or absence of windows and doors, and similar information. The reader has had previous experience with the letters of which the word is composed and he is able to pronounce it, but he has never before encountered the word *hogan*, nor has he ever seen a hogan. How can this curious visual symbol have meaning for him?

Hogan acquires meaning for the reader because he has had direct experience with other words and ideas in the sentence. These words arouse images in his mind because he has encountered in personal experience the ideas and images they represent. He has seen a circle, and he has had experience with houses. Encountering the concepts of *house* and *circle* in a specific relation to each other, the reader is enabled to create a new image in his mind—an image approximating a hogan—which he has never seen. Thus, through the combination and recombination of familiar words, images, and concepts, the reader builds new meanings, which in turn provide the basis for further understandings.

It becomes apparent that the fundamental elements in reading comprehension derive from direct experience. References to such concepts as anger, love, hate, reconciliation, warmth, pain, light, and dark can have meaning for the reader only in the degree to which he has in one way or another had experience with them. Not only does direct experience facilitate the acquisition of meaning from the printed page but it also creates the conditions for that keen interest in reading that is so essential to reading growth. For example, a person who has visited the headquarters of the United Nations will read with redoubled insight and pleasure a story in *The New Yorker* about a reporter's visit to the same place; a boy who is assembling a stamp collection will read a book about stamp issues with an intensity of interest that would most likely not exist in a boy who does not pursue this hobby. Thus the reading of recent history also takes on significance and life as the reader recognizes in historical scenes the flesh and blood realities he knows from his own past. The depth and range of his comprehension will depend in part upon the length and richness of that past.

Basic to all the reading experience through which children learn is the direct contact with things, people, and events. It has been argued that the concepts usually encountered in reading material are common to the experience of most or all children and that the instructor's primary task is to teach the recognition of the printed symbol. Such argument overlooks the wide diversity of the environments of children in the country or in the city, in mining or industrial towns, in slums or wealthy suburbs, in cattle country or fishing villages. For example, an excellent story, "Black Storm," by Thomas C. Hinkle,[3] begins as follows: "Near a frontier cattle town of old Kansas on the memorable morning, John McDonald, the cattle-owner of the Chisholm Range, stood in the center of a corral holding the reins of a beautiful horse—a coal-black gelding." Consider the difference in the understanding that a country boy, especially one from the West, and a city boy would bring to this passage!

Consideration of the bearing of an individual's background on his ability to read with comprehension forces one to recognize the handicaps that a child from a culturally deprived environment experiences in the process of learning to read. Problems of such boys and girls are discussed in Chapter 15.

Reading is, of course, in itself an important kind of experience. Through the synthesis of the direct impressions that can be brought about in the process of reading, the reader develops new images

[3] In E. M. Orr, E. T. Holston, and Stella S. Center, *Discovering New Fields in Reading and Literature*. New York: Charles Scribner's Sons, 1955.

and concepts that enable him to extend the range of his vision of reality. The amount of direct experience that even the most privileged person may enjoy is necessarily limited. Through reading we may range in imagination over the globe, over the known universe, and over the centuries, and each new reading experience provides the background for further understanding in reading.

KNOWLEDGE OF LANGUAGE

If direct experience is to be of substantial aid in reading, it must be accompanied by an adequate fund of experience with language. Children who visit a fire station and see the engines, the ladders, the fire extinguishers, and the other equipment, but do not hear the words that identify the objects, have not been adequately prepared for reading about firemen and fire fighting. It is necessary to introduce them to the verbal symbols in association with the observation of the objects and the processes. Much discussion and explanation of terms should therefore accompany the direct experiences the school provides.

That a good knowledge of language is necessary in preparation for the reading experience illustrates the close interrelations of the various aspects of language communication. Evidence shows that there is a strong relation between linguistic ability and reading achievement, and that a child's ability to understand and use language orally is an important factor in beginning reading. All we know about children's language learning points to the interrelatedness of the four facets of language—reading, writing, speaking, and listening. We may conclude, therefore, that wide experience with all kinds of language, including extensive contacts with words and sentences in meaningful situations, contributes effectively to the improvement of reading. Growth in reading usually is best produced not from a program of isolated drills but from a rich, diversified, and stimulating language environment and a curriculum that provides for many kinds of highly motivated language experiences.

DESIRE AND PURPOSE

The *desire* to read is the motivating force that leads to reading. It may simply be the desire to do what others around us are doing. It may be the desire to have needed information or to spend a pleasant leisure hour. In any case, the desire to read arises from a sense of need for reading. The sense of need can be cultivated by creating the necessary conditions.

Desire eventuates in purpose, which clarifies the direction effort shall take. Thus the emphasis in reading guidance should be placed not upon arbitrary teacher-direction, but upon the awakening of pupil desire, the release of pupil energy, and the development of pupil self-direction. The teacher's aim is to guide, to lead—not to coerce; but the pupil must supply the voluntary effort if real learning is to take place.

Especially in the initial stages of reading, the factor of good motivation is of prime importance. Motivation is not a mere mechanical preliminary to the reading itself, but is the result of the teacher's providing or helping the pupil to discover clear goals. If the child's first experiences with reading are purposeful, he will be started on the road to meaningful reading. We cannot start him with a set of skills, mechanically acquired without reference to meaning, and then expect him later to put them to use in meaningful reading.

The principle of reading with a purpose, of *active* reading, has clear implications for reading assignments. We must not send children to the printed page without adequate preparation for the reading. A good assignment, as a rule, includes a discussion that will orient the pupil to the material he will encounter. It helps him to formulate questions to be answered and to visualize clearly the uses to which the information is to be put. It gives him some notion of the nature of the material to be read and the manner in which the material is to be approached. It helps him to anticipate some of the key words and perhaps the pronunciation of unfamiliar proper names. In short, the good assignment helps the pupil to establish clear purpose for the reading. Perhaps the best assignments are self-assignments. Such assignments arise out of problems, discussions, and activities that call for further information. The search may be initiated by the individual himself, by a committee, or by the class as a whole.

The reading connected with a unit of instruction may involve various purposes. Reading may be done as preliminary exploration, or browsing, in a variety of books for the purpose of general orientation to the subject of the unit. This would be a period of "sampling," a get-acquainted period to indicate the nature of the area to be studied. It may be done as differentiated research, where each pupil pursues some special aspect of the main topic. Reading may also be done for the purpose of outlining and organizing what has been read in various sources.

The number and types of purposes for which individuals read are almost unlimited. Children and young adults have many things that they want and need to know. They want to know what the good radio and television programs and movies are, and what makes them good; how to apply for a position and how to behave in an interview; what makes wars and how they can be prevented; how they can be more popular among their friends; what they can believe in the newspapers; how they can get along better at home; where they can get the truth about the trouble spots around the world. They want to know about labor, prices, employment, and new scientific advances. They want to know what they must do to be safe when riding a bicycle, driving a car, or repairing a light switch. They want to know what attitudes they should assume toward sex, courtship and marriage, ethics, and religion. Many would like to know how they can help to secure more and better schools and libraries for all children and youth.

The task of the school is to assist the reader in carrying out his purposes. If he is frustrated by obstacles too numerous and too great in the form of vocabulary burden or complexity of thought, he will soon give up his purposes or seek to achieve them by means other than reading. Too many young readers have abandoned the spontaneous search for meaning in books because they did not receive appropriate guidance. But if they are given the encouragement and opportunity, they will often avidly explore every aspect of experience, asking more questions than the wisest and most learned can answer.

INTEREST IN READING

Closely related to purpose in reading is interest. Children are most likely to read with comprehension those materials that deal with topics of interest to them. In fact, it has been found that some pupils are able to read stories at a level of reading difficulty far beyond their normal abilities if the subject is one in which they are vitally interested. Thus a boy who follows professional baseball closely may successfully read a sports story in a newspaper even though it is several years beyond him in reading difficulty.

Children's interests are at least in part the result of the experiences they have had. They are closely related to the activities of play and work which constitute their daily living. Many of these interests are common to all boys and girls. Others are common only to boys or only to girls. Some are related to the earlier, others to the later, ages. Still others arise out of individual experience and are affected by the special aptitude or background of the individual. Since interests are learned, rather than inherited, it is possible to extend both their range and their quality. Any activity that will open new fields of exploration to children can help to expand a pupil's reading interests and his mastery of the printed page. Reading should, therefore, be taught in the setting of a wide variety of purposeful enterprises designed to expand the child's range of interests. Radio, television, films, field trips, class projects, group discussion involving the exchange of experiences —all these are methods by which the ground may be prepared for ever more zestful and meaningful reading.

READING SKILLS

The omission thus far of a discussion of the specific skills involved in the act of reading itself has been intentional. We felt that because so much of formal reading instruction has stressed the mechanical skills of word recognition and sentence comprehension, a heavy emphasis upon the background factors in reading growth was needed here. Nevertheless, no consideration of the development of reading competence would be complete without careful attention to the matter of specific reading skills. Later chapters will discuss these in detail.

Some children, of course, acquire the necessary skills without formal instruction. Given the various conditions described earlier in this chapter and an environment that is in every respect conducive to reading growth, they learn from the beginning to get meaning from the printed page and almost unconsciously develop the habits of word recognition and comprehension of sentences and longer units. For such children the analytical reading drills can be more harmful than helpful.

Most children, however, can be materially aided by specific instruction in reading skills. They can make more rapid improvement if they can be shown how to recognize letters and phonic elements, how to discover familiar elements in the longer unfamiliar words, how to use context clues, how to note details, how to find the main idea of a longer passage, how to compare, evaluate, and visualize the author's meaning, how to locate and utilize needed information, how to follow printed directions, and how to adapt approach and speed of reading both to the nature of the material read and to their purpose. These skills can be learned through guided practice. In no case must there be neglect of either the factor of interest or the factor of skill in reading.

The preceding survey of growth factors has illustrated how intimately reading is related to the total development of the child. When we speak of "developmental" reading, therefore, we may be referring to any one of three aspects of the problem of reading instruction. First, we may be considering the effect of the various growth factors on the child's progress in reading. Second, we may be thinking of the ways in which reading affects the child's general intellectual, emotional, and social growth. Third, we may have in mind the orderly progression of reading skills as new needs emerge from the growing life of the child. In whatever sense the term is used, it focuses attention on the fact that reading is a continuous process, that it is a part of an intricate pattern of growth, and that each factor and each specific skill must be considered in relation to all others.

FOR FURTHER STUDY

Chall, Jeanne, *The Great Debate*. New York: McGraw-Hill, Inc., 1967. Chapter 1, "The Conventional Wisdom and Its Challengers," pp. 13–52; Chapter 2, "Challenged and Challengers Speak Their Minds," pp. 53–74.

Dawson, Mildred A., and Henry A. Bamman, *Fundamentals of Basic Reading Instruction*. New York: David McKay Company, Inc., 1963. Pages 17–28.

Durr, Williams K., *Reading Instruction: Dimensions and Issues*. Boston: Houghton Mifflin Company, 1967. "Perception Skills and Beginning Readings," pp. 253–258; "Major Approaches to Word Perception," pp. 258–263; "Perceptual-Motor Aspects of Learning Disabilities," pp. 263–271; "More Than Remedial Reading," pp. 330–334; "Characteristics of Dyslexia and Their Remedial Implications," pp. 344–349.

Frost, Joe L., *Issues and Innovations in the Teaching of Reading*. Chicago: Scott, Foresman and Company, 1967. "Language Development in Children," pp. 3–16; "Oral Language Proficiency Affects Reading and Writing," pp. 16–19; "The Sub-Strata-Factor Theory of Reading: Some Experimental Evidence," pp. 19–28; "Research on the Processes of Thinking with Some Applications to Reading," pp. 28–39.

Holt, John, *How Children Fail*. New York: Pitman Publishing Corporation, 1964. Party II, "Fear and Failure," pp. 37–69; Part IV, "How Schools Fail," pp. 133–161.

Schubert, Delwyn G., and Theodore L. Torgerson, (eds.). *Readings in Reading*. New York: Thomas Y. Crowell Company, 1968. Chapter 11, "How Children and Adults Perceive Words in Reading," pp. 75–88; Chapter 17, "Laying the Foundation for Word Perception," pp. 133–136; Chapter 48, "Identifying Readers Who Need Corrective Instruction," pp. 325–333; Chapter 51, "Understanding and Handling Reading-Personality Problems," pp. 343–347.

PART TWO

CULTIVATING GROWTH IN READING ABILITIES

CHAPTER 4A

Readiness for Reading

When should reading instruction begin? That is an unsettled question.

Although in the twenties and thirties there were staunch advocates favoring postponement of reading beyond the first grade, their recommendation was never widely adopted. Typically in the past it has been assumed that reading instruction should start in the first grade. Until rather recently it was advocated by many persons in the forefront of educational thinking that systematic reading instruction in that grade should be preceded by a so-called reading readiness period. Often this period extended over a month or six weeks or more for all boys and girls. Frequently it was even longer for some pupils. It was not unusual for one or more first-grade children in a room to spend the entire year in "getting ready to read." Now, however, many educators are seriously questioning the need for a period of reading readiness for many boys and girls in the first grade.

Another assumption on which kindergarten programs have been planned ever since the rise of the kindergarten movement is now the subject of marked, at times bitter, disagreement. The argument centers around the role of the kindergarten in teaching reading, as well as its proper place in helping the child to become ready to learn to read.

A more radical position is highlighted as the controversy revolves around the question of whether reading instruction should start even in prekindergarten days, in the home. It should be noted, too,

There is satisfaction in books. (Photo courtesy Anne Arundel County, Maryland, Public Schools.)

that among those who argue that the home is the logical place for beginning reading instruction for many boys and girls, there is disagreement as to the age at which the child should be given instruction.

BASES FOR THE CONTROVERSY ABOUT THE TIME TO BEGIN READING INSTRUCTION

One reason for the debate concerning the optimum time to begin reading instruction is that there is a lack of unanimity in differentiating between *readiness for reading* and *reading*. For example, some teachers consider learning the letters of the alphabet and the sounds represented by them as part of reading readiness. Others refer to this process as reading. Work with experience charts—records of the experiences of the children—is thought of by some as reading, by others as reading readiness procedure.

Another factor that complicates discussion of the question as to when reading instruction should begin is that teachers differ in the extent to which they will continue into the learning-to-read period some of the types of work begun during the period of reading readiness. One teacher might, for example, at first during the learning-to-read period continue to help the boys and girls differentiate between the appearance of words—visual discrimination—a practice she may have emphasized during the reading readiness period. Another teacher, utilizing a similar procedure before beginning reading instruction, might discontinue it after the children begin to read.

Arguments for Earlier Instruction

Keeping in mind the difference in interpretation of what constitutes reading readiness, let us examine the arguments advanced for each of the positions favoring earlier instruction in reading to which reference was made in the introductory paragraphs of this chapter.

THE READING READINESS PERIOD IN FIRST GRADE Opponents of the practice of having a reading readiness period as customary procedure in the beginning weeks or months of the first grade point out that first-grade children of today differ greatly from boys and girls of a few decades ago in their readiness for reading as far as factors amenable to environmental stimulation are concerned. These persons state that the average six-year-old has traveled more extensively, has viewed television programs more frequently, has been in closer contact with people who have seen more of the world, has had more out-of-the-home experiences than children of the preceding generation. Since much of the usual readiness program has consisted of efforts to broaden the pupils' backgrounds, it is claimed that a major purpose for postponement of reading at the beginning of the first grade has already been met by today's entrants to first grade. Furthermore, those favoring elimination of a reading readiness period at the beginning of the first grade for the average child point out that a greatly increased number of boys and girls now attend kindergarten and that kindergartens avowedly have had as an objective, concomitant with the major aims of the kindergarten, to help boys and girls through ongoing activities to get ready to read. Moreover, many persons opposed to a reading readiness period for all or almost all beginning first-grade pupils claim that the somewhat formalized instruction boys and girls have often been receiving in the form of reading readiness exercises, such as discriminating between sounds, between letters, and between words, is either below the learning level of the child or is somewhat irrelevant to the task of learning to read.

It should be noted that the argument as usually advanced against a reading readiness period in first grade is not against such a period for any one child or group of children in that grade. It is in opposition to a requirement that all or almost all children go through such a stage after they enter first grade. The claim is that only a minority of first-grade entrants are not ready to begin to read. That a sizable number have previously started to read is also pointed out to support the argument against a reading readiness period for all.

THE ROLE OF THE KINDERGARTEN IN LEARNING TO READ   In the not very distant past it was rather universally conceded that reading instruction had no place in the kindergarten. Furthermore, it was also generally agreed that the activities in the kindergarten that were included, in part at least, to help the child become ready to read, should be limited to activities such as helping the child develop emotionally and socially, assisting him in expanding his experiences, and guiding his language development. Efforts to assist him in becoming ready for reading through a systematic program for the development of reading readiness were generally looked upon with disfavor. Learning the names of the letters of the alphabet and the sounds they commonly represent was considered entirely inappropriate at the kindergarten level. All of these assumptions are now being attacked by those educators who claim that there is no need for a universal reading readiness period in the first grade and who also support the position that the kindergarten should play a significant role in getting the child ready to read. Some also affirm that a considerable number of boys and girls in kindergarten are ready to learn to read while still on that rung of the educational ladder.

Arguments for initiating reading instruction in kindergarten for some children include references to studies of experimental set-ups in which kindergarten children have been taught to read. One often quoted is the Denver study,[1] conducted with the aid of a grant from the Cooperative Research Branch of the U.S. Office of Education, in order to ascertain the effectiveness of reading instruction in the kindergarten. Brzeinski, reporting on that study, states:

> The pilot program of systematic instruction in beginning reading skills [which included work on learning the letters of the alphabet and the sounds represented by them] appeared to be more effective than the regular kindergarten program, which incidentally provided opportunity for the development of reading readiness.

Brzeinski also points out that at the end of the first-grade program the

[1] Joseph E. Brzeinski, "Beginning Reading in Denver," *The Reading Teacher*, 18, pp. 16–21 (October 1964).

children in the experimental group were better readers than those in the control group.

Other studies dealing with reading in the kindergarten that are quoted as indicating the seeming effectiveness of reading instruction at that level include the Glenview Study,[2] of Glenview, Illinois, and the Livermore experiment,[3] conducted in the Livermore, California, school district.

Among persons endorsing a somewhat formalized readiness-for-reading program in kindergarten are those who believe that beginning reading instruction should be primarily a code-deciphering process in which the pupil learns the words through "translating" letters or combinations of letters into the sounds commonly represented by them. They place emphasis on learning in kindergarten the letters of the alphabet and the sounds commonly represented by them. Some would include exercises of various types designed to help boys and girls acquire some of the other skills necessary, in their opinion, for beginning reading. To accomplish the aims of a program of this type workbooks are frequently used. Commonly found among such published materials are, among others, exercises to develop skill in discriminating between letters and between words, to increase vocabulary, and to follow directions.

READING INSTRUCTION IN THE PRESCHOOL PERIOD
Of late books and magazine articles have been appearing in abundance in which the claim is made that the best time to teach a child to read is in preschool days. An extreme position is that taken by Doman, Stevens, and Orem in an article that appeared in the *Ladies Home Journal* entitled, "You Can Teach Your Baby To Read." In it the following often-quoted paragraph appears:

> The best time to teach your child to read with little or no trouble is when he is about two years old. Beyond two years of age, the teaching of reading gets harder every year. If your child is five, it will be easier than when he is six. Four is easier still, and three is even easier. If you are willing to go to a little trouble, you can begin when your baby is 18 months old or—if you are very clever—as early as 10 months.[4]

[2] Robert L. Hillerich, "Kindergartens Are Ready! Are We?" *Elementary English*, 42, pp. 569–573 (May 1965).

[3] Marjorie Kelley, "Reading in the Kindergarten," pp. 20–25 in Ralph Staiger (ed.), *New Directions in Reading*. New York: Bantam Books, 1967.

[4] Glenn Doman, George L. Stevens, and Reginald C. Orem, "You Can Teach Your Baby To Read," *Ladies Home Journal*, 80, p. 62 (May 1963).

Doman expanded this article into the book *How To Teach Your Child To Read*, published in 1964.[5]

Books and articles such as those to which reference has been made argue for an earlier start in reading by citing evidence that reading has been learned by young children. The work with Montessori materials used in teaching three- and four-year-old children to read in the Whitby School in Whitby, Connecticut, is also presented as evidence of effectiveness of early reading (see page 556). It must be remembered, however, that the teaching in Whitby School was not done by parents in the home but by teachers in a school situation. O. K. Moore's work with children three and four years of age at the Responsive Environment Foundation in Hamden, Connecticut, and the longitudinal study of Dolores Durkin in the Denver experiment (see page 576) are also frequently quoted. (In Chapter 16 the work of Moore is discussed.)

Comments on Arguments for Earlier Instruction

Although an increasing amount of research deals with the question of an early start in reading and although a sizable number of experimenters have concluded that on the basis of their work an early start in reading seems desirable, the evidence has not been conclusive. More longitudinal studies will need to be completed before many educators are willing to take anything as a final answer. Evidence undoubtedly shows that children—at least some children—can learn to read earlier than most boys and girls now do. However, whether or not it is desirable for many of them to start learning to read at an early age has not been established.

AT THE BEGINNING OF THE FIRST GRADE   It is being more generally conceded than formerly that a school program should not be planned around a reading readiness period of weeks or months for all boys and girls at the beginning of their first year of school. Some children can read before they start school. A period of reading readiness for them might, indeed, lead to boredom. Furthermore, in many instances it would be a waste of time. Some of the children who cannot read when they begin school are, however, ready for beginning reading instruction on their level of maturation and of ability. For these individuals, too, reading should not be postponed.

IN THE KINDERGARTEN   There has been strong opposition by many kindergarten teachers and by leaders in the field of child growth and development to systematic reading instruction in the

[5] Glenn Doman, *How To Teach Your Child To Read.* New York: Random House, Inc., 1964.

kindergarten. Opponents of reading instruction in the kindergarten argue that because a child of kindergarten age can learn to read is not sufficient reason to conclude that he should be taught reading at that period of his life. James L. Hymes, Jr., for example, sounds this warning: "Everyone loses if we produce early readers but in the process weaken humans. Everyone loses if we produce early readers but in the process kill the joy of reading."[6]

Questions such as these must be considered in connection with teaching reading in the kindergarten: (1) Does teaching reading require time that should be spent on other types of activities? (2) Are methods used in teaching reading to the beginner in violation of the principles that should govern learning at that stage of the development of the child? (3) Are the children who learn to read in the kindergarten superior in their reading achievement to others by the time they leave the elementary school? (In answering this question care must be taken that children who learned to read early are compared with children equated for intelligence, home conditions, and other factors that may have contributed to making the pupils who learn to read early a selected group even though it has been claimed that high intelligence is not an attribute of early readers as a group.) (4) Is there danger that the child who learns to read early may in later years lose, if he has acquired, a love for reading?

Some of these questions will be difficult, if not impossible, to answer conclusively with known methods of measurement. However, it is important that they be seriously considered before drastic steps are taken to change the kindergarten program. Whether or not reading should be taught in the kindergarten should be determined only after a careful reevaluation of the desired objectives and goals of the kindergarten. The aims of the kindergarten should not necessarily be those that seemed best decades ago. Unless such a reappraisal of the kindergarten program is made, there is danger that the question of reading on that level may be settled unwisely.

IN PRESCHOOL DAYS   As a group first-grade teachers have been quite vocal in their opposition to teaching reading at home to the preschool child. One argument frequently advanced by teachers is that many parents are not trained to teach reading. However, it would seem doubtful that a child who wants to learn to read before he enters school would be harmed much, if at all, through lack of professional training in the field of reading by his tutor, his parent. Undoubtedly, if preschool reading instruction is proved to be desirable, then it may

[6] James L. Hymes, Jr., "Early Reading Is Very Risky Business," *Grade Teacher,* 82, p. 88 (March 1965).

well be the province of the school or some other agency to provide parents with information on the subject. Some literature is already on the market advising parents as to how to teach their children to read or how to prepare them for reading. The book *Preparing Your Child for Reading* supplements assistance given to parents of kindergarten children in the Denver experiment who viewed a sixteen-lesson television series on that subject. Whether one agrees or disagrees with the methods recommended in any one publication, it cannot be denied that many books could be published to help parents. Furthermore, the schools could sponsor workshops, provide lecture series, give demonstrations, and circulate bulletins designed to assist parents to guide their children in learning to read. One point that should be emphasized in a program of parent education is that no preschool child should be forced to learn to read.

Another contention of many first-grade teachers is that parents should not help boys and girls of preschool age with reading because a parent may use a different method of teaching reading than the one that will be employed in the school. The child may, the argument continues, encounter greater difficulties in reading at school than he would be likely to meet if he had not had parental guidance. However, it seems difficult to imagine that a child taught at home by, let us say, a whole-word method would be handicapped if later at school he were taught by a phonic method, or vice versa. In fact, it might be argued that the two methods may be found to reinforce each other.

Still another reason why many first-grade teachers object to teaching the child to read before he comes to school is that they claim the child will then become bored if he needs to be in a reading group of children who cannot read. That argument is a poor one for the school to offer. A drastic change needs to be made in a lockstep program that requires a child who can read when he enters school to be treated as if he had no knowledge of reading. The school should not discourage a boy or girl from achieving success in any area while he is still at home on the grounds that if the child could read upon entrance to first grade the school would not know how to adapt instruction to his needs. If there are others in the room who can read, he can be placed in a group with them alone. If he is the only one who can read, he can be given individualized instruction.

Even though in the preceding paragraphs an attempt has been made to refute the common arguments teachers propose against preschool learning to read, there are serious questions to be raised about preschool reading. It is not primarily a matter of "Can a child be taught reading before he enters school?" as some popular publications seem to indicate, but "Should he be taught to read before first grade?" "What is to be gained by an early start?'' too, needs to be investigated. More than parental pride in the achievement of a child at an early age must be the underlying purpose. Whether or not the child who learns to read in preschool days is spending on learning to read the time that should advisedly be used for other activities is a point to be considered seriously. What effect learning to read at an early age may have on his reading later on, in terms of both reading skills and attitudes toward reading, should also be studied carefully, not only in connection with reading in the kindergarten but also in relation to reading at home on the part of the prekindergarten child.

The extensive research literature on reading readiness now available proves, if nothing else, that the problem related to the time for beginning reading instruction, like all questions associated with human learning in general, is complex and that the need for further investigation is imperative. We must remember, however, when interpreting the research now available and that to be done in the future that we are not dealing with objects on an assembly line but with human beings. The principal object is not to achieve efficiency in putting out a better product, in this case a child who makes better scores on standardized tests. The fullest development, well-being, and happiness of the child are the ultimate ends, and reading is but a means to those ends. In spite of some of the trends in our national life, we must remember that children are worthwhile for their own sake and that they must not be used to try to prove that our nation and our society are stronger and more intelligent than other nations and other societies. It is a deeply ingrained principle of democracy that the school, and society itself, exist for the welfare of the individuals who comprise them, not the reverse. This principle has pertinence to the problem of reading readiness.

IS THIS CHILD READY TO READ?

When all arguments have been exhausted as to when reading instruction should begin, in the final analysis the decision needs to be made not for boys and girls collectively but for each child individually. The question, therefore, is not, "When are children ready to read?" but, "Is *this child* ready to read?"

One significant indication of a child's readiness is his initial attitude toward reading.

On the opening day of school the first-grade teacher will find that her pupils vary greatly in their attitudes toward reading. Probably there will be one or more boys and girls, like Carol, who are already reading material of the difficulty of primers and who are eager to read more and more books. There will be boys and girls like Tommy, who, pencil and tablet clutched tightly, go to the teacher and exclaim enthusiastically, "I want to learn to read. I want to learn to read." Fathers, mothers, and possibly sisters and brothers have been reading fascinating stories to them. So they come to school, wanting to learn to read in order to be independent of others for their stories. They may have discovered, too, that a great deal of information is found in books. They will insist on being taught to read in a hurry.

But not all the children in the room will be like Tommy. There will probably be a Susan, who has enjoyed hearing others read or tell stories to her, but who has not looked forward to learning to read. She prefers not to learn, because she thinks it more fun to have her mother read to her than to read by herself. However, the teacher may wonder whether, in spite of lack of interest at the time, Susan may not become ready for reading before Tommy.

Then, too, there is Peggy, who enters school with fear and trepidation because she has heard disconcerting tales about what happens at school. The teacher may ask herself, "If I can get Peggy to overcome her fear, will it be wise to put her into a reading group?"

Another familiar figure in a first-grade room at the beginning of the year is Jim, who is greatly disturbed at the thought that now he can no longer spend the entire day playing cowboy. He is in no mood to be interested in what is done at school, for he anticipates only boring experiences.

In the average first grade, then, the children's attitudes toward learning to read may range from disinclination to indifference to anticipation. There are many other respects, however, in which first-grade children reveal great differences. They differ in mental, physical, social, emotional, and other educational or psychological factors of great importance in beginning reading.

Numerous factors, therefore, contribute to reading readiness. The presence of any or even all of them will in itself not guarantee reading success. Moreover, it is not necessary that all these factors be present in equal degree, although most of them should be present in at least moderate degree.

Mental Age

For several decades after Washburne and Morphett[7] reported that, in the words of Washburne, "It is safer not to try to teach begin-

---

[7] Mabel Morphett and Carleton Washburn, "When Should Children Begin to Read?" *Elementary English Journal,* 31, pp. 496–503 (March 1931).

ning reading to most children until they are mentally six and a half,"[8] their recommendation, though not unchallenged, was widely accepted. It was put into practice in many schools. The validity of the conclusion of the two investigators is now seriously questioned, in fact frequently categorically denied.

Whether or not a child is ready to read undoubtedly should be answered not only in reference to his mental age but also in consideration of many other factors. The decision should be based in part upon the reading program of the school. Children with mental ages considerably below six years and six months are being taught to read effectively if the methods and materials are suitable to their level of intellectual maturity. For the teacher to know that level is important.

One method of obtaining information on mental maturity is through the use of dependable mental tests. However, it should be remembered that even the best mental test provides an imperfect measure of native ability or intelligence. A child who had many rich and intellectually stimulating experiences will do better on an intelligence test than a child of equal innate ability who has been brought up in a very limiting environment.

Tests should not ordinarily be given a child immediately upon his entrance into the first grade, when he is still unaccustomed to the school environment. Many teachers like to wait until several weeks after school starts before they give any kind of standardized tests. The practice of having pupils come before the opening day of school, sometimes in the preceding spring, to take tests to determine their fitness for entrance into the first grade or to aid in their placement is probably quesionable, chiefly because the accuracy of the test results is doubtful. Furthermore, if taking a test is the child's first or one of his first school experiences, he may think of going to school as a not especially intriguing adventure.

STANDARDIZED TESTS OF MENTAL ABILITY   Perhaps the best-known individual test of mental ability is the *Terman Revision of the Stanford-Binet Intelligence Scale*, available in two forms, published by Houghton Mifflin Company, Boston. Since this test involves some knowledge of language, it may not fully reflect the real abilities of children with language handicaps.

Another now frequently used individual intelligence test is the *Wechsler-Bellevue Intelligence Scales*, published by the Psychological Corporation, New York. In it, as in the *Terman Revision of the*

[8] Carleton Washburne, "Individualized Plan of Instruction in Winnetka," in William S. Gray (ed.), *Adjusting Reading Programs to Individuals*, Supplementary Education Monographs, No. 52 (October 1941), pp. 90–95.

Stanford-Binet Intelligence Scale, the factor of language ability is involved.

On the market, too, are individual non-language psychological tests designed to reduce the invalidity of the test results that might, with language psychological tests, be due to lack of proficiency in the use of the English language on the part of the person being tested. An example of such a test is the *Arthur Performance Scale*, published by C. H. Stoelting and Company, Chicago. It can be used effectively with children from non-English-speaking homes as well as with children with other language problems. The use of the *Arthur Performance Scale*, however, is not restricted to children with language difficulties.

A much-used group test is the *Pintner-Cunningham Primary Test*, Form A, Form B, and Form C, published by Harcourt, Brace & World, Inc., New York. The subtests, which together are devised to test general mental ability, give an indication of the nature of the abilities tested. They are: Test 1, Common Observation; Test 2, Aesthetic Differences; Test 3, Associated Objects; Test 4, Discrimination of Size; Test 5, Picture Parts (in which the pupil is tested in ability to find among several pictures one like a designated one); Test 6, Picture Completion (in which the pupil is asked to indicate which of a number of parts is needed to finish an incomplete picture); Test 7, Dot Drawing (in which the pupil is asked to connect dots so that a picture like a given one will be drawn). Although all seven tests are composed entirely of pictures, an understanding of language is required for taking the test, since all the directions are given verbally.

The California Test of Mental Maturity, Pre-Primary Battery, published by the California Test Bureau, Los Angeles, California, is available in a long and short form. Certain of the subtests require a minimum use of language, while other sections reveal how adequately the child understands relations expressed in words. Since a pupil's score in non-language test may be higher or lower than in language tests, it is of great value to obtain test scores on the types of mental ability tested both by language and by nonlanguage tests. *The California Test of Mental Maturity, Pre-Primary Battery* is concerned with the following mental factors: memory, spatial relations, logical reasoning, numerical reasoning, and verbal concepts.

The *Davis-Eells Test of General Intelligence or Problem-Solving Ability, Primary-A*, for grades one and two, called *Davis-Eells Games* on the pupils' booklets, is published by Harcourt, Brace & World, Inc., New York. Mental capacity is considered synonymous in this test with problem-solving ability. In constructing the test the authors took special care to choose content equally familiar to all economic-social cultures within an urban environment. No reading skill is required, for all the exercises consist of pictures to be checked in answer to thought questions given orally by the examiner. Rate of response is not checked in the test.

The Pintner Non-Language Primary Mental Test, published by the Bureau of Publications, Teachers College, Columbia University, New York, can also be used with children with language handicaps.

Other widely used group intelligence tests are the *Kuhlmann-Anderson Intelligence Test, Grade IA*, published by the Educational Test Bureau, Inc., of Minneapolis, Minnesota, and the *Detroit Beginning First Grade Intelligence Test*, distributed by Harcourt, Brace & World, Inc., New York.

SUBJECTIVE DATA ON MENTAL ABILITY Intelligence tests, however, are not the only means by which the teacher can gain insight into the child's intelligence. Long before psychological tests were available there were rough methods of estimating a person's intelligence. Although mental tests are probably more reliable indexes of intelligence than more informal methods, the latter should also be used. Informal observation may serve as a valuable check on the accuracy of test scores. If no mental test has been given, the observant teacher may compare the child's reactions with those usually expected of children of his age. By consulting books on child growth and development the teacher can find out what types of behavior are characteristic of children at various age levels. Information about an individual child's customary behavior can also be obtained from others who know him well, especially his parents. And, of course, the teacher should realize that environmental deprivations may make the child seem less intelligent than he is.

Physical Fitness

The teacher of the beginning reader should always consult such data as may be available in the offices of the school doctor or nurse. Information that can be obtained through conferences with parents is also often helpful. Through observation of the child the teacher can frequently get clues to the child's physical well-being which may alert her to the need for referral to the nurse or doctor. If there is no school nurse, symptoms of illness or handicap may be discussed with the parents, who may be encouraged to consult a physician, dentist, or eye specialist. Rather easily observable factors like sleepiness, listlessness, irritability, and languor often are signs of difficulties that may seriously interfere with learning to read.

Unfortunately, during the critical period of getting ready to read and of beginning reading, children are often absent from school because of illness. Not much can be done by the teacher to prevent such illness, except to provide frequent rest periods and frequent periods of physical activity, to check room temperature and ventilation, and to suggest that a child be sent home at the first sign of a cold or other illness. Since frequent interruptions are to be expected, the teacher should plan her work accordingly. Much repetition and review of earlier activities are necessary. When a child returns after an absence of several days, the teacher should do everything possible to make him feel that he still belongs, has his own seat, and follows the familiar routine. He should be greeted with pleasure by teacher and class.

VISION   Since probably no phase of the physical well-being of the child affects reading as much as eyesight, the vision of a child who is about to learn to read should be checked as carefully as possible.

The screening test for vision that is most commonly used in schools is the Snellen Letter chart or the Snellen Symbol E chart, which is an adaptation of the letter chart, for use with nonreaders. On the letter charts are seven rows of the letters printed in various sizes, decreasing from the top row to the bottom. While the examinee is being tested, he stands twenty feet from the chart and reads as far down the Snellen Letter chart as his vision permits. On the Snellen Symbol E chart the pupil indicates by the fingers of one hand the positions, like **E**, **m**, **Ǝ**, and **ɯ**, in which the letter E occurs on that chart. If the rating on a Snellen chart for either eye is below 20/20, referral should be made to a competent eye doctor. Teachers should guard against concluding, if a child's vision for reading at the "far-point" is good, that his vision for reading at the "near-point," as required when reading books, is satisfactory. Many persons see well at a distance but have difficulty at the near-point. The Snellen charts commonly test only the clearness of vision at a distance of twenty feet. Nearsightedness, which is the only visual anomaly detected by the Snellen chart, is more commonly associated with good rather than poor reading ability. Consequently, use of the Snellen test as part of a reading readiness check-up is questionable.

The Visual Sensation Tests of the Betts Ready to Read battery make a more comprehensive visual analysis than is possible through the use of the Snellen charts. Like the latter, they test clearness of vision at the far-point, and they also make it possible to detect some problems of binocular vision. By means of a telebinocular, a stereoscopic machine developed by Emmett A. Betts and associates, with accompanying stereoscopic slides or stereographs, these tests check distance fusion, binocular visual efficiency at a far-point (clearness of vision), left-eye efficiency, right-eye visual efficiency, vertical balance, depth perception, lateral balance, fusion at the reading distance, and sharpness of image. Other tests of near-point vision are:

The *Keystone Visual Survey Tests.* Keystone View Company, Meadville, Pennsylvania.
The *Orthorater.* Bausch and Lomb Optical Company, New York.
The *Sight Screener.* American Optical Company, Southbridge, Massachusetts.
Spache Binocular Reading Test. Keystone View Company, Meadville, Pennsylvania.

Before choosing any test for checking visual efficiency teachers are advised to study carefully the literature furnished by the publishers of the tests to note what they purport to test and how the tests operate. In no case should the teacher or school nurse use vision tests to try to *diagnose* eye defects. The tests should be used in the schools merely as screening tests. If the results of the testing indicate that there is a possibility of a difficulty in vision, a referral for diagnosis and possible remediation should be made to a competent specialist in the field of vision.

Even without tests some symptoms of visual difficulties, like inflamed eyelids, scowling, and frowning, can be detected. The distance from the eye at which a child holds his books may also be a sign of trouble. Complaints of headaches after reading, too, are frequently significant in discovering vision problems.

One argument that has frequently been given against early reading instruction is the assumption that the eye of a preschool-age child is not mature enough for him to read without danger of injury to his eyesight. However, in a report on a study of vision of five-year-olds, Thomas Eames states that the vision of every child in that group was such that he could begin to learn to read at that time without fear of resulting damage to the eye.[9] Nevertheless, there is also research to substantiate the claim that an early heavy reading load can be damaging to the eyes.

HEARING   The hearing ability of a child may have an important effect on his reading. It is believed that even a fairly small loss in hearing acuity may cause problems with reading. In many schools an effort is made to secure accurate information about children's auditory acuity. In these schools the health service often checks

[9] Thomas Eames, "Physical Factors in Reading," *The Reading Teacher,* 15, p. 432 (May 1962).

hearing by means of an audiometer. Some audiometers are made for group, others for individual, testing. Audiometers are obtainable from:

The Maico Company, Minneapolis, Minnesota.
Aurex Corporation, Chicago, Illinois.
Medical Acoustic Instrument Company, Minneapolis, Minnesota.
Dakon Corporation, New Hyde Park, New York.
Otarion Listener Corporation, Ossining, New York.
C. H. Stoelting Company, Chicago, Illinois.
Sonatone Corporation, Elmsford, New York.[10]

The use of an audiometer requires specialized training. Moreover, in many schools teachers do not have access to clinics in which audiometers are used. They should therefore be alert to observable signs of hearing loss, which frequently goes undetected and which can seriously interfere not only with reading progress but with learning in general. Inattention, monotonous or unnatural pitch, lack of clear and distinct speech, frequent requests for repetition of questions, turning one ear to a speaker, head tilting, and rubbing of the ear are among the indications of possible defects of hearing.

The classroom teacher can also make a rough check of children's hearing by means of the "watch-tick" test. The examiner holds a watch of medium size and quietness in the palm of his hand and stands behind the child being examined. The child covers one ear with the palm of his hand. The watch is held about three feet from the child and moved closer until the child indicates that he hears its tick. Both ears are tested in this way. By comparing one child's responses with another's, the teacher knows which children should be examined by a nurse or doctor. Whisper tests and low-voice tests may also offer clues as to whether hearing difficulty may be suspected.

PERCEPTUOMOTOR ORGANIZATION OF THE LEARNER
In the book *Predicting Reading Failure,* DeHirsch, Jansky, and Langford present the results of their search for a more valid prediction of reading success than commonly obtained by schools basing their appraisal of readiness chiefly on intelligence tests, reading readiness tests, and teacher observation and estimation. In the book the authors present a predictive index that they have worked out. They state: "We ... put together a battery of tests which we hoped would reflect the children's preceptuomotor and linguistic status at kindergarten level." [11]

[10] Further information on audiometers is given in Emmett A. Betts, *Foundations of Reading Instruction.* New York: American Book Company, 1950.

[11] Katrina DeHirsch, Jeannette Jansky, and William Langford, *Predicting Reading Failure, A Preliminary Study,* p. 5. New York: Harper & Row, Publishers, Inc., 1966.

It may be that a battery of tests of the type recommended can constitute a better guide to assessment of readiness for reading as well as a basis for helping boys and girls overcome those problems that otherwise might interfere with success in reading.

Social and Emotional Development

The social maturity of a child can be determined in part by observing his "at-homeness" in group situations. It is of special importance to note his ability to cooperate with others in a group. Emotional maturity can roughly be gauged by the child's reaction to conditions that to him are unpleasant, his willingness to consider the rights of others, and his ability to sacrifice immediate pleasures for future gains.

To the child in the prereading period, school is still a strange place calling for many adjustments which had not been required of him at home or even in the kindergarten. Teachers will often observe signs of fear, anxiety, withdrawal, or belligerence in children as a result. Getting ready to read requires the growth both of self-confidence and of confidence in the teacher.

Educational Factors

Educational factors that have decided bearing upon beginning reading can be measured through the use of tests frequently referred to as reading readiness tests as well as by means of a variety of non-standardized procedures.

READING READINESS TESTS　Many, though not all, of the educational factors related to beginning reading are being measured by means of reading readiness tests. However, such tests are far from perfect predictions of reading successes, with some, of course, decidedly better than others.

Many reading readiness tests appraise the child's background of information, either in a subtest so labeled or in one by some other name in which other characteristics of reading readiness are also tested. The breadth of background of a pupil's information, which reflects the richness of experience he has had, can be tested by asking him such questions as "How many cents are there in a nickel?"

The ability to discriminate between objects, words, and letters is also measured in many reading readiness tests. A common method for evaluating the ability to discriminate among objects is to present a series of four or five pictures in a row, all but one of which is like the first one. The series may consist of pictures of five houses all alike except one in which no chimney is shown. The child is asked to cross out the one that is unlike the first one. Similar exercises are devised for testing the pupil's ability to discriminate between letters or words. Pupils are not expected to read the words or letters; all they are to do is to recognize which letter or word is different from others in the same row, or which are alike.

Comprehension of the meaning of words is also tested in many reading readiness tests. In some tests the pupil is asked to give words that mean the opposite of the words named by the examiner. If, for example, the teacher says *summer,* the pupil is to answer *winter;* if the teacher says *up,* the pupil is to say *down.*

One widely used readiness test is the *Gates Reading Readiness Test,* published by the Bureau of Publications, Teachers College, Columbia University, New York. It is divided into five subtests which measure specific skills important in learning to read. The skills tested are the ability to follow directions, to discriminate between words that are similar, to differentiate between sounds, and to identify letters and numbers by name. The ability to follow directions is tested by asking the pupil to mark pictures as instructed. Two subtests measure the ability to discriminate between words. One does so by requiring the child to indicate which two words in each group of four are alike. The other asks the child to state which word in a series of four is like the one shown to the child on a word card. In the fourth subtest the pupil marks the picture the name of which rhymes with a word the examiner names. The first four subtests are group tests, but the fifth subtest, in which the pupil names as many of the capital and small letters and the given numbers as he can, must be given to one pupil at a time.

The Van Wagenen Reading Readiness Test, published by the Betts Reading Clinic, Haverford, Pennsylvania, has two forms, both within the same test booklet. It tests range of information, perception of relations, vocabulary, memory span for ideas, word discrimination, and word learning. The subtest entitled "Perception of Relations" evaluates the child's ability to make analogies of this type: "Birds, sing: dogs, _____." Under "Memory Span for Ideas" the child is asked to repeat verbatim after the examiner sentences of increasing length and complexity. The "Word Discrimination" section tests visual discrimination, which is the ability to differentiate between two or more forms. The subtest "Word Learning" tests the rapidity with which a child can learn a new word when symbols with which the word is to be associated are given. Cards with a series of symbols (not letters of the alphabet) are shown to the pupil, and he is told what word to associate with that card. After a series of cards has been presented several times, the pupil is asked to name the words as he looks at the cards. The *Van Wagenen Reading Readiness Test* is usable only as an individual test.

The *Metropolitan Readiness Tests,* which are group tests published by Harcourt, Brace & World, Inc., New York, and available in two forms, consist of six subtests, entitled "Word Meaning," "Sentences," "Information," "Matching," "Numbers," and "Copying." All six subtests are made up of pictures, which the pupil is asked to mark or copy according to oral instructions by the teacher. The first subtest is a test to measure the child's ability to understand words. In the second subtest the pupil's comprehension of phrases and sentences is checked. The informational background of the child is tested in the third test. In the fourth test his power of visual perception is measured as revealed by his ability to select the letter, figure, word, or picture that is similar to a specified one. The fifth subtest measures many abilities related to numbers, such as knowing the vocabulary of numbers, writing numbers, recognizing written numbers, understanding number terms, telling time, and knowing the meaning of fractional parts. In the sixth subtest, "Copying," the pupil's power of visual perception and his motor control are tested. One special value of this subtest, in terms of reading skills, is that it helps detect tendencies toward reversing parts of letters or words that may be indicative of difficulties in reading.

The *Lee-Clark Reading Readiness Test,* published by the California Test Bureau, Los Angeles, is a group test printed in only one form. The three subtests measure the ability to match letters, to follow directions, to understand the meaning of words, and to note similarities among given words.

The *Classification Test for Beginners in Reading,* by Clarence R. Stone and C. C. Grover, distributed by the Webster Publishing Company, St. Louis, Missouri, is a group test, in which the pupil's ability to observe likenesses and differences between word forms is tested. No more than about twenty minutes is required for giving the test.

In the choice of reading readiness tests, as in the selection of other kinds of standardized tests, attention needs to be given to validity, reliability, ease of administering and of scoring, availability in more than one form, and reasonableness of cost. Since many teachers find it valuable to know a child's achievement in a variety of abilities related to beginning reading, they welcome the fact that many readiness tests are divided into subtests. When averages or norms are computed for the subtests, the teacher can determine in which of the characteristics tested each child is average, above average, or below average.

Although readiness tests alone are far from perfect means of determining whether a pupil is ready for beginning reading, the use of sufficiently reliable and valid ones is an asset in evaluation. However, the results must be interpreted with caution. The correlation of scores made by groups of children who have taken several readiness tests has not been very high. Nevertheless, it is probably true that a teacher can learn more about how ready a child is for beginning reading by giving him a reading readiness test than she could learn by spending the same length of time on other means of evaluation. Further value in the use of readiness tests is that the teacher can find them a diagnostic tool by means of which she can plan subsequent work for the child.

INFORMAL MEANS OF EVALUATION   Even though standardized tests throw considerable light on factors that are important in deciding whether it is advisable to begin the teaching of reading to a child, much can be done without them in trying to make that decision wisely. Informal tests, constructed by the teacher, can also be of decided help.

1. *Testing visual and auditory discrimination.* The ability to discriminate between letter and word forms and between letter and word sounds, which constitutes an essential to reading, can be tested in a variety of ways through teacher-made tests. In devising these tests the teacher must have clearly in mind the meaning of the terms *visual discrimination* and *auditory discrimination* and the importance to reading of the development of these skills. She must not confuse *visual discrimination* with *vision* nor *auditory discrimination* with *hearing.* By *visual discrimination* is meant the ability to *differentiate* between two or more forms, such as objects, written words, or written letters. Although a child's vision may be excellent, he may be unable to make fine differentiations between similar objects, pictures, words, or letters presented in visual form. In order to succeed in reading, the child should be able to differentiate between forms as nearly alike as *m* and *n*. If an individual cannot see such differences readily, he is likely to be greatly handicapped when learning to read. Some entering pupils do not possess this ability to the extent needed for beginning reading, but fortunately it can be developed through training.

By *auditory discrimination* is meant the ability to note the differences between sounds. A high degree of correlation has been found between auditory discrimination and success in reading.[12] A child's hearing may be excellent, even though he is unable to distinguish between the sound of the bells of the Presbyterian church and the Lutheran church. In order to be successful in reading, especially when

[12] Bertha Boyd Thompson, "A Longitudinal Study of Auditory Discrimination," *Journal of Educational Research,* 56, pp. 376–378 (March 1963).

it is taught chiefly by means of phonetic approaches, pupils should be able to recognize the difference between sounds as similar as the *b* and the *p* sounds as they occur in words. As in the case of visual discrimination, auditory discrimination may be improved through practice.

To test visual discrimination the teacher may make a test similar to one used frequently in standardized reading readiness tests. She may ask the pupils, for example, which word in the following row is different from the others:

man man man men man.

Or she may ask the boys and girls to find the word, in a row like the following, that is different from the first one in the row:

fine fine find fine fine.

A test of this type can be duplicated for the pupils on sheets of paper containing many rows of words arranged like those in the examples.

To test auditory discrimination the teacher can ask the pupils to indicate, for example, which of these pairs of sounds which she gives are alike and which are different: *m,n; n,m; n,n; m,m; b,p; p,p; p,b; b,b.* Or she can ask the pupils to name other words that begin with the same sound as the one with which, for example, the word *mother* begins. Another variation is to ask the pupils which pairs of words like the following begin with the same sound: *mother, man; cat, came; bark, pie.*

2. *Appraising other factors.* Through teacher-made tests, in many cases similar to those found in standardized tests, the teacher can get an approximation of the child's vocabulary, his ability to follow directions, his ability to remember, his power to do critical thinking, as well as of many other skills or abilities related to reading.

A significant test to determine a child's ability to retain words presented in written form can easily be devised. The teacher can present on cards a series of three or four or more words and spend several minutes providing the pupil with practice on them. She can give the practice by first naming the words and then asking the pupils to repeat them. Then she may have the pupil match the cards with words written in manuscript writing on the board. Further practice can be provided by having a pupil point to the words on the list on the board as the teacher or another child names them in an order different from the one in which they are written. To check the ability to remember the words the teacher can ask the pupil, after an interval of an hour or longer, to name the words earlier presented as the teacher points to them on the board or shows cards on which they are written.

Valuable information can also be collected through careful observation of the children. To get insight into a child's background of experience, the teacher may wish to talk with him concerning his interests. A rough measure of his attitude toward reading can be gained by observing how often he looks at books on the reading tables, whether he asks for stories to be read to him, and whether he is interested in finding out what the written word says. Whether he has acquired the top-to-bottom and left-to-right sequence can be determined in part by observing him as he looks at pictures and as he "reads" captions and other labels. An index of his vocabulary can be gained by listening to him talk and by gauging roughly how well he understands what he hears. Many teachers keep a written record of those characteristics of a child that have a bearing upon his ability to learn to read. Whether a written record is kept or not, informal observation of children in classroom and school ground situations serves as a useful supplement to standardized reading readiness tests.

Thus, during the first weeks of school, the teacher will want to study the characteristics of each child that relate to success in beginning reading. She can do so by means of mental tests, reading readiness tests, informal observations of children, conferences with children, consultation with parents and others, and examination of records. Some factors that she should consider are intelligence, hearing, vision, visual and auditory discrimination, experience background, vocabulary, emotional and social maturity, ability to remember, ability to follow directions, power to do critical thinking, and interest in reading. On the basis of her best judgment, as she weighs all the data that she has collected, the teacher will decide which pupils are ready for reading and which pupils are not.

GUIDELINES FOR HELPING THE CHILD GET READY TO LEARN TO READ

After the first-grade teacher has decided whether her pupils are ready to learn to read, she is confronted with the problem of what to do with those who are not ready for systematic instruction in reading. Should she have them postpone participation in all activities that pertain to reading in the hope that as they mature they will overcome their shortcomings? Clearly the answer is "No."

It is true that some children who are not ready for reading at the beginning of the school year will be ready in a few months even without special instruction. They need merely to wait for the further maturing of their various powers. Others, however, will respond quickly to specific guidance. There is no justification for the attitude of the teacher who, when asked why one child sat by himself in the back of the room throughout most of the school day, answered, "Oh, he is waiting for his reading readiness."

What then are the guidelines that the teacher should follow when planning a program for the prereading period?

The teacher should have clearly in mind the objectives of the prereading period. The general purpose of the prereading period is, of course, to guide the child in such a way that he will become better prepared for beginning reading. More specifically, the objectives of the prereading program can be stated as follows:

1. To determine whether the child is ready to learn to read, and if he is not ready, to find out how he can best be helped.

2. To assist the child in becoming adjusted to life in school.

3. To broaden the child's background of experience.

4. To help the child to gain greater emotional and social maturity.

5. To help the child increase his speaking and understanding vocabulary.

6. To provide an environment in which the child will have an opportunity to develop the skills essential to beginning reading.

7. To increase the child's interest in reading and to make him aware of the functions of reading.

Unless the child is cognizant of needs that can be satisfied through reading, he is not likely to be strongly motivated to read. In many ways the teacher can help him see that through reading he can learn to increase his store of information and that reading can be a source of pleasure for him.

Reading readiness activities should be an integral part of the total first-grade program. By means of many of the activities that the children carry on in any good first-grade program many of the goals of the prereading period can be attained. For example, characteristic activities of a first grade, such as storytelling, the examination of picture books, music and art activities, and excursions, can contribute greatly to the development of readiness for reading.

Direct help in the form of practice activities should be provided for some boys and girls. Although many of the activities of a good first-grade program, even when not designed specifically to prepare children for reading, are instrumental in fostering reading readiness, some boys and girls seem to require additional practice on certain skills which are essential to beginning reading. For example, practice periods set up to help children gain proficiency in discriminating between word forms are valuable when not enough meaningful repetition can be provided by incidental means. Such practice should not, however, replace abundant incidental instruction, which is afforded, for instance, when the children look for a name on a chart listing the children who have special responsibilities for the week. The teacher may at that time say, "No, that word is not *John* (as the teacher points to *Jim* and then *John*), although it begins like *John*. It is *Jim*." "Find Mathilda's name. Is it longer or shorter than Mary's?"

The activities of the prereading period should provide background for the initial reading tasks. Unfortunately, the reading textbooks, which must be written for the child population as a whole, cannot take account of the many variations in the social, cultural, geographical, and vocational backgrounds of all the children. The characters and situations portrayed in most reading textbooks are, therefore, usually drawn from the environments of fairly typical middle-class homes and communities. To be sure, the popularity of television has had an equalizing effect upon the background information that many boys and girls have. The city child who watches television has a better understanding of the farm and the farm child of the city than was formerly the case. Nevertheless, this knowledge as obtained through television is often superficial. The slum-dwelling child or the child living on a Wyoming ranch or an Indian reservation is still likely to have some difficulty in recognizing the Bob and Sue of the suburbanite family in the basal reader. Furthermore, to the country child the incidents may be quite dull in comparison with the killing of a rattlesnake or the rounding up of cattle escaping through a break in the fence.

Nor can it be taken for granted that the city child will understand references to a farm. He may not ever have seen a cow, and the illustration in the book may give him a misleading impression of her size.

Preparing the children for the basal reading series can therefore, in some instances, be a formidable task. Storytelling, discussion, and the use of various audiovisual aids may be used to prepare the child for the situations encountered in the readers. A rich "experience" program in the prereading period, including possibly a visit to a farm, will provide the foundation upon which the initial reading skills may be built.

Even in schools where no basal reading series is used and the program is individualized as the teacher attempts to help every child read material on his level, problems similar to those mentioned in relation to the textbook program persist. In such an individualized reading program it is still necessary to provide appropriate experiences in preparation for reading. Experiences such as field trips, discussions, and at times word study can help assure greater effectiveness for an individualized reading program as well as for one based in part on textbooks.

The length of the reading readiness period, if one is needed, should vary. Some of the boys and girls will possibly be reading when they enter first grade. Others, though not reading, may know the alphabet and the sounds commonly associated with the letters or combinations of letters. Reading readiness for these children can often prove to be worse than a waste of time unless preparation can help reduce possible lacks that might persist, even though in most respects the child is ready to read or is already reading.

Many boys and girls can begin to read almost as soon as they start school. Others will be ready to begin within a few weeks of that time. Some will probably not be well equipped for reading until some months have passed. For others, occasionally, it may be desirable to wait still longer. However, in a school system in which the teaching of reading is part of the first-grade curriculum, as it almost always is, a child should not be deprived of reading instruction throughout the school year unless he is clearly too immature to undertake the task with facility and pleasure. If he is not learning to read at some time during the year when most of his classmates are doing so, he may develop a poor attitude toward reading or serious feelings of inferiority. Usually, after sufficient preparation for the reading task, the child will find experiences of success in reading if the teacher employs methods and materials appropriate to his needs.

In explaining to parents why reading instruction has been delayed for their children, teachers sometimes use the analogy of infants' teething, walking, and talking. They point out that some children start later than others, but that after they have their teeth and have learned to walk and to talk they get along as well as the others. They explain that it is not in the child's interest to bring pressure upon him to read before he is ready. There is merit in this analogy, because maturational factors play a part in reading readiness. However, one important difference should be recognized. Parental guidance plays a relatively small part in determining when a child begins to walk, and none at all in determining when his first teeth make their appearance. On the other hand, parent and teacher guidance and environmental conditions generally have an enormous effect on the cultivation of genuine reading readiness. Reading readiness cannot be brought about before a child is mature enough to read, but it can be delayed by failure to provide the necessary guidance early enough.

A child should be taught to read as soon as he is ready. If he is ready before he starts school he should be permitted, even encouraged, to learn to read. The experience of reading, for the child who can read with success and pleasure, enriches his life and contributes to his general development. On the other hand, it is an error to assert, as some writers have done, that it is an established fact that a child who starts to read late has lost one or more years of his life and that he will always be one or more years behind in his capacity to read. First, there are many experiences besides reading that a young child can have to enrich his life. Second, although evidence has been presented indicating that an early reader may be able to maintain his superiority, there is also evidence to show that some children who do not receive reading instruction until the second year of school outstrip their counterparts who learned to read in the first grade, even before the end of the elementary school period.

A large variety of appropriate materials should be made available during the prereading period. Since one important objective of the prereading period is to develop and maintain an interest in reading, the children should have access to a large number of attractive books. Some of these may be placed on a library table, of height appropriate for the first-grade child, while others may be arranged on low bookcases. Included should be books to which the pupils have been introduced as the teacher showed them or talked about them or read from them to the class. The display should not, however, be limited to books with which the pupils are familiar. There should also be some that are new to the children, so that through them interest in exploring books can be developed. To help the boys and girls realize that books are valuable not only for the stories but also for the information they contain, the book collection should include both stories and informational material.

Books that boys and girls have made can also stimulate interest in reading. On the library table may be placed large books that other children have made in preceding years. For example, if the first grade the year before made as a class project a big picture book telling about a visit to a farm, the children can see how by means of the book it is possible to share information with others. Such a book is especially helpful if there are captions or simple story material accompanying the pictures. The new class, too, might bring pictures on a subject like "Our School" or "Our Pets" and mount them to form a big book. Under each picture the teacher might write a sentence or two suggested by the children. It is easy to interest children in a book they have helped to make.

Displays on bulletin boards can be of much value. A bulletin board on which are mounted leaves, with captions telling the kind, may help extend the experiences of some of the children. It can also give them further proof that learning to read is worthwhile, since the words below the leaves give significant information. Pictures of the means of transportation that some of the boys and girls have used, like the bicycle, the truck, the automobile, and the airplane, can serve similar purposes.

Many publishing companies that sell textbooks for elementary school reading also have reading readiness booklets that can serve a helpful purpose for some children. Some of the booklets provide specific preparation for a certain series of readers, while others can be used profitably by some boys and girls regardless of the reading books that will be used later.

Duplicated materials made by the teacher can also be valuable. For example, exercises in noting likenesses and differences among groups of pictures or geometric designs or letters or words can be provided in this manner.

CHAPTER 4B

Developing Readiness
for Reading

So far we have discussed in some detail the theory basic to a sound prereading program. Now let us see how it can be applied in the classroom.

FOSTERING EMOTIONAL AND SOCIAL MATURITY

As the first-grade teacher adjusts her procedures to the emotional and social maturity of her pupils and strives to help them reach higher levels, she will keep certain principles in mind: (1) The teacher herself should act like an emotionally and socially mature person. (2) An atmosphere of calm, courtesy, industry, and happiness should prevail in the room. (3) Respect should be shown for the personality of each person. (4) Restrictions should serve a purpose and be relatively few in number. (5) Directions and suggestions should generally be positive rather than negative. (6) Praise is usually more effective than blame, but praise must be deserved to be of value. (7) In all school activities, the development of the entire child should be taken into consideration. (8) Every individual needs security, approval, success, and means of self-expression. (9) The help and cooperation of parents should be secured whenever possible. (10) The teacher should not necessarily postpone reading instruction until a child is well adjusted socially and emotionally, because success in reading can contribute greatly to a feeling of security.

The teacher will encounter numerous problems of emotional and social maturity which directly affect a child's readiness for reading. Some children are shy, others overaggressive; some are "spoiled" or overprotected. What can the teacher do for them?

Often the shy child is the immature child. Insecurity may result from many causes. One of the common characteristics of the shy child is his fear of not being accepted by his peer group. If he has had little previous experience with participation in group activity, he may need gradual and patient introduction to group enterprises of many types. Certainly he should be made to feel, by every possible means, that he is liked. He should be brought into contact with other children who are friendly to him. He should receive praise for successful efforts at social adjustment. He should be encouraged to contribute constructively to the work of the group and thus secure the approval of his peers.

In the case of the child who cries easily or loses his temper on slight provocation, careful attention should be given to his general physical well-being. Has he been getting enough rest and wholesome food? Does he show signs of illness? Where the crying may have become a habit, the teacher should be ready to supply suitable distractions and try to avoid situations that may give rise to crying. The positive approach is usually the more effective. Thus when a child exhibits self-control in a situation, the teacher, instead of ignoring such desirable behavior, may say, "I noticed that Phyllis did not become angry when George broke her clay bowl. She helped George pick up the pieces and said she would make another bowl."

Although the aggressive child may be the most troublesome, he usually presents a less serious problem than the shy and retiring one. Tactful discussions with the group as a whole about respecting the rights of others may be helpful, and it may be necessary to provide experiences that teach the child he cannot get what he wants through aggressive behavior. Most aggressive children are merely seeking to gain recognition which they cannot get by more constructive methods. They should be given frequent opportunities to obtain such recognition by means that are socially approved.

The teacher will also encounter the overprotected and the "spoiled" child. Wherever possible, she should seek the cooperation of the oversolicitous parents. The overprotected child, while feeling secure in the affections of the teacher, should be encouraged to assume ever-increasing independence in making and carrying out decisions. The teacher should insist on his doing for himself the things he can learn to do without adult assistance and should praise him when he succeeds.

The "spoiled" child usually insists on having his own way in all matters. When thwarted, he may engage in pouting, crying, or various forms of aggressive behavior. Most "spoiled" children can be taught to "take turns" in group activities. They can be made to understand that no one is able to have his own way at all times and that thoughtfulness of others creates pleasant relationships. In extreme cases it may be necessary to isolate the child temporarily from the group, if only for the sake of the other children. Such disciplinary measures should, however, be regarded as exceptional.

The following is a list of ways in which the teacher can help boys and girls develop emotional and social maturity important in the learning-to-read period:

1. Providing the shy child with opportunities to become increasingly involved in activities well graded for him.
2. Helping the overly aggressive child take a rightful place in the social scene of the classroom.
3. Using praise when deserved but resorting to criticism sparingly.
4. Adapting the curriculum to the needs of each child so that he is likely to have a maximum of success and a minimum of frustrations.
5. Helping boys and girls appreciate the difference between license and liberty.
6. Giving responsibilities to all pupils.
7. Helping boys and girls in self-evaluation.
8. Helping boys and girls become more self-reliant.
9. Avoiding much competition with others.
10. Placing a child in a group in which he is likely to be happy.
11. Encouraging the child to do without assistance chores that he can do alone.
12. Encouraging a child to express his own opinions.
13. Encouraging every pupil to develop his special talents.[1]

DEVELOPING EDUCATIONAL READINESS

As the teacher pays attention to the emotional and social development of boys and girls, she can at the same time help them grow in other characteristics that have a marked bearing upon success in beginning reading. How this can be done through attention to the experience background, auditory and visual discrimination, and other factors is explained in the remaining pages of this chapter.

[1] Martha Dallmann, *Teaching the Language Arts in the Elementary School*, p. 180. Dubuque, Iowa: The William C. Brown Company, 1964.

Enriching the Child's Background of Experience

One way in which children's readiness for reading can be cultivated is through the extension of their experience background. Experience is important, not merely because children must get ready for reading, but because appropriate, wholesome, and varied experiences are an important part of ₁ach person's life, at any age. Even for the many children in the primary school who have already enjoyed a wide variety of experiences with places, persons, things, processes, and events, new and interesting school experiences are desirable. The school should provide all children with an interesting environment in which to grow up. Although many—perhaps most—of the children who enter first grade have a sufficient experience background to learn to read, the school should continue to open new worlds of experience to all children. For those children whose experiences have been severely limited, it may be desirable to postpone formal reading instruction until they have had the opportunity to enjoy a variety of direct experiences.

For all children it is well to make sure that the situations encountered in their first reading books are familiar. Most children's books, especially reading textbooks, present scenes and incidents familiar to the great majority of children. A boy and a girl, parents, a dog or a cat, simple toys, and perhaps a tractor or a mechanical crane constitute the major "props" of the primers. Nevertheless, the wider and richer the child's previous experience has been, the greater his chances of approaching the reading with confidence and pleasure. Building background should therefore not be limited to the kinds of situations encountered in the first reading book.

Experienced teachers are familiar with the wide variety in the range and types of backgrounds found among school children. They know it is necessary to study the children carefully in order to meet the multifarious individual needs. In some cases it will be possible to distinguish between different groups in the first-grade class. Thus, for example, those children who have not attended kindergarten may be selected for an exploratory trip through the school building. If an individual child has never had a pet, the teacher may talk with him about animals, show him pictures of pets, or better still, arrange for the class to acquire one.

Socioeconomic level will often affect the nature of the child's previous experiences, but not necessarily their extent. Children from middle class homes have often traveled considerably, even to distant countries. They are likely to see more movies, have more toys and books at home, and have more opportunity for gardening, experimentation with pencils, crayons, and paper and construction materials than lower class children. On the other hand, the slum-dwelling child knows a world that is quite unfamiliar to his more fortunate classmate. He may have developed, through the necessities of his life, a greater maturity and independence and often even a tragic sophistication about the ways of the adult world.

The ideal school environment for preparing boys and girls for reading, then, is one in which many things are going on. A primary class may be building a large model airplane, operating a store, viewing a film, making a terrarium, or caring for a pet. The child's background of experience can be extended by going on field trips, examining objects, looking at pictures, observing or participating in demonstrations and experiments, and listening to stories.

GOING ON FIELD TRIPS   The eagerness of most first-grade children to learn more about the part of the world near them should be fully utilized. There are many places in or near school that boys and girls enjoy seeing. Trips through the school, examination of playground equipment, walks to gather leaves or stones, trips to look at trees and birds—all can be made real learning experiences, contributing not only to reading but also helping the child find out more about the world in which he lives. But such trips must be carefully planned if the maximum value is to be obtained. Part of the planning should usually involve preparing the pupils for the trip so that they will know better what to look for. For example, before the boys and girls go on a walk to gather leaves, some pictures of pretty leaves may be shown and brief comments made. The purpose of the children in going on the walk, possibly to see how many different kinds of leaves each child can find, should be one that is wholeheartedly accepted by the group. During the trip itself help should also be given frequently in the form of suggestions or questions or directions. At this time the teacher may ask the pupils to notice if many leaves have fallen, and whether more green leaves are on the trees than on the ground. After the trip it is important to have a follow-up, when the pupils may engage in one or more activities such as showing their leaves, expressing rhythmically how the leaves fall, mounting them, drawing pictures suggested by their walk, making up a poem about leaves, or planning the sentences for a chart telling about their trip.

EXAMINING OBJECTS   By means of objects displayed in the room or otherwise brought to the attention of the boys and girls, the pupil's fund of information can be greatly extended. Discussion of material on a science table can be encouraged. The children can be encouraged to bring to school objects in which they are interested, such as stones or model airplanes or toy boats, and to explain them to the other children. Thus through wise direction many significant facts can be learned as the children show a new doll, a strange-looking acorn, or a knife that was recently received as a birthday present.

LOOKING AT PICTURES   Pictures serve as an important means of broadening the experience background of the children. If motion-picture equipment is available, the teacher can select motion pictures that will fit the needs and interests of her group. Slides and filmstrips, too, some of which are specifically planned for several of the basic reading series, can be used to make concrete the things that might otherwise be rather meaningless abstractions. Mounted pictures, postcards, and snapshots, brought either by the pupils or the teacher, can be a source of pleasure and of learning. Exhibiting them attractively will encourage children to study them and can also serve as a means of teaching them how to display pictures effectively. If the children share the responsibility of arranging the materials in an orderly fashion, they can develop skill in mounting pictures and arranging attractive displays.

OBSERVING OR PARTICIPATING IN DEMONSTRATIONS AND EXPERIMENTS   Demonstrations and experiments are of special interest to many children, and they can be the source of much information. Many experiences in science lend themselves well to use in the first grade; these include finding out what happens to plants when they have and when they do not have sunlight, discovering what effect salt has on ice, noticing how steam becomes water, and discovering that air is necessary for a candle to burn. Often the teacher can let the pupils take part in the experiments.

LISTENING TO STORIES   Storytelling at all ages can open a variety of vistas to the child. Realistic stories, in particular, are appealing to children of five and six. Although children should share in the storytelling and self-expression for the child telling a story is important, the welfare of the listener should also be considered. Consequently, the quality of the story and the method of telling it should be matters of concern not only for the sake of the storyteller but also for that of the listener.

ENGAGING IN OTHER ACTIVITIES   The teacher has at her disposal many other means of preparing boys and girls for beginning reading through extending their experiences. She can do this by providing records to which the children can listen, encouraging creative expression through music and art, interesting the children in putting on plays or puppet shows, and making provisions for discussions and conversation that is interesting, elevating, and informative.

Stimulating Growth in Language Abilities

Since there is a close relation between reading and other language abilities, much can be done to help the pupil develop in all of the linguistic skills. Both during the prereading period and after the child has begun reading in books, his development in language can be stimulated in a variety of ways so that he will become more ready for reading or will become a more efficient reader. The teacher can effect growth in reading skill or in abilities related to reading by wisely guiding activities that deal with speech, listening, and writing.

One period of the school day that can contribute richly to the development of language efficiency is the "sharing period." In a large number of primary grades a short period, popularly called "show and tell" time, is set aside daily so that the pupils will have an opportunity to "share" some of their experiences with others in their group. They do so by telling their classmates and the teacher experiences of interest to them. During this period many teachers like an informal seating arrangement, often in circular or semicircular formation.

Typically during the sharing period one pupil at a time, either while seated or while standing at a place where others can see him, tells in a sentence or more something that he thinks will interest others. At times he has something to show to the class as he makes his explanation. A child showing a stone that he found on his way to school may say, "I found a pretty stone." With or without questioning by the teacher or the rest of the group he may add, "I found it on the way to school. I am going to keep it." Other typical bits of information given by first-grade pupils are:

> We have a new baby. It is a baby sister.
> Mother is taking me to the five-and-ten-cent store tonight. I will buy a doll.
> I fell yesterday. This is where I hurt my leg. A dog chased me.

In conducting a sharing period these are points many teachers find profitable to observe: (1) Good English should be encouraged but not to the point of inhibition of spontaneity in talking. (2) Participation should be well distributed. Although frequently not every child can have a "turn" during every sharing time, no one should be slighted day after day and nobody should monopolize the time. (3) Opportunities to increase the pupils' vocabulary should be utilized. This can often be done if after a pupil has used a word unfamiliar to many, the teacher makes the term clearer. For example, if one child says, "I found this piece of marble," the word *marble* can be explained through comments or questions by the teacher. (4) Sharing time should be a happy time. (5) The sharing period should not be a long period, probably not more than about twenty minutes in length. (6) A good time for a sharing period is the beginning of the day when the pupils are eager to tell what has happened since they were last with the others.

Many values can be gained through effective use of sharing time, some of which are directly related to reading abilities. Besides having an opportunity to improve the understanding vocabulary, the children can grow in self-confidence, in power to relate events in sequence, in ability to predict outcomes, in attentiveness when listening, in number and complexity of concepts, in interest in reading more about some of the topics discussed, and in many other ways. The relation of many of these learnings to getting ready for reading is evident.

Increasingly the interrelation between reading and writing is being stressed. One of the major gains possible from the use of the experience chart (discussed in the last part of this chapter) is that it highlights that relation.

Oral expression can serve as an aid to reading. (Photo courtesy Cleveland, Ohio, Public Schools.)

The adverse effect upon reading of growing up in a culturally and economically disadvantaged environment is caused in part, it seems, by the poor quality of oral expression on the part of the majority of children in such areas. This problem and related ones are the topic of Chapter 15.

DEVELOPING SPEECH   A chief objective of first-grade programs, before and after reading instruction is begun, is to help the pupil express himself well orally. Skill in speech plays a significant part in learning to read. The child embarrassed by ridicule because of baby talk is not likely to want to participate freely in group discussions based on reading activities. The boy or girl unable to talk in short, simple sentences is frequently unable to anticipate the meaning of a sentence, even of the type found in beginning reading books. In these and other ways skill in reading and in speech often go hand in hand.

The following points should serve as guidelines in the selection of procedures for the development of speech:

1. Most speech improvement comes about through informal classroom activities.
2. Provision should be made for a large number of enriching experiences that give opportunity for improved oral expression.
3. Attention should be given to various phases of speech, such as proper enunciation and pronunciation, adequate speaking vocabulary, and interest in speaking with or to others, with an understanding of courtesies and proprieties in speaking.
4. Pupils who need help in speech should be given opportunity for special practice.
5. The teacher's own speech habits should be a suitable model for the children.
6. Poor speech habits may be caused by feelings of insecurity.
7. Special attention should be given to children who come from homes where a foreign language is spoken.
8. The teacher should not talk too much.
9. The physical features of the room and the activities carried on by the class should be made so interesting that the children will have vital topics for discussion and conversation.
10. The atmosphere of the classroom should encourage children to converse freely at appropriate times.

The following are some ways in which the teacher can help pupils to improve the pattern of their expression:

1. Providing many opportunities for free discussion during various activities, such as planning a project or making the schedule for the day.
2. Encouraging the pupils to tell stories that they have heard or experienced or made up.

3. Asking pupils to explain pictures they have drawn.
4. Placing on the bulletin board pictures the pupils can interpret orally to others.
5. Setting aside time for dramatizing some of the stories read or told by the teacher to the group.
6. Helping the boys and girls put on simple puppet shows.
7. Providing opportunities for dramatic play—for example, playing house.
8. Helping the children do choral reading or otherwise saying poems in unison.
9. Making provisions for many opportunities for singing.
10. Talking individually to the boys and girls when they come to school in the morning, during the noon hour, when they leave in the afternoon, or during periods set aside for individual or committee work.
11. Encouraging all pupils to participate in a "sharing period."
12. Asking pupils to talk about group experiences, like class trips to the bakery or the post office or the fire station, or to report on trips they have taken when not under the supervision of school.
13. Displaying in the room objects that are likely to stimulate discussion.
14. Setting time aside for the children to tell about what they enjoy doing, like caring for an animal, playing a game, or doing some cooking.

IMPROVING LISTENING   One aspect of the language arts that has not been emphasized sufficiently in many schools is listening. Frequently it has been taken for granted. Because of its close relation to reading and to many other significant activities both in and out of school, increased attention should be given to this ability.

In trying to help children develop better habits of listening, the teacher should utilize regular classroom activities whenever possible. The following are ways in which children can be helped to become better listeners:

1. The pupils can play games in which the children, who are blindfolded, try to identify sounds such as the tapping of a pencil on a desk, the crushing of paper, writing on the chalkboard.
2. The children go on a "listening walk" with the teacher, on which they try to discover as many sounds as they can while on the walk. Later a composite list of the sounds heard might be made.
3. As the teacher tells or reads stories to the boys and girls, she can stop occasionally to ask questions that test their attentiveness—for example, "Why did Bobby want to get some apples for his mother?"
4. After the teacher has told or read part of a story to the class, she may say, "When I have finished the story, see if you can tell what happened to the snowman."
5. Before the teacher reads a story to the class, the pupils can be told

There is an interrelationship among the language arts. (Photo courtesy Riverside, California, Unified School System.)

that after the reading they will be asked to arrange in order pictures that illustrate the action of the story.

6. The pupils can be encouraged to listen carefully to stories so that they can tell them to others.

7. The pupils can draw up standards for good listening, such as looking at the person talking, not talking while someone else talks, and not playing with anything while someone is talking.

8. Evaluations of how well the pupils are listening, according to standards like those mentioned in (7), can be made by the class.

9. Listening can be encouraged by means of dramatization of stories or incidents.

10. At times some pupils may be given exercises in improving and testing their ability to listen.

IMPROVING THE SPEAKING AND UNDERSTANDING VOCABULARY   Closely related to the improvement of both speaking and listening is the development of the speaking and understanding vocabulary. Since the vocabulary of beginning books and the sentence structure used in these books are necessarily below the understanding and speaking level of many of the children, it is important to extend their knowledge and use of words through listening and talking. Although much of the work on vocabulary development may be carried on by incidental instruction, it should nevertheless be carefully planned. Direct practice may sometimes be needed. Growth in children's speaking and listening vocabulary can be fostered in many ways:

1. Providing opportunity to engage in activity when working on significant units of work. New words should be introduced as need for them arises.
2. Reading or telling stories that include some unfamiliar words. The meaning of new words should, of course, be explained.
3. Writing a group letter.
4. Dramatizing words like *walked, ran, crept, raced.*
5. Calling attention to children's use of new or especially colorful words.
6. Drawing pictures illustrating such new words as *funnel, burrow, tractor.*
7. Playing games in which children make up sentences that refer to a new word. A sentence might be, "I am thinking of something a rabbit does. He does it when he makes a hole. The word begins with the *b* sound."
8. Using motion pictures, slides, and filmstrips.
9. Bringing interesting objects to the room. If a rock exhibit is set up, for example, children may enlarge their vocabulary by learning terms like *marble, granite, sandstone.*
10. Taking children on excursion and helping them become familiar with terms that give more meaning to their trip, like *cash register, sales, customer.*
11. Introducing songs and poems that contain new words.

In helping children to add words to their understanding and speaking vocabulary, the teacher may follow these steps:

1. Introduce the word in a meaningful situation.
2. Draw attention to the new word by giving its meaning, asking someone in the group who knows the word to give the meaning, or questioning the others so that they can tell what the word means.
3. Let some of the children use the word in a sentence.
4. Make certain that the pupils pronounce the word correctly.
5. Use the word in later conversation or discussion.
6. Encourage the pupils to use the word.

DEVELOPING A READING VOCABULARY   Even during the prereading program the teacher can help the pupils acquire a reading vocabulary that will assist them greatly when they begin reading in a book. She can do so by labeling shelves where articles like scissors, paste, and crayons are kept. Attaching the children's names to their lockers and desks can also be of value. But merely labeling articles is not enough, for looking at a word, without the intent to remember it, frequently does not result in learning on the part of the child. For this reason, attention should be called to the labels and the children should be given an opportunity for associating the words with objects. At times the pupils may be asked to match the appropriate cards with the labels or they may name cards containing the words without comparing them with the cards used as labels. Labeling objects like a table, a desk, or a chair is of little value unless a real purpose is served thereby. It may be profitable, for example, to place words on a table to show what is to be exhibited on it.

Picture-word cards, cards on which the picture and the name of the item pictured are given, like *mother, father, sister, brother, cat, dog, school,* and *home,* can be displayed and used in practice exercises for pupils who seem to need such repetition. On the back of the card may be written the word that goes with the picture, so that pupils may practice recognizing words without looking at the illustrations. Sets of small cards like these, possibly four inches by six inches, can be used by the pupils individually. Similarly, both large cards for group use and small cards for individual practice can be made, with the names of the primary and the secondary colors corresponding to the color illustrated on the reverse side.

There are many other means of adding words to the children's vocabulary. The teacher may put on the chalkboard or on large sheets of paper directions often used in the classroom, such as "Please get your wraps," or "Please form a circle." Instead of giving the directions orally, the teacher may sometimes point to these. Plans for the day may also be written on the board daily before school: "We will take a walk," or "We will hear a good story today." A chart with the names of the children in the room can be used in a game in which one child points to a name while another says it.

LEARNING TO WRITE   The simple writing experiences of children during the prereading period can be of help in later reading instruction. Usually their writing during this stage is confined to the writing of their names or the copying of sentences from the board or from sheets of paper. Brief invitations to parents or short sentences to accompany illustrations they have made may be copied. Through writing of this type, children can be made more aware of the function of the written word both as writing and as reading. Moreover, as the pupils are writing they can become familiar with the configuration of words, by noting which words are short words, which are long words, and which begin or end in the same way. Since many children enjoy reading what they have written, they should have opportunity to read to others in the room or to their parents the captions under their pictures or the notes they write.

LEARNING THE LETTERS OF THE ALPHABET AND THEIR SOUNDS   As indicated in Chapter 4A, many teachers do not believe that part of the reading readiness period should be devoted to learning the letters of the alphabet and the sounds that they commonly represent. Those who do favor this practice will find many suggestions for teaching the letters and their sounds in workbooks and teachers' manuals of series of readers that emphasize early learning of the "code" (the letter-sound or the grapheme-phoneme relation) on which the English language is based. However, a few suggested procedures are also indicated below.

1. The boys and girls are given cards on each of which is written a letter of the alphabet. As the teacher names a letter, the pupils hold up the card on which it is written.
2. As the teacher or a pupil points to a letter of the alphabet written on the chalkboard, a pupil gives the name of the letter.
3. The children write the letter of the alphabet with which the name of the word representing an illustrated object begins. For example, the pupils write the letter *b* as the beginning letter of the word for a picture of a boy.

Developing Auditory and Visual Discrimination

Among the most important prerequisites for successful reading are the ability to differentiate between sounds of words and letters and the ability to see the differences between written words and between letters. Since improvement in making such discriminations can be brought about through training, suggestions for their development are given in the following pages.

AUDITORY DISCRIMINATION   In helping children to discriminate between sounds they hear, teachers should remember that:

1. *There is great variation among first-grade children in powers of auditory discrimination.* The difference is not necessarily due to degrees of auditory acuity. Two children, for example, may plainly hear the words *weather* and *whether*, but only one may be able to note the difference in the sound.

2. *Instruction in auditory discrimination should take individual differences into account.* Many children will have developed the needed skill in auditory discrimination before they first come to school. For them the exercises in discrimination would be wasteful and stupid.

On the other hand, the child who cannot tell whether *dog* and *cat* begin with the same sound or with different sounds needs help in learning to discriminate between sounds that are quite unlike. The same is true of those children who have little difficulty in distinguishing sounds at the beginning of words but have trouble with sounds at the end of words.

   3.   *Instruction in auditory discrimination should be an integral part of the regular classroom activities.* As children take part in the usual classroom activities, like playing with their toys or pets, their attention can be drawn to the differences in sounds. When, for example, a child fails to distinguish between *car* and *cars,* the teacher may try to help him detect the difference. At times there is value in providing separate exercises in noting which pairs of words are alike and which different, as in the case of *car* and *cars* and *car* and *car.* Or a child may be asked to supply the last word of the second line of a jingle in order to make it rhyme with the first line.

   Some of the ways in which auditory discrimination can be developed during the prereading period consist of having the pupils do the following:

1.   Giving orally words beginning with the same sound with which another word begins. The teacher may write on the board the words named by the pupils, even though the pupils cannot read them.
2.   Drawing a circle around each picture in a group, the name of which begins with a specified sound.
3.   Telling whether a sound that the teacher specifies is found at the beginning, near the middle, or at the end of each of a group of words named by the teacher.
4.   Telling which pairs of words named by the teacher, like *mother, man* or *little, ball,* begin with the same sound.
5.   Naming the word in a list given by the teacher, like *mother, man, many, few, market,* that does not begin with the same sound as the others.
6.   Telling which pairs of words given by the teacher end in the same sound, like *walks, sings* or *runs, play.*
7.   Naming the word in a list, like *at, talk, fit, get,* that does not end with the same sound as the others.
8.   Telling which pairs or words, like *rat, sat* or *bat, sit,* are rhyming words.
9.   Telling which word in a list does not rhyme, as in *cat, bat, sat, sit.*
10.   Naming rhyming words.
11.   Telling which pairs of sounds, like *m, n* or *m, m,* are alike.
12.   Making up rhymes.
13.   Playing the game, "I spy." In this game, pupils guess what object a child refers to in a statement like "I spy something that begins with the same sound as *Mary,*" or "I spy something that ends with the same sound as *took.*"

14. Naming the objects in a picture that begin with the same sound as a word that is named by the teacher.
15. Naming the objects in a picture that rhyme with a word that is named by the teacher.
16. Supplying the last word for a two-line jingle of which the teacher gives all but the last word. The pupils would name the words that rhyme with the last word of the first line.

VISUAL DISCRIMINATION   In planning procedures for the development of visual discrimination during the prereading period, certain general observations should be kept in mind: (1) Some beginning first-grade pupils do not have enough skill in visual discrimination to undertake the reading task with ease. (2) Instruction should be adapted to individual differences. (3) So far as possible, skill in visual discrimination should be furthered in connection with meaningful classroom activities. (4) Not all deficiencies in visual discrimination need to be removed before reading instruction is begun. As the child learns to read, opportunities for making finer discriminations will present themselves.

Some suggestions for methods of providing growth in the ability to distinguish between word forms and letter forms during the prereading period are:

1. Asking the pupils to find the word in a written series, like *big, boy, big, big, big,* which is unlike the other words.
2. Asking the pupils to draw a line under each word in a written series, like the following, which is the same as the first word in a row:

    man   mother   man   man   man.

    At first, practice should be given in differentiating between words that are decidedly different in appearance, like *man* and *mother*. Later, the pupil should be asked to discriminate between words almost alike in appearance, like *man* and *men*.
3. After pupils have dictated to the teacher a record of some experience they have had, like taking care of a pet, asking one child to draw a line under all the words in the story that begin with the same letter as a word indicated by the teacher.
4. Listing two parallel columns of words, in which the same words are used but in a different order. The pupils may draw lines connecting the like words in the two columns.
5. Asking the pupils to cross out a given word, like *dog,* each time that it occurs in a group of sentences in which the word is used several times.
6. Having the pupils match tagboard cards, on which single words are written, with words as they are written on the board.
7. Having the pupils draw a circle around a word in a list on the board that is the same as a word on a card shown to the class.

8. Having the children find on a chart all the names of pupils in the room that begin with a specified letter.
9. Having the pupils arrange cards in groups that end with the same letter. The words on the cards might be sing, jump, running, pup, duck, thing, black, dog, back, rug.
10. Asking the boys and girls to draw a line under the words in a list that contain a given combination of letters such as in, in listings such as the following: tin, tan, it, inside, win.
11. Asking the pupils to match word cards with words in a cardholder or on the chalkboard.
12. Having the pupils find the part of a longer word that is like a shorter word. For example, the boys and girls might be shown, on the chalkboard the words walk and walking and be asked to underline in the second word the part that is like the first.

      walk   walking

13. Helping the boys and girls judge the length and shape of words by means of configuration clues as lines are drawn around each of two words that have been written on the chalkboard. The pupils could then tell whether the outline of the two words is alike or different. For example, the "boxes" drawn around the words run and see would be similar, but those drawn around the words sing and play would be different.

      run   see   sing   play

Improving the Ability To Remember

The ability to remember plays an important role in reading. One cause of inadequate retention in reading is found in poor habits of attentiveness. A child who does not pay careful attention to what is going on cannot be expected to remember. The teacher can attack this problem by assisting boys and girls to become more attentive. Some ways in which children can be helped to attend better, and therefore to remember better, have been discussed earlier in this chapter under the related topic, "Improving Listening." Here are some additional suggestions for increasing a pupil's memory span:

1. Making the work interesting enough so that the pupil will have reason to want to pay attention.
2. Making sure that the work is on the level of the pupil.
3. Varying the activities frequently enough so that the child's power of attention will not be overtaxed. At the same time children should be helped to develop an ever longer span of attention.

4. Developing in pupils the desire to remain with an activity until it is completed, unless there is good reason not to do so.
5. Keeping in the room reasonable orderliness conducive to good attention.
6. Requiring pupils to keep to the topic of discussion.
7. Keeping each child responsible for remembering the answer to a question that he asked a community helper on a trip to the post office or police station or fire department.

REMEMBERING A SEQUENCE OF IDEAS   To help the boys and girls to remember a sequence of ideas encountered in reading or listening, the teacher may wish to follow some of these suggestions:

1. After the teacher or a pupil has told a story, the teacher may ask such questions as, "What was the first thing Nancy did when she saw that her dog had followed her?" "What did she do next?"
2. After the teacher has given directions for a simple experiment, like showing that plants need light, she may ask the pupils, "What is the first thing we need to do?" and "What do we need to do next?" After the experiment has been completed, the pupils may be asked to enumerate the steps that were followed.
3. Retelling stories can be a helpful means of developing the ability to remember a sequence of ideas. The pupil should relate the incidents in the correct order.
4. The boys and girls, with the assistance of the teacher, might build a topical outline for the dramatizing of a story. The pupils could decide upon the events to be included in the dramatization and the teacher lists these on the chalkboard. They could then arrange these events in logical sequence.
5. The teacher might place on a flannel board, in mixed-up order, a series of pictures illustrating a story known to the boys and girls and then ask the pupils to rearrange the pictures in correct order.
6. The group may make a "movie" either to illustrate a story that the teacher has told or read to them or to portray activities in which they have engaged. Such an activity furnishes excellent practice in remembering events in sequence and cultivates other abilities important in reading, such as critical thinking, good work habits, skill in following directions, and ability to work with others.

A "movie" theater can be simply constructed. A large cardboard box can be used as the stage. An opening can be cut into one side of the box, possibly twelve inches high and eighteen inches wide, through which the "movie" is viewed. The roller can be two ends of broom handles to which the "movie" roll is attached. Each of the rollers can be inserted into the "theater" through two holes, one cut at the top and the other at the bottom of the box near the front corners of the "theater." Flaps of the box at the two sides of the "theater" (as it stands with the "stage" side to the front) through which the "movie" is put into it can be closed by means of a string at each opening tied around two brass fasteners. The "theater," when placed on a table, will need to project far enough over the edge so that the bottom parts of the rollers are free of the table.

Steps in planning a "movie" on a story told to the class may be these:

1. Discussing the story.
2. Deciding to make a "movie" of the story.
3. Retelling the story.
4. Deciding on pictures to include.
5. Working out a sequence of the pictures to be drawn.
6. Assigning pictures to be drawn.
7. Drawing the pictures.
8. Deciding on captions or longer explanations of the pictures to be written for the "movie" by the teacher.
9. Arranging the pictures and the writing in the proper sequence.
10. Fastening the pictures to a roll.
11. Practicing telling the story of the "movie."

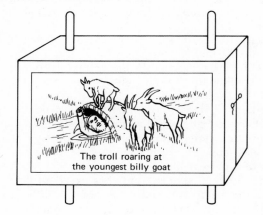

The troll roaring at
the youngest billy goat

If the story of "The Three Billy Goats Gruff" were made into a "movie," these are pictures that might be drawn: (1) three billy goats at the side of the hill, (2) the green hill that they saw in the distance, (3) the stream they would have to cross, (4) the bridge they would have to cross, (5) the ugly troll who lived under the bridge, (6) the youngest billy goat starting to cross the bridge, (7) the troll roaring at the youngest billy goat, (8) the youngest billy goat talking with the troll, (9) the youngest billy goat feeding on the hillside, (10) the second billy goat starting across the bridge, (11) the troll roaring at the second billy goat, (12) the second billy goat talking with the troll, (13) the second billy goat going across the bridge, (14) the first and the second billy goats feeding on the hillside, (15) the big billy goat starting across the bridge, (16) the troll roaring at the big billy goat, (17) the big billy goat talking with the troll, (18) the fight between the big billy goat and the troll, (19) the end of the troll, (20) the big billy goat going across the bridge, and (21) the three billy goats feeding on the hillside.

If there are fewer pupils than pictures to be drawn, some children could draw two. If the number of pictures is less than the number of pupils, two children could each draw a picture on the same topic. In that case one of the pictures, not necessarily the better, could be used in the "movie" and the other displayed with pride elsewhere, possibly as part of a big book or on the bulletin board.

FOLLOWING DIRECTIONS   The ability to follow directions involves considerable skill in remembering. So many directions are given to children in school that, as a rule, no special exercises are needed for practice in this skill. Usually the problem is to reduce rather than increase the number of teacher mandates. To facilitate learning, the teacher's directions should be clear. Although at first the directions should be very simple, they should become more complex as the pupils develop. At times the teacher may need to demonstrate how to follow a rather involved set of directions. At other times she can help pupils by having the class follow directions together.

Stimulating Growth in Critical Thinking

There are several methods of stimulating the power of critical thinking among children. The teacher can help the pupils increase in ability to think critically by means of the questions she asks when she reads or tells stories to them. For example, as she reads the story *Millions of Cats* by Wanda Gág, she may ask, "What do you think the little old woman will say when the little old man comes home not with one cat, but with millions of cats?" Or after she has told "The Tale of Peter Rabbit," she may ask, "Why was Peter Rabbit happy at the end of the story even though his mother had punished him?" Questions about what will happen next force children to think as they listen. Pantomine or dramatization of stories also calls for certain kinds of critical thinking, as does interpretation of a story by drawing pictures. The teacher can further encourage critical thinking by giving the boys and girls a part in planning activities, in deciding upon the better course of action in a given situation, and in determining why some of their actions were wise or unwise.

One excellent opportunity for the development of the power to think is provided by the "planning period," which is part of the daily program in some primary grade rooms. During this period, which is usually at the beginning of the school day, the pupils, with the direction and guidance of the teacher, make plans for the day. The role of the teacher in planning will vary, depending upon the ability of the pupils to map out a good schedule, the complexity of the planning, and other factors. Always, however, without seeming authoritarian, the teacher maintains her role as a leader responsible in major part for the planning of the day's adventures.

The teacher may write on the board the suggestions of the class along with her own. Often the teacher starts the planning period by inquiring what items of business were not completed during the preceding day or days. Decision can then be reached as to what should be on the agenda for the day. Other suggestions can be made and discussed. The teacher may want to make a chart for a check list of the schedule for the day. Such a chart might contain items like these:

What Should We Do Today?

1.	Listen to a story.	7.	Look at picture books.
2.	Tell stories.	8.	Make things.
3.	Play house.	9.	Sing.
4.	Draw or paint.	10.	Rest.
5.	Write.	11.	Have lunch.
6.	Play games.	12.	Go to the washroom.

At first, as each item is considered the teacher will usually need to read it, but before long some of the children will be able to read at least some of the items orally to the rest of the group. As the schedule for the day is planned, the teacher may find it best to have more specificity in the items than the check list offers. For example, instead of stating one point of business for the day as "Play games," it may be stated, "Learn a new game and play some we know."

After the teacher thinks a justifiable listing has been completed, she and the pupils can decide on the sequence or the time of day when each activity shall take place. Frequently it will be found that too many activities have been planned.

The planning period offers a variety of ways by which the children can develop readiness for reading. Some of these are: noting the left-to-right and top-to-bottom sequence in reading; being aware of the fact that reading helps one know what to do next; learning to read some words that are used often in a written list; developing self-expression; and listening to others.

Increasing Skill in Handling Books

Skill in handling books, another ability to which attention should be given in the prereading period, can be developed in the following ways through precept and practice:

1. The teacher should handle all books with care.
2. The teacher may help the boys and girls draw up a list of specifications for taking care of books, such as:
   a. Have clean hands when you handle a book.
   b. Do not fold the pages of a book.
   c. Do not tear the pages of books.
   d. Do not put pencils or other objects in a book.
   e. Do not write in a book.
   f. Turn the pages of a book carefully.
3. The pupils may demonstrate proper ways of holding books.
4. The desirability of arranging books neatly on shelves and on the library table may be discussed and demonstrated.
5. Responsibility for care of books can be developed by rotating appointments of pupils serving as librarians.
6. The teacher might make a little bookman, whose body is in the shape of a book, who at times "speaks" to the boys and girls about how he likes to be treated.
7. Two pupils might present a short skit in which one child takes the part of a well-handled book and the other of a poorly-handled one. The two characters might tell how people treat them.
8. The teacher might take the class to a room in a library where books are being mended. An explanation of the process in very simple terms, with emphasis on the length of time it takes to mend books and the skill required to do it well may, it is hoped, encourage the boys and girls to take good care of books.

Orienting to Left-to-Right and and Top-to-Bottom Sequence

Some children entering first grade require help in observing a left-to-right and top-to-bottom sequence in reading pictures or print. Some need to be shown which is their right and which is their left hand. Others, who do know left from right, have not yet discovered that reading, in English, proceeds from left to right and from top to bottom.

Special practice in left-to-right and top-to-bottom reading may sometimes be needed.

The following are suggestions for helping children develop this directional orientation to reading:

1. As the teacher reads a book to the class, she can point out where she starts reading and in what direction she progresses.
2. As the teacher or children reread from charts or the chalkboard stories that have been dictated, the teacher can run her hand rhythmically under the lines. Or she can ask a pupil to point to the word with which she should begin reading. In time, a pupil can sweep his hands below the line he is reading from a chart or from the chalkboard. Care must be taken in the latter case that word pointing with consequent "word calling" does not result.
3. At times, when the teacher writes on large sheets of paper or on the board, she can ask the pupils where she should begin writing and in what direction she should proceed.
4. As some pupils are placing a picture story on a flannel board, they should be guided to arrange the pictures from left to right in each row and from top to bottom by rows.
5. To emphasize the left-to-right order, boys and girls could be shown a series of possibly three pictures illustrating different actions, with the pictures not in the sequence of the activity illustrated. For example, the pictures might illustrate a boy leaving his home. The first one might show him outside the door of his home, the second running when he is already a distance from home, and the third running when he is farther from his home. The pupils could then be asked to arrange the pictures in order in a left-to-right sequence on a chalkboard tray.

Developing and Maintaining Interest in Reading

The importance of access to an abundance of interesting reading materials has already been stressed in this book. Other ways in which the teacher can try to interest the children in books are taking them to the school or public library where they can browse among the books and where, probably, the librarian will be willing to tell them a story; inviting one or more children from a second or third grade to entertain the first grade by reading an interesting story to them; taking boys and girls to other rooms in the elementary school in which they can see books being used for various purposes; reading stories and informational material to the class.

The sharing period, discussed earlier in this chapter, can serve to interest children in reading. They can be encouraged to show and talk about books they like. Some of these may be picture books for which the child reporting makes up the story. Or the books may contain a simple text, which someone has read beforehand to the pupil reporting.

　　Use of little booklets containing children's stories, written by the teacher at the dictation of the pupils, gives added incentive to learning to read. In these booklets may be recorded reports planned by the class as a whole on an activity in which they have engaged, such as a trip to a farm. Or the material may consist of individual accounts about each child—for example, reports on the work of each child's father. Some teachers, too, for recording in these books, make up stories in which the vocabulary is well controlled. Although making such a book is time-consuming, it is worthwhile in the long run, since the book can often be used not only once with a given group but also later on with classes of succeeding years.

　　Keeping records on charts of some of the experiences of the group, such as visiting the grocery store, can also stimulate interest in reading. How these charts can be constructed and utilized is explained below.

USING THE EXPERIENCE CHART IN THE PREREADING PERIOD

　　The term *experience chart* ordinarily refers to a written record of an experience a class has had, is having, or is intending to have. An experience chart is planned cooperatively by the pupils and the teacher and, in the primary grades, is usually recorded by the teacher. First-grade children who found pretty leaves may make an experience chart telling about their leaves, or those about to have a party may plan a chart to help remember points about the proposed party. Two examples of such charts follow:

LEAVES
We found many pretty leaves.
We found them on our walk.
We found some red leaves.
Some of our leaves are brown.
Some of our leaves are yellow.

OUR PARTY
We will have a party.
We will have the party on Monday.
We will have it in the afternoon.
Mary and Susan will bring cookies.
We will drink milk.
We will play games.

Experience charts serve a variety of purposes. The teacher's objective in helping plan a chart may be primarily to give children an opportunity to learn to express themselves well. Sometimes they are used chiefly to provide an opportunity for cooperative planning. Such charts are called language charts. Experience charts that are used primarily for reading purposes, either to get the child more nearly ready for beginning reading or to supplement the reading experiences that he has already had, are known as reading charts. Various purposes can, however, be served by the same chart. As the pupils construct and use a reading experience chart, they can also improve their expression and learn to plan cooperatively. The differentiation between the two kinds is made because in the so-called language experience chart it is not as important to restrict the vocabulary as in the chart that serves primarily as a prereading or reading experience. The following discussion of experience charts refers essentially to those that help in reading, either in the prereading period or later.

Many children profit from reading charts when they begin first grade. The exceptions are those children who have had a rich background of experience and are therefore ready to do the simple reading provided in preprimers without the aid of reading charts. Their work with experience charts can be largely limited to language charts, in which reading is not the primary objective.

Experience charts are frequently recorded on large pieces of paper, often 24 by 36 inches or 18 by 24 inches. They can, however, be made on smaller sheets, as they often are when they are designed for individual use rather than for group purposes. If the chart is to be preserved for a considerable time, it is often made on tagboard or mounting board. A record that is to be used for only a short time may well be kept on less expensive paper, like newsprint. Sometimes the charts are assembled, punched at the top, fastened by rings, and attached to a chart holder, which often is on a tripod base. Upon the tripod there is frequently an adjustable metal pole, across the top of which is a crossbar which holds the chart. Some experience records are kept in large notebooks, often made of butcher paper, probably 24 by 36 inches. The records kept in a notebook usually are on one theme, such as "Our Pets" or "Our Schoolroom" or "The First-Grade Boys and Girls."

Steps in Making and Using Experience Charts

Experience charts are used in a variety of ways during the prereading period. Outlined below are steps similar to those that many teachers follow when detailed study of the chart is done as a prereading exercise. The chart is set up for two successive school days, although a shorter or longer time may be devoted to work on it. In considering these steps, the reader must bear in mind that many stories on charts or on the chalkboard have usually been made and utilized in a class before any one chart is given the detailed study that is here described.

First Day

1.   The boys and girls participate in an interesting and significant experience.

2.   The children discuss the experience.

3.   The pupils, with the help of the teacher, plan the title, general content, and the exact sentences for the chart as the teacher does the writing on the board.

4.   The chart as a whole is read first by the teacher, then by the pupils and the teacher together, and finally by the boys and girls alone.

Second Day

5.   Before class the teacher has copied onto chart paper the writing for the experience chart that she had put on the board the preceding day. The teacher has also copied on separate strips of tagboard each of the lines of the chart, so that they can be matched later with the writing on the chart. These are placed on the chalk tray or in a word-card holder. On word cards made of tagboard the teacher has also written a few of the words, on which she plans to give special practice.

6.   The new chart is then read by the teacher and pupils together.

7.   The teacher reads sentences for the pupils to find, and they point to each one as they read it.

8.   After the teacher has read the sentences out of the regular order, the pupils match the sentence strips with the sentences on the chart and read them.

9.   As the teacher shows the boys and girls each of the several word cards, containing those words on which she thinks it is important to provide practice, she pronounces the word and has the pupils say it after her. A pupil then matches the word on the card with the same word on the chart. Further practice on the words can be given if before class the teacher writes these words on the board. In that case the pupils can name the words as the teacher points to them.

10.   Review of words used in the chart that the boys and girls have studied earlier can then be made.

11.   Before the period is over one or more pupils can read the chart alone.

Description of Some of the Steps in Making and Using Experience Charts

Since some of the steps already outlined need no further explanation, they are not included in the comments that follow.

1. *Motivation for making a chart.* After the pupils have engaged in an experience and have discussed it, there are many ways in which the teacher can interest the pupils in making, and then reading, an experience chart. The teacher may suggest to the pupils that they make a chart so that visitors coming into the room can read, or have read to them, what the class has done. Or the boys and girls may make one so that they can go to other rooms to read the chart to the children.

2. *Planning the chart.* In planning the chart, the teacher should keep in mind that: (a) Care needs to be taken that many, preferably all, of the children take part in the planning. (b) The teacher can, by questioning, help the pupils suggest significant items. (c) She can be of assistance in helping formulate sentences that are correct in structure. (d) She can help decide on the sequence. (e) She can guide the work so that the vocabulary used in the chart is fairly simple. She can also see to it that some words, on which she wants children to have practice, are used more than once and that appropriate "review words" also appear in the text. (f) She can give the pupils help in vocabulary building by asking for more colorful or more descriptive words to be substituted for given ones. (g) After the first draft is written, she can assist the children in revising the sentences so that they may create a more unified composition.

3. *Constructing the chart.* Care should be taken to make the manuscript writing as nearly perfect as possible in the time available. Neatness, letter form, alignment, size, slant, and spacing between letters, between words, and between lines should receive adequate attention. If a picture is needed, it can be supplied by the teacher or a pupil or taken from a discarded publication.

4. *Making the sentence strips and the word cards.* The precautions given in connection with the writing of the chart should also be observed in the making of sentence strips and word cards. Teachers find it desirable to keep sentence strips of the same width, often about four inches wide, for uniformity when they are used with other cards and for ease in filing. For the same reasons some teachers also cut most of the word cards of the same length, approximately ten inches. Words that cannot be written without crowding on this size of paper are written on longer cards.

Usually no more than three or four "new words," for special study, should be included on one chart. These should be selected on the basis of their likely usefulness to the children. Some teachers prefer to choose words from the pupils' first reading books.

5. *Follow-up activities.* In addition to the culminating activity, already suggested, of reading the chart to visitors or pupils in other rooms, the teacher may make copies available to the children. She may leave space near each of the words that can be illustrated, so that the pupils can draw a picture that goes with the word; for example, opposite the word *leaves,* the pupils may draw a picture of leaves. This activity may help the children recall the word more easily later. The children can make the sheets into a booklet and draw an appropriate picture for the cover. After a child has learned to "read" the chart, he may take his booklet home and read it to his parents.

Illustration of Work on an Experience Chart

The following is an imaginary description of possible procedures in the development of an experience chart.

Early in the year, after the first-grade boys and girls had been on a listening walk, they made an experience chart, on which were recorded some of the sounds they heard while on the walk. At that time the teacher suggested that they might want to make a chart of all especially interesting activities in which they would take part during the year. The idea received an enthusiastic reception. The teacher pointed out that such charts could help them remember what they had done during the school year. She also suggested visitors might like to read them. Consequently, the day after the Halloween party, it was easy to interest the boys and girls in making a chart reporting on it.

The teacher helped the boys and girls plan the report for the chart. When "Our Party" was suggested as the title, she asked if anyone could think of a title that would tell what kind of party it was. When a boy responded by suggesting "Our Halloween Party," she wrote the title on the chalkboard. Then the pupils discussed some of the points they wanted to include in the report. Comments such as these were made:

> We will want to tell that we had a Halloween party.
> We should tell that we had candy.
> We want to tell that we were dressed up.

As the pupils suggested the wording of the sentences, the teacher helped them with sentence structure. Furthermore, she watched the vocabulary used on the chart so that some of the "new words" were repeated frequently enough to assure the pupils' increased likelihood of learning them. She also guided the children so that their thoughts were recorded in logical sequence. Thus the following sentences, which the teacher wrote on the chalkboard, evolved:

OUR HALLOWEEN PARTY

We had a Halloween party.
We had the party in our room.
We played games at our party.
We had candy at our party.
It was Halloween candy.
We also had cookies.
We wore Halloween costumes.

The, a, at, and *in* were words used on the chart that the children had previously acquired as part of their reading vocabulary. "New words," which the teacher planned to teach in connection with the work on this chart, were *we, had, our,* and *Halloween.* These words, excepting *Halloween,* were found in the first-grade reading books that the children would later be reading.

Next followed practice in "reading" the chart. First the teacher read it alone. Then she and the pupils read it together.

For an illustration on the chart several suggestions came from the children. Someone recommended cutting a picture of a goblin out of an old magazine. Another pupil suggested that a picture of a goblin be cut freehand. Still another child thought that drawing a picture would be better. After further discussion it was agreed that each pupil should cut out of construction paper, freehand, a picture of something that would go well with the chart. It was also agreed that each pupil could then decorate his cut-out as he saw fit. A committee, it was decided, was then to select one for the chart that the teacher agreed to have ready by the following day.

The next day the teacher brought to class with her the chart, separate strips of tagboard on which were written the title and each of the sentences used on the chart, and cards on which the "new words" *we, had, our,* and *Halloween* and the "review words" *the, a, at,* and *in* were written.

Practice was then given in reading the new materials. First, the teacher alone read the chart as she moved her hand across each line of writing. After the pupils had read it twice in concert, several children read it alone. Thereupon the pupils matched the sentence strips with the chart, by holding each strip next to the corresponding sentence on the chart and reading it. As the teacher read a sentence out of its normal order in the story, a pupil found the correct strip and read it orally.

To give practice on the words on the cards, the teacher began by asking someone to find the word *our* in the title. Then the pupils pronounced the word *our* as the teacher showed the class the word card for it and as she placed it in a card holder. A pupil pointed to the word *our* as it appeared in some of the sentences of the report and pronounced it. In a similar manner the teacher presented the words *we* and *Halloween*. When she introduced the word *had,* before telling the pupils the word, she wrote *house* and *had* on the chalkboard, explaining that the "new word" began with the same sound as the word *house,* which the class had already learned to read. After the class had identified the *h* sound in *house,* the teacher pronounced the word *had* and asked the pupils to note that both of these words began with the *h* sound. Next, the pupils named other words beginning with the same sound, such as *hat, home,* and *Harry,* which the teacher wrote on the chalkboard. As the teacher showed the cards for the "review words" *the, a, at,* and *in,* the pupil named them and found them on the chart. The word cards containing the new words and the review words were then mixed, and pupils, individually, named them as the teacher showed the cards. Before the period was over several children again "read" the chart.

For follow-up work, on the third day of the lesson the teacher brought to class duplicated copies of the chart, one for each child, on paper 8½ by 11 inches. She also had sheets of paper of the same size on which were the four "new words" *we, had, our* and *Halloween.* Above the word *Halloween* space was provided in which the pupils then drew illustrations of things that might suggest Halloween. The teacher also distributed to each boy and girl a piece of construction paper on which the pupils could paste the freehand drawings they had cut out of paper two days before. Thereupon the pupils made all the sheets into booklets, fastening them with brass fasteners. Several children then read the story orally. The rule was made that, as soon as a child could read the story without error, he could give his booklet to his parents and read it to them. The boys and girls who did not have an opportunity to read the booklet orally on that day were given a chance to do so within the next few days, either during class time or at other times. When need for additional practice was indicated, it was provided.

Arguments for and against the Use of Experience Charts

There is disagreement concerning the use of experience charts. Most of the controversy centers on the question, "To what extent should experience charts be used in first-grade reading?"

Especially controversial is the question as to whether they should be used as substitutes for the commercial reading readiness books.

Some of the arguments given for the use of experience charts as reading readiness materials are these: (1) The valuable experiences that boys and girls get can be made more meaningful by basing charts on them. (2) Reading about their own experiences is more interesting to them than using reading readiness books. (3) The relation between reading and two other language arts, talking and writing, is made evident to the boys and girls. (4) The children acquire a reading vocabulary, the value of which they easily recognize.

Persons who do not favor the extensive use of experience charts try to refute the arguments given for their frequent use by claiming that: (1) The valuable experiences that boys and girls get will enrich their background of information and understanding without their necessarily writing a chart about the experiences. (2) Reading one's own story is not as interesting, in some cases, as reading the published prereading materials. (3) The relation between reading and the other language arts can be made evident to the boys and girls without using experience charts extensively. (4) The pupils are able to recognize the value of the reading vocabulary they acquire when reading well-graded and well-written reading readiness books.

Among the most significant arguments advanced against extensive use of experience charts as reading materials is that the words that appear in the charts are not as well selected as those that are found in published reading readiness books. Writers of textbooks in reading for the primary grades have spent much time and energy in attempts to secure a suitable vocabulary. An effort is made by them to use words that pupils will meet frequently in other reading, to introduce only a few new words in each selection, and to give systematic review of words learned, by providing for repetition in the reading, at spaced intervals, both in the book in which the word is presented and in later books in the series. Those favoring the use of experience charts claim that the teacher can help in selecting words for a chart so that there will be included those that the children will be likely to encounter in other reading. However, if the teacher does much of the selecting of the words for a chart, it is evidently the teacher's, rather than the pupils', account.

Another argument against extensive use of experience charts as reading material in the first grade is that boys and girls do not get practice of the type needed for independent reading later on. Reading should be, it is argued by persons opposed to the wide use of reading experience charts, a process of thought getting, not a process of "reading" what one already knows—as is the case in experience charts when used as outlined on pages 86–91. Furthermore, criticism is directed at the fact that there is memorization of what is written on the chart, not reading in the true sense of the word.

A point the teacher must consider when deciding upon the number of experience charts to use is the fact that to make many charts is very time-consuming.

No one formula can be given for the proportionate amount of emphasis that should be placed on experience' charts. There will, in many classes, be some boys and girls who will need few, if any, reading experiences with charts or with published reading readiness materials before they begin regular book reading. With others it will be advantageous to use either or both types. What the proportion of charts and reading readiness books should be with those children for whom either type or both are indicated will vary with the skill of the teacher, the books available, and the needs of these pupils.

These, then, are some of the ways in which the first-grade teacher can help boys and girls become ready for the great adventure of the school, learning to read.

FOR FURTHER STUDY

Barbe, Walter B., *Teaching Reading.* New York: Oxford University Press, 1965. Chapter 3, "Getting Ready for Reading," pp. 75–97.

Burton, William E., *Reading in Child Development.* Indianapolis, Ind.: The Bobbs-Merrill Company, Inc., 1958. "The Importance of Readiness for Reading," pp. 166–208.

Dechant, Emerald V., *Improving the Teaching of Reading.* Englewood Cliffs, N.J.: Prentice-Hall, Inc., 1964. Chapter 7, "Developing Reading Readiness," pp. 127–168.

DeHirsch, Katrina, Jeannette Jansky, and William S. Langford, *Predicting Reading Failure: A Preliminary Study.* New York: Harper & Row, Publishers, Inc., 1966.

Durkin, Dolores, *Children Who Read Early.* New York: Teachers College Press, Columbia University, 1966. Pages xiv–174.

Gans, Roma, *Common Sense in Reading.* Indianapolis, Ind.: The Bobbs-Merrill Company, Inc., 1963. Chapter 3, "Beginning To Be a Reader at Home," pp. 38–53; Chapter 4, "How Kindergarten Helps the Beginning Reader," pp. 54–70.

Harris, Albert J., *Readings on Reading Instruction.* New York: David McKay Company, Inc., 1963. Part III, "Reading Readiness," pp. 58–90.

Herrick, Vergil E., and Marcella Nerbovig, *Using Experience Charts with Children*. Columbus, Ohio: Charles E. Merrill Books, 1964.

Ilg, Frances L., and Louise Bates Ames, *School Readiness: Behavior Tests Used at the Gesell Institute*. New York: Harper & Row, Publishers, Inc., 1965.

McKim, Margaret G., and Helen Caskey, *Guiding Growth in Reading*. New York: Crowell-Collier and Macmillan, Inc., 1963. Chapter 3, "What Makes for Success in Beginning Reading," pp. 31–63; Chapter 4, "Providing Pre-Reading Experiences," pp. 64–97.

Monroe, Marion, and Bernice Rogers, *Foundations of Reading: Informal Pre-Reading Procedures*. Chicago: Scott, Foresman and Company, 1964. Chapter 1, "Where Reading Begins," pp. 2–23; Chapter 2, "Teacher Meets Pupil," pp. 24–48; Chapter 3, "Pupil Meets Print," pp. 50–63; Chapter 8, "Organizing for Action," pp. 180–208.

Morrison, Ida E., *Teaching Reading in the Elementary School*. New York: The Ronald Press Company, 1968. Chapter 3, "Analyzing Reading Readiness," pp. 53–81.

Spache, George D. and Evelyn B., *Reading in the Elementary School*. Boston: Allyn and Bacon, Inc., 1969. Chapter 7, "Readiness Training," pp. 189–233; Chapter 8, "The Combined Program for Primary Grades."

QUESTIONS FOR THOUGHT AND DISCUSSION

1. What unfortunate consequences are probable if the concept of reading readiness is not accepted and the formal teaching of reading is begun with all children upon their entrance to school?
2. Some writers have pointed out that just what constitutes readiness for reading depends to a degree on what the program in any given school is. Thus it is believed that a child may be ready for the materials and methods used in one school but not nearly so ready for the program found in another school. How does a teacher deal with the problem of the pupil who has been caught, through no fault of his own, in such a predicament?
3. A mental test may give some indication of a child's probable success in beginning reading. In general, it will not give the teacher the specific suggestions for methods of work with the individual which she may get from a readiness test. If you were asked to devise some sort of mental test or reading readiness test, how would you start?
4. Some schools use reading readiness tests instead of mental tests to help teachers place first-grade pupils in the group where they will make most progress. Wherever possible a combination of both a reading readiness test and an intelligence test is likely to produce better results. Some would argue that the observation of behavior by the skilled teacher is more important than either a readiness test or a mental test at the beginning stages of reading. What is your opinion?

5. No skill in education is more fundamental than reading. The issue arises as to when organized instruction in reading should begin. Because systematic teaching of reading is usually started in the first grade, the issue may be stated as follows: *What should be done with reading in the kindergarten? At home?* How would you answer that question?
6. It is not always realized by younger and less experienced teachers that children do not necessarily learn what the teacher intends. As a child acquaints himself with a fact, a skill, or an idea, he may at the same time modify his goals, his values, or his attitudes. Would you prefer to defend or attack this statement? How?
7. In the book *Predicting Reading Failure* by DeHirsch et al., the authors attempt to develop diagnostic criteria of future failure at early ages. What do you regard as some of the criteria that would help teachers identify at kindergarten level "high-risk" children—those in danger of failing when they are exposed to formal education?
8. Educators would like to try to find out why a sizable number of first- and second-grade children dislike school. This information can probably often best be secured from parents, since a child does not necessarily reveal his dislike at school. What kinds of questions should such investigators pose to parents?
9. In the middle 1960s the Educational Policies Commission proposed that school extend downward to the age of four, but, in so doing, the commission did not intend a simple downward extension of, or preparation for, the program now offered in most first grades. The commission stated:

> We envision a program uniquely adapted to children of ages four and five; the program for six-year-olds would be altered to take into account the earlier schooling of the children, rather than vice versa. The program suitable for four- and five-year-olds differs in basic ways from the traditional first grade, for it is not focused on reading, writing, and arithmetic, and it need not be an all-day program.

What kind of program do you think the commission might have had in mind when it made its proposal?

CHAPTER 5A

Word Recognition

Reading involves much more than word recognition, although the ability to recognize recorded words is basic to the reading process. Without skill in associating word forms as given in writing with word sounds and meanings, no one can be an effective reader. Persons in the field of reading accept without question that this ability to thus recognize words is essential to the development of maturity in reading. On this point there is no argument. There are, however, many points of controversy concerning how word recognition should best be taught.

THE BASIC ISSUE

The current debate among those in the reading field primarily focuses on the question of how word recognition should be taught in beginning reading instruction. The issue concerns whether the emphasis in the initial stages of reading instruction should be on learning the sounds represented by the written letters or whether, without much or any attention to the letter-sound relation, the effort should be concentrated on helping pupils to acquire the meaning of the written message.

Clarification of Terms

The terms frequently applied to the two approaches to teaching word recognition are the *code approach* and the *meaning approach.* The code approach emphasizes the need of the child in beginning reading instruction to learn the sounds represented by each letter or combination of letters. It is so named because the aim of the teacher employing the method is to help the learner acquire facility in the use of the code of the letter-sound relation. The meaning approach, on the other hand, places major emphasis on the meaning of what is read and gives little, if any, attention to developing in pupils skill in recognizing relations between the letters and the sounds they represent. This approach is also known as the *whole word approach.* There are also various combinations of the two approaches, with some placing almost equal emphasis on the deciphering of the code and the acquisition of meaning. In fact, in practice, rarely, if ever, is either the code or the meaning approach used to the exclusion of the other.

Many people, both professional and lay, would state that the issue in beginning reading instruction is the *phonic approach* versus the *"look-say" approach.* The phonic approach is a code approach, since it is by means of phonics that the child learns what sounds are represented by the letters of the alphabet. The "look-say" method refers to the practice by which the pupil, without learning to focus on the letters of the alphabet and their sounds, centers his attention on the whole word. Typically he looks at the word as someone tells it to him and then he repeats it ("says" it), hopefully so he will remember it from its appearance. When the "look-say" method is used, emphasis is usually placed on the meaning of what is read. Consequently, for practical purposes this approach is classified as a meaning approach. Thus the question of the phonic versus the "look-say" approach can be thought of as roughly paralleling that of the code versus the meaning approach.

Historical Perspective

In the history of reading instruction in the United States at times one approach and at times another has been the prevailing one. In Colonial times and throughout much of the nineteenth century and even into the twentieth, a code-deciphering approach to reading instruction was generally used. The child learned the names of the letters of the alphabet and the sounds they most commonly represented. Thereupon he combined sounds to make syllables and words of more than one syllable. Thus a synthetic phonic approach was used, in which the learner synthesized the sounds of a syllable or word as procedure in learning to recognize a word.

A strong reaction to the use of phonics, especially phonic

synthesis, then set in. The criticisms leveled against the phonic method were numerous. Important among them were the following: (1) The English language is not based on an easily acquired letter-sound relation, for some letters have more than one sound (for example, *c,* with its soft and hard sounds) and some sounds are represented by more than one letter or letter combination (for example, the sound of *s,* which is represented not only by the letter *s* but also frequently by the letter *c*). (2) Phonics when used as the initial approach to reading instruction tends to produce slow word-by-word readers. (3) Use of phonics as a beginning method places the emphasis on the mechanics of reading rather than on thought getting. (4) A phonic approach is likely to make learning to read an uninteresting experience.

Beginning about 1915 the whole-word method or sight method became popular. Some teachers advocated using a sentence method, in which an entire sentence was read to a child and then his attention drawn to some of the words that comprise it. Others advocated a story-method approach, with a very short story read to the pupil and subsequently his attention directed to some of the sentences and words comprising the story. The experience chart, which the pupils help make (described in Chapter 4B), has been used extensively as representative of the story method. The whole-word method, the sentence method, and even the story method, including the experience chart, became popular during the period when the progressive education movement was at its height in this country. In addition, the word method gained substantiation from research which was interpreted to indicate that since it was as easy, if not more so, to learn a whole word as a part of one, a meaning unit, the word, should be used as the basic element in beginning reading instruction. It was popularly suggested that the beginner should learn about fifty to seventy-five words by the sight method, with someone telling him each word, before beginning work on phonics. It was also recommended that when phonics was used it should be as phonic analysis rather than synthesis. In other words, instead of beginning with the sounds of the letters and combining them into syllables (synthesis), the learner should start with the word and from it derive the phonic elements that make it up. For example, when the child knew the word *mother* because he had been told the word, the teacher might through phonic analysis have him identify the sound with which the word begins and then ask him to name other words that begin with the same sound.

Proponents of the phonic method for beginning reading instruction have not been lacking at any time during the century.

However, little attention was paid to them by leaders in the field of elementary school education until the publication of *Why Johnny Can't Read.*[1] In this book, the word method was severely criticized and a phonic approach strongly advocated. Widely read and highly acclaimed by the public, Flesch's book was the target for much criticism by professional educators. It would seem, however, that in spite of the renunciation of the book by various professional persons, it had a significant effect on the teaching of reading. Undoubtedly it has been instrumental in causing phonics to be given greater attention in educational literature.

Another factor resulting in the more widespread use of phonics at the present time might well be the fact that in general the emphasis in American education, rightly or wrongly, in recent years has become more academically centered and less child centered. What a child learns in terms of subject matter has been stressed in many educational circles, to the regret of a large number of specialists in the area of child growth and development, rather than factors related to the pupil's emotional and social development.

During the last two decades, too, several widely publicized innovations in the teaching of reading, some of which are described briefly later in this chapter, fit in well with a phonic approach. Undoubtedly some of them have played their part in causing increased attention to be given to code deciphering as a method of beginning reading instruction.

Recent Studies

Although an exceedingly large amount of research has been done in the reading field, with much of it dealing with approaches to reading instruction, most of these studies have been rather piecemeal. The studies have typically been isolated ones made by individuals working independently without the financial backing for authoritative investigations in the field. Four studies that are an exception to this rule, however, are (1) *Learning To Read: A Report of a Conference of Reading Experts;*[2] (2) *The First R: The Harvard Report on Reading*

---

[1] Rudolph Flesch, *Why Johnny Can't Read and What You Can Do About It.* New York: Harper & Row, Publishers, Inc., 1955.

[2] *Learning To Read: A Report of a Conference of Reading Experts.* Foreword by James B. Conant. Princeton, N.J.: Educational Testing Service, 1962.

in Elementary Schools;[3] (3) *The Final Report: Project No. X-001;*[4] and
(4) *Learning to Read: The Great Debate* by Jeanne Chall.[5]

LEARNING TO READ: A REPORT OF A CONFERENCE
OF READING EXPERTS   So great was the general concern as to the
place of phonics instruction that Dr. James B. Conant, who was engaged
in a nationwide study of American public education, called a conference of well-known writers on the teaching of reading to discuss
the matter. Thus, on September 22 and 23, 1961, a group of reading
specialists, representing a divergence of views on the question of
phonics in reading instruction, met in New York to discover areas
of agreement among them on this subject. The conference was financed
by the Carnegie Corporation of New York, and its report was later
distributed by the Educational Testing Service.

Twenty-seven members of the committee signed the report;
one submitted a minority report. The group consisted of university
professors, school superintendents, supervisors of reading instruction,
and authors of widely used specialized phonics materials. It is reasonable to assume that it was representative of the opinions of leaders
in research and teaching throughout the country.

What were the major generalizations about phonics that the
members of the conference found that they could agree upon? The
following quotations from the report provide an answer:

> It is not true that our schools, in general, use primarily a "sight-
> word" method. It is not true that our schools, in general do not
> teach phonics.
>
> We hold that reading cannot be taught by "sight-words" (look-
> say) alone. Such teaching would require our children to memorize,
> word by word, the mass of printed words. No reading authority
> advocates so impossible a procedure. . . .
>
> It should be remembered that when children come to school
> they want to learn to read. It is good sense to capitalize on this
> desire at once. Therefore, as the children begin to learn the read-
> ing skills, it is rather standard practice for good teachers to see
> to it that they simultaneously learn a few printed words that are

---

[3] Mary C. Austin and Coleman Morrison, *The First R: The Harvard Report on Reading in Elementary Schools.* New York: Crowell-Collier and Macmillan, Inc., 1963.

[4] Guy L. Bond and Robert Dykstra, *Final Report, Project No. X 001.* Washington,
D.C.: Bureau of Research, Office of Education, U.S. Department of Health, Education and Welfare, 1967.

[5] Jeanne Chall, *Learning To Read: The Great Debate.* New York: McGraw-Hill Book
Company, Inc., 1967.

common in children's speaking vocabularies and that they will thereafter recognize when they see them. With these few words as a base, the children can begin utterly simple reading almost immediately—for instance, a sentence of only two or three words. . . .

The learning of these few initial words is not a mere feat of memory but is the result of the composite procedure by which in the very early stages of reading instruction children begin to learn how to identify printed words. Because of their use in the very beginning reading, these words are usually called "sight-words"— that is, they are words that once learned will thereafter be recognized whenever they are seen. They are the beginning of the "reading vocabulary" that all persons must possess who are going to read well. . . .

However, many children at that age do not know what *sounds* are represented by the *letters* in the printed word. Therefore, they have to learn to relate the letters in the printed word to the sounds in the spoken word. With the variety of sounds that most letters have, this is not a small task. It is here that phonics enters in, for phonics is the study of the relationship of the letters and letter combinations in words on the printed page and the sounds in the spoken words. . . .

But the whole purpose of reading is to get meaning. That is why good teachers insist upon uniting phonics instruction with instruction in the word recognition skills through which meaning is ascertained.

The mastery of the skills that lead to recognition and meaning of words may not be left to chance or haphazard practice. If this seems obvious, then it should be equally obvious that learning the word recognition skills should be carefully planned and expertly guided if it is to be effective. This means that the heart of the reading instruction program really is a competent, dedicated teacher who knows both the theory of reading instruction and the ways different children learn. . . .

The following statements express the beliefs of the members of the Conference concerning the nature of the primary and elementary reading program as it exists in schools today and ways to strengthen it.

1. From our experience, we know that the constituent parts of the reading instruction program throughout our country are those that we have presented in this report as indispensable to a good, acceptable program. We know this, also, from the results of a survey made especially for our Conference by the Bureau of Applied Social Research, Columbia University.

   The evidence from the Columbia Survey shows that:

   a. classroom teachers of reading are in practically unanimous agreement on the importance of these constituent parts, and they report that they practice them in the classroom;

b. extremes of "no-phonics" or "all-phonics" programs are exceptions;

c. a predominantly sight-word method is practically non-existent.[6]

THE FIRST R: THE HARVARD REPORT ON READING IN ELEMENTARY SCHOOLS   This is the report of an intensive study sponsored by the Carnegie Foundation for the Advancement of Teaching. Referring to the report in the Foreword of the book, Herold C. Hunt of Harvard University states:

> Reflected are reading practices in more than a thousand of the nation's public school systems enrolling a large segment of our country's elementary school population. Combining questionnaire with observational techniques, the validity of the findings has been accurately established.[7]

The report concerns itself with various reading problems, one of which deals with the issue discussed in this chapter, namely, whether a code-emphasis (phonic) program should serve as the approach to reading instruction. In substance, the writers of this report answer in the negative. While they do not question the importance of phonics in teaching reading, they are opposed to it as the initial approach to reading. In regard to the phonic programs that they found in many schools, the authors of *The First R* state:

> They [the staff members] were concerned over the long postponement of meaningful reading materials, the overemphasis upon phonics and phonic principles at early stages of reading progress (usually for all children), and the lack of evidence of the value of the methods, either in isolation or in conjunction with basal readers.[8]

The following quotation from the report has bearing on the question of phonics not only in the initial stage of teaching word recognition but also in later phases:

[6] *Learning To Read, A Report of a Conference of Reading Experts.*

[7] Austin and Morrison, p. v.

[8] Austin and Morrison, p. 25.

While the ability to unlock new words through phonics is an essential skill, children need to acquire and apply a number of word recognition techniques in attacking unfamiliar words. Mastery of any one of these does not insure ability to recognize all new words; some may be more useful than others in specific instances. Therefore, it is recommended: *that continued emphasis be placed on helping children develop proficiency in word recognition through the use of meaning clues, visual analysis of word forms, sounding approaches, and the dictionary.*[9]

FINAL REPORT, PROJECT NO. X-001   The *Final Report* is the summary of the findings, with recommendations, of what is commonly known as the First Grade Reading Study, sponsored by the U.S. Office of Education. It is a coordinated study utilizing the findings of twenty-seven projects supported by the government with the understanding on the part of the directors of the projects that the studies would constitute an integral part of the Cooperative Research Program wih Guy L. Bond as coordinator. Two of three major questions that the program staff investigated are as follows:

> Which of the many approaches to initial reading instruction produces superior reading and spelling achievement at the end of the first grade?
>
> Is any program uniquely effective or ineffective for pupils with high or low readiness for reading?[10]

Basic conclusions from the *Final Report* relevant to the question of whether the initial approach in reading instruction should be a code-deciphering process, in which letters of the alphabet are matched by the learner with the sounds they represent, are indicated in the following quotations from that report:

> From the evidence reported concerning the use of phonics in teaching children to read earlier there can be little doubt that phonics should be an important part of the reading program. However, there is disagreement on the type of phonic approach which should be used and on the amount of phonics which should be included in the reading program. It seems apparent, from the studies reviewed, that phonics does not contribute much to children's comprehension of what is read.

[9] Austin and Morrison, p. 221.

[10] Bond and Dykstra, p. 41.

Indications are that the initial reading vocabulary should be selected with a greater balance between phonetically regular words and high utility words. It is likely that introducing words solely on the basis of frequency of use presents an unusually complex decoding task for the beginning reader.

Word study skills must be emphasized and taught systematically regardless of what approach to initial reading instruction is utilized.

Combinations of programs, such as a basal program with supplementary phonics materials, often are superior to single approaches.[11]

Further discussion of the First Grade Reading Study sponsored by the U.S. Office of Education is found in Chapter 16.

LEARNING TO READ: THE GREAT DEBATE   In this book Jeanne Chall reports on the results of her extensive investigation made under a grant from the Carnegie Foundation for the Advancement of Teaching. To gather data as bases for her report, the author (1) read the literature in the field that deals with descriptions of various methods of beginning reading instruction and that reports on relevant research; (2) visited classrooms in widely scattered areas in different types of school situations in this country and in England to acquire firsthand information as to how beginning reading instruction is being provided and to discuss methods with the teaching and/or supervisory staffs of the schools visited; (3) studied books used as basal reading textbooks; and (4) consulted with advocates of various methods of teaching beginning reading so as to obtain a clearer interpretation of each method.

Jeanne Chall's findings are revolutionary in that they are in rather direct opposition to many of the points of view about beginning reading instruction commonly held by specialists in the reading field. She throws a bombshell among those who believe that a code-deciphering approach, one in which the grapheme-phoneme relation is emphasized from the very beginning, is undesirable. In fact, the author even makes it seem rather professionally embarrassing that, according to her claims, her investigation indicates that Rudolph Flesch as well as the many laymen—often irate parents—urging a phonic approach to reading instruction are probably right, and that many professional writers on the teaching of reading are, for the most part, wrong in their premise that learning to read in the initial stage of reading instruction through a code approach is undesirable.

[11] Bond and Dykstra, pp. 19, 212, 210, 210, respectively.

The following quotation from *Learning To Read: The Great Debate* gives Jeanne Chall's point of view:

> My review of the research from the laboratory, the classroom, and the clinic points to the need for a correction in beginning reading instructional methods. Most schoolchildren in the United States are taught to read by what I have termed a meaning-emphasis method. Yet the research from 1912 to 1965 indicates that a code-emphasis method—i.e., one that views beginning reading as essentially different from mature reading and emphasizes learning of the printed code for the spoken language—produces better results, at least up to the point where sufficient evidence seems to be available, the end of the third grade.
>
> The results are better, not only in terms of the mechanical aspects of literacy alone, as was once supposed, but also in terms of the ultimate goals of reading instruction—comprehension and possibly even speed of reading. The long-existing fear that an initial code emphasis produces readers who do not read for meaning or with enjoyment is unfounded. On the contrary, the evidence indicates that better results in terms of reading for meaning are achieved with the programs that emphasize code at the start than with the programs that stress meaning at the beginning.[12]

In spite of the author's strong statements such as the above setting forth the alleged superiority of a code approach over a meaning approach, she tempers her report by such statements as the following:

> My recommendation for a methods change does not apply to all pupils. Some pupils may have a unique or uncommon way of learning. Insisting on one method for all may complicate things further.
>
> My recommendation for a change in beginning reading methods does not apply to school systems that have been getting excellent results with their present methods and materials that the teachers use with confidence. Many factors may make existing methods and materials better suited to these schools than new ones. What is effective for a class of thirty-five may be too slow-moving for a class of ten or fifteen. The functional type of learning that leaves the programming pretty much up to the individual pupil may work perfectly for a small class of able children with a creative teacher who already knows what to teach and when. Imposing a set, systematic program on a teacher who is knowledgeable about

[12] Chall, p. 307.

reading and keenly attuned to the strengths and weaknesses of her pupils may very well destroy the beauty of what she has already achieved.

A beginning code-emphasis program will *not* cure all reading ills. It cannot guarantee that *all* children will learn to read easily. Nor have the results of meaning-emphasis programs been so disastrous that all academic and emotional failures can be blamed on them, as some proponents and publishers of new code-emphasis programs claim. But the evidence does show that a changeover to code-emphasis programs for the beginner can improve the situation somewhat, and in this all too imperfect world even a small improvement is worth working for. I believe that method changes, if made in the right spirit, will lead to improved reading standards.[13]

INNOVATIVE PROGRAMS

As is to be expected in an era in which there is sharp controversy as to how reading can be taught most effectively, new programs have been advocated for teaching reading. In some of the programs the aim is to decrease the difficulties involved in learning to read by providing a code with a single symbol-sound relation. In others the problem of word recognition in beginning reading instruction has been attacked by means other than an attempt to provide an invariable grapheme-phoneme equivalence.

The advocates of some of the new programs have reported on them with perhaps undue enthusiasm. It is well, therefore, in making evaluations to keep in mind the following statements by Bond and Robert Dykstra:

> In conclusion, the superiority of a single method of reading instruction is yet to be determined. It appears that a composite of methods would produce the best results and that an effort should be made to determine what each method would contribute to the reading program.[14]

Jeanne Chall, who as the result of her investigation favors code-emphasis programs, states:

> I cannot emphasize too strongly that the evidence *does not endorse any one code-emphasis method over another*. There is no evi-

[13] Chall, p. 309.

[14] Bond and Dykstra, p. 20.

dence to date that ITA is better than a linguistic approach, that a linguistic approach is better than a systematic-phonics approach, or that a systematic phonics approach is better than ITA or a linguistic approach. Neither do we have any evidence to date that one published code-emphasis program is superior to another, although some undoubtedly are.[15]

The following statements also have bearing on the evaluation of new programs:

> Nor can I emphasize too strongly that I recommend a code emphasis only as a *beginning* reading method—a method to *start* the child on—and that I do *not* recommend ignoring reading-for-meaning practice. Once the pupil has learned to recognize in print the words he knows (because they are part of his speaking and listening vocabulary), any additional work on decoding is a sheer waste of time.[16]

Initial Teaching Alphabet

The initial teaching alphabet, commonly referred to as i/t/a came into prominence in England in 1961. It was introduced into this country by John Downing, from England, in 1963. Advocates of i/t/a propose to simplify the process of learning to read by circumventing a serious difficulty of written English, namely, that some letters or combinations of letters represent more than one sound and that some sounds are symbolized by more than one letter or combination of letters. I/t/a provides a forty-four letter alphabet in which each character allegedly represents only one sound and in which each sound is represented by only one character.

Of the forty-four–letter alphabet of i/t/a, twenty-four letters are found in the alphabet commonly used in writing English, which is referred to as traditional orthography. The remaining characters are either combinations of letters in the traditional alphabet or new symbols.

Proponents of i/t/a stress that they do not consider the system a method of teaching but a way of writing and therefore a means of reading. They claim that with this alphabet a code or a meaning approach can be used. However, it would seem that if a code approach is not used, there would be little if any reason for having a variation from the traditional orthography. After all, the advantage claimed by

[15] Chall, p. 307.
[16] Chall, p. 307.

The Initial Teaching Alphabet.

adherents of any symbol-sound equivalence system is that such a system provides a simplified code with a consistent grapheme-phoneme relation.

It should be noted that leaders of i/t/a advocate the use of their alphabet only for beginning reading. They suggest that as soon as the child has considerable proficiency in reading materials written in i/t/a he should begin making the transition to material in traditional orthography. The time when this stage of readiness occurs varies, it is claimed. Some children may be ready to make the transition fairly early in the first grade while others may not reach that point until varying times during the second and third grades.

I/t/a enthusiasts claim such advantages as the following:

1. It is much simpler for the child to learn to read by means of a symbol-sound code in which every character has but one sound and in which every sound is represented by but one symbol.
2. Children learn to read much more rapidly with i/t/a than with traditional orthography.
3. Making the transition from reading i/t/a to reading traditional orthography is relatively easy, so that soon after making the changeover the learner can read even in traditional orthography more effectively than one who started reading in that orthography.
4. Pupils being taught with i/t/a have greater skill in written self-expression than boys and girls using traditional orthography.
5. Children with speech defects who are taught with i/t/a as a beginning method of reading instruction are likely to be helped more than other children toward lessening or overcoming their speech difficulties.

I/t/a also has its critics. A chief contention of those who are unconvinced that it is the most effective means of beginning reading instruction is that it has not been used long enough in this country to justify the claims for superiority made by its proponents. Since there is lacking the completion of longitudinal studies through which children are observed from the time of beginning instruction in reading through the grades of the elementary school and beyond, they argue that the long-time comparative effect of reading with initial use of this alphabet versus other approaches to reading instruction has not been established. Furthermore, critics of the system point out that the number of pupils participating in often-quoted experimental set-ups involving use of i/t/a has been too small to establish the validity claimed for the studies. Other arguments advanced by the critics of i/t/a are as follows:

1. In addition to disadvantages resulting from the small number of children used in experiments, these experiments have not been set up with adequate attention to other factors essential for obtaining valid generalizations of worth. Critics of the system have pointed out shortcomings in the experimental pattern of the most quoted i/t/a experiment in this country, that of Albert J. Mazurkiewicz in the Lehigh-Bethlehem study. Lack of control of variables in the experimental and control groups constitutes a major source of criticism.
2. Some of the superiority claimed by experimenters with i/t/a may be due to the so-called Hawthorne effect, which operates to the advantage of an experimental group in that attention given to individuals as participants

in a new experimental program tends to increase the learning that takes place.

3. It has not been established that the problems involved in making a transition from i/t/a to traditional orthography is not so great that it might more than counterbalance the advantages in other respects that are claimed for the system.

4. The spelling of children taught to read with i/t/a is, according to some studies, poorer than that of other children.

Words-in-Color

The words-in-color program, like i/t/a, aims to decrease reading frustrations and increase reading power by providing a reliable symbol-sound code. The following explanation of the words-in-color program is given in one of the brochures of the company that publishes the materials, Learning Materials, Inc., Encyclopedia Britannica Press.

> Each of the 47 sounds of English is printed in a distinctive color on wall charts. Alphabet letters or groups of letters (280 signs of English) are colored according to how they sound in a given word. Thus color is used to make English phonetic without in any way changing traditional spellings.
>
> A sound is always represented by *one* color—regardless of its spelling. If it is the short sound of *a*, it is white whether it is in *pat* or *laugh*. Children use these color clues to help them fix the image in their minds.
>
> From the beginning, the pupil writes and reads in *black and white* each colored sign that he is introduced to so that there is immediate and constant transfer. Since he carries the images of these signs in color in his mind, the pupil can evoke and re-evoke the images if he needs them for reading or writing. Thus he is not dependent on printing in color.

It will be noted that, like i/t/a, the method is recommended for use only in beginning reading instruction. Also like i/t/a, it has not been used long enough in this country to give validity to the claims for superiority over other systems, for it was not until 1959 that Caleb Gattegno, who originated the system, made application to the English language of his studies with it in Spanish and in Hindi languages.

Diacritical Marking System

The diacritical marking system (DMS) that is here described, like words-in-color and i/t/a, is planned for use in beginning reading only. Also like words-in-color and i/t/a, it is based on the principle that a single grapheme-phoneme (written symbol-sound) relation greatly simplifies the problems of beginning reading instruction. The near-equivalence is secured by adding diacritical marks to the letters in the traditional alphabet. Basic rules for markings in this system are listed below, as given in the article by Edward Fry.

BASIC RULES

1. Regular consonants and short vowels are unchanged.

2. Silent letters have a slash mark. (writ¢ ri𝑔ht)

3. Long vowels have a bar over mark. (mād¢ mā𝑖d)

4. Schwa vowels have a dot over mark. (ȧgo lemȯn)

5. Other consistent sounds than those above are indicated by the bar. (is̲ a𝑢tō)

6. Digraphs have a bar under both letters. (s̲h̲ut c̲h̲at)

7. Exceptions to the above stated basic rules have an asterisk above the letter. (ȯ̇f ȯ̇nc¢)[17]

A specimen of DMS writing is given below.

TḢE LITTL¢ RED HEN

Once upon ȧ tīm¢ Littl¢ Red Hen liv¢d in ȧ ba̲r̲n wit̲h̲ h¢r fīv¢ chi¢ks. Ȧ pig, ȧ cat, and ȧ du¢k mād¢ the𝑖r hōm¢ in tḣe sām¢ ba̲r̲n. E𝑎ch dāy t̲h̲e littl¢ red hen led h¢r chi¢ks ou̲t to lo̲o̲k fo̲r̲ fōo̲d. But t̲h̲e pig, t̲h̲e cat, and t̲h̲e du¢k wo𝑢ld not lo̲o̲k fo̲r̲ fōo̲d.

Edward Fry claims superiority for the DMS over other systems devised to simplify the grapheme-phoneme relation for beginning reading. He asserts: (1) other systems have devised alphabets too unlike the traditional alphabet to assure maximum ease in making the transition from the new forms to the regular alphabet; and (2) the grapheme-phoneme relation in other alphabets is less nearly constant than in DMS.

Linguistic Approach to Reading

Suggestions for the application of phonetic principles to the teaching of reading have recently been made by a number of eminent linguists. The linguist emphasizes the fact that reading and writing are

[17] Edward Fry, "A Diacritical Marking System To Aid Beginning Reading Instruction," p. 73 in William K. Durr (ed.), *Reading Instruction: Dimensions and Issues.* Boston: Houghton-Mifflin Company, 1967.

relatively recent inventions and that they are derivative from the spoken language. He therefore regards the study of speech sounds, or phonetics, as central to any defensible theory of reading instruction.

For example, the late Leonard Bloomfield described a plan for initial reading instruction which is based upon the reproduction of speech sounds through the use of visual symbols.[18] In Bloomfield's theory, the early stages of reading instruction should be concerned exclusively with mastery of the mechanics of reading. Nonsense words may serve very well in fixing the skills required for later meaningful reading. He suggests the following four stages in a sequence designed to promote the development of the essential mechanical skills that will lead eventually to fluent, effective reading:

1. The recognition of the letters of the alphabet. These are to be presented in two-letter and three-letter words, in groups arranged according to the five vowel letters. Each letter in a group should represent a single phonetic value. Thus only the short *a* or only the hard *g* should be included in a word group. Work in this stage should be continued until the pupils are thoroughly trained.
2. Learning regular spellings in which double consonants and other digraphs appear in consistent uses.
3. Learning words whose spellings may be called *semi-irregular,* as in the word groups *line, shine, mile,* and *while,* or *bone, stone, hole, pole.*
4. Learning irregularly spelled words, such as *father, mother, night, all, rough, cough,* and *through.* Unfamiliar words may be used. At this stage, however, each word is a separate item to be memorized so that it may be available for reading.

Bloomfield's ideas have more recently been more fully developed in a book by Barnhart.[19] Barnhart has carried on Bloomfield's work with the intention of facilitating the experimental use of his method. However, the one classroom experiment in which the Bloomfield approach was compared with a conventional phonic approach revealed no significant differences in pupil achievement. Clearly further experimentation would be desirable.

Another well-known linguist, C. C. Fries, advocates a procedure not unlike that of Bloomfield's. Reviewing the history of linguistic science over a long period and of changes in theories of reading instruction, he outlines the implications of modern linguistics for the teaching

[18] Leonard Bloomfield, "Linguistics and Reading," *The Elementary English Review,* 19, pp. 125–130, 183–186 (April, May 1942).

[19] Leonard Bloomfield and Clarence Barnhart, *Let's Read: A Linguistic Approach.* Detroit: Wayne State University Press, 1961.

of reading.[20] Although he recognizes that the ultimate purpose of reading instruction is reading for meaning, Fries believes that the child's introduction to reading should not be complicated by the search for meaning in words. The child's primary task is to make a transfer from auditory language signs in speech to a set of corresponding visual signs in reading. The ability to identify and distinguish the graphic shapes that supply the visual symbols must first be brought to the level of instant and automatic response to the visual signals. Substituting visual for auditory signals implies clearly that the early reading experiences should be confined to words and meanings already a part of the child's speaking repertory.

Fries distinguishes three steps in teaching a child to read:

> The first stage in learning the reading process is the "transfer" stage. It is the period during which the child is learning to transfer from the auditory signs for language signals, which he has already learned, to a set of visual signs for the same signals. This process of transfer is not the learning of the language code or of a new language code; it is not the learning of a new or different set of language signals. It is not the learning of new "words," or of new grammatical structures, or of new meanings. These are all matters of the language signals which he has on the whole already learned so well that he is not conscious of their use. This first stage is complete when within his narrow linguistic experience the child can respond rapidly and accurately to the visual patterns that represent the language signals in this limited field, as he does to the auditory patterns that they replace.
>
> The second stage covers the period during which the responses to the visual patterns become habits so automatic that the graphic shapes themselves sink below the threshold of attention, and the cumulative comprehension of the meanings signalled enables the reader to supply those portions of the signals which are not in the graphic representation themselves.
>
> The third stage begins when the reading process itself is so automatic that the reading is used equally with or even more than live language in the acquiring and developing of experience—when reading stimulates the vivid imaginative realization of vicarious experience.[21]

When evaluating the possible contributions of linguists to the teaching of reading, it should be kept in mind that not all agree with

[20] Charles C. Fries, *Linguistics and Reading*. New York: Holt, Rinehart and Winston, Inc., 1963.

[21] Fries, p. 132.

either Bloomfield or Fries. Of the various schools of linguists the two whose impact upon the elementary school program has been markedly felt are the phonologists and the structuralists. The former are interested primarily in the study of the language through its sounds. The structuralists emphasize the structure or syntax of the language. Even among adherents to either one of these groups there are numerous differences as far as the implications of their suggestions on teaching reading are concerned.

While teachers of reading can learn much from linguists about the science of the language, the responsibility of deciding upon the characteristics of the reading program should not rest with the linguist. What the linguist should do is criticize current programs in the light of any violation of linguistic principles inherent in them and suggest principles that should be followed in the light of learnings in his field.[22] The reading program should be determined by the educator who considers not only recommendations from linguists but also those from other fields—child psychology and the psychology of learning among them.

On the market are many materials that claim to be linguistically oriented. Before a school system decides upon the use of any of these materials, consideration should be given to these points: (1) the linguistic principles upon which it is claimed the material is based; (2) the soundness of these principles in relation to what is known from other areas such as child growth and development and the psychology of learning; (3) the way in which these principles are put into operation in the material; and (4) the extent of the agreement of the practices outlined with the basic principles of teaching reading which the persons making the evaluation accept.

A major difference between the plans proposed by the linguists and the conventional initial phonics approaches is in the manner in which the phonic elements are first presented to the child. The linguists introduce the phonetic elements in whole words, either real words or nonsense words, presumably on the ground that the phonetic values of letters, especially vowels, cannot be determined in isolation. In both cases, however, the basis is laid by means of drills on language form and structure and on spelling patterns rather than on meanings.

To the linguist, concerned with the spoken language, it seems logical to begin with the phoneme. Many educators hesitate to subject the young child, eager to read stories for himself, to long periods of drill with isolated letter sounds and nonsense syllables. They regard the

[22] Kenneth S. Goodman, "The Linguistics of Reading," *Elementary School Journal,* 64, pp. 355–361 (April 1964).

visual associations with specific sounds as only one kind of aid, along with configuration and context and whole-word perception, in converting graphic signs accurately and speedily into meanings.

The question is not whether children can learn to read by either or both of these methods. Under suitable conditions and with intelligent teaching most children can learn to read, as they have done through the years, by any of a great variety of methods. What concerns educators most is which method or methods over the long run will help the greatest number of readers to make the greatest progress in reading, develop keen and continuing interest in reading, and achieve the highest possible levels of comprehension. Quite possibly for some children the phonetic approach is the most effective, while for others another approach or combination of approaches is the most effective.

SKILLS FOR DEVELOPING INDEPENDENCE IN WORD RECOGNITION

Five major skills are considered by many persons in the field of reading as important to the development of independence in word recognition: (1) recognizing whole words by means of the sight method; (2) using context clues; (3) studying words phonetically; (4) analyzing words structurally; and (5) using the dictionary. Many of those who favor a code approach to reading, however, deny the value of the first two skills listed.

All five skills are here discussed in turn, although often more than one is employed simultaneously in an attack upon a given word. For example, in the sentence "Susan is playing with her doll," the child may use several clues for recognizing the word *playing*. If the word is not already a part of the child's sight vocabulary, he can use context clues, study the word phonetically, and note the structure of the word as he takes cognizance of the *ing* suffix.

Learning Words by the Sight Method

As noted earlier in this chapter, the predominant method of teaching reading fifty and more years ago was to teach the child the individual letters first and then to teach him how to combine these letters into syllables and words. The reading of phrases and sentences was presumed to follow naturally. This method seemed the simplest and most logical. In the terminology of today, a code approach was used, namely, phonic synthesis. In fact, the approach had marked similarity to code approaches used today by an increasing number of persons.

Justification for teaching words as wholes has been based in part on research on perception, which, many claim, revealed that most people tend to recognize the larger visual shapes first and examine details only when the total configuration cannot be readily identified. Thus it is claimed by advocates of the whole-word method that it is easier for a child to recognize the word *cat* as a unit than to discover the phonetic values of the letters and to combine them. The theory is that much as the child recognizes his pet Puff without adding up the colors and characteristics of the individual parts—legs, ears, eyes, and the like—so can he learn to recognize a word. Furthermore, the claim is that only when two cats resemble each other in most details does one look more closely at the parts to make an identification; thus the learner needs to analyze the difference between words only when it is not marked.

Confirmation of the value of a whole-word method came from early eye-movement studies in reading by Dearborn, Judd, Buswell, and others. Their investigations indicated that in a single fixation the reader recognizes whole words and even phrases that have become familiar to him through frequent exposure to them. Consequently, many reading systems begin with whole words and introduce the child to them through telling the words, associating the words with pictures, using experience charts, and similar methods. An obvious advantage claimed for this approach is that the child is immediately started on the road to reading for meaning. The words so taught at the outset are said to be taught by the sight method.

Presentation of new words to be added to the pupil's sight vocabulary is generally made both in meaningful context and out of context. The purpose is to make the pupil's response automatic when he sees the word. In this connection the chalkboard and teacher-made or commercial charts are most useful. Labeling of objects in the room is helpful if it is made functional. Thus the shelves in the cupboard may be labeled *Scissors, Paste, Brushes,* and *Cloths* to aid the child in finding materials. Words learned out of context should as soon as possible be encountered in context. Reading-card drills in which whole words are presented should be preceded and followed by the use of these words in speaking and reading. The task is made easier if the words are selected from those the child uses in his own speech and from those "service words," such as prepositions, pronouns, and connecting verbs, that account for a majority of all words read.

The basis of the procedure is repetition of the desired words in different situations. If the child's reading vocabulary is consequently impoverished, as many of the critics of the sight-word method complain, the use of abundant voluntary reading in children's trade books can serve as supplement and corrective, the adherents of the meaning approach claim.

It used to be recommended rather universally by persons favoring the sight method that a stock of between fifty and seventy-five words learned by this method is necessary before work in phonics can be successfully begun. However, currently many people favoring the sight method agree that there is no reason why teaching by this method cannot be accompanied earlier by some help from phonics. In fact, many recommend that the sight method be supplemented almost from the beginning with work on one or more phonic elements of many words being learned.

If the sight method is used, it is important that only a rather limited number of new words be presented at one time. Individual differences among the children should determine the number attempted, and the teacher should not inhibit the gifted reader in a successful quest for a growing reading vocabulary, whatever the method of teaching. For the average pupil, however, a firmer foundation is laid if only a few words are thoroughly fixed in mind from day to day.

Some persons advocating a sight-method approach draw attention to the value of noting the general configuration of a word as an aid to recall. After a pupil has been told a word, it is claimed, he may at times find it helpful in recognizing it when he encounters it again if he observes the outline of the word or other matters of form.

Observation of the configuration of a word can be a valuable procedure, it is asserted, not only during the periods of reading readiness and initial reading instruction but in all stages of reading, including adult reading. In fact, for rapid reading it may be essential. Through noting the outline of the word the reader is saved, it is argued, from the necessity of painstakingly deciphering many words that he meets, especially if this clue is used in conjunction with the verbal context in which a word appears. Frequently, too, people favoring this procedure claim that attention to the configuration can be given to good advantage along with a study of phonics. One way in which the child in the early stages of learning to read can be aided in developing skill in the use of the configuration clues is through questions and comments by the teacher concerning the length of a word. If a child reads *mother* when he sees the word *man*, the teacher may say, "This word could not be *mother*, for *mother* is a longer word than this."

The following cautions should be observed in using the configuration of a word as a method of recognition: (1) Pupils should not be expected to remember a large number of words through configuration clues only, for many words closely resemble one another in general appearance. Overuse of this practice is likely to result in guessing. (2) The teacher should be on guard against making wrong use of the striking characteristics of a word as a means to word recognition. Not infrequently a teacher tries to help a child remember the word *monkey* by the "tail" letter on *monkey*. This is a most confusing practice, since many words other than *monkey* end in y.

Use of Context Clues

Like the sight method, the use of context clues is severely criticized by many advocates of a code approach to beginning reading instruction. It has been ridiculed as a "guessing method," but its adherents persistently claim that intelligent guessing is often a desired procedure. Let us note how the method is frequently used.

A teacher may use the sight method plus the method of visual context when she helps a pupil learn the word *mother* as it appears with a picture of a woman. When using both of these procedures in teaching a child to identify the word, she may tell him the word is *mother* and then lead him to notice that the word goes with the picture. Or she may ask him what the word under the picture might be. If he says *mother*, she needs to let him know that he is right.

A word can also be presented by the sight method combined with the use of verbal context clues. For example, if the pupils know all the words except *bat* in the sentence "Bob has a ball and a bat," the teacher might tell them that she thinks many of them can figure out the new word in the sentence as they read it to see what word would fit where the new word appears. If the pupils suggest that the word might be *bat*, she will need to tell them that they are right. If the pupils do not name the correct word, the teacher should tell them the word and help them to see that *bat* fits with the meaning of the rest of the sentence.

In spite of the critics of the use of context clues, many persons consider skill in making use of verbal context clues significant to all stages of reading instruction, even to adult reading. Arguments for use of context clues in word recognition include: (1) In the earlier stages it is of great help in providing boys and girls with needed practice on words they have identified at a previous time but which they still do not recognize instantly without other aids. (2) Before the pupils have learned to identify and remember words through word analysis or synthesis, they can, by means of skill in the use of verbal clues, frequently get from the context the aid in recalling the word that they need. (3) Even after the readers have developed facility in the use of structural and phonetic analysis and synthesis, they can be aided in increasing their rate through efficient use of verbal context clues; often through the context a reader can recognize a word faster than through analytic methods. For example, a person who comes across the sentence, "Geometry is one branch of mathematics in which I am greatly interested" can use a context clue in recognizing the word *mathematics*. (4) There are many words in English whose pronunciation depends upon the context, such as *read, lead, bow, refuse*.

As indicated in the illustration in the preceding paragraph, an adequate background of experience is essential for success in the use of context clues. A person who does not know what geometry is would receive little help from context in the sentence, "Geometry is one branch of mathematics in which I am greatly interested." Consequently, it is the teacher's responsibility to provide sufficient experiences with the subjects about which the pupils will be reading. The teacher can help boys and girls get the needed background by a variety of means—discussions, explanations, demonstrations, experiments, field trips and other visual aids, and reading. Once he has read fairly easy material on a given subject, the pupil can often be helped to understand more difficult reading done subsequently on the same topic. At times, guidance can be given just before the class begins reading a selection in which concepts are discussed with which the pupils are not familiar. At other times, preparation for the reading may have taken place days or even weeks before. A wide background of experience is one assurance that the child will have less difficulty not only in reading in general but also in making intelligent use of verbal context clues.

If a reader is to be expected to get help through the verbal context in the identification of a word, the proportion of unfamiliar to familiar words should be kept small. If a first-grade child comes to the sentence, "The boy has a ball and a bat," without recognizing either *boy* or *ball* or *bat*, no intelligent use of context clues can be made. The exact ratio of unknown to known words, as far as recognition of the word is concerned, cannot, of course, be ascertained because it will differ according to difficulty of the concepts discussed, the intelligence, maturity, background, and reading ability of the reader, and the skill of the teacher.

The identification of a word does not necessarily have to take place in context in order that the pupil may recognize it later by context clues. A teacher may write on the board the word *mother* when she tells the child the word, and later on, when he again encounters the word in his reading, help him make use of the context to recall the word. Sometimes it is desirable first to present a word in isolation, since more attention can be given it then.

Use of Phonics

The place of phonics in reading instruction, as noted earlier, has been the subject of heated controversy and of much experimental research. Not only has the subject been discussed by teachers for many years but it has also in recent times excited partisan interest not only within the teaching profession but among the public at large. This increased participation in the controversy is undoubtedly due in part to the publication of such books as *Why Johnny Can't Read.*

Probably few persons in the field of the teaching of reading would disagree with the point of view that no one becomes an efficient reader who has not learned—either by himself or with the aid of another person, most likely the teacher—at least part of the code giving the relation between the written symbols and the sounds represented by them. Furthermore, a number of people in the field of reading contend that many boys and girls will greatly profit from help in acquiring this complex skill. The dispute about phonics, therefore, is not over the *whether* but over the *how*, the *when*, and the *what.*

A point of much debate is whether or not a phonic approach rather than a meaning approach should be the basis for beginning reading instruction. (For arguments pro and con on this important issue see pages 98–106.)

A second question is whether the approach to word recognition should be *synthetic* or *analytic*. Advocates of the synthetic method favor teaching letters and graphemes, or phonograms, first, and then teaching children to combine the sound elements into words. Those who believe in the analytic method favor presenting children with whole words first and then teaching them to analyze words into the sound elements that comprise them. This second method is sometimes called the whole-part-whole method.

Over the years, children have learned to read by various methods, including the synthetic. The problem has been one of finding a general approach that would be effective with the largest possible number of children and that would lead to strong and continuing interest in good reading throughout life. On this ground, the numerous methods that may be described as analytic have been widely accepted. There is no meaning in phonemes. Only when they have been combined into word parts, whole words, phrases, and sentences do they yield meaning. And since there can be no true reading without the apprehension of meaning, adherents to the meaning approach argue, the process should begin with the perception of the larger units—words and their affixes. Moreover, they claim that as soon as possible, the child

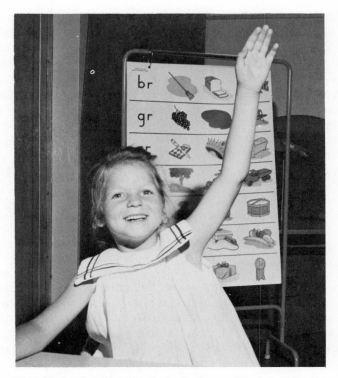

Knowledge of blends is important. (Photo courtesy Boise, Idaho, Public Schools.)

should be confronted with phrases and sentences in order to avoid the habit of word-by-word reading. Quick perception of the larger units is considered important, not primarily for the development of speed but for the development of comprehension.

Most people will concede that an intelligent, able, sympathetic teacher, one who is flexible enough to adapt her procedure to individual needs, is more important than the method, but this fact in no way relieves us of the necessity of weighing the relative advantages of one method over another.

A third point of difference, which arises among those not subscribing to a code approach to beginning reading instruction, is the question of whether instruction in phonics should be systematic or incidental. Granted that there is an essential body of phonics skills to be mastered, should these skills be taught sequentially to all children, with whole words deliberately chosen to illustrate a phonics principle?

Or should the phonics principles be taught to each child as the need arises in his reading? Many reading specialists and classroom teachers prefer a combination of these two approaches.

An objection to the sequential, isolated teaching of phonic principles is the fact that many good young readers discover the principles themselves in the course of highly motivated meaningful reading, and for them class instruction in phonics tends to be wasteful. On the other hand, in guided individualized reading programs there is danger that many children will fail to encounter or to master essential phonic elements.

In an important study Durrell and others found that:

> Most reading difficulties can be prevented by an instructional program which provides early instruction in letter names and sounds, followed by applied phonics and *accompanied by suitable practice in meaningful sight vocabulary and aids to attentive silent reading* . . .[23]

To overcome or decrease the frustrations that may result from the lack of consistency between letters and sounds is the purpose of i/t/a, words-in-color, the diacritical marking system, and other methods advocated for beginning reading instruction that have close letter-sound relations. However, many teachers through a variety of teaching methods also meet the challenge presented by the somewhat unphonetic nature of the English language in ways other than using systems based on a consistent letter-sound equivalence.

It is feared by many that prolonged work on phonics independently taught not only diverts the child from the process of getting meaning from the printed page but also reduces the amount of time available for genuine reading. It is also argued that emphasis on phonics may cause lack of interest in reading. It should be noted, however, that Jeanne Chall arrived at the following conclusion in her report on her extensive investigation of primary-grade reading:

> Under a meaning emphasis, the child has an early advantage (in the middle of grade 1) on reading-for-meaning tests (standardized silent reading tests of vocabulary and comprehension). However, he has an early disadvantage in accuracy or oral word recognition (pronunciation) and connected oral reading tests (when rate is not included in the score), which ultimately dissipates the early advantage on the standardized silent reading tests. At about the

[23] Donald D. Durrell and others, "Success in First Grade Reading," *Journal of Education*, p. 140 (February 1958). Italics added.

Learning can be fun. (Anne Arundel County, Maryland, Public Schools. Photo by Ken Abenschein.)

end of the first grade (or the beginning of the second grade), and continuing through about the third grade, meaning-emphasis programs tend to affect comprehension and vocabulary test scores adversely, mainly because the child does less well in word recognition.[24]

PRINCIPLES OF TEACHING PHONICS   With the great divergence of opinion concerning the role of phonics in reading instruction, there are few generalizations having to do with teaching by this method that will be accepted by the two opposing factions other than that phonics is important in learning to read. Other principles, though less commonly accepted, to which, however, a large number of educators adhere, are here listed.

1. *Instruction in phonics should be functional.* Only those

[24] Chall, p. 127.

generalizations about differences and likenesses of words should be taught which apply to the simple words the beginner encounters in his reading or in presentations by the teacher.

2. *For most pupils, instruction in phonics should be systematic.* The progression should be from the simpler, more widely used elements and generalizations to the more difficult and less generally applied learnings, with well-distributed practice.

3. *The work in phonics should be adapted to individual differences.* Any program in word recognition should be geared to the developmental level of the children. Pupils within a given grade may be expected to be on varying levels in many respects, including the various phases of phonetic analysis. Some will not be ready as soon as others. Some will be able to deal with simple abstract learnings; others will profit more from concrete experiences. Moreover, progress will vary greatly after initial instruction has begun. Some pupils will need practically no help beyond that provided by the material they are currently reading, while others will benefit greatly from additional practice in workbooks or teacher-made materials and games or drills that focus attention on certain needed skills.

4. *Rules and generalizations should frequently be taught inductively.* By presenting three or more familiar words that have the same initial, medial, or final letter, the teacher can call attention to the similarity and help the pupil to fix the appropriate sound in mind in such a way as to enable him to recognize the same sound in another word. For example, if the pupil has learned the similar beginning of the words *make, mother,* and *man,* he is equipped to attack the word *mouse* by applying a generalization to a new grouping of letters. Chalkboard, chart, and workbook can supply practice in making such applications, and of course the rule, which the pupil himself has been led to formulate, can then be used in his own "silent" reading. Similar generalizations can be made and applied with the medial vowel in words ending in a silent *e.*

It should be noted that it is probably unwise to expect that all generalizations about phonics should be learned inductively. Children can also learn through deductive teaching. While it seems desirable that often they should be helped in reaching conclusions in the form of rules or generalizations, to follow the inductive procedure at all times may slow the process of learning. Furthermore, much learning in life outside of school takes place without use of an inductive method. Children, too, learn to profit from deductions made from generalizations presented to them.

ELEMENTS OF PHONICS TO BE TAUGHT   One major point of disagreement concerning the teaching of phonics is the question of what should be taught. It is not the purpose of the writers to state authoritatively what the phonic content of the reading program should be. Most reading systems emphasizing phonics and most basal readers indicate clearly what they recommend as the minimum of phonics that should be taught. The listing given here includes only those elements that are rather commonly accepted as important.

For convenience in studying the list that follows a few definitions are here given. (1) *Digraphs* are written or printed symbols made up of two letters representing one phoneme or speech sound. They are of two kinds, consonant digraphs, such as *th, ng, ck*, and vowel digraphs, such as *ei, ie, ea, ay*. (2) *Diphthongs* are written or printed symbols representing two vowels so nearly blended that they almost produce a single speech sound, such as *oy, ou, ew*. (3) Consonant blends are combinations of two or three consonants, such as *br, gr, str*, blended in such a way that each letter in the blend keeps its own identity.

1. *Outline of subject matter.* Included in many programs of reading instruction are the following elements of phonics: (a) single consonants in monosyllabic and polysyllabic words, found in initial, final and medial positions of words; (b) consonant blends, such as *st, gr, br, cr, tch, pl*; (c) consonant digraphs, such as *ch, th, sh*; (d) single vowels ("short" and "long " vowels, vowels modified when preceding *r*, the *a* when preceding *l* or *w*, and other vowel sounds); (e) vowel digraphs, such as *ea, oa, ai, ay, ee, oo*; (f) diphthongs, such as *oy, oi, ou, ow*; and (f) silent letters.

2. *Generalizations to be learned.* It should be noted that several of the generalizations here stated are not without exception as far as the universality of their application is concerned.

A single vowel in a syllable is usually short unless it is the final letter in the syllable. (Examples: b*a*t, b*a*by)

If there are two vowels together in the same syllable, the first vowel is often long and the second silent. (Example: b*oa*t)

If a final *e* in a syllable is preceded by a single consonant, a single vowel preceding the consonant is usually long and the *e* is silent. (Example: r*a*te)

The sound of a single vowel preceding an *r* is usually modified by the *r*. (Example: color)

The sound of a single *a* preceding an *l* or a *w* is affected by the *l* or *w*. (Examples: f*a*ll; cl*a*w)

A final *y* in words of more than one syllable is usually short. (Example: baby)

A *c* before *e, i,* or *y* has, as a rule, the soft sound. (Example: city)

A *g* before *e, i,* or *y* has, as a rule, the soft sound. (Example: gem)

SEQUENCE   One caution needs to be expressed at this point. The listing of phonic elements and generalizations in the preceding section of this chapter is not to be considered as the sequence in which they are to be taught.

Grade levels are an undesirable criterion for determining sequence. Since the accomplishments of boys and girls and their readiness for any phase of reading instruction varies so much from grade to grade, it is better to express in terms of levels of achievement the sequence of phonic skills to be studied.

There is no one best sequence for teaching the various aspects of phonic analysis. Numerous acceptable orders of presentation have been worked out. The succession should be based on principles such as these: (1) There should be progression from the simple to the more complex. (2) Other things being equal, the more frequently used elements and generalizations should be taught before the less frequently used. (3) Provisions should be made on each level for the maintenance of skills acquired, at least in part, on the preceding level.

One of the best sources of suggestions as to the sequence to follow in phonic programs is to be found in the teachers' manuals accompanying the series of readers. Any teacher using one of these should acquaint herself with the program outlined in the manuals. However, the suggestions should not be followed slavishly. The recommendations are, for the most part, made in terms of the average child in a grade. The teacher must make adaptation to individual differences. A suggested sequence for phonics instruction follows:

1. Provide needed work on auditory and visual discrimination.
2. Teach the sounds of consonants before those of vowels. Start with the single consonant sounds that have but one sound, namely, *b, h, j, l, m, p, t,* and *v.* Teach them as they occur in initial and then in final positions in words, before teaching them in medial positions. Finally, teach common consonant digraphs, then two-letter consonant blends, then, three-letter consonant digraphs, then two-letter consonant blends, then three-letter consonant blends.
3. Teach the vowel sounds, the short sounds first, then the long.
4. Teach vowel digraphs and diphthongs and silent letters.
5. Teach rules governing "long" and "short" vowels.

Although exact stipulations as to the grade in which an element should be taught cannot be given, in general it should be noted that it is probably wise to complete almost all of the new work on phonetic elements and generalizations by the end of the third grade. However, much should be done in the intermediate grades to maintain and to make further application of learnings acquired earlier.

Use of Structural Analysis

Phonetic analysis is not the only type of word analysis. A second method of analyzing words is through the use of structural analysis. While in phonetic analysis the reader deciphers a word by means of sounds represented by the letters or combination of letters in a word, in structural analysis he recognizes the meaning or pronunciation units of a word.

Structural analysis deals with both word variants and word derivatives. By a word variant is meant a word that deviates from the root word according to grammatical usage. Word variants show inflections according to the case, number, and gender of nouns, the tense, voice, and mood of verbs, and the comparison of adjectives and adverbs. Thus variants of the noun *prince* are *princes* and *princess;* of the verb *walk* are *walks, walked, walking;* of the adjective *small* are *smaller* and *smallest.* Word derivatives are words formed from root words through the addition of prefixes and/or suffixes—for example, *likeable* and *uncomfortable.* Learning compound words—for example, *something*—through identification or recognition of the parts, and polysyllabic words through the aid of syllabication, is also part of structural analysis.

The question may be asked, "Why teach structural analysis of word variants or word derivatives when these words could be studied through phonetic analysis?" To be specific, "Why should the teacher bother teaching children to use structural analysis when learning the word *unhappy* after they can recognize the root *happy* and can analyze the word phonetically?" The answer is that phonetic analysis is a slower form of word analysis than structural analysis. The child who has learned to recognize instantly the prefix *un* in *unhappy* does not have to engage in the uneconomical procedure of first analyzing *un* phonetically. The reader who can quickly identify the common prefixes and suffixes reads with more speed than the one who has to use phonics in this process.

In succeeding paragraphs the following questions will be discussed: (1) What are the basic principles that should be observed in teaching structural analysis? (2) What should be taught to boys and girls in the elementary school about structural analysis? (3) In what sequence and at what levels should the various elements of word structure be taught? (4) What are some additional suggestions for teaching children to identify and recognize words by means of structural analysis? The fourth question will be answered primarily in Chapter 5B, where many specific illustrations are presented.

PRINCIPLES OF TEACHING STRUCTURAL ANALYSIS
The following principles warrant special emphasis in relation to analyzing words by means of their structure.

1. *Overemphasis on structural analysis should be avoided.* Structural analysis should be seen in relation to other methods of word recognition. When a word can be recalled by means of quicker methods, such as configuration or context clues, the reader should not resort to word analysis. If too much attention has been paid to locating root words, prefixes, and suffixes, it is possible for reading to become ineffective because the reader approaches too many words by trying to locate word parts. Consequently, it is undesirable to have all "new words" analyzed either phonetically or structurally.

2. *As a rule, the reader should examine a "new word" to see if he can analyze it structurally before he tries to unlock it by means of phonics.* This principle is sound because structural analysis is usually a quicker method of word recognition than phonetic analysis. Consequently rate in reading as well as quality of comprehension can be improved if the more tedious methods involving phonics are employed only when other means fail.

3. *The analysis of "new words" should not be isolated from reading as a meaningful process.* Frequently it is advisable to present in context a "new word" that is to be analyzed structurally. The context can help the reader decide what the word is. For example, if the reader comes across the sentence, "Sam is walking home," and he knows the root word *walk*, he can often tell without really studying the ending that the "new word" is *walking*, not *walks* or *walked*.

4. *The sequence in teaching a "new word" by means of structural analysis should, as a rule, be from the whole word to the word part and then back to the whole word.* Specifically, it is usually desirable to present the word first—for example, *walking*—next to ask the pupils to identify the root word and the ending, and then to have them combine the root with the ending. This procedure is recommended because it more nearly resembles the situation in which the pupil is likely to encounter a word. Nevertheless, occasional special practice in

which a child forms variants or derivatives of a word are helpful, as, for example, having the pupils form the words *walks, walked,* and *walking* from *walk.*

5. *Structural analysis should not be confused with "finding little words in big words."* One rather common method used to help boys and girls analyze words structurally is to ask them to "find little words in big words." This practice may be misleading. For example, finding *at* in *mat* could lead a child also to look for *at* in *mate* and therefore confuse him. Furthermore, even in *mat,* if the reader looks for *at,* he is likely to pronounce it *mu-at.* Anyone accustomed to searching for "little words in big words" might easily pronounce *together* as *to-get-her* or *some* as *so-me,* and in the word *furthermore* he might be led to a wrong identification if he isolates *the* or *he* or *her.*

6. *Generalizations should be developed with pupils.* They should not be presented as rules to be memorized. For example, when teaching that words ending in *y* preceded by a consonant change the *y* to *i* before adding *es,* the teacher may write on the board a few nouns ending in *y,* some preceded by a consonant, others by a vowel, like *boy, boys; lady, ladies; day, days; candy, candies;* and *toy, toys.* The pupils may observe how the plural of each of the singular nouns in the list was formed, writing in one column the singular words ending in *y* preceded by a vowel and in the other the singular words ending in *y* preceded by a consonant. Next the pupils may summarize their observation that to the words in the first column ending in *y* preceded by a vowel, an *s* only was added. The teacher may then explain that this summarization holds true in other cases. Similarly the boys and girls may summarize their finding that in the words in the second column—those ending in *y* preceded by a consonant—the *y* was changed to *i* before *es* was added. The teacher may then explain that this summarization, too, holds true in other cases. To make this original learning permanent, the pupils should be helped to note the application of these rules in their later reading and in their spelling. This method of procedure in developing a generalization is much more likely to be effective than that in which the teacher gives the rule and the pupils memorize it.

7. *There should be a developmental program that provides for training in structural analysis.* Skill in analyzing words structurally is such a significant phase of skill in word recognition that it cannot be left to chance. While incidental methods should be used whenever they help foster a better understanding of words on the part of boys and girls, the teacher should make certain that all the essential elements of structural analysis are presented and that provisions are made for the

maintenance of these skills through meaningful distributed practice. Suggestions as to the elements to include in such a program are given in the next paragraphs.

A DEVELOPMENTAL PROGRAM   Exactly which elements and generalizations in structural analysis should be taught in the elementary school is a question that has not been determined. In trying to decide on the points to be studied, the teacher should keep these criteria in mind: (1) the frequency of occurrence of the structural form, (2) the ease with which the learner can identify the form, and (3) the value of the element to the development of speed and independence in word recognition.

The following elements in structural analysis of words are frequently considered important enough to be taught somewhere in the elementary school:

1. *Skill in identifying or recognizing words ending in* able, ance, d, ed, er, es, est, ful, ible, ies, ily, ing, ish, less, ly, ment, ness, *and* s *in words in which the root is known to the reader.* Pupils should be familiar with the application of the following generalizations about the endings of words:

Words ending in y preceded by a consonant change the y to i before adding
   es to form a variant of the root word.
Words ending in y preceded by a consonant change the y to i before ed, er,
   est, or ly is added.
Many words ending in a consonant double the final consonant before ed or
   ing is added.
Many root words ending in e drop the e before adding ing to form a variant.

2. *Skill in identifying or recognizing words with the prefixes* ab, ad, com, de, dis, ex, im, in, pre, pro, re, sub, *and* un *in words in which the root is known to the reader.* The more advanced pupils in the elementary school may also be helped to recognize the fact that a variation of the prefix im occurs in words like illegal and illegible, where instead of the m of the prefix im the first consonant of the root of the word is doubled so that the consonant preceded by i forms the prefix to the root of the word.

3. *Skill in identifying or recognizing compound words where one or both parts of a compound or hyphenated word are known to the reader.*

4. *Skill in identifying or recognizing the possessive form when the word without the possessive ending is known to the reader.*

5. *Skill in identifying or recognizing common contractions*

like he'll, I'll I'm, it's, there's, they're, that's, she'll, we'll, we're, what's where's, *and* you'll *and those ending in* n't, *like* don't.

6. *Skill in identifying or recognizing polysyllabic words part-ly by means of syllabication.* Syllabication can aid in the identification and recognition of words. It is usually helpful to pupils to understand that there are as many syllables in a word as there are vowel sounds. It is not essential to the recognition or pronunciation of a word to know exactly where some of the breaks between syllables occur. For instance, a child does not have to know whether the division of syllables in the word *tumble* comes before or after the *b* in order to pronounce the word correctly, even though, of course, for written syllabication that knowl-edge is essential. However, if rules for syllabication are to be studied, these are some that may be helpful to elementary school children:

If the initial vowel in a word is followed by two consonants, the first of the two consonants usually ends the first syllable of the word, as in *big' ger.*
If the initial vowel in a word is followed by a single consonant, the conso-nant usually begins the second syllable of the word, as in *ma' jor.*
If the last syllable of a word ends in *le,* the consonant preceding *le* usually begins the last syllable, as in *ta' ble.*

SEQUENCE AND ALLOCATION TO LEVELS OF READING
The order in which the elements significant in structural analysis should be taught cannot be stated authoritatively for all grades or for all indi-viduals within a grade. Factors like the following will need to be taken into consideration in working out the sequence in which the elements should be taught: (1) The items included in a list of points to be devel-oped in stressing facility in word recognition through structural analysis should not, as a rule, be taken up in the order in which they occur in this book. (2) One factor that should help determine the order of development is the occurrence or presentation in the reading textbook of words representative of the form to be studied. Most reading books for the elementary school provide definite guidance in the teachers' manual for a program of word recognition. (3) The difficulty of a point to be learned should be one of the criteria for deciding the order in which the items should be taught. Other things being equal, those points easier to learn and to apply should be taught first.

Use of the Dictionary

Effective use of a dictionary for purposes of word identifica-tion, pronunciation, and meaning is one of the most important skills in word recognition that need to be acquired in the elementary school. In

Chapters 8A and 8B, dealing with the locational skills, a somewhat detailed account is given of how to help pupils develop skill in the use of the dictionary.

THE READING VOCABULARY

Writers of reading textbooks have tried to include only those words that are a part of the understanding or speaking vocabulary of the primary school child. Unfortunately, they have not found it possible to include the many dialects and linguistic variations employed by children in so vast and diverse a country as ours. For this reason, the reading textbook necessarily fails to meet the needs of children in the many geographic sections of English-speaking countries. How, for example, can the youngster on a Nebraska farm, in a New York slum, or on an Alabama plantation meet on common terms with a boy or girl who has grown up in a Cleveland suburb? All this is not to suggest that a reading series designed for the children of a large nation must provide a homogeneous reading diet. The effort has been to find a common denominator.

The selection of words for inclusion in the pupil's reading vocabulary, especially in the primary grades, is a matter of considerable consequence. It is for this reason that makers of textbooks in reading have spent time and effort in the selection of words used in their books. In publishing reading books for the beginning primary grades they have tried to choose words whose meaning the boys and girls know. They have rightfully insisted that it is unwise to try to teach children in the first grade to read words with which they are unfamiliar, when there are several thousand words in their understanding vocabulary that they cannot recognize in print. It is not until the later primary grades that most authors of basal reading books try to introduce words that will extend the child's understanding vocabulary. In order to provide a vocabulary suitable for the child to read, authors of reading series have based their vocabulary selection in part on carefully compiled lists of words.

Less attention, however, is currently given to word lists. Furthermore, many persons in the field of reading, especially those favoring a code approach, insist that words for primary grade reading should be selected less on the basis of the utility of a word (in terms of frequency of use) and more on the value of the word in terms of phonic learnings that can be acquired and in terms of opportunity provided for unlocking other words with the same phonic elements. In early grades, too, persons who hold this view recommend that many of the words used in children's reading be phonetically regular words.

Description of Word Lists

One of the earliest studies of children's vocabulary was "The Kindergarten Union" list published in 1928 by the International Kindergarten Union, which is now the Association for Childhood Education International.[25] It contains the 2,596 words which, according to that study, were used the most frequently by the young children whose parents or kindergarten teachers recorded the words the boys and girls used. Although this list does not indicate which words are encountered most in reading by beginning readers, it does throw light on the problem of vocabulary selection for first-grade books, since the words in the early reading materials should be chosen from the words whose meaning presents no problem to the children.

The much-used *A Teacher's Wordbook of 20,000 Words*, compiled by Edward L. Thorndike,[26] contains words selected from a large variety of sources of reading material, some for children, others for adults. Thorndike tabulated these so that the frequency with which each word is used is indicated by its placement in groups of 500 or 1,000. It is of only limited value for work on vocabulary control for the primary grades, however, since the frequency with which words are used by adults in reading is not a good index of the words that can best be used in primary grade reading. *A Teacher's Wordbook of 30,000 Words,* by Edward L. Thorndike and Irving Lorge,[27] published in 1944, includes not only the results of the research reported in the earlier *A Teacher's Wordbook of 20,000 Words* but also three other counts made of more than four million running words. Since it indicates the frequency with which some of the words are used in reading materials for children, it is more useful than its predecessor for writers of children's books and for teachers who construct some of their own instructional materials.

One of the most widely used lists by makers of textbooks for children in grades one through three is *A Reading Vocabulary for the Primary Grades* by Arthur I. Gates.[28] It is based in part on Thorndike's

[25] Association for Childhood Education International, "The Kindergarten Union List." New York: Bureau of Publications, Teachers College, Columbia University, 1935.

[26] Edward L. Thorndike, *A Teacher's Wordbook of 20,000 Words.* New York: Bureau of Publications, Teachers College, Columbia University, 1926.

[27] Edward L. Thorndike and Irving Lorge, *A Teacher's Wordbook of 30,000 Words.* New York: Bureau of Publications, Teachers College, Columbia University, 1944.

[28] Arthur I. Gates, *A Reading Vocabulary for the Primary Grades.* New York: Bureau of Publications, Teachers College, Columbia University, 1935.

studies and gives 1,811 words frequently used in primary grade reading materials. The relative frequency of words arranged in groups of 500 is shown.

A more up-to-date list, *Stone's 1941 Graded Vocabulary for Primary Reading*,[29] contains 2,164 words selected on the basis of a vocabulary study of textbooks from the preprimer level through the third reader and of other lists compiled earlier. All the readers used in the study were published between 1931 and 1941.

The Author's Word List for the Primary Grades[30] is based on the study of the vocabulary of 84 preprimers, 69 primers, 84 first readers, 85 second readers, and 47 third readers. Among the preprimer and primer words were included only those that were found in one third or more of all the books studied on that level. The words are graded and their frequency of use is indicated.

A list that is based on words used in writing by children of the elementary school, through grade eight, is Rinsland's *A Basic Vocabulary of Elementary School Children*.[31] It consists of 14,571 words, each of which occurred at least three times among the 6,112,359 words that the children in the elementary school used in their writing.

A Basic Sight Vocabulary by E. W. Dolch[32] consists of 220 words, exclusive of nouns, which are used with greatest frequency in reading books for the primary grades. Although no nouns are given in this list, Dolch has compiled a separate list of 95 nouns commonly used in the lower grades in basal reading books. Dolch's study shows that approximately two-thirds of the words in reading material for the primary grades are among the 220 words listed by him. Almost as large a percentage of words found in the intermediate grade reading books that were examined in the Dolch study are in the list. Because of the frequency of the use of the words, they are words that many teachers think every child should learn to recognize with facility during the initial period of reading instruction.

---

[29] Clarence R. Stone, *Stone's 1941 Graded Vocabulary for Primary Reading*. St. Louis, Mo.: Webster Publishing Company, 1941.

[30] L. L. Krantz, *The Author's Word List for Primary Grades*. Minneapolis, Minn.: Curriculum Research Company, 1945.

[31] Henry Rinsland, *A Basic Vocabulary of Elementary School Children*. New York: The Macmillan Company, 1945.

[32] Edward W. Dolch, *Methods in Reading*, pp. 373–374. Champaign, Ill.: The Garrard Publishing Company, 1955.

Use of Word Lists

Although a great service has been done by the compilers of word lists, these points should be considered:

1. When making use of word lists based in part or in entirety upon occurrence of words in writing of or for adults, the teacher should not conclude that the words used most frequently in writing for adults are the ones that should appear in the books for children in the lower grades.
2. If a word list is based on the material written for adults as well as on some for children, unless the two parts of the study are kept discrete, it is questionable to what extent the list is useful in determining the vocabulary that should be used in reading material for children.
3. The words that boys and girls should be taught to read should not be confined to a list of words that they write. The reading vocabulary of a child is almost invariably greater than his writing vocabulary.
4. Whenever a new reading series bases its vocabulary extensively on a list that expresses current practice in vocabulary selection among materials already in print for children, there is the likelihood that whatever imperfections in vocabulary there are in other books will be perpetuated.
5. There is danger of lack of rich content if the vocabulary is too strictly controlled. This is true especially in books in the content areas like social studies and science. As a rule, the children's books in these fields have a greater vocabulary burden than those in basal reading series. While in many respects this is fortunate, cognizance must be taken of the resulting reading problems.

The Vocabulary Burden

When deciding upon the reading materials for boys and girls, particularly in the lower grades, the teacher should consider not only the choice of words included but also the proportion of new words and the amount of repetition provided at appropriately spaced intervals. The tendency has been to reduce the number of different words used in readers during the initial stage of reading instruction. Recently, however, an increase in the number of running words has been advocated. It is claimed that if the words are phonetically regular words, more words can be learned by the child than when he is unable to unlock the new words by means of phonics.

No conclusive research is available on the optimum number of new words per page, but it is questionable whether it is desirable to introduce on the average more than one new word per page in pre-primer material and more than two per page in the primer and first reader stages. The number of new words to be presented on a page, however, is dependent upon so many factors that it is doubtful whether research can establish the optimum number for either the primary or the intermediate grades. It is usually conceded that as the child progresses in his ability to read, he can encounter, without reaching a level of frustration, more new words in proportion to the running words than he could earlier. In this connection it is important to bear in mind that while the number of new words given on a page in an intermediate grade book is often considerably larger than the number in first-grade books (one reason being, of course, that the average length of the page increases from the primary to the intermediate grades), in reality many of the so-called "new words" in the intermediate grade reader are new only insofar as they have not been used before in the series; they may be words which the pupils have identified through other reading.

A bright child may not need nearly as many repetitions as the average child. Furthermore, the method of presentation of a new word by the teacher determines in part how many repetitions are desirable. It would seem that probably in the books for the primary grades adequate repetition is provided for the average child. However, many reading textbooks for the intermediate grades do not repeat words often enough for many boys and girls to be able to learn them without undue difficulty. This point is particularly serious when the words are new not only to the child's reading, but also to his understanding, vocabulary. A teacher can, however, solve this problem in part by supplying significant supplementary practice on the words, most of which should as a rule be done in context.

The proportionate number of new words and the amount of repetition desirable, too, should not be determined mechanically, without reference to the individual, to the method of presentation of words, and to the supplementary reading that the child does. The learning of words should not be dependent solely upon repetition in a textbook. If considerable emphasis is put in reading instruction on developing power to decipher new words and upon meaning, it becomes less important to rely greatly on word lists.

CHAPTER 5B

Developing Skill
in Word Recognition

.

Specific suggestions for classroom practices in developing skill in word recognition are presented in this chapter.

TEACHING WORDS AS SIGHT WORDS

The following suggestions may be helpful to teachers who use the whole-word method as one of the means of helping boys and girls grow to independence in word recognition.

1. *Presenting new words before reading a selection.* Let us assume that the new word to be encountered is *summer.* The teacher has written it on the chalkboard in manuscript and now points to it, saying it clearly. She invites the class to repeat it with her in unison. She turns next to a cardholder or to word cards placed on the chalk ledge and asks individual children or the class as a whole to select the word *summer* from the numerous words on view. On the board are several sentences, one or more of which include the word *summer.* Children are called upon to select those sentences containing the word and to point to the word. They then find the word in the selection to be read.

2. *Studying new words after a selection has been read.* At times the teacher may prefer to have the children read a selection before she helps them with the new words in it. She is justified in doing so if she has reason to believe that most of the pupils will be able to figure

out the new words by themselves. If the selection to be read contains many new words, however, it is usually advisable not to rely upon children's ability to deal with them independently. After the reading, the children may be asked to identify the words with which they had difficulty, so that the teacher may present them in the manner suggested in the preceding paragraph. When using this procedure, however, the teacher should keep in mind the fact that frequently boys and girls, especially those with many problems in the recognition of words, may not respond to the suggestion that they designate the words they do not know. The teacher will, therefore, frequently want to select for practice words with which she thinks one or more children may have difficulty.

3. *Presenting new words before reading a selection and providing further practice on them after the reading.* In many instances work on words either before or after reading a selection may be insufficient to assure needed control of the new vocabulary. Consequently, at times the teacher will want to present the "new words" before the reading and then provide additional practice on them after the reading. The latter reinforcement of the learning may frequently be planned in such a way that the boys and girls become more familiar not only with the word in question but also with other forms of the word and of words that have elements in common with it. For example, if the "new word" *walk* has been presented before the reading, after the selection has been read the boys and girls might work on variants of the word, such as *walks, walked, walking.* Or if the word *cat* has been presented, after reading the story or part of it the pupils might work on words similar to *cat* in all respects except the initial letter, such as *hat, fat, pat, rat, sat.*

4. *"Telling" the word to save time.* After a child has acquired some efficiency in analyzing words phonetically and structurally, it may still at times be desirable to present a word to him as a "sight word." Stopping to decipher the sound of a word may interfere seriously with the flow of the narrative and thus produce irritating interruptions in what should be a pleasurable process of getting meaning. In such instances the sensible teacher supplies the word so that the pupil may get on with the story.

5. *Reading "new words" orally from the board.* A list of numbered words written on the board may sometimes be used as a brief exercise in the building of a sight vocabulary. Members of the class volunteer to indicate by number the words they know. Thus the presentation of new sight words by the teacher is supplemented by class participation. Obviously such an exercise should be both very brief and relatively infrequent.

6. *Distinguishing between words of similar length and shape.* Words that bear a general resemblance to each other in the eyes of a young child may be placed on the board in a row, with all the words alike except the one that is to be distinguished from the others. Or in the following list of words

when   where   where   when   where   when

pupils may be asked to draw a circle around each word that says *where*. The exercise may be repeated for the identification of the word *when*. Brief exercises may be arranged for other words of similar general appearance, such as *say* and *may*, *man* and *can*, *make* and *cake*, *mat* and *sat*.

7. *Distinguishing between words presented in pairs.* Words often confused by young readers may sometimes be presented in pairs. Thus the following words may be written on the board together:

when, where	thought, through
why, what	on, no
then, there	went, want.

The teacher points to each pair in turn, saying the words and calling on pupils to draw a line under the appropriate word or pair of words. Or she may write an incomplete sentence, calling on pupils to supply the missing words:

I＿＿＿a new ball. *(went, want)*

8. *Matching words and pictures.* Both to provide practice in recognizing words and to test the ability to do so, the teacher can give each pupil a sheet of paper giving a column of words and another of pictures. Pupils are then asked to draw lines from the words to the matching pictures. Or, instead of single words, groups of words or whole sentences can be supplied along with matching pictures. For example, pupils may be asked to draw a line from a picture of a boy with a ball to the one of three sentences that is illustrated by the picture as shown below.

Tom has a ball.
Tom has a bat.
Mary has a ball.

9. *Copying the word to be learned.* Some children who have

difficulty in remembering the appearance of a word by means of the sight method find it helpful to get practice in writing the word. There are many ways in which practice can be provided through a visual-motor approach. For example, the child is presented with the written or printed word *sister*. He is told what the word says and then proceeds to copy it. If he has made an error, he draws a line under the part of the model word that he did not copy correctly. Then he takes a second look at the word, thinking of its sound as he does so. He knows that next he will be asked to write the word without looking at the model. After he has written the word from memory, he compares it with the original copy and takes note of any differences. After a certain amount of such practice, he tries to identify the word in a list and in context.

By no means do all children need to use this slow and rather cumbersome method for learning new words. Nevertheless, it has been used successfully when other methods have failed. It is useful also with children who normally respond readily to the sight method but have difficulty with certain words, such as *them, then, why, what, where,* and *when.*

10. *Using individual word cards.* When pupils have individual cards similar to the larger ones suitable for group work, for practice on the words they might hold up their word cards that correspond to the ones the teacher shows. Then one of the pupils could name the word on the card.

11. *Labeling objects in the room.* After the teacher has made labels for various items in the classroom, the pupils can be asked to place the labels with the objects. In some cases the labels may be placed on or near the objects and in other instances they may be attached to the objects with tape. Labels can be used to designate objects in an exhibit, owners of lockers, contents of shelves or cupboards, library books, and the like.

12. *Pantomiming words.* Pantomime can be used effectively for practice on sight words that are difficult to illustrate in some other ways. Verbs and prepositions are among such words. The pupils might illustrate by actions, as the teacher points at the written words, verbs such as *hop, walk, run, smile, laugh* and prepositions such as *under, between, over.*

13. *Using a flannel board.* To a flannel board might be attached, for practice on sight words, various cut-outs illustrating "new words." These may be selected in terms of words "new" in a given story or in terms of those used in connection with a given topic, such as Christmas, Thanksgiving, birds, or space. On a table near the flannel board might be placed word cards (backed by a strip of flannel or felt)

to accompany each of the cut-out figures. The pupils could attach the cards to the appropriate illustrations. They could check their work by referring to a chart that is provided, on which the words are given next to the illustrations of them.

14. *Using "helper charts."* "Helper charts," on which are indicated lists of duties to be performed by members of the class, possibly illustrated, could have a parallel column with names of persons to perform the tasks. For example, the direction *Water plants* in the first column could have a card to the right of it with the name *Sally* attached to the chart. Or the only words on the chart could be the children's names. In that case a picture of a waste basket, for example, could indicate that David is to pass it during the week that his name is on the chart opposite the illustration.

15. *Following directions given on a chart.* Practice in learning some words or groups of words by sight can be provided by listing on a chart some directions that the pupils have frequent occasion to follow, for example: *Get ready to go home; Put on your wraps; Get ready for storytelling.* As the teacher, with her hands, "frames" a direction or otherwise points at it, the pupils respond to it by following it.

16. *Using "new words" in sentences.* To insure remembering words learned by the sight method, the teacher may ask the boys and girls to dictate to her sentences containing the words, which she writes on the chalkboard. Underlining of the words by the pupils may further aid recall.

17. *Illustrating words for a booklet.* To help the pupils remember words that can be illustrated, the teacher might prepare a worksheet for every child on which in each quarter of the sheet is written in manuscript a word to be illustrated. These sheets can be assembled in a booklet.

18. *Distinguishing between homonyms.* The sight-word method can be used in teaching homonyms. To gain practice in using newly acquired knowledge of the words, the pupils might be given exercises in which they are to supply the correct homonyms. In sentences such as the following the pupils might be asked to write the correct word given in parentheses.

> John_____the ball to the catcher *(threw, through)*
> _____you please open the window? *(wood, would)*

19. *Saying words written on slips of paper.* After the "new words" for a story have been presented, the teacher may pass out slips of paper on each of which is written one of the "new words." When

each child has chosen a slip of paper, one after another the pupils pronounce the words they drew. If a child does not recognize the word he has, he passes it on to the next person. A game could be made from this procedure.

DEVELOPING WORD RECOGNITION
THROUGH CONTEXT CLUES

Context clues are often most effective when they are employed along with other methods of word attack. The following suggestions should be read with this principle in mind.

1. *Using pictures in connection with the presentation of a word.* If the teacher wishes to present the word *ball* to the young child, she may first show a picture of a ball and carry on a brief conversation about it. In this way she is able to create in the child's mind the impressions of reality that give meaning to the verbal symbols. First comes the referent, then the symbol for it. The symbol can then evoke the referent when the reader encounters it in verbal context. To reinforce the context clues, the teacher may call attention to the length and contour of a word and confront the reader with sentences in which it is used.

2. *Introducing new words, in advance of reading, with the aid of pictures.* Before either the class or a single pupil begins to read a selection, the attention of the children may be called to an accompanying picture in the book. Discussion of the picture can naturally lead to the new word in the text, which can be pointed out and emphasized. In such preliminary discussion, the teacher may encourage the class to anticipate the story from an examination of the pictures.

A variation of this method is for the pupils to find the picture, among various ones placed on the chalkboard, that completes a part of a sentence that the teacher has written on the board. Thereupon the teacher can write the word with the rest of the sentence or show a word card with it.

3. *Using picture-word cards.* Some teachers have quite successfully made extensive use of picture-word cards in teaching word recognition. Sets of cards, each one of which carries on one side a picture with the appropriate label and on the other the word alone, are given to all pupils. Sometimes larger versions of the picture cards are mounted along the walls, and the children make a game of matching their own cards with those they find there. It should be emphasized that such games in word recognition should be combined with abundant experience in encountering the words in sentence context.

4. *Using picture dictionaries.* In this connection the reader is referred to pages 158–160 for a discussion of the great value of the many new picture dictionaries.

5. *Using picture clues on the bulletin board.* The bulletin board should be a source of constant pleasure and stimulation to the pupils. Pictures, clipped from magazines, drawn, or contributed by pupils or secured from various other sources (not from library periodicals!) are a most effective means of introducing children to the printed word. For example, a picture of a Christmas tree, attractively labeled, is a powerful device for drawing attention to the appearance of familiar words and for leading into a brief study of the structure of those words.

6. *Anticipating meaning through examination of pictures in a series.* Since logical thinking can be an important aspect of the use of context clues, pupils might be provided exercises in which they tell what they think will happen next in a series of events represented by pictures. For example, the first picture might be of a dog following a boy to school; the second might be of the boy stopping en route to school trying to persuade the dog to return home; the third might be of the boy and his dog approaching the door of the schoolhouse. Then the children could be asked to state which one of two pictures is the more likely to be the next in the sequence, one showing the dog running home as soon as they neared the schoolhouse door or one showing the dog managing to get into the school as the boys and girls enter the building even though the owner tried to prevent him from entering. A variation of this exercise is one in which the pupils are asked to describe a suitable picture to follow the pictures in the series that were shown.

7. *Selecting words that are already in the child's vocabulary.* The new word to be learned in the lower primary grades should preferably be one that is already a part of the child's speaking or understanding vocabulary. To make certain that the word and its meaning are familiar to the pupils, the teacher may arrange for direct experiences and group discussions which will help to establish the needed word or words in the working vocabulary of the children. Thus if the word *zoo* is to be encountered in the reading, it may in some classes be desirable to arrange a trip to a zoo, look at a film or filmstrip about a zoo, look at pictures of animals in a zoo, or at least talk about zoos. Some of the fine picture books describing unfamiliar animals should be displayed on the book table or on the shelves of the classroom library.

8. *Using questions to help pupils learn words.* If, for example, in the sentence, "Betty bought a present for her mother" all words but *bought* are known by the reader, the teacher may ask, "How do you think Betty got the present that she gave her mother?" If the child says

that she found it, the teacher may ask him to name other words than *found* that could fit into the sentence or she may tell the pupil that the word used begins with the letter *b* as a clue to the "missing word."

9. *Anticipating meaning through completion exercises.* Pupils can be asked to supply words that might fit in a blank in an incomplete sentence, such as, "Dick —— home after school." The word to be supplied is *ran.* If the pupils suggest *walked, ran, hurried,* or *hopped,* the teacher may say, "Yes, all those words would fit into the sentence, but this one begins with the *r* sound. Which word is it?" The correct word is then written in the blank. A variation from this type of exercise is one in which the pupils choose from a group of words the one that fits the meaning, for example,

Sam played_____. *(ball, boy, bat, work, sing)*

10. *Anticipating words when listening.* Training in the use of context clues may occur if the teacher pauses at suitable spots as she reads orally and asks the class to tell what they think the next word is. For example, she may read a sentence such as, "The cat climbed up a" and then ask what word might come next.

11. *Discussing with the class appropriate techniques of identifying words through context.* Although the suggestions will necessarily vary with the pupil's stage in learning to read, certain general hints may prove helpful to children in various grades: (a) Read the entire sentence before trying to determine the meaning of the new word. (b) Look at the beginning and ending sounds of the word to note whether these match a word that would make sense in the context. (c) Read for meaning. If your first impression of a word, derived from its appearance, does not make sense, give it a second and more careful look. (d) If sentence clues do not help, read the whole paragraph. The broader context may provide the key.

12. *Becoming acquainted with words related to the theme of the selection.* If the teacher will introduce children to interesting new words in advance of the reading, vocabulary difficulties may be substantially diminished. Thus in a story about Eskimos, a preliminary discussion of such words as *igloo, kayak, whale, walrus, glacier,* and *frigid* may markedly reduce the child's word-recognition problems.

13. *Learning to recognize synonyms and antonyms.* Word meanings may frequently be obtained from reference to neighboring words. Thus in the sentence, "These are the nomothetic, or institutional, dimensions of our goal-structure, as distinguished from the idiographic, or individual dimensions," we have both synonymic and antonymic

clues to the unusual words, *nomothetic* and *idiographic*. Phonic and structural clues are essential, and an elementary knowledge of Greek would help us a great deal, but the sentence contains its own built-in keys to the new words. At the child's level, the following sentences illustrate the value of contextual clues in the form of synonyms and antonyms:

> The picture showed an *ocelot*, a member of the cat family, in a charming pose.

> While the princess moved among the guests with a friendly smile for everyone, the prince offended many with his *dour* expression.

> As the game was about to begin, the principal announced over the loud-speaker that the coach and *mentor* of the team would be present, after all.

> Unlike the *torrid* winds of his homeland, the cool breezes from this picturesque harbor invigorated and inspired Sapu.

> For various and *sundry* reasons, the squire delayed building his new home.

> Neither the rich nor the *indigent* failed to find a welcome at the bishop's home.

14. *Using a word in a sentence to summarize the thought of a preceding sentence or group of sentences.* If this method is used, the pupil must know the words in the sentence(s) preceding the one containing the word that is unfamiliar in print.

The word *friends* in the second of the two sentences given below is clarified by the sentence that precedes it.

> Mary and Ann like each other.
> They are good *friends*.

15. *Having pupils find the word in a group of words which means the opposite or almost the opposite of the first word in the row.*

> *kind:* sad   happy   good   mean

16. *Writing on the chalkboard a sentence with a "new word" that a pupil has given orally.* As the teacher writes the sentence on the board, she might underline the "new word" and ask someone to read the sentence and to name the underlined word.

17. *Giving riddles, in written form, for the pupils to solve.* A number of simple riddles like the following might be written on the chalkboard:

> I give milk.
> I eat grass.
> What am I?

Opposite the riddle might be placed a series of words, like *apples, cow, house,* from which the children are to select the one that answers the riddle.

18. *Providing pupils with pictures to complete so that they fit sentences that accompany them.* Each child could be given a sheet of paper on which there is a series of sentences or groups of sentences, each containing an indication as to what needs to be done to a picture in order to have it fit the sentence containing the new word, which is underlined. For example, one group of sentences might be:

> Ted likes to play *ball.*
> His *ball* is red.

To the right of these two sentences might be given an outline picture of a ball.

19. *Giving the pupils duplicated pictures on which various words that they are learning are illustrated.* For example, there could be a picture of a Christmas scene, with these words illustrated in it: *mother, father, tree, book, doll, candy, ball.* The words could be written along the sides and bottom of the picture. The pupils could then draw a line from each of the words to the part in the picture illustrating that word.

20. *Using transparencies with an overhead projector.* On a transparency the teacher may write before class a series of sentences in each of which a blank has been left for a "new word." To the right of each sentence can be a picture illustrating the word. The children can be instructed to read the part of a sentence given, look at the accompanying picture, and name the missing word. The teacher can then, after a sentence has been taken up in this manner, write the word in color on an overlay so that it completes the sentence on the original transparency. After each sentence has been completed, the boys and girls may be given practice in naming the "new words," first, as they occur when the overlay is placed on the first transparency and then when only the overlay is shown.

21. *Using other visual aids.* Some reading series are accom-

panied by films and filmstrips that introduce children to new concepts and new words. Teacher-made slides, based upon the reading materials, can also prove to be effective in helping children to cope with new vocabulary.

22. *Taking advantage of typographical aids.* Among the various types of context clues, some of the most helpful are the mechanical typographical devices. Punctuation marks, italics, bold print, parentheses, indentations, footnotes, and other similar devices provide helps in the recognition and interpretation of new words.

23. *Making effective use of context to aid in pronunciation.* Children may be given practice in recognizing the correct one of alternative pronunciations of words. In the following two sentences the context provides the essential clue:

> The *lead* in my pencil is broken.
> *Lead* the way, please.

Boys and girls enjoy making up sentences in which words like the following are pronounced in two different ways, depending upon the context: *read, tear, use, wound, wind, bow.*

DEVELOPING WORD RECOGNITION THROUGH THE USE OF PHONICS

Suggestions given here for the use of phonics in the teaching of word recognition are intentionally confined to a relatively small number. The teachers' manuals that accompany the better reading series contain many excellent suggestions for applying the phonics principles stated in Chapter 5A. These suggestions are based upon the special vocabularies which are a part of the developmental programs described in specific series. Methods of teaching phonic skills described in the following paragraphs should, of course, be adapted to the specific needs of children, whether a basal reading series is used or not.

1. A child should not receive phonics instruction before he is "ready"— that is, until he is able to make the necessary visual and auditory discriminations with ease. The stage of readiness will vary with different children and with the difficulty of phonics instruction to be given. It is important to remember that the initial experiences with phonics should be successful ones.
2. One of the most elementary of the phonic skills is that of knowing the sounds commonly associated with single consonants in initial position in a word. In the first work on phonics, the teacher should teach consonants that, unless they are silent letters or blended with others, can

be depended upon to have the same sound always—namely, *b, h, j, l, m, p, t,* and *v.* Practice can be provided by means of procedures like these:

a. After the pupils have had some practice in, for example, associating the letter *m* in the initial position in a word with the corresponding sound, they may name words in addition to the ones already mentioned that begin with the same letter. These words may then be listed on the board and attention drawn to the letter *m* in those words.

b. The teacher may wish to write on the board two letters, such as *m* and *h,* with which the pupils have had some familiarity and illustrate them as they occur in initial position in a word. Then a pupil may point to the correct letter as the teacher names words that begin with either the sound of *m* or *h*—for example, *man, mother, hat, hair, many, had, has.* As a variation of this procedure, if the boys and girls can write the letters, each child could number a paper—possibly from 1 to 10—and then write *h* or *m* as the teacher names words beginning with these letters.

c. The boys and girls might make sentences in which the initial sound is alike in many of the words in a given sentence, like:

Polly picked peas and put them near the flower pot.

d. As the teacher names a word, the pupils might write the letter representing the sound with which the word begins.

e. As the teacher names a word beginning with a consonant in initial position, the pupils might point at objects in the room, the names of which begin with the same sound. The game "I Spy," in which the leader says, "I spy something that begins with the same sound as the word ____" can be played.

f. A phonic tree may be made by placing a small branch of a tree in a jar of sand. The "tree" could be whitewashed and the stand, if not colorful, painted green. To the top of the tree could be attached a card with a letter to be emphasized. If the letter *t* is used, the boys and girls may hang to the branches of the tree pictures of words beginning with that letter. Similarly, a tree could be used for practice on consonants in ending positions, on blends, on various vowel sounds, and on phonograms such as *ake, air, at.* The children can look for the pictures or they can choose appropriate ones from a box containing many pictures selected on the basis of use for help in phonics. The tree should be changed frequently if maximum learning is to be achieved through use of this device.

3. To get practice in application of what they know about consonants in initial position in a word, as well as about the use of context clues, pupils could tell what word fits into sentences like this one, where only the initial consonant of the word is given:

Susan fed her d____.

Or the boys and girls might draw pictures to illustrate words missing in sentences of that type.

Similar types of practice might be provided for pupils to strengthen their recognition of the sounds of consonants in final position in a word.

4. Practice could be provided in making substitutions of consonants in words. For example, if the pupil knows the word *fun*, he has merely to substitute the consonant *r* for *f* to be able to recognize the word *run*. The teacher can ask boys and girls who know the word *man*, when they come to the "new word" *can*, "What word that we know looks the same as this word except for the beginning letter?" When the boys and girls have replied *man*, the teacher can write *man* on the board directly below the word *can* and then ask with what sound that word (pointing at *can*) begins. She can continue by saying, "Let's name a word that begins with the *c* (hard *c*) sound and rhymes with *man*." Opportunity might also then be given for the boys and girls to name other words that are like *man* and *can* except for the beginning letter, like *tan* and *ran*. Attention needs to be drawn not only to the possibility of substitution of consonants in initial position but also in ending and medial position in a syllable as a possible means of deciphering a new word. In such cases, a similar procedure may be applied. The same method can be used with words in which substitution of a vowel in medial position in a syllable is a possible means of deciphering a new word, as when *bit* is recognized when the word *bat* is known, by a substitution of the *i* for the *a*.

If special practice is needed to develop skill in identifying words through substitution of letters, an exercise like this might be used:

> *Direction:* Draw a line under all words in each row that are exactly alike except for the beginning letter.
> man   men   can   pan   ran   map

The following directions might be given with a page consisting of rows of words like those that are here listed.

> *Direction:* Draw a line under all words in each row that are like the first word except for the ending letter.
> has   hat   was   ham   had   his

5. Some boys and girls who can use phonetic clues secured through the recognition of consonants at the beginning and ending positions of a word are uncertain what to do when a consonant comes in a medial position within a syllable, for example, in the word *late*. What can be done in the case of polysyllabic words is briefly described later in this section in the part on syllabication in connection with structural analysis of words. As a rule, in the case of monosyllabic words not much practice is needed on consonants in medial position if the pupils know

well the role of the consonants in the initial and ending positions. Nevertheless, an indication should be given to the child fairly early in his training in phonics that consonants can occur in other than beginning and ending positions, as suggested in paragraph number 4 on page 149.

6.   As boys and girls meet in their reading consonant blends like *st, gr, tr, cr,* and *str,* they should learn that these and other consonant combinations are sounded in such rapid succession that they do not make two entirely separate sounds. They could be asked to name words beginning with whatever blend they are then studying or have studied. A phonic wheel like the one illustrated can help provide occasional practice not only on beginning consonant blends but also on initial single consonants.

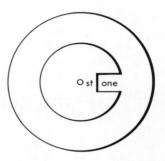

The wheel can be made of two circles of tagboard, one a little smaller than the other, fastened together in the middle by a brass fastener so that the smaller wheel can spin around. Since the wheel here illustrated is to give practice on *st* in initial position in a word, the letters *st* are written on the inner circle next to an indentation in that circle made by cutting out a piece of the tagboard. The cut-out part should be of sufficient size so that endings like *ore* (to go with the *st* to form *store*), *one, op,* and *ick* written on the outer circle can be seen when the slot is moved in such a way that the opening in the smaller circle is opposite the place where the ending in the larger wheel occurs. Then as the child spins the smaller circle, he can read the words that begin with *st,* like *store, stone, stop,* and *stick.*

7.   Another phonic device that helps provide practice needed by some pupils is that of listing either consonant blends or single consonants on slips of tagboard about 1 by 2 inches, with the consonant or consonant blend written at the right of each of these cards. Attached by brass fasteners to the bottom of the pile of these smaller cards could be a larger one, possibly 1 by 4 inches, that contains all of the letters of a word except the beginning consonant or consonant blend. If on the longer card the ending *ake* were given, then on the smaller cards

might be written *b, r, c, t, m, f, l, s,* and *w.* To form different words for recognition, the pupils can lift up one card at a time and thereby make a number of words ending in *ake.*

8. After boys and girls have learned the sound of *th,* both voiced as in *there* and voiceless as in *thin,* the teacher may wish to write on the board a list of words beginning with *th,* some with the voiced and some with the voiceless sound, such as *the, that, thick, think.* Then as the pupils pronounce each word they could, for example, put a star in front of every word that begins with the sound of the *th* in *thin.*

9. When teaching vowel sounds the teacher may, for example, ask the pupils to identify the sound of the *a* in words like *at, bat, man, sand.* Or she may ask the boys and girls which words in a series like the following has an *a* with the same sound as the *a* in *at: ate, cat, am, air, can, arm, late, bat.*

   Another, but similar, type of practice could be provided by asking the children to indicate which in a series of words listed on the chalkboard or on paper contains a given sound that is identified as the long sound or the short sound of a vowel. For example, the pupils might select words with the long *e* sound from among a group of words like the following, included among which are words with the long *e* sound, words with the short *e* sound, words with other sounds of *e,* and words with the silent *e: be, set, late, been, he, she.*

   Another procedure is to have the pupils make new words by changing the vowel in a word to form other words, as when they substitute for the *a* in *hat,* the letters *i, o,* and *u* to form *hit, hot,* and *hut.*

10. To provide practice in identifying the sound of a vowel—for example, the sound of long and short *a*—the boys and girls could be given a sheet of paper on which are drawn squares about 2 by 2 inches. In each of the squares is a picture illustrating a short word containing the long or short sound of the letter *a.* Also in each square the teacher writes four or more words some of which contain the long *a* and some the short *a* sound. The pupils could then be instructed to draw a line under every word in a square that contains the same sound of the *a* as in the word illustrated by the picture. One row of the pictures with accompanying words might look like this:

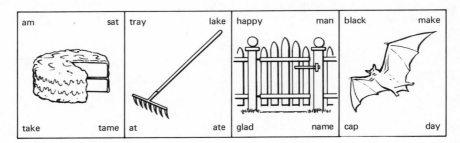

As a variation of the exercise just described, the pupils could indicate which words in a row like the following have the same sound of the vowel *a* as the first word in this row has: <u>*bat*</u>   *rat*   *rate*   *made*   *sat.*

11. The pupils may write on small slips of paper the vowels on which practice is needed, one vowel per piece of paper. If the practice is to be on the vowels *a* and *e*, the pupils may hold up the one of these two letters that is represented by a sound in each word as the teacher names it. For example, when the teacher says *name*, the pupils will hold up their papers with the letter *a* written on them.

12. Further practice on vowels could be provided through procedures such as the following:

   a. After the teacher has written on the board a word containing one vowel, for example, *bell,* she asks questions that involve changing the vowel of the given word so that another word is formed. For example, if the word *bell* has been written on the chalkboard, the teacher might ask the pupils what change would need to be made in that word so that the "new word" names something with which boys and girls play.

   b. In two columns could be listed words containing various vowel sounds, with one word in each column having the same vowel sound as a word in the other column. The pupils are to match the words with similar vowel sounds.

take	at
and	end
eat	seat
ten	say

13. To teach the boys and girls the sound of *ar, or, er, ir,* and *ur* as used in standard American speech, the teacher could have them give the sound of these letters as she pronounces them and writes words such as these on the board: *color, murmur, burglar, fir, orator.* Next the pupils can give the sound of those combinations of vowels with r. Then they

can name other words containing an *ar, or, er, ir,* or *ur* combination. They should be helped to realize that a vowel preceding an *r* does not necessarily indicate such a combination, for example, in the case of *rare, figure, mire, deer, clear.*

In a similar way the teacher can proceed to develop inductively the generalization about the sound of *a* when it precedes a *w* or an *ll,* as in *claw* and *fall.*

14. After the boys and girls have learned that in vowel digraphs, like *ea, oa, ai, ay, ee,* and *ei,* the sound of the first letter forming the digraph is often long and the second silent, the teacher may list on the board examples that the pupils name. Then they can mark words, given on a list distributed to each child, that contain one of the digraphs that follow the rule. Some of the words on this list might be *each, oats, may, eel.* What words are used will depend in part on the reading level of the learner. In a similar manner the pupils could practice on diphthongs like *oy, oi, ou,* and *ow.*

The pupils should be cautioned that the generalization regarding vowel digraphs is not, by any means, an invariable rule.

15. Although it is usually easy to develop the concept that some letters are silent, it is likely to be more difficult to teach the pupils *when* letters are silent. In this connection it is desirable that boys and girls recognize the difference between vowel digraphs, in which one letter is silent, and diphthongs, in which two letters together form one sound unlike either of the vowels. Practice may be provided by having the pupils tell in which words, in a list like the following, one of two letters in Roman type is silent: *about, oil, boat, clean, cow, rail.*

To teach inductively the generalization that a final *e* in a syllable preceded by a single consonant is usually silent, the teacher could place on the board a numbered list of three or four words that are in harmony with the rule: (1) rate, (2) tame, (3) hope, (4) rule. For each word the pupils could be asked to (1) pronounce the word, (2) tell with what letter the word ends, (3) tell whether the *e* is silent or not silent, (4) indicate what kind of letter—vowel or consonant—precedes the vowel, and (5) state how many consonants precede the vowel. As a summary, the pupils could answer these questions about all the words in this list:

1. With what letter does each word end?
2. Is the *e* silent?
3. What kind of letter—vowel or consonant—precedes the final *e*?
4. How many consonants precede the final *e* in each of the words in the list?

Next the teacher could tell the pupils that usually when the final letter in a syllable is *e,* the *e* is silent if it is preceded by a single consonant.

Thereupon she could give the pupils opportunity for applying the rule. They could tell in which words in a list of words like these this rule applies: *came, ride, male, riddle, table.*

16.   To help the pupils remember sounds of letters, the teacher could make a chart that gives the letters or combinations of letters that produce a sound and a word illustrating each sound that the boys and girls have learned. Pictures that illustrate words containing a given sound are sometimes helpful. For example, the word *mother* with a picture of a mother would serve to help with the sound of *m.* Often, instead of using one big chart, tagboard cards, about 5 by 8 inches, are used, on each of which is one picture, one word, and one letter.

Another device is to have the boys and girls make individual books in which there is a page for each letter or letter sound that they have studied. On these pages they could paste pictures illustrating words that contain these sounds.

To get further practice in associating the written symbol and the sound, a box containing various consonants or consonant blends on slips of paper might be used. As a child draws a letter out of the box, he might name it and find objects in the room the names of which begin with that letter. Or the pupils might match the written symbols with pictures arranged around the room that begin with a given sound. Or as the teacher holds up a picture, the children might hold up a card with the letter or letters with which the name of the object in the picture begins.

17.   Rhyming words can be used in teaching phonics with procedures such as the following:

   a.   The teacher repeats a nursery rhyme and asks the pupils to listen for words that rhyme.

   b.   The boys and girls complete jingles that the teacher makes up, such as:

> At recess time on this day
> All the children will want to _____.

   c.   The pupils name pairs of rhyming words.

   d.   As the teacher names various words in pairs, some of which rhyme and some of which do not rhyme, such as *meat, seat* and *take, talk,* the pupils tell which pairs rhyme.

   e.   The teacher presents orally sets of three words, two of which rhyme. The pupils tell which pairs rhyme.

   f.   The pupils make card files of rhyming words. For example, one card could consist of words rhyming with *play,* such as *day, hay, lay, may, pay, ray, say, stay, today, way.* Pupils may wish to refer to the cards when writing original poetry.

   g.   The teacher places on the chalkboard ledge a series of pictures, the name of each of which rhymes with the name of some other object or person pictured in the collection. For example, she might place on the chalkboard pictures of a boy and of a toy, of a hat and of a bat. As a leader points to one of the pictures, another pupil finds a picture the name of which rhymes with the name of the one at which the leader pointed. These two pictures can then be removed from the collection as practice continues on other rhyming words.

18. To provide practice in becoming conscious of the position of sounds in a word the teacher could tell the pupils, for example, that all the words she will give will contain the sound of *t*. After the teacher has given a word, a pupil tells whether the sound of *t* comes at the beginning or end of a word or within it. Words like these can be pronounced: *hat, Tom, little.*

19. After the boys and girls have had work on blends, the teacher may draw four large circles on the chalkboard, in one of which she has written, for example, the word *clock,* in another the word *tree,* and in still another *store.* Then as she gives, from a word card, the name of a word beginning with the sound of the *cl* in *clown,* a child can take the card and put it on the chalkboard ledge near the circle in which the word *clock* is written. Similarly, when the teacher pronounces the word *stove,* a pupil should place the word card under the circle.

20. When the boys and girls are ready to learn the diacritical markings of words, it is important to begin slowly enough so that the work will not be confusing to them. After they have worked on the long and short sounds of the vowels, the teacher may tell them that there is a way of indicating the sound of a letter in writing. Then she can tell them the marking frequently used for the long and short vowels and provide practice in their interpreting and writing these markings for words. At this time she may also wish to draw attention to the fact that in some systems of marking the short vowel sounds are not indicated by markings and explain that the assumption is that when words are marked diacritically, if no marking occurs over a vowel, the vowel is short. One way in which she may wish to help the boys and girls use diacritical marks is by asking them to mark all the long and the short vowels in a list of words of which they already know the pronunciation. Later they can learn to decipher words by means of markings.

Since more than one set of diacritical markings is in common use, the system selected for practice should be the one most used in the pupils' glossaries or dictionaries. In the intermediate grades, however, boys and girls should be helped to decipher words when a system different from one they have been employing is used. They should know that at the bottom of the pages of a dictionary is given the guide to pronunciation that will help them interpret the markings of the words in that book.

DEVELOPING WORD RECOGNITION
THROUGH THE USE OF STRUCTURAL ANALYSIS

Without resorting to the undesirable practice of having boys and girls "find little words in big"—for example, *as* in *has*—the teacher can in many ways aid the pupils in developing through structural analysis a method of identifying and recognizing some words more rapidly than through phonetic analysis. A few such methods are listed here.

1. As the teacher refers to a compound word on the board, like *grandmother*, she may tell the boys and girls that the word is made up of two words and ask them to find these two words.

2. Use can be made of two columns of words in one of which is the first part of a compound word and in the other, the second part. The boys and girls can then draw lines connecting the words in the two columns that together form one word—for example:

grand	basket
worth	room
waiting	while
waste	mother

As variation of this procedure the teacher may put into a cardholder a group of words in mixed-up order that might be used in forming compound words, like the following, which pupils will combine into compound words: school, stairs, book, story, up, mother, grand, house.

3. The boys and girls can make a collection of compound words for posting on the bulletin board. To the right of each compound word the words of which it is composed can be written.

4. A crossword puzzle could be made by the teacher or pupils in which only compound words would serve as answers. Part of each word could be supplied in a numbered list while the other part could be chosen from an unnumbered list that is supplied with the puzzle.

5. Each pupil in the room might be given a card on which is written part of a compound word that can be combined with the word on another pupil's card to form one word. The children find their word partners and then each pair tells the class what was formed.

6. The boys and girls can get help in unlocking words by looking for the root of a word that contains a suffix. For example, in the word *sings* the teacher may wish to draw a line under *sing*, stating that that much of the word the pupils already know. Then she can ask them to pronounce the root word and thereafter the new word.

7. The boys and girls can make a list of words containing a given root, like *walk, walks, walked, walking.*

8. When the pupils come to a word like *unwise,* if they have had the word *wise,* the teacher can draw a line under *wise* and ask what that part of the word is. The pupils can then give the prefix and, next, combine the prefix with the root of the word. Having the boys and girls make a list of common prefixes, like *mis, im,* and *ir,* with words in which they form a prefix, like *misuse, impossible,* and *irresponsible,* can help them both in word recognition and in word meaning.

9. On a sheet of paper each child can write the base words of a list of words containing either prefixes or suffixes or both that have been written on the board.

10. The teacher may write on the board a list of words with prefixes that mean *not,* like *unhappy, impossible,* and *irresponsible.* Then the boys and girls could name words to add to the list. Next they could draw a line under the different prefixes that mean *not.*

11. The boys and girls can supply the correct prefix for each word in a list, like the following, for which the meaning of the word to be formed has been given:

       _____ known   not known
       _____ like   not to like
       _____ kind   not kind

12. The pupils can be helped in the development of the generalization that many root words ending in *e* drop the final *e* before adding *ing,* like *make, making.* They can give examples of words to which this generalization applies.

13. Each pupil can be given a card with a prefix or suffix, while the teacher has a series of cards containing root words to many of which a prefix or a suffix on a pupil's card could be added. As the teacher holds up a card, all pupils who have a card with a prefix or suffix that can be combined with the root word stand. Next the pupils who have the appropriate prefixes or suffixes can write on the chalkboard the words that can be formed from the root word with the addition of their prefixes or suffixes.

14. The class might make a chart with three columns, in the first of which are listed common prefixes. In the second column could be given a meaning of each prefix and in the third column, examples of words in which the prefix has the designated meaning.

15. The pupils may be given two columns of words, with words with prefixes in the first column and synonyms for them, in a different order, without prefixes in the opposite column. The instruc-

tions would be to draw lines connecting each word in the first column with its synonym in the second.

> unhappy   hate
> dislike   mean
> unkind   sad

16. The pupils could be asked to draw a line from a root word given in one column to a prefix that goes with that word in another column.

> form   dis
> happy   re
> interested   un

17. Another matching exercise is one in which the pupils draw a line from each prefix given in one column to a common meaning of that prefix found in the second column.

> un   back
> ex   under
> re   out
> pre   before
> sub   not

18. As the boys and girls acquire the essentials of syllabication, they should learn to divide words into syllables—first of all, as an aid to word recognition and, second, as a help in writing words when it is necessary to divide them into syllables. Some generalizations about syllabication, of value in word recognition, are given in Chapter 5A.

To give help in syllabication, the pupils might be given a list of words, some with one, others with two, and still others with more than two syllables. The boys and girls could indicate after each word the number of syllables it contains.

19. The class could make a list of contractions, with the words that were combined to form each contraction given opposite each contraction. Or a crossword puzzle could be made, the answers to which are contractions. The words from which the contractions are formed could constitute the numbered list of words for the puzzle.

USING PICTURE DICTIONARIES

The term *picture dictionary* usually refers to books in which a picture is used with every word entry to help the child identify and recall words. Often, but not always, the words are arranged in alphabetical order. To illustrate the letter *a*, a large picture of an apple, along with the word *apple*, and a sentence containing the word may be given.

The following are some of the more widely used picture dictionaries:

Clemons, Elizabeth, *Dixie Dictionary*. New York: Holt, Rinehart and Winston, Inc., 1961. 62 pages.

Courtis, Stuart, and Garnette Watters, *Illustrated Golden Dictionary*. New York: Simon and Schuster, Inc., 1961. 544 pages.

MacBean, Dilla W., *Picture Book Dictionary*. Chicago: Children's Press, Inc., 1962. 48 pages.

McIntire, Alta, *The Follett Beginning-to-Read Picture Dictionary*. Chicago: Follett Publishing Company, 1959. 32 pages.

Monroe, Marion, and W. C. Greet, *My Little Pictionary*. Glenview, Ill.: Scott, Foresman and Company, 1964.

O'Donnell, Mabel, and Wilhelmina Townes, *Words I Like to Read, Write, and Spell*. New York: Harper & Row, Publishers, Inc., 1963. 224 pages.

Parke, Margaret B., *Young Reader's Color-Picture Dictionary for Reading, Writing, and Spelling*. Illustrated by Cynthia and Alvin Koehler. New York: Grosset & Dunlap, Inc., 1958. 93 pages.

Scott, Alice, and Stella Center, *The Giant Picture Dictionary for Boys and Girls*. New York: Doubleday & Company, Inc., 1958. 316 pages.

Watters, Garnette, and Stuart Courtis, *The Picture Dictionary for Children*. New York: Grosset & Dunlap, Inc., 1958. 383 pages.

Wright, Wendell W., ed., *The Rainbow Dictionary*. Cleveland: The World Publishing Company, 1959. 434 pages.

Some suggestions for the use of picture dictionaries are:

1. For younger children, stress simplicity of arrangement of words and of illustrations of the words.
2. Take time to help children in the use of the picture dictionary.
3. Use the picture dictionary primarily as a self-help device.
4. Make the picture dictionary easily available to the children, display it attractively, and have numerous copies on the reading table.
5. Be sure to make ample time available for the use of the picture dictionary.

Pupil-made picture dictionaries are especially valuable, perhaps more than the commercial ones, certainly as supplementary materials. One type of picture dictionary is one in which the children either draw or paste a picture representing an entry word and then write the word, often used in a simple sentence, on the same page with the picture. These pages are arranged to good advantage in alphabetical order by means of a looseleaf notebook. As the pupil meets a new word that can be illustrated, he writes it on a sheet of paper and pastes on the same sheet a picture that he has found or drawn himself. Sometimes the picture dictionary is a group project; at other times each pupil makes his own.

A picture dictionary may be in the form of cards, instead of sheets of paper, that contain the words and the illustrations of words. These cards can be arranged in a file, which can be expanded as the class progresses in knowledge of words. Another variation of the picture dictionary is often made in connection with the words that can be illustrated that occur in a story or a section of a book. As the pupil meets new words that can be illustrated in a given story or unit in a reader, he illustrates each one; he then can refer to the word as he finds the need of doing so. For example, if in a story the child meets the words *rabbit, tree, ran, squirrel,* and *into* he may divide a sheet of paper into four parts, using one of the four parts for the word *rabbit* under a picture of a rabbit and reserving another of the four parts for each of these words: *tree, ran,* and *squirrel. Ran* he may illustrate by a boy, a dog, or a rabbit running. Since words like *into* do not easily present themselves in a pictorial illustration, that kind of word usually is omitted from a picture dictionary.

Another teacher-pupil-made adaptation of the picture dictionary deals only with words used in a science or social studies unit.

As the pupil uses the picture dictionary to recognize words, the teacher can help him derive other benefits from it. Some of these values are: (1) help in spelling, (2) development of interest in words, and (3) development of skill in finding words in alphabetical order. If the picture dictionary is pupil-made, these are additional values: (1) practice in arranging words in alphabetical order, (2) development of ability to draw, cut out, and paste pictures, and (3) development of skill in arranging words and pictures neatly on a page.

WORKBOOKS AS AN AID
TO WORD RECOGNITION

Workbooks of various types, when not used as busywork, can be of service in helping the child develop from dependence to independence in word recognition. One type, and probably the more useful, is that which accompanies reading series. The better reading series have a well-developed sequence of workbooks designed to be used in conjunction with the hardback books, the regular readers. Most of these are written to give the boys and girls practice after the material in the textbook has been read. In such instances the new words are presented in connection with the work in the reading books. After a story or part of a story has been read, the pupil is given more practice in recognizing the words in that and other selections by using the words in a variety of ways. At times the pupils are asked to draw a line under the word that completes the meaning of a sentence in which one of the new words has been left out. At other times the pupils may draw a line from a word to the picture that is used to illustrate it. An examination of any workbook accompanying a reader will reveal a variety of ways in which it provides practice on words and makes possible a test on the skills as well.

But not all workbooks published as part of a reading series are planned to be studied by the child after he has read a corresponding section in the textbook. Some are designed so that a child studies a number of pages in the workbook before he reads the material that corresponds to it in the reader. In that case the new words for the selection in the reader are presented in the workbook and practice on their recognition is provided. In this type of arrangement the child thus meets in the workbook, before he even starts the regular book, all the new words in the story. The words are not, however, presented as a list of words but are given in context, frequently in material of interest to the boys and girls.

Some teachers prefer making material of the workbook type themselves, believing that it is better suited to the needs of the particular boys and girls than that given in the workbooks. Although this practice has merit, it is time-consuming and not really necessary today. It is true, however, that when workbook materials were sterile in content and poor in selection of objectives to be accomplished, it was not difficult to justify the large amount of time that many teachers, especially in the lower grades, spent in devising and duplicating materials to provide practice beyond that given in the reader on various skills of reading.

In using workbooks that are not made to accompany any one series of readers, there is the danger of lack of unity in objectives and procedures between reader and workbook. If the authors of the textbook series have in mind one program for the development of word recognition and the writers of the workbook follow a different sequence and observe other criteria, the articulation when using these two types of materials is often poor. This difficulty is especially likely to exist if the teacher is under pressure to require every pupil to do every page in a workbook, regardless of the appropriateness of the material to the rest of the program and to the needs of the boys and girls. Nevertheless, judicious use of workbooks that are made independently of any one series of readers can be helpful if the workbooks are based on sound principles of teaching reading.

GAMES AND WORD RECOGNITION

In connection with the role of games in relation to the development of power in word recognition, these questions frequently concern teachers: (1) Under what conditions are games desirable? (2) What are some games that can aid in word recognition?

Criteria for Selection of Games

In determining the role of games in developing power in word recognition, the teacher needs to have her purposes clearly in mind. If the major purpose is to help the boys and girls become more skillful in identifying and remembering words, then a game, to be acceptable, must satisfy the requirements for good drill. If the chief aim is to furnish recreation, then, of course, it is not essential that the characteristics of effective drill be present. Games that are not primarily designed to give help in reading can be scheduled during times of the school day set aside for recreational activities, such as before school, during the noon hour, during recess when better use of the time cannot be made, and during other periods when recreation is the primary aim.

One criterion for effective drill that is often not observed when games are used in learning to read is this: "Other things being equal, that drill is the better of two that provides the more practice on the skill in question in a given length of time." Other criteria of good drill for a game used primarily as a learning activity are: (1) The boys and girls should be cognizant of the purpose served by the drill. (2) The game should be on the interest level of the participants. (3) The game should not interfere with the development of good citizenship. (4) If competition is an element of the drill, it should be primarily competition with self rather than with others. (5) The game should be a means to an end, not an end in itself.

List of Games Commercially Available

Some of the reading games are available through publishing companies, in variety stores, and in department stores. Use of most of these can be justified chiefly as recreational activities that may, however, provide opportunity for growth in reading. Many teachers like to place such games on a reading table, so that they will be accessible to the children in free periods during, before, or after school time.

The following list of games is merely illustrative of the large number now available.

1. *"Phonic Lotto," by E. W. Dolch. Champaign, Illinois: The Garrard Publishing Company.*

"Phonic Lotto," a game for two to ten players, consists of ten cards 7¹/₂ by 5¹/₂ inches, and sixty smaller cards, 2¹/₄ inches square. Each of the larger cards is divided into six squares, on which there is printed a vowel or vowel combination accompanied by a picture, the name of which contains the vowel or vowel combination given in the square. The sixty smaller cards show pictures of objects whose names contain one of the vowel sounds found on the squares of the large cards. The sounds on which there is drill are the long and short vowel sounds, *a, e, i, o, u;* the digraphs, *ai, ay, ee, oa;* the diphthongs, *oi, oy, ou, ow, ew, oo;* and the vowels with the letter *r,* namely, *ar, er, ir, or, ur.* In the game the purpose is to match the small cards so that the pictures on them are placed on the pictures on the large card the names of which contain the same vowel sounds.

2. *"Group Word Teaching Game," by E. W. Dolch. Champaign, Illinois: The Garrard Publishing Company.*

The game consists of nine sets of cards each containing six like cards. On the cards of each set are listed 24 of the 220 basic sight words compiled by Dolch. The game is played much like Lotto. As a word from a printed list is read by the leader, the players cover the word on their cards with small oblong pieces of paper.

3. *"Group Sounding Game," by E. W. Dolch. Champaign, Illinois: The Garrard Publishing Company.*

There are six cards, similar to Lotto cards, in each of the following sets: Set A—initial consonants; Set B—short vowels, *a, e,* and *i;* Set C—all short vowels; Set D—harder consonants; Set E—blended consonants; Set F—consonant digraphs; Set G—long vowels; Set H—vowels with *r;* Set I—diphthongs; Set J—miscellaneous consonants; Set K—closed syllables; Set L—open syllables; Set M—prefixes and suffixes; Set N—three syllables; and Set O—three syllables. The game can be played by six players, who cover the words the leader calls from a list of words on a given "set" that he is furnished.

4. *"What the Letters Say," by E. W. Dolch. Champaign, Illinois: The Garrard Publishing Company.*

This game, also called "A Beginning Sounding Game," consists of cards on which one sound for each letter is illustrated by a picture and a word. In the game the child gets practice in associating the name of a letter with one of its sounds and with three different words, on different cards that illustrate the sound.

5. *"Take," by E. W. Dolch. Champaign, Illinois: The Garrard Publishing Company.*

This is a self-teaching phonics game in which the pupils match the sounds of the beginning, middle, or ending of words with cards on which a picture and the name of that picture are given. This game is for boys and girls in the third grade and up.

6. *"The Syllable Game," by E. W. Dolch. Champaign, Illinois: The Garrard Publishing Company.*

In "The Syllable Game" there are three decks of sixty-four cards each, with two-syllable words in two decks and with words up to four syllables in the third deck. It is a game that a child can play either alone or with another person while learning to recognize many common syllables.

7. *"Phonic Rummy." Buffalo, N.Y.: Kenworthy Educational Service, Inc.*

"Phonic Rummy" comes in four sets: one for grades one and two; another for grades two and three; still another for grades two, three, and four; and a fourth for grades three, four, and five. In each set there are two packs of 60 cards. With these cards can be played a game in matching vowel sounds.

8. *"Junior Phonic Rummy." Buffalo, N.Y.: Kenworthy Educational Service, Inc.*

This game, similar to "Phonic Rummy," is also a matching game in which words used widely in first-grade readers are matched for vowel sounds.

9. *"Doghouse Game." Buffalo, N.Y.: Kenworthy Educational Service, Inc.*

"Doghouse Game" comes in twelve game envelopes, on the face of each of which are printed thirty-five phonograms as well as rules for pronunciation and sixty-four consonants and consonant blends. A variety of games can be played with these cards.

10. *"A B C Game." Buffalo, N.Y.: Kenworthy Educational Service, Inc.*

This game, designed for teaching letter, word, and picture recognition, is played by matching the cards in the set, on each of which are a picture, the name of the picture, and the letter with which the word begins. The game is played somewhat like "Old Maid," as the players try to find the mate for every card that they have until every player, excepting the person who has the card entitled "Mr. ABC," has given up all of his cards.

11. *"Phonic Quizmo." Chicago: Beckley-Cardy Company.*

This is another game that is similar to Lotto. The pupils cover on their cards the words beginning with the same letter or letter combination found in words that the teacher reads from a list supplied with the game.

12. *"Phonetic Word Wheel." Chicago: Beckley-Cardy Company.*

Various games can be devised with the phonetic word wheel in which the pupils are provided with practice in recognizing vowels, consonants, and blends.

13. *"Make-a-Word Game." Chicago: Beckley-Cardy Company.*

With the sixty-five green cards with consonants or consonant blends and the sixty-five orange cards with phonograms that are supplied in this game matching games can be played.

14. *"Go Fish." Washington, D.C.: The Remedial Education Center.*

"Go Fish," a consonant sound game, consists of a series of three cards of each consonant, of three different colors, with a picture on each, the name of which begins with a consonant sound, the letter for which is also given on the card. Each player is given six cards, while the remaining cards are placed into the fish pile in the center. Each player in turn asks any other player for a card that begins with the consonant sound that he gives. If the player is unsuccessful in his attempt to get the desired card from a player, he goes to the fish pile to see if he can draw it from that. If he does not get the card at his first attempt, he loses his turn. Whenever a player has acquired all three cards beginning with the same consonant sound, he places the three cards in a pile in front of him, forming a "book." The person with the largest number of "books" wins the game.

15. *"Vowel Dominoes." Washington, D.C.: The Remedial Education Center.*

To play this game cards $1^1/_2$ inches by $2^1/_2$ inches, resembling dominoes, are used. On half of each card is a vowel and on the other half a picture of a word containing a vowel sound. For example, on half of one card is the letter o and on the other half a picture of a drum, to represent the u sound. The game can be played much like dominoes. For example, a card with the letter a and a picture of a safety pin can be placed next to a card with the letter i and a picture of a top, so that the half of the first card on which the safety pin is drawn is next to the letter *i* of the second card, thereby placing the picture of a word with the *i* sound next to the letter *i*.

Other Reading Games

Many games other than those produced commercially can be used to develop reading skills. It is hoped that those listed here will suggest to the teacher many others that might be particularly suitable to the needs of her pupils.

1. *Pollyanna.* A board similar to the one pictured below can be made, with spaces marked off large enough so that a small word card can be placed on each, perhaps fastened to the board by "Ace" corners. The player spins the arrow, which will indicate the number of

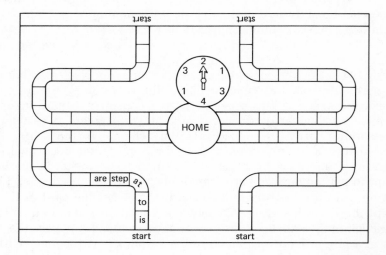

steps he can advance during his turn. The game can be played in a variety of ways, of which the following is one: If a player can pronounce each word in the steps that he is entitled to take, he places a button or other small marker with which each player is supplied on the last word in his "turn." If he cannot pronounce all the words in the steps he is allowed, he is told the first word that halts his progress. Then he is required to place his marker on the word preceding the one he missed. The first player to arrive at "home" wins.

2. *Word Baseball.* One way in which to play "word baseball" is to designate one corner of the room as "home" and the other three corners as first, second, and third base. If the pupil who is "up for bat"

can pronounce the word that the teacher shows him, he can go to first base. If he can say the next word, he may go to second base. If he can go on through third base to home, he scores a "home-run." However, if he is unable to pronounce his first word, he is "out" and an "out" is recorded for his team. If he cannot pronounce a word, other than the first one given to him when his turn comes, he proceeds to second base when the next batter on his side has pronounced the first word given to him. A similar procedure determines the length of his stay on third base. Scoring can be done in a variety of ways.

3. *A Reading "Spelldown."* The class can line up in two teams as they do for spelldowns. One child can be appointed scorekeeper. The teacher should have a large number of word cards with words that the pupils have studied but on which they need further practice. As the teacher holds up the first card, the first pupil tries to pronounce it and use it in a sentence. If he is able to pronounce the word and use it in a sentence, he scores a point for his team; he then takes his place at the end of his line. If he cannot pronounce a word and use it in a sentence, he stays where he is and a score is recorded for the opposing team. In that case the card is shown to a member of the other team. If he, too, does not know the word or cannot use it in a sentence, the word "comes back" to the next pupil on the team who was first given the word. Each time a word is missed, the opposing team gets a point.

4. *Action Sentences.* The leader, who may be the teacher, places in a word holder or on a chalk ledge several sentences with directions such as "Get a book from the table." After a pupil has performed one of the directions, another child points to the sentence that tells what the other child did. He reads the sentence as he points to it.

5. *Checkers.* For this game a checkerboard about 16 by 16 inches may be used. "Ace" corners are fitted to each square on the board. On separate squares, the same size as the squares on the board, one word is written twice on each, in this manner:

The game can be played in a variety of ways. One is to have the player pronounce the word on the card he draws and then place it on the board.

6. *Ten-pins.* Ten-pins can be set up on the floor. From a stack of word cards placed face down, players take turns in picking up the

top card. If a player can pronounce the word on his card, he gets a turn at trying to knock pins over with a ball. If he cannot pronounce a word, the person whose turn it is next pronounces it. Score is kept in terms of the ten-pins that are dislocated. This game is chiefly for recreational, not reading, purposes.

7. *Ring-toss.* A variation of ten-pins is ring-toss. In this game, the person pronouncing his word correctly gets a turn at trying to toss a ring onto a hook. The winner is the one who has hooked the most rings by the time the hooks are filled. The chief value of this game is recreational.

8. *Flinch.* On cards similar to the one illustrated below may be written words from science, social studies, or a general word list. There need to be as many sets of cards, each containing the same number, as there are players. After the cards have been dealt face down, the first player turns over the top card. The cards numbered 1 are played in the center of the table while all others are played on the stack of an opponent if the number is consecutive, either up or down.

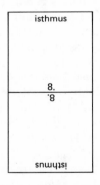

If a player is unable to play, he places the card in front of him face down at the bottom of his stack. If a player misses seeing a play, each opponent places a card face down on the player's stack. As he plays, each player says the number and word on the card.

9. *Sentence Game.* After word cards have been passed out to the class, the teacher reads a sentence using only words appearing on the cards. Each pupil who has a card on which a word used in that sentence is written goes to the front of the room. A pupil designated as "sentence maker" makes the sentence by arranging the children with their cards in the proper order as the teacher repeats the sentence. If a sentence maker forms the sentence incorrectly, another pupil is appointed in his place. The pupil who does not recognize that he has a needed word in his possession, or who thinks that he has one when he

does not, can be "penalized" by his having to put his card into a center pile from which, with future sentences, the "sentence maker" selects the word if it is again needed for a sentence.

Distributors of Games

Teachers interested in securing reading games may, in addition to canvassing stores, wish to write to publishing companies for catalogues describing their reading games. Some companies that distribute games are: (1) Beckley-Cardy Company, Chicago, Illinois; (2) Cadaco-Ellis Company, Chicago, Illinois; (3) The Garrard Publishing Company, Champaign, Illinois; (4) Houghton Mifflin Company, Boston, Massachusetts; (5) Judy Company, Minneapolis, Minnesota; (6) Kenworthy Educational Service, Inc., Buffalo, New York; (7) Kraeg Games, Inc., St. Louis, Missouri; (8) Milton Bradley Company, Springfield, Massachusetts; (9) Remedial Education Center, Washington, D.C.; (10) Simon and Schuster, Inc., New York, New York; (11) Training Aids, Inc., Los Angeles, California; and (12) Whitman Publishing Company, Racine, Wisconsin.

FOR FURTHER STUDY

Austin, Mary C., and Coleman Morrison, with others, *The First R: the Harvard Report on Reading in Elementary Schools.* New York: Crowell-Collier and Macmillan, Inc., 1963. Pages 27–35.

Barbe, Walter B., *Teaching Reading.* New York: Oxford University Press, 1965. Chapter 4, "Word Perception and Meaning," pp. 98–105; Chapter 5, "Primary Grades Programs and Methods," pp. 126–181.

Bond, Guy L., and Eva Bond Wagner, *Teaching the Child To Read.* New York: The Macmillan Company, 1960. Pages 149–199.

Burton, William E., *Reading in Child Development.* Indianapolis, Ind.: The Bobbs-Merrill Company, Inc., 1956. Pages 232–309.

Chall, Jeanne S., *Learning To Read: The Great Debate.* New York: McGraw-Hill Book Company, Inc., 1967.

Clymer, Theodore, "The Utility of Phonic Generalizations in the Primary Grades," *The Reading Teacher,* 16 pp. 252–258 (January 1963).

Dechant, Emerald V., *Improving the Teaching of Reading.* Englewood Cliffs, N.J.: Prentice-Hall, Inc., 1964. Chapter 12. "Developing a Meaningful Vocabulary," pp. 322–352.

Deighton, Lee G., *Vocabulary in the Classroom*. New York: Teachers College Press, Columbia University, 1962.

Durr, William P. (ed.), *Reading Instruction: Dimensions and Issues*. Boston: Houghton Mifflin Company, 1967.

Durkin, Dolores, *Phonics and the Teaching of Reading*. Practical Suggestions for Teaching, No. 22, Alice Miel, ed. New York: Teachers College Press, Columbia University, 1962.

Fries, Charles C., *Linguistics and Reading*. New York: Holt, Rinehart and Winston, Inc., 1963.

Gans, Roma, *Common Sense in Reading*. Indianapolis, Ind.: The Bobbs-Merrill Company, Inc., 1963. Chapter 8, "Making Gains in Independent Reading Power," pp. 136–162.

Gans, Roma, *Fact and Fiction about Phonics*. Indianapolis, Ind.: The Bobbs-Merrill Company, Inc., 1964.

Harris, Albert J., *Readings on Reading Instruction*. New York: David McKay Company, Inc., 1963. Part IV, "Beginning Reading Programs," pp. 91–113; Part IX, "Development of Vocabulary," pp. 236–265.

Hildreth, Gertrude, "New Methods for Old in Teaching Phonics," *Elementary School Journal*, 57, pp. 436–441 (May 1957).

Kirk, Samuel A. and Winifred D., "How Johnny Learns To Read," *Elementary English*, 33, pp. 266–269 (May 1956).

McKim, Margaret G., and Helen Caskey, *Guiding Growth in Reading*. New York: Crowell-Collier and Macmillan, Inc., 1963. Chapter 6, "Planning the Reading Program in the Primary Grades," pp. 182–215; Chapter 9, "Helping Primary Children Learn To Work with Words," pp. 216–256.

National Society for the Study of Education, *Innovation and Change in Reading Instruction*. Chicago: University of Chicago Press, 1968.

Russell, David H., "Teaching Identification and Recognition," *Handbook of Research on Teaching*, N. L. Gage, ed. Skokie, Ill.: Rand McNally & Company, 1963.

Stauffer, Russell G., *Directing Reading Maturity as a Cognitive Process*. New York: Harper & Row, Publishers, Inc., 1969. Chapter 6.

Stern, Catherine, and Toni S. Gould, *Children Discover Reading*. New York: Random House, Inc., 1963.

Tinker, Miles A., and Constance M. McCullough, *Teaching Elementary Reading*. New York: Appleton-Century-Crofts, 1968. Chapter 7, Chapter 8, pp. 130–184.

QUESTIONS FOR THOUGHT AND DISCUSSION

1. Workbooks are a part of the basic reading program according to some authorities. But from other quarters comes severe criticism, which may be the result of the misuse of the workbook rather than the material itself. How would you use the workbook in your program? If you would not want to use a workbook, be able to state your reasons.

2. There is and has been a wide divergence of opinion about teaching phonics. Some teachers claim that multiple approaches to word recognition are more appropriate than an all-phonics approach. Can you accept this position? Be able to defend your position.

3. Teachers, especially those of children who are beginning to learn to read, often wonder what they should do about teaching the alphabet. They are in doubt as to whether they should set about this task deliberately and at a specified time or delay introducing the letters. What would you do about teaching the alphabet?

4. Many teachers have been concerned about the use of charts in the primary grades and their relation to the reading program. What do you regard as the proper place of experience charts in the primary program? What purposes might such charts serve and what are their uses as learning instruments?

5. There are several word lists that are useful to elementary teachers even though they are not, for the most part, studies of the actual vocabulary of elementary school children. How would you use a list you might select in your classroom?

6. Several factors contribute to the simplicity or difficulty of reading material. Several are listed for you. What are important factors to consider in connection with each?
    a. Familiarity of experience described.
    b. Concreteness of words and concepts.
    c. Length and complexity of sentences.
    d. Effective use of words.
    e. Inclusion of vivid details.

7. Any modern reading program consists of much more than reading from one book. Although the use of a basic series is only part of the complete reading program, sets of basic readers are so commonly used in most schools that a few suggestions about their use are important for an overview of reading activities. What, in your estimation, are some of the principles upon which the basic reading series should be constructed?

8. Some individuals argue that pictures should be omitted from beginning reading materials. Their assumption would appear to be that children might use the pictures for solving some unrecognized words and thus would not come to grips with the printed symbols themselves. Can a child become overly dependent on pictures? What would you do to prevent this problem if you think it is a possibility? If it did occur, how would you help the child overcome his overreliance on pictorial clues?

CHAPTER 6A

Reading with Comprehension

The importance of skill in recognizing words has been pointed out in the preceding chapters. While it is impossible for a person to read without being able to recognize words, word recognition does not constitute all of reading. It is merely a tool for reading. Unless the reader comprehends what is recorded on the page, he is engaging in an exercise in recognizing words, not in reading as the word *reading* is used in this book.

VIEWS CONCERNING COMPREHENSION

Although there is general agreement that by reading with comprehension is meant getting meaning from what is being perceived in writing, there are various additional commonly accepted points of view, a statement of which may add to an understanding of the term *comprehension*. Let us at this point examine some of those on which there is general agreement. Reference to others, including some that are controversial, will be made in connection with topics discussed later in this chapter.

1. *A passage can properly be read with varying degrees of understanding.* The scale of comprehension ranges from practically no meaning to what might be referred to as complete understanding. The degree of comprehension will depend not only upon the physical condition of the reader, upon his skill in reading, and upon the diffi-

culty of the material but also upon his purpose. All he may want as he reads a selection is to get the general idea of what is written. On the other hand, he may set out to read the material in order to test every point made in terms of its applicability to a problem confronting him. He may read every detail of the directions for performing an experiment, but may read a newspaper article only to find out whether anyone he knows is mentioned in it. One of the marks of the efficient reader is the extent to which he can adjust the degree of his comprehension to his objective.

A term that has been much used in recent years is *critical reading*. There is no general agreement on the meaning of this expression. Martha King states:

> Some writers have described critical reading narrowly and negatively, limiting the concept to the selection and rejection of material. Others have defined the term broadly enough to include many skills that are frequently classified as literal comprehension skills. Still other writers have categorized critical reading as one level in a hierarchial order of reading skills and placed it above literal comprehension and interpretation but below assimilative or creative reading.[1]

Among the views on critical reading discussed in the book *Critical Reading* is that by E. Elona Sochor, which is summarized as follows:

> She [E. Sochor] makes the point that the thinking process has not yet been structured into a hierarchial order and that critical and literal reading cannot be differentiated on the basis of thinking processes or language-experience relationships. The differentiation that can be made is on the basis of the reader's purpose.[2]

However we may define *critical reading* and in whatever way we may subdivide activities we call by that name, the concern of educators, in general, when they use the term is that boys and girls learn to read effectively beyond the level of merely comprehending what is read.

2. *The degree or type of comprehension that takes place in reading can be classified in a variety of ways.* One classification is that

[1] Martha L. King, Bernice D. Ellinger, and Willavene Wolf (eds.), *Critical Thinking*, p. 2. Philadelphia: J. B. Lippincott Company, 1967.

[2] King, Ellinger, and Wolf, p. 3.

the reader may be (1) reading the lines, (2) reading "between the lines," or (3) reading "beyond the lines." *Reading the lines* refers to understanding what is actually written on the page, that is, knowing the exact meanings that are definitely expressed. *Reading between the lines* designates reading in which the reader comprehends the meaning that is not expressed "in so many words," but that is implied. In *reading beyond the lines* the reader is stimulated to think of applications that he can make beyond those suggested by the author. It is in this type of reading that the reader definitely associates what he is reading with his own experiences, past or contemplated.

The reader may also be thought of as reading passively or actively. If he reads passively, he obtains the factual, the literal meaning. If he reads actively, he reacts to the material; he reads "between the lines" or "beyond the lines." The understanding with which a person reads may be thought of as being on one of three levels: (1) getting the facts, (2) making inferences from what he reads, and (3) applying what he reads by means of associational processes. Yet another means of classifying the type of comprehension is to divide it into (1) the factual level; (2) the level of generalization, where the reader generalizes on what he reads; and (3) the critical level, where the reader evaluates what he reads in terms of the purpose of the author and the reliability and validity of the material.

In the classifications given above there is no basic contradiction concerning what reading comprehension should include. All of these classifications throw light on the process of reading with understanding. It should be noted that one trend in current thinking, which is reflected in the categories into which comprehension has been divided, is the placing of increased emphasis on the nonfactual phases of comprehension.

3. *Thinking is an essential part of reading with understanding beyond the level of merely getting the factual meaning expressed.* Anything that is done to help the learner develop in power to think can be beneficial to him in reading if he has acquired skill in word recognition and in reading on the lowest level of comprehension.

4. *There seems to be a rather marked relation between ability to listen and ability to comprehend what is read.* Teachers have long recognized a relation between listening and phonics. Recent studies have noted that there seem to be many elements in listening that are common to some phases of comprehension even though, of course, there are also decided differences. For example, the listener cannot immediately ponder a statement made in a talk without danger of not comprehending what is said next. The reader, however, can

take time off to grasp a point before he continues. Furthermore, he can reread parts that he wishes to understand better; the listener, on the other hand, does not have a similar opportunity unless the speaker repeats what he has said. In spite of such differences, some of the skills required for good listening seem to be linked with some of those important in reading comprehension to such an extent that research seems to indicate that training in listening can favorably influence comprehension.[3]

5. *Reading should serve as a means to an end.* The ultimate goal of reading instruction should go beyond simply the development of a good reader. The objective should be the development of the individual. Instruction should be so geared as to achieve this goal.

RELATIONS BETWEEN COMPREHENSION SKILLS AND OTHER READING SKILLS

The skills involved in reading with understanding are related to other reading skills. Understanding of these relations is of value for intelligent guidance of the pupil through successive stages of growth in reading.

Comprehension and Word Recognition

Although word recognition is a prerequisite to comprehension, it does not guarantee comprehension. Moreover, full recognition of all words in a passage is not always necessary for the degree of comprehension required. While reading a selection in order to give a detailed account of the contents may depend upon recognition of most or all of the words, reading to determine relevance to a given topic may not call for this amount of word recognition. Experience, background, interest, and native intelligence may also play a part in determining how many and which individual words a reader may miss and still achieve the desired degree of comprehension.

Comprehension and Retention

It is not at all uncommon for a reader to remember verbally some material that he does not understand. A fifth-grade girl, who lived far from a large body of water, was studying about New England

---

[3] Melvin Lubershane, "Can Training in Listening Improve Reading Ability?" *Chicago Schools Journal,* 43, pp. 277–281 (March 1962).

and could glibly reproduce this sentence, which she remembered verbatim from her textbook: "New England has many good harbors." However, when the teacher asked her what the sentence meant, her ignorance of the meaning of the word *harbor* was revealed. The girl's retention of the sentence had been perfect, but her comprehension was zero. It should also be noted that the reader may comprehend what he reads but not retain it, possibly not even for a matter of minutes.

Comprehension and Rate of Reading

The rate of reading and the degree of comprehension are not highly correlated. Although there is a positive correlation between rate of reading and quality of comprehension, it cannot be automatically assumed that because a person reads fast he necessarily comprehends well. The problem of the relation between the two factors is complicated by the fact that an efficient reader will vary his rate of comprehension according to the type and difficulty of the material and according to his purpose in reading. Yet it is clear that in general, allowing for flexibility of approach, the better readers are also the faster readers.

Comprehension and Skill in Using Reference Materials

The reader with poor comprehension is also usually lacking in "locational skills." He is not likely to make efficient use of an index. His ineffectiveness will often be caused, in part, by the fact that he has only a hazy idea of the material he has read. Furthermore, after he locates the needed data in a book, he may be unable to select the main points and the supporting details in what he reads or to follow the directions given. He may also have trouble when trying to summarize what he has found in reference books.

Comprehension, a Complex of Many Skills

A reader who is deficient in some aspects of comprehension may not necessarily have difficulty with all types of comprehension. He may be able to find the main idea of a selection with accuracy and dispatch, but have difficulty in selecting and organizing supporting details. Some children have accurate knowledge of word and sentence meanings but fail to understand longer selections such as paragraphs or stories or articles. Others show proficiency in reading stories but cannot effectively read material in the areas of the social studies or science or mathematics. Thus it becomes the responsibility of the teacher to discover the strengths and weaknesses in comprehension of her pupils.

CAUSES OF DIFFICULTIES IN COMPREHENSION

The teacher must understand the causes of difficulties in comprehension if she is to help individuals overcome their shortcomings in comprehending what they read. Moreover, knowledge of the causes may help the teacher to prevent the occurrence of serious deficiencies.

These are typical comments made by individuals who have difficulty in understanding what they read: "I am not able to concentrate as I read." "I have difficulty in figuring out the meaning of a selection because there are so many words that I do not recognize." "I often have trouble getting the meaning of the first page or two when I start reading. Often I have to read for a few minutes without really knowing what I am reading before it makes sense to me." "I can understand what I read but I cannot give a satisfactory summary of it."

Limited Intelligence

As we have seen, there is a substantial correlation between intelligence and reading ability. It is true that a child who is intelligent enough to go to school is intelligent enough to learn to read simple materials. Nevertheless, a child's ability to comprehend in reading is limited by the conceptual "load" that his mental ability enables him to carry. All the mechanical reading skills in the world will not enable him to read materials involving abstractions beyond the level of his mental development. While we should never underestimate a child's powers, we should adjust the task to his capabilities. The slowest learner can grow in comprehension, but in some cases we must expect the growth to be slow. The reader whose IQ is 65 may learn how to find the answer to a simple question, but he should not be required to interpret a complicated graph.

Environmental Influences

Noisy surroundings, inadequate lighting, high or low temperatures, and stimulating or distracting surroundings may interfere with maximum comprehension. The extent to which the environment affects comprehension varies with individuals. The same person, too, may at one time not be bothered by factors that other times decidedly decrease his comprehension. Interest on the part of the learner is one of the determinants of the effect of potential distractions.

Physical Factors Inherent in the Reader

Such matters as fatigue, malnutrition, or undernutrition may have an unfavorable bearing on comprehension. Factors related to the perceptuomotor organization of the learner (see Chapter 4A) also have bearing on his ability to comprehend what he reads.[4] (See pages 50–51.)

Overemphasis on Word Recognition

Methods of teaching that concentrate on the recognition of individual words but neglect attention to meanings that can be derived from connected discourse may account for deficiencies in comprehension. Bright children normally make the transition from word to phrase to sentence to paragraph with ease and with little aid from the teacher. Many boys and girls, however, are baffled by the task of finding meaning in word groups. They need to be encouraged to move rapidly on the line in order to discover what happened, or to find the answers to their questions. Exclusive use of phonic methods, for example, may result in mere word calling rather than intelligent reading. The aim is to equip the pupil with a variety of methods of attacking new words and at the same time to develop in him the power to get larger meaning from the printed page.

Overemphasis on Oral Reading

Oral reading can have either a desirable or a detrimental effect on comprehension. Often oral reading of a selection that is particularly difficult for the reader increases his understanding of it, since he not only sees but also hears what he reads. Furthermore, in effective oral reading, if there is an audience, the reader is required not only to understand what he reads but also to interpret his understanding to others. In this process increased attention needs to be placed on comprehension.

Unfortunately oral reading, if not done well, can have an undesirable effect on comprehension. The reader can become so con-

[4] Katrina DeHirsch, Jeannette Jansky, and William Langford, *Predicting Reading Failure, A Preliminary Study.* New York: Harper & Row, Publishers, Inc., 1966.

scious of his audience that he will fail to understand what he is reading. Overemphasis on oral reading may also make a child so self-conscious while reading to others that his concentration may be on how, rather than on what, he is reading. There is a point to the familiar story of the child who, after he had read a passage orally, was asked by his teacher a simple question about the content of the selection. His response was, "I don't know. I wasn't listening; I was reading."

Insufficient Background for Reading a Selection

Another frequent cause of poor comprehension is lack of an experience background essential to the understanding of what is being read. A city child who has never been on a farm may have difficulty in fully comprehending a story about country life. A sixth-grade boy who has never worked with science materials may not be ready to follow the directions given for an experiment. Lack of understanding of the concepts involved in reading materials and of the words used is an additional limitation to comprehension. Semantic problems of pupils who know only one meaning of words like *fair, spring,* and *plain* also cause difficulties in comprehension.

Failure To Adjust Reading Techniques to Reading Purpose and Type of Reading Material

Good reading comprehension requires a flexible approach to the printed page. Stevie, for example, had been reading a great deal of fiction and had derived great pleasure from the experience. However, when he encountered arithmetic problems, he had difficulty because he read them as if he were reading a story and so moved too rapidly over the lines. On the other hand, Bobby was a meticulous reader of science materials. When he tried to read stories, he failed to derive real satisfaction from his reading because he used the same reading methods for narrative that he was accustomed to employ with factual and expository prose. Similarly, a child may be unable to recognize the main idea of a passage because he is too absorbed in noting concrete details. The need is for versatility in adapting the reading method to the reading purpose and to the nature of the material read.

Lack of Appropriate Teacher Guidance

Difficulties in reading comprehension may frequently be overcome with the aid of a teacher skilled in observing the causes of the difficulties. Some of the possible causes have been suggested in the preceding paragraphs. They are, of course, only illustrative.

Alert teachers put forth great effort to find and eliminate or prevent the obstacles to meaningful reading. Problems of comprehension among pupils can sometimes be reduced by the effective use of questioning. By asking suitable questions before the pupils read a selection or after they have completed it, the teacher can help make otherwise obscure meanings clear. However, when teachers are unfamiliar with the nature and extent of the pupil's difficulties, the problems tend to multiply. The use of appropriate standardized reading tests (see Chapter 13), informal teacher-made tests such as those suggested in Chapter 7B, as well as frequent oral reading by individual readers to the teacher are the common means of discovering some of the causes of poor comprehension. Careful observation of a pupil's reading behavior may offer valuable clues. The teacher may ask, "What type of material does the pupil read outside of class?" "How much spare time does he spend in reading?" "How does he attack new words?" "Does he have a limited vocabulary for his stage of development?" "Does he know how to get the main thought of a passage?"

School records are an essential source of information about the causes of poor comprehension. Attendance records, health records, previous school history, anecdotal records concerning the child's attitudes, problems, and earlier behavior, and similar records can give the teacher insight into his difficulties.

COMPREHENSION SKILLS

There is controversy among leaders in the field of the teaching of reading as to whether or not reading is a general ability. Some claim that it is, while others think of reading as a combination of various specific skills, such as getting the main idea or predicting outcomes, which should be identified for the purpose of helping the learner improve in ability to comprehend what he reads. Part of this argument is probably one of semantics, since comprehension could be described as a general ability even by those who believe that there are specific skills that comprise the general ability. Where the point of view does make a difference, however, is in the application of it to a teaching-learning situation. Those who believe that there are specific abilities that constitute effective comprehension will probably want to pay definite attention to these skills in their instructional procedures; others who do not share this view are likely not to place much, if any, emphasis on the acquisition of these various abilities.

To the authors of this book it seems important that help be given to many boys and girls in acquiring such skills as noting details that support the main idea of a selection, judging the authenticity of a report, and making generalizations on the basis of what is read. Consequently, these skills are here identified and briefly described.

Earlier in this chapter reference was made to various ways in which comprehension skills have been classified. None of those enumerated is comprised of more than three main categories. Disagreement as to the best categorization and the overlapping between the divisions of the various classifications make it desirable in the following description of needed skills to avoid the division suggested in any of the classifications given earlier. It will be noted that some of the skills described below are directed at acquiring the factual meaning of what is read while others are primarily of the "reading-between-the-lines" type and still others are largely or entirely of the "reading-beyond-the-lines" type (see pages 173–174).

The specific skills that form a part of the ability to comprehend what is read may be classified rather loosely according to (1) the purpose of the reader and (2) the length and nature of the selection read. We consider first the skills dependent upon the reader's purpose.

Reading To Find the Main Idea

One of the most common reasons for reading is to get the general idea of a selection. Reading of fiction is usually done for this purpose. Even in other types of reading, like science, it may often legitimately be the goal. In that field the primary grade pupil may read a page to find out whether it tells about helicopters. The more mature reader in an elementary school may read to find out whether it is advisable to include a certain chapter in a bibliography that he is preparing on "Our Solar System." The ability to determine the main idea of a part read is basic also to many other comprehension skills, such as the ability to summarize and organize. Skill in finding the main idea in a paragraph or a longer selection, and in not mistaking a detail for the major point, needs to be developed in many pupils not only through incidental means but often also through practice exercises.

Reading To Select Significant Details

The ability to note important details is closely related to skill in finding the central thought or main idea of a selection. To be proficient in this respect, the reader needs to do more than differentiate between main points and supporting details; he must also be able to decide what points are important for the purpose he has in mind. In *Miss Hickory* by Carolyn Sherwin Bailey, the story about the little doll whose body is a twig of an apple tree and whose head is a hickory nut, the person who tells the story may want to remember exactly where the story takes place. However, the child who is reading the book solely for his own enjoyment may satisfy his purpose without taking special note of this detail. The reader who gives equal attention to all details that are presented may find himself so encumbered that he loses perspective. Practice may be needed to help him decide which details are worthy of special note and which should be ignored. Their relation to the main idea of the selection will usually determine their value; the purpose of the reader will be another determinant. As the pupils work for improvement in noting details, they should be helped to realize that details are of value as they support a main idea or assist in arriving at a conclusion or serve some other purpose of the reader beyond that of merely taking note of details.

Care must be taken that practice in noting details does not decrease the ability to find the main idea or to generalize. Constant emphasis should be placed on the fact that details must be fitted into a setting in which they serve a purpose.

Reading To Follow Directions

The ability to follow directions is usually a combination of many reading skills. The ability to note details, to organize, and to note the sequence of events are among the learnings essential to this type of reading skill.

Reading To Summarize and Organize

Both the ability to select the main idea and to choose significant details are basic to another commonly sought goal of reading—that of summarizing and organizing. However, to make an adequate summary or to organize what has been read, it is not enough for the reader to know what the main idea is and what the significant details are. He must also be able to sense the relation between the main point and the details as well as the relation among the details. Furthermore, he often needs to know either how to make these relations clear to others or how to record them for later rereading.

Frequently the efficient reader makes summaries and organizes what he reads without doing any writing. The person who reads a chapter and then asks himself what the main points are, what material constitutes significant details, and how all these parts are woven together is making a summary and organizing what he reads. In fact, skill in organizing or summarizing is ordinarily put to use without the writing of summaries or outlines. Practice in summarizing and organizing may lead to such skill in these activities that frequently the reader almost unconsciously summarizes and organizes what he reads.

Reading To Arrive at Generalizations

Formulating generalizations is in a sense a specialized form of summarizing. To arrive at generalizations the reader needs to note specific instances and then decide whether the data presented are sufficient to warrant a significant conclusion. If they are of the type on which a sound conclusion can be based, he must determine what the deduction from the instances discussed should be. If, for example, he reads about children in Holland who wore wooden shoes, he should realize that he would be wrong if he made the decision that Dutch children always wear wooden shoes. On the other hand, if a typical scene in a schoolroom in China were described and if the author indicated that the scene is representative, the reader may correctly conclude that Chinese schools in many respects are unlike the school he is attending.

One danger for the person not skillful in making generalizations is that he may generalize without sufficient evidence. Another is that he will make too broad a generalization. To avoid errors due to both of these causes a teacher can give specific guidance not only with material read but also with observations made in other situations.

Reading To Predict Outcomes

Another important comprehension skill is that of predicting outcomes. This skill may manifest itself in a variety of ways. For example, if the reader sees the sentence, "The farmers set no traps for any of the animals on the grounds, for they like animals," he can anticipate (unless a break in thought is indicated by words like *but* or *however* or *nevertheless*) that the next sentence in the paragraph will not contradict the thought that the farmers were kind to the animals. This skill is in effect an aspect of what we call "active" reading, in which the reader assumes an attitude of anticipation.

Skill in predicting outcomes is useful in helping the reader note when he has misread a word or a sentence. It is also of value because the person who is adept at predicting outcomes as he reads can usually get the thought more quickly than others. This skill is helpful also in remembering what is read, for it enables the reader to take special note only of those points that are new to him or are different from what he would have expected, and the burden of recall is thereby lessened.

Reading To Evaluate Critically

One of the most significant comprehension skills is that of making critical evaluations of what is read. By critical evaluation is not meant the attitude of suspecting every statement read of being false. The power of critical evaluation in reading involves numerous factors. The reader needs to learn to ask such questions as these: Is the material relevant? Can the facts alleged be verified? Is the author qualified to discuss the subject? Do the statements harmonize with what I know to be true? Does the author draw valid conclusions from the facts? Is the author omitting or suppressing any important facts? Are the statements expressions of fact, or inferences? Does the material contain any unstated assumptions? Can I accept these assumptions? Should I revise my own assumptions in the light of what I have read?

Critical discrimination in reading calls for a wide background of knowledge concerning the subject under discussion. Literally, the word *criticism* means the application of criteria, or standards of judgment. Such criteria can come only from some previous contact with the subject. The reader has no way of judging the truth of the statement, "Polio is seldom fatal" if he has not had some previous knowledge about polio. He must then be entirely dependent upon the reliability, competence, and honesty of the author. Moreover, critical reading involves the capacity for making comparisons and appraisals. Critical reading is active, creative reading. Children should begin developing the skills of critical independence in reading at the outset.

The levels of criticism will vary with the age and maturity of the pupil. A primary school child may be asked to pick out a false statement in a series, such as "Horses can fly," while a sixth-grade pupil may be called upon to find editorial statements in a news story. Critical discrimination in reading can be cultivated through skillful training.

A recent study by Willavene Wolf and others listed the following abilities to read critically:

(1) General abilities.

A. The ability to recognize reading material as one important source of ideas or information and to relate other sources such as television, pictures, etc., of the child's own personal observations of his world.

B. The ability to read and understand a variety of reading materials which represent differing interpretations or viewpoints.

C. The ability to question as one reads, to phrase possible answers, and then to read further for the information that will act as a guide for the conclusion that: (1) there is more than one answer to the question, (2) there is no conclusive answer to the question, or (3) there is one answer to the question.

D. The ability to continue reading until one has gathered enough information to reach as complete an answer or to make as sound a judgment as he can presently make.

(2) Specific abilities.

E. The ability to analyze what is read for the purpose of indentifying the author's purposes, point of view or prejudices (and then determine how the purposes, etc., relate to one's own set of values and opinions or to the values and opinions of others).

F. The ability to analyze what is read for the purpose of identifying the publisher's purposes, point of view or prejudices; to determine how these influence the publisher's selection and promotion of materials; and finally to relate these to one's own values and opinions or to the values and opinions of others.

G. The ability to determine the author's reputation as a knowledgeable and reliable source of information in a specific field or as a recognized writer of quality material.

H. The ability to see relationships while reading that are not directly stated by the author (draw inferences): for example, to read the author's description which indicates but does not directly state that the setting is a spring morning; or, to read the author's subtle wording which hints at but does not directly state his opinion, and then to relate that opinion to the reader's own, perhaps for forming a new opinion.

I. The ability to tell the difference between an author's factual statements and the author's opinion or personal interpretation of fact.

J. The ability to follow the sequence of an author's presentation and to determine how logical or illogical the sequence was.

K. The ability to compare and contrast various (reading) sources in related content areas and determine, on the basis of sound judgment, the worth of each in contributing to one's increase in that area.

L. The ability to form an opinion of what one reads, relating what is read to one's past knowledge, and identifying those areas where one lacks enough knowledge for forming a sound opinion.

M. The ability to locate and select the reading materials that will provide the information related to the topic of the study.

N. The ability to recognize when the author has omitted facts or information that are necessary for an honest and complete understanding of some situation or issue.

O. The ability to identify and analyze the devices authors sometimes use to persuade or influence the reader:

1. Appealing to emotion over reason (name calling), (appealing to sympathy).
2. Using glittering generalities.
3. Getting endorsement from some prominent person (testimonial).
4. Inferring a relationship between two objects, or persons, or events which does not exist (identification, transfer).
5. Omitting facts (card stacking).
6. Avoiding source of information.
7. Encouraging one to join the band wagon.
8. Plain Folks approach.

P. The ability to analyze and determine the accuracy and the clarity of information presented through such graphic presentations as cartoons, maps, charts, graphs, pictures.

Q. The ability to identify and then analyze the literary form used by the author: fiction, historical fiction, non-fiction, biography, autobiography, fantasy, fable, myth or legend, folk tale, satire, allegory, etc.

R. The ability to analyze and then form a personal opinion about the literary quality of the material read. Such analysis might concentrate on one or more of the following:

1. Story structure.
2. Character development.
3. The story atmosphere, setting, or mood.
4. The author's style or literary devices used: figurative language, symbolism, repetition, understatement, exaggeration, personification, foreshadowing, irony, pun, alliteration.[5]

[5] This discussion of critical reading is reproduced by permission from the study of Willavene Wolf *et al., Critical Reading Ability of Elementary School Children,* pp. 133–135. Columbus, Ohio: Ohio State University Research Foundation, 1967. Project No. 5–1040 supported by the U.S. Office of Information. The section is quoted at length because in our opinion it is one of the best statements available concerning the elements involved in critical reading. It is necessarily theoretical, and students are encouraged to devise creative ways of translating it into specific classroom practices.

It should be noted that critical reading is essential, too, to some of the comprehension skills discussed in this chapter, such as *reading to find the main idea, reading the predict outcomes, doing associational reading.*

Doing Associational Reading

Unlike the skills described so far, the ability to do associational reading, in a sense, cannot be classified under comprehension according to the purpose of the reader. When doing this type of reading, the reader does not, as a rule, set out to want to do associational reading. However, he is probably more likely to be doing this type of reading if he approaches reading with a desire, though not clearly formulated, to make use of what he reads. When an individual does associational reading, he applies what he is reading to his background of experience, real or vicarious. Often he makes connections, too, between what he reads and what he may do in the future. It is one of the higher types of reading, beyond the level of merely fact-getting. How it can be encouraged by the teacher is explained in Chapter 6B.

Reading Graphs, Tables, Charts, and Maps

Many readers do not recognize the value of tables, charts, graphs, and maps. Special instruction in the interpretation of these useful tools is often necessary. With the increasing production of materials of this kind, this skill has become important as never before.

We turn now to another kind of classification of comprehension skills. Getting meaning from or through the printed page involves the ability to perceive and understand words *in relation* to other words. It is hoped that the application of learnings from the science of linguistics will throw light on the complex problems connected with comprehending the relation between words and groups of words so that the reader can be helped more adequately to comprehend phrases, sentences, paragraphs, and longer selections.

Phrase Meanings

Since a phrase can be said to be more than the sum total of the words in it, skill in comprehension of phrases is not synonymous with skill in word meaning. The expression *in the long run* means more than *in* plus *the* plus *long* plus *run,* even though the meaning of each

Vocabulary development as an aid to reading. (Photo courtesy Alameda County, California, Public Schools.)

of the words contributes to the total thought. Especially in the case of idiomatic expressions is there need to examine the words carefully in their composite setting in the phrase. Another cause of difficulty in phrase comprehension is that frequently an immature reader does not recognize a phrase as such and, therefore, does not read it in a meaningful grouping. In the sentence, "At long last the tired men arrived," if the reader pauses after the word *long* because he does not recognize the word *last* as belonging to the phrase, he will not get the meaning. Therefore it is necessary in the case of many learners to focus attention on the recognition and meaning of phrases.

Sentence Meaning

What has been said about a phrase being more than the sum total of the words comprising it can also be said about a sentence. While the comprehension of many sentences is often almost automatic with persons who are reading on their proper level, with others it is not. Often a reader can understand every word of a long or involved sentence without getting the meaning of the sentence. The understanding that sentences are thought units is often fundamental to the comprehension of a complex sentence. For this reason, a study of the interrelationships of the parts of a sentence is frequently of value. Because sentence comprehension is more than word recognition and because an understanding of sentences is essential to the comprehension of longer selections, the reader should become skillful in reading sentences as whole units.

Paragraph Meaning

Many of the problems that are involved in the comprehension of paragraphs have already been referred to in the discussion of such skills as finding the main idea, selecting important details, answering questions, arriving at generalizations, and following directions. Some of the suggestions given in connection with predicting outcomes, evaluating critically, and summarizing and organizing also apply to paragraph comprehension. Frequently it is through reading a paragraph that the outcome is to be predicted. The paragraph may be one to be evaluated critically or to be summarized. Some problems of comprehension involve skills that are peculiar to the paragraph rather than to phrases or longer selections. Finding the topic sentence, if there is one, is one such problem. Another is that of seeing the relation between the topic sentence and the other sentences. A realization of the purpose of each sentence in a well-constructed paragraph is still another. Because of these and other considerations unique to paragraph comprehension, special attention should be given to the means of understanding the paragraph.

Comprehension of Longer Selections

Selections longer than paragraphs, such as articles, stories, chapters, or books, may present special problems. Among these are questions as to how to get the most value from center headings, side headings, and transitional words and phrases, or how to study the interrelationships between various types of paragraphs. Problems of sustained attention, too, arise with reading of this type. Since there are skills peculiar to comprehension of longer selections, special attention needs to be paid to the means of reading stories, articles, chapters, and books.

GENERAL PROCEDURES FOR IMPROVING COMPREHENSION

Improvement in comprehension skills can be brought about in the same manner that growth in almost all other reading abilities can be stimulated. It can be achieved through reading in context during the regular reading period, through reading activities during other parts of the school day, and through reading out of class, as well as through the use of practice exercises specifically set up to provide improvement in the skills. Activities other than reading, too, can serve as an important means of improving comprehension in reading. Because of the close relation between comprehension of material presented orally and comprehension of material in written form, some procedures beneficial to the former type are also valuable in the development of the latter.

Improvement through Incidental Means

If the term *incidental means* is used to refer to all types of reading situations other than those involving practice exercises, there are many ways in which comprehension skills can be improved during the regular reading period by incidental means. Much of the reading in the primary grades, for example, deals with reading to answer questions. The boys and girls may read a story in their textbooks in order to answer a question that either the teacher or a pupil has raised. Or after the pupils have read a story they may practice selecting the main point by suggesting titles for a puppet show that they plan to base on the story. Similarly, practice in summarizing can be given when a pupil who has time to finish reading a selection summarizes the ending of the story for a child who has not completed it. During the process of reading a story there can be discussion as to what the children think will happen next. Skill in predicting outcomes can also be acquired by discussion of why certain developments in a story were the ones likely to take place. If the child reads the story of "The Three Billy Goats Gruff," after he knows how the little Billy Goat Gruff was allowed to cross the bridge, he can be asked what he would imagine the middle-sized Billy Goat Gruff would say when the troll threatened to eat him.

In classes other than reading, much opportunity can be given for improvement of comprehension skills simultaneously with learning the content. In the social studies there is almost unlimited chance for meaningful practice in reading maps. Boys and girls can be helped not only in reading political maps but also physical maps, temperature maps, rainfall maps, population maps, product maps, and others. Growing out of the work in social studies may be projects like one in which one fifth grade engaged. The teacher placed on a big bulletin board a variety of maps and a sheet of paper on which were listed significant and interesting questions under the caption, "Can You Find the Answers to These Questions?" The boys and girls were also encouraged to bring to school other types of maps, which, if appropriate, were posted.

The many tables given in geography books can be made to serve an important purpose in comprehension. Boys and girls who need to learn when to use a table and how to use it can be helped to acquire that learning during classes in the social studies and science. In these classes they can learn the importance of noting the titles of tables and the significance of the names of the columns and rows in a table. They may at times be asked to see how many of the questions that they have raised are answered in a table or graph or map in their own textbooks. They may also look into a reference book, such as a young people's encyclopedia, to find out what information bearing on their problems they may find there either in maps, tables, charts, or graphs. Use of literary maps in phases of literature for children can improve skill in using pictorial materials and at the same time enhance the study of the literature.

There are also many ways in which the teacher can encourage the pupil to acquire skill in various types of comprehension outside of the classroom. She can stimulate the pupil to read widely and extensively. Incentive to note main points and significant details and to organize and summarize can be given by providing the children opportunity to report on some of the outside reading in a variety of ways. The reports may take the form of telling in a few sentences the gist of a book they have been reading or by describing in detail some favorite scene. Planning dramatizations based on books, giving puppet shows or television programs, or making "movies" can all help the learner to read with more comprehension.

The teacher can develop many of the comprehension skills through activities other than reading. She can ask the children to predict events in stories that she is telling or reading to them. She can encourage them to summarize reports they have heard, to enumerate in order the steps they followed in performing an experiment, to make plans for a project in which they are about to engage, to come to valid conclusions when they have listened to a series of remarks on related topics, and to decide whether certain information given to them orally is factual or a matter of opinion. The teacher's insistence on better concentration on whatever the children are doing can also bring about rewarding results. The individual who is in the habit of not concentrating when not reading is likely to find it difficult to refrain from letting his mind wander while reading.

Improvement through Practice Exercises

For some boys and girls a program of improvement in comprehension skills similar to the type just described will be sufficient. However, many will profit greatly if they are also given direct practice in the form of exercises to help them develop skills in comprehending what they read. Some pupils may need direct practice on all of the major types of comprehension skills, while others will require such help with only some or one of the skills. Ability in diagnosis on the part of the teacher is therefore necessary as she tries to determine which boys and girls need special practice in developing some or all of the comprehension skills.

In the use of practice exercises, the teacher must keep in mind certain basic principles. (1) *The teacher should have a clearly defined goal to be accomplished with each of the practice materials she uses.* She should decide what skills require direct practice and then provide the best type of exercises possible for achieving her goal economically. (2) *The boys and girls should know the purpose of each practice exercise.* Unless they know why they are doing a certain exercise, they are likely to get inferior results and lose interest. (3) *The boys and girls should be helped to see the importance of the skill to be developed by means of a given exercise.* Unless the pupils are helped to appreciate the worthwhileness of an activity, they are likely to perform it halfheartedly and consequently achieve poorly. In fact, it is often valuable to let them help determine, with teacher guidance, the number and types of exercises they need. (4) *Both the teacher and the pupil should know what, if any, progress is being made.* Knowledge of results, especially if they are encouraging, seems to be real incentive for learning. Through a study of results the teacher can also profit directly by securing evidence on the effectiveness of methods and procedures used.

CHAPTER 6B

Developing Comprehension
in Reading

This chapter suggests ways in which the ideas on reading with comprehension presented in Chapter 6A can be put into practice. The fact that a long listing is given for various skills to be developed should not, however, indicate to the teacher that she should use many of them at one time. Rather, the lists should be used as a reference from which the suggestions that appear appropriate for use at the time can be selected. It is hoped that many will suggest to the teacher additional practices that might be valuable for use in the classroom. Some of the suggestions can be followed either when systematic or incidental instruction in reading is given; others are of value primarily during the phases of the reading program that deal with the development of skills.

PROCEDURES FOR DEVELOPING COMPREHENSION

Suggestions for developing the following types of skills are given: (1) finding the main idea, (2) selecting significant details, (3) reading to answer questions, (4) following directions, (5) making summaries and organizing material, (6) arriving at generalizations and coming to conclusions, (7) predicting outcomes, (8) evaluating what is read, (9) doing associational reading, (10) reading graphical material, (11) getting the meaning of phrases, (12) comprehending sentences, and (13) comprehending paragraphs.

Developing Skill in Finding the Main Idea

Activities such as the following may help the learner to find the main idea of a passage:

1. Matching a series of pictures with the paragraphs they illustrate.
2. Stating the main idea of a selection.
3. Selecting from a list of sentences one that best expresses the main idea of a paragraph.
4. Selecting from a list of questions one that the entire paragraph answers.
5. Writing below a paragraph the question answered by the entire paragraph.
6. Selecting the best title from a list.
7. Naming a title to fit a given paragraph or longer selection.
8. Following directions, such as:
    a. Find the sentence that gives the main idea of the article.
    b. Draw a line under the words in the second paragraph that give the topic of that paragraph.
    c. Draw a line under the words that best describe the character discussed in the selection.
9. Reading a story to find out whether it is suitable to tell or read to others for a given purpose or to dramatize.
10. Reading a story a second time in order to determine what scenes should be dramatized.
11. Skimming a series or a group of trade books to decide which one to read, either for pleasure or some other purpose.
12. Telling which word of a series describes a character in a selection.
13. Making a "movie" or mural showing the main events in a story.
14. Noting certain phrases such as *the first* and *the most important* to see if they point out a main idea.
15. Matching a picture that illustrates a main idea with a paragraph that it illustrates.
16. Selecting topic sentences in paragraphs that contain topic sentences.
17. Changing each of the side headings of a longer selection to a question answered by the part following.

ADDITIONAL ACTIVITIES   The following are illustrations of practice exercises based on the preceding suggestions:

1

Direction: After you have read the story, write an x on the line to show which one would make the best title.

We made many plans for Christmas. We decided to trim our Christmas tree. Each boy and girl will make a decoration. We also decided to have a party. We will place our presents under the tree. At our party we will play games. We will also sing songs.

_____(a) Our Plans for Christmas
_____(b) Our Christmas Tree
_____(c) Decorations for Our Tree
_____(d) Christmas in Our Town

2

Direction: On the line below the story write a good title for it.

Sir Edwin Landseer was one of the greatest animal artists of modern times. When he attended art school, he divided his time between his classes and the zoo, where he studied animals and drew pictures of them. Although Landseer drew pictures of many animals, probably his most famous ones are those of dogs. The best-known one undoubtedly is the one named "The Old Shepherd's Chief Mourner." It is the picture of a devoted dog sadly guarding the coffin of his master, a shepherd.

Learning To Select Significant Details

By performing activities like the following, boys and girls can get practice in noting details and choosing those that are significant for their purpose:

1. Indicating which of a series of ideas listed are brought out in a given selection.
2. Telling which of a series of details support the main idea of a selection.
3. Reading to note as many details as possible that support a main idea.
4. Making a list of details included in a selection.
5. Answering questions on details in a sentence, paragraph, or longer selection.
6. Completing sentences, copied by the teacher from a reading selection, in which blanks were left for words that test the comprehension of details.
7. Matching a series of details with a list of main ideas.
8. Giving a list of words to describe a character whose actions have been discussed in a story.
9. Taking special note of details of a story to be told to others.
10. Showing which word in a series of sentences or paragraphs does not belong in a paragraph.
11. Checking a list of materials to indicate which are needed for an activity or project.
12. Studying the regulations for use of equipment for the playground, the reading table, or the playhouse.

13. Looking at a picture and then describing it.
14. Drawing a picture illustrating details of what has been read.
15. Deciding what actions in a story should be performed by characters in a "movie" or play that the class plans to put on.
16. Making a list of details that occur in a story, as preparation for dramatizing the story.
17. Composing a paragraph by supplying details to support a main idea that has been selected as theme.
18. Deciding which details are important to remember in terms of a stated purpose.
19. Preparing charts based on material that has been read—for example, a chart showing the growth in population in a state.
20. Taking notes on points read in order to report them to others in a group in connection with a unit of work.
21. Reading reference materials to answer questions raised by the class or by a committee in order to get information needed for a project.
22. Showing through outlining the relation between details and a main point.
23. Indicating which details belong and which do not belong in an outline that has been made on a selection.
24. Reading material in science and mathematics in which careful note needs to be taken of many points in order to comprehend the meaning, and then answering questions on the material or using it in other ways.
25. Reading directions and then following them.
26. Doing editorial work on a class newspaper.
27. Deciding whether the facts given by a reporter include sufficient details to justify a given headline in a newspaper.
28. Discussing whether the author relates details through his own comments, by the characters' actions, or by reports by characters as to what happened.
29. Listing the details in a description of a room, a landscape, or some other setting, in preparation for making a drawing.
30. Writing a main idea for a paragraph and then writing details to support it.
31. Writing a paragraph describing a given object, which other pupils are to guess.
32. Keeping a news record.
33. Keeping a weather chart.

ADDITIONAL ACTIVITIES   Two types of procedures that can be used in order to develop skill in selecting details are illustrated in the following exercises.

1

Directions: After you have read the following paragraph,

write *M* on the line to the left of the topic listed that expresses the main idea of the paragraph. Write *D* to the left of each topic that expresses a detail mentioned in the paragraph. Write *O* to the left of any item not mentioned in the paragraph.

One of the most interesting animals in the world is the great gray kangaroo, found in great numbers in Australia. One of its characteristics of special note is its size and shape. It is sometimes ten feet in length from the tip of the nose to the end of the tail and weighs as much as 200 pounds. Its long, strong tail is used as a prop when the kangaroo stands on its two hind legs. The kangaroo is a very swift runner. It can clear as many as twenty feet at one leap. It runs on its hind legs only. The development and care of the young is very interesting. Upon birth the baby kangaroo is only about an inch in length. It is then taken care of in the pouch to the front of the mother's hind legs. In this pouch it receives its nourishment from the milk of the mother. After the baby has lived in the pouch for about four months, it leans out of the pouch to eat grass while its mother, too, is grazing. Then for months thereafter, usually till the baby is about ten months old, the young kangaroo returns to the protection of the pouch even though it spends much of its time in the world outside. In fact, the baby likes the pouch so much that it stays in it until its mother refuses to carry it any longer.

_____(a)   The claws of the kangaroo.
_____(b)   The kangaroo, an interesting animal.
_____(c)   Australia, the home of the kangaroo.
_____(d)   How the kangaroo takes care of its young.
_____(e)   The leap of the kangaroo.
_____(f)   The value of the kangaroo.

2

Directions: The main topic of a paragraph is the food of the camel. Some of the sentences that are listed below are on that topic. Others do not deal with the topic and therefore should not be included in a paragraph on the food of the camel. Write *yes* on the line to the left of each sentence that can correctly be included in the paragraph and write *no* on the other lines.

_____(a)   The camel eats thistles that grow in the desert.
_____(b)   The camel is a lazy animal.
_____(c)   The mother camel is very tender toward her baby.
_____(d)   The camel can live for a long time without food.
_____(e)   The camel likes to eat baskets or saddles or newspapers.

Learning To Read To Answer Questions

Proficiency in finding the answer to a question can be helpful in a variety of reading situations. It is important at times in order to choose the main idea, to note details, to predict outcomes, to form generalizations, to follow directions, and to perform other activities connected with reading.

Answers are relatively easy to find when the questions are partly couched in the exact words of the writer. With the immature reader or the one who has difficulty in reading to find the answer to a question, this type of question may be used at first. If the writer says, "Susan's father gave her a kitten for her birthday," the teacher may ask, "What did Susan's father give her for her birthday?" A sample of a question to which the answer can be found less easily is, "What reasons can you find for the actions of the heroine?" or "Why do you think the heroine acted as she did?" The formulation of questions the teacher asks can encourage or discourage critical thinking.

Not only should the pupils gain skill in finding answers to questions that are stated by others but to avoid overdependence on the teacher they also need to develop in ability to formulate significant questions for themselves as purposes for reading. Questions by the teacher should serve chiefly as steppingstones to questions that the reader raises himself.

Practice that can be of value in developing skill in answering questions can be secured by performing activities such as the following:

1. Reading to answer questions stated by the teacher.
2. Indicating which of a series of questions listed by the teacher are likely to be answered in a given selection and then checking the responses after reading the selection.
3. Stating questions the reader would expect to find answered in a given selection and then checking to find the responses after reading the selection.
4. Indicating which of a series of questions that may possibly be answered in a given selection are formulated clearly, and rewording those that are not.
5. Reading to answer questions stated at the end of a selected reading.
6. Reading to answer questions brought out by viewing a film or filmstrip.

ADDITIONAL ACTIVITIES   The following exercises indicate two ways in which the pupils can get practice in deciding which questions are likely to be answered in a given selection. Since frequently it is important that the pupil rather than the teacher set a question or questions that he hopes will be answered in a selection, an exercise like the first one is often of value.

1

Directions: Before you read this selection on [title stated], make a list of questions that you may expect to find answered in it. Then read the selection to find the answer to as many questions as you can. After you have read it, on the lines provided after each question, write the answer to the questions that were answered in the paragraph. If a question was not answered, write the words *not answered*. (The selection may be chosen from the pupils' textbooks in social studies or science.)

1. Question 1. _____
     Answer: _____
                 _____

2. Question 2. _____
     Answer: _____
                 _____

3. Question 3. _____
     Answer: _____
                 _____

4. Question 4. _____
     Answer: _____
                 _____

2

Directions: Which of the following questions would you expect to find answered in the article on [title stated] given below? Before you read the selection, write *yes* on the line to the left of each question that you think may be answered. On the other lines write *no*. After you have read the selection, correct your *yes-no* answers by putting an *x* to the left of each of your answers that is incorrect. Then write the answer to each question that was discussed in the paragraph. Write it on the lines provided below the questions. (The selection may be chosen from the pupils' textbooks in social studies or science.)

1. _____(Question 1 by the teacher is listed here.)
    Answer: _____
             _____

2. _____(Question 2 by the teacher is listed here.)
    Answer: _____
             _____

3. _____(Question 3 by the teacher is listed here.)
    Answer: _____
        _____
        _____

Learning To Follow Directions

These methods may be helpful for an individual who is trying to improve his skill in following directions:

1. Repeating directions.
2. Observing written directions, such as, "Make one ball yellow. Make the other ball blue."
3. Following directions that the teacher has written on the chalkboard or on cards, such as, "Get ready for music" or "Come to the reading circle."
4. Answering questions about a set of directions, such as, "What should you do after you have cut the paper the correct size?"
5. Acting out an individually assigned sentence from a reading selection and then having the rest of the class tell which sentence it is.
6. Following written or oral directions for making things, such as a folder for papers or a papier-mâché globe.
7. Drawing a picture from directions given.
8. Drawing pictures based on descriptions that the boys and girls read.
9. Carrying out plans made by the class or committee for work on a unit.
10. Writing directions for doing or making something.
11. Reading directions for a game and then following them.
12. Reading directions for doing tricks and then performing them.
13. Arranging in correct order the sentences for directions to do or make something.
14. Reading directions for work-type activities in various subject fields and then following them.
15. Finding directions for experiments and carrying them out in front of the class.

ADDITIONAL ACTIVITY   This type of exercise may be helpful to persons having difficulty either in giving or following directions for going from one place to another.

Directions: Draw a diagram showing how a person who is at the post office could get to the city hall.

From the post office walk north until you come to the end of the block. Then turn left and walk west for two blocks, crossing the street before you again turn right to walk another half block north. There in the middle of the block you will find the city hall.

Making Summaries and Organizing Material

Skill in summarizing and organizing what is read can be developed through activities like these:

1. Telling which of several summaries best summarizes a paragraph or longer selection.
2. Answering questions like these: "What explorers helped Spain establish her claims to the New World? What did each of them do to give her a claim to the Americas?"
3. Organizing materials gathered from a variety of sources for an oral or written report.
4. Taking note of words like *first, second,* and *third* as they occur in context.
5. Classifying materials in the room for functional purposes—for example, putting all the books on one topic on a specified table or assembling, for use on two or more bulletin boards, pictures on different topics.
6. Telling what items belong in classifications like *food, clothing, shelter.*
7. Drawing pictures to tell the story of the main events in a story.
8. Arranging pictures in the order in which events pictured by them occurred in a story.
9. Organizing steps in a process demonstrated on a field trip, under topics such as "Steps in Baking Bread" or "The Manufacture of Flour."
10. Filling in main topics and subtopics of a selection when suggestions are given as to the number of main topics and the number of subtopics under each main topic.
11. Listing the questions on which information is needed to solve the problem of a unit, and then grouping the questions on similar topics.
12. Listing the topics on which information is needed to solve the problem of a unit, and then putting the list into outline form.
13. Placing subtopics, which are given in mixed-up order, under a list of main topics that are specified.
14. Learning the form for making outlines, including numbering and lettering, indentation, and capitalization and punctuation.
15. Making an outline, either in a group or individually, of parts of a story that one of the pupils will tell to another group of boys and girls.
16. Telling what is wrong with an incorrect outline that some pupil has made or one that the teacher has intentionally written incorrectly.
17. Arranging in correct order paragraphs dealing with one topic given in mixed-up order.
18. Selecting the sentences that do not belong in a paragraph that is set up so that it contains some irrelevant sentences.
19. Writing headlines for a class paper.
20. Making a list of actions of characters to show what traits they possess.
21. Making charts giving information about topics studied, such as "Our

Community Helpers," "How We Travel," "Famous Americans," "Greek Contributions to Civilization."

22. Studying the table of contents to note the organization of a book.
23. Learning where in a well-constructed paragraph a topic sentence, if there is one, is often found.
24. Reading to plan a dramatization.
25. Planning pictures for a "movie" or mural on a story or article read.
26. Telling under which of a series of circumstances outlining is of value.
27. Outlining the papers written by others in the group.
28. Checking a series of true-false statements like the following, to indicate which give good advice for making notes: (1) "Take your notes in your own words, not in those of the writer." (2) "If you do not understand what something means, be sure to include the point in your notes."
29. Before a child is able to write an outline, drawing illustrations to use as notes when planning a report or story. For example, as illustrated notes on the story of "The Three Little Pigs," sketches such as these might be made:

> The three little pigs.
> The houses of the three pigs.
> The wolf blowing in the first house.
> The wolf blowing in the second house.
> The wolf trying to blow in the third house.
> The wolf trying to catch the third pig.
> The death of the wolf.

30. Taking notes on points needed for a report.
31. Making an outline, such as the following, of points to be included in book reports:

> The title and author of the book.
> What the book is about.
> Two or three interesting parts of the book.
> How the reporter liked the book.
> Where the book can be found.

32. Checking a list of notes to determine which are appropriately recorded and which are not.

ADDITIONAL ACTIVITIES   Three additional ways in which practice can be given in summarizing or outlining are shown in these exercises.

1

Directions: Make an outline that will give the information shown in this chart.

PURPOSES OF SETTLEMENT

For religious freedom	Jamestown
To help debtors	Plymouth
For commercial reasons	Pennsylvania
	Georgia
	New Amsterdam

2

Directions: The sentences in this paragraph are not in the correct order. Write 1 on the line to the left of the sentence that should come first. Write 2 on the line to the left of the sentence that should come second. Number the rest of the sentences in the same way.

_____ Stephen heard something call, "Caw! Caw!" _____ There lay a baby crow. _____ Stephen looked around. _____ One day Stephen went to the woods with his father. _____ When Stephen saw that the crow could not walk, he took it home with him. _____ The crow had a broken leg. _____ Stephen always took good care of his crow.

3

As the boys and girls are studying about the Missouri Compromise, they could be asked to fill in subtopics in this beginning of an outline.

THE MISSOURI COMPROMISE

A. Events leading up to the compromise
    1.
    2.
B. Provisions of the compromise
    1.
    2.
C. Effects of the compromise
    1.
    2.

Developing Ability To Arrive at Generalizations and Come to Conclusions

In addition to the following suggestions for activities that can be valuable in developing the ability to arrive at generalizations and come to conclusions, some of those recommended under "Making Summaries and Organizing Material" can be used.

1. Making and guessing riddles.
2. Checking which ones of several conclusions are warranted by data given and explaining why the unsound conclusions are invalid.

3. Stating as specific a conclusion as possible after reading data presented in a paragraph or longer selection and explaining, in some cases, why no broader conclusion could be reached.
4. Discussing questions like the following after reading a story: (a) "Why do you think _____ made his decision to go West?" (b) "Under what conditions do you think _____ would have been friendly to strangers?"
5. Telling which of a list of statements are generalizations and which are specifics.
6. Listing facts heard or read that justify a given generalization or that prove that a given generalization is unsound.
7. After making a generalization based on what has been heard or read, checking the generalization against experiences or finding additional support for the generalization or experimenting to see if the generalization applies.
8. Discussing the effect that certain events in a story or in history had on individuals.
9. Stating the generalization that is justified on the basis of given facts.
10. Discussing the ideas contained in several stories to see if they give generalizations that were brought out in a story.
11. Formulating titles that indicate the generalization brought out in a series of stories.
12. Drawing a series of pictures that illustrate points leading to a generalization developed in a story or article.

ADDITIONAL ACTIVITIES   These exercises indicate how some of the above suggestions can be carried out.

1

After the teacher has read the following paragraph to the class, she asks the pupils, "What was Sally holding in her arms?"

> It was Christmas Eve. Everybody in the family, Father, Mother, Bobby, and three-year-old Sally, were in bed, or were supposed to be in bed. Suddenly Mother awoke. She thought she heard the creak of a stair. Then she heard nothing. So she fell asleep again. Later she heard a sound that seemed to come from the living room. She thought she heard a thin voice say, "Ma-ma! Ma-ma!" It was not Sally's voice. It was not Bobby's voice. Then all was quiet again. But this time Mother did not fall asleep. She awoke Father. Father went downstairs to see what was happening. When he opened the door into the living room, he saw that the big Mamma-doll that Santa Claus had left for Sally to find the next morning was gone. Then he looked into Sally's playroom. There he saw Sally sitting in her little rocker holding a bundle in her arms.

2

Pupils can make up and guess riddles like the following:

(a) I have two legs and two wings. I can fly high into the air. I sing songs. I lay eggs. What am I?

(b) I lived in Minnesota when I was a boy. I am an aviator. I made one of the most famous airplane flights that has ever been made. My wife enjoys flying. Who am I?

3

Directions: Below the following paragraph is a list of statements in the form of conclusions. On the blank to the left of each statement write *yes* if you think the reader can correctly come to that conclusion after reading the paragraph. Otherwise write *no*. If a conclusion is not correct for the paragraph, in the space provided state why you think it is not a sound conclusion. When you give your reasons, make certain to write the number of the conclusion to which you are referring.

On my last visit to the zoo, I spent part of my time watching two mother camels and their little colts. Both of the mothers stood near their young as if they wished to protect their babies from all harm. It seemed to me that there was a look of tenderness on the mothers' faces as they were looking at the little camels. I then remembered that my father had told me that the mother camel is often very kind to her young.

_____1. The camel is very gentle toward other animals.
_____2. The camel is very gentle toward people.
_____3. The mother camel is often very kind to her baby.
_____4. The mother camel is a very gentle animal.

Reasons. _____

_____

_____

_____

_____

Improving Ability To Predict Outcomes

Some the suggestions given under "Developing Ability To Arrive at Generalizations and Come to Conclusions" may be added to the following list of activities for improving the ability to predict outcomes.

1. While looking at pictures of a story, stating what the outcome of the story is likely to be.

2. Indicating by means of multiple-choice questions what is likely to happen next in a story or article.
3. Telling what is likely to happen next in a story or article, without help of multiple-choice questions.
4. Discussing why things happened as they did in a story or other account.
5. Making up endings for stories, orally or in writing.
6. Estimating the answer in some types of arithmetic problems.
7. Comparing our present situation with a previous one in history and deciding what might happen as a result of present conditions.
8. Indicating what is likely to happen at the time when work on a science experiment is begun.
9. Evaluating plans the class is making, in terms of expected outcomes.
10. Predicting what will happen next after having listened to part of the account of an experience another pupil has had.
11. Listing on the board known points about a situation and possible outcomes and then discussing the probability of certain results and the unlikelihood of others.
12. Arranging in order pictures illustrating a story that the pupils have not heard or read in entirety.
13. Upon arrival at school, predicting the weather and giving reasons for prediction, and later checking the prediction.
14. Predicting, after reading a current news report, what will happen and then the following day checking to see if the prediction was correct.

Developing Skill in Evaluating What Is Read

The ability to evaluate critically what is read may require any one of the following skills: (1) distinguishing between fact and opinion, (2) telling what is real and what is fanciful, (3) determining the qualifications of the author and his purpose and attitude, (4) noting the up-to-dateness of the information presented, (5) deciding whether propaganda is being spread, and (6) examining critically the generalizations made. The last-named of these skills is discussed on pages 203–204. Below are suggestions for developing each of the other skills listed. It should be noted, too, that some suggestions applicable to critical evaluation of what is read are listed on preceding pages under ideas presented for developing other comprehension skills. The reader is also referred, for additional suggestions on procedure, to the quotation from Willavene Wolf on pages 185–186.

FACT OR OPINION   To gain proficiency in distinguishing between fact and opinion, the pupils might do the following:

1. Analyze newspaper reports to determine whether they present facts or opinions.

2. Study news reports and editorials to determine the essential differences in the two types of writing.
3. Locate statements of opinion found within a given selection.
4. Indicate which of a series of statements express facts only and then rewrite those that are not purely factual so that they do not express an opinion.
5. Rewrite statements of fact that are mixed with statements of opinion in such a way that instead of showing sympathy toward a person or event they will show antipathy (and vice versa).
6. Delete from paragraphs or longer selections statements that are not entirely factual.

ADDITIONAL ACTIVITY   Directions like the following may be given to provide practice in discriminating between statements that are based entirely on facts and those that are based, in part at least, on opinion.

Directions: Some of the following sentences are statements of fact; others are, at least in part, expressions of opinion. On the line at the right of each sentence that is only a statement of fact, write an *F*, for *fact*. Write an *O*, for *opinion*, on the line if the statement is, at least in part, an expression of an opinion. Then in the space following the last sentence in this exercise, rewrite those sentences which reveal the writer's opinion. Rewrite them in such a manner that the rewritten sentences are statements of fact only. Number your sentences to correspond to the numbers of the printed sentences.

1. Lake Michigan cuts the state of Michigan in two parts. 1._____
2. The best place to be in winter is Florida.   2._____
3. The road from here to the next town is a gravel road. 3._____
4. The most beautiful place in the United States is Mount Rainier.   4._____
5. The best vacation spot in the Northwest is Portland, Oregon.   5._____

REAL OR FANCIFUL   In order to become more adept at judging whether or not written material is of a fanciful or factual nature, pupils might perform activities such as these that follow:

1. Find examples in stories of means by which the author indicated that the story is fanciful.
2. Draw up a list of expressions often used in stories to show that the stories are fanciful, for example, "Once upon a time."
3. Decide whether a story is real or fanciful and indicate the reason for the decision.
4. Read a story that is fictional but based in part on fact and then determine which statements are likely to be true and which are more likely to be fictional.

THE AUTHOR   In order to decide upon the qualifications of an author or his purpose or attitude, the reader might engage in activities such as these:

1. Deciding how each of two persons, both qualified to speak or write on a given subject but with a different experience background, might express himself on that subject.
2. Discussing which of two authors whose qualifications are stated would be better qualified to write on a given topic.
3. Deciding with classmates upon questions that, if answered, might help a reader decide upon the qualifications of an author; for example, (a) Does the author have much information about the subject? (b) Has he a good reputation as a writer? as a person? (c) Is there a reason why he would be likely to push one point of view over another?
4. Deciding upon the purpose of an author in writing a given selection.
5. Indicating which of a list of sentences reveal a sympathetic attitude and which an unsympathetic one toward a person or a situation.

UP-TO-DATENESS   Activities such as these might be of value in helping boys and girls decide upon the up-to-dateness and the need of up-to-dateness in regard to writings:

1. Noting the copyright date of books.
2. Indicating which books written long ago are valuable for a stated purpose and which are not.
3. Finding an item of information as it is reported in a book with an old copyright date and in one with a recent copyright and comparing the two.
4. Making a list of questions on which information in a book with an old copyright date would be as useful as one with a recent copyright.

PROPAGANDA TECHNIQUES   Activities such as the following may help a person in detecting propaganda when he sees it in print or hears it:

1. Indicating which statements present only so limited a part of the truth that an incorrect impression is given.
2. Indicating which of a series of words, such as *native land, house, home folks,* arouse emotion.
3. Noting types of words often used to arouse emotions of sympathy or love or anger.
4. Writing a report employing propaganda techniques.
5. Noting how an author who says he is presenting both sides of a controversial matter slights one side of the question.
6. Reading a report on an event in two newspapers, one of which is known to be sensational, and then comparing the reports.
7. Writing headlines that might be included in a newspaper or magazine known for sensationalism and rewriting these headlines as they might appear in a paper or magazine not given to sensationalism.

ADDITIONAL POINTS   The following are additional suggestive activities for increasing in power to evaluate critically what is read:

1. Indicating which of a series of statements are relevant and which are irrelevant to a given purpose.
2. Locating inconsistencies in a series of paragraphs or longer selections.
3. Matching a series of abstract statements with items in a list of incidents that illustrate the abstractions.
4. Asking, or, in other cases, answering, thought-provoking questions about something that has been heard or read.
5. Choosing from a list of chapter titles those chapters that are most likely to be valuable in connection with a given problem.
6. Setting up standards for a story to be chosen, such as listing points to consider when selecting a story to be read to a given group for a stated purpose.
7. Giving book reviews in which emphasis is placed on the evaluation of the book rather than on the story itself.
8. Checking the validity of a statement in terms of agreement with other statements in the same book.
9. Determining how to decide upon the likely truth when two contradictory statements are found.
10. Bringing to class an editorial from a newspaper and a news item and then listing the differences in writing style, giving reasons why each type is written as it is.

Developing Ability To Do Associational Reading

Associational reading can be thought of as a process in which the reader applies what he is reading to his past experiences, real or vicarious, as well as to possible future situations. He makes associations. Like other types of reading abilities, the ability to do associational reading can be improved through environmental stimulation. Ways in which a teacher can be of help in stimulating the pupils to grow in power to do associational reading follow:

1. Asking the pupils after reading a selection how they would feel if they had been in the same position.
2. Telling the boys and girls some of her own experiences that parts of a story remind her of.
3. Giving the pupils the opportunity to tell experiences of their own that certain parts of a selection remind them of.
4. Asking the pupils what application they can make of what they read to future situations that they may encounter.
5. Encouraging the boys and girls to use various senses to make clearer the image of what they are reading. At times they might illustrate by a drawing part of a story; at other times music expressing the mood of a story might be correlated with the written accounts. Oral reading, too, can make more vivid what is read. Choral reading of a selection is particularly valuable for this purpose.
6. Giving the boys and girls the opportunity to discuss their reactions to a story. The interchange of ideas may frequently make more vivid the message gleaned from the written material.

Learning To Read Graphical and Tabular Material

The following types of activities can prove helpful in teaching boys and girls to read graphs, tables, charts, and maps with greater comprehension:

1. Answering questions about data on a calendar, such as "How many Thursdays are there in June?" or "On what day of the week is June 11?"
2. Making a calendar to record weather conditions.
3. Making graphs on individual or group achievements.
4. Making a map of the classroom or community.
5. Studying a map and map legend and then answering questions based on them.
6. Showing information of various types—for example, surface features, population centers, and political divisions—on maps that have been duplicated.
7. Making, in answer to a question, a list of important points that can be gained for a stated purpose from a given map, table, graph, or chart.

ADDITIONAL ACTIVITY   An exercise of this type may be

used before pupils start keeping a similar record of their own achievement.

Directions: The graph shows how many spelling words out of the fifteen in each weekly test Harold had correct during the first ten weeks of the school year. Answer the questions or follow the directions given below.

1. How many times did Harold have a perfect score?
2. What was the largest number of words that Harold had wrong on any test?
3. During which week did Harold have the largest number of words wrong?
4. For how many more records of tests is there room on this graph?
5. Mark the graph for the eleventh week to show that Harold had two words wrong.

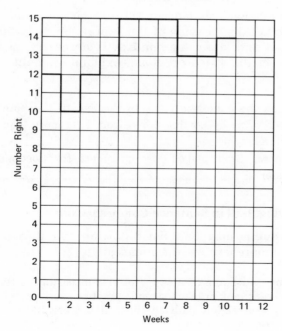

MY SPELLING RECORD

Developing Skill in Getting the Meaning of Phrases

Skill in the comprehension of phrases can be developed by means of the following activities:

1. Giving the meaning of expressions used in sentences.
2. Matching phrases in one column with words with similar meaning in another column.
3. Finding in a selection phrases that answer certain questions, such as, "What group of words tells that Frank is happy?"
4. Discussing the meaning of commonly used idiomatic expressions.
5. Interpreting figures of speech.
6. Underlining the complete phrase in an exercise where the first word of the phrases is underlined.
7. Playing a game in which pupils read what is written on a phrase card.
8. Locating a phrase that is illustrated by a picture.
9. Making up a phrase that expresses the meaning of a given phrase.
10. Completing sentences by matching the beginnings of sentences given in one column with appropriate endings in a column of phrases.

ADDITIONAL ACTIVITY   An exercise like this may be used in the intermediate grades.

Directions: Each sentence in this exercise contains an expression in italics. To get the meaning of the expression, note the meaning of each word in it and study the context. If necessary, consult your dictionary. Then, in the space provided, explain what the expression means.

1. When the explorers came to the end of the path, they saw *a veil of spray* coming down from falls more than a hundred feet in height. _____
2. General Grant asked his opponents for *unconditional surrender.* _____

Improving Skill in Sentence Comprehension

Some pupils may find the following activities of value in improving their comprehension of sentences:

1. Drawing a line under one of a series of sentences that is illustrated by a picture in a workbook or teacher-made practice exercise.
2. Picking out in connection with an illustrated story the sentences that are well illustrated by a picture.

3. Answering, with *yes* or *no,* questions on which readers will agree if the meaning is clear to them, such as, (a) Is winter a colder season than summer? (b) Do all good people live in warm houses?
4. Arranging in correct order the parts of scrambled sentences.
5. Listing the sentences in a selection that help prove a given point.
6. Indicating which sentences in a series mean almost the same as specified sentences.
7. Making up sentences that describe a picture.
8. Finding in a book a sentence that suggests an appropriate title for a story or picture.
9. Getting practice in phrasing while reading so as to avoid difficulty in understanding a sentence. Difficulty would be likely to occur when a reader does not know, for example, that the end of a phrase in the following sentence comes after *happenings,* not after *unusual:* "One of the most unusual happenings occurred this morning."
10. Making sentences that show variety in structure, such as, (a) "Quickly the boys ran home." (b) "The boys ran home quickly."
11. Studying the thought of sentences in which the subject and predicate are in inverted order, and constructing some of that type.
12. Finding sentences that answer given questions.
13. Making up sentences that describe the same idea in different ways.
14. Studying sentences in which many adjectives or adverbs or phrases or clauses modify the subject and the predicate.
15. Interpreting the meaning of conjunctions and prepositions as they are used in sentences.
16. Answering questions about a sentence with which the pupils have difficulty and indicating which part of a sentence answers each question.
17. Making, in connection with a long sentence that presents comprehension difficulties, a sentence for every idea contained in it.
18. Establishing the relation in meaning among the parts of a sentence.
19. Deciding on the meaning of some sentences through the study of punctuation marks.

Developing Skill in Paragraph Comprehension

Many suggestions for improved comprehension of paragraphs have been given under various skills listed earlier in this chapter, as under "Developing Skill in Finding the Main Idea", and in "Making Summaries and Organizing Material." A few additional ones are given here.

1. Locating a paragraph on a stated page by means of directions such as, "Place a finger under the paragraph that begins with the words 'Evelyn ran home as fast as she could,'" or "Read the last sentence of the first paragraph on page _____ ."

2. Finding the paragraph that answers a question or contains a specified thought.
3. Finding the topic sentence of paragraphs that contain topic sentences.
4. Studying the topic sentence of a paragraph to help get the main idea of the paragraph.
5. Using the topic sentence of a paragraph as an aid when organizing as well as when skimming.
6. Studying the relation of sentences within a paragraph.
7. Writing paragraphs on specified topics.
8. Arranging in order paragraphs that are not in the correct sequence.
9. Matching a series of paragraphs with summaries of these paragraphs.

ADDITIONAL ACTIVITY   An exercise like this can be particularly helpful, since it is based on reading in the pupils' books. At least one of the paragraphs used in this exercise should have a topic sentence and at least one should not.

Directions: Read the three paragraphs in your [name of textbook supplied] on page _____ to answers these questions and to follow these directions. (The same questions as those given for the first paragraph should be asked about the other paragraphs.)

Paragraph 1. Does it contain a topic sentence? _____ If so, write the first three words of the sentence. _____

If there is a topic sentence in the paragraph, do all the details given in the paragraph support the topic sentence? _____

If the paragraph does not contain a topic sentence, would the paragraph be improved if it had one? _____ Give reasons for your answer. _____

_____

If the paragraph has no topic sentence and if the paragraph could be improved if it contained one, write a sentence that would make a good topic sentence for the paragraph. _____

_____

_____

Developing Skill in Understanding the Meaning of Longer Selections

Since many suggestions for development of skill in comprehending longer materials were given under a variety of topics earlier in this chapter, we list here only the following three additional types of activities that pupils could profitably perform to gain more skill in comprehending materials of this type.

1. Finding the place in a story or article or book where specified parts begin.
2. Reading a story or article to decide where it can be divided into parts.
3. Taking a pretest, before reading a selection, on questions based on the selection and then, after reading it, taking the test again.

ADDITIONAL ACTIVITY   To help boys and girls make adequate use of center heads and sideheads, an exercise like this may prove of help.

Directions: Read the headings given in this exercise. Study them to find out what questions you would expect to find discussed under each. Then in the space to the right of each question write the number of the center head and the letter of the sidehead under which you would expect to find the question discussed. Write an N, for *not discussed*, in the space to the right of each question that you do not expect to find discussed under any of these headings.

CHRISTOPHER COLUMBUS

Center head: 1. *The Boyhood of Columbus*
Sideheads: a. Birthplace
                    b. Work of his father
                    c. His early interest in the sea
Center head: 2. *The Plan of Columbus*
Sideheads: a. His beliefs about the shape of the earth
                    b. His disbelief in the stories of the dragons of the sea
                    c. His belief that India could be reached by water
Center head: 3. *Columbus in Search of Aid*
Sideheads: a. Refusal of Spain to help him
                    b. Plan to ask France for aid
                    c. The help of the abbott
                    d. Promise of help by Queen Isabella and King Ferdinand
Center head: 4. *Getting Ready for the First Voyage*
Sideheads: a. Getting men
                    b. Getting ships and supplies
Center head: 5. *First Voyage*
Sideheads: a. Fears of the sailors
                    b. Scarcity of food
                    c. Length of the voyage
                    d. Threat of mutiny
                    e. Seeing land
                    f. The landing
                    g. Exploring the land
                    h. Return to Spain

Center head: 6. *Later Voyages and Death*
Sideheads: a. The second, third, and fourth voyages
                  b. Return to Spain in chains
                  c. Last days and death

1. Why were the sailors afraid they would fall off the edge of the earth? _____
2. How did the Spanish court treat Columbus upon his return after his fourth voyage? _____
3. Did the Norsemen discover America? _____
4. What did Columbus believe, even before 1492, was the shape of the earth? _____
5. Why did Spain at first refuse to give aid to Columbus? _____
6. Why was it hard to secure good men for the first voyage? _____
7. How many ships did Columbus have with him on his first voyage? _____
8. When was land first seen? _____
9. What did Columbus do to keep his men from mutinying on the first voyage? _____
10. Where did Columbus die? _____
11. What parts of America did the French explore? _____

THE DEVELOPMENT OF COMPREHENSION SKILLS THROUGH READING LESSONS

All of the comprehension skills can be developed in part through reading lessons without recourse to definite practice exercises. This section of the chapter is devoted to demonstrating how growth in the various skills can be encouraged in these lessons. The material is based on selections from a second-grade, a fourth-grade, and a sixth-grade reader. The comprehension skills that a teacher will decide to develop in any of these lessons will depend upon the total developmental reading program based upon the needs of the boys and girls. The suggestions enumerated in connection with any of these lessons are not necessarily the ones to be used. They are merely suggestive of the many possible ones from which a selection may be made. Nor should nearly all of the recommendations be used for any one selection, for the number is too large and there is overlapping among them. Excellent suggestions for the development of power in comprehension are also listed in the manuals for the teacher accompanying the basal textbooks.

A Second-grade Lesson

In the second-grade reader *We Are Neighbors*[1] is the story "The Red Shoes," written by Maj Lindman. It tells of three little boys who, after they found out that their mother would like some red shoes for her birthday, went out in search of work so that they could earn money to buy the gift. All three found work. Snipp finished painting a fence red, Snapp helped a man clean his chimney, and Snurr worked in a flour mill. When the boys had completed their work, they used the money they had earned to buy a beautiful pair of red shoes for their mother. Snipp in his clothes red with paint, Snapp in his suit that was black with soot, and Snurr looking like a snowman in his clothes that were covered with flour, rushed home happily to give their delighted mother the red shoes that they had purchased for her.

FINDING THE MAIN IDEA   The pupils may read the story in order to decide whether it would be a good one to read to another group or whether it would be suitable for using for a dramatization or a home-made "movie," if they had been planning to engage in one of these activities.

SELECTING IMPORTANT DETAILS   If the pupils decide to dramatize the story or to make a "movie" of it or to give a puppet play, they may read the story carefully in order to decide what scenes to include in the dramatization or "movie."

SUMMARIZING AND ORGANIZING   Although most work in writing summaries is usually postponed till grades later than the second, with some second-grade groups a simple file, possibly in the form of a looseleaf notebook, of stories that they like particularly may be kept. For such a file the group could cooperatively plan a brief summary on this order: "Three boys, Snipp, Snapp, and Snurr, wanted to buy some red shoes for their mother for her birthday. They worked to earn the money. They earned enough money to buy her some red shoes. Their mother liked her present."

If the pupils decide to put on a play, they can help determine what the main parts of the play should be. The division might be as follows:

1. The boys ask their mother what she wants for her birthday.
2. The boys look for work.
3. The boys find work.
4. The boys buy the shoes.
5. The boys give the shoes to their mother.

[1] Odille Ousley and David H. Russell, *We Are Neighbors*. Boston: Ginn & Company, 1966. Ginn Basic Readers.

Then the pupils can decide on the details to be portrayed in connection with each main part.

ARRIVING AT GENERALIZATIONS   After discussing why the boys were so happy when they had spent their money to buy a gift for their mother, the teacher may guide the discussion, without undue moralizing, so that the boys and girls will tell of times when they, too, were happy when they had done something for someone else. It may be unwise in many instances to ask the pupils to state the generalization, that often a person becomes happy if he has made someone else happy; however, the teacher may make a statement that would serve as a generalization—for example, "Often people find that they become happy when they have done something nice for others."

PREDICTING OUTCOMES   During the course of the reading of the story, the teacher may at appropriate places make comments and ask questions like this: "Snipp's clothes were red after he had painted the fence and Snapp's were black after he had helped clean a chimney. What color do you imagine Snurr's were after he had finished working?" Then the boys and girls could be asked to read to find out whether they were right in the prediction.

EVALUATING CRITICALLY   The pupils may discuss whether they think the story is a fanciful tale. The likelihood of boys getting work of the types mentioned may be discussed in this connection.

ANSWERING QUESTIONS   The pupils may read the entire story, after a proper introduction by the teacher, to find out whether the boys were able to get some red shoes for their mother. After the pupils have read the part that tells that Snipp asked a man if he could paint the fence for him, the teacher may say, "Read the rest of the page to find out whether Snipp painted the fence for the man." After the pupils have read the parts that tell what kinds of work Snipp and Snapp had found, the teacher may say, "Read the next page to find out whether Snurr was able to find some work."

FOLLOWING DIRECTIONS   The teacher may write on the board directions like these:

1. Finish reading the story.
2. Study the questions on the board.
3. Use your book to find answers to questions that you do not know.

SENTENCE COMPREHENSION   If the pupils have difficulty in comprehending the rather long sentence, "They were still thinking of ways they could earn money to buy red shoes," the teacher may ask them to tell in their own words what the boys were thinking about as they walked along. Or, after the children have read the sentence, she may ask them, "Of what were the boys thinking as they were walking along?" Practice in formulating good sentences as they discuss what they read or as they make a summary can also indirectly help boys and girls in the comprehension of the meaning of the written sentences.

PARAGRAPH MEANING   To help the pupils become more familiar with the term *paragraph*, the pupils can be given a direction like this: "Read the second paragraph on page 140 [of the reader] to find out why the boys were happy."

COMPREHENSION OF A LONGER SELECTION   On the basis of a story like this one the pupils can be helped in learning to read longer selections more effectively by performing such activities as these: (1) finding where each of the parts of the story that were enumerated earlier under "Summarizing and Organizing" begins (see page 217) or (2) telling the story to another group of boys and girls.

A Fourth-grade Lesson

In the fourth-grade reader *Meeting New Friends*,[2] "The Wonderful Spectacles" tells how two Dutch children, Jan and Gretchen, had an important part in the invention of the telescope. One day while their father, a spectacle maker, had gone to another town, the two children accompanied by Malkin, the cat, had gone into their father's workshop and had examined many articles, his magnifying glasses among them. When they had looked at things in the shop through the magnifying lenses, they decided to go outdoors to examine things there. They noticed that a magnifying lens was helpful only when they looked at objects close to them. Then Jan, who happened to look at a weather vane through the two magnifying lenses held a distance apart, noticed that it seemed much larger and closer. When toward evening the children heard their father's voice, they rushed back into the shop to return the glasses before their father would miss them. In their hurry they knocked down and broke a pair of spectacles. Afraid of the punishment they would receive from their father, they were relieved momentarily when they noticed that again the cat was in the workshop, for they thought they might be able to let Malkin take the blame for the broken spectacles. When later in the evening the father reported that the spectacles had been broken and that evidently Malkin had caused the accident, Jan and Gretchen were still more relieved. But before long

[2] Guy L. Bond, Marie C. Cuddy, and Leo C. Fay, *Meeting New Friends*. Chicago: Lyons and Carnahan, 1962. The Developmental Reading Series.

their consciences hurt them. Therefore they decided they would tell their father the truth. They also told him of their discovery of the effect upon the visibility of an object in the distance if it is viewed through two lenses held a ways apart. How the children's observation led to the invention of the telescope and what use Galileo made of their discovery are reported in the rest of the story.

This story is suited admirably to the development of any of a variety of comprehension skills. The following are a few possible ways in which improvement in comprehension can be brought about in connection with a reading lesson based on this story.

FINDING THE MAIN IDEA   The boys and girls may decide to share some of the information they would get through the study of the section in their reader entitled, "It Happened This Way," of which this story is the first. In that case they may, first of all, read this story and the others in the section in order to find out how they can best present to their audience the information gleaned from their reading. After they have read all the stories, they may decide that one would be suitable for telling, another for dramatizing, and another for a "movie." Still another may be used to demonstrate a process.

SELECTING IMPORTANT DETAILS   In connection with any of the activities suggested above it is important for the pupils to select important details.

SUMMARIZING AND ORGANIZING   The pupils may make a chart on which they summarize or organize important information they receive while reading this and other stories in this section of the textbook. Skill in organizing and in summarizing can also be developed in connection with activities suggested earlier under "Finding the Main Idea."

ARRIVING AT GENERALIZATIONS   The story provides excellent opportunity to help boys and girls develop in the ability to make generalizations. Attention can be drawn to the fact that after Jan had noticed that the lens made a near-by fly look big, he had incorrectly concluded that the glass could make everything look big. Later, he rightly concluded that the lens made near-by, but not distant, objects look bigger. Discussion could also center around the question, "Besides looking at a weather vane what should the children do before they should come to the conclusion that looking through two lenses, one close to the eye and the other farther away, makes a distant object seem larger and closer?" Practice in testing a generalization could also be given by letting some of the pupils look at a distant object through two lenses held a distance apart.

PREDICTING OUTCOMES   After the pupils have read to

the point where the children in the story let the cat take the blame for the broken spectacles, the pupils may tell whether they think Jan and Gretchen will tell their father that they had broken the glasses. They may be asked to give reasons for their answer.

After the pupils have finished reading the story, they may read aloud the parts that hint that the children will not let the cat take the blame.

EVALUATING CRITICALLY   The pupils can enumerate the happenings that led to the discoveries of Galileo by arranging the events into a cause-effect relationship. For example,

1. Because the father accidentally left the door in his shop open, Jan and Gretchen had an opportunity to look through a lens at things inside the shop.
2. Because they looked at things inside the shop through lenses, they became interested in looking at things outside through lenses.
3. Because they wanted to look at things outside through lenses, they took the lenses out of the shop.
4. Because they took the lenses out of the shop, they had an opportunity to look at the rooster on the weather vane through two lenses held a distance apart.
5. Because they looked at the rooster, they had the chance to observe the effects of looking through two lenses at objects at a distance.
6. Because they discovered the effect of looking through two lenses at the rooster, they were able to tell their father the effect of looking through the two lenses.
7. Because the children had told their father of their discovery, he was able to make the first crude telescope.
8. Because of their father's work with the telescope, Galileo was able to find out much about stars.

The ability to evaluate critically what is read may also be developed by asking the pupils whether they think comments like these made in the story, which show the effect of a guilty conscience, are true to life: "But somehow getting presents seemed to be much less fun than usual." "At supper the food did not taste very good to them, either." "Their mother's cookies tasted like dry paper in their mouths."

The boys and girls can discuss whether they think the story is true or fanciful and then decide on ways of trying to find out to what extent it is true.

ANSWERING QUESTIONS   The boys and girls could read the story to find out how the telescope was invented. Or, if they read the story part by part, they could read to answer questions like these as they proceed: "What did Gretchen do when Jan invited her to come into the workshop with him?" "What did Father do after the children had gone to bed?"

FOLLOWING DIRECTIONS   After reading the story the pupils could write directions for making a simple telescope and then follow them.

WORD MEANING   Here are several ways in which the meaning of some of the words used in the story could be made clearer:

1. To help the pupils understand the meaning of the term *magnifying lenses,* they could be asked to see whether by studying the picture on page 101 of the reader and reading the text on that page they could decide what a magnifying lens is. The meaning could further be clarified for the children by letting them look through a magnifying lens.
2. By looking at the picture on page 101 the pupils may be helped to understand the meaning of the word *workbench* as used in the sentence: "A fly was on the workbench and Gretchen bent over it, staring through the magnifying glass."
3. Through the picture given on page 104 of the reader and the sentence, "Jan looked up at the weather vane on top of the church steeple across the square," the pupils may be able to get help in deciding on a synonym for *steeple.*
4. In helping the boys and girls understand the word *courage,* the teacher may ask them what word the father used when he said he thought his children were brave to confess what they had done.
5. Examination and use of a small telescope could help the boys and girls attach more meaning to the word *telescope.*
6. Reference to weather vanes in town could make that term clearer.

SENTENCE MEANING   Development in skill in sentence comprehension could be brought about through questions and directions like these:

1. "What do you think Father meant when he said, 'Perhaps all men will see better because of what you learned today'?"
2. "Explain this statement by Gretchen: 'The weather vane came close to us, really close.' "
3. "Give in your own words this sentence, 'He looked at the moon and no longer saw the face of a man, but the outlines of mountains and valleys.' "

A Sixth-grade Lesson

The story by Mary Macleod, "Arthur Wins the Sword and Slays the Giant," found in the sixth-grade reader *Into New Worlds*[3] can

---

[3] Albert Harris, Marion Gartler, Caryl Roman, and Marcella Benditt, *Into New Worlds.* New York: The Macmillan Company, 1966. The Macmillan Reading Program.

be used in a variety of ways to develop comprehension skills. It tells about the birth of the legendary hero King Arthur, of his boyhood spent under the care of Sir Ector, of his winning of the sword Excalibur which proved he was the rightful heir to the English throne, of his code of ethics for the knights of the order of his famous Round Table, of his refusal to pay tribute to Rome, and of his slaying of a fearful giant.

The following are some of the ways in which comprehension skills can be developed in connection with the reading of this story.

SUMMARIZING AND ORGANIZING   To make certain that the pupils comprehend the literal meaning of the story, they might be asked to list in order of occurrence the main events in the life of King Arthur to which reference is made in the story. The list might be something like this:

> His birth.
> His delivery to Merlin.
> His father's death.
> The winning of Excalibur.
> The formation of the order of the Round Table.
> The decision not to pay tribute.
> Starting out for Rome.
> Killing the giant.

Or to help the boys and girls recall the sequence of events, they could be given a list of topics such as the above, in mixed-up order, and be asked to arrange them in sequence.

ARRIVING AT GENERALIZATIONS   To help the boys and girls arrive at generalizations they might be asked:

1. What words they think describe King Arthur and then to find sentences or groups of sentences on which they based their characterizations.
2. To read the last sentence of the story again, the one that states: "But all men of honor said it was merry to be under such a chieftain who would risk his person in adventures as other poor knights did." Thereupon the pupils might be asked why knights might like to serve under King Arthur—other than the reason stated in that sentence.

PREDICTING OUTCOMES   The boys and girls might consider the question, "Where did we get the first hint that King Arthur was going to be successful in his fight with the fearful giant?" Then they might list additional bases for the prediction that King Arthur would be able to overcome the giant.

REAL OR FANCIFUL   After the teacher has told the class that there seems to have been a character with some of the traits of

King Arthur in the fifth or sixth century but that in part at least he is a legendary figure, the boys and girls might select those points in the story that seem to be fanciful. Thereupon the teacher might refer a pupil to the account in *Compton's Pictured Encyclopedia* to note the answer there given to the question, "What is real and what is fanciful about the tales of King Arthur and his knights?" A pupil could then report his findings to the class.

ASSOCIATIONAL READING   Preliminary to drawing a mural representing important events in King Arthur's life, some of the boys and girls might be reading other accounts of King Arthur and his knights of the Round Table, for example:

Pyle, Howard, *The Story of King Arthur and His Knights.*
Robinson, Mabel, *King Arthur and His Knights.*
Schiller, Barbara, *The Kitchen Knight.* (This book gives the story of Gareth and Lynette.)

Questions such as these to help the boys and girls develop in ability to do associational reading might be asked: (1) "What do you think you might have said or done if you had been a knight or a lady in King Arthur's court when the messengers from Rome demanded tribute?" (2) "Undoubtedly King Uther felt very sad when he had to give up young Arthur on the night of his birth. If you had been one of the members of King Uther's court, how would you have tried to comfort him?"

COMPREHENSION OF WORD MEANING   Questions and comments to help build word-comprehension skill might include some of the following:

1. What do you imagine the word *realm* means in the sentence, "He had asked the Archbishop to tell all the lords of the *realm* to come to London at Christmas?"
2. Note the sentence that states: "At the time, he said, a *miracle* would show who should be rightly king of all the realm." How would you explain what is meant by a miracle?
3. What words could be used instead of the word *vanquished* in the second of the following sentences?

"Beware," said the widow. "Approach him not too near, for he hath *vanquished* fifteen kings, and made a coat of precious stones, embroidered with their beards."

ADDITIONAL SKILL   It might be pointed out to the pupils

that even though the stories about King Arthur are in large part fictional, like other stories with a historical setting they give us an idea of the life of the time they represent. Then the boys and girls could make a list of points brought out in the story that they think give an idea of the life of the times represented.

FOR FURTHER STUDY

Barbe, Walter B., *Teaching Reading*. New York: Oxford University Press, 1965. Chapter 33, "Teaching Critical Reading in the Middle Grades," pp. 277–281.

Bond, Guy A., and Eva Bond Wagner, *Teaching the Child To Read*. New York: Crowell-Collier and Macmillan, Inc., 1966. Chapter 13, "Reading Content-Subject Materials," pp. 253–286.

De Boer, John J., "Creative Reading and the Gifted Student," *The Reading Teacher,* 16, pp. 435–441 (May 1963).

Dechant, Emerald V., *Improving the Teaching of Reading*. Englewood Cliffs, N.J.: Prentice-Hall, Inc., 1964. Chapter 13, "Advancing the Pupil's Comprehension Skills," pp. 353–402.

Gans, Roma, *Common Sense in Reading*. Indianapolis, Ind.: The Bobbs-Merrill Company, Inc., 1963. Chapter 9, "The Expanding Function and Power of Reading in the Intermediate Grades," pp. 163–187; Chapter 10, "Comprehension—Probing with Reasons," pp. 188–212; Chapter 11, "Learning To Extend Comprehension through Discussion," pp. 213–228.

Harris, Albert J., *Readings on Reading Instruction*. New York: David McKay Company, Inc., 1963. Chapter 13, "Materials for the Reading Program," pp. 358–386.

Hester, Kathleen B., *Teaching Every Child To Read*. New York: Harper & Row, Publishers, 1964. Part 5, "A Teacher Plans To Further Reading as a Thinking Process," pp. 251–269.

King, Martha L., Bernice D. Ellinger, and Willavene Wolf (eds.), *Critical Reading*. Philadelphia: J. B. Lippincott Company, 1967.

McKee, Paul, *Reading: A Program of Instruction for the Elementary School*. Boston: Houghton Mifflin Company, 1966. Chapter 11, "Improving Reading through Instruction in the Content Subjects," pp. 405–435.

McKim, Margaret G., and Helen Caskey, *Guiding Growth in Reading*. New York: Crowell-Collier and Macmillan, Inc., 1963. Chapter 10, "Planning the Reading Program in the Intermediate Grades," pp. 259–289; Chapter 11, "Developing Reading Skills through On-going Classroom Activities in the Intermediate Grades," pp. 289–328; Chapter 12, "Developing Reading Skills through Special Practice Activities in the Intermediate Grades," pp. 329–379.

Smith, Nila B., *Reading Instruction for Today's Children*. Englewood Cliffs, N.J.: Prentice-Hall, Inc., 1963. Chapter 23, "Practice and Maintenance Activities for Use in Developing Study Skills in Content Areas," pp. 563–571.

Spache, George D., and Evelyn B., *Reading in The Elementary School*, 2d ed. Boston: Allyn and Bacon, Inc., 1969.

Stahl, Stanley S., Jr., *The Teaching of Reading in the Intermediate Grades*. Dubuque, Iowa: William C. Brown Company, Publishers, 1965. Pages 15–25, 46–72, 73–92.

Stauffer, Russell G., *Teaching Reading as a Thinking Process*. New York: Harper & Row, Publishers, 1969.

Strang, Ruth, Constance McCullough, and Arthur Traxler, *The Improvement of Reading*. New York: McGraw-Hill Book Company, Inc., 1967. Chapter III.

Tinker, Miles A., and Constance M. McCullough, *Teaching Elementary Reading*. New York: Appleton-Century-Crofts, 1968. Chapter 13, "Reading in the Content Fields," pp. 258–284.

Veatch, Jeannette, *Reading in the Elementary School*. New York: The Ronald Press Company, 1966. Chapter 11, "Teaching Skills for Reading," pp. 358–433.

QUESTIONS FOR THOUGHT AND DISCUSSION

1. Why is it essential to use children's own backgrounds of experience and known oral vocabularies in vocabulary development?
2. What factors may affect the meanings of words in total context? Why is it often necessary to look beyond standardized, or dictionary, meanings in order to discover these meanings?
3. In some instances children can ascribe no meanings to terms that are used in materials at hand. Or they may ascribe wrong, vague, or partially correct meanings to such words. Thus what has been termed verbalism develops. What harm can verbalism do as both teacher and pupil strive for meaning?
4. Some writers think of meaning-getting skills in reading as falling into three levels: literal comprehension, interpretation, and critical reading. Precisely what do these terms mean to you?
5. Since teaching in the social studies certainly demands more than relating facts and figures, reading for good comprehension has to be a concern of the teacher. What are some of the reading skills that must be an integral part of the social studies? What might you as a teacher do to assure development of these in your pupils?
6. In the past teachers and research workers in reading have given a great deal of attention to word perception and general reading comprehension skills. But in recent years the development of critical reading skills has come to be of increasing concern. Do you believe that critical reading

can be taught in the early grades? how early? Be able to describe a situation in which conditions would appear to be conducive to the development of critical reading ability in an early grade.

7. The term *creative reading* has come to mean many things. For one writer it means an attitude of suspended judgment with regard to reading materials, the ability to read above and beyond the obvious, the ability to see or perceive relations, the ability to recognize authors' intentions. At what level would you try to develop such abilities? How would you embark on such a venture?

CHAPTER 7A

Reading Rates

"How fast should I be able to read?" is one of the questions about reading most frequently asked of teachers. It is asked from the elementary school through college. Not only are pupils and students concerned about the rate of reading, but parents, too, may want to know how many words a minute their child reads and how he compares with the average for his grade. Inquiries concerning the reader's rate of reading are often accompanied by the question, "How can I improve my rate?"

The concern about rate of reading is understandable. The person who can read a selection rapidly and still accomplish his purpose has a distinct advantage over the one who cannot. In school the slow reader is often unable to do the work required of him. In the professional and business world, too, the ability to perform activities quickly—and these include reading—is an important asset. The individual who always reads slowly will not have time to read as much interesting and significant material as the one who reads rapidly. The sheer volume of printed matter available today, much of it essential to a knowledge of new developments in the world of ideas and of events, makes extensive reading mandatory for the educated person and the responsible citizen.

Ideally, one's rate of reading would approximate one's rate of thinking. Obviously such a standard would be unrealistic in the case of difficult material, but a serious lag between rate of reading and rate of thinking not only results in waste of time but tends to reduce a person's pleasure and interest in reading. Slow, cumbersome methods of reading start a vicious circle from less reading to less efficient reading to still less reading.

Professional interest in speed of reading first rose sharply in the 1920s with the shift of emphasis from oral to silent reading. It was discovered that the average child entering the intermediate grades could read more rapidly silently than orally. At first it was widely believed that reading speed was a unitary ability and that improvement in rate was automatically reflected in all kinds of reading. Only gradually did the relation between rate and type of reading material come under intensive study.

The difference in rate between oral and silent reading is dramatically illustrated in the eye-movement studies of Judd, Buswell, and others. Buswell's study of the "eye-voice span," for example, showed that in oral reading the eyes of the good reader run well ahead of his voice. In studies of silent reading it was found that the eyes of the efficient reader move across the line in a series of rhythmical leaps. He makes few, if any, aimless regressions. He makes relatively few fixations per line, and these are of short duration. He is not delayed, as in oral reading, by the mere physical act of articulation. The silent reading rate of the efficient reader exceeds that of his oral reading. In the intermediate grades the average pupil may read silently from one-and-a-half times to twice his oral reading rate or even more.

The reference to eye movements in relation to rate of silent reading would hardly be complete without mention of the fact that in some of the programs of "speed reading" currently in vogue, the advocates claim that the eye can be trained to "take in" the printed page much more rapidly if the usual eye movements are discontinued and new ones adopted. Of one such method, that used by Evelyn Wood and her associates, of Salt Lake City, Robert Hermann states the following, relevant to eye movements:

> Basically the Wood method abandons conventional eye movements and trains the eye to move vertically down the center of the page. Some Wood readers use a swinging, zigzag, downward movement. Some literature indicates that a few Wood readers can take a whole page or even two pages in a single look, and that some of them read down one page and up the next.[1]

[1] Robert Hermann, "The Speed Reading Controversy," Chapter VII in Ralph Staiger and David A. Sohn (eds.), *New Directions in Reading*. New York: Bantam Books, 1967, p. 152.

It is a matter of heated controversy what interpretation should be given to the claims concerning eye movements in speed reading programs such as that proposed by Mrs. Wood.

So-called "controlled reading" needs also to be considered in terms of eye movements. Controlled reading is described briefly and evaluated later in this chapter. (See pages 235–237.)

READING RATE AND COMPREHENSION

Much discussion has centered on the question of the relation between rate of reading and comprehension. The question would be clarified if we substituted the term *rate of comprehension* for *rate of reading*. Reading without adequate comprehension cannot properly be called reading. Therefore, if we believe that a good reader is one who can most quickly grasp the meaning of a passage, the fast reader is necessarily the good reader. We can then dispense with any debate about rate versus comprehension.

Good readers differ in their rates of comprehension. It takes some good readers a little longer than others to discover the literal and implied meanings of a passage. An individual's temperament and rhythm of learning sometimes account for these differences. Standardized tests of reading are usually based on the assumption that speed of comprehension is an essential aspect of reading competence. For this reason they may frequently obscure a pupil's real reading potential. Standardized test scores should be interpreted with this fact in mind. In order to assess the reader's true capabilities we need to go behind the scores and analyze the specific nature of his performance on a test.

There are important interrelations between speed and comprehension in reading. On the one hand, improved comprehension facilitates growth in speed. On the other hand, habits of more rapid reading often aid comprehension by shifting attention from individual words to the larger word patterns that carry the meaning. The development of comprehension, which is primary, may therefore be cultivated in some children, especially in the intermediate and upper grades, by encouraging faster reading.

While the teacher's aim should be to develop maximum speed of reading within the limits of the child's comprehension, a special effort should be made to teach him how to adjust his rate to his purpose and to the type of material he is reading. When the material is difficult and a high degree of accuracy is required, a very slow rate is appropriate. Many readers, even very good ones, assume that all materials must be read at a "normal" rate. They must be taught how to "shift gears" when they attack a verbal problem in arithmetic or a difficult passage in science. Thus, although superior readers tend to excel in both speed and comprehension with ordinary narrative material, they employ slower rates when these are needed for maximum comprehension.

CAUSES OF UNDULY SLOW READING

The rate at which a person reads is by various factors. Low intelligence, which leaves its impact on all reading skills, can have a marked effect upon rate of reading. Poor health also seems to have a detrimental influence on the rate at which an individual reads, although it must be noted that some people in poor health are among the most prodigious and fastest readers. Additional causes of unduly slow reading are lack of skill in word recognition, vocalization, pointing to words, overemphasis on oral reading, and lack of interest and purpose.

Lack of Skill in Word Recognition

The person who has difficulty in recognizing words quickly and accurately is likely to be a very slow reader. He is at a special disadvantage when he wishes to find the answer to a question. He is also handicapped when he tries to read study-type materials that contain words not easily recognized by him.

Often the methods by which an individual has been taught to recognize words play an important role in reading rate. The person who habitually analyzes all words phonetically will have slower habits of word recognition than one who has learned to analyze words only if he cannot quickly identify them as wholes. This fact should not be interpreted to mean that a knowledge of phonics is detrimental to speed of reading. Rather, it suggests that misuse of phonics may have an undesirable effect on rate of reading. Phonics is an important aid to word recognition only when faster methods fail to bring results. Moreover, the person who can identify a large number of words through effective use of methods of word attack other than phonics, such as recognition of a sight word or use of context clues or structural analysis, is more often the one who can more speedily accomplish his purpose in reading.

Vocalization

Early stress on speech sounds in reading instruction inevitably creates strong associations in the mind of the child between the sight of a word and its sound. The sound image is intended to serve as a bridge between visual perception and the apprehension of meaning, and normally the child becomes less and less conscious of language sounds as he seeks meaning on the printed page. Exclusive preoccupation with sounding in the initial stages of reading tends to cause lip movements and possibly excessive subvocalization in later stages. Speed of reading is then frequently restricted to the rate of oral reading. Under these conditions the child is obliged to unlearn habits deeply fixed in the beginning. Suppressed oral reading is not conducive to the development of desirable rates of silent reading.

Closely related to the habit of vocalization is the feeling some readers have that they must "read" every word in order to comprehend. In many types of reading, as in skimming and scanning, the good reader finds the key words and supplies the intervening words with sufficient accuracy to derive the meaning intended by the author. In these cases the reading materials are not simply a continuity of symbols intended to correspond to the spoken language; they are, rather, a set of clues, a sort of shorthand, designed to communicate meaning without the need for vocal articulation of all the words.

Pointing to Words

Another practice likely to arrest development in rate of reading is pointing to each word as it is being read. In early reading instruction in the first grade, when it usually takes the reader longer to recognize a word than to say it, pointing with the finger may not reduce reading rate. However, the practice can have a detrimental effect later on speed of reading, for the habit may become established, with the result that the pupil persists in its use after he should be reading at faster rates than are possible with pointing.

Many first-grade teachers supply the children with markers in the form of heavy strips of paper, often about the length of a line of print and about an inch in width. With these markers, which the boys and girls keep under the line being read, the children can often keep their place more easily than they otherwise could. Probably if a marker is used only for a very limited length of time it can serve as a helpful crutch. The danger is that children may get into the habit of needing some means other than their eyes and mind to keep the place. Like all other crutches, markers should be discarded as soon as they have helped a person over a difficult situation.

Overemphasis on Oral Reading

Oral reading has its proper place in reading programs, but a program dominated by oral reading practice is almost certain to produce habits of slow silent reading. Even in the initial reading period children should be encouraged to read words silently much of the time. In general, it is recommended that children be asked to read a passage silently before they are called upon to read it orally. By this means silent reading habits are established, and the subsequent oral reading will be improved because of increased comprehension of the material read. The practice of children following in their books while someone is reading the same material orally to them is to be discouraged after the pupils have learned to read more rapidly silently than orally. Otherwise they may tend to reduce their silent reading rate to be more equal to their oral reading rates.

Lack of Interest and Purpose

The ability to read rapidly is only in part a matter of habit and skill. Perhaps even more important is the attitude of the reader. If the pupil knows what he is looking for on the printed page, he will be impatient until he finds his quarry. He will not dawdle over the passages that are only secondary to the goals he is seeking or that are irrelevant to them. Clear purposes are therefore basic to the improvement of both comprehension and rate.

The daydreaming pupil makes little progress in reading. But when his interest has been kindled, when the action in a story moves toward a climax, when the narrative brings smiles or tears, he races down the lines to learn the outcome. The scene before him will not be obscured by laborious struggles with printed words. With the well-selected story, the words, the page, even the immediate environment, fade from consciousness and only the people and the places and the actions in the story remain. For many children the key to reading speed is interest. Abundant, highly motivated reading will do what no tachistoscopes or flashmeters can.

APPRAISAL OF READING RATES

In order to plan an effective program of reading instruction that will help each child learn to read at appropriate rates, careful appraisal should be made of every pupil's reading rates.

Since an effective reader has more than one reading rate, it is not a simple matter to make an appraisal. Consequently, a variety of means needs to be used. *Informal observation* is one. The classroom teacher has many opportunities to note the characteristics of a pupil's reading rates. She can observe whether the child wastes time while reading. By studying the child in reading situations she can gather evidence as to whether the pupil is able to adjust his rate of reading to his purpose and to the difficulty of the material. She can note whether he skims parts of it and reads other parts more carefully.

Sometimes important evidence about a pupil's reading habits as they affect rate of reading can be secured through *conferences*. The teacher can often discover by this means whether the pupil knows that variations in rates are necessary to good reading. Answers to questions as to the type of situations in which skimming or slow reading is required can also be illuminating to the teacher desirous of learning more about a pupil's rate of reading.

Tests, too, can furnish valuable data. Some of the standardized reading tests contain subtests for determining rate, among them the following: the *Sangren-Woody Reading Test* (Harcourt, Brace & World), the *Iowa Silent Reading Tests: Elementary Test* (Harcourt, Brace & World), the *Gates Reading Survey* (Bureau of Publications, Teachers College, Columbia University), and *Diagnostic Reading Tests* (Committee on Diagnostic Testing). However, tests in which rate is measured in only one type of situation do not give a clear index of an individual's rate of reading. For this reason tests need to be supplemented by other means of appraisal. Because of these limitations in the measurement of rate, many teachers like to make tests of their own. One type is described in Chapter 7B. Tests similar to the one there described can be used to record the pupil's reading rate in a variety of situations.

Whenever a pupil is timed while reading, whether he is taking a standardized or nonstandardized test, allowance should be made for the fact that the results may be inaccurate because the pupil knows he is being timed. No matter how hard a teacher may try to keep the testing situation free from strain, some children, as soon as they know they are being timed, show the effects of working under pressure. There are many children who cannot do their best under such conditions.

One type of record that the teacher may find it advantageous to keep is a *checklist* on which she indicates change or persistence in attitudes or habits or skills concerned with the improvement in reading rates. By means of a checklist the teacher can be spared the necessity of depending upon her memory as to the reading skills of each of her pupils. On such a checklist may be questions like the following: (1) Does the child recognize the need of variation in rate? (2) Is he able to adjust his rate to his purpose and to the material he is reading? (3) Does he know when to skim?

Charts, graphs, and tables are useful in appraising growth in the ability to employ appropriate reading rates. In keeping this type of record, the teacher should be sure to compare only those data that are truly comparable. Rate in skimming an article should not be compared with rate in reading a selection of similar difficulty when more detailed examination is required. For skimming, a reading rate of 400 words per minute may be slow, while a work-type rate of 200 words per minute may be fast. Rate of reading two selections that are unlike in difficulty or type cannot be directly compared.

Another point is that if rates in reading are charted, they should be recorded over a relatively long period of time. In many situations there are too many rather insignificant variations in rate from day to day to make a short-term study of rates of reading of much value. It often takes more than a few days of successful practice to show measurable improvement, even when real progress is being made from the beginning.

Furthermore, the learner himself should be informed of his progress. If a child is old enough to try to improve his rate of reading, he is old enough to understand the simple record of his performance. The learner's concern should be the improvement of his own skill, not a desire to equal or surpass others or to attain a norm.

National norms on standardized tests are not extremely helpful to teachers who wish to evaluate their pupils' reading rates. Different tests show different median rates for the various school grades, probably because of the wide variation in the difficulty and type of content they present.

Because of the wide range of individual differences among children even within the same grade, it is inadvisable to prescribe specific goals for individuals or even whole classes. The reading rate of the average adult reader, with nonstudy-type materials, has been estimated at approximately 250 words per minute, and this figure can be substantially raised through deliberate practice in reading speed. Pupils who approach this standard by the end of the sixth grade can therefore not be regarded as deficient in reading speed. Many pupils will exceed it. The teacher of the primary grades should not be concerned with speed in terms of words per minute.

CONTROLLED READING

Various machines for regulating the speed at which the printed page is exposed to the reader are commercially available. The basic principle of most of these devices is that of an instrument known in psychological laboratories as a tachistoscope. This is a contrivance that flashes words or phrases on a screen at a controlled rate. The use of the tachistoscope and similar instruments in reading instruction is sometimes called controlled reading.

The chief purpose of these instruments is to increase the reader's ability to perceive whole words and phrases quickly in a single fixation. Through intensive and prolonged practice a child may be able to perceive—that is, recognize and identify—words and phrases with progressively greater speed. The theory is that such training will transfer to the printed page and will result not only in improved reading rate but also in better comprehension, because meaning is usually derived from whole words and words in combination rather than from individual letters.

Among the well-known pacing devices are the Harvard Reading Films, developed by Walter F. Dearborn and his colleagues. These films, however, have not as yet been made in an edition usable in the elementary school. The films present reading material through bright exposures of part or all of a line of print at a time. Regressive movements of the eyes are thus discouraged, since the reader is forced to move his eyes more and more rapidly in left-to-right movements in order to comprehend the meaning. Tests are available with each film to test the reader's comprehension.

Other devices that employ "pressure methods" are the SRA Reading Rate Accelerator (Science Research Associates, Chicago), the Keystone Reading Pacer (Keystone View Company, Meadville, Pennsylvania), the Renshaw Tachistoscopic Trainer (Stereo Optical Company, Chicago), and the Shadowscope Pacer (Lafayette Instrument Company, Lafayette, Indiana). The Keystone Tachistoscope, also available through the Keystone View Company, is a popular device for increasing rate of perception of individual letters and words. All of these and similar machines present printed matter at controlled rates of speed. Faced with a gradually increasing rate of exposure, the reader is pressed to "take in" meaningful units on the line at a pace that can be constantly accelerated. For a description of mechanical aids of this type, the reader may wish to consult the book *Improving the Teaching of Reading*[2] and *The Reading Improvement Handbook*.[3]

[2] Emerald V. Dechant, *Improving the Teaching of Reading*. Englewood Cliffs, N.J.: Prentice-Hall, Inc., 1964.

[3] John S. Simons and Helen O'Hara Rosenblum, *The Reading Improvement Handbook*. College Station, Pullman, Wash.: Reading Improvement, 1965.

Unquestionably, the reading machines have been effective in improving reading rate in many cases. How permanent the improvement has been is a matter of conjecture. Quite possibly the machines have an initial advantage in that they provide novelty and interest in the improvement of reading. Unfortunately, after a time the novelty may wear off, and consequently one of the chief reasons for the success reported with instruments of this type may no longer operate.

In controlled reading emphasis is placed primarily upon the improvement of rate. Programs of improvement in reading should also place stress on comprehension. Although research studies indicate either that there was no loss in comprehension or that slight gains were made, the little increase in power in comprehension has not been commensurate with the amount of time and energy spent on attempts at improvement of reading.

The use of mechanical aids for controlling the rate of reading does not eliminate the need for an attack on the underlying causes of inappropriate rates of reading. The machines may discourage dawdling habits of reading, but in themselves they do not eliminate the chief causes of unsatisfactory rate of comprehension, such as lack of skill in methods of word recognition, lack of skill in selecting details, difficulty in organizing what is read, failure to read material critically, and inability to locate information rapidly. In fact, controlled reading can even have a detrimental effect upon some of these factors. For example, the person whose chief cause of slow reading is a difficulty in recognizing words may develop even poorer habits of word recognition because he is not given time to apply sound means of word identification. Nor can the efficient reader employ the flexible habits of reading that are needed to get meaning quickly. When he comes to a word that he must analyze, he wants to stop for a longer pause. He may find it advisable to make regressive movements if he discovers that he has just finished reading a point that he should note carefully. He will want to vary his rate in accordance with his purpose in reading, rather than follow the operation of mechanical shutters that compel him to read every line or part of a line in the same time as preceding ones.

Undoubtedly the eye movements that are forced by controlled reading resemble, to some extent, those of successful readers. Simulating these movements, however, will not necessarily produce good reading. The positive correlation between efficient reading and efficient eye movements is not caused by the effect of eye movements upon reading; rather, good eye movements are the result, not the cause, of efficient reading. The attack, consequently, should not be made directly upon eye movements.

GUIDELINES FOR IMPROVING RATE OF READING

To assist the teacher further in helping boys and girls to read at appropriate rates, guidelines that should be kept in mind by the teacher are now discussed. Only those generalizations are presented on which there is little, if any, disagreement among specialists in the teaching of reading.

1. *Growth in ability to read at appropriate rates is subject to training.* Assistance can be given the person who is not reading at appropriate rates. Studies show that remarkable increases in rate have been achieved in a brief period of time in many clinical situations, supervised reading courses, and classroom situations where this phase of reading has been stressed. In fact, there is reason to think that almost all readers could make valuable increase in the speed with which they read, without loss in comprehension, if they were given appropriate help. Emphasis, however, on increase of reading rates should usually be postponed until the intermediate grades, when pupils have ordinarily gained proficiency in reading skills basic to the development of greater speed where desirable.

2. *Reading rates should vary with the purpose of the reader and the type and difficulty of the material.* In fact, the desirable rate may vary even within a given selection from one part to another. Both the teacher and the learner should be aware of this fact. In the first grade the teacher will usually set the purpose of reading. She may tell a pupil to read the next page to find out what Bobby did when his mother told him what she wanted for her birthday, or she may ask him to glance over the next page to find the new word *mother*, which has been presented on the board or on a word card. She may show the pupil that in the latter assignment it is not necessary for him to read every word and that consequently it should not take him as long to read that page as it would if he read the page to answer a question about it. Thus an early beginning can be made in helping boys and girls read at different rates for different purposes.

Later in the development of skill in reading, the learner should be given increasing opportunity to decide on suitable purposes himself and to determine what rate of reading he will need in order to accomplish his objective.

A somewhat arbitrary classification of the rates of reading may help to clarify for pupils the ways of adapting speed to the nature of the reading material and the purpose for reading it. Reading rates have often been divided into three categories: rapid reading, moderately

fast reading, and slow reading. What is known as skimming is considered by many to be the fast type of rapid reading. In skimming, as the
term is thought of by many, the reader glances rapidly over a page
without reading every word and moves his eyes quickly along the lines
and down the page. He may be skimming in order to see if a certain
topic is discussed or to find out what topic is taken up. Skimming is
also needed when a person glances through a table of contents to find
a given chapter title so that he can tell on which page the chapter
begins, or when he looks over the words on a page in the dictionary in
order to locate an entry word. It should be noted that Robert Hermann
makes a distinction between *skimming* and *scanning*. He states, "Scanning is different from skimming. In scanning, you have in mind certain
specific facts or words you are looking for. . . . (Some experts call this
process skimming.)"[4] In this book the two terms are used interchangeably.

    Fast reading is also appropriate, usually, when the reader
looks at a newspaper to find out what is going on in the world or reads
a magazine article just for fun. Moderately fast reading is called for
when the reader wishes to note some details. Slow reading is advisable in a study-type situation or when appreciation of the beauty of
style or of the unfolding of the details of a situation or the personality
of the characters is desired.

    3. *Teachers and pupils should have clearly defined goals for
the improvement of reading rates.* General objectives are not enough.
The teacher should try to find out the needs of the pupils in order to
help them overcome their difficulties. The aims should be specific—for
example, to learn when to read at the different rates, to read study-type
material more slowly so as to have an opportunity to get the thought of
the selection, and to read fiction rapidly while maintaining the desired
amount of comprehension.

    The pupil, too, should have clear-cut objectives. Results are
better when the learner is consciously seeking specific goals.

    4. *Development of ability to read at appropriate rates should
not interfere with development of other reading skills.* Rates of reading
should not be increased at a sacrifice of comprehension. To be sure,
when a pupil has been reading more slowly than his immediate purpose
warrants, rate should be increased. Increase in rate sometimes brings
about a better degree of comprehension, if teaching methods eliminate
defects in rate and comprehension simultaneously. It requires insight on

[4] Hermann, p. 149.

the part of the teacher to know when rate and when comprehension should be stressed the more.

Much of what has been said about the effect of improvement in rate on comprehension can also, in general terms, be said of the relation that should exist between increase in rate and other reading skills. In the case of skill in locating information, for example, it would be unfortunate if greater speed in finding an entry in an index caused the reader to become less accurate in doing so. The goal is to spend less time in finding an entry without sacrificing accuracy.

5. *Neither haste nor undue tension should characterize the efforts to read at appropriate rates.* All practices in an effective program of developmental or remedial reading should be in harmony with the principles of mental health. Studies of child development have shown the harmful effects of creating pressures which result in anxiety and fear of failure. However, this does not mean that at times measures should not be taken to prod a person whose poor achievement, below his expected level, is due to dawdling habits or to lack of effort. Not only are haste and undue tension undesirable from the point of view of maintaining an emotional equilibrium but they are also detrimental because they interfere with success in learning. Consequently, the child should be encouraged to do his best without becoming frantic when he fails to achieve his goal.

6. *The marked difference in children's ability to read at appropriate rates should be recognized.* Part of the variation among children results from differences in training received in school and practice outside of school. A further cause lies in the variations in innate capacity of individuals to master the intricacies of learning to read at the appropriate rates. Some will never become as skillful as others in reading at desirable rates.

An effective program for helping pupils to acquire skill in reading at appropriate rates recognizes these variations among individuals. The teacher needs to know what stage of learning to read each child has reached, and she must work out a program that is adapted to the needs of individual children. She should not be satisfied with averages. Some children who read with less than average speed for their grade in all types of reading situations may still be working up to capacity or even straining themselves to do good work beyond their capacity. On the other hand, some children, although surpassing norms in rate of reading, may still be reading below their potential.

CHAPTER 7B

Developing Appropriate
Reading Rates

The purpose of this chapter is to demonstrate how the teacher can help children to develop reading rates appropriate to the various types of materials and purposes for reading.

METHODS OF DEVELOPING APPROPRIATE RATES

In this chapter reading rates are grouped for convenience into three categories: rapid reading, moderately fast reading, and slow reading. Each of these types of reading is desirable under certain circumstances and undesirable under others. The efficient reader knows not only how to use these but also when.

Some of the following suggestions are given for the improvement of rate in connection with the regular reading lessons in the basal reading textbook. Also included are recommendations that can be used in the content fields, and others that can serve as practice exercises. Samples of a few practice exercises are given. No attempt has been made, however, to designate the type of situation in which the suggestions can best be used. Nor are all the methods recommended for use with all groups or individuals. Selection should be made on the basis of the principles set forth in the preceding chapter. It is hoped that the list of recommendations will suggest to the teacher many others that are especially adapted to her pupils.

Some activities performed by pupils can be helpful for

increasing rate whether fast, moderately fast, or rather slow reading is called for by the purpose of the reader and the material. The following are illustrative:

1. Discussing the importance of reading at the fastest rate possible in keeping with the aim of the reader and the nature of the material.
2. Discussing the importance of maintaining a desired level of comprehension as rate is increased.
3. Explaining that some readers read too fast to achieve the comprehension level they wish to attain.
4. Explaining the importance of purpose in reading, in order to help pupils understand the optimum speed at which the material should be read.
5. Explaining the relation between type and difficulty of material and the optimum speed at which the material should be read.
6. Estimating the speed (in terms of fast, moderately fast, and slow) at which materials of designated types and difficulty should be read.
7. Reading while being timed and later checked for comprehension.
8. Practicing reading of words, phrases, or sentences that are exposed for varying lengths of time either by a commercially produced reading machine or by a teacher-made tachistoscope. The teacher can make a tachistoscope by cutting a slit in a piece of tagboard and sliding the words or groups of words, listed in column form, through the slit, at varying intervals.
9. Listing in one column possible speeds at which the pupils might read and in a second column topics on which they may be reading for stated purposes. Lines can then be drawn between the columns, matching the speed with the corresponding topic.
10. Listening to the teacher read in meaningful phrases.
11. Reading silently material in which the phrases have been marked or separated.
12. Matching words given in two columns which when combined make meaningful phrases.
13. Marking the meaningful phrases that occur in a selection.
14. Indicating orally the meaningful phrases in a selection.
15. Keeping a record of progress in reading at appropriate rates.
16. Reading a selection in which varying rates are appropriate and indicating where and why the variations should occur.
17. Discussing importance of freedom from interfering movements such as vocalization in supposedly silent reading and pointing to words when reading.
18. Engaging in any activities that help improve skill in word recognition. (For suggestions see Chapter 5B.)
19. Engaging in any activities that help attain the level of comprehension demanded by a situation. (For suggestions see Chapter 6B.)

Developing Skill in Reading at a Fast Rate

Skill in skimming can be developed through additional activities. It should be noted, however, that it is doubtful that speed of reading should be encouraged in the primary grades when children usually lack in many of the basic reading skills.

1. Explaining in what situations skimming can properly be used—for example, when the reader wishes to get only a general impression of a passage or when he wishes to glance at it to see if it furnishes a certain item of information.
2. Explaining how the eyes move across the page when skimming. (It may help some of the boys and girls to know that in skimming the eyes do not always need to move from the end of one line to the beginning of the next. The eyes often take in only a part of each line as they move rapidly across and down a page.)
3. Skimming a selection while consciously moving the eyes rapidly across and down a page, without stopping to note details.
4. Skimming a table of contents to find out on what page a chapter on a given topic begins.
5. Skimming parts of an article in an encyclopedia to find a desired fact.
6. Skimming a page in a book to find a given "new word" that has been presented.
7. Skimming a page to find the answer to a question based on that page.
8. Skimming a page to see if it gives information on a given topic.
9. Skimming a page to find a sentence to be quoted.
10. Skimming a newspaper to find a report on a social activity which took place.
11. Skimming through books in the library to find one dealing, at least in part, with a specified topic.
12. Skimming a book to find out whether one would like to read it.
13. Finding as rapidly as possible the topic sentences of paragraphs.
14. Skimming a selection in order to find answers to a list of questions as quickly as possible.
15. Skimming a selection after a more thorough reading to see if any points to be remembered have been forgotten.
16. Timing oneself or being timed while engaging in many of the types of activities that have been suggested.
17. Skimming the index of a book to locate an entry in order to secure a specified item of information.
18. Finding a word in a dictionary.
19. Skimming a telephone directory to find the name of a person whose telephone number is desired.
20. Reading a paragraph in which some words have been omitted, words without which a reader can get the general thought of the paragraph. The pupils can be told not to try to guess the missing words but to see

if they can understand the paragraph as it is written while reading it rapidly.
21. Skimming a story after previous reading to determine what characters are needed for a dramatization of the story.
22. Skimming a selection to find proof for a point made.

The following are ways in which improvement may be brought about in reading at an effective rate when fast reading, but not skimming, is desired, as is often when reading a magazine or a book of fiction:

1. Explaining when fast reading other than skimming should be used.
2. Identifying situations in which fast reading, other than skimming, is desired.
3. Getting practice in reading rapidly easy material or material with which the reader has some familiarity.
4. Getting practice in selecting the main idea of a paragraph, without intent to note details, as rapidly as possible.
5. Timing oneself or being timed while reading rapidly.

PRACTICE EXERCISES   Some pupils can be helped to acquire appropriate reading rates by means of practice exercises. Many workbooks, some accompanying basal textbooks and others independent of them, provide such practice exercises. However, the teacher may often find it desirable to construct exercises of her own. The teacher will find suggestions of possible practice exercises in the lists in this chapter and in preceding B chapters.

The following samples of exercises are representative of some that may encourage either skimming or rapid reading without skimming.

1

An exercise such as the following, especially if timed, is particularly helpful to pupils inclined to use too much time in locating the main thought in a paragraph or longer selection.

Directions: This exercise is to help you learn to locate rapidly a certain sentence in a paragraph. You will be timed while you are doing this exercise. Preceding each paragraph there is a sentence. You are to find the sentence in the paragraph that expresses the thought of that sentence. When you have located the sentence in the paragraph, draw a circle around the first word of it and continue with the next paragraph.

1. Sentence: The Indian elephant has a lighter skin than the African.

There are many differences between the two kinds of elephants, the African and the Indian. The African elephants grow larger than the Indian elephants. As a rule both the male and the female of the African elephant have tusks, but only the Indian male has them. The tusks of the African elephant are larger than those of the Indian. The ears of the African elephant are also larger. The elephant in Africa has two knobs at the end of its trunk, but the Indian has only one. The elephants from Africa are darker than those from Asia. Even the texture of the skin of the two animals is different, for that of the Indian elephant is not as rough as that of the African.

2

An exercise like the following, in which the child's rate during the first two minutes is checked, is valuable in stimulating him to begin reading promptly and to read at his maximum rate. The figure at the beginning of each line indicates the cumulative number of words that the child has read by the end of the line, not including the title. It should be explained that the pupils do not need to read the figures. The teacher may wish to tell the class what the numbers represent. The beginning or all of a selection like the following may be read by the pupils. If only part of a story is included in the exercises, the teacher should tell the pupils how it ends.

Directions: The following exercise is to help you get started reading rapidly when the material is easy for you and when all you need to know is the general idea of what you are reading. When you are told to begin, read as rapidly as you can while still getting the general idea of what you are reading. At the end of two minutes you will be asked to stop. As soon as you hear the word *stop*, draw a circle around the last word you read. Then finish the story and answer the questions given at the end of the story.

THE BUNNY WHO DIDN'T BELIEVE IN SANTA[1]

6	Once there was a little Bunny
12	named Winkie who didn't believe in
19	Santa Claus—if you can imagine such
26	a thing! Of course this made his
34	mother feel very sad, and, for a time,
41	it looked as if Winkie might feel
49	worse than sad. In fact, he got into

[1] Mabel Harmer, "The Bunny Who Didn't Believe in Santa," *Grade Teacher*, 72, p. 25 (December 1954). (Adapted.)

55   very serious trouble and might even
64   have lost his life if it hadn't been for
70   _____. But that part should come at
76   the very end of the story.
82   It was Christmas Eve and Mother
88   Cottontail and her nine bunnies were
95   doing all the things that everyone else
102 does on that jolliest of eves. They
107 were trimming the Christmas tree,
113 hanging up the stockings and singing
115 Christmas carols.

Developing Skill in Reading at a Moderately Fast Rate

In order to develop skill in reading moderately easy material with the purpose of finding the main ideas as well as numerous details, activities like the following may prove helpful:

1. Discussing in what situations moderately fast reading should take place.
2. Identifying situations in which reading of this type is appropriate.
3. Getting much practice in reading this type of material.
4. Getting practice in selecting the main ideas and some supporting details rapidly.
5. Timing pupils or letting them time themselves as they read material of this type.
6. Reading a page of a book to find the words that complete sentences written on the chalkboard or on a sheet of paper.
7. Reading a paragraph in which one or two words do not fit the meaning of one or more sentences. When these words are located, the children should circle each incorrect word and write a more suitable word in the margin.
8. Telling for which of a series of listed purposes one would ordinarily engage in moderately fast reading. The list might be similar to this:
   a. Reading to get the general idea of the living conditions in the South during the last year of the Civil War.
   b. Looking for a word in the dictionary.
   c. Reading a report in the society column of a newspaper to find out where a certain party was held.
   d. Studying in a science book about how heat travels in order to be able draw a series of pictures for an accordionlike folder that would illustrate conduction, radiation, and convection.
9. Using handmade or commercially produced tachistoscopic devices that are being operated at a moderately fast speed.
10. Answering questions that the teacher asks about something read to or by the pupils that can be answered in phrases. For example, the question might be, "Why did Snipp, Snapp, and Snurr want to find work?" The pupils could choose the correct phase from a list such as this and

read it out loud: (1) "to go to the show," (2) "to buy a present," (3) "to buy a dog."

11. Reading a list of words in which some letters have been omitted, such as: (1) Ch ist s, (2) sc ool, (3) t ch r. The teacher could explain to the pupils the relation between this exercise and the fact that it is not necessary for effective readers to look at every letter of a word when reading some types of materials.

PRACTICE EXERCISE   Stories are well adapted for use as exercises—for example, the following—in fairly rapid reading of rather easy material. The story should be one that the children do not already know.

Directions: Read as rapidly as you can the story of "The Shoemaker and the Elves" so as to be able to answer fairly easy questions that you will be asked on it. Your teacher will time you while you are reading the story.

Questions on the story. (These questions are to be answered in as few words as possible.)

1. How many pairs of shoes did the shoemaker find the morning after the night when he had cut out leather for just one pair of shoes? _____
2. Why did the shoemaker and his wife decide to sit up one night shortly before Christmas? _____
3. Where in the room were the shoemaker and his wife hiding the evening when they sat up? _____
4. How many elves came to do the work for the shoemaker? _____
5. What did the shoemaker and his wife do to show their gratitude to their elves? _____
6. How did the elves like their presents? _____

Developing Skill in Reading at a Relatively Slow Rate

Many elementary school children, especially in the intermediate grades, need help in reading for study purposes. Often they also need to learn how to adjust their reading rate for directions which they are asked to follow. Although the rate of reading for such purposes necessarily is relatively slow, the pupils should be helped to read as rapidly as possible to attain their objectives. Many can profit from taking part in activities like the following:

1. Discussing in what situations slower reading is called for.
2. Identifying situations in which slower reading should take place.

3. Reading, under timed conditions, materials that require careful understanding of what is read.
4. Finding quickly a statement that proves or disproves a given statement.
5. Selecting all points that support a stated main topic.
6. Outlining a selection that has been read.
7. Finding a word or group of words that expresses a detail stated by the teacher.
8. Repeating directions that have been exposed for a relatively long time.
9. Following directions that have been exposed for a relatively long time.
10. Reading, under timed conditions, a difficult work-type selection on which detailed questions are later to be answered.
11. Reading a selection to determine whether the writer is sympathetic or unsympathetic toward a particular cause or person.
12. Reading a selection in order to find a generalization developed in the writing.
13. Reading a selection in order to answer a thought question on it.
14. Reading a selection in order to report on it.
15. Reading literary material in order to find points particularly interesting to the reader.
16. Answering questions on the details of an arithmetic problem.
17. Arranging in correct sequence the details of a story that have been listed out of order.
18. Contrasting an editorial with an objectively written news article.
19. Memorizing a significant line or longer part of a paragraph.

READING LESSONS AND THE DEVELOPMENT OF APPROPRIATE RATES

The teacher has many opportunities to help pupils develop appropriate rates of reading through the use of the basal textbook. Excellent suggestions are given in the manuals that accompany basal reading series.

Improving Reading Rates in the Second Grade

Although less emphasis should generally be placed on speed in the primary than in the intermediate grades, some attention should nevertheless be paid to it even in the earlier grades.

The story chosen here for illustration is "He Would Not Listen," pages 2 to 11 in *Just for Fun*.[2] It is the story of a rooster who gets into trouble again and again because he does not follow the solid advice of his good friend, a little hen, who keeps helping him out of his difficulties. Because the rooster does not listen to the little hen, he becomes sick from eating green strawberries and later from drinking cold water when he is very hot. He gets pelted with cobs of corn when,

[2] Guy L. Bond and others, *Just for Fun*. Chicago: Lyons and Carnahan, 1962. Developmental Reading Series.

against the advice of the little hen, he goes into a barn into which men are throwing corn for storage. Another time he might have been drowned while trying to walk on ice that was too thin if the little hen had not rescued him.

In connection with this story, the teacher may use techniques such as the following that will help pupils read some parts rapidly, some with moderate speed, and others slowly enough to note important details. The teacher should always aim to promote the greatest speed possible without sacrificing comprehension.

1. After the word *sometimes* has been presented on the board, the teacher may ask the pupils to glance at page 2 to see how quickly they can locate the places where the word is used.
2. The teacher may tell the class to read pages 2 through 5 as rapidly as they can to find out what was the first thing that the rooster did against which the little hen had warned him.
3. After the pupils have read silently pages 6 and 7, which tell how the rooster became sick from drinking water that was too cold, they may be asked to find the exact words with which the little hen warned the rooster not to drink the cold water.
4. The pupils can be asked to read page 8 carefully in order to tell in their own words exactly what happened when the men decided to throw corn into the barn for winter storage.
5. The teacher can ask the pupils to read pages 9 through 11, which tell about the rooster's experiences on the ice, in order to answer questions like the following: (a) How did the rooster feel when he looked out of the window and saw that winter had come? (b) Where did he decide to go? (c) What did the little hen say when the rooster said he would slide on the ice? (d) What happened after the rooster went on the ice? (e) Who kept the rooster from drowning?
6. Before the pupils read pages 9 and 10, they may be told to read the pages as rapidly as they can while still reading them carefully enough to find the answers to the questions. They may be asked to answer the questions orally. Or they may be asked to answer multiple-choice statements like these:

> One morning when the rooster looked out and saw that winter had come, he was
> > happy
> > sad
> > tired.
> The rooster wanted to slide on the ice
> > on the lake
> > on the river
> > in the back yard.

After the answers have been checked, a pupil may be asked to reread silently the part that gives the answer to any question he may have missed.

The following are suggestions for group activities that involve reading at various rates:

1. The teacher can place on a library table other stories about roosters or other animals that had adventures like those of the rooster. Time can then be provided for the pupils to skim these stories to decide which one each would like to read.
2. If the pupils decide to dramatize parts of the story, they may choose the main events that should be included in their dramatization. First they may dictate, as the teacher writes on the board, the points that they remember that should be in the play. Then they may reread the story rapidly to see if they have omitted any that they think should be included.
3. After reading the story, the group may decide to make a "movie" of it. When the pictures drawn for the story have been chosen and the sequence determined, the class may be asked to find as quickly as possible the parts in the story on which the pictures are based. Slower reading will be needed to get the full benefit of suggestions for drawing suitable pictures.

Improving Reading Rates in the Fifth Grade

In order to teach intermediate grade pupils to note details, the following procedure may be helpful. One teacher who taught lessons of this type, on an average of about one a week, based them on the selections within the basal reading textbooks. The first time that the reading period was devoted to work like this the boys and girls discussed some ways in which they could read at the optimum rates materials that were fairly easy for them when they wished to note rather carefully quite a number of details. Some points discussed were: (a) need for concentration; (b) suitable posture; (c) reading as fast as possible while maintaining or increasing the ability to understand at the required level of comprehension; (d) timing oneself while reading; and (e) reading a great deal. In later lessons reference was again made to these points and further suggestions were given for making effective use of them.

A SUGGESTED TEACHING PLAN   In order to make clear how a lesson like this can be taught in such a way as to test the boys and girls on rate and comprehension in reading material of the type indicated for a specified purpose, a copy of a plan that could be used for teaching the story "The Forty-Niners," pages 37 to 44 in *Adventures Here and There*,[3] is described here. It is followed by further explanation of the plan.

[3] Emmett A. Betts and Carolyn M. Welch, *Adventures Here and There*. New York: American Book Company, 1963.

The plan for using the story "The Forty-Niners" for a silent reading test lesson should not be followed rigidly. Instead, whatever procedure is followed for this or any other story should be determined by the needs of the pupils. This plan is merely to serve as a sample of one way in which a story could be used to help children test themselves and improve in ability to read at an appropriate rate rather easy story material with the aim of remembering details.

A. *Topic:* Silent reading of "The Forty-Niners"
B. *Pupils' Aims*
  1. To test our rate in reading a story such as "The Forty-Niners" when wanting to remember details
  2. To get practice in improving our rate of reading easy material while at the same time reading with comprehension
  3. To find out how the forty-niners fared on their trip westward and after their arrival in California
C. *Materials*
  1. Material on the chalkboard
     a. Words for pronunciation: *Sutter, Sierras, Sacramento, frontier*
     b. Sentences for study of meaning.
        Digging in rocks and boulders, men *struck* gold wherever they dug.
        The men brought news of the California gold *strike.*
        It's *free for the taking.*
        Indians *descended upon* the wagons.
     c. Names of places to be located: *Sierras, San Francisco Bay, Sacramento, Panama, Panama City, Cape Horn*
     d. Directions
        (1) Read from page 37 to the bottom of page 43.
        (2) Record your rate.
        (3) Answer the questions.
        (4) If you have time, finish the story.
     e. Reading rates for a 1,000-word passage (beginning with three minutes and ending with twelve, with erasing of figures to be done every quarter of a minute)

333	200	143	111	91
308	190	138	108	89
286	182	133	105	87
267	172	129	103	85
250	167	125	100	
235	160	121	98	
222	154	118	95	
211	148	114	93	

  2. Outline map of the western hemisphere
  3. Books dealing with the Gold Rush
  4. Paper and pencil
  5. Individual graphs (See illustration.)

MY PROGRESS IN READING
TESTS

	1.	2.	3.	4.	5.	6.	7.	8.	9.	10.	11.	12.	13.	14.	15.
10.															
9.															
8.															
7.															
6.															
5.															
4.															
3.															
2.															
1.															
0.															

NUMBER
RIGHT

TEST NUMBER	NUMBER RIGHT	RATE
1.	————	————
2.	————	————
3.	————	————
4.	————	————
5.	————	————
6.	————	————
7.	————	————
8.	————	————
9.	————	————
10.	————	————
11.	————	————
12.	————	————
13.	————	————
14.	————	————
15.	————	————

6.   Duplicated tests questions

SILENT READING TEST ON "THE FORTY-NINERS"

Directions: After you have read from page 37 to bottom of page 43, number from one to ten on the slip of paper given to you. After each number, write the letter to the left of the word or group of words in parentheses that will make the corresponding sentence correct.

1.   (a. John Sutter, b. One of John Sutter's neighbors, c. One of John Sutter's workmen) discovered the gold near Sutter's mill.

2. Gold was discovered at Sutter's sawmill in (a. 1847, b. 1848, c. 1849).
3. (a. Some, b. None, c. All) of Sutter's men made tremendous fortunes.
4. John Sutter became (a. an extremely wealthy, b. a rather wealthy, c. a poor) man as a result of the discovery of gold on his land.
5. (a. The governor of the territory, b. The editor of the San Francisco newspaper, c. A missionary from a nearby mission) went to the scene of the gold rush to find out whether the reports he had heard were true.
6. By (a. 1848, b. 1849, c. 1850) all of the United States and many countries across the seas had learned of the discovery.
7. The fastest of the three routes to California was (a. the overland route, b. the route across Panama, c. the route around Cape Horn).
8. (a. Only a few, b. About half, c. Most) of the people who had the "California fever" took the overland route from the Middle West through the divides in the mountains.
9. The people taking the overland route tried to plan their trip so that they would be traveling during (a. late spring and summer, b. the summer, c. the fall).
10. The people who took the overland route to California were never able to travel more than (a. five, b. ten, c. twenty) miles a day.

D. *Procedure*
   1. Introduction
      a. Introduction to the story
         (1) Review of reasons why people settled the West that the pupils had previously learned
         (2) Reference by the teacher to the fact that some went West to get riches (if the pupils did not mention this point)
      b. Statement by the teacher of the third aim listed under *Pupils' Aims* (See *B-3.*)
      c. Statement by the teacher of the first two aims listed under *Pupils' Aims* (See *B-1* and *B-2*).
   2. Word study
      a. Pronunciation of words (See *C-1-a.*)
         (1) Presentation through these methods: phonetic analysis, syllabication, sight-word method
         (2) Practice on pronunciation
      b. Study of meaning of the words written in italics in sentences under *Materials,* through study of context clues and explanation by the pupils and/or teacher (See *C-1-b.*)
   3. Location of places (See *C-1-c.*)
   4. Directions for taking the test

     a. Reference is made to the directions listed under *Materials* (See C-1-d.)
     b. Pupils place a marker between pages 42 and 43 and note that they are to stop reading for the test at the bottom of page 43.
5. Taking the test
     a. Reading from page 37 to the bottom of page 43, while the teacher erases rates on the chalkboard every quarter of a minute, beginning with three minutes and ending with twelve (See C-1-e.)
     b. Recording the time
     c. Answering the questions
     d. Doing the additional work, namely, reading silently the rest of the story, if time permits
6. Correcting the papers. Pupils check their papers as the teacher does the following:
     a. Gives the number of the sentence
     b. Gives the letter preceding the word or group of words that forms the correct answer
     c. Names the word or group of words that forms the correct answer
     d. Reads the sentence supplying the correct answer
7. Recording marks on individual graphs, showing rate and comprehension (See C-5.)
8. Report on page 44 by a pupil who has finished the story
9. Forward look
     a. Discussion of plans for further progress in development of adequate reading rates
     b. Reference to books on library table (See C-3.)

EXPLANATION OF THE TEACHING PLAN   Below is given further explanation of the plan outlined for teaching "The Forty-Niners."

1. *Length of the selection tested.* The test, both for rate and comprehension, is only one part of the selection chosen for the teaching plan. A reason for, at times, limiting a test to only part of a story is to make the selection for testing no longer than, hopefully, every child can read during the allotted time. The number of words that a teacher will want to include in the part tested will vary with the selection and with the length of the class period. In some instances the teacher may wish to include the whole story, if it is not very long. On the other hand, she may not want to exclude a story containing only about 800 words. If, however, a much shorter number of words is chosen for the selection on which the class is to be tested, it may be difficult to select enough significant points for testing comprehension.

In estimating the number of words for the selection, the following procedure was used. The average number of words in the first ten full lines of the story was found to be 10.4 words. If, as in this case, a selection of about 1,000 words is decided upon, the number of lines on which the test should be given could be found by dividing 1,000 by 10.4, which is 96. In counting the lines, it is recommended that at times part of a line be counted and at other times a fractional part not be counted, so as to keep the estimate of words approximately correct. When the entire selection is to be used for the test, the average number of words per line can be multiplied by the number of lines to obtain the approximate number of words in the selection.

2. *Computation of rate.* The rates listed under *Materials* in this plan are the rates per minute for a 1,000-word selection, beginning with three minutes and extending through twelve, exact to the quarter of a minute. The count was begun with three minutes, because in many fifth-grade classes there are few who would read material of this type at more than 333 words per minute. The counting was discontinued after twelve minutes because only very few fifth-grade pupils would be likely to read material of this type for the purpose indicated at a rate slower than 83 words per minute. If it takes a pupil longer than this time or if he finishes reading in less than three minutes, the teacher should, of course, take note of that fact.

In the table given under *Materials* the first entry, 333, is obtained by dividing 1,000 by 3. Thus the rate is secured for a person who requires only three minutes to read the selection. The next entry, *308*, is the quotient when dividing 1,000 words by $3^1/_4$, and so on.

If the teacher writes on the chalkboard before class a table similar to the one given in the teaching plan, she would erase a figure every quarter of a minute. She would begin erasing when the pupils had read for three minutes. She would start with the first entry in the column farthest to the left, continuing down that column and then proceeding similarly with the next column. The boys and girls should be given the instruction that as soon as they have completed the required reading, they should look at the chalkboard and copy the highest remaining figure as their reading rate. If anyone finishes the selection in less than three minutes, the starting time for the recording of rate, he may be asked to write on his paper a plus sign after the number of words per minute computed for three minutes. In this instance he would then write *333+*. If anyone has not completed the assigned part at the end of twelve minutes, he could be instructed to place a minus sign to the right of the figure he copies, in this case writing *83—*.

3. *The test.* If a test of this type is to be given more than once and if the results are to be compared from one test to another, as

suggested earlier, it is desirable to keep the questions on all the tests of the same type. Multiple-choice questions were selected for this plan because they are easier to check than completion statements and because they usually form a more reliable test than a small number of true-false statements. To be comparable, the number of choices pro- vided in each multiple-choice statement should be kept the same. Ten was chosen for the number of questions because ten is so small a number that many significant questions can quite easily be asked on a selection. For purposes of comparison of results, it is suggested that the number be kept constant from test to test.

4. *Keeping a record.* Suggestions for using a graph like the one given on page 252 of this chapter have already been given. These, or similar graphs, should not be posted, for each pupil should be com- peting with himself, not with others. Frequent conferences between the teacher and each pupil should be held so that the pupil can get aid in interpreting the results of his efforts and so that he can receive sugges- tions for further improvement. The pupil should recognize the fact that a slight fluctuation in the score for rate is not necessarily significant, because of the inaccuracy of the tests and the fact that the rate of learning varies with circumstances.

5. *Additional work.* If the test is on only part of the selection, pupils should be encouraged to finish the story for themselves or the teacher or a pupil may tell the ending.

Other types of additional work for those pupils finishing earlier may be: (a) checking, by rereading parts of the selection, on any question in the test about which the pupil was not certain, (b) engaging in additional interesting and significant activities based on the story read, or (c) reading in a "library book" that the pupil already has at his desk.

6. *Supplementary reading.* If the teacher wishes to encourage children to read more on a topic related to the theme of the selection studied, she should have some additional books at hand. Telling the boys and girls briefly about the books and making provisions for their withdrawal can help stimulate more reading. Sometimes reference can be made to books in the library. If the books are not at that time in the classroom, it is recommended that the titles and the authors be written on the chalkboard or bulletin board so that the pupils will not forget the names by the time they go to the library.

FOR FURTHER STUDY

Barbe, Walter B., *Teaching Reading.* New York: Oxford University Press, 1965. Chapter VII, "Developing Rate and Comprehension," pp. 233–258.

Bond, Guy L., and Miles A. Tinker, *Reading Difficulties: Their Diagnosis and Correction.* New York: Appleton-Century-Crofts, 1967. Chapter 16, "Improving Rate of Comprehension," pp. 421–443.

Mazurkiewicz, Albert J., *New Perspectives in Reading Instruction.* New York: Pitman Publishing Corporation, 1964. Chapter 65, "Instrument Techniques in Reading Programs," pp. 525–538.

Schubert, Delwyn G., and Theodore L. Torgerson, *Readings in Reading.* New York: Thomas Y. Crowell Company, 1968. Chapter 29, "Speed Reading: Its Value and Place in a School Program," pp. 203–208; Chapter 30, "Machines and Reading: A Review of Research," pp. 214–218; Chapter 32, "Rate of Comprehension—Needed Research," pp. 218–222; Chapter 78, "Speed Reading," pp. 528–530; Chapter 79, "Speed Reading," pp. 530–532; Chapter 80, "Vision and Rapid Reading," pp. 533–543.

Smith, Nila B., *Reading Instruction for Today's Children.* Englewood Cliffs, N.J.: Prentice-Hall, Inc., 1963. Chapter 11, "Reading Rate," pp. 353–383.

Staiger, Ralph, and David A. Sohn (eds.), *New Directions in Reading.* New York: Bantam Books, 1967. Chapter VII, "The Speed Reading Controversy."

Tinker, Miles A., and Constance M. McCullough, *Teaching Elementary Reading,* New York: Appleton-Century-Crofts, 1968. Chapter 12, "Speed of Reading," pp. 237–257.

QUESTIONS FOR THOUGHT AND DISCUSSION

1. Today, there are over twenty commercial devices on the market that mechanize the act of reading in some fashion or other. It is often implied, if not stated, that speed of reading is our primary goal. Is this so? What are reasons for your stand?

2. A case is made by some who would teach us speed reading that rate and comprehension are positively related, or that comprehension increases with increase of speed in reading. Do you agree? If you do agree, what evidence can you give to support your position?

3. Skimming is a reading technique for securing rapidly the more important information in a selection in order to get a fairly complete idea of the content. If you think that you know how to skim, how would you describe the process as you see it? If you do not skim, can you state why you do not engage in this type of reading?

4. Educators have been interested in eye movements in reading for over fifty years. Considerable emphasis has been placed upon the relation of eye-movement patterns to speed of reading. What do the following terms mean: *fixation pause; return sweep; regressions?*

5. Can you defend the following statement? How?

The pupil who tends to read all material at about the same rate, as many do, is a poor reader. A goodly number of readers at all educational levels have not acquired the ability to adjust their speed of reading appropriately.

6. A recent study analyzed "bright" and "dull" students and their reading performances. The study revealed what you might suspect: the bright student reads a passage to extract the main ideas expressed by the writer, but the dull student approaches it as an assignment in the mechanics of reading. What might cause the difference in approach?

7. From a recent research study, pronounced contrasts became evident when the fastest readers are compared with the slowest. It would appear that a different set of abilities must be acquired in order to improve the speed of an already fast reader from those needed to improve the speed of a slow reader. Imagine you are a teacher and you have identified a very rapid reader in your class, as well as a very slow reader. How might you go about trying to improve the rates of *both* readers?

8. In properly conceived and executed classroom programs to speed up reading, few pupils will achieve relatively small gains, many will make moderate gains, and a few will make relatively great gains in rate of reading. An occasional pupil will achieve exceptional improvement. The degree to which the gains are maintained or to which they are transferred to reading work-type material is not well established. What suggestions do you have for maintenance and for transfer?

9. The term *flexibility* as applied to reading rate has been interpreted in a number of ways, and there still is some ambiguity surrounding the term—what it is, how it may be measured, and how it may be developed. Writers in the field have observed that flexibility does not just "happen," but is a composite of many factors that are trained, taught, and encouraged through an individual's reading career. What are some of these factors?

10. It has been asserted that a flexible reader selects the speed best suited to his purpose and to the reading material. Sometimes teachers direct students to vary their rate, shifting to a higher or lower rate when encountering easier or more difficult ideas or when comprehension needs differ. Does saying, "speed up," "slow down," "shift gears" really accomplish much? How would you go about achieving your ends?

CHAPTER 8 A

Locating Information and Using It

The development of the ability to locate information in printed sources has become an increasingly important concern of the school. In earlier, simpler days, pupils used relatively few books and were usually directed to the exact locations of the material to be studied. In our day of abundant newspapers, magazines, encyclopedias, dictionaries, almanacs, and other kinds of printed matter, skill in finding information is becoming ever more imperative. The increasing complexity of modern life, too, has brought this new need into focus.

Unfortunately, many children as well as adults, including college graduates, have only limited skill in locating information. For this reason, many people simply make no effort to look for information which they need or desire. Often people who have access to dictionaries and who want to know the meaning of a word do not look it up because they have difficulty in making efficient use of this indispensable reference aid.

Happily, teachers are beginning to meet the challenge presented by changing needs, by making a persistent effort to help boys and girls receive the needed information and practice in locating materials economically and efficiently. Almost all professional books on the teaching of reading stress the importance of these skills and make suggestions for their development. Basal textbook series for boys and girls provide for growth in these skills, and the teachers' guidebooks which accompany the children's books abound in excellent recommendations as to how these skills can be developed. Many of the workbooks provide helpful exercises.

The abilities to be developed in relation to the location of material are here classified under four categories: (1) the ability to find information in nonreference books, (2) the ability to use the dictionary, (3) the ability to use reference books other than the dictionary, and (4) the ability to locate books and magazine articles in the library.

BASIC LOCATIONAL SKILLS

Several of the locational skills basic to effective use of reading materials deal with the finding of information.

Skill in Finding Words Arranged in Alphabetical Order

One of these basic skills, that of finding words that are arranged in alphabetical order, is needed in many types of situations, as in locating information in the index of a book, in the card catalog, in the dictionary, in an encyclopedia, and in other reference books. Unfortunately, elementary school teachers have often wrongly assumed that the pupil has the following skills or learnings essential to locating words arranged in alphabetical order:

1. Knowledge of the sequence of letters in the alphabet.
2. Ability to tell which letter precedes and which follows another without repeating part of the alphabet either orally or silently.
3. Instant knowledge of the part of the alphabet—the first, middle, or last— in which a letter occurs.
4. Knowledge of the fact that in indexes, dictionaries, and card catalogs the words are arranged in alphabetical order.
5. Understanding of and skill in arranging words in alphabetical order when the first letter of each word is different.
6. Understanding of and skill in arranging words in alphabetical order when the first letter of the words is alike but the second different.
7. Understanding of and skill in arranging words in alphabetical order when the first two or more letters of the words are alike but subsequent letters are different.
8. Knowledge of how to arrange words in alphabetical order when problems like these and others exist: (a) words beginning with the syllable *Mc* or *Mac*; (b) titles beginning with *the*, *a*, or *an*; (c) words like *grand* and *grandmother*, in which all the letters of one word are given in the same sequence in the first part of a second word; (d) names of persons if both the first and the last names are given.

Skill in Finding a Specified Page

Another skill basic to many types of reading is finding quickly a given page in a book or magazine. Many pupils need to be taught that there are quicker ways of finding a page than to start at the beginning of the book and leaf through it until they came to the page they want. They also need practice in opening a book in the vicinity of the page they want. Development of this skill should be encouraged, as a rule, early in the first grade. Much of the practice in finding a specified page can be provided in the ongoing instructional program without the use of practice exercises.

Skill in Finding an Entry Word

Skill in finding an entry word is needed in using a dictionary, an encyclopedia, and other reference books. In order to find an entry word quickly, pupils should know the following facts about guide words: (1) In dictionaries, guide words are listed on each page of the book proper, usually in the columns at the top of the page. (2) These words indicate the first and the last entry words listed on a given page or, in the case of some dictionaries, on two facing pages. (3) By glancing at the guide words in a dictionary the reader can tell whether the word for which he is looking is on that page or, in some dictionaries, on one of the two facing pages. (4) Similar provisions are made in some of the other reference books, so that the reader can quickly ascertain whether the topic for which he is looking belongs between the first and last topics discussed on a given page.

It is not enough, however, for children to know what guide words are and where they are found. They should also develop skill in using guide words to locate entries quickly.

Skill in Deciding on Key Words

Another locational skill needed is that of knowing under what word to look for the desired information. This skill is often referred to as the ability to decide on key words. Lack of it causes much waste of time and frequently is the reason why reference books are not used more. Skill can be developed step by step through a gradation of difficulties, beginning with work on finding a topic in an index or reference book when the topic is worded in the same manner as the entry in the book. Later, pupils should be given practice in deciding which one of a variety of words is the most likely entry under which the needed information would be found. Use of subtopics in indexes should also be taught as an aid in finding the key words.

Knowledge of Content of Reference Books

Many pupils need guidance in learning what type of information is contained in different kinds of books and magazines. For example, a pupil will need to learn what types of information to look for in geography books, in history books, in science books, and in health books. He will also need to learn what types of information he can expect to find in various encyclopedias for children, in the *World Almanac*, in an atlas, in a dictionary, and in other reference books. As he develops skill in the use of these books, he will continue to discover new types of information. He cannot, of course, learn about them all at once. In the case of the dictionary, for example, he will usually first learn that it yields the meanings of words. Only later will he discover that he can find the pronunciation of words in it and, still later, that it contains information about syllabication and other matters.

Interpreting Information

After the reader has located information, he must be able to interpret it. Sometimes interpretation is an easy process, requiring neither special effort nor skill. At other times particular alertness is needed.

Pupils need to develop skill in learning to interpret the abbreviations given in reference material. Knowledge of many abbreviations is essential to effective reading of reference books. Furthermore, the pupils should know where to look for a key to the abbreviations and how to apply the information given in the key.

Common to several types of reference materials are the references to additional material designated by *See* or *See also*. The boys and girls need to know before they leave the elementary school what is meant by these directions as well as how to use them. It is also important for them to know when they should follow the *See* or *See also* direction. Speed in locating the cross reference and in deciding whether it contributes to the topic also needs to be developed.

Another problem in the use of reference materials is selecting the points that have bearing on the purpose that the reader has in mind. How to interpret charts, tables, maps, graphs, and diagrams given in reference books is only part of the task. The pupil needs to know also how to find speedily and correctly the information given in words, groups of words, sentences, or paragraphs.

Making Use of Information

After the reader has found and interpreted the information he wants, he may use it for a variety of purposes. He may compare what he has learned in one reference with what he has read in another or with what he already knows. He may take notes on it, write a summary, or make an outline in order either better to remember the data himself or to assist him as he tries to impart the information to others through informal conversation, reports, panel discussions, or illustrations. Sometimes he may compile a bibliography for his own or others' use. How to take notes, make summaries and outlines, and perform some of the other activities for purposes of retention and comprehension are discussed in other parts of this book.

ABILITY TO FIND INFORMATION IN NONREFERENCE BOOKS

Elementary school children should learn to use the following parts of books or features in books effectively in order to locate information quickly in their textbooks and in trade books:

1. The preface.
2. The introduction.
3. The table of contents.
4. Lists of maps and illustrations.
5. Chapter headings, center headings, and side headings.
6. The index.

The pupils should know where each of these parts is found, what its function is, and how to make effective use of it. Furthermore, the teacher should try to develop in them the desire to make effective use of the several parts.

The Preface

The boys and girls should learn the following facts about the preface: (1) It is found in the front part of the book. (2) It is written either by the author or the editor of the book. (3) It tells the author's purpose in writing the book and often indicates any special features of the book. (4) It is useful in indicating whether a given topic or question is likely to be treated in the book.

The Introduction

If the introduction is studied, the pupils should know that the terms *introduction* and *preface* are sometimes used interchangeably. They should learn that some books contain both a preface and an introduction. As they examine these two parts of a book, they should know that, although a study of the introduction may help them to decide whether information that they want is given in the book, its primary purpose is not to serve as a locational aid.

The Table of Contents

The pupil can use the table of contents almost as soon as he begins reading books. If a new book has no table of contents, the teacher can indicate what the book deals with. When a simple table of contents is given, as in many primers, the pupil can find the new story in the table of contents with the help of the teacher. Reference can also be made to the page, if the pupil cannot read the page number by himself. The teacher may say, pointing to the page, "This number 10 tells us that our story is on page 10." Thereupon she can help the pupils find the page.

Lists of Maps and Illustrations

Pupils should acquire the following learnings about maps and illustrations: (1) A list of maps and illustrations included in a book may be found either in the front part of the book or in the back. (2) Textbooks in social studies, science, and health are more likely to provide a list of maps or illustrations than trade books. (3) The list of maps and illustrations gives the titles used with the maps and illustrations and also the page on which they are found.

Chapter Headings, Center Headings, and Side Headings

Pupils should be taught the value of various kinds of headings in locating material and given practice in their use. As soon as side and center headings are given in the textbooks that the pupils read or in the reference books they use, simple help should be given in making effective use of these aids as means of locating information.

The following are some of the points that pupils should learn about the index of a book: (1) The index is in the back of the book. (2)

The topics are arranged alphabetically, not in order of appearance in the book, as in a table of contents. (3) In many books subtopics are given under the main entries.

The following skills should be developed: (1) deciding under what entry information on a given topic or question is likely to be given; (2) speed in finding an entry; (3) locating a topic when it appears as subtopic in the index; (4) ability to turn quickly to the pages on which the information, according to the index, is given; and (5) ability to find quickly the lines on a page that give the information on the desired topic.

ABILITY TO USE THE DICTIONARY

One of the outstanding developments in materials of instruction for the elementary school in recent years has been the dictionary for children. Before that, if boys and girls used any dictionaries, they had to use those planned for adults. Pupils in the early part of this century often had access only to a large, unabridged dictionary or to one or two less complete ones that were also compiled for adults. In some schools the children in the intermediate grades were urged or required to have their own abridged dictionary. Because of the price and the convenience of handling, many children brought to school pocket-sized dictionaries that in many respects were more difficult to understand than the unabridged dictionaries. Those who thought that these abbreviated dictionaries would be suitable for children were wrong, for often only one short line was allowed per entry. Obviously there was little chance for explanation when no more space than this was devoted to a word. At times the entry word was defined by a synonym even more difficult for the child to understand than the word he had looked up.

Dictionaries for the Elementary School

In addition to the picture dictionaries to which reference is made in Chapter 5B, "Developing Skill in Word Recognition," the following are commonly used in the elementary school:

Giant Golden Illustrated Dictionary, Stuart A. Courtis and Garnette Watters, eds. New York: Golden Press, Inc., 1961. Six volumes.

The Holt Basic Dictionary of American English. New York: Holt, Rinehart and Winston, Inc., 1966.

The Holt Intermediate Dictionary of American English. New York: Holt, Rinehart and Winston, Inc., 1966.

Illustrated Golden Dictionary for Young Readers, rev. ed., Stuart A. Courtis and Garnett Watters, eds. New York: Golden Press, Inc., 1956.

Thorndike-Barnhart Beginning Dictionary, Edward L. Thorndike and Clarence
L. Barnhart, eds. Chicago: Scott, Foresman and Company, 1964.
Thorndike-Barnhart Junior Dictionary, Edward L. Thorndike and Clarence
L. Barnhart, eds. Chicago: Scott, Foresman and Company, 1959.
Webster's A Dictionary for Boys and Girls. New York: American Book Company, 1962.
Webster's Elementary Dictionary. New York: American Book Company, 1961.
The Winston Dictionary for Schools, Thomas K. Brown and Wiliam D. Lewis, eds. New York: Holt, Rinehart and Winston, Inc., 1963.

Dictionary Skills

The skills to be learned in using a dictionary even in the elementary school are so complex that the teacher should have clearly in mind the subskills about which she should give information and for which she should provide practice. The following skills are needed for the efficient use of the dictionary in the elementary school:

1. Ability to locate a word quickly.
2. Ability to learn the pronunciation of a word.
3. Ability to find the spelling of a word and related abilities.
   a. Spelling.
   b. Syllabication.
   c. Hyphenation.
   d. Abbreviations.
   e. Capitalization.
4. Ability to learn the meaning of a word.
5. Ability to use the parts of the dictionary preceding and following the main parts of the dictionary, both in the pupil's dictionary and in an unabridged dictionary.

LOCATING A WORD IN THE DICTIONARY   In order to locate a word in the dictionary quickly, the pupil needs to know more than how to find a word in a list arranged alphabetically and how to make use of guide words. The difficulty in which one fifth-grade girl found herself illustrates the need for more information. This girl's teacher had told her pupils that the unabridged dictionary in their room contained every word in the English language. One day, while the teacher was busy with another group, this girl ran across the word *busied* in her reading and was puzzled as to the meaning of the word. Had the word been *busy* she would have recognized it in print, and had she heard the word *busied* pronounced, she would have had no difficulty with its meaning. However, when she saw the word *busied* in context, she thought it would be pronounced *bu si' ed*, giving the *s* an *s* instead of a *z* sound and the *i* a long sound. She therefore went to the big dictionary and looked for the entry *busied*. When she could not find *busied* listed as an entry word, she had no idea that she might find it under another form. Consequently, she could hardly wait until she could tell her teacher about her amazing discovery that the dictionary did not contain every word in the language. When the teacher asked her which word she did not find, she told her *busied*, pronouncing the word as *bu si' ed*. Many boys and girls have difficulty in finding a word in a dictionary when it is not given as an entry word in the form in which they meet the word in their reading. However, teachers are increasingly trying to show pupils how inflected forms can be located in the dictionary. In some schools, too, more emphasis is being placed on structural analysis, which serves as an aid in recognizing the inflected forms.

LEARNING THE PRONUNCIATION   The elementary school child should learn to find the pronunciation of a word by means of respellings and diacritical marks, as interpreted in the key to pronunciation at the bottom of the page in a dictionary. The significance of the syllabication of words and the markings of the accent should be clear to him. He should understand that if two pronunciations are given for the same word, each pronunciation is used, as, for example, in the word *record*, which as a noun has the accent on the first syllable but as a verb on the second. Furthermore, he should bear in mind that if no specification is given as to which of two pronunciations should be used under given circumstances, in most dictionaries the first of two indicated is usually the preferred one. However, it should also be made clear that often two pronunciations are equally acceptable, but, since one has to be written before the other, the pronunciation indicated first is not always a preferred pronunciation.

FINDING THE SPELLING   It is a difficult feat for many individuals, even adults, to find a word in the dictionary without being sure of the spelling. The pupil should therefore be given guidance and practice in this skill. Merely to say to a child, "Look up in the dictionary the word that you do not know how to spell," is inviting frustration. Pupils should learn how the plurals of nouns and other inflected forms are indicated. They need to know that some words pronounced alike—homonyms—have different meanings for different spellings. For spelling purposes it is also often necessary to know how words can be divided into syllables and whether they are hyphenated. Consequently, the pupil needs to know the key for the division into syllables and hyphenation. Some dictionaries show syllabication by means of a space left between syllables; others show it by a hyphen, which must not be interpreted as a sign that the word is a compound word. The symbols for hyphenation also vary. In some dictionaries the hyphen is used to show hyphenation, and in others the double hyphen, one line above the other, is used for that purpose. Often the pupils need help in finding out what the symbols in a given dictionary indicate.

Another problem in spelling deals with the abbreviation of a word, if it can be abbreviated. Boys and girls should know that the dictionary gives the abbreviations of words, and they should learn where they can be found.

By means of the dictionary the pupils in the elementary school should be able to find out whether a word is always written with a capital letter. They should know where and how the dictionaries give information about capitalization.

LEARNING THE MEANING   Pupils need to develop the following skills for understanding the meaning of words through the use of a dictionary:

1. They should, when the word is used in context, be able to select the meaning that fits into the setting in which it is used.
2. They should be able to make effective use of the pictorial illustrations given for some words.
3. They should be able to make effective use of the verbal illustrations given, knowing which meaning of a word a given illustration fits.
4. They should understand information given about inflected forms.
5. They should know the interpretations of the symbols for the parts of speech they have studied.
6. They should know how to make use of information given about idiomatic expressions in which some words are commonly used.
7. They should understand what is meant by synonyms and antonyms, and they should know how the dictionaries they use give this type of information.

MAKING USE OF INFORMATION GIVEN IN THE PARTS THAT PRECEDE AND FOLLOW THE MAIN PART OF THE DICTIONARY   If there is an unabridged dictionary in the schoolroom, the teacher in a fifth or sixth grade may wish to introduce the pupils to some of the types of information given in the part preceding and following the main section of the dictionary. They will be interested to know that by turning to an unabridged dictionary they can find illustrations of flags of all the countries of the world, that the dictionary gives biographical data on important persons, and that it has a very helpful section dealing with geographical locations. Even some of the dictionaries designed for boys and girls in the elementary school contain materials of great value in the front and back portions. Familiarity with all the parts of one's own dictionary should be an objective that is accomplished some time during the elementary school.

ABILITY TO USE REFERENCE BOOKS OTHER THAN THE DICTIONARY

Encyclopedias and other suitable reference materials for boys and girls can serve at least two very important purposes—that of helping the child gain needed information and that of opening for him a source of information that can continue to serve his needs throughout life. More and more schools are ordering for the various rooms in their school system sets of encyclopedias as well as other reference material. If there are no adequate reference books in an intermediate-grade room, the teacher should discover whether some can be obtained for her classroom. However, even if the desired reference books are not available in the classroom, they may often be found either in school or public libraries. Some boys and girls have sets of encyclopedias or other reference books at home which they should utilize.

The quality of reference materials for boys and girls in the elementary school has greatly improved. There are the well-known *Compton's Pictured Encyclopedia, The World Book Encyclopedia, Junior Britannica,* and *Our Wonderful World.* One set of encyclopedias that is filling a real need for children in the primary and lower intermediate grades as well as for the teachers of those grades is *Childcraft,* published by Field Enterprises, Incorporated. All of these encyclopedias give information on persons, places, and things, as well as on important events. An encyclopedia limited in scope, but excellent, is the *Junior Book of Authors,* written on a level that many boys and girls in the intermediate grades can comprehend. It contains biographies or autobiographies of the famous writers of books for children, illustrated with a picture of the writer. It also gives a list of the works of each author.

There are several types of reference materials other than encyclopedias or dictionaries that boys and girls in the upper elementary school grades can learn to use effectively. One is the *World Almanac,* published yearly, which gives concise data, chiefly in the form of isolated facts, on a large variety of topics, such as government, sports, and industry. It is especially valuable for the statistics recorded in it. The child can find the answer to many questions of interest to him, for example, "What is the population of the United States?" or "Which is longer, the Mississippi River or the Congo River?" Parts of *Goode's School Atlas,* with its variety of types of maps, constitute an excellent supplement to maps given in geography books. Familiarity with the *Subject Index to Poetry,* if a copy of it is available, can also serve the needs of many boys and girls in the fifth and sixth grades. Many pupils in the intermediate grades would profit from an introduction to *Who's Who* and *Who's Who in America.*

In the first part of this chapter there is an enumeration of skills basic to the use of many types of reference material—for example, ability to find words when they are arranged in alphabetical order, ability to use cross references, and ability to utilize information found in reference books. All of these skills are needed for effective use of encyclopedias and other specialized reference books. In addition to these skills, pupils need the following in order to use materials of this type efficiently:

1. Knowledge of what is contained in the reference books.
2. Knowledge of the organization of the reference books.
3. Ability to decide in which reference book the desired information is likely to be found.
4. Skill in finding the information.

ABILITY TO LOCATE MATERIALS IN THE LIBRARY

In order to be able to locate materials effectively in a library the pupil needs to know how to use the card catalog, how to locate books on the shelves (if the library has open shelves), and how to use sources like the *Reader's Guide to Periodical Literature.* The help given in learning how to locate books in a library should be in terms of the library to which children have access. If none is located in the community, a miniature classroom library can serve as substitute.

Using the Card Catalog

Almost all libraries have card catalogs that serve as indexes to their book collections. Pupils should know that the term *card catalog* is applied to the collection of drawers in which are filed three-by-five-inch cards which give data on all the books in the library. They should learn that the cards are arranged alphabetically in the drawers and that the progression of the drawers is from the top toward the bottom drawer of one stack of drawers to the top drawer in the next stack.

In order to have skill in the use of a card catalog, boys and girls must be familiar with the common types of cards used. They should know at least three of the cards that the card catalog contains— namely, the author card, the title card, and the subject card. They also

Learning to use the library. (Photo by William Dippel.)

need to know that on an author card the alphabetical arrangement is according to the last name of the author, on a title card according to the first significant word of the title, and on a subject card according to the subject of the book. The pupils should also realize that if an individual knows the first and last names of the author of a book, it may be timesaving to look for the book under the author card. If the name of the author is not known but the exact title is known, it is often expedient to look for the title card. If neither the name of the author nor the exact title is known, it is usually best to look for the subject card. The children should also learn that by means of the subject card they can find out what other books are available in the library on a given subject. These statements will seem quite obvious to the college student and the young teacher, but they often need to be explained to elementary school pupils.

Guidance should be given in observing the data found on all three types of cards. The terms *B* for *biography* and *J* for *juvenile*, if these are used, should also be explained. The pupils should learn the significance of the call number and the use they can make of it in locating a book in the library.

Finding Books on Shelves

If the library accessible to the child has open stacks, the pupil should learn something about the arrangement of the books.

Most small libraries use an adaptation of the Dewey decimal system of classification. If the library has that system of classification, the pupil should learn to use it. While pupils should not be asked to memorize the categories, they should have general familiarity with the system and know where in a library they can find the classification chart. The Dewey decimal system employs the following number classifications:

000–099   General works, including bibliography and general periodicals
100–199   Philosophy, psychology, ethics
200–299   Religion, Bible, mythology
300–399   Sociology, economics, education, political science
400–499   Philology, dictionaries, grammars
500–599   Natural science, including mathematics, chemistry, physics
600–699   Applied science, including useful arts, medicine, agriculture, manufacturing
700–799   Fine arts, music, recreation
800–899   Literature
900–999   History, biography, travel

Using the Reader's Guide to Periodical Literature

Some boys and girls in the upper grades of the elementary school can be taught how to locate magazine articles by means of the *Reader's Guide to Periodical Literature*. The teacher, possibly with the help of the librarian, may decide to teach the child such facts as the following:

1. Where the *Reader's Guide to Periodical Literature* is located.
2. How often it is published.
3. Method of cumulation.
4. Type of information it contains.
5. How to locate information in it.

Pupils should also find out where a list of the magazines the library has is posted and where both the bound and unbound periodicals are kept.

Locating Other Materials in the Library

Increasingly there will be an urgent need for boys and girls even in the elementary school to learn to locate materials other than books and magazines both in their classroom and in central libraries. With the greater supply of films, filmstrips, slides, tapes, and records, those in charge of libraries are finding it imperative to store these aids according to a system that will facilitate their use. With growing individualization of work in many schools and with libraries increasingly being used as learning centers, it is becoming all the more important that boys and girls know where to find these materials. If time is to be saved and use of the materials encouraged, many pupils will need help in learning the plan of organization followed in the storage of these aids to learning. What system of storage is used will vary considerably from library to library. Elementary school pupils should be familiarized with whatever method of organization is used in libraries to which they have access.

Undoubtedly in the near future the need of guidance in the use of newer types of materials will be an essential in a program of helping boys and girls locate information, if predictions concerning the library of the future come true. Then skill in locating materials, at least in larger libraries such as those to which reference is made in the following quotation, will be an asset to learning.

> Wonderful developments in libraries are taking place and each year will bring dramatic changes.
> Libraries of the future will be amazingly efficient. Microfilm, computer analysis, central storage banks, dial access, and on-demand printing will revolutionize research and note-taking. Reading and creating of tomorrow will be enhanced greatly by technology.[1]

PRINCIPLES UNDERLYING THE TEACHING OF LOCATIONAL SKILLS

For teaching boys and girls how to acquire skill in locating information, there is a large variety of procedures from which to choose. They should be selected in terms of principles like the following.

1. *Readiness for a locational skill facilitates learning.* In part, readiness for this type of skill, as for other learnings, is a matter of maturation. However, to a considerable extent it is closely related to the experience background of the learner. Fortunately, the background of experience can be broadened, and the teacher is in a key position to

[1] Verna D. Anderson, *Reading and Young Children*, p. 321. New York: The Macmillan Company, 1968.

help. No teacher needs to wait complacently for a child to become ready to learn how to locate material in print. Readiness can be achieved through a well-planned sequence of activities, preferably those that relate to problems for functional use of printed sources.

Readiness can also be thought of in terms of a felt need to learn a skill. Because of the role of purpose in arousing a state of readiness, the teacher should set the stage for the acquisition of the skill. She can do this either by making use of a situation or by creating one in which the child feels a need for a given skill. For example, if the class is uncertain as to the pronunciation of a word, an occasion could be provided for teaching how the pronunciation of a word is indicated in the dictionary. Or if the pupils are planning to make a list of the persons in the room, in connection with the assignment of responsibilities, the teacher may give the pupils instruction and practice in writing words in alphabetical order.

The optimum grade placement of a skill either for initial presentation or for practice purposes has not been ascertained. It is generally agreed, however, that although the bulk of the work in developing skill in locating information should be done in the intermediate grades, work in the primary grades can make a significant contribution in this area. In the first three grades, help can be given in locating some of the information that children wish to find in books and magazines. Furthermore, in the primary grades a stable foundation can be laid for skills that can be developed in the intermediate grades.

The following are some of the skills in locating information that are developed, at least in part, in many primary grades:

a. Looking at the pictures to get an idea as to the content of a book.
b. Noting the titles of stories as they appear in the main part of the book.
c. Finding page numbers.
d. Reading the titles of stories as listed in the table of contents.
e. Looking at the titles of stories in order to see which ones are likely to deal with a given topic.
f. Knowing where, in the room or school or public library, books of interest can be found.
g. Learning alphabetical order.
h. Arranging letters and words in alphabetical order.
i. Knowing how to use a picture dictionary.
j. Using a glossary in a textbook.
k. Learning a few facts related to using a dictionary for children.
l. Finding material and looking at pictures in an encyclopedia for younger children—for example, *Childcraft*.
m. Looking at pictures and getting information through the teacher's read-

ing from encyclopedias like *Compton's Pictured Encyclopedia, The World Book Encyclopedia, Britannica Junior,* or *Our Wonderful World.*
n. Getting information from atlases, yearbooks, and the *World Almanac.*

2. *Opportunity should be provided to make use of skills learned.* Closely related to the problem of readiness for learning a skill is that of making use of what is learned. Since the pupil is, as a rule, more receptive to learning if he knows he will find it of value, only those abilities of real worth to a child before he is an adult should be developed. Fortunately, many skills that are needed by adults are also important to children. By providing the child with opportunity to make real use of his skill, the teacher helps furnish the child with distributed practice, important in the learning of any skill.

The children should be stimulated to make use of the skills that they are acquiring and to recognize situations in which they can do so. The teacher can also lead discussions in which the group decides what use can be made of the skills. In addition, as the teacher sees boys and girls make application of the recently acquired skills, she can call such activities to the attention of the class. She can also encourage pupils themselves to report ways in which their new abilities proved helpful to them.

Since the skills to be learned should generally be limited to those that the pupils can use in the near future, the *Reader's Guide to Periodical Literature* should not be stressed in the teaching unless it is generally available to children. Of course, the teacher may explain to the pupils that such a guide exists, but detailed information on its use would under most circumstances be inappropriate.

3. *Provision should be made for evaluating skill in locating information.* One way of appraising the skill of intermediate-grade boys and girls to locate information is by means of standardized tests. Unfortunately, most standardized reading tests for the elementary school do not test skill in locating information. Two tests that do devote sections to this skill are the Iowa Silent Reading Test and the Iowa Every Pupil Test.

The teacher can also appraise skill through more informal means, such as teacher-made tests, observation of pupils while doing practice exercises designed to develop skills in locating information, and observation of pupils when they look up information while not taking tests or doing practice exercises. An advantage of the teacher-made tests over the standardized tests is that the locational skills not tested in the commercially produced tests can be included. A further point in favor of teacher-made tests is that the teacher has the opportunity to devise test items that apply specifically to what the pupils are or will be studying. As she observes the boys and girls in nontesting situations, she can note not only their skills but also their attitudes toward finding information and utilizing it. Expressions, for example, showing dislike of looking up words in a dictionary tell the teacher something she ought to know for planning future strategy.

In making evaluations it is important to observe these criteria: (1) Evaluation should be made in terms of the objectives. To be sure, before a teacher begins instruction in locating information a survey test giving information on the pupil's abilities in a variety of locational skills may be given. (2) Both teacher and pupils should take part in evaluation procedures. If the pupil has a voice in planning the means of appraisal, he is more likely to try to improve in the skills that are being taught. Furthermore, his attitude toward the tests will probably be more favorable. (3) Evaluation should be a continuous process. It should not be confined to appraisal when work on a skill is begun and when the time to be spent on working on it systematically is ended. Throughout the period of learning, checks should be made on how successful the teaching and learning have been.

4. *Systematic instruction should be given in the development of the locational skills.* While possibly for a small minority of the boys and girls in the elementary school no instruction beyond the incidental will be essential, in many instances even these children will profit from lessons definitely planned to help them acquire greater facility in the locational skills. For a large number of pupils, much floundering and inefficiency will result unless they are given direct help in the development of the ability to locate information. How these skills can be developed incidentally in the content subjects is discussed in part of Chapter 11. To supplement such instruction, direct assistance can, and in most cases should, be given by providing presentation lessons in which the pupils are taught locational skills and practice exercises in which they can strengthen their command of the skills. In the following chapter suggestions as to types of practice desirable are given.

5. *Materials of instruction should fit the needs of the individuals.* Many teachers are not aware of the excellent materials that are available for the development of locational skills. Through the sensible application of the many suggestions given in the teachers' guides accompanying most of the basal textbook series in reading, the teacher can utilize many stories and articles in the reading books. Textbooks and workbooks in the language arts also frequently devote a sizable number of pages to the development of these skills. Of late some of the publishers of dictionaries for children have supplied exercises to help develop skill in the use of the dictionary.

CHAPTER 8B

Developing Ability To Locate
Information and Use It

Anyone with ordinary intelligence and average reading ability should have no difficulty in acquiring the locational skills. Unfortunately, however, because of inadequate instruction, many persons who have graduated from high school are deficient in this area. A teacher who puts into practice the principles set forth in the preceding chapter can do much to help pupils attack their problems of finding information in printed materials. The following pages will illustrate ways of putting these principles into effect.

DEVELOPING THE BASIC SKILLS

Basic to the development of skill in locating information in various types of books and magazines are skills in (1) finding words in alphabetical order, (2) finding a given page in a book quickly, (3) deciding on key words, and (4) utilizing information gained.

Finding a Given Page in a Book Quickly

Pupils can be given help in quickly finding a given page in books of various types by means of activities like the following:

1. Telling the pupils in the first grade where to find page numbers in a book.
2. Teaching the pupils how to turn the pages of a book.

3. Having the pupils try to open a book as near as possible to a given page before they begin turning pages.
4. Giving the pupils practice in finding a given page quickly by having them keep a record during a short period of time of how many attempts they had to make before getting the right page.
5. Having the pupils estimate to which page you have opened a book.

Finding Words in Alphabetical Order

Finding words in lists arranged alphabetically is a basic skill in locating information. The following methods are illustrative of the means by which this skill may be developed:

1. Having the pupils memorize the letters in alphabetical order.
2. Writing the letters in alphabetical order on the board with some letters missing and asking the pupils to supply the missing letters.
3. Asking pupils to name or write the letter that immediately precedes or follows a given letter.
4. Having the pupils state in what part of the alphabet—first, middle, or last—given letters are found. Some teachers may prefer making the division of the alphabet into the first, second, third, and fourth quarters.
5. Having the pupils arrange letters in alphabetical order.
6. Asking the pupils to arrange in alphabetical order a series of words in which the first letters are different; in which the first and second letters are different; and in which the first three or more letters are different.
7. Explaining to the pupils that persons' names are usually listed according to the last names, and that when two or more persons have the same last name, their names are arranged according to the first names.
8. Asking the pupils to arrange in alphabetical order the names of the boys and girls in their class.
9. Explaining to the class that as the teacher shows each word card of a set, a pupil is to respond by naming a word beginning with the letter immediately preceding, in alphabetical order, the letter with which the word on the card begins. A variation of this procedure is to have a pupil give a word beginning with the letter immediately following, in alphabetical order, the letter with which the word on a given card begins.
10. Explaining to the pupils that on each page of the dictionary and in many other reference books words known as guide words are given. The pupils should learn that the first guide word, written in the upper left-hand corner, designates the first entry word on that page and that the second guide word, usually appearing in the upper right-hand corner, indicates the last entry word on that page. They should also learn that looking at the guide words can help the reader to determine quickly which words are found on given pages.
11. Having the pupils indicate whether a given word comes between two stated guide words.

12. Asking the pupils to name words that are expected to be found as entry words on a page in the dictionary for which the guide words are stated.
13. Providing the pupils with a list of numbered sets of guide words from a dictionary, opposite which there is a list of words, arranged in a different order, each of which appears between one of the pairs of guide words. On the line to the right of each word in the second column the pupil writes the number of the matching guide words.

PRACTICE EXERCISES   Practice exercises can be used to advantage in teaching boys and girls to find words in alphabetical order. Samples of a few follow.

1

Explanation. Preparatory to finding words in alphabetical order is skill in knowing the arrangement of letters in alphabetical sequence.

Directions: Write the letters that come immediately before and after, in ABC order, each of the letters.

LETTERS

1. ——— *t* ———   5. ——— *o* ———
2. ——— *f* ———   6. ——— *w* ———
3. ——— *d* ———   7. ——— *v* ———
4. ——— *q* ———   8. ——— *k* ———

2

Directions: Supply the missing letters.

1. a ——— c d ——— f ——— h i ———
2. r s ——— u ——— w ——— y z

3

Directions: Write *yes* on the line to the left of each number if the words in that item are arranged in alphabetical order. Otherwise write *no.*

WORDS

———1. camel; cat; lion; fox
———2. bay; gulf; lake; ocean
———3. talk; tear; tease; take
———4. James; Jones; Johnson; Jacobson

4

Directions: Put an x through each word that is not in alphabetical order in the lists that follow.

WORDS

1. apples, bananas, pears, oranges, plums
2. stone, brick, granite, marble, wood, stone

5

Explanation. In providing pupils with practice in arranging words in alphabetical order, the easiest type of exercise is one in which the first letters of the words are different. More difficult is an exercise in which only some of the first letters of the words are different, so that the alphabetical order of the word needs to be determined in part by the second letter of the words; still more difficult is an exercise in which the third and fourth letters of a word help to determine the alphabetical order. (In the exercise that follows the third letter of *bluebirds* and *blackbirds* determines which word comes first.)

Directions: Write 1 to the left of the word that should come first in alphabetical order, 2 to the left of the word that should come second, and so on.

_____bluebirds	_____doves
_____blackbirds	_____chickadees
_____bobwhites	_____cardinals
_____ducks	_____cranes

6

Directions: Each of the following lists of names is in alphabetical order. Number the words as they should appear if the two lists were to be combined into one alphabetical list.

_____Albright, Marian	_____Alexander, Marjorie
_____Ayres, Harold	_____Douda, Helen
_____Fleischer, Susan	_____Foster, Arthur
_____Fleming, Gertrude	_____Gordon, Evelyn
_____Manton, Cecil	_____Miller, John
_____Meier, Roberta	_____Nelson, Nels
_____Otto, Charles	_____Nelson, Samuel
_____Owens, James	_____Sutton, Maria
_____Spoerr, Geraldine	_____Wright, Jean
_____Staples, Daniel	_____Young, Richard

7

Directions: On one page of a dictionary the guide words are *Nashville* and *nature.* Write *yes* to the right of the following words that you would expect to find on that page. Write *no* to the right of the others.

WORDS

1.	narrow⎯⎯	6.	net⎯⎯
2.	nail⎯⎯	7.	neck⎯⎯
3.	nature⎯⎯	8.	needle⎯⎯
4.	nation⎯⎯	9.	nurse⎯⎯
5.	name⎯⎯	10.	navy⎯⎯

Deciding on Key Words

One of the more difficult locational skills is to decide on the key words under which certain information can be found. Through a progression of activities from the less to the more difficult and from the known to the unknown, this ability can be developed. Some methods that can prove helpful in developing this skill are:

1. Asking the pupils to tell under what key word in an index a reference may be found for a question such as, "In what year did George Washington become president of the United States?"
2. Providing the boys and girls with an exercise in which they will choose the one of three or four words under which a reference is the most likely to be listed that gives information on a stated topic.
3. Having the pupils explain the relevancy of cross references to the subject matter being read.

PRACTICE EXERCISES   These samples show several ways in which practice in deciding upon key words can be provided. The value of such exercises can usually be greatly increased if the pupils are given a chance to discuss their reasons for making their selections.

1

Directions: Draw a line under the key word in each of the following questions that seems to you is the most likely entry word in an index of a nonreference book or in a reference book such as an encyclopedia under which you would find an answer to the question.

QUESTIONS

1. What is one of the chief exports of the Philippines?
2. What was the color of the uniform of the soldiers of the South during the Civil War?

2

Directions: Draw a line under the word or group of words in parentheses that you would choose as the most likely key word in an index to give information about the question.

QUESTIONS

1. In what year did George Washington become president of the United States? (Washington; George; president; United States)
2. In what year did the Mexican War, which was fought between the United States and Mexico, begin? (wars; Mexican War; United States; Mexico)
3. What were the provisions of the Kansas-Nebraska Bill? (Kansas-Nebraska Bill; Nebraska; provisions; bill)

Discovering What Types of Information Are Given in Various Kinds of Books

As each new type of reference book is introduced, help should be given to the boys and girls to decide what type of information they should look for in it. Possible procedures are:

1. Encouraging the pupils to look through the various parts of a reference book to find out what information it contains.
2. Having the pupils make a chart to indicate in what reference books they would try to locate information on specific problems.
3. Asking the pupils in what reference books they would look if they wanted stated types of information—for example, data on the life of Hans Christian Andersen.
4. Having the pupils look up data on a given topic in a variety of books to compare the type of information given in each.
5. Asking the pupils to read parts of the table of contents or index of several reference books, and to note the various types of information given.
6. Explaining the differences between an encyclopedia and a dictionary.
7. Asking the pupils when giving reports to tell from what references they received their information if reference books were consulted.
8. Providing the pupils with opportunity to report on any topic of interest to them on which they found information in a reference book and to state what reference book they consulted.
9. Having a "quiz program" based on information found in reference books. It would be helpful, in some instances, to have the pupils indicate in which reference book the answer to each question was found.
10. Explaining the means used to keep a reference book up-to-date, such as supplements to encyclopedias.

PRACTICE EXERCISES   After the boys and girls have had experiences in learning what types of information are given in various kinds of books, they might do an exercise similar to the following. The books listed should be those with which the pupils are familiar.

Directions: Below the questions is a list of different kinds of books that are lettered from (a) through (g). On the line to the right of each question, write the letter or letters given to the books in which you would expect to find an answer to the question.

QUESTIONS

1. What was the population of Delaware, Ohio, during the past year? _____

2. What were the chief exports of France during the past year? _____

3. How often should a person clean his teeth? _____

4. What causes a dental cavity? _____

5. What is the origin of the word *belfry*? _____

6. What part of speech is the word *produce* when the accent is on the second syllable? _____

BOOKS

a. *Compton's Pictured Encyclopedia*
b. *The World Almanac*
c. *Junior Book af Authors*
d. *Reader's Guide to Periodical Literature*
e. a dictionary
f. an atlas
g. a hygiene book

Interpreting Punctuation Marks, Diacritical Marks, Abbreviations, and Symbols

Since in indexes, dictionaries, and other reference books punctuation marks are used in different ways, and since the abbreviations and symbols used vary somewhat from one book to another, it is suggested that, although there are common problems, most work on this topic be taken up as each new reference book is studied. The following are ways in which these interpretative skills can be developed:

1. Helping the pupils find out how syllabication of words is indicated in their own dictionaries and how the hyphen between compound words is written.

2. Asking the pupils to look up in the dictionary words like *bluejay, Sunday school,* and *good-by* to find out which are hyphenated.
3. Helping the pupils to find the key to the diacritical marks, abbreviations, and symbols used in a reference book.
4. Providing practice in pronouncing words according to the respelling indicated in a dictionary.
5. After helping the pupils learn how division into syllables is shown in their dictionaries, asking them to divide words into syllables after consulting a dictionary.
6. Providing practice in interpreting accent marks by having pupils pronounce words that are not always accented in the same way, like *pres' ent* and *pre sent'.*
7. Asking the pupils to give words illustrating the various sounds of letters and of letter combinations like *a, e, c, th.*
8. Teaching the abbreviations for words commonly used and then testing the pupils on them.
9. Explaining to the group that when a word has two correct pronunciations, both are usually indicated in a dictionary, and that if one is preferred, that is given first. Also, however, it should be pointed out that it must not be taken for granted that if there are two pronunciations given, the second one is not as desirable as the first, for the two may be equally desirable.
10. Explaining to the boys and girls that if every letter in the alphabet stood for but one sound and every sound were represented by but one letter, there would probably be no need to have the pronunication of a word indicated in a dictionary.
11. Helping the boys and girls discover that one and only one vowel sound is heard in each syllable. The pupils might give the vowel sound in each syllable of a group of words listed on the chalkboard.

Selecting Points That Have Bearing on a Given Problem

After the necessary reference pages have been located, skill in selecting points that have bearing on a given problem can be developed through various activities, such as:

1. Asking the class questions that are phrased in words similar to those used in the text that serve as an answer to them and asking questions when the answers are not phrased in the same way.
2. Asking the pupils to find the answer to a question or a direction like the following, in which the answer consists of two or more sentences referred to in various parts of a paragraph: "Name three reasons why many cranberries are produced in Massachusetts."
3. Providing practice in formulating problems, so that the pupils know specifically what information they are looking for. This might be done by

having the boys and girls write the question or questions that they want answered.

4. Providing practice in skimming by having the pupils read as rapidly as possible, while they are being timed, a selection to spot certain words, sentences, or thoughts.
5. Asking the pupils to list items they would expect to find under a certain topic.

PRACTICE EXERCISES   To provide practice in deciding which points have bearing on a given problem, the teacher might ask the pupils to write an x on the line to the left of each sentence that gives information on the topic stated.

1. Topic: How to make molds of footprints
   _____a. Before making a mold, clean the footprints.
   _____b. Detectives often study the footprints of human beings.
   _____c. Plaster of Paris can be used to make a mold.
   _____d. The footprint should be thoroughly dry before the plaster of Paris is poured onto it.
2. Topic: Where the robin migrates in winter
   _____a. The robin is larger than the house wren.
   _____b. Robins usually breed more than once during a season.
   _____c. In the winter robins fly as far south as Mexico.
   _____d. Robins stay in the northern states till November.

Utilizing Information Gained

After the exact information needed has been located, skill in utilizing it can be acquired through activities such as the following:

1. Having the pupils judge whether a statement is reliable by considering who wrote it or in what book it appeared.
2. Giving the pupils practice in deciding which of a series of statements are relevant to their problem.
3. Having the pupils compile a bibliography of information helpful on a topic.
4. Providing opportunity for the pupils to give a talk or write a paper on information they have gathered.
5. Giving the pupils opportunity to explain to others what they learned, by putting on puppet shows or making friezes or "movies."
6. After the pupils have looked up a topic in an encyclopedia, giving them time to write a small number of interesting and significant facts that they learned and then having others in the class read those sentences.

7. Giving the pupils an opportunity to compare facts read in an encyclopedia with their own experiences.
8. Having pupils compare the information on a given subject gained from one encyclopedia with that on the same topic in another encyclopedia.

DEVELOPING SKILL IN USING NONREFERENCE BOOKS

Skill in using the various parts of a book for locating information can be acquired by means of the following methods:

1. Having the pupils examine the various parts of a book to find out where they are located, what they contain, and how the data given in them are arranged.
2. Providing practice for the pupils in examining the preface of a book to see if the book is likely to contain information needed on a given topic.
3. Having the pupils find answers to questions about the various parts of a book, for example, "What is the purpose of the preface?"
4. Helping the pupils make a chart on which they list the important points to remember about each part of a book, for example, "The index is found in the back part of the book."
5. Even in the first grade, having the pupils turn to the table of contents of their reader to find the page of the story they will read.
6. Giving the pupils the opportunity to answer questions like the following as they examine the table of contents in their textbook in the social studies: "How many chapters are there in the book?" or "In which chapter would you expect to find information about the fire department?"
7. Through examination of the table of contents of several books, having the pupils make a list of books in which information is given on a topic in which they are interested.
8. Asking the pupils to tell the chief differences between a glossary and a dictionary.
9. Explaining to the boys and girls the meaning of the word *appendix*.
10. Having the pupils look up cross references quickly.
11. After making and distributing duplicate copies of a table of contents and an index, asking the pupils questions answered in these.
12. When discussing a place of special interest, having the pupils look in the index of their social studies books to find out where, if at all, it is shown on a map in these books.
13. Having the pupils make a table of contents and an index for a class notebook they are making—one on "Famous Modern Americans," for example.
14. Helping the boys and girls write a preface for a class notebook on a topic such as "Autobiographies of Boys and Girls in Our Fifth Grade." They could also include in it an appendix giving name, date of birth, and place of birth of each pupil.

15. Having the pupils compile a list of words that have interesting origins (*neighbor* is such a word) and letting them explain the etymology of these words to the class. An illustrated chart might be made to help the pupils remember the information.

Practice Exercises

These three samples of exercises show how practice exercises can be used to develop skill in locating information in nonreference books.

1

Although work on the table of contents can be begun in the first and second grades, in these lower grades, as a rule, the work should be done only as it is a help in finding an entry in the table of contents. In the intermediate grades, however, exercises such as the following can be used. Since the questions are based on the table of contents given in *Shining Hours*,[1] if this specific exercise were used, each pupil would have to have access to a copy of this reader. The exercise can, of course, be easily adapted for use with any reader.

Directions: This exercise is to help you learn to make good use of a table of contents in a book. Find and write the answers to these questions by using the table of contents of *Shining Hours*. Your teacher may decide to time you while you are doing this exercise.

QUESTIONS

1. Into how many parts are the stories and poems divided? (Do not count the Glossary or Little Dictionary as one part). _____
2. What is the first word of the third story listed under "The World's Children"? _____
3. Who wrote "The Legend of Betsy Ross"? _____
4. On what page does the story "The Dragon Chair" begin? _____
5. On what page does a poem by Edward Lear begin? _____

2

Directions: To help you find out what types of material are found in appendixes of books, study the appendixes of three books and fill out the following form.

1. *Name of author:* _____*Title:* _____

[1] Nila Banton Smith, Hazel Hart, and Clara B. Baker, *Shining Hours.* Indianapolis, Ind.: The Bobbs Merrill Company, Inc., 1964.

Type of materials: _____

_____

_____

2. *Name of author:* _____ *Title:* _____
   Type of materials: _____

_____

_____

3. *Name of author:* _____ *Title:* _____
   Type of materials: _____

_____

_____

3

After the boys and girls have studied the parts of a book, a list of questions similar to the following might be used as a means of review and evaluation.

Directions: Draw a line under the correct word or group of words in parentheses.

1. The index of a book is arranged (alphabetically; by chapters; in the order in which the points are taken up in the book).
2. The preface is found in the (front; middle; back) part of the book.
3. The glossary (tells the purpose of the author in writing the book; gives the list of chapters in a book; gives the pronunciation and meaning of some of the words used in the book).
4. The table of contents is arranged (alphabetically; by chapters; in the order in which the points are taken up in the book).

DEVELOPING SKILL IN USING THE DICTIONARY

Some procedures that can help in the development of skills essential to the effective use of the dictionary are listed under "Finding Words in Alphabetical Order," on page 278, and under "Interpreting Punctuation Marks, Diacritical Marks, Abbreviations, and Symbols," on page 283. Additional suggestions follow.

1. Providing practice in deciding which inflectional forms are likely to be treated as distinct words in a dictionary and given separate entries and which forms are likely to be treated as run-on entries.
2. Having the pupils make a list of the types of information given for an entry word.

3. Providing practice in which the pupils select from a dictionary the meaning of a word that is appropriate in a given context.
4. Providing practice in looking up the spelling of a word in the dictionary by helping the pupils decide on probable spellings of it and then looking for these in the dictionary.
5. Providing practice in pronouncing words that according to the dictionary have two correct pronunciations.
6. Helping the pupils really learn the meanings of words they look up, so that they are not satisfied with knowing a synonym without knowing the shade of difference in meaning between the two synonyms.
7. Providing the pupils with sentences in each of which a word is underlined and asking the boys and girls to restate each sentence without using the underlined word, An example of such sentence is: "The boys and girls did not *anticipate* a big crowd."
8. Providing practice in using the abbreviations and arbitrary signs in the dictionary.
9. Helping the pupils discover how the thumb index may help them in locating a word.
10. Having a pupil from one of two teams into which the class is divided give two guide words from a page in a dictionary and write them on the chalkboard while a pupil from the other team names a word that would be expected to be found on that page of the dictionary and writes it on the board. This practice could be provided in somewhat the same way that spelldowns are sometimes conducted.
11. Providing practice in finding out through the dictionary the possible parts of speech of a word like *effect* and in using it in those ways in sentences.
12. Giving help in finding the various definitions of a word that may be used as different parts of speech, for example, *effect* as a noun or as a verb.
13. Asking the pupils to find the answers to questions like the following through using the dictionary: "Are the American robin and the European robin alike?"
14. Having the pupils make a composite list of sentences illustrating all the meanings of a word of that they can think or that they can find in a dictionary, for example, "I can *run* fast" or "I have a *run* in my stocking."
15. Having the pupils explain with the help of the dictionary the meanings of words that are homonyms and then having them use the words in sentences.
16. Asking the pupils to look up the meaning of the words *prefix* and *suffix* and then asking them to learn the meaning of common prefixes and suffixes.
17. Having the pupils give words containing common prefixes and suffixes.
18. Asking the pupils to look up in the dictionary a list of words often mispronounced, like *handkerchief,* and giving them practice in pronouncing them correctly.

19. Having the pupils make their own picture dictionaries or make one as a class project.
20. Asking the pupils to look up words like the following to find out which should begin with a capital letter, whatever their use in a sentence may be: *river, history, Bible, Indian.*
21. Having the pupils find the meaning of words that are often confused— for example, *suppose* and *expect.*
22. Teaching the pupils the most frequently used rules for syllabication and having them divide words according to these rules and check their work in the dictionary.
23. Helping the children get meaning from illustrations in a dictionary by asking them questions about a picture or by having them explain how a given picture supplements the verbal explanation.
24. Drawing the attention of the pupils to aspects of an illustration that give an indication of the size of what is pictured.

Practice Exercises

The following are six samples of exercises for developing skill in using the dictionary.

1

Directions: Decide in which part of the dictionary you would look for each of the following words. Write a *B* (for Beginning) if it is found near the beginning of the dictionary. Write an *M* if it is found near the middle and an *E* if it is found near the end.

1. shoemaker _____   4. theater _____
2. memory _____   5. discovery _____
3. correct _____   6. whales _____

2

Directions: Look up in your dictionary the following list of words that are often mispronounced. On the line to the right of each write the respelling of the word with markings, including the accent, as given in the dictionary. Your teacher may give you an opportunity to pronounce some of the words to your classmates.

1. athletic _____
2. adult _____
3. handkerchief _____
4. little _____
5. often _____
6. library _____

3

Directions: To the right of each sentence write the spelling of the italicized (or underlined) word. If necessary, consult your dictionary to get the correct spelling.

1. I think that this trip was really necess___ry. _____
2. Did you *rec___ve* my message? _____
3. The boys and girls will leave in two *sep___rate* groups. _____

4

Directions: Some of the following compound words, which are here divided into syllables, should be separated by a hyphen and others should not. Consult your dictionary before you write the words correctly on the lines left for the purpose. Study the spelling of the words so that you can write them if your teacher dictates them to you.

1. an y bod y _____
2. green house _____
3. out of date _____
4. sis ter in law _____
5. shell fish _____
6. steam ship _____
7. two edged _____
8. ex pres i dent _____

5

Directions: Here are some of the meanings and illustrations given for the word *way* in a dictionary.[2] (1) Road, or any passage: *The way was muddy after the rain.* (2) Route (from one place to another): *the way to Boston; the way home.* (3) Direction: *Everyone face this way!* (4) Distance: *She lives a long way from here.* (5) Away; far: *to be way behind in a race.* (6) Room; space for action: *Make way for the parade.* (7) Progress; advance; headway: *We pushed our way through the crowd. He made his way to business.* (8) Manner: *The child has winning ways.* (9) Means or method: *Sailors know many ways of tying a knot.* (10) Habit; customary manner: *The ways of another country are different from our own.* (11) Wish; desire; will: *Little Cyril's mother always lets him have his way.* (12) Characteristic; respect; feature: *In*

[2] From *The Holt Basic Dictionary of American English.* New York: Holt, Rinehart and Winston, Inc., 1966.

many ways she is like her father. (13) Condition: *The old dog is in a bad way.*

Use the word *way* in thirteen sentences of your own to show each of the thirteen meanings given above.

6

Directions: Here are some of the meanings found in a dictionary for the word *head*.[3] On the line to the left of each sentence given below write the letter appearing before the meaning of the word *head* that that word has in each of the sentences.

- a. The part of the body of man and most animals that contains the brain, mouth, eyes, ears, etc., and is located at the top of the upright body or the front of a four-legged or crawling body in ordinary motion
- b. The enlarged part of something resembling [the part of the body known as *head*]
- c. Top or upper part
- d. Front end
- e. The round, firm part of a plant
- f. Portrait
- g. Topic or little
- h. Mental ability

SENTENCES

_____ 1. Mother bought a head of lettuce.
_____ 2. Our teacher asked one of the boys to be at the head of the line.
_____ 3. Mr. Jones carved a granite head of the President.
_____ 4. The head of the hammer was securely fastened.
_____ 5. Jimmy has a good head for numbers.

7

Directions: Look up the answers to the following questions in your dictionary and answer them by writing *yes* or *no* on the line to the left of the questions. On the line to the right of each question write the page in your dictionary on which you found the answer.

_____ 1. Did the English obtain the Magna Carta from King Alfred? _____
_____ 2. Should the word *English* always begin with a capital letter? _____

[3] From *The Holt Basic Dictionary of American English.*

_____ 3. Can the word *affect* be used as a noun? _____
_____ 4. Is *gotten* a word? _____
_____ 5. Is it correct to place the accent on the second syllable in *theater*? _____

DEVELOPING SKILL IN USING REFERENCE BOOKS OTHER THAN THE DICTIONARY

Skills needed in order to locate material in reference books other than the dictionary can be developed through activities like the following:

1. Providing opportunity to use as many as possible of the following reference books: *Childcraft, Compton's Pictured Encyclopedia,* the *World Book Encyclopedia, Junior Britannica, Our Wonderful World,* the *Junior Book of Authors,* the *Index to Poetry,* the *World Almanac,* and a standard atlas.
2. Providing the pupils with a list of topics on which they are to check those that are likely to be found in an encyclopedia.
3. Having the pupils answer a list of questions, the answers to which are to be found in one or more of the reference books listed in the first item above.
4. Having the pupils give information found on one or more of the maps contained in an atlas to which they have access.
5. Asking the pupils to tell in which volume of a set of encyclopedias information on a specified topic would be likely to be given. For this purpose the information on the labels on the back of the encyclopedias should be written on the board or duplicated on paper.
6. Showing the pupils the filmstrip, "How To Use an Encyclopedia."[4]
7. Explaining the use of the index volume of a set of encyclopedias and providing the pupils with practice in using it.
8. Giving the pupils a list of questions to answer in one word or a few words after consulting an encyclopedia.

Practice Exercises

The following are three of the many types of practice exercises that can be used in order to develop skill in using reference books.

1

Directions: Find the answers to these questions in the *World Almanac.*

[4] "How To Use an Encyclopedia." New York: Popular Science Publishing Company.

1. Is the population of the village, town, or city in which you are living given in the *World Almanac*? If so, what was it according to the last edition of the *World Almanac*?
2. Where was Thomas Edison born? _____
3. What is the state flower of Minnesota? _____
4. What state leads in the production of cotton? _____
5. When was Florida admitted to the Union? _____
6. What is the state bird of Ohio? _____
7. In what building did Abraham Lincoln die? _____

2

Directions: Below each entry taken from the *Reader's Guide to Periodical Literature* are given some parts of the entry. On the lines provided explain what each means or represents.

1. *Entry:* Another spring project: birdhouse building. S. Miller. il Audubon Mag 57:94 Mr '55
   a. Another spring project: birdhouse building _____
   b. S. Miller _____
   c. il _____
   d. Audubon Mag _____
   e. 57 _____
   f. 94 _____
   g. Mr _____
   h. '55 _____
2. *Entry:* ABC's of flower arrangement. F. Hullenlocher. il Bet Hom & Gard 24: 62-5 Je; 74-7 Jl '56
   a. F. _____
   b. 62-5 _____
   c. 74-7 _____

3

Directions: Place an x on the line to the left of each of the following topics that you would expect to be found in an encyclopedia.

_____ 1. The population of your home town
_____ 2. An account of the Battle of Gettysburg
_____ 3. The early attempts at aviation
_____ 4. The spelling of the word *necessary*

DEVELOPING SKILL IN LOCATING MATERIAL IN THE LIBRARY

Some procedures effective in learning to locate material in the library are:

1. Taking the children on a trip to the library.

2. Helping the pupils draw a diagram showing the location of materials in their library.

3. Displaying and explaining to the children a chart giving the Dewey decimal system of classification if that method of classification is used in their library.

4. Asking the pupils to write a subject card, an author card, and a title card card as you give them the necessary bibliographical data on a book.

5. Asking the pupils to list the facts given in a card catalog in addition to the author and title of a book.

6. Asking the pupils to suggest subjects under which they may be able to find on a subject card references to the answer to a given question, for example, "What was travel like in the country in 1865?"

7. Having the pupils put on a skit that illustrates "do's" and "don't's" of library behavior.

8. Having a pupil act as librarian and explain to his audience the meaning and use of a call number.

9. Explaining to the boys and girls the plan of cumulation followed in the *Reader's Guide to Periodical Literature* and having them find entries on articles included in various volumes.

10. Asking the pupils to explain every part of an entry found in the *Reader's Guide to Periodical Literature.*

11. Helping the pupils make a card catalog of the books in their own room library. Guide cards should be included in the catalog and "see also" cards.

12. Having the pupils gather from reference books information needed for work on a unit in science or social studies.

13. Providing time for pupils to examine and read various magazines in the library and then to give reports on them.

Practice Exercises

Following are suggested activities for developing skill in locating material in the library.

1

Explanation: After the teacher or one or two pupils have drawn a diagram of a card catalog on a chart, the pupils could be asked questions concerning it.

QUESTIONS

1. In which drawer would you look for a book by Louisa M. Alcott?

2. In which drawer would you look for the title of another book by the author of *Doctor Doolittle?*

3. What uses can you make of a card catalog besides finding out what books are in the library?

2

Directions: Find the answer to the following questions by consulting the card catalog in your library.

1. What is the call number of the book *Heidi?* _____
2. What books written by the author of *The Singing Tree* are in your library? _____
3. What is the title and call number of a book in your library on early pioneer life? _____
4. What facts other than the title and author are given on the subject card for the book *Little Women?* _____

3

After the pupils have finished the following exercises, opportunity should be provided for their checking the correctness of their answers by consulting the card catalog.

Directions: What is a broader subject under which you might find a reference listed in your card catalog on each of the following subjects?

1. Thomas Edison _____
2. Description of Yellowstone National Park _____
3. Tennis _____
4. Recipes for cakes _____
5. The settlers of Plymouth, Massachusetts _____

4

The pupils could be given a diagram of the library they are using that shows the location of the various stacks and tables and racks where books or magazines are kept. The various positions should be numbered so that the pupils can refer to them by number. Make certain that the pupils understand the diagram.

Directions: On the diagram showing the arrangement of your library, the bookshelves and tables are numbered. Answer the following questions by writing the number of the bookshelf or table used in the diagram. If you do not know the answer to a question, study the arrangement of the library before you try to write an answer.

1. Where are the books for the very young children kept? _____
2. Where are the books on biography kept? _____
3. On what table are some of the newest books for boys and girls placed? _____
4. Where are books on American history placed? _____
5. Where are the encyclopedias for boys and girls kept? _____

FOR FURTHER STUDY

Dechant, Emerald V., *Improving the Teaching of Reading.* Englewood Cliffs, N.J.: Prentice-Hall, Inc., 1964. Chapter 12, "Developing a Meaningful Vocabulary," pp. 322–352; Chapter 13, "Advancing the Pupil's Comprehension Skills," pp. 353–402.

McKim, Margaret G., and Helen Caskey, *Guiding Growth in Reading in the Modern Elementary School.* New York: Crowell-Collier and Macmillan, Inc., 1963. Pages 363–376.

Mazurkiewicz, Albert, J. (ed.), *New Perspectives in Reading Instruction.* New York: Pitman Publishing Corporation, 1964. "How To Teach Dictionary and Index Skills," by Mary E. Coleman, pp. 425–436.

Morrison, Ida E., *Teaching Reading in the Elementary School.* New York: The Ronald Press Company, 1968. Chapter 17, "Reading for Thought in Intermediate and Upper Grades," pp. 392–434.

Perkins, Ralph, *Book Selection Media: A Descriptive Guide to 170 Aids for Selecting Library Materials.* Champaign, Ill.: National Council of Teachers of English, 1967. Pages xxiii–168.

Schubert, Delwyn G., and Theodore L. Torgerson (eds.), *Readings in Reading.* New York: Thomas Y. Crowell Company, 1968. Chapter 45, "Whose Brand of Reading Methods Is the 'Best Buy'?" pp. 307–308; Chapter 47, "Locating, Introducing and Using Easy-to-Read, High-Interest Reading Matter," pp. 316–321.

QUESTIONS FOR THOUGHT AND DISCUSSION

1. Some very useful criteria which if used by the classroom teacher can help in the matter of dictionary selection: the first of these is *scope;* the second, *reliability;* the third, *format;* and the fourth and fifth, *word treatment* and *balance.* How would you evaluate an elementary school dictionary with which you are familiar, according to these criteria?

2. How would you respond to the following quotation which appeared in a recent magazine article?

    How do we set about working with a child in such a way that he will find in the dictionary not only the spelling, the pronunciation, or the meaning of an unfamiliar word but, more important, that he will come to regard the dictionary as a source of much interesting and informative data about our language?

3. In one classroom we have thirty pupils, each of whom has his own dictionary. Down the hall in another classroom we have six or eight copies of several different dictionaries. How do you account for these two quite differing practices at the same grade level?

4. What is your position on the following controversial statement? Be able to state your case.

> Dictionary skills are an inseparable part of the language arts program in general and the reading program specifically and need not, in fact, should not, be taught in isolation.

5. Some writers have urged that we pay more attention to the concept of "dictionary readiness." They name as prerequisites such matters as readiness for locating words; readiness for deriving the meaning; readiness for pronunciation. What constitutes each of these facets of readiness?

6. When children learn how to use reference books certain problems almost inevitably arise. For example, there is the problem of children copying when gathering data in a reference work. Or there is the concern that children not use the encyclopedia until they know how to outline or write material in their own words. Imagine you are a sixth-grade teacher and you have to deal with one of these problems. How would you proceed?

7. It has been contended that comprehension is the important factor to consider when selecting encyclopedias for children. Since many children have interest levels higher than their reading ability, it is claimed that definite training in use of encyclopedias is important for helping children to absorb the information given in them. Do you agree? Be able to defend your answer.

8. In considering the role and function of the elementary school library, certain problems of terminology arise. Should the library be called an instructional materials center, a learning resource center, an educational media center, or just a library? Be able to give reasons for your preference?

9. Several questions come to mind as we are placing more emphasis on the use of the dictionary in developing better word usage. How soon can children begin to use dictionaries other than picture dictionaries? How valuable would a thesaurus be in an intermediate-grade classroom?

CHAPTER 9A

Oral Reading

Fifty years ago, reading instruction in most elementary schools was instruction in oral reading. Numerous educators had, indeed, called attention to the sterility of the exclusively oral approach. Thus Edmund B. Huey wrote in 1908:

> Reading as a school exercise has almost always been thought of as reading aloud, in spite of the obvious fact that reading in actual life is to be mainly silent reading. The consequent attention to reading as an exercise in speaking . . . has been heavily at the expense of reading as the art of thought-getting . . .[1]

In this statement he confirmed the views of earlier educational leaders such as Horace Mann and Francis W. Parker. It was not until the early 1920s, however, that a widespread shift of emphasis from oral to silent reading took place. In this period a great quantity of published materials, including a yearbook of the National Study for the Study of Education, numerous research reports, textbooks on the teaching of reading, reading manuals, and series of basal readers, stressed the need for instruction in silent reading.

The arguments in favor of silent as against oral reading were based chiefly upon two considerations: (1) Most reading outside of

[1] Edmund B. Huey, *The Psychology and Pedagogy of Reading*, p. 359. New York: The Macmillan Company, 1908.

school is silent reading and (2) silent reading emphasizes meaning rather than sound. Psychologists of many schools—behaviorist, gestalt, organismic, and others—were concerned with the ways in which communication takes place between the writer and the reader. Experimentation with various methods of teaching reading, and the rise of the tests and measurements movement, further strengthened the trend toward silent reading instruction.

THE IMPORTANCE OF ORAL READING

As teachers began to emphasize silent reading, many of them, unfortunately, began to neglect oral reading. Especially in the intermediate grades little attention was paid to oral reading. It may be true that not more than about 1 percent of out-of-school reading is oral. However, frequency of use should by no means be the sole determiner of the emphasis to be placed on the development of any ability. Such factors as the value of the skill and the relative difficulty of mastering it should also play an important part in any decision concerning what is to be included in the curriculum. Oral reading is a valuable skill, one that is not automatically learned in an effective program of silent reading instruction. Rather, in the case of a large number of boys and girls—probably the great majority of them—specific attention is required on the part of the teacher if skill in oral reading is to be acquired.

Values of Oral Reading

One important value of oral reading that is often not given due attention is that it can produce beneficial results in the social and emotional development of children. The growth in literary appreciation that can come as boys and girls read orally to each other is in itself justification for oral reading instruction. Furthermore, sympathetic relations among members of a group may often be created or strengthened by means of the oral reading experience. A boy or girl may acquire a much-needed feeling of acceptance in his group by being able to contribute a story, a joke, or an interesting fact by reading aloud from a book, a magazine, or a newspaper. Pupils who do not excel in other activities may find recognition in superior performance in oral reading. Moreover, oral reading may help them develop self-assurance and poise.

Many additional values can be achieved through oral reading. The following are some of the ways in which oral reading can help pupils

1. To communicate ideas
2. To provide enjoyment for others
3. To add to the reader's understanding of what he reads
4. To diagnose problems in silent reading
5. To increase vocabulary
6. To improve speech

Functional Situations for Oral Reading

At all times when oral reading is included in the day's program it should serve a purpose that is considered worthwhile not only by the teacher but also by the pupils. Frequently the function may be in relation to the ongoing activity of the classroom. Opportunities for purposeful oral reading are exemplified by the following activities, which are merely suggestive of many others.

1. Giving oral reports or reading stories orally, including original ones by the boys and girls, to another group, possibly within the context of a program consisting of a variety of activities.
2. Putting on a make-believe radio or television program.
3. Rereading orally short selections that have been read silently with the purpose of clarifying the meaning.
4. Reading orally to prove a point.
5. Reading orally to give one's interpretation of a selection.
6. Participating in a panel that is reading a series of short stories or one longer story in parts.
7. Giving a puppet play in which the "conversation" is read.
8. Reading reports.
9. Taking part in choral reading. (Suggestions for choral reading are given on pages 319–324.
10. Putting on a program in which a narrator reads orally the "conversation" of "characters" made by pupils through *origami* (the Japanese art of paper folding).[2]

Sometimes the main function of oral reading practice may be to increase the pupils' skill in that activity. At such times, too,

[2] Two books helpful to the teacher who wishes to learn more about origami are *All about Origami,* by Isao Honda, published by Toto Bunka Company, Tokyo, 1960; and *Folding Paper Puppets,* by Shari Lewis and Lillian Oppenheimer, published by Stein and Day, New York, 1962, but distributed by J. B. Lippincott Company, Philadelphia.

it is usually advisable that the boys and girls recognize the objective to be served by that practice. Attention might be focused on maintaining or acquiring contact with the audience, on effective phrasing, and on skillful interpretation of the mood the writer seems to wish to portray. Exercises in the form of practice in pronunciation, enunciation, and modulation of voice are also valuable for many boys and girls. Among the suggestions listed under "Instructional Practices" (page 313), are included some that provide specific practice in attaining these and other desirable skills of oral reading.

RELATION BETWEEN ORAL AND SILENT READING

Almost all the skills that are important in silent reading are also needed in effective oral reading, because in a certain sense all oral reading is preceded by silent reading. A word in print cannot be given orally unless the reader has recognized the word and by that very act has read it silently. Consequently, skill in word recognition, possession of a suitable meaning vocabulary, and the ability to comprehend what is read are essentials of both oral and silent reading. Even rate of reading is a factor in both types, because the individual who cannot read silently as rapidly as he can say the words he is reading is handicapped in his oral reading.

The effective oral reader possesses many of the silent reading skills and, in addition, many abilities peculiar to oral reading. One of these is correct pronunciation of words. In silent reading the pupil must recognize the word and know its meaning, but it is not essential that he know how to pronounce it. Clear articulation, a pleasing and well-modulated voice, and proper contact with the audience are additional concerns of the oral reader. Furthermore, in oral reading, thought getting, common to both oral and silent reading, must be followed by vocal interpretation, because it is necessary to convey to the audience the reader's grasp of the meaning of the passage. Thus oral reading, if done well, becomes a highly complex skill.

A convenient term frequently used to describe what goes on in oral reading is the "eye-voice span." The eye-voice span is the distance between the word the reader is uttering and the word on which his eyes rest at the same moment. In good oral reading the eyes run ahead of the voice. This is necessary if the reading is to be connected, fluent, and meaningful. Many children can learn to avoid "word calling" by being encouraged to let their eyes move ahead of their voices.

Oral reading, when well done, can serve as an aid to silent

reading in many ways, some of which are illustrated later in this chapter and in the B chapter that follows. Oral reading, for example, helps in the diagnosis of difficulties in silent reading. As a pupil reads a selection orally, the teacher can frequently detect the types of errors that keep the pupil from reading well silently. Difficulties such as the following, common to both oral and silent reading, often are revealed: omission of words or phrases; insertion of words or phrases; substitution of letters, words, or phrases; skipping lines; repeating lines; and phrasing so inadequately that it interferes with thought getting and interpretation.

Learning to read well orally, then, is more difficult than learning to read well silently. Not only must the oral reader have a good grasp of the meaning of the material he reads but he must have many abilities besides. He needs not only, as in silent reading, to get the thought but he must also interpret or convey it to his listeners. He must know his listeners—their interests and probable attitudes toward the material read as well as their capacity to understand it—and he must be sensitive to their reactions as he reads to them. He must be fluent enough to focus his mind on the thought rather than the recognition and pronunciation of individual words. He must reproduce in his reading the mood and intention of the author, recognizing irony or pathos, happiness or depression, excitement or pensiveness. To accomplish his purpose he must know how to use pauses effectively. He must have skill in using his voice. He must be free of mannerisms that might detract attention from the message he brings. He must make a poised appearance.

It is important that the person who is to read orally to a group be given, as a rule, the opportunity to read the material silently before he reads it to others. Silent reading preceding oral reading is desirable in order that the reader be given the opportunity in his first reading to solve problems of word recognition and pronunciation that he may have. Furthermore, the reader will be likely to interpret the meaning of the writer more accurately if he has the chance to get the meaning himself before he is confronted with the task of interpreting. In oral reading the reader is in the limelight in a social situation, and he may become uncomfortable unless he has the security of knowing the material he is to present to his audience. Even the adult reader usually likes to read beforehand that which he is to read to others, whether the material consists of minutes of a meeting written by someone else, a story from a magazine, or an article from the newspaper. However, there is also a legitimate place for sight reading.

The term *sight reading* is here used to refer to oral reading when the reader has not previously read the material either silently or orally, that is, when he reads at first sight. As indicated in the preceding paragraph, such procedure is usually undesirable for the reasons given. However, it can be used advisedly at times, for example, when the teacher is the only listener. The purpose in having a pupil read to the teacher might be diagnostic. Through hearing the child read orally material that he has not previously read, the alert teacher can detect problems that cannot be isolated through tests on the child's silent reading, such as reversals of letters or words, omission of letters or words, or repeating lines. Sight reading, too, can be justified in a small group if the pupils are intent on helping one another practice reading stories or other material that they later will read to another group of boys and girls or to visitors.

Occasionally, too, sight reading may be justified for still another purpose. The boys and girls may be reading orally without previous practice in silent reading in order to have practice in sight reading in an audience situation. The teacher may want to explain to the pupils that sometimes people do get called on to read something orally without having had the opportunity to read it beforehand. It can be made clear to the boys and girls that practice in sight reading may help them to feel at ease if sometime someone asks them to read orally without their having the chance to precede the oral reading by silent reading. It is important when pupils do sight reading in front of their peers that an atmosphere of understanding and good will permeate the situation.

A child required to read by sight to an audience, unless the situation is one that is well controlled to eliminate problems, is in a precarious position. In an atmosphere lacking in good will and mutual understanding, he may become frustrated and otherwise emotionally upset to the extent that he develops a dislike for reading. Such an attitude may result in serious reading retardation.

ORAL READING IN THE INITIAL STAGE
OF READING INSTRUCTION

The role of oral reading in the early phases of learning to read has been and continues to be a point of argument. The debate, however, no longer centers on whether there should be any oral reading at that time. Nor does it turn on the question of whether there should be silent reading in the first grade. The issue is primarily how oral reading, as part of the developmental program of the first grade, should be conducted.

It is poor practice during the initial period of reading instruction to have children read a selection orally before they have read it silently. Sight reading should not be done in the first grade in an audience situation and it should be done only sparingly, if at all, when the pupil reads only to the teacher. Before a pupil is asked to do sight reading to an audience he should have developed basic reading skills to the extent that he will not, with easy material, be bothered by problems of word recognition or of comprehension of what he might be called upon to read to a group. If he lacks such skills, he will have difficulty in interpreting the written message to an audience, and when required to perform this task in front of others, the pupil may suffer emotionally. The needed proficiency in the fundamental skills of reading is seldom acquired in the first grade.

There are further reasons why a pupil in the initial stage of reading instruction should not be asked to read material to an audience if he has not had the opportunity to read it silently beforehand. In fact, this argument also gives the reason for not requiring the child to do sight reading even when only the teacher is the audience. When the beginning reader reads orally material he has not previously read silently, he may read it word by word and thus develop into a person who habitually reads in that manner. It is also argued that he may establish the habit of reading orally without expression even if he ceases later to be a word-by-word reader.

Another argument against sight reading in the early primary grades has to do with the effect of this type of reading upon the audience. When the material is read haltingly, as the immature reader is likely to do if his oral reading has not been preceded by silent reading, the interest of the audience will be low. In fact, the listeners will frequently be bored. Anything that may cause lack of interest in any phase of reading during the initial period of reading instruction should indeed be eyed with serious misgivings. The gravity of the situation will be obvious as one recalls that one of the main objectives of beginning reading instruction is to interest boys and girls in reading.

Another undesirable practice followed in many first grades is that of having the pupils read around the class orally while the rest of the boys and girls are supposedly following in their books. The word *supposedly* is well included in the preceding sentence. Often a pupil has his book upside down while presumably reading silently or is on a different page than the person reading orally. Frequently, too, a child who has a paper marker for keeping his place has the marker under the wrong line of print. Furthermore, even when the boys and girls have read the selection silently beforehand, if considerable time has elapsed between the silent reading and the oral reading, the reading is likely to be done in a halting manner. Such reading is harmful to the oral reader and uninteresting to the pupils reading silently. Moreover, when a pupil reads orally to others who are reading silently, incentive for interpretation of the written message by the oral reader is not likely to be strong. Also, the members of the audience are in danger of getting practice in half listening and half reading, since they lack incentive for both effective listening and significant reading. It should be noted that when boys and girls are asked to read silently while someone is reading orally to them after they have learned to read more rapidly silently than orally, even greater harm is likely to be done to them than earlier. When the learner has reached that stage, which is frequently reached during the second half of the second grade, there is danger that his silent reading will be reduced to the speed of his oral reading.

There is, however, an important place for oral reading in the first grade. It has been pointed out that probably many boys and girls in the first grade do not get the feeling that they are reading unless they are reading orally. At a stage in reading instruction when attitudes concerning reading are of the greatest significance, to deprive the child of the opportunity to do oral reading may prove disastrous as far as his future success in reading is concerned. It may even affect adversely his personality development when the importance of reading is emphasized as much as it usually and rightly is in the typical first-grade room.

How then does oral reading fit into the beginning reading program? Here are a few suggestions.

1. The boys and girls can read silently in short segments the story in a basal reader. For example, in the beginning days of reading instruction, possibly when the pupils are reading preprimers or primers, the teacher may ask them to read only one sentence at a time silently. She may ask them, for example, to read the next sentence silently to find out what Tom then said to his mother. Thereupon she may ask a pupil to read the sentence as he thinks Tom said it. To be sure, every sentence that is read silently should not be read orally. At times the teacher may ask questions about what was read. At other times she may ask the boys and girls to point to a word or words she names. At still other times the pupils might discuss what

they have just read. Or they might predict what they think will happen next.

2. Reading a selection by parts is also, after previous silent reading of the selection, good reason for oral reading. It is advisable that the pupils to whom parts have been given have the opportunity to reread the material silently after the assignment of lines has been made.

3. Even in first grade, occasionally one or more pupils might read to the class material the group has not read. The persons doing the reading should practice beforehand both silently and orally the material they will read. The teacher can do much to make such reading a real occasion, a program for the listeners.

4. Oral reading at home by the pupils should be encouraged. For suggestions as to how parents can help in the oral reading program, the reader is referred to page 312.

PROPORTION OF TIME FOR ORAL AND SILENT READING

What should be the proportion of oral to silent reading? To this question a precise answer cannot be given for each grade, for the apportionment depends upon a variety of factors. One of these is the length of the reading period in schools that set aside time daily for reading instruction. There is wide variation in the same grades in various schools, and often there are differences within the same building if there is more than one room of the same grade. Moreover, even when the reading periods in the two rooms of the same grade are of equal length, the time spent in oral reading may vary greatly. In one room more time may be spent in silent reading during study periods than in the other. Furthermore, the amount of oral and silent reading done during other class periods, such as social studies or science, will influence the question of the proportion of time to be devoted to each. Reading at home, too, will affect the division of the reading period between the two types of reading. Factors like individual differences among children, their past training, the methods used by the teacher, and her skill in teaching reading will also need to be considered.

In the first grade and in the first part of the second grade, when most children cannot read more rapidly silently than orally, oral reading will not ordinarily affect the rate of silent reading unfavorably. However, even in beginning reading an undue amount of vocalization in silent reading may result from overemphasis on oral reading.

Oral reading in the lower grades is abundantly justified by the extreme pleasure that many children experience when they read to others or listen to others read to them. Although oral reading exercises can prove boring to all concerned, most children look forward to the opportunity to read aloud to the teacher or classmates when there is an atmosphere of approval. It would seem unwise to deprive children of a satisfying experience that strengthens the desire to learn to read. Every avenue to genuine reading interest should be utilized.

A teacher may ask a child to read aloud to her in order to learn the child's specific needs in reading. Children may read aloud to each other to share a pleasurable reading experience or to pass on desired information. Group drills in oral reading, however, with all members of the group following on the page, should generally be avoided.

APPRAISING SKILL IN ORAL READING

Before the teacher attempts to appraise the oral reading skill of her pupils, she will advisedly have in mind the characteristics of the efficient oral reader.

Characteristics of the Effective Oral Reader

The teacher who undertakes to evaluate children's growth in oral reading skill will look for such familiar signs as these:

1. The pupil recognizes the common words at sight.
2. He pronounces the words correctly.
3. He shows that he knows the meaning not only of the words but of the entire selection.
4. He uses variety and appropriateness of tone, pitch, force, and speed.
5. He enunciates clearly.
6. He appears at ease while he reads.
7. He is free from interfering mannerisms.
8. He is responsive to the reactions of the audience.
9. He exhibits interest and enthusiasm when he reads.
10. He gives his own interpretation of the selection through his oral reading.
11. His posture is erect and dignified without being overformal.
12. He handles his book effectively.

Comprehension is, of course, a primary requisite to efficient oral reading. As explained earlier in this chapter, this fact constitutes one important reason why pupils should not ordinarily be encouraged to read a passage aloud until they have first read it silently and understand it. Good phrasing, effective expression, and appropriate emphasis all depend upon the reader's grasp of the meaning. It is sometimes possible for a skillful reader to read orally without giving full attention to the content, but for most children good comprehension is a first requirement for accurate, intelligible oral reading. Meaning will determine the correct selection of word accents, the sound values of letters, and the intonation appropriate to the purpose of the writer.

The physical behavior of the oral reader, while distinctly secondary to the problem of comprehension, requires some attention on the part of the teacher. Formal restrictions that were once imposed with respect to the position of the feet and hands are no longer observed. Children are encouraged to stand erect, to assume a natural, relaxed position, and to avoid leaning against a desk, table, or chair. The book or magazine should not shield the face of the reader. Ideally, contact with the audience is maintained by frequent upward glances toward the listeners, but such contact is the result of a feeling of ease and an eagerness to communicate rather than conscious effort or deliberate drill.

It is recommended that the pupils know what traits are considered important for effective oral reading. In the intermediate grades and probably even in the upper primary, the boys and girls can take part in drawing up a checklist of the qualities of a good oral reader. These points may be recorded on a chart. If there is not enough display space in a classroom to keep the chart up all the time, it could be stored until it is to be used, namely, when the pupils are reading orally or are preparing for oral reading.

The points to be included in a checklist for use by the boys and girls will necessarily vary from grade to grade. In the lower grades a brief listing couched in simple language will be all that is desirable. In the intermediate grades the list of items may be similar to the one recorded on the sample on page 329.

Checking the Oral Reading

Informal observation of a pupil's performance in the oral reading situation, especially with the aid of a checklist, is one of the best methods of evaluating growth in the skills peculiar to oral reading. Defects such as bad posture, finger pointing, and poor intonation are easily noted by the alert teacher who is interested in improving the oral reading performance of her pupils. A record may be kept of the diagnosis, in a manner similar to that suggested on page 329. Boys and girls, too, can participate in the appraisals made. It is recommended that the suggestions for improvement given in class be leveled not at any one individual but that they serve as points for consideration by all the pupils who have read orally on a given day.

Mention is frequently made of standardized oral reading tests. Such tests, however, are in reality devices to determine a pupil's skill in silent reading. They are valuable in revealing to the teacher the specific difficulties that a pupil encounters when dealing with words and sentences. Valuable data can be obtained for use in diagnosis of reading problems from reading tests such as the following, though these tests do not measure the specific skills of *oral* reading: (1) the Gray Oral Reading Check Tests (Bobbs-Merrill Company); (2) the Gates Oral Reading Test (Bureau of Publications, Teachers College, Columbia University); (3) the Durrell Oral Reading Test (Harcourt, Brace & World); (4) the Jenkins Oral Reading Test (The C. A. Gregory Company); and (5) the oral sections of the Diagnostic Reading Tests (Committee on Diagnostic Reading Tests). These tests measure points such as reversals of letters and words, substitution of letters or words, omissions, and inadequate return sweeps of the eye to the succeeding line of reading. For an indication of the pupil's skill in reference to points peculiar to oral reading such as phrasing, expressiveness, and reaction to the audience, the teacher must rely on her own careful observation of pupil performance and such cumulative anecdotal records as she may find time to keep.

CAUSES OF DEFICIENCIES IN ORAL READING

Reference was made earlier in this chapter to some of the manifestations of pupil difficulties in oral reading. These overt signs of trouble, such as omission of words, reading at too rapid a rate for effective interpretation, or nervousness while reading, are often indexes of underlying problems. Among the factors that frequently contribute adversely to oral reading are: (1) an undesirable audience situation; (2) unsuitable material; (3) lack of skill in some abilities important in silent reading, such as skill in recognizing words and power of understanding what is read; (4) need of specific help in development of skills peculiar to oral reading, such as desirable posture, correct handling of the book, or effectiveness of interpretation; and (5) insufficient preparation for the reading of a given selection.

GENERAL SUGGESTIONS FOR THE IMPROVEMENT OF ORAL READING

Chapter 9B presents specific suggestions for procedures planned to help boys and girls become better oral readers. In this section of the present chapter are listed and discussed some general recommendations on which the details of procedure can be based. The discussion that follows includes suggestions for alleviating the causes of deficiencies in oral reading which are listed in the preceding section.

1. *Children should be given many opportunities to do oral reading and they should be encouraged to make use of these opportunities.* The fact that apparently it is possible for children to learn to read for meaning without oral reading experiences in the classroom does not justify depriving them of the chance to engage in oral reading. Children's motives for oral reading, on which the teacher can build, are of many kinds. The boys and girls may read aloud to the teacher to show their progress in mastering the printed page; they may do so to share a poem or a story with other children; they may read orally to prove a point or to raise a question. They may engage in additional activities of the type suggested on pages 313–315.

2. *The skills of oral reading can be improved through instruction.* Successful experiences in oral reading will give needed self-confidence to the shy child. Approval by teacher and class will help him to take further, perhaps timid, steps toward self-assured oral reading. Teachers can help boys and girls to overcome monotony of rate or pitch and to read literary materials aloud with feeling and animation.

3. *Most instruction in oral reading is preferably incidental.* There is a proper place for formal exercises in oral reading in rehearsal for assembly programs or for special events in the classroom, but throughout the year the instruction is likely to consist of helpful suggestions as the child undertakes to communicate with his classmates from the printed page. Such suggestions are, of course, always made in such a way as not to embarrass the reader. Usually they are made privately. They should always be given along with praise for those good qualities the child displays.

4. *The teacher's example can be a model for the oral reading of the boys and girls.* Not all teachers are skillful oral readers, but all can learn to read aloud with good enunciation, appropriate volume and emphasis, and an interesting variety of pitch and rate. Teachers in all grades should cultivate this ability.

5. *Ordinarily the pupils should be encouraged to listen to the reader without following him in their own books.* Reasons for this generalization were given earlier in this chapter.

6. *Children should have access to a wide variety of suitable materials for oral reading.* Such materials should be easy and interesting and often include dialogue. They should include stories and poems, both published materials and the children's own work. Stories or articles cut out of discarded books and magazines make excellent material for oral reading. On special occasions, such as holidays or the birthdays of famous persons, stories about the exploits of national heroes and the meaning of the holidays may be used. Humorous anecdotes are especially suitable for oral reading.

7. *Oral reading should take place only when there is a receptive audience.* The reader must be eager to communicate, and the audience must be eager to listen. Until such conditions exist, it would be better to postpone the oral reading. Adverse criticism by members of the audience should usually not be directed against one individual reader but should be stated as applicable to some or all of the group. Occasional favorable comment on specifics by the teacher is desirable, and certainly suggestions given privately by the teacher are in order.

8. *The cooperation of the parents should be enlisted whenever possible.* Although parents should not be expected to help teach the skills of oral reading, they can encourage children to read aloud to them and to other children in the home. Such experiences effectively supplement the limited opportunities the school can provide for oral reading. At meetings of the Parent Teacher Association teachers might well suggest ways in which parents can help with reading, oral reading included. At these meetings suggestions can be given as to what standards in oral reading should be expected from the boys and girls. Recommendations for a program of home reading, where the parent reads to the child and the child to the parent, can also profitably be given. Since problems in reading differ from grade to grade, home room meetings of the PTA are especially suitable for group conferences with parents about how they can be of help. Brief bulletins to parents, too, about their possible role in the program of oral reading can be of value.

CHAPTER 9B

---

*Developing Skill
in Oral Reading*

In order that the child may learn to interpret the written page effectively to others, he should be given abundant opportunity to read aloud meaningful materials. Providing the boys and girls with this opportunity is one of the most important ways in which the teacher can help them become skillful oral readers. However, although experience in reading in purposeful situations is basic, some direct instruction is also usually valuable and at times necessary.

INSTRUCTIONAL PRACTICES

Following are some illustrative teaching practices which may prove helpful as direct instruction in oral reading.

1. Stressing the importance of correct pronunciation through class discussion and comments by the teacher.
2. Requiring pupils to check pronunciation before reading orally, and giving them help when necessary.
3. Teaching the interpretation of diacritical marks in the dictionary.
4. Stressing the importance of clear enunciation.
5. Practicing the enunciation of words in which the endings *ing, ed,* and *t* are often slurred.
6. Teaching pupils to note the number of syllables in a word, using a dictionary if necessary.
7. Having pupils divide assigned words into syllables.

8. Using rhyme to illustrate correct pronunciation, as: *"Just rhymes* with *must,* not with *best!"*
9. Having pupils make a list of words they habitually enunciate poorly.
10. Listening to records to note examples of excellent enunciation.
11. Having pupils make tape recordings of their voices to note the quality of enunciation.
12. Having pupils listen to the teacher read a sentence with good phrasing and say it back to her. (This should, as a rule, be done individually, with different sentences.)
13. Contrasting good and poor phrasing in the reading of a sentence.
14. Exposing for very short duration phrases to be read orally.
15. Having pupils read passages silently to note proper places for pausing and then read them orally.
16. Teaching the use of punctuation marks in determining where the pauses should come.
17. Reading orally a selection without pausing for punctuation marks and asking the class to supply them where they are needed.
18. Having pupils look for answers through silent reading of a passage and then read the appropriate parts aloud.
19. Having pupils summarize a selection after reading it aloud.
20. Preparing in advance questions to be answered by the pupil after reading orally.
21. Explaining to the pupils the role of the reader as interpreter.
22. Explaining some of the rules of good interpretation, such as (a) reading a selection beforehand, (b) making certain that one understands what is to be read, and (c) reading with expression.
23. Choosing materials that pupils will be able to interpret adequately.
24. Emphasizing the importance of having a clear purpose for the oral reading.
25. Helping pupils overcome individual mannerisms that draw attention away from the message.
26. Providing pupils for oral reading with sentences that express strong emotions, such as love, fear, sadness, surprise, anxiety.
27. Demonstrating to the class the need for variety of tone, pitch, and rate in oral reading, by contrasting monotonous with varied expression.
28. Demonstrating and having pupils practice the use of different types of tone, pitch, and rate with different materials.
29. Giving practice in expressing different moods through changes in voice qualities.
30. Having pupils listen to speakers who use their voices effectively.
31. Having pupils find the words in a sentence that are especially significant in the context and then read the sentence to emphasize the important words.
32. Arranging for pupils to read in concert with others, as in choral reading.
33. Having the class formulate standards for good oral reading, including ways of holding a book or magazine.

34. Making and encouraging the pupils to help make displays that will emphasize points to observe in oral reading.
35. Getting class participation in deciding upon appropriate times and materials for oral reading.
36. Listening to pupils, individually, read for diagnostic purposes.
37. Having pupils reread a short selection orally as an aid to comprehension.
38. Discussing with a class what a reader can do to make it easy for an audience not to be restless.
39. Encouraging pupils to prepare a sketch in which varying inflections are used to say the same expression in order to produce different meanings. For example, the sentence, "What a day!" could be given so as to express more than one reaction to the day.
40. Helping the class draw up standards for oral reading of the minutes of a club meeting.

ORAL READING BY THE TEACHER

Some persons insist that a day should never pass during which the elementary school teacher does not read something orally to the class. While this may be an extreme view, certainly frequent oral reading by the teacher is highly desirable. By means of such reading, pupils can be acquainted with literature of genuine worth that is too difficult for them to read by themselves. Moreover, the teacher is able by this means to set standards of performance to which the pupils can aspire.

Naturally, not all teachers are equally skillful in oral reading. For many, it is desirable to precede the reading with careful preparation through prior silent reading of the selections, or even rehearsal of the oral reading activity itself. Such preparation includes also a careful consideration of the material to be used. Stories read to children should be of high quality but on the level of the children. They should be of the kind that lend themselves to oral reading. For younger children, especially, stories with much conversation in them are likely to have the greatest appeal. In addition to fiction, the reading material may include selections from poetry, social studies, current events, and even science.

A procedure that the intermediate-grade teacher may find valuable is one in which the boys and girls alternate with her in reading a rather lengthy story, possibly an entire book. Fifteen or twenty minutes daily might be spent thus. The pupil or pupils whose turn it is to read orally on a given day should beforehand have practiced carefully reading orally the part of the selection assigned to them. Often it is advisable in reading of this type that the teacher serve as reader most of the time in order that the interest of the audience will not be lost.

Teachers sometimes ask, "When and how should the pictures be shown when a book is read to the class?" The answer must, of course, depend upon the circumstances. Many picture-story books are poorly adapted to reading to a group. Such books are more suitable for individual reading or reading shared by two or three children. Most of the modern picture books for young children have more illustrations than text; indeed, the central message is in the pictures while the text is only commentary. In such cases, it is best to have the pupils grouped as closely as possible around the teacher. The teacher reads the text material on a page and holds up the book to show the picture, turning it in all directions so that everyone may see. The children should have time to see and enjoy each scene as the story progresses. To help the pupils' observation, the teacher may at times decide to point out details in some of the pictures as the story goes along. If the class is too large for convenient showing of the pictures to all pupils, the story should be read to children in smaller groups. No child should be made to feel neglected because he was unable to see the pictures. And, of course, after the reading, the book should be added to the room collection, where individual pupils can reexamine it at leisure.

ORAL READING BY CHILDREN IN SMALL GROUPS

In both primary and intermediate grades, the children can be divided into small groups of three or four or five who will meet in various parts of the room to read orally to one another. If this procedure can be carried out effectively in a room, much of the problem of finding time for everyone to get as much practice in oral reading as is desirable can be solved. Care must be taken that the material read is very easy and very interesting. Furthermore, in each group there should be at least one person who can serve as chairman and help the others with words they cannot recognize. So that an orderliness conducive to work prevails, it is usually necessary to work out rules of procedure for the group reading, designating such points as order of reading, responsibilities of the chairman, responsibilities of the reader, and duties of the listeners. If possible, there should be a rotating chairmanship, but no child who is unable to perform the duties of a chairman should be appointed to the post. The teacher can spend her time going from group to group, observing points that she may wish to bring up at a later time so as to provide for improvement in routine. This plan works only when pupils can read fairly well the material they have and when the teacher is able to maintain the desired orderliness even when she is not at all times in direct contact with each group.

Practice in reading in small groups can be especially valuable when the various groups read in order later on to give information to the rest of the class on a problem that the class is studying. At times the boys and girls as they are working in small groups might be practicing reading selections, possibly stories in a basal reading textbook, that later on they will want to read at home to their parents.

Miss Marguerite Goens, formerly first-grade teacher in Indianapolis, worked out an excellent plan for small-group reading through the help of the third grade in her building. In this cooperating third grade several of the best readers went to the first-grade room twice a week for twenty minutes to take charge of oral reading groups consisting of three or four pupils each. While the assistants were working with the children, the room teacher circulated from group to group giving needed assistance. In order to make certain that the reading material was of worth and on the level of the readers and that it fulfilled the requirements for oral presentation, everything that was to be read, including material that pupils brought to school, had to be approved by the teacher before it was read orally. The group work did not take the place of the developmental reading classes, but it did serve as a very vital adjunct to it.

READING POETRY ORALLY

One of the neglected areas of oral reading in many schools is that of poetry reading by the boys and girls. It is an art so filled with rich opportunities for developing appreciation that much more emphasis should be placed upon it than is commonly the case. Unfortunately, when poetry is read orally, it is often done so poorly that the results actually interfere with its enjoyment.

As a rule, the child who does the reading should be well prepared. There are occasions when the boys and girls might read, without preparation beforehand, in order to be given specific help in reading poetry more effectively. But when the aim of the teacher is to have the audience get enjoyment from the reading, the pupils should be able to read the poetry so as to arouse appreciation in their listeners. At all such times the pupil should practice reading his poem orally before he appears in front of his audience. If possible, the teacher should help him while he is practicing. She can do so by assisting the reader to get the meaning of the poem through questioning, through comments, and through reading orally part or all of the poem herself. All the other elements essential to effective oral reading of prose, such as skill in word recognition and handling the book with facility, are also requirements for reading poetry. Because pupils are more accustomed to prose than poetry and because difficulties in interpretation of poetry are often greater than those in interpretation of prose, to achieve as good results when reading poetry as when reading prose is difficult for many boys and girls. The child must have a feeling of confidence and poise as he comes in front of his audience, a becoming self-assurance that results from knowledge of being well prepared and having a worthwhile contribution to make. Some pitfalls in reading poetry that the teacher must try to help the child avoid are "sing-song" reading, lack of discrimination between commas that represent grammatical structure and those that represent rhetorical phrasing, and overdramatic reading.

The poetry should be well selected. Even for young children there is much poetry of superior quality. An examination of the excellent anthologies of literature for children will suggest many poems and will give the names of poets whose work, other than that quoted in the anthology, is worth investigating. At times the teacher may choose the poems to be read, but no pupil should be forced to read a poem that he himself does not enjoy or one that he does not want to read to the group. When a girl or boy has a voice in choosing the poem, however, the selection should not be left entirely up to him. The teacher is responsible for seeing that no poem chosen is of poor quality. Furthermore, in the choice of poems the ability of the reader to interpret and of the audience to enjoy must be considered.

The reading of poetry should be done in a suitable setting. Sometimes the teacher will need to help create the mood needed for enjoyment even before the pupil begins reading. The teacher can at times do this by means of questions or discussion. For example, before a child reads the poem "The Swing" by Robert Louis Stevenson, the teacher may give the audience a chance to tell whether they like to be up in a swing and how they feel when they are swinging. At other times a picture may help the children get into the right mood for a poem. Before a pupil reads orally "The Duel" by Eugene Field, a picture of a gingham dog and a calico cat, with a discussion as to how the two look at each other, may get the pupils interested in finding out how the gingham dog and the calico cat in the poem got along. Printed pictures that express the mood of the poem well are sometimes available. At other times the reader may wish to draw beforehand a picture that he thinks will help the audience want to hear his poem. Interest in the poem may be aroused by posting the picture on a bulletin board even as long as a few days before the poem will be read. A question written near the picture, such as, "What is happening in this picture?" might arouse curiosity.

The audience should often have more access to a poem than is afforded by one reading. The poems that are read orally may be posted on a bulletin board so that everyone can read them. Or they may be put into a booklet placed on the literary table, easily accessible to all the children. Oral rereading of the poem by the person who had prepared it is often effective. When a series of poems has been read, the pupils may be asked to specify a few that they would like particularly to hear again.

CHORAL READING

Choral reading, in its simplest terms, can be defined as the speaking of poetry or prose by several or many voices either in unison or by parts, as solos or as group work.

Values of Choral Reading

Many values may be found in choral reading at its best. One of these is the beneficial effect it can have on personality development. The shy child becomes more self-confident when he can quite inconspicuously, in group work, get the assurance that comes from knowledge of a contribution to a shared undertaking. Similarly the "show-off," even in solo parts, can learn to submerge himself for the good of the group and find satisfaction in so doing. Another value that can result from choral reading is an understanding and appreciation of poetry and poetic prose. This, obviously, can be expected only if literature of enduring quality is used for choral reading purposes.

A third value is the beneficial effect choral reading can have on the speech and the oral reading of the child. The emphasis placed in choral reading upon voice quality, interpretation of meaning, enunciation, and articulation can affect oral reading favorably. Furthermore, the poise and self-assurance that it aims to develop, and under favorable conditions achieves, are essentials of effective oral reading of any type.

It is not the purpose of this chapter to give a comprehensive treatment of how to teach choral reading. The description that is given, as well as the suggestions for teaching it that are included, will serve chiefly to help make clear the relation between choral reading and other oral reading.

Background for Choral Reading

Before the teacher begins choral reading with her class, whether she teaches in the primary or intermediate grades, it is advisable that she ascertain whether or not the boys and girls have been introduced to a variety of worthwhile poems. If the field of their appreciation of poetry is narrow, her first step should probably be reading or—better yet—saying poems to the class. As she repeats a poem, the pupils may wish to join her on whatever lines or parts of lines they remember. At other times she may want to precede the reading of a poem by giving a brief background for the poem, to set the mood for it or to provide valuable information that will add to the appreciation of the poem. She may accomplish this purpose by comments she makes or by class discussion. After reading a poem or saying it to the class, if the boys and girls are able to read it, they might read it orally with her. Help can be given with the rhythm of the poem so that it adds to the words, not detracts from them through sing-song. To some poems children could beat time or walk or run or skip as the poem suggests. Music that harmonizes with the theme of a poem could be played. Pictures in the room suggesting the mood of some poems, books of poetry in which the illustrations add to the significance of the words, flowers or other objects of beauty through the sight of which the pupils may catch the spirit of a poem could be used to help interest boys and girls in good poetry. Flannel boards and bulletin boards can serve as means of displaying illustrations of some favorite poems. A poetry corner in the classroom may serve as further motivation. In the upper primary and in the intermediate grades the pupils might bring to school poems that they find particularly enjoyable. In one class every boy and girl selected a favorite poem, which the teacher typed and then combined into a class booklet. The table of contents gave not only the title of the poem but also the name of the person who selected it. Enthusiasm for reading the booklet ran high, partly because the boys and girls wanted to read the choices of their classmates.

To succeed in laying a suitable background for the appreciation of poetry, the spirit of the classroom must be one in which thoughts of poetry are encouraged. It must be one in which creativeness and imaginativeness have a place. It must be one in which teachers and pupils work together cooperatively, one in which, to paraphrase Samuel Crothers in his book *The Gentle Reader,* the birthright of imagination is not sacrificed for a mess of knowledge.

For further suggestions on reading poetry orally the reader is referred to the section of this chapter entitled "Reading Poetry Orally."

Grouping for Choral Reading

While a background for choral reading is being laid, it is usually advisable with beginners in the art to have the pupils attain some skill in saying poems in concert before any attempt is made at grouping for choral reading. It is wise at that time for the teacher to take note of the characteristics of the voices of the various individuals as she hears them talk or read—usually, if not always, without the boys and girls being conscious of the fact that she is testing for grouping. Since the simplest grouping is a two-part division of voices, into the high and the low, the teacher will want to note mentally which voices belong in each group. Sometimes she may also employ a more direct method as she tests voices by having the pupils repeat a sentence or sing a tune or count to ten. She may wish to enlist the help of the boys and girls in doing the grouping. After the pupils have had some practice in two-group speaking, the teacher may wish to organize a third group, including in it the pupils whose voices are on the borderline between high and low.

Care must be taken when grouping that no misunderstandings result. Some girls may be inclined, unless caution is exercised, to think that it borders the disgraceful to have a low voice and be in a group with many of the boys. The teacher should point out that in the elementary school in two-part grouping there are usually some boys and some girls in each of the groups. She could also point out that the blend of the voices of both boys and girls in each division contributes much to choral reading, as it does to singing. It should be made clear that the grouping done before much time has been spent on choral reading is subject to change later. Reasons for change may be that the child's voice has changed or that the testing situation produced inaccurate results. The need for more pupils in one of the groups with different poems may also result in reassignment of groups. It is important that a pupil be happy in the group to which he has been assigned. Better that the reading of a poem be poor than that one child be made unhappy by his role in an activity that should bring joy to all participants!

Casting

After grouping comes casting. By casting a poem is meant dividing the lines of a poem or prose selection into parts and assigning these parts to individuals or groups of individuals.

It should probably be pointed out that a poem can be read in unison for choral reading, with high and low or with high, intermediate, and low voices saying the same lines. Such reading is more difficult than that in which the several groups speak different lines. Reading in unison as choral reading is not to be confused with concert reading in which there is no division into types of voices. Because of the difficulty of effective reading in unison, that type of choral reading is usually not attempted in the elementary school, although, of course, all boys and girls saying the same lines without grouping of voices is common practice.

There are several types of casting commonly used in the elementary schools. The reading may be done in a solo-chorus combination, as, for example, when the teacher or other leader reads alone all parts excepting the chorus parts, in which the entire class participates. The dialogue type of choral reading can be done either by two individuals who take the parts or by two choruses saying alternate lines or groups of lines. The line-a-child casting differs from the dialogues by two persons in that lines are assigned to three or more individuals. Similarly, line-a-choir reading differs from dialogues participated in by two choruses in that three or more groups say the lines. The use of various combinations of these types in reading a single long selection makes possible considerable variation of pattern of reading. Which type should be used will be determined in part by the ability of the group, the selection itself, and the objectives to be accomplished. Frequently the children, under the guidance of the teacher, should have a voice in deciding upon the type of casting to be done and the assignment of parts.

Selection of Material

The final responsibility for selecting material for choral reading lies with the teacher. While it is desirable that boys and girls, especially those somewhat experienced in choral reading, be encouraged to help in the choice, it should be clear to them that their recommendations will not necessarily be accepted. The teacher will not want to subject the class to poorly chosen verse or prose for choral reading because one or more pupils suggested it.

There are certain standards that should be observed in the selection of material. If the boys and girls participate in the selection, standards should be applied by them, too. However, in a pupils' checklist the wording might be different from that in a list such as the following, which is prepared for the teacher. These points should be noted about a poem to be used for choral reading.

1. The poem should have literary value.
2. It should be on the pupils' level of understanding.
3. It should be one the boys and girls will enjoy.
4. It should be one that the teacher will enjoy teaching.
5. It should have rhythm.
6. It should fill a need of the class.
7. It should be adaptable to choral reading of the type that the boys and girls are capable of doing.

Books containing poems chosen for their suitability for choral reading, with suggestions for casting, can be of value to both teachers and pupils. Some such books are *Choral Speaking Arrangements for the Lower Grades* by Louise Abney and Grace Bowe (The Expression Company), *Verse Choir in the Elementary School* by Clifford Barton (Teachers Publishing Corporation), *Choral Reading for Fun and Recreation* by Helen A. Brown and Harry J. Heltman (Westminster Press), and *Let's Say Poetry Together* by Carrie Rasmussen (Burgess Publishing Company). Poems listed in such books, however, are not necessarily the most suitable for any given group of boys and girls. Wide acquaintance with poetry, access to the best anthologies of poetry for children, as well as books of poetry by single authors, will keep the teacher and, to some extent, the pupils from being limited by poems suggested in books designed specifically for choral reading.

Additional Suggestions

Following are additional points that the teacher should bear in mind as she helps boys and girls in choral reading.

Choral reading should be fun. If it is not, the major reasons for doing it will probably not be accomplished. This does not mean that hard work may not be necessary in order to get the desired results, but it does mean that if appreciation of good literature is to result, the pupils must enjoy the work.

Boys and girls should be helped, if help is indicated, to comprehend the meaning of the material they use for choral reading. This does not mean that the child must know every word in a selection or that he must have the depth of insight into a poem that an adult might have. However, problems in vocabulary should not be allowed to interfere with the interpretation of meaning. Nor should comprehension of the poem be limited by lack of sufficient insight to make it meaningful to the child. Fortunately there is no reason why the teacher cannot help boys and girls with problems of word meaning and of comprehension of poems which but for difficulty in these two respects might be highly suitable for choral reading. She can frankly approach the pupils with the thought that attention to some of the words will enhance their understanding and hopefully their enjoyment of a poem. Upon such a comment might follow a brief period of word study. Similarly, through questions and comments, the teacher can help the members of the class with the meaning of a poem as a whole.

Boys and girls should be aware of the importance of good posture in choral reading and they should be stimulated to want to assume such posture. The teacher's posture should be exemplary. Practice in desirable posture might be valuable. Discussion of the need of good breath control and of the relation between breath control and posture might be helpful.

The teacher might well emphasize with the boys and girls the importance of good speech. She can show them, through illustration and demonstration, the difference between slovenly and clear enunciation. In fact, a group of boys and girls could put on an informal dramatization depicting both faulty and good enunciation.

A good leader is essential to effective choral reading. The leader can show the speakers or readers when the different parts should come in, when the voices of a group should be softer or louder, happier or sadder, faster or slower. Use of a baton is probably rightfully frowned upon, since it seems better that the leader use his hands or his body as a whole to communicate with the group. During practice periods at times a pupil might serve as leader. When there is an audience, the teacher should be the leader so that she can deal inconspicuously and competently with any problem that may come up.

Costuming is to be discouraged in choral reading. The wearing of costumes might detract from the beauty of the interpretation as presented by children's voices. Some teachers like to have their pupils when engaging in choral reading wear uniform apparel, having the boys wear light shirts and dark trousers and the girls white blouses and dark skirts. But what in costuming could be as effective as boys and girls dressed in their better school dresses as they interpret in their unsophisticated ways a worthwhile message from a poem that is of lasting value to them!

DRAMATIZATION AND ORAL READING

Dramatization can serve various important purposes in the elementary school, one of which is improvement in oral reading. It is true that oral reading is not a part of some types of dramatizations by elementary school children. In many of the plays planned by boys and girls, acting is somewhat impromptu, without any lines recorded, and without any reading to be done. Frequently, too, commercially written plays are dramatized by pupils with the only reading experience being silent rather than oral reading. However, under some circumstances oral reading has a part in the dramatization. Some situations in which oral reading is used are as follows.

1. Sometimes when boys and girls make up their own plays the lines are recorded, the parts assigned to children, the lines practiced as the children read their parts orally, and finally the play is read to an audience.
2. Some basal reading series contain dramatic selections not designed for memorization, but planned for oral reading.
3. Some printed plays, later to be memorized by the pupils, in early practice periods are read by them orally.
4. Narrators of plays often read their parts to the audience.
5. Frequently the lines for a puppet play are read orally. Sometimes they are read by characters behind the scene. At other times they may be read by a person in view of the audience, who plays a role similar to that of the narrator.

PUPPETRY AND ORAL READING

Since puppetry affords many excellent opportunities for oral reading, it is here discussed in greater detail than the other points to which reference was made in the preceding paragraph.

Values of Puppetry

Puppetry can serve many valuable objectives, among them the following.

1. It can be used as a means of motivation for schoolwork in various areas. For example, a puppet show based on some phase of colonial life, such as the colonial school, can play a significant role in interesting the boys and girls in that period of history.
2. It can be a means of giving information. For example, a well-planned and well-executed puppet show featuring some important phases of Benjamin

Franklin's life may give the members of the audience and the participants in the puppet play valuable information about Franklin.

3. It can be used when giving oral reports. In a report on *Miss Hickory*, the child giving the report may decide to have puppets tell the last part of the story, where Squirrel finally gets the hickory nut head that he had so long coveted.

4. It can serve as a means of self-expression.

5. It can provide boys and girls with the experience of making puppets, designing and making the stage, sewing or painting the backdrop, and making the furniture.

6. It can develop into a happy leisure-time activity for the child who will make of puppetry a hobby.

7. It can provide opportunity for oral reading in a functional and interesting setting.

Puppets and Puppet Stages

A few suggestions are here given as to kinds of puppets and puppet stages that can be used in puppet plays. For more suggestions on the topic, the teacher is referred to books on literature for children and on the teaching of the language arts, which frequently include a section on puppetry. Additional references include *The Puppet Theater Handbook* by Marjorie Batchelder (Harper & Row); *Puppets and Plays —A Creative Approach* by Marjorie Batchelder and Virginia Comer (Harper & Row); *Puppets into Actors* by Olive Blackham (The Macmilland Company); *Shadow Puppets* by Olive Blackham (Harper & Row); *A Handbook of First Puppets* by Alexander Ficklen (J. B. Lippincott Company); *Puppet and Pantomime Plays* by Vernon Howard (Sterling Publishing Company); *First Book of Puppets* by Moritz Jagendorf (Franklin Watts); *The Puppet Book* by Shari Lewis (Citadel Press); *Easy Puppets* by Gertrude Pels (Thomas Y. Crowell Company); *The Puppet Do-It-Yourself Book* by Lois Pratt (Exposition Press); *Puppetry, Marionettes, and Shadow Plays* by Loren Taylor (Burgess Publishing Company).

Puppets should be distinguished from marionettes. It is customary to apply the term *marionette* to those lifelike creatures that are controlled by strings; the term *puppet* is often reserved for figures that are not manipulated by string. Because of the difficulties of handling marionettes, they are not commonly used in the elementary school. However, the same opportunities for oral reading that are here pointed out can be achieved as well through marionettes as through puppets.

Puppets can be classified in a variety of ways. One division is that of (1) stationary or table puppets, (2) rod puppets, and (3) hand puppets. Of these the stationary puppet is the simplest. Stationary or table puppets can be placed on a table and left there, without motion, throughout a short play when the puppet is the chief actor. The parts can be read orally. The puppet can represent the entire body or the head only. Examples of stationary puppets are a puppet head made from a bottle, with features pasted or painted on; the head of a puppet made from a tin can onto which eyes, ears, mouth, nose, and hair are attached or painted; a paper doll made to stand erect by a tripod made of stiff paper attached to the back side of the base of the puppet.

A rod puppet is one that is controlled by a rod. Any two-dimensional or three-dimensional object, such as a block of wood or an apple or a balloon, with a rod attached to it for manipulation of the puppet may serve as a rod puppet. Another frequently made rod puppet is one in which a paper bag serves as head and body, to which a tongue depressor or other type of rod is attached. As one or more pupils read the parts of the play, the rod puppets can be shown either in full view of the audience or on a puppet stage.

The term *hand puppet* is applied to puppets that are controlled directly by the hand, without a rod. They are of endless variety. Paper bag puppets, puppets made of socks, balloon puppets, tin can puppets, light bulb puppets, and papier-mâché puppets are examples of hand puppets. In most cases the head of such puppets is made of the material designated in the name of the puppet while the body is often represented by a "dress" made of paper or cloth. Hand puppets are usually used on stage, but they can be shown without a stage as one or more of the pupils read or speak the lines.

A table top, a curtain supported by a rod resting on the back of two straight chairs, a box placed on a table, a doorway with a curtain across the bottom half—all these and many others may serve as temporary stages. Stages can also be constructed from paper cartons or from wood.

Even when the puppets are crude and the stage setting simple, boys and girls through excellence of reading can make the little dolls "come to life."

A PREPARED ORAL READING PROGRAM

In this section is presented a teaching plan that illustrates how a class period devoted to oral reading that has been prepared beforehand can be conducted. An explanation of phases of the plan follows.

Teaching Plan

This plan for a fourth-grade class, like all other teaching plans, should not be thought of as a model that should be followed exactly; rather it is hoped that it will serve as one concrete illustration of what can be done. The needs of the boys and girls should determine the procedure to be followed in any one situation.

A. *Topic:* Prepared oral reading of Christmas stories
B. *Pupils' aims*
  1. To see if we will like the Christmas stories that will be read to us
  2. To try to read so that our listeners will enjoy hearing us read
  3. To be good listeners
C. *Materials*
  1. Board work
    a. "Old Hans and the Toyshop Twins"
       Kenneth Jackson
       Betty Thurston
       Lois Roth
       Jean VanSickle
    b. "The Christmas Tree"
       Jimmie Reed
       Beverly Myers
    c. "The Snow Santa Claus"
       Doris Gale
       Ted Hershey
    d. "A Christmas Friend"
       Ted Gardner
       Norma Staley
  2. Copies of the stories listed under 1 above
  3. Chart entitled "Oral Reading" with these points listed on it:
     Posture
     Voice
     Pronunciation
     Enunciation
     Getting the message across
     Remembering the audience
     Listening
  4. Individual cards like the one illustrated on page 329
D. *Procedure*
  1. Motivation
     The teacher says: "How many of you like to hear or read Christmas stories? A committee has prepared several stories which they will read to you."
  2. Noting points to watch when reading orally
    a. The teacher, referring to the chart mentioned under C-3 above,

Gardner, Ted		Oral Reading						
Dates:								
1. Posture								
2. Voice								
3. Pronunciation								
4. Enunciation								
5. Getting the message across								
6. Remembering the audience								
7. Listening								

states that the boys and girls have tried hard to watch those points as they practiced their reading.

b. Two pupils put on a two-minute skit in which they demonstrate good and poor posture while reading orally, and the class briefly names points of excellence and of criticism in the two types of posture demonstrated.

c. The pupils tell what "remembering the audience" means, stressing the fact that while "looking at the audience" is important, it should not be done mechanically.

d. The pupils indicate what a good listener does.

3. Statement of the procedure to be followed in reading the stories

The teacher explains to the boys and girls that after a few introductory remarks the boys and girls whose names are written on the program on the board, under C-1, will read the stories listed there.

4. Reading of the stories by the children preceded by an introductory remark or a question on each story by the teacher or by the reader

5. Brief discussion of the content of the stories

6. Pupils' evaluation of the reading

a. Pupils name the points on the chart that they think were watched particularly well.

b. Pupils name the points on the chart that they think need to be improved upon.

c. Group discusses means by which they can improve upon the points referred to under b above.

d. Teacher explains that individually later on she will discuss with those who read the quality of their reading.

At that time cards like the one illustrated above can be used for making an analysis of each pupil's reading.

Explanation of the Plan

In a lesson of this type the following procedure might be followed: (1) preparation before class, (2) deciding upon the aims for the period, (3) reference to the points to be observed in the oral reading, (4) announcement of the plan of procedure in the reading, (5) reading of the selections, (6) discussion of the story, and (7) evaluation of the reading. Each of these points is here discussed to clarify it in relation to the teaching plan presented and to indicate a few of the possible variations from it that the teacher may wish to make.

1. *Preparation before class.* Preparation should include choosing the readers, selecting the materials to be read, practicing reading the selections, providing for the materials needed during classtime, and making seating arrangements.

    a. Choosing the readers. The teacher who helped make plans for the reading program described earlier was in the habit of choosing no pupil for a second turn at participating in an oral reading program before everyone in the room had had the opportunity to take part in one. She also made certain that pupils of varying ability appeared on each program. She took this precaution because she realized that while it would be relatively easy to keep a program interesting if all participants were good readers, it would be difficult to hold the interest of the audience if only the poorer readers performed.

    The question is often asked, "Should the poor reader really be expected or allowed to take part in an audience reading program?" The answer is, "Yes, as a rule." If a pupil is not permitted to read because he has decided difficulties in reading, he may feel slighted, even though often he may act as if he were pleased that he did not have to read. Moreover, it is the poorer reader, rather than the excellent one, who needs the practice. The teacher can help save the former from feelings of inadequacy in the oral reading situation by giving him shorter selections than most others in the group so that he can prepare thoroughly what he reads. It is probably good policy to give some of the better readers relatively brief selections, too, so that the one who is less able will not think of the brevity of his reading as a stigma attached to his performance. Also, the teacher can see to it that the child who cannot read as well orally as the others has very easy material to read. Help from the teacher in preparation for the reading can often preserve the ego of the reader, with a minimum of undesirable emotional reactions. At the same time, in this way the pupil can get real help in becoming a better reader. Some teachers, rather than depriving a poor reader of the opportunity to read orally, wisely help him all but memorize his selection before class so that he may perform well before his peers.

    There are, however, undoubtedly some pupils in the intermediate grades who should be excused at least for a part of the year from participating in oral reading. A child who is so shy that he will be harmed rather than helped through reading orally should not be required to read. Great care should be taken, of course, in deciding when a child should not be asked to read. For example, Jim, a fourth-grader with approximately third-grade reading ability, complained to his tutor that his teacher never called on him to read orally.

b. Selection of material. The material to be read orally should be selected with particular care. Sometimes the teacher will make the selection by herself, always remembering that the material should be at the level of the pupils' interest. At other times pupils should have the opportunity to select from a variety presented by the teacher. When children make their own suggestions, the teacher, perhaps in consultation with a pupil committee, will advise as to the suitability of the selections.

The material selected should be easy for the reader to read orally and easy for the audience to comprehend. Often it is advisable to select material for audience reading that is a grade or so lower in difficulty level than the reader's silent reading level. Effective oral reading requires ability in silent reading plus the complex skill of interpreting to others what is read.

A variety of suitable materials is available. Stories, both humorous and serious, fanciful and realistic, are one source. Anecdotes make very good reading. Work-type materials of the kind that requires more than one reading or very careful attention have no legitimate place in an oral reading program. Sometimes each child on the program may have a separate, very short, selection to read. At other times a longer one may be apportioned to two or more, or even all, of the persons who will be reading. Appropriate selections are easily available in most situations because only one copy of a book or magazine article is needed. This is true even if more than one pupil is preparing material out of the same book or magazine, since they can practice at different times and since no one should be reading silently while someone is reading orally. Many teachers like to cut materials out of books that are ready to be discarded or magazines that are not being saved. The stories used in the teaching plan were cut out of a magazine in columns and then mounted on tagboard 9 inches by 12 inches. Mounted material can often be handled better while it is being read and can be kept in better condition when filed for later use.

c. Preparation of the reader. Each reader should be thoroughly prepared for the reading. As a rule, silent reading of the selection beforehand is not enough. The pupil should read it orally one or more times, either to the teacher or to someone else who can help him not only with word recognition but also with problems of interpretation. If several children are to read parts of the same selection, at times they can help each other during the practice period. But the teacher is always responsible for seeing that no one comes before the class inadequately prepared. Furthermore, each pupil should know exactly where his selection is to begin and end if he is to read only part of an article or story.

d. Provision for materials. Careful provision should be made, often with the help of the boys and girls, so that supplies and equipment needed during the class period will be available. Included may be material placed on the board, as in the case of the plan reproduced in this chapter. If a plan like this one were used, the program for the period could be listed on the board, with the title of each story to be read and the names of the persons who were to read each, in the order of appearance. Sometimes, instead, boys and girls like to make duplicates of the program on paper to distribute to the audience at the beginning of the class period.

A chart similar to the one referred to in the plan, giving the points the pupils will watch in their oral reading, can be displayed. So that the pupils may wholeheartedly accept the skills for the improvement of which they will work, it is usually advisable to have the list worked out cooperatively by the pupils and the teacher. The wording should be meaningful to the pupils. If the word *enunciation* is used, as it is on the list given in the plan, the teacher should make certain that the boys and girls know what it means. The list can be drawn up early in the school year and then it can be reproduced on chart paper. For easy reference, it could be either kept posted in the room at all times or else exhibited whenever the pupils give reading programs.

Each pupil could be provided with a card similar to the one illustrated on page 329. These cards could be kept by the teacher or the child. The record should not be kept for competitive purposes, and only the teacher and the owner of a card should have access to it. A check can be placed on the chart after each item on which the child does well and a minus sign after each item on which he needs to improve. Although on the card reproduced provision is made for checking seven different times, the number could vary. A place is left for the date of each reading. Space for comments is on the back of the card.

Sometimes other materials may be needed. A map often adds to the value of the reading by enabling the pupil to locate places about which he reads. At times pictures help the audience to visualize what will be read. Realia, too, may profitably be exhibited, if they help accomplish the purpose set for the oral reading. For example, pupils in the fifth or sixth grades can be aided in getting into the mood of the story about Nancy Hanks, the mother of Abraham Lincoln, if a replica of a log cabin is shown as representative of the type in which Lincoln lived when he was a boy.

e.   Room arrangements. Arrangements should be made before class for proper seating of the audience and of the participants in the program. Sometimes all that is needed is to reserve seats near the front of the room for those who will read. At times, if there are portable seats, they can be rearranged so as to make it as easy as possible to have a desirable audience situation. If, as in the plan that is reproduced,

Christmas stories are being read, someone can see to it that the shades are pulled and the lights are lit on the Christmas tree in the room before class begins.

2. *Deciding upon the aims for the period.* The aims can be suggested by the pupils who prepare the oral reading or by the teacher. No matter who states them, it is important that they are objectives that the class can wholeheartedly accept. In the teaching plan given on page 328 three aims were listed. The second aim, the aim of the readers, "To try to read so that our listeners will enjoy hearing us read," should be determined before class as the boys and girls practice reading. The first and last are suggested objectives for the members of the audience. It will be noted that the first aim, as stated, is not that each child should enjoy the story. There can be nothing mandatory about appreciation. A person does not enjoy something because he sets out to enjoy it or because he is told to enjoy it. In the plan described, the aim that deals with appreciation leaves the final choice explicitly with the audience, for all that is suggested is that they find out whether or not they will enjoy the stories. That is as far as the recommendation should be made when appreciation-type of teaching is done. The third aim is brought out in 2-*d* under "Procedure," which states, "The pupils indicate what a good listener does."

The audience is entitled to have a reason for listening. If the children have no purpose, they will often pay inadequate attention to what is read. Therefore, a suggestion as to what the purpose might be should be given either by the pupils who will read or by the teacher. At times the purpose may deal with entertainment and at other times it may be to get information. It is not necessary that in every oral reading lesson the audience specifically decide that they will try to be good listeners. After a while it should be taken for granted that that will always be an objective. Nevertheless, occasionally additional elements may well be stressed for observation as far as the conduct of the audience is concerned. It is often advisable that each person who reads have in mind a particular point that he wishes to observe especially well.

As a rule, the number of expressed aims should be greatly limited, probably to three at the most. It is to be assumed that the pupil will always have certain objectives in mind in reading of this type, without mention being made of them. A large number of stated aims is likely to result in diffusion of effort. There is much to be applied to educational practice in the quotation that says, "This one thing I do." Multiplicity of aim can be decidedly disadvantageous under some circumstances.

3. *Reference to the points to be observed.* It is not necessary that the points to watch in oral reading should be discussed in each audience reading situation before the boys and girls begin reading. Sometimes they may be taken up after the reading only, and at other times no class mention needs to be made of them. Several factors should enter into the decision as to whether they should be discussed, either before or after the

reading. One is the time available for discussion during the lesson. Another is whether the mood to be portrayed through the reading can better be created if no mention is made of the skills to be developed.

4. *Announcement of the plan of procedure.* Although in the plan given the teacher made the announcement, often the teacher can remain entirely in the background and a pupil, appointed as chairman of the meeting, can make the announcement. At other times, when the pupils are handed copies of the program, no mention of the order needs to be made.

5. *Reading of the selections.* It is essential that the atmosphere of a program should be maintained throughout the time set aside for reading. The teacher should not correct or prompt the reader unless it is absolutely necessary for the continuance of the program. Interruptions should probably be made no more often than in an assembly program. Possibly the only occasion when the teacher is justified in intervening arises when the child stops reading because he does not know the next word even though previously he had been instructed to proceed as best he could.

6. *Discussion of the story.* Sometimes the discussion of the story may be omitted—certainly in cases in which the mood created by the story might be destroyed by talking about it. Usually, if there is discussion, it should be brief. It might be led by the teacher or by a pupil. Occasionally, if the aim is to see how well the boys and girls have acquired the information given, they might check themselves on their ability to answer written questions on what was presented.

7. *Evaluation of the reading.* It is not recommended that the teacher check the individual "score" card while the child is reading. Some pupils may not be made self-conscious by such a practice, but others will surely either concentrate on technique rather than thought or become tense. It is just as easy for the teacher to check the cards periodically after class and discuss the record with the pupils individually.

Hard and fast rules about evaluation should not, of course, interfere with occasional informal comments upon the success with which a pupil has mastered specific skills of oral reading. However, usually it is most effective to discuss group progress in general terms at the end of the reading period. Individual pupils should be encouraged to keep their own scores and compare them with the teacher's judgments in private conference. No child should feel that he is going on trial when he rises to read.

FOR FURTHER STUDY

Bond, Guy A., and Eva Bond Wagner, *Teaching the Child To Read.* New York: Crowell-Collier and Macmillan, Inc., 1966. Chapter 12, "Oral Reading," pp. 240–249.

Burton, William, *Reading in Child Development.* Indianapolis, Ind.: The Bobbs-Merrill Company, Inc., 1958. Chapter 10, "The Place of Oral Reading," pp. 347–359.

Harris, Albert J., *Readings on Reading Instruction*. New York: David McKay Company, Inc., 1963. Chapter XIV, "Oral Reading," pp. 388–411.

Huckleberry, Alan W., and Edward S. Strother, *Speech Education for the Elementary Teacher*. Boston: Allyn and Bacon, Inc., 1966. Chapter 7, "The Solo Reader," pp. 159–169.

Tinker, Miles A., and Constance M. McCullough, *Teaching Elementary Reading*. New York: Appleton-Century-Crofts, 1968. Chapter 11, "Reading Aloud," pp. 224–236.

Veatch, Jeannette, *Reading in the Elementary School*. New York: The Ronald Press Company, 1966. Chapter 10, "Reading at the More Advanced Levels," pp. 302-357.

QUESTIONS FOR THOUGHT AND DISCUSSION

1. What values do you see in choral reading?
2. Be able to name six or eight criteria of good oral reading—that is, six or eight requirements oral reading must meet if it is to be called good reading. How may a list of these be used to advantage in teaching? (Consider their possible value to both the teacher and the pupils.)
3. What is your reaction to the following statement which is sometimes heard among reading instructors?

    > Oral expression may be improved among all children in the ideal classroom of the future. Here the teacher will accept individual differences, plan for and with the children, supply quantities of interesting materials, and provide many real opportunities for speaking and reading aloud.

4. To develop all aspects of oral reading, the teacher must use both systematic instruction and highly motivated practice. What are some middle-grade activities that offer good opportunities for the development of oral reading skills?
5. The proficiency with which children are able to use oral language when they come to school will vary markedly from individual to individual. But no matter how capable a child is in the use of oral language when he comes to school, his skill in this area can always be improved or extended. Can you suggest some techniques that may help the school discharge its responsibilities during the child's primary years.
6. One objective of teaching listening should be to develop the ability to listen appreciatively. Many opportunities arise during the school day to use this important listening ability. Teachers should be aware of ways to cultivate and improve it. What are some effective ways?
7. What is meant by dramatic reading? What advantages has it?
8. What is the difference between interpretative and imitative reading?
9. The teacher in the elementary grades is interested in the practical problem of how we can help children toward better expression in reading. What are suggestions for attaining this end?

CHAPTER 10 A

Children's Interests in Reading

The development of keen and continuing interests in reading is not only one of the basic aims of reading instruction but also an essential condition for sturdy growth in reading ability. Successful reading depends on the drive that comes from within the learner. The use of outward compulsion achieves little in the way of reading progress and may in fact inhibit the growth of reading interest. Only as the abundant energies that are resident in all normal children are released may we expect rapid and enduring gains in reading skill and interest. We must, therefore, discover and nurture the interests that impel the child to seek meaning from the printed page.

For this reason, what is variously called "free" reading, "recreational" reading, and "personal" reading has come to occupy a place of first importance in the school program. While not long ago teachers tended to regard this kind of reading as peripheral to the instructional program—a kind of extracurricular activity—today "reading for fun" is considered a legitimate and desirable activity for school hours. The systematic study of children's interests has thus become a central part of the instructional program in reading.

THE AIMS OF GUIDANCE IN WIDE, VOLUNTARY READING

How great the importance of wide, voluntary reading is can be seen from an examination of some of the major purposes of this type of reading.

1. *Providing leisure-time activities.* Perhaps the first, though not necessarily the most important, purpose is the development of the habit of reading in leisure time. Children should have much leisure time, and they should have abundant resources for its constructive use. Certainly some of these resources should take the form of sports, hobbies, and social activities. But there are many occasions when children and young people do not have the opportunity to pursue hobbies or take part in games and social activities. These are the times when good books and good magazines should be a source of pleasure. Developing the love for good reading is one of the greatest benefits that we can provide for children.

The leisure hour is the time for fairy tales, folk tales, fables, myths, tall stories, and the sagas of heroes. It is the time for *Winnie the Pooh*, for the stories of Dr. Seuss, for *Mary Poppins*, for *Mother Goose*, for *Alice's Adventures in Wonderland*, for the *Arabian Nights*. For some children it is the time for poetry—for the nonsense verse of Lewis Carroll and Edward Lear, the humor and pathos of Rose Fyleman and Eugene Field. The leisure hour can be an hour of magic, enchantment, relaxation, and relief. It can help the child to see the wonder and the beauty in the "commonplace" world all around him.

2. *Expanding the horizons of children in space and time.* Most children, like most adults, live in a circumscribed world. It is true that radio, television, and motion pictures have expanded the world measurably in our generation, but the new media have not supplanted print as a means of broadening our horizons. Each of the new media has something unique to give, but each has its limitations. Only the printed word can offer to the reader the world of the past in the mood of reflection and reminiscence and interpretation. New symbols evoke, through the various electronic media, the excitement of the possibilities of the future. But only the book can fully unfold the meaning of that future in words which supply the reader with the means to communicate to others his aspirations for the life of tomorrow.

We should prefer Bob or Sue to visit Rome or the English Lake Country or New Orleans or Mexico City rather than merely to read about these places. But even when they are fortunate enough to do so, their direct observation of the new scenes will have clearer purpose and yield more abundant rewards if they have first read about them, and their subsequent reading will in turn be heightened in vividness and color.

Some day perhaps our schools will be supplied with air buses to take classes on guided tours to Gettysburg and Valley Forge, perhaps even to Jerusalem and the Nile Valley. For the present we are grateful if the schools have a few books with settings in these places. Since most boys and girls cannot see all of their world firsthand, it is of the greatest urgency that they be given the key to the medium of books, through which they can learn about that world. Eleanor Hoffman's *Mischief in Fez* can take them in spirit to Morocco to share in the enchantment of its hypnotic folklore. Evelyn Stefansson's *Here Is Alaska*, Reba Mirsky's *Seven Grandmothers*, Leonard Clark's *Explorers' Digest*, Augusta Baker's *Talking Tree: Fairy Tales from Fifteen Lands*, Beatrice Liu's *Little Wu and the Watermelons*, Anna Louise Strong's *Peoples of the U.S.S.R.*, Irmengarde Eberle's *Big Family of Peoples*, Ann Nolan Clark's *Secret of the Andes*, and Denis Clark's *Life of a Kangaroo* are examples of the many hundreds of books that can lay the foundations of a broad world view. Sonja Bleeker's factual accounts of several American Indian tribes, such as *The Navajo*, extend the horizons of children with respect to a subject often obscured by distorted narrative or fanciful inventions.

So also the child's vision of the world of science can grow through the reading of the many fine new educational books. The numerous nature books of Herbert Zim, Reed's *Stars for Sam*, Schneider's *You Among the Stars*, Lewellen's *You and Atomic Energy*, and Selsam's *Play with Plants* are illustrative of the type. Informational books on subjects other than science are increasing in number and variety each year. They serve for fortunate children as "windows upon the world" of people and things. They help boys and girls to dwell in a constantly expanding world and to achieve a constantly expanding comprehension of that world.

3. *Providing vicarious experience.* Closely related to the objective of the widening horizon is that of the vicarious enrichment of experience. The materials and methods employed in the achievement of this objective will be substantially the same as those used in the effort to expand young people's intellectual horizons, but the direction the instruction will take will vary in essential particulars. Here the purpose will be to build a stock of impressions that the child's direct experience cannot provide. It is by means of the rapidly growing, well-organized mass of experience with people, places, things, and processes that the child or youth develops the ability to comprehend what he reads, to converse interestingly, to discuss intelligently, to make constructive use of his leisure, to live comfortably with himself in hours of solitude.

We are dealing here with a fundamental principle of learning, one that emphasizes the overriding importance of a wide contact with the best in children's literature. The generalized concepts that the learner encounters in history and geography textbooks are the products of the author's systematic experiences. They cannot become the child's unless the child has first had an abundance of firsthand experiences on which generalized notions can be built. Textbooks, because they must be comprehensive, cannot supply these, or at best they can supply only a few of them. The chronology of the life of Lincoln will have little meaning for the reader unless he has first lived vicariously with Lincoln in his log cabin at New Salem, accompanied him on his circuit in Central Illinois, paced the floor with him in the White House, or visited General Grant with him in the general's tent. Reading the D'Aulaires' *Abraham Lincoln*, Enid Meadowcroft's *Abraham Lincoln*, Carl Sandburg's *Abe Lincoln Grows Up*, Augusta Stevenson's *Abe Lincoln: Frontier Boy*, Genevieve Foster's *Abraham Lincoln's World*, Clara Ingram Judson's *Abraham Lincoln, Friend of the People*, or the picture book *Abe Lincoln and His Times, 1809–1865* will be worth a hundred readings of a section of a chapter in a history text, however useful the text may be. These can provide the wealth of personalized contacts with the man Lincoln which will illuminate the larger patterns of history with which the textbook deals.

The peculiar advantage of children's literature is that it can offer an emotionalized approach to reality which enables the reader to identify himself personally with his subject. Carol R. Brink's *Caddie Woodlawn* and Laura Ingalls Wilder's "Little House" books do not merely list the facts about frontier life; they enable young readers actually to live it, endure its hardships, and rejoice in its simple, homely, but authentic delights. Statistics about casualties in the American Civil War will have significance in the development of a unit in the social studies, but they will not have personal meaning for young people until the pupils have read such books as Delight Ausley's *Sword and the Spirit: A Life of John Brown*, Arna Bontemps' *Chariot in the Sky*, Samuel and Beryl Epstein's *Andrews Raid*, or, in the case of early adolescents, Elsie Singmaster's *Swords of Steel*, a story of Gettysburg. Figures about exports take on meaning when young readers share in spirit in the life of the farmer or factory worker who produces them, the railroad or airplane worker who transports them, the stevedore who trucks them on the dock, the seaman who looks after their safe delivery. Children's literature is a means of seeing the world through other people's eyes for a time, and it multiples a hundredfold the experiences and insights of each person who reads.

4. *Developing esthetic sensitivity.* Many complaints have been made about the general level of taste of the American people. The banality, transparency, and even venality of typical radio and television

programs have been widely commented upon. The public taste in motion pictures has been criticized with equal severity. The run-of-the-mill picture makes its appeal to people of limited intelligence and crude taste, and producers say that these are the only films that can profit at the box office. There is reason to believe that the case has been overstated, since the public has often responded enthusiastically on those rare occasions when a really superior picture is offered. Nevertheless, it is clear that for multitudes of people the area of esthetic sensitivity has scarcely been cultivated. Good literature for children can help in the development of discrimination among esthetic values if the children can be introduced to it in an atmosphere conducive to such development.

Many boys and girls will at first find it difficult to obtain a deep pleasure from such a lovely but quiet, somewhat slow-moving book as Kenneth Grahame's *Wind in the Willows*. For some children, especially if it is read to them a chapter at a time, its humor, its receptiveness to the more subtle physical sensations, and its beautiful, simple style will prove irresistible. For others, it should be preceded by other stories more obvious, more dramatic. Hugh Lofting's *Dr. Dolittle*, Pamela Travers' *Mary Poppins*, Louisa May Alcott's *Little Women*, Dr. Seuss' *The 500 Hats of Bartholomew Cubbins*, or Robert Lawson's *Rabbit Hill* will for some boys and girls be worthy preliminaries. For each child, certainly each group, the "literary escalator" will be different.

The development of esthetic appreciation was the earliest of the school's stated objectives in the teaching of literature, and for a long time it was the only one. Today, although we see many other valuable uses for literature, literary judgment, enjoyment, and appreciation remain among the most important.

5. *Helping children to understand themselves and others.* Evelyn Wenzel, in *Elementary English*, discussed the "Little House" books of Laura Ingalls Wilder. This fine series of stories certainly possesses great literary merit, but Professor Wenzel in this article considers these books from another viewpoint. She has recognized them as being a means of helping young people to accomplish their developmental tasks and to recognize how to meet their personal needs. She finds in Mrs. Wilder's work many situations dealing with (1) young people's need for security: material security, emotional security; (2) young people's need for achievement: physical, intellectual, spiritual, and moral achievement, growing up, overcoming fears and misunderstandings, overcoming sister troubles, meeting the problems of an expanding world, dealing with adolescent problems and the problems

of courtship and marriage, and gaining insight into some of the mysteries of life; and (3) young people's need for change and escape. Professor Wenzel's is a valuable analysis—one that might be made of many other writers whose mark has hitherto been considered from the point of view of literary excellence alone.

While this function of literature—that of promoting self-understanding—has been referred to as *bibliotherapy*, there is legitimate objection to the use of this term, just as there is to the term *remedial reading*. Therapy implies illness, and the existence of personal and interpersonal problems in the life of children is not an illness, but a normal condition. When the problems become serious enough they may require therapy, but the teacher is not a therapist.

Almost any kind of book can help young people in gaining insight into themselves and others, provided it is written at the level of their abilities and is an honest and skillful portrayal of life. Helen Sewell's *Jimmy and Jemima* portrays with appropriate humor for primary grade children the destructive effects of sibling rivalry. Even Eleanor Estes' "Moffat" stories, with their delicate nonsense, have their value in steadying the emotions of children who have frustrations and troubles great enough to test adult endurance.

As children grow up, they have the need to understand and accept differences in others. They must learn to accept the handicapped member of the class without derision or condescension. Actually, most children can do this quite unconsciously, but often their attitudes have been poisoned by adults. Teaching good human relations, therefore, is not so much a matter of developing new attitudes as of having children unlearn acquired ones.

The problem is, of course, especially serious in the case of differences in race and national origin. Many fine books have been written for children of various ages to develop an appreciation of differences and a respect for other cultures. Lorraine and Jerrold Beim's *Two Is a Team*, for the primary level, and Jesse Jackson's *Call Me Charley*, for the intermediate-grade level, illustrate the many excellent books portraying the Negro. Laura Armer's *Waterless Mountain*, for younger children, and Florence Crannell Means' *Whispering Girl*, and Sonja Bleeker's well-written anthropological studies, for older children, are examples of sympathetic portrayals of the American Indian. Many of us are familiar with Mrs. Means' *Moved-Outers*, about a Japanese relocation camp in California, and with Eleanor Estes' *Hundred Dresses*, a poignant story of an immigrant girl. Books about people in other countries are constantly increasing in number and improving in quality.

Fortunately for the teacher, there are now appearing many

new guides to children's literature dealing with personal and human relations problems. *Reading Ladders for Human Relations*, published by the American Council on Education, provides a graduated list of children's and young people's books dealing with eight human relations themes. The Children's Book Center of the University of Chicago publishes a monthly list of the best new children's books, annotated and classified according to theme. Charlemae Rollins has written an excellent brochure, called *We Build Together*, listing young people's books about the Negro and suggesting criteria for the evaluation of such books.

STUDYING THE INTERESTS OF CHILDREN

In order that we may effectively guide the reading of children, we must know a great deal about their interests. Reading interests are the product of the general interests of children and youth. Often, therefore, the process of stimulating reading interests involves the expansion and enrichment of the child's general interests. In the following sections we shall examine the various interests that have been found to be characteristic of boys and girls at various age levels.

Hobbies

Many children progress through a series of hobbies and diverse intellectual interests. One talented boy, for example, was successively preoccupied with the following topics from ages five to fourteen: animals, stamps, rocks, magic, chemistry, medieval heraldry, military strategy, photography, maps, hunting and fishing, navigation, locksmithing, and science fiction. Subsequently he developed an interest in hot rods, but fortunately pursued it only in magazines. In the fishing stage, his involvement was limited to the purchase of equipment with the small sums he earned as a newspaper carrier, because no fishing waters could be found in a reasonable distance from his home. His fishing hobby was strictly an activity of the imagination. But what is important is that during this phase he read *Field and Stream* and other outdoor-life magazines. In each of these stages his hobby was enriched through the reading of weekly armloads of library books which opened new worlds to him in his chosen field of interest. Only in his sports interests did he confine himself generally to the physical activities themselves.

Play Interests

Many studies have been made of the play interests and reading interests of boys and girls in the successive stages of their development. These studies reveal that while the individual differences among children are wide, certain interests tend to be persistent at given age levels from one generation to another. For example, many adults will recognize the lists of leisure-time interests given in Tables I and II on pages 344–345 as characteristic of most normal, able-bodied boys and girls. Only the newer media of mass communication are peculiar to the interests of children today.

Television

The mass media of communication, especially television, are extremely popular with children of all ages. In summarizing a series of annual reports on television viewing, Witty and Kinsella noted that, contrary to what many expert observers anticipated, television has maintained its popularity with elementary school children throughout the years that it has been available on a large scale.[1] It is the favorite leisure-time activity of young boys and girls. Regardless of intelligence or school success, children spend upwards of 20 hours a week in staring at the television screen. The continued hypnotic effect of this new medium has caused justified concern among those who believe that reading is still the most rewarding of all the methods of making vicarious contact with reality and of spending one's leisure time.

Complaints about the quality of television offerings for both children and adults are numerous and vigorous. For example, in 1954 the National Association for Better Radio and Television found that crime and violence on children's programs had increased 400 percent during the preceding three years. However, in 1955 it was able to point to the increased availability of other types of programs. Teachers and parents also blame television for such problems as neglect of homework, mealtime interruptions, increased nervousness, lack of sleep, impoverishment of play, lack of interest in school, reduction in reading, and eyestrain.

Does television stimulate or inhibit the development of interest in reading? The answer probably is that for some children it stimulates and for others it inhibits such interest. While many parents and teachers report that children on the whole read less today than they did before the advent of television, many librarians report an increase in the reading of children's books. Certainly the many long hours that children spend with television each week are diverted from time that in an earlier day might have been spent with good books. On the other

[1] Paul Witty and Paul Kinsella, "Televiewing: Some Observations from Studies, 1949–1962," *Elementary English*, 39 (December 1962), pp. 772–779, 802.

TABLE I
INTERESTS OF PUPILS IN GRADES 1 AND 2

BOYS	PERCENT	GIRLS	PERCENT
Activity Preferences (95 Percent Return)			
Play outdoors	29.7	Play outdoors	28.7
Watch TV	27.7	Watch TV	22.5
Go to the movies	15.6	Go to the movies	16.7
Read stories	9.9	Listen to stories	13.7
Listen to stories	9.9	Read stories	10.3
Read comics	5.6	Read comics	6.1
Listen to radio	1.6	Listen to radio	2.0
Pets Owned (60 Percent Return)			
Dog	50.0	Cat	47.0
Cat	16.1	Dog	37.9
Bird	15.3	Bird	19.1
Fish	14.4	Fish	15.4
Turtle and parakeet	13.5	Parakeet	13.2
Attendance at Movies (88 Percent Return)			
Seldom or never	32.7	Seldom or never	29.6
Three to six times a year	22.9	Three to six times a year	22.9
Once a month	15.8	Once or twice a year	20.8
Once or twice a year	14.5	Once a month	16.1
Twice a month	8.8	Once a week	6.8
Once a week	5.3	Twice a month	3.8
Vocational Choices (97 Percent Return)			
Policeman	32.0	Nurse	36.5
Doctor	20.0	Teacher	33.9
Pilot	12.0	Mother and housewife	15.2
Baseball player	12.0	Ballerina	6.1
Scientist	7.3	Secretary	1.8
Fireman	3.3	Airline hostess	1.8
Things Feared (95 Percent Return)			
Snakes	19.2	Dogs	22.2
Dogs	18.6	The dark	14.9
The dark	13.8	Storms	11.8
Fire	10.8	Snakes	11.3
Wild animals	5.4	Wild animals	9.5
Games Liked Best (96 Percent Return)			
Baseball	27.6	Playing house	14.6
Cowboys and Indians	14.9	Playing school	12.6
Tetherball	7.5	Hide-and-seek	9.3
Monopoly	6.0	Tag	6.0
Checkers	6.0	Checkers	5.3
Duck-duck-goose	5.2	Playing with dolls	5.3

TABLE II
INTEREST OF PUPILS IN GRADES 3 THROUGH 6

BOYS	PERCENT	GIRLS	PERCENT
Activity Preferences (95 Percent Return)			
Watching TV	29.4	Watching TV	24.8
Playing indoors	21.7	Reading	24.8
Reading	20.8	Playing indoors	15.9
Playing outside	13.5	Playing outside	7.0
Playing baseball	4.0	Ice skating	2.9
Playing football	4.0		
Movie Attendance (86 Percent Return)			
Once a week	34.5	Once a week	26.8
Once a month	24.4	Once a month	24.3
Twice a month	12.5	Less than once or twice a year	13.2
Three to six times a year	9.6	Three to six times a year	12.3
Once or twice a year	9.6	Twice a month	10.9
Less than once or twice a year	6.6	Once or twice a year	7.7
Twice a week	2.8	Twice a week	4.8
Vocational Preference (96 Percent Return)			
Doctor	13.2	Teacher	22.7
Scientist	8.6	Nurse	18.7
Baseball player	7.0	Secretary	10.9
Engineer	5.4	Mother and housewife	6.4
Soldier	4.9	Airline hostess	6.2

Source: The data in Tables I, II, III, and IV are selected, by permission of the author and the publishers, from a report by Professor Paul A. Witty, "Studies of Interests of Children," in *The Packet,* 16 (Winter 1961–1962), pp. 15–23. *The Packet* is a Heath Service Bulletin for elementary teachers, published by D. C. Heath and Company, Boston, Mass.

hand, some television programs open new avenues of interest to children, who thereupon seek books on these subjects and read them with increased interest and comprehension. The relation between television and reading appears to depend upon the nature of the program and the nature of the individual child. *Zoo Parade, Disneyland,* travelogues, science programs, and biographical and historical presentations probably serve to encourage some children to read more widely.

Witty and Kinsella point out:

> We should, of course, not close our eyes to some unfortunate weaknesses in TV. Too many children's programs feature crime, horror and violence. Commercials, too, are sometimes not only absurd, but misleading. Too few programs are developed with a concern for the interests and welfare of children. Greater re-

sourcefulness and imagination are certainly needed in planning and developing children's programs. The scheduling of children's programs is often unfortunate since adult programs, frequently inappropriate for children, predominate at the favorite viewing times.

Despite limitations, this gigantic new instrument can provide worthwhile entertainment. There are some genuinely informative programs and occasionally inspiring presentations of great beauty. There are untapped possibilities for utilizing the interest engendered by TV to foster constructive individual and group endeavor. It is well to remember that the pleasures and satisfactions children derive from TV afford strong motivation for worthy accomplishment. For it often follows as John Mansfield has said: "The days that make us happy are the days that make us wise."[2]

TABLE III
READING INTEREST OF PUPILS IN GRADES 1 AND 2

BOYS	PERCENT	GIRLS	PERCENT
Kinds of Books Preferred (95 Percent Return)			
Animals	34.2	Animals	52.4
Stars, planets, space	28.2	Children of other lands	28.6
Pilots	17.1	Children at home	21.7
Children at home	5.3	Fairy tales	9.7
Children of other lands	4.6	School	9.0
Series Books Read (61 Percent Return)			
Golden Books	58.4	Golden Books	62.5
I Want To Be Books	14.3	True Books	5.5
True Books	7.8	I Want To Be Books	4.2
Oz Books	6.5	Wonder Books	2.8
First Books	46.3	Oz Books	2.4
		First Books	2.4
Magazines Preferred (51 Percent Return)			
Humpty Dumpty	46.3	*Humpty Dumpty*	46.8
Jack and Jill	20.4	*Jack and Jill*	26.6
Highlights	9.3	*Highlights*	7.6
Children's Digest	5.5	*Children's Digest*	3.8
Boys' Life	3.7	*Child Life*	2.5

[2] Witty and Kinsella, pp. 779, 802.

TABLE IV

READING INTERESTS OF PUPILS IN GRADES 3 THROUGH 6

BOYS	PERCENT	GIRLS	PERCENT
Kinds of Stories Liked (92 Percent Returned)			
Adventure	20.3	Mystery	18.3
Westerns	17.1	Adventure	16.1
Mystery	17.0	Animal	14.3
Science fiction	12.9	Humor	10.8
Humor	9.3	Westerns	10.3
Preferred Storybooks (93 Percent Return)			
Black Beauty		Little Women	
Davy Crockett		Cinderella	
Daniel Boone		Snow White	
Robin Hood, Thirty Seconds over		Heidi	
Tokyo, and Custer's Last Stand		Black Beauty	
Nonfiction Reading (84 Percent Return)			
Space travel	28.7	Famous people	25.0
Famous people	18.5	People from other lands	17.7
Handicrafts	12.8	Handicrafts	16.1
Travel	12.7	Travel	12.7
Careers	10.3	Space travel	11.5
Series Books Read (99 Percent Return)			
Landmark	28.0	First Books	12.8
First Books	16.3	Landmark	7.8
Teen-Age Tales	10.2	Bobbsey Twins	7.8
Magazines Read by Pupils in Grades 3 Through 6 (86 Percent Return)			
Life	28.8	Life	26.3
Boy's Life	22.5	Look	14.1
Look	12.0	Saturday Evening Post	6.9
Saturday Evening Post	6.5	Jack and Jill	6.7
Sports Illustrated	3.0	American Girl	4.6
Ebony	3.0	Better Homes and Gardens	4.6

Reading Interests

Tables III and IV indicate reading interests of pupils in the elementary school reported in Paul Witty's article, "Studies of Interests of Children." [3]

[3] Paul Witty, "Studies of Interests of Children," *The Packet*, 16 (Winter, 1961–1962), pp. 15–23.

COMICS   The popularity of comic books is properly deplored by parents and teachers. Nearly one billion copies of comic books are distributed every year in the United States alone. They range from the informative type to the amusing and harmless type to the Western, mystery, detective, and crime type to the horror and pornography type. Contrary to the popular notion, there are comic book series that make harmless reading. Nevertheless, the ready availability of comic books which depict horror, violence, vulgarity, invasion of civil liberties, and contempt for law is rightly considered a menace. Even when a comic book does not openly portray killing, maiming, torture, stealing, or frightening monsters and machines, it may reflect, directly or by implication, unwholesome attitudes and ideals such as greed, unworthy ambition, selfishness, and the worship of material success.

There has been much debate as to the effects of the crime comics upon the personality of the child and upon juvenile delinquency. A number of serious writers have held comics responsible for misbehavior and crime on the part of children. For example, Fredric Wertham, senior psychiatrist at Bellevue and Queens General Hospitals in New York City, has associated much cruel or criminal behavior of children with the reading of comic books. On the other hand, juvenile court judges appear to be divided as to the influence of the comic book upon the actual behavior of children.

We cannot be led to the conclusion that all comic books should be outlawed. Even the legal censorship of comic books raises serious constitutional questions. Parental and public pressure may help a great deal in cleaning up the magazine stands, but in the final analysis the solution lies in developing among children genuine interests in the better reading materials—of which there is such a rich abundance—and in the better things of life.

Comic book reading generally passes through three stages. Children under eleven like the "funny animal" comics, the Donald Ducks and Bugs Bunnies who walk and talk and act like human beings in familiar situations. This age group tends to read more comic books than older children. Eleven- and twelve-year-olds specialize in fantastic adventure comics—"Superman," "Batman," "Captain Marvel," "Captain Video." Children over twelve increasingly read *True* and *Classic* comics, if they read comics at all. Since the total amount of comic book reading declines sharply after ages eleven and twelve, these, then, are the critical ages in the reading of comics, from the standpoint of both the number and the quality.

Sports and crime comics are, of course, more popular with boys than with girls. Both sexes like humor when it is available.

Strangely enough, there is little difference in the amount and character of the general reading of those who read comic books extensively and those who do not. Nor is there any great difference in comic book reading habits between good readers and poor. Vocabulary development is on the whole no less rapid among comic book readers than among nonreaders of these books.

The popularity of comic books may probably be attributed in large part to their low cost and ready availability. New and used copies may be purchased for a few cents; a flourishing exchange market exists in many schools. On the other hand, good books, attractive books, may cost upwards of $2 each. When libraries and classrooms provide boys and girls with well-illustrated books about adventure, animals, space travel, science, humor, and other themes that appeal to them, the battle with the comic book can often be won. More books of literary quality produced as paperbacks may also serve to reduce the reading of comics.

MAGAZINES   Since comic books appear in magazine form, one valuable method of combating undesirable comics is to introduce the children to the many fine magazines addressed to them. Children's magazines have many features in common with comic books. The selections are short and usually well illustrated. Like comic books, they are expendable, timely, varied. It is therefore not astonishing that magazines are very popular with elementary school children beyond the second grade. They represent a much-neglected resource of the school.

Periodicals for Children

The following list of selected periodicals is an adaptation of that given by Professor Thomas Horn and associates.[4] Only those are included that were judged by Horn to be on the interest level of boys and girls in the elementary school. In the original list an annotation is given for each magazine, and magazines of interest to pupils beyond the elementary school are included. However, even the original list does not include the many excellent children's magazines published by religious organizations.

Adventure

Amazing Stories, Ziff-Davis Publishing Company, 434 South Wabash Ave.,
    Chicago, Ill. 60605. $3.50 yearly, single copy $.50. (5–12)
Child Life, Child Life, Inc., 1100 Waterway Blvd., Indianapolis, Ind. 46202.
    $5 yearly. (K–7)

[4] Thomas D. Horn, Audrey Fisher, and James L. Lanman, "Periodicals for Children and Youth," *Elementary English,* XLIII (April 1966), pp. 341–358, 399. Reprinted with the permission of the National Council of Teachers of English, and Thomas D. Horn, Audrey Fisher, and James L. Lanman.

Agriculture

American Forests, American Forestry Association, 919 Seventeenth St., N.W.,
   Washington, D.C., 20006. $6 yearly, single copy $.50. (5–12)
National 4-H News, National 4-H Service Committee, Inc., 59 E. Van Buren,
   Chicago, Ill. 60605. $2 yearly. (4–12)

Animals and Pets

Animal Kingdom, New York Zoological Society, Bronx Park, New York, N.Y.
   10460. $3.50 yearly. (5–12)
Aquarium, The, Aquariums Publishing, Inc., P.O. Box 832, Norristown, Pa.
   19404. $4.50 yearly, single copy $.50. (5–12)
Audubon Magazine, National Audubon Society, 1130 Fifth Ave., New York,
   N.Y. 10028. $5 yearly, single copy $1. (5–12)
Horse Lover's Magazine. Horse Lover's Magazine, Box 1432, Richmond, Calif.
   94802. 38 yearly, single copy $.40 (5–12)

Art

Design, Design Publishing Company, 1100 Waterway Blvd., Indianapolis, Ind.
   46202. $4.50 yearly. (1–12)
Ideals, Ideals, Milwaukee, Wisc. 53226. $7.50 yearly, single copy $1.50. (1–12)

Aviation

Flying, Zeff-Davis Publishing Company, 434 South Wabash Ave., Chicago,
   Ill. 60605. $8 yearly. (5–12)

Business or Economics

Consumer Reports, Consumers Union of U.S., Inc., 256 Washington St., Mt.
   Vernon, N.Y. 10553. $6 yearly, $4 yearly to an educator. (5–12)

Current Events

Africa Report, The African-American Institute, Inc., 500 Dupont Circle Building, Washington, D.C. 20036. $6 yearly, single copy $.75. (5–12)
Life, Time, Inc., 9 Rockefeller Plaza, New York, N.Y. 10020. $7.75 yearly,
   single copy $.35. (4–12)
Look, Look Building, Des Moines, Iowa, 50304. $5 yearly, single copy $.50.
   (4–12)

General

American Girl, Girl Scouts of the U.S.A., 830 Third Ave., New York, N.Y.
   10022. $3 yearly. (5–12)
Boy's Life, Boy Scouts of America, New Brunswick, N.J. 08903. $3 yearly,
   $1.50 for Boy Scouts; single copy $.25. (5–12)
Calling All Girls, The Better Reading Foundation, Inc., 52 Vanderbilt Ave.,
   New York, N.Y. 10017. $5 yearly, single copy $.50. (3–9)

Children's Digest, The Better Reading Foundation, Inc., 52 Vanderbilt Ave., New York, N.Y. 10017. $5 yearly, single copy $.50. Braille edition: American Printing House for the Blind, Louisville, Ky. 1–6)

Children's Playmate, Children's Playmate Magazine, Inc., 6529 Union Ave., Cleveland, Ohio 44105. $3.50 yearly, single copy $.35. (1–6)

Highlights for Children, incorporating *Children's Activities,* Highlights for Children, Inc., 2300 West Fifth Ave., Columbus, Ohio 43216. $5.95 yearly. (1–6)

Humpty Dumpty's Magazine, The Better Reading Foundation, Inc., 52 Vanderbilt Ave., New York, N.Y. 10017. $5 yearly.

Jack and Jill, The Curtis Publishing Company, Independence Square, Philadelphia 19105. $3.95 yearly, single copy $.35. (1–6)

Reader's Digest, Reader's Digest Services, Inc., Educational Division, Pleasantville, N.Y. 10570. $2.97 yearly, single copy $.35. (3–12)

Hobbies

American Modeler, Conde Nast Publications, Inc., 420 Lexington Ave., New York, N.Y. 10017. $3 yearly, single copy $.30. (5–12)

American Pigeon Journal, American Pigeon Journal Company, Warrenton, Mo. 63383. $3 yearly, single copy $.35. (5–12)

Hobbies, Lightner Publishing Company, 1006 Michigan Ave., Chicago, Ill. 60605. $4 yearly. (5–12)

Model Airplane News, Air Age, Inc., 551 Fifth Ave., New York, N.Y. 10017. $3.50 yearly, single copy $.35. (5–12)

Model Railroader, Kalmbach Publishing Company, 1027 North Seventh St., Milwaukee, Wisc. 53203. $6 yearly, single copy $.50. (5–12)

Pack-O-Fun, Clapper Publishing Company, Inc., P.O. Box 568, Park Ridge, Ill. 60068. $3 yearly. (1–6)

Scott's Monthly Journal, Scott Publications, Inc., 461 Eighth Ave., New York, N.Y. 10001. $4 yearly. (5–12)

Home Economics

Parents' Magazine and Better Homemaking, Parents' Institute, Inc., 52 Vanderbilt Ave., New York, N.Y. 10022. $4 yearly, single copy $.50. (5–12)

Music

Keyboard, Jr., and *Young Keyboard, Jr.,* Keyboard, Jr., Publications, Inc., 1346 Chapel St., New Haven, Conn. 06511. $1.50 yearly, single copies $.70 for five or more. (4–12)

Plays

Plays, Plays, Inc., 8 Arlington St., Boston, Mass. 02116. $6 yearly. (1–12)

Science

Earth and Sky, Outdoor Publishing Company, P.O. Box 589, Pasadena, Calif. 91102. (5–8)

Mechanics Illustrated, Fawcett Publishers, Inc., Fawcett Place, Greenwich, Conn. 06830. $3 yearly, single copy $.25.

Natural History Magazine, The American Museum of Natural History, Central Park West at 79th St., New York, N.Y. 10024. $5 yearly. (5–12)

Popular Mechanics Magazine, The Hearst Company, 250 West 55th St., New York, N.Y. 10019. $4 yearly, single copy $.50. (4–12)

Popular Science Monthly, Popular Science Publishing, Inc., 355 Lexington Ave., New York, N.Y. 10017. $4 yearly, single copy $.50. (4–12)

Review of Popular Astronomy, The, Sky Map Publishers, Inc., 111 South Meramac, St. Louis, Mo. 63105. $4 yearly, single copy $.65. (4–12)

Social Studies

American Heritage, American Heritage Publishing Company, 551 Fifth Ave., New York, N.Y. 10017. $15 yearly, single copy $3.95. Annual index $1. (4–12)

American Junior Red Cross News, American National Red Cross, National Headquarters, Washington, D.C. 20006. $1 yearly. (1–6)

Arizona Highways, Arizona Highway Department, Phoenix, Ariz. 85009. $4 yearly. (1–6)

Focus, American Geographical Society, Broadway at 156th St., New York, N.Y. 10032. $1.25 yearly. (4–12)

Frontier Times, Western Publications, Box 3668, 709 West 19th St., Austin, Tex. 78704. $3 yearly, single copy $.35. (4–12)

Gopher Historian, Minnesota Historical Society, Historical Building, St. Paul, Minn. 65100. $1.50 yearly. (5–9)

Holiday, Curtis Publishing Company, Independence Square, Philadelphia, Pa. 19105. $5.95 yearly. (6–12)

Hoosier Historian, Indiana Junior Historical Society, 140 N. Senate Ave., State Library and Historical Building, Indianapolis, Ind. 46204. Free to members of affiliated clubs. (5–9)

Montana, Michael Kennedy, Historical Society of Montana, Roberts and 6th Aves., Helena, Mont. 59601. $1.50 per issue. (5–12)

National Geographic Magazine, National Geographic Society, 17th and M Sts., N.W., Washington, D.C. 20036. $4 yearly, single copy $1. (3–12)

National Geographic School Bulletins, National Geographic Society, 17th and M Sts., N.W., Washington, D.C. 20036. $2 yearly. (4–12)

UNESCO Courier, UNESCO Publication Center, U.S.A., 317 East 34 St., New York, N.Y. 10016. $5 yearly, single copy $.50. (5–12)

In a study of children's choices of magazines, George Norvell asked 3,280 children of grades four through six (half boys and half girls) and 2,720 children of grade three (half boys and half girls) to indicate on a list of magazines their degree of interest in each magazine with which they were familiar. The results of the study in grades four through six are summarized in Table V.[5] The figure in the "No." column indicates how many pupils checked a magazine as one they knew. The "Score" column gives the interest score arrived at through application of a statistical formula.

One of the best-known and most reliable sources of information about children's magazines is Laura K. Martin's *Magazines for School Libraries*.[6] *101 Magazines for Schools,* by Ruby E. Cundiff, is available from the Tennessee Book Company.[7] The National Council of Teachers of English has published a committee report entitled *Using Magazines*.[8] A monthly mimeographed periodical called *Subject Index to Children's Magazines* serves as a kind of juvenile *Reader's Guide to Periodical Literature*. It is edited by Meribah Hazen at 301 Palomino Lake, Madison, Wisconsin.

BOOKS As every teacher knows, children differ widely in the degree to which they are interested in the reading of books. Some children read no books at all on their own, while others read several books a week. In order to discover what kinds of books will interest children, it is necessary to examine the voluntary choices of those who do like to read. Many such studies have been made.

As one might expect, pictures help a great deal to interest children in books. Children especially prefer colored pictures. However, the picture merely serves as a bridge to the content of the book. If the subject of the picture interests the reader, it will lure him to the book; if it does not, it will be ineffective.

In judging whether a book will interest a child, we must be careful not to be limited to adult standards. Children obviously do not always like books that adults consider superior. It is possible for adults to remember books they liked as children, and to assume that modern children will like them too. In some cases, of course, this is true. *Little Women, Heidi, Black Beauty, The Five Little Peppers,* and *Treasure Island* are perennially popular with children; *Robinson Crusoe, A Christmas Carol, Hans Brinker,* and *Tom Sawyer* also fall into this category. But other children's books of the past deal with topics and express attitudes that were of interest in their day but seem inappropriate or even ludicrous in our time. The same holds true for the element of literary style.

[5] For the results of the study in grade three see *Elementary English,* XLIII, p. 404 (April 1966).

[6] New York: The H. W. Wilson Company, 1950.

[7] Nashville, Tenn., 1954.

[8] Champaign, Ill., 1950.

TABLE V

THE INTERESTS OF BOYS AND GIRLS, GRADES 4 TO 6,
IN 31 MAGAZINES LISTED IN THE ORDER OF POPULARITY (1962)

BOYS

MAGAZINE	NO.	SCORE	MAGAZINE	NO.	SCORE
Boys' Life	1263	89.3	Look	1172	66.9
National Geographic	895	89.2	My Weekly Reader	1336	66.5
Popular Science	591	86.7	Modern Screen	76	65.8
Popular Mechanics	640	85.9	Time	739	65.7
Hot Rod	669	85.4	Junior Red Cross News	193	62.7
Junior Natural History	208	81.7	Children's Activities	122	61.7
Scouting	453	81.6	Child Life	211	60.4
Model Airplane News	227	80.1	Photoplay	88	60.2
Explorer	319	79.9	True Confessions	102	52.9
Junior Scholastic	525	79.1	Seventeen	127	49.6
Saturday Evening Post	772	73.6	American Girl	50	48.0
Life	1377	72.8	Calling All Girls	68	47.8
Reader's Digest	1049	70.9	McCall's	600	47.6
Newsweek	472	69.0	Better Homes & Gardens	411	44.0
Current Events	201	68.4	Good Housekeeping	355	39.4
Children's Digest	905	67.0			

GIRLS

MAGAZINE	NO.	SCORE	MAGAZINE	NO.	SCORE
National Geographic	760	86.5	Junior Red Cross News	221	71.0
American Girl	706	86.0	Boys' Life	256	70.9
Calling All Girls	834	84.2	Look	1167	70.9
Seventeen	433	84.1	Children's Activities	169	69.8
Junior Scholastic	518	80.2	My Weekly Reader	1330	67.5
Modern Screen	98	79.1	Newsweek	329	67.3
Junior Natural History	112	76.8	True Confessions	100	67.0
McCall's	1062	75.9	Child Life	264	66.7
Scouting	117	75.2	Better Homes & Gardens	650	62.6
Saturday Evening Post	649	74.8	Good Housekeeping	595	61.6
Life	1354	74.4	Hot Rod	104	61.5
Children's Digest	1029	72.7	Time	659	60.0
Reader's Digest	1058	72.1	Popular Science	144	59.7
Photoplay	111	71.6	Popular Mechanics	148	51.7
Current Events	137	71.5	Model Airplane News	24	50.0
Explorer	156	71.5			

BOYS AND GIRLS

MAGAZINE	NO.	SCORE	MAGAZINE	NO.	SCORE
National Geographic	1655	87.9	Newsweek	801	68.2
Boys' Life	1519	80.1	American Girl	756	67.0
Junior Scholastic	1043	79.7	My Weekly Reader	2666	67.0
Junior Natural History	320	79.3	Junior Red Cross News	414	66.9
Scouting	570	78.4	Seventeen	560	66.9
Explorer	475	75.7	Calling All Girls	902	66.0
Saturday Evening Post	1421	74.2	Photoplay	199	65.9
Life	2731	73.6	Children's Activities	291	65.8
Hot Rod	773	73.5	Model Airplane News	251	65.1
Popular Science	735	73.2	Child Life	475	63.6
Modern Screen	174	72.5	Time	1398	62.9
Readers' Digest	2107	71.5	McCall's	1662	61.8
Current Events	338	70.0	True Confessions	202	60.0
Children's Digest	1934	69.9	Better Homes & Gardens	1061	53.3
Look	2339	68.9	Good Housekeeping	950	50.5
Popular Mechanics	788	68.8			

Source: George W. Norvell, "The Challenge of Periodicals in Education," *Elementary English*, XLIII (April 1966), p. 403. Reprinted with the permission of the National Council of Teachers of English and George W. Norvell.

When we read these generalizations about children's interests in books and reading, we must always keep in mind that each child has his own individual pattern of voluntary reading. Some average children read more than some bright children. Some boys read more than some girls. Some able readers read very little; some children of limited reading ability read a great deal. Some children continue to increase in the amount of reading as they reach adolescence. Some children read excessively, or compulsively, because of emotional maladjustment; others avoid reading for the same reason. It is the particular combination of cultural and personality factors that come together in the life of an individual child that determines his voluntary reading habits. There can be no substitute for the painstaking study of individual children to discover the extent and nature of their reading interests.

CHAPTER 10B

Developing Children's Interests in Reading

The preceding chapter discussed the importance of the interest factor in the teaching of reading, the purposes of the voluntary reading program, and the developmental stages in the unfolding interests of boys and girls. In this chapter we shall consider ways in which the classroom teacher can extend the range and elevate the quality of children's interests in reading.

Although the term *free reading* is commonly used to distinguish it from assigned reading, in a sense it is a misnomer. The child who reads freely and widely in the pulps and worthless or harmful books is in great need of guidance by teachers and parents. It is one of the aims of the reading program to influence his preferences so that he will choose more worthy and more rewarding books to read. Perhaps the term *voluntary reading* or *personal reading* would be better. In *directed reading* the teacher guides the reading choices of children in the direction of books of specific types or books that have certain themes. Such guidance may be desirable in the case of children who are too steadily absorbed in a single subject or who have never discovered that poetry or biography can be fun, too. In this chapter, for the sake of uniformity, we shall employ the term *voluntary reading*.

PRINCIPLES UNDERLYING THE VOLUNTARY READING PROGRAM

Before describing specific classroom practices in the guidance of voluntary reading, we shall enumerate certain principles that will help us to devise and evaluate our procedures. There are no doubt others, but these are among the most fundamental of the governing principles:

1. Interests are acquired and, like other acquired traits, are amenable to training or teaching. They are responsive to the home and school environments and are conditioned by experience.
2. In any group of children, there will be wide variations in the children's tastes and interests. It is the task of the teacher to discover, so far as possible, what these tastes and interests are.
3. Reading interests and life interests bear a reciprocal relation to each other. A child will read, or can be induced to read, about the things he is interested in; through reading he will become interested in more things.
4. In order that we may improve a child's interests and tastes in reading, we must begin at his present level. No matter how limited or immature his interests may be, they are all we have to build upon. We cannot usually advance the child from Mickey Mouse to *Robinson Crusoe* in one leap. Normally we progress by easy stages. The speed will depend upon the child and the circumstances.
5. The program in voluntary reading should be a balanced program. It should include many themes and areas of interest, many literary types, many media, and both factual and imaginative material. It should appeal to many different types of pupil purposes.
6. Many children who read widely will oscillate between books of high and of low literary merit. All printed matter is grist to their mill. The measure of their growth is the highest literary level to which they respond with comprehension and pleasure. The reading of material of lesser quality is in itself no evidence of immaturity.
7. In the evaluation of children's reading interests, every effort should be made to ascertain the child's genuine preferences rather than his perception of what the teacher considers worthwhile.
8. The techniques of improving a child's voluntary reading habits should in general be those of enticement and persuasion rather than those of coercion.
9. The aim of the voluntary reading program should not be the reading of certain specific books or a certain number of books but the development of enduring interests in reading.
10. Home and school cooperation is of great value in the cultivation of desirable reading interests on the part of children.

CONDITIONS NEEDED FOR EFFECTIVE GUIDANCE

To effective guidance in reading the teacher, the environment, and the curriculum can contribute.

The Teacher

In the development of reading interests, as in all other instruction, the teacher is the key factor. If the teacher feels affection for the children, exhibits a sincere interest in their problems and their interests, is accepting, gives encouragement, and demonstrates genuine enthusiasm for books, she can create an atmosphere that is favorable to voluntary reading. The teacher who exercises a rigid discipline will get from many only such reading as she demands, and no more. The reading is unlikely to be accompanied with pleasure, and it will end when the assignments end.

The teacher's attitude toward the pupils should be, within limits, a permissive one. Children should be free to go from their seats to the book table or to read a story to a classmate or to go to the teacher with a comment or a call for help. All this presupposes, of course, a class size that will permit mobility and a certain amount of intercommunication. Crowded classrooms necessarily require a degree of regimentation and formal "discipline."

A generalized attitude of friendliness and good *rapport* with children are not enough. Since the task of the teacher is to bring child and book together, she must know a great deal about the child, and she must have a wide acquaintance with children's books. Her knowledge of the child should include information about his home background, his intelligence, his general maturity, his personal adjustment, his reading ability, his play interests, and his reading interests. School records, tests, interviews with parents and other teachers, and particularly a careful observation of individual children are ways through which the teacher can know the child.

The teacher's preparation for the cultivation of children's interests in books includes a wide acquaintance with the rapidly growing supply of juvenile literature. While a good background in the reading of adult literature and acquaintance with the best in the theater, movies, radio, and television will be of great assistance, wide reading in children's books is essential. Reliance upon recollection of favorite books of one's own childhood will not do. So much has happened in this field, even in the last ten years, that a new look at children's books is imperative. The reading of the new books can be a really delightful experience. It is impossible for a teacher to be familiar with even a small fraction of the new titles, but she should be on speaking terms with the best of them. Fortunately she may have access to numerous publications which will acquaint her with recommended children's books. A list of such publications is found in the latter part of this chapter.

The Physical Environment

No studies, to our knowledge, have been made of the effect of the physical environment in the classroom upon the development of reading interests in children. Nevertheless, experienced teachers believe that attractive surroundings help in encouraging children to read. For most children, especially those who have little interest in reading, an attractive room provides a setting in which reading seems the natural thing to do. Some children will, of course, develop strong reading interests almost regardless of the physical surroundings. An inviting reading corner, with table, comfortable chairs, and perhaps a reading lamp, may attract children who have completed their other work. Movable tables and chairs, plenty of shelf space, a book display table, a bulletin board, and above all, a colorful display of books, frequently changed, will help to create the reading environment in which the love of books can flourish.

The Curriculum

When we speak of voluntary reading, we refer to reading that is personal, individual, and therefore not necessarily related to any units of work that may be in progress in the classroom. Nevertheless, the kind of curriculum that is pursued may have a great influence upon children's voluntary reading activities. If the curriculum is inflexible, totally prescribed, and textbook centered, it is likely to dampen the enthusiasm of many children for books and to blunt the edge of their curiosity. On the other hand, if the curriculum is vital and stimulating, if it encourages child initiative, if it encourages exploration in many directions, it will provide an abundance of "leads" for pleasurable personal reading. In this process almost every subject of study may have a part.

ACTIVITIES THAT PROMOTE WHOLESOME VOLUNTARY READING The teacher who is both a lover of books and a lover of children will be resourceful in finding new ways of bringing children and books together. However, there are many standard techniques that skillful teachers frequently use on appropriate occasions. Here are some of them.

1. *Utilizing children's experiences.* Young children in modern

schools enjoy a great variety of experiences. In some classrooms there is a "discovery" table on which may be found a constantly changing collection of interesting objects, contributed by both teacher and pupils—shells, rocks, tropical fish, twigs, models of trains or planes, textile samples, parts of Indian or foreign costumes, and the like. Each day the children go to the table to see what is new there. Questions come thick and fast, and the teacher is ready to suggest and to display fine children's books that will help to answer them.

Class visits to places of interest in the community or in nearby towns may also be a source of inspiration for voluntary reading. Classes, under the supervision of a teacher and with the consent of the parents, often go to the zoo, the museum, historical shrines, the bakery, the dairy, the farm, a factory, a newspaper plant, an airport, a railway station (sometimes children may talk with trainmen or inspect the cab of the engine), and radio and television stations. The alert teacher will arrange to have many good books about these places ready for children to read on their return. If children have become really interested, they will usually not be deterred by vocabulary which would ordinarily be too difficult for them.

The active classroom provides the setting for many other kinds of experiences. Primary grade children are fascinated by many kinds of pets. Hamsters, kittens, raccoons, white mice, goldfish, snakes, and rabbits have all found comfortable homes and eager audiences in primary grade schoolrooms. Fortunately on all of these there is much interesting material for children to read.

2. *Reading and telling to children.* Perhaps the most popular time of the school day is the story hour. If it is to be successful, however, it requires careful thought and preparation on the part of the teacher. The story chosen for the day should possess literary merit. It should be one that the teacher herself enjoys and can read aloud with enthusiasm. The children should be grouped about the teacher, sitting on the floor or on comfortable chairs, not too crowded but close enough to the teacher to hear with ease. The group should not be too large; if necessary, the class should be divided into subgroups to help create an atmosphere of intimacy and to permit the teacher to read in a quiet though animated voice. The teacher first shows the children the book—the jacket, the cover, the title page. As she reads, she will pause occasionally to ask a question, make a comment, or answer the inevitable exclamations and questions of the children. She will take time to show the illustrations as the story proceeds, and she will accede to the noisy requests to look at them again after the

story is over. She will take pains to make it possible for *all* the children to have a good view of the pictures.

Sometimes, especially with older children, the teacher will stop short of the climax and invite the children to read for themselves how the story turned out. Or she will stop and ask the children to guess at the outcome before she reads to the end. If she asks the pupils to finish the story by themselves, she will arrange, if possible, to have several copies of the book available in order to avoid the tantalizing and frustrating effect of indefinite suspense.

In the lower grades children are often encouraged to read stories to each other. The reader should be a fairly good oral reader, enthusiastic about the story, and the listener must be a willing one.

Storytelling by the teacher is one of the most ancient of all the means by which young people become aware of the heritage of books. While good storytelling is an art, it is one that can be successfully cultivated by any teacher of young children. Valuable hints may be found in the recent pamphlet, *Once upon a Time,* prepared by the Picture Book Committee of the Children's and Young People's Section of the New York Library Association. It may be obtained for 25 cents from Anne Izard of the New York City Public Library. Also, the entire March 1957 issue of the magazine *Elementary English* is devoted to the subject of listening and storytelling. Another source is *Stories To Tell to Children,* compiled by Laura E. Cathon and others (Pittsburgh: Carnegie Library, 1949). An excellent book on the subject of storytelling, containing many examples of good stories to tell to children, has been written by Ruth Tooze, director of the Children's Book Caravan.[1]

3. *Using the browsing table.* One of the most influential factors in the development of reading interests is that of accessibility. Perhaps the widespread popularity of the paperbacks, both good and bad, is attributable to the fact that they may be secured so easily and inexpensively at any drugstore. Many people will not make the effort to go to the library and the bookstore to get a book, but will purchase a paperback along with a newspaper, a railroad ticket, or a candy bar. Thus, unfortunately, we seldom find a queue at the charging desk of a library.

So it is with children. Until a keen appetite for reading has been aroused, it is necessary to bring the books to the children. The book display on a browsing table should be attractive and colorful.

---

[1] Ruth Tooze, *Storytelling: How To Develop Skills in the Art of Telling Stories to Children.* Englewood Cliffs, N.J.: Prentice-Hall, Inc., 1959.

Story hour. (Zimbel—Monkmeyer Press Photo Service.)

It should be varied in subject matter and changed frequently to lend new interest from week to week. At appropriate times during the school day, the children should be permitted and encouraged to go to the table, page through the books, look at the pictures, and select a book to read in school and to borrow for home use. When new books are added to the collection, the teacher should take a few minutes to call the children's attention to them.

4. *Pupil selection and management of books.* Nowhere does the principle of teacher-pupil planning operate with more effectiveness than in the guidance of voluntary reading. If the children have a voice in the selection of the books for the room collection, they are more likely to feel a proprietary interest in them and may be motivated to read them, or at least to become acquainted with them.

Methods of acquiring books for the room collection vary from one school system to another. In some schools a certain sum of money is periodically allotted to each teacher, who may order the book titles she believes she needs. In other schools all general book purchases are made through the principal's office or the school library. In almost all instances, when books are available for room collections, the teacher has the opportunity to make the selection of titles. In any case, whether the books are newly purchased or borrowed from a central collection, the teacher has the opportunity to consult her pupils about the books to be requested.

Preparing the book order is an exciting event in the elementary school classroom. Children who have enjoyed books by certain authors will ask about other titles by the same writers and request that they be included in the order. "May we have some more books about dogs (horses, sports, adventure, fairy tales, magic, space travel)?" will be a common question. The teacher herself, of course, should have many titles to recommend. She will describe these to the children, telling them something of the theme and story of each. When the final order is ready to send in, the teacher makes a last-minute inspection to be sure that all the selections are appropriate for her class.

The children will be impatient for the books to arrive. The time when they finally come is a red-letter day. If they are new and arrive by mail, the children should have the pleasure of opening the packages. In any event, the arrival of the books should be some kind of ceremony, followed by a quiet period of browsing.

Children will take pleasure, too, in preparing the books for the shelves. (It is to be hoped that the room is equipped with an abun-

Interesting children in books through a variety of activities. (Photo courtesy St. Mary's School, Delaware, Ohio.)

dance of open shelf space). Under the guidance of the teacher, they will arrange the books on the shelves and on the browsing table. Pupil committees will assist in the work of charging out books and keeping the records. They will help in returning books to the central library and in bringing back new titles. Through taking care of and handling books, children will come to regard them as precious possessions.

5. *Book discussions and informal book reports.* When a child likes a book, he wants to talk about it with someone. He should, therefore, have an opportunity to talked with the teacher about it and be encouraged to tell the class about it during the discussions in story hour. Sometimes he can be encouraged to stand before the group and recapitulate the story.

Care should be taken not to allow the oral book reports to become a tedious succession of routine summaries. First, there should probably be no more than two or three reports in a period. Second, children should be taught how to make an effective report. It is possible to explain to them how to select the significant details of a story, to arrange them in proper order, and to build up suspense. Third, the class should be given opportunity to ask questions and to discuss the story. Such oral reports are not intended to serve as a check on whether the boys and girls have read the minimum number of books. Their purpose is to introduce other children to new books they will like.

6. *Dramatizations.* Children who have read the same book may wish to dramatize scenes from it. The dialogue may be taken directly from the book, or it may be improvised. This latter, "creative" kind of dramatics is usually more fun and is less likely to be stilted and overformal. However, the nature of the story and especially the vocabulary employed in the quotations should determine the type of dramatization selected. Other children may wish to reproduce in costume a particularly striking illustration from a book. Guessing games, too, are popular with children. A pupil, or a group of pupils, will act out characters from a story with the aid of pantomime and simple costume, while the rest of the class guesses the identity of the characters. If large sections of a book or an entire book is made into a play, it may be possible to record the final performance on tape, to be replayed for other classes.

7. *Use of audio-visual aids.* Visual aids are a very effective means of awakening the children's desire to read. These aids may include phonograph records, radio and television programs, films, filmstrips, slides, and pictures.

Dramatic recordings of books that have won the Newbery Award are now available. The discs, which are 33⅓ r.p.m., sell for

Audio-visual materials are effective aids to reading. (Photo courtesy Boston, Massachusetts, Public Schools.)

$5.95 and may be obtained direct from Newbery Awards Records, New York. Complete teaching aids, including background information, vocabulary lists, suggestions for prelistening and follow-up activities, and other data, accompany the records. The dramatizations are expertly directed and are performed by professional actors. The famous Landmark Book Series, published by Random House, is accompanied by dramatizations based upon the books. The records may be secured from Enrichment Records, Inc., New York. Other publishers similarly produce records that dramatize children's books. Thomas Y. Crowell, for example, has issued a record of *Harriet Tubman, Conductor on the Underground Railroad,* by Ann Perry, and Ginn and Company has an album of LP recordings entitled, "Let's Listen." Record companies have issued recordings of many of the children's favorites. Camden (R.C.A.-Victor) has one on *The 500 Hats of Bartholomew Cubbins,* by Dr. Seuss, read by Paul Wing, and another on *A Christmas Carol.* Spoken Arts Records provides unusual recordings of literature. Of particular interest to teachers of young children are the *Just So Stories* of Kipling, *You Read to Me, I'll Read to You,* by John Ciardi, and *Grimm's Fairy Tales.* A catalog may be obtained from Spoken Arts, New Rochelle, New York. Folkways Records presents songs, folktales, and poetry. A catalog may be secured from Folkways Records, New York.

The playing of such records, both before and after the

reading of the books, gives the children a sense of the reality of the story and often makes the reading itself an irresistible activity.

The use of records and recordings has numerous advantages. First, it is possible for the teacher to listen in advance to a record in order to determine its suitability for a class. Second, it is possible to stop a record at any time to discuss aspects of a story or to answer children's questions. Third, it is possible to play a record over and over, as often as the teacher or the children may desire.

As the record appeals to the ear, so the slide, filmstrip, and film appeal to the eye. Like the phonograph record, however, the visual media require careful preplanning by the teacher. Especially in the case of the slide and the filmstrip, the teacher should be familiar with the content in advance. While some filmstrips are accompanied by a record that is synchronized with the pictures on the screen, for others, the teacher must supply the sound element that is lacking—the explanation and the commentary. Often the filmstrips come provided with a teachers' manual, which explains each frame and focuses attention upon the significant ideas in the series. As a rule, it is desirable to discuss with the class in advance what is to be looked for in the still or moving pictures and to follow up the presentation with questions, interpretations, and summaries.

An example of filmstrips suited to the elementary grades is the series "Our American Heritage of Folk Music," produced by the Society for Visual Education, Inc., Chicago, Illinois. This is a series of long-playing records accompanied by filmstrips on Songs of the Sea, Songs of the Cowboy, Songs of the Mountains, Songs of the Plains, Songs of the Railroads, and Songs of the Civil War. Each filmstrip consists of about fifty frames. The records and filmstrips together provide a pleasant stimulus to the reading of children's books dealing with these themes.

Certain radio and television programs can be recommended in connection with developing children's interest in reading. Many stations throughout the country conduct regular "book hours" to which we can call children's attention.

Although television is a new medium, it has grown with unprecedented speed. The annual surveys by Paul Witty in *Elementary English* effectively dramatize the phenomenal development of this industry. Already a large body of professional literature on the subject of children and television has come into being. Two interesting pamphlets may be recommended: *Children and TV—Making the Most of It*, a publication of the Association for Childhood Education International,

Washington, D.C., and *Your Child, Radio, and TV,* by Paul Witty, published by Science Research Associates, Chicago, Illinois.

Not all audio-visual aids are as formal as those described in the preceding paragraphs. Many miscellaneous aids may be used to good advantage. Attractive bulletin board displays, colorful wall maps, pictures, and book jackets may frequently be used to serve as an avenue to the reading of books.

Following are some lists of sources for audio-visual materials. These lists are highly selected, for the field of audio-visual methods in teaching has become so large that a whole book would be required to do justice to it. Fortunately there is a growing supply of literature on the subject. A comprehensive book concerning it is the attractive volume by Edgar Dale, *Audio-Visual Methods in Teaching,* rev. ed., published by Holt, Rinehart and Winston, Inc.

Audio-Visual Materials—General

Audio-Visual Materials for Teaching Reading. A very extensive listing of films, filmstrips, slides, pictures, recordings, and special devices for the teaching of reading. Compiled by Robert Leestma of the Audio-Visual Education Center of the University of Michigan. Slater's Bookstore, Inc., Ann Arbor, Mich.

Audio-Visual Catalog. Materials for Learning, Inc., Brooklyn, N.Y.

Selected Information Sources for Educational Films

Choosing a Classroom Film. McGraw-Hill, Inc., New York.

Film and You. Bailey Films, Hollywood, Calif.

Catalog of Frith Films. Hollywood, Calif.

Instructional Films and Filmstrips. 16 mm. Catalog of Universal-International and J. Arthur Rank features. United World Films, New York.

Library of Congress, Card Division, Washington, D.C. Price lists of catalog card service for films and records.

UCLA Children's Film Series. Children's Theatre Committee, Theatre Arts Department, University of California, Los Angeles. Self-addressed, stamped envelope.

Selected List of Sources of Educational Films

Bailey Films, Hollywood, Calif.

Coronet Films, Chicago.

Education Film Library Association, New York.

Encyclopaedia Britannica Films, Inc., Wilmette, Ill.

Folkways Record and Service Corporation, New York.

International Film Bureau, Chicago.

Jam Handy Organization, Detroit.

McGraw-Hill Filmstrip Catalog, McGraw-Hill Text-Films, New York.
Teaching Film Custodians, New York.
United World Films, New York.
Weston Woods Studios, Weston, Conn.
Many state universities also operate rental libraries of educational films.

Selected Information Sources for Educational Records and Recordings

Annotated List of Phonograph Records. Materials for Learning, Inc., Brooklyn, N.Y. (10 cents)
Catalog of Recorded Tape and Catalog of Children's Records. M. and N. Harrison, Inc., New York.
Folkways Record and Service Corporation, record catalog, New York.
National Council of Teachers of English, Champaign, Ill.
National Tape Recording Catalog, 1962–1963. Department of Audio-Visual Instruction, N. E. A., Washington, D.C.
Spoken Arts Records, New Rochelle, N.Y.
The Tape Recorder in the Elementary Classroom. Minnesota Mining and Manufacturing Company, St. Paul, Minn.

Selected List of Sources of Educational Recordings

American Friends Service Committee, Philadelphia.
American Library Association, Chicago. (Folk tales)
Children's Record Guild, New York.
Columbia Records, Inc., New York.
Decca Records, New York.
Educational Record Company of Illinois, Charleston, Ill.
Enrichment Landmark Records, to accompany Landmark Books (Random House). Enrichment Teaching Materials, New York.
Instructional Films, Wilmette, Ill.
Library of Congress, Washington, D.C.
National Council of Teachers of English, Champaign, Ill.
World Wide Records Corporation, New York.

Selected Information Sources for Educational Filmstrips and Slides

Educational Filmstrip Catalog. Society for Visual Education, Inc., Chicago.
Educators Guide to Free Slidefilms. Educators Progress Service, Randolph, Wis.
Enrichment Filmstrips. Enrichment Teaching Materials, New York. Based on such Landmark Books (Random House) as *Paul Revere and the Minute Men, The Winter at Valley Forge, The California Gold Rush.*
Eye Gate House, Inc., Jamaica, N.Y.
Filmstrip Catalog. From 21 companies, arranged by subjects. Also a catalog of educational record albums. Stanley Bowmar Company, Valhalla, N.Y.

Filmstrip Guide. The H. W. Wilson Company, New York. Classified by subjects. Alphabetical index. Found in many libraries.

Jam Handy Organization, Detroit.

Keystone View Company Catalogs. Meadville, Pa. Extensive listing of slides.

Society for Visual Education, Inc., Chicago.

Young American Filmstrip Catalog. Young America Films, New York.

Miscellaneous Audio-Visual Aids

Baited Bulletin Boards, prepared by Thomas A. Koskey. Fearon Publishers, San Francisco, Calif. Design, color, grouping, eye movement, texture, shape. Illustrated. Examples.

Better Bulletin Board Displays, by J. Preston Lockridge and Ernest F. Tiemann. Bridges for Ideas Series, Visual Instruction Bureau, Division of Extension, University of Texas, Austin, Tex. Designed so that every page can be used as resource material for the preparation of bulletin boards.

Bulletin Boards, by Martha Dallmann. Teachers Publishing Corporation, Darien, Conn., 1959. Planning, use, materials, procedures; suggestions for various subjects. 114 illustrations.

Graphic Tools for Teachers, by R. A. Frye. E. and J. Printing Company, Austin, Tex. Using graphic materials in the classroom.

Portrait of the real Davy Crockett, by S. S. Osgood, lithographer. 10" x 15". State Teachers Magazines, Inc. Chicago.

Free and Inexpensive Materials—General

Catalog of Free Teaching Aids. Riverside, Calif.

Choosing Free Materials for Use in the Schools. AASA, Washington, D.C.

Educators Guide to Free Films. Educators Progress Service, Randoph, Wis. Annual.

Educators Guide to Free Slidefilms. (Same as above)

Elementary Teachers Guide to Free Curriculum Materials. (Same as above)

Free and Inexpensive Learning Materials. Division of Surveys and Field Services, George Peabody College for Teachers, Nashville, Tenn.

8. *Book programs by children on radio and television.* Radio and television stations, especially in the smaller communities, welcome school groups to their programs. The opportunity to present a discussion of children's books on radio or television can serve as powerful motivation for children to read the best of the current books for young people. Both large city schools and schools in smaller towns have successfully produced children's book programs in this manner, sometimes as single projects and sometimes in a regular series during the winter months.

With primary grade children it is sometimes effective to have a storytelling period with a make-believe microphone. Such simulated "broadcasts" may serve to encourage the shy child who normally would hesitate to speak before a group. Programs may take the form of dramatizations, interviews, or direct storytelling. Visits to local radio studios will furnish ideas for procedures and physical settings. Later on, the children will be ready to participate in real broadcasts on radio and television. Meanwhile the focus will be on the books themselves and on the exciting activity of sharing book experiences.

9. *Book Week activities, book festivals, and book fairs.* In order to stimulate interest in children's books on a nation-wide scale, the Children's Book Council each year sponsors the National Children's Book Week. The Council, composed of the children's book editors of 60 leading publishing houses, is located in New York. It supplies schools with a Book Week poster, usually designed by a distinguished illustrator of children's books, streamers with children's book themes, full-color bookmarks reproducing the Book Week posters, records, picture quizzes, and other Book Week aids. Local schools throughout the country celebrate Book Week with special assemblies, open house, plays, radio programs, and other activities.

Recognizing that fall Book Week activities often tended to result in neglect of book projects during the rest of the year, the New York *Herald Tribune* established in 1937 the Spring Book Festival. It began by awarding two prizes of $250 each, one for the best book for younger children and one for older children. The newspaper issues each May a special Spring Book Festival number corresponding to the Children's Book Week number in the fall. Spring Book Week is observed in cooperation with bookstores from coast to coast.

Another development in the field of children's books is the book fair or book bazaar. The book fair is usually a community project involving the schools, libraries, churches, civic groups, and various organizations interested in literature and the arts. Interest in local book fairs has been stimulated by the Children's Book Council, which also publishes a volume, *The World of Children's Books,* that includes a chapter on "How To Run a Book Fair." The book fair is usually set up in cooperation with a local bookseller or jobber who supplies the books and allows a commission on direct sales and orders taken at the fair. Such proceeds from book sales are commonly applied to some educational project, often the expansion of the school library. An extensive list of books for display in the fair has been compiled by the Publisher's Liaison Committee. It may be secured without cost from the Children's Book Council.

In 1954 the first Midwest Book Fair, with 2,600 titles, was co-sponsored by the Children's Book Council, the *Chicago Tribune,* and the Chicago Public Library. Held at Chicago's Museum of Science and Industry, it attracted 44,000 visitors. Trained children's librarians were on hand to answer questions. One booth exhibited a model children's home library. Other book fairs were held that same year in New York (the *Times'* "Reading Is Fun" exhibit toured the schools in the New York area), Cleveland, Buffalo, Detroit, Washington, Minneapolis, Philadelphia, and Hampton, Virginia. Distinguished children's authors appeared at some of the fairs. Storytelling programs were held mornings and afternoons.

Book fairs need not be planned on the grand scale of those held in the great cities. In one school[2] the project is sponsored annually by two fourth-grade classes. One year, library tables usually arranged for small groups were placed around the room for displays of new books. Book Week posters and pupil-made murals of scenes from the books lined the walls of the room. Prize-winning books, along with displays of jackets and facsimiles of the medals, were featured. Original new-book illustrations loaned by the publishers were mounted on the upper shelves, and the exhibit also included photographs of authors and illustrators. A puppet show featuring characters from favorite books was shown to the children of other grades and to parents. In all these activities, the PTA cooperated closely.

10. *Miscellaneous procedures.* The teacher who is enthusiastic about books and reading will, of course, find many new ways of interesting children in books. Teachers can cooperate with children's librarians who organize reading clubs that meet regularly in the public library or branch library. The activities of such reading groups may include film showings, book reviews by the members or by adult counselors, tours of historical sites or places of local interest, record sessions, arranging for guest speakers, parties, and the discussion of reviews in magazines and newspapers.

Classroom activities may include recommending favorite books to children in lower grades, conducting imaginary conversations among well-known characters from different books, visiting the public library, writing letters of appreciation to authors of books that were especially well liked, writing brief reactions to stories that had a special impact, identifying story sites on a world map, making theme posters from books, and having each child assemble his own poetry anthology.

Other activities that have been suggested include decorating book jackets; writing a movie script for an adventure story; giving

[2] Gladys Jacobson, "Book Fair at Daniel Webster," *Elementary English*, 27 (October 1950), pp. 356–367.

an illustrated lecture about a travel book, using postcards, slides, magazine clippings, and other pictorial matter; making a "movie" of a book by means of a series of pictures on a paper roll attached to rollers; supplying a different ending to a story; selecting the most humorous or exciting incident from a book to tell to the class; writing a letter to the librarian or a friend recommending a book; making a scrapbook about a subject treated in a book; giving a puppet show based on a book; stretching a cord across the room and mounting on it paper cloths decorated with titles and pictures of book characters; modeling clay or soap figures from illustrations in books; making a diorama on a sand table to reproduce the setting of a story; making a mural from a story; listening to radio or television reviews of children's books; selecting poems for choral reading; collecting pictures to illustrate a book of verse.

Puppet shows can be very effective, but they require advance planning and some specialized knowledge. The following are some reference sources for work with puppets and marionettes:

Fletcher, Helen Jill, and Jack Deckter, *Puppet Book.* Philadelphia: Chilton Company—Book Division, 1947.

Hoben, Alice M., *The Beginner's Puppet Book.* New York: Noble & Noble Publishing, Inc., 1938.

Howard, Vernon, Puppet and Pantomime Plays. New York: Sterling Publishing Company, 1962.

Nau, Elizabeth, "Making Marionettes for the Classroom," *Elementary English,* 29, p. 19 (January 1952).

Pels, Gertrude, *Easy Puppets.* Illustrated by Albert Pels. New York: Thomas Y. Crowell Company, 1951.

Pratt, Lois H., *The Puppet Do-It-Yourself Book.* New York: Exposition Press, 1957.

Rhodes, M., "Pupils and Puppets," *The Grade Teacher,* 69, p. 48 (November 1951).

Taylor, Loren E., *Puppetry, Marionettes, and Shadow Plays,* Minneapolis: Burgess Publishing Company, 1965.

Although cumulative reading records are commonly regarded as evaluation devices, they can serve also as incentives to reading. Cumulative records take many forms. Some teachers ask children to keep card files of books they have read. Others provide each child with a large card with spaces for authors, titles, and a one- or two-sentence description of each book. A four-page leaflet called *My Reading Design* provides for listing of book titles and insertion of numbers in a pie graph representing different themes and types of books.[3]

[3] Published by *The News Journal,* North Manchester, Ind.

DEVELOPING INTEREST IN POETRY

Leland B. Jacobs, in an article, "Making Poetry Live with Children," in *Literature with Children,* edited by Margaret Rasmussen, a publication of the Association for Childhood Education International, has many valuable suggestions for the development of children's interest in poetry:

POETS EVERY CHILD SHOULD MEET

Perceptive teachers constructively set about to enrich school living through poetry. In the first place, they know intimately the appeals of many poets whose work is attractive to children. Such teachers are well acquainted with the writings of poets with whom children should have the opportunity to get acquainted:

Dorothy Aldis	Aileen Fisher
Mary Austin	Frances Frost
Harry Behn	Rose Fyleman
Rosemary and Stephen Benét	Edward Lear
William Blake	Vachel Lindsay
Margaret Wise Brown	Myra Cohn Livingston
Lewis Carroll	A. A. Milne
Marchette Chute	Laura E. Richards
John Ciardi	James Whitcomb Riley
Elizabeth Coatsworth	Elizabeth Madox Roberts
Walter De La Mare	Christina Rossetti
Paul Laurence Dunbar	Carl Sandburg
Ivy O. Eastwick	Robert Louis Stevenson
Eleanor Farjeon	James S. Tippett
Eugene Field	Winifred Welles
Rachel Field	Annette Wynn

Of course, there are many other poets whose one or two or handful of poems are appealing to children and should be at the teacher's fingertips for use at the right time. In addition, if the teacher possesses several outstanding anthologies for children, he will be rich in resources for making poetry time a happy time for youngsters.

Anyone who is well read in poetry for children soon discovers that there never can be graded poetry lists. To say "There are fifth grade poems" is unfair to children and to poetry. The teacher should not be concerned with "leveling" poetry. Rather, he should select poetry, whether it be primarily written for children or adults, which meets children's mind and spirits at the present gradients of their development as personalities, as thinking persons and as consumers of the arts.

WHAT CHILDREN ENJOY IN POETRY

A perceptive teacher knows that children develop taste in poetry only as the adults in their lives guide that development of taste. The teacher capitalizes on what children like in poetry but at the same time whets their taste with good poetry which is the work of sensitive, original writers. Children enjoy good poetry that:

gives them an exhilarating sense of melodious movement
makes the everyday experiences of life vibrant
tells wonderful stories
releases health-giving laughter
carries them into extravagant or fanciful situations
extends their appreciation of their natural world
creates memorable personages or characters
sings its way into their minds and memories.

Pleasurable responses to poetry are evoked when poetry selections are neatly gauged to the maturity and interests of the youngsters. In the poetry of their workday world, children respond well to poems about pets, play activities, occupations, transportation and interesting people. In their natural world they enjoy poems about seasons, weather, animals, flowers, trees. In humorous poetry they respond to ludicrous situations, peculiar people, tongue-tickling words, absurdities, oddities and nonsense. In narrative poetry they listen enthusiastically to adventure on sea and land, patriotic achievements, courageous deeds, historical personages and events and rousing heroism. In the fanciful, they enjoy fine make-believe, the poetic interpretation of preternatural creatures, and at times the grotesque. In lyric poetry they feel akin to poetry that is rich in sensory imagery, creates moods, calls forth pictures in the mind, makes the commonplace distinctively uncommon.

POEMS MUST BE READ WELL

Then, too, the modern teacher knows that poems do not look particularly inviting on a printed page. But when the poem is read well, all its melody, its vibrance, its feeling tone, its movement, its unique quality leap into life. So the teacher learns how to read poetry well. A good reader is one who:

appreciatively comprehends the psychological content and emotional intent of the poem which he is reading
knows that as he reads a poem to children he must both reveal what seem to be the poet's thoughts and communicate the poet's moods and nuances of meaning to the listeners
helps the listener to think, sense, and feel with the poet
sympathetically interprets the full esthetic appeal and quality of mood which the poem possesses

takes his clues for the actual oralization from the patterning of
the poem: its variety, its images, its symbols, its rhythms, its
rhymes, its symmetry

employs effective variety in timing in his reading and uses the
eloquence of appropriate pauses

so utilizes tonal quality in volume, pitch, and force that, through
cadenced reading, enjoyment is enhanced

avoids elocutionary, declamatory or other forms of artificial oral
interpretation in favor of wholesome naturalness

acts as a medium through which the ideas and feelings of the poet
touch deeply the ideas and feelings of the listener. . . .[4]

THE SCHOOL LIBRARY

Since the textbook has ceased to dominate instruction in
modern elementary schools, greater reliance than ever is being placed
upon the library. The library provides an extensive and well-selected
variety of recreational books, geared to many interests and levels of
reading ability. It has fine reference books such as *Compton's Pictured
Encyclopedia*,[5] *The World Book*,[6] and the *Britannica Junior*,[7] as well
as such sets as *The Pictorial Encyclopedia of American History*.[8] The
library helps children to develop new interests and hobbies, and introduces them to the use of community libraries and bookstores. It serves
also as a central repository for books that are loaned to teachers for
classroom use.

The mere existence of a school library is no guarantee that
it will be effectively used. Wherever possible, it should be administered
by a full-time, trained librarian, not left to some teacher to care for
after school. The librarian should have as many assistants as are
necessary to take care of mechanical and routine details so that she
can devote her main energies to book selection and reading guidance.
A good system of classifying and cataloguing should be put into operation. The librarian should be a member of school-wide curriculum
committees in order that she can cooperate fully in carrying out edu-

[4] Reprinted by permission of the Association for Childhood Education International,
3615 Wisconsin Avenue, N.W., Washington, D.C. From Bulletin No. 3-A, *Literature
with Children*, Copyright 1961; "Making Literature Live with Children," by Leland
B. Jacobs. The student is urged to read this entire excellent pamphlet.

[5] F. E. Compton Company, Chicago.

[6] Field Enterprises, Educational Division, Chicago.

[7] *Britannica Junior*, Chicago.

[8] Childrens Press, Inc., Chicago.

cational policy. Provision should be made for all pupils to go to the library regularly. Children should feel that they are welcome in the library and that the librarian is a very useful friend and helper.

In some schools the library has been made into a "materials center" for the school. This means that it serves as a central clearing house for all instructional materials, including audio-visual aids, pamphlets, textbooks, and the like. Since library books are only one kind of instructional material, it seems logical that the library should be a center for all kinds of teaching aids. The library should be a vital, busy educational unit, not a museum.

Some objections, however, have been raised to the use of the library as a materials center. It is pointed out that the work of a materials center may become chiefly a mechanical and routine activity and will add to the already great burden of the librarian. Moreover, fears are expressed that appropriations for audio-visual and other materials will be deducted from the expenditures for books. Further, the expert handling of instructional material will add to the training needed by the qualified librarian. These are valid objections. The idea of the materials center should, therefore, not be introduced unless the school is prepared to add a specialist in audio-visual aids and sufficient clerical staff and to provide the necessary additional space and equipment without reducing in any way the appropriation for library books and library maintenance.

In view of the great importance of the school library in every good reading program, it is regrettable that so large a percentage of American elementary schools have inadequate libraries, or none at all. When pressures from increased enrollments call for ever more classroom space, the library room, if one has been provided, is often the first to go. Administrators and teachers should do all in their power to convince boards of education and the public that a good library is essential to a good school. Far from being a luxury, it is a facility without which the school cannot function efficiently.

Requirements for an elementary school library will vary with the size of the school. If the school has no library, the staff should see that a beginning, however modest, is made and that improvement and expansion are provided for each year. The school should be provided with the statement of school library standards of the American Library Association (*Standards for School Library Programs,* by the American Association of School Librarians, Chicago). This report describes standards for personnel, equipment, and materials for school libraries in schools of various enrollments.

The American Library Association recommends, for example,

that schools with 200 to 1,000 pupils have a library of 6,000 to 10,000 books, and that schools with 200 to 250 pupils appropriate $1,000 to $1,500 per year to the library, exclusive of reference books, binding costs, and salaries. It recommends that six-grade elementary schools subscribe to twenty-five magazines. It advocates the employment, in schools of small enrollment, of a librarian one day per week; provision for the storage and classification of pamphlets, newspapers, films and filmstrips, pictures and slides, and realia; a professional collection for teachers, including books and magazines, supported by an annual appropriation of not less than $200; in larger schools, in addition to the reading room, one or more conference rooms and a workroom.

Choosing Books for the Room and School Libraries

With the exception of those who are experts in children's literature, few teachers are able to keep up with the great outpouring of children's books, and fewer still can judge with ease which of the new titles are suitable for children. Teachers are, therefore, dependent in great degree upon the recommendations of the specialists. Two excellent references that discuss and list books for children are *Children and Books* by May Arbuthnot (Scott, Foresman, and Company, 1964) and *Children's Literature in the Elementary School* by Charlotte Huck and Doris Young Kuhn (Holt, Rinehart and Winston, Inc., 1968). The numerous booklists now available will therefore be sources or valuable aids to teachers in planning their periodic requests for books. There are a few standard lists that should be part of the reference collection of every elementary school library. These include:

A Basic Book Collection for Elementary Grades. Chicago: American Library Association, 1960.

Children's Books for Schools and Libraries, Phillips B. Steckler, editor. New York: R. R. Bowker Company, 1967.

The Elementary School Library Collection by Mary Virginia Gaver, et al. Newark, N.J.: The Bro-Dart Foundation, 1968.

Subject Index to Books for Primary Grades. Mary K. Eakin and Eleanor Merritt. Chicago: American Library Association, 1961.

Subject Index to Books for Intermediate Grades. Mary K. Eakin. Chicago: American Library Association, 1963.

The Children's Catalog. Compiled by Ruth Giles and others. Standard Catalog Series. New York: The H. W. Wilson Company. Supplements.

A comprehensive list of references and booklists is found

in an article by Barbara V. Olson in *Elementary English* for May 1961, "Aids for Librarians in Elementary Schools." Other lists are published by the American Library Association and many other organizations. The following compilation, which includes many book lists commonly employed by teachers and librarians, is not intended to be comprehensive. By reading such magazines as the *ALA Bulletin, Bulletin of the Center for Children's Books, Childhood Education, The Library Journal, The Horn Book,* and *Elementary English,* among other magazines of library and educational organizations, the teacher may keep abreast of the new publications in the field of children's literature. The children's book sections of such newspapers and magazines as the *New York Times* and the *Saturday Review* report many of the best new publications in the field of children's literature. Since the output (more than 1,200 new titles per year) is so great, it is not possible for any of these periodicals to report upon and evaluate more than a small fraction of the year's products. Every elementary school should seek to be included in the regular mailing lists of the leading publishers. The professional library of every elementary school should include at least some of the following book lists.

Miscellaneous Lists

A Basic Book Collection for Elementary Grades. Chicago: American Library Association, 1960.

Adventuring with Books. Champaign, Ill.: National Council of Teachers of English, 1960.

A Bibliography of Books for Children. Washington, D.C.: Association for Childhood Education International, 1962.

Booklist Books: A Selection. Chicago: American Library Association.

Books for Beginning Readers. By Elizabeth Guilfoile. Champaign, Ill.: National Council of Teachers of English, 1962.

Books of the Year for Children. New York: Child Study Association of America, latest edition.

Children's Books: Awards and Prizes. New York: Children's Book Council, revised annually.

Children's Books for $1.25 or Less. Washington, D.C.: Association for Childhood Education International, latest edition.

Children's Books To Enrich the Social Studies. By Helen Huus. Washington, D.C.: National Council for the Social Studies, 1961.

Children's Books Suggested as Holiday Gifts: New York: New York Public Library, revised annually.

Children's Books Too Good To Miss. By May Hill Arbuthnot and others. Cleveland: The Press of Western Reserve University, 1966.

Current Books: Junior Booklist of the Secondary Education Board. Prepared by the Committee on Junior Booklist. Secondary Education Board, Milton, Mass.

"Distinguished Children's Books," *ALA Bulletin,* annual. Chicago: American Library Association.

Fifty Years of Children's Books. By Dora V. Smith. Champaign, Ill.: National Council of Teachers of English, 1963.

Gold Star List of American Fiction, annual. Syracuse, N.Y.: Syracuse Public Library.

Growing Up with Books. New York: R. R. Bowker Company.

Notable Children's Books of—. Chicago: American Library Association, latest edition.

Paperbound Book Guide for Elementary Schools. New York: R. R. Bowker Company, 1966.

Recommended Children's Books of—. New York: R. R. Bowker Company, latest edition.

Starred Books from the Library Journal. Edited by Peggy Melcher. *Library Journal.* New York. Arranged by grade and subject with author-title index.

Stories: A List of Stories To Tell and To Read Aloud. Compiled by Eulalie Steinmetz. New York: New York Public Library, Alphabetically arranged, followed by a subject index.

Story Telling. By Ruth Tooze. Englewood Cliffs, N.J.: Prentice-Hall, Inc., 1959.

Summary of Junior Book Awards Program. Boys' Clubs of America, New York.

A Parent's Guide to Children's Reading. By Nancy Larrick. New York: Pocket Books, 1964.

A Teacher's Guide to Children's Books. By Nancy Larrick. Columbus, Ohio: Charles E. Merrill Books, Inc., 1960.

Treasure for the Taking: A Book List for Boys and Girls. By Anne Thaxter. New York: Viking Press.

Wisconsin Reading Circle Annual. Issued by the State Reading Circle Board. Supplements. State Reading Circle Board, State Department of Public Instruction, Madison, Wis.

The following are among the award-winning books in various competitions:

Newbery Winners

1923   *The Voyages of Dr. Dolittle,* Hugh Lofting. J. B. Lippincott Company.

1924   *The Dark Frigate,* Charles Boardman Hawes. Little, Brown & Company.

1925   *Tales from Silver Lands,* Charles J. Finger. Doubleday & Company, Inc.

1926   *Shen of the Sea,* Arthur Bowie Chrisman. E. P. Dutton and Company, Inc.

1927   *Smoky, the Cowhorse,* Will James. Charles Scribner's Sons.

1928   *Gayneck: The Story of a Pigeon*, Dhan Gopal Mukerji. E. P. Dutton & Company, Inc.

1929   *The Trumpeter of Krakow*, Eric P. Kelly. The Macmillan Company.

1930   *Hitty: Her First Hundred Years*, Rachel Field. The Macmillan Company.

1931   *The Cat Who Went to Heaven*, Elizabeth Coatsworth. The Macmillan Company.

1932   *Waterless Mountain*, Laura Adams Armer. David McKay Company, Inc.

1933   *Young Fu of the Upper Yangtze*, Elizabeth Foreman Lewis. Holt, Rinehart and Winston, Inc.

1934   *The Story of the Author of Little Women: Invincible Louisa*, Cornelia Meigs. Little, Brown and Company.

1935   *Dobry*, Monica Shannon. The Viking Press, Inc.

1936   *Caddie Woodlawn*, Carol Ryrie Brink. The Macmillan Company.

1937   *Roller Skates*, Ruth Sawyer. The Viking Press, Inc.

1938   *The White Stag*, Kate Seredy. The Viking Press, Inc.

1939   *Thimble Summer*, Elizabeth Enright. Holt, Rinehart and Winston, Inc.

1940   *Daniel Boone*, James Daugherty. The Viking Press, Inc.

1941   *Call It Courage*, Armstrong Sperry. The Macmillan Company.

1942   *The Matchlock Gun*, Walter D. Edmonds. Dodd, Mead & Company, Inc.

1943   *Adam of the Road*, Elizabeth Janet Gray. The Viking Press, Inc.

1944   *Johnny Tremain*, Esther Forbes. Houghton Mifflin Company.

1945   *Rabbit Hill*, Robert Lawson, The Viking Press, Inc.

1946   *Strawberry Girl*, Lois Lenski. J. B. Lippincott Company.

1947   *Miss Hickory*, Carolyn Sherwin Bailey. The Viking Press, Inc.

1948   *Twenty-one Balloons*, William Pene du Bois. The Viking Press, Inc.

1949   *King of the Wind*, Marguerite Henry. Rand McNally & Company.

1950   *Door in the Wall*, Marguerite de Angeli. Doubleday & Company, Inc.

1951   *Amos Fortune: Free Man*, Elizabeth Yates. Aladdin.

1952   *Ginger Pye*, Eleanor Estes. Harcourt, Brace & World, Inc.

1953   *Secret of the Andes*, Ann Nolan Clark. The Viking Press, Inc.

1954   *And Now Miguel*, Joseph Krumgold. Thomas Y. Crowell Company.

1955   *The Wheel on the School*, Meindert de Jong. Harper & Row, Publishers.

1956   *Carry on, Mr. Bowditch*, Jean Lee Latham. Houghton Mifflin Company.

1957   *Miracles on Maple Hill*, Virginia Sorensen. Illustrated by Beth and Joe Krush. Harcourt, Brace & World, Inc.

1958   *Rifles for Matie*, Harold Keith. Thomas Y. Crowell Company.

1959   *The Witch of Blackbird Pond*. Elizabeth George Speare. Houghton Mifflin Company.

1960   *Onion John*, Joseph Krumgold. Thomas Y. Crowell Company.

1961   *Island of the Blue Dolphins*, Scott O'Dell. Houghton Mifflin Company.

1962   *The Bronze Bow*, Elizabeth George Speare. Houghton Mifflin Company.

1963   *A Wrinkle in Time*, Madeleine L' Engle. Farrar, Straus & Giroux, Inc.

1964   *It's Like This, Cat*, Emily Cheney Neville. Harper & Row, Publishers.

1965   *Shadow of a Bull*, Maia Wojciechowska. Atheneum Publishers.

1966   *I, Juan de Pareja*, Elizabeth Borton de Trevino. Farrar, Straus & Giroux, Inc.

1967   *Up a Road Slowly*, Irene Hunt. Follett Publishing Company.

1968   *From the Mixed-up Files of Mrs. Basil E. Frankweiler*, E. L. Konigsburg. Atheneum Publishers.

1969   *The High King*, Lloyd Alexander. Illustrated by Evaline Ness. Holt, Rinehart and Winston, Inc.

Caldecott Awards

1938   *Animals of the Bible*, Dorothy Lathrop. J. B. Lippincott Company.

1939   *Mei-Li*, Thomas Handforth. Doubleday & Company, Inc.

1940   *Abraham Lincoln*, Ingri and Edgar Parin D'Aulaire. Doubleday & Company, Inc.

1941   *They Were Strong and Good*, Robert Lawson. The Viking Press, Inc.

1942   *Make Way for Ducklings*, Robert McCloskey. The Viking Press, Inc.

1943   *The Little House*, Virginia Lee Burton. Houghton Mifflin Company.

1944   *Many Moons*, James Thurber. Illustrated by Louis Slobodkin. Harcourt, Brace & World, Inc.

1945   *Prayer for a Child*, Rachel Field. Illustrated by Elizabeth Orton Jones. The Macmillan Company.

1946   *The Rooster Crows: A Book of American Rhymes and Jingles*, Maud and Miska Petersham. The Macmillan Company.

1947   *The Little Island*, Golden MacDonald. Illustrated by Leonard Weisgard. Doubleday & Company, Inc.

1948   *White Snow, Bright Snow*, Alvin Tresselt. Illustrated by Roger Duvoisin. Lothrop, Lee & Shepard Co.

1949   *The Big Snow*, Berta and Elmer Hader. The Macmillan Company.

1950   *Song of the Swallows*, Leo Politi. Charles Scribner's Sons.

1951   *The Egg Tree*, Katherine Milhous. Charles Scribner's Sons.

1952   *Finders Keepers*, William Lipkind and Nicolas Mordvinoff. Harcourt, Brace & World, Inc.

1953   *The Biggest Bear*, Lynd Ward. Houghton Mifflin Company.

1954   *Madeline's Rescue*, Ludwig Bemelmans. The Viking Press, Inc.

1955   *Cinderella*, Marcia Brown. Charles Scribner's Sons.

1956   *Frog Went A-Courtin'*, John Langstaff. Illustrated by Feodor Rojankovsky. Harcourt, Brace & World, Inc.

1957   *A Tree Is Nice*, Janice May Udry. Illustrated by Marc Simont. Harper & Row, Publishers.

1958   *Time of Wonder*, Robert McCloskey. The Viking Press, Inc.

1959   *Chanticleer and the Fox*, Barbara Cooney. Thomas Y. Crowell Company.

1960   *Nine Days to Christmas*, Marie Hall Ets and Aurora Labastida. Illustrated by Marie Hall Ets. The Viking Press, Inc.

1961   *Baboushka and the Three Kings*, Ruth Robbins. Illustrated by Nicolas Sidjakov. Parnassus Press.

1962   *Once a Mouse*, Marcia Brown. Charles Scribner's Sons.

1963   *The Snowy Day*, Ezra Jack Keats. The Viking Press, Inc.

1964   *Where the Wild Things Are*, Maurice Sendak. Harper & Row, Publishers.

1965   *May I Bring a Friend?* Beatrice Schenk de Regniers. Illustrated by Beni Montresor. Atheneum Publishers.

1966   *Always Room for One More*, Sorche Nic Leodhas. Illustrated by Nonny Hogrogian. Holt, Rinehart and Winston, Inc.

1967   *Sam, Bangs, and Moonshine*, Evaline Ness. Holt, Rinehart and Winston, Inc.

1968   *Drummer Hoff*, Barbara Emberley. Illustrated by Ed Emberley. World Publishing Company.

1969   *The Fool of the World and the Flying Ship*, Retold by Arthur Ransome. Illustrated by Uri Shulvitz. Farrar, Straus & Giroux.

The Charles W. Follett Award

1950   *Johnny Texas*, Carol Hoff.

1951   *All-of-a-Kind Family*, Sydney Taylor.

1952   *Thirty-One Brothers and Sisters*, Reba Paeff Mirsky.

1953   *Tornado Jones*, Trella Lamson Dick.

1954   *Little Wu and the Watermelons*, Beatrice Liu.

1955   *Minutemen of the Sea*, Tom Cluff.

1956   (No manuscript submitted in the competition for the 1956 Follett Award was found worthy of the Award.)

1957   *Chucho, The Boy with the Good Name*, Eula Mark Phillips.

1958   *South Town*, Robert Willis.

1959   *Model "A" Mule*, Robert Willis.

1960   *What Then, Raman?* Shirley Arora.

1961   (No Award)

1962   *Me and Caleb*, Franklyn E. Meyer.

1963   (No Award)

1964   *Across Five Aprils*, Irene Hunt.

1965   (No Award)

1966   (No Award)

1967   *Lions in the Way*, Bella Rodman.

1968   *Marc Chagall*, Howard Greenfield.

1969   *Banner over Me*, Margery F. Greenleaf.

Child Study Association Award

1943   *Keystone Kids*, John R. Tunis. Harcourt, Brace & World, Inc.

1944   *The House*, Marjorie Hill Allee. Houghton Mifflin Company.

1945   *The Moved-Outers*, Florence Crannell Means. Houghton Mifflin Company.

1946   *Heart of Danger*, Howard Peace. Doubleday & Company, Inc.

1947   *Judy's Journey*, Lois Lenski. J. B. Lippincott Company.

1948   *The Big Wave*, Pearl Buck. The John Day Company, Inc.

1949   *Paul Tiber*, Maria Gleit. Charles Scribner's Sons.

1950   *The United Nations and Youth*, Eleanor Roosevelt and Helen Ferris. Doubleday & Company, Inc.

1951 (No Award)
1952 *Twenty and Ten*, Claire Huchet Bishop. The Viking Press, Inc.
Jareb, Miriam Powell. Thomas Y. Crowell Company.
1953 *In a Mirror*, Mary Stolz. Harper & Row, Publishers.
1954 *High Road Home*, William Corbin. Coward-McCann, Inc.
The Ordeal of the Young Hunter, Jonreed Lauritzen. Little, Brown & Company.
1955 *Crow Boy*, Tara Yashima. The Viking Press, Inc.
Plain Girl, Virginia Sorensen. Harcourt, Brace & World, Inc.
1956 *The House of Sixty Fathers*, Meindert de Jong. Harper & Row, Publishers.
1957 *Shadow Across the Campus*, Helen Sattley. Dodd, Mead & Company, Inc.
1958 *South Town*, Lorenz Graham. Follett Publishing Company.
1959 *Jennifer*, Zoa Sherburne. William Morrow & Company, Inc.
1960 *Janine*, Robin McKown. Julian Messner, Inc.
1961 *The Road to Agra*, Aimee Somerfelt. Criterion Books, Inc.
1962 *The Trouble with Terry*, Joan M. Benjie Lexan. The Dial Press, Inc.
1963 *The Rock and the Willow*, Mildred Lee. Lothrop, Lee & Shepard Co.
The Peaceable Revolution, Betty Schechter. Houghton Mifflin Company.
1964 *The High Pasture*, Ruth Harnden. Houghton Mifflin Company.
1965 *The Empty Schoolhouse*, Natalie Savage Carlson. Harper & Row, Publishers.
1966 *Queenie Peavy*, Robert Burch. The Viking Press, Inc.
Curious George Goes to the Hospital, Margaret and H. A. Rey. Special award. Houghton Mifflin Company.
1967 *The Contender*, Robert Lipsyte. Harper & Row, Publishers.
1968 *What It's All About*, Vadim Frolov. Doubleday & Company, Inc.

Book World Children's Spring Book Festival Awards

1937 Younger age: *Seven Simeons*, Boris Artzybasheff. The Viking Press, Inc.
Older age: *The Smuggler's Sloop*, Rob White, III. Little, Brown & Company.
1938 Younger age: *The Hobbit*, J. R. R. Tolkien. Houghton Mifflin Company.
Older age: *The Iron Duke*, John R. Tunis. Harcourt, Brace & World, Inc.
1939 Younger age: *The Story of Horace*, Alice N. Coats. Coward-McCann, Inc.
Older age: *The Hired Man's Elephant*, Phil Strong. Dodd, Mead & Company, Inc.
1940 Younger age: *That Mario*, Lucy Herndon Crockett. Holt, Rinehart and Winston, Inc.
Older age: *Cap'n Ezra Privateer*, James D. Adams. Harcourt, Brace & World, Inc.

1941   Picture Book: *In My Mother's House*, Ann Nolan Clark. The Viking Press, Inc.
Eight to Twelve: *Pete*. Tom Robinson. The Viking Press, Inc.
Older boys and girls: *Clara Barton*, Mildred Mastin Pace. Charles Scribner's Sons.

1942   Picture Book: *Mr. Tootwhistle's Invention*, Peter Wells. Holt, Rinehart and Winston, Inc.
Eight to twelve: *I Have Just Begun to Fight*, Commander Edward Ellsberg. Dodd, Mead & Company, Inc.
Older boys and girls: *None but the Brave*, Rosamond Van Der Zee Marshall. Houghton Mifflin Company.

1943   Picture Book: *Five Golden Wrens*, Hugh Troy. Oxford University Press.
Eight to twelve: *These Happy Golden Years*, Laura Ingalls Wilder. Harper & Row, Publishers.
Older boys and girls: *Patterns on the Wall*, Elizabeth Yates. Alfred A. Knopf, Inc.

1944   Picture Book: *A Ring and a Riddle*, M. Illin and E. Segal and the illustrator, Vera Bock. J. B. Lippincott Company.
Eight to twelve: *They Put Out to Sea*, Roger Duvoisin. Alfred A. Knopf, Inc.
Older boys and girls: *Storm Canvas*, Armstrong Sperry. Holt, Rinehart and Winston, Inc.

1945   Picture Book: *Little People in a Big Country*, Norma Cohn. Oxford University Press.
Eight to twelve: *Gulf Stream*, Ruth Brindze. Vanguard Press, Inc.
Older boys and girls: *Sandy*, Elizabeth Janet Gray. The Viking Press, Inc.

1946   Picture Books: *Farm Stories*, Kathryn and Bryan Jackson, shared with illustrator, Gustaf Tenggren. Simon and Schuster, Inc.
Eight to twelve: *Thirteenth Stone*, Jean Rothwell. Harcourt, Brace & World, Inc.
Older boys and girls: *The Quest of the Golden Condor*, Clayton Knight. Alfred A. Knopf, Inc.

1947   Picture Book: *Oley: The Sea Monster*, Marie Hall Ets. The Viking Press, Inc.
Eight to twelve: *Pancakes—Paris*, Claire Huchet Bishop. The Viking Press, Inc.
Older boys and girls: *Twenty-one Balloons*, William Pene Du Bois. The Viking Press, Inc.

1948   Picture Book: *My Father's Dragon*, Ruth Stiles Gannett. Random House, Inc.
Eight to twelve: *Daughter of the Mountains*, Louise Rankin. The Viking Press, Inc.
Older boys and girls: *Crimson Anchor: A Sea Mystery*, Felix Riesenberg, Jr. Dodd, Mead & Company, Inc.

1949   Picture Book: *Bonnie Bess: The Weathervane Horse*, Alvin Tresselt and Marilyn Hafner. Lothrop, Lee & Shepard Co.

Eight to twelve: *Bush Holiday*, Stephen Fennimore. Doubleday & Company, Inc.

Older boys and girls: *Start of the Trail*, Louise Dickinson Rich. J. B. Lippincott Company.

1950   Picture Book: *Sunshine*, Ludwig Bemelmans. Simon and Schuster, Inc.

Eight to twelve: *Windfall Fiddle*, Carl Cramer. Alfred A. Knopf, Inc.

Older boys and girls: *Amos Fortune: Free Man*, Elizabeth Yates. Aladdin.

1951   Picture Book: *Jeanne Marie Counts Her Sheep*, Françoise. Charles Scribner's Sons.

Eight to twelve: *Ginger Pye*, Eleanor Estes. Harcourt, Brace & World, Inc.

Older boys and girls: *Americans Before Columbus*, Elizabeth Baity. The Viking Press, Inc.

1952   Picture Book: *Looking for Something*, Ann Nolan Clark. The Viking Press, Inc.

Eight to twelve: *The Talking Cat*, Natalie Savage Carlson. Harper & Row, Publishers.

Older boys and girls: *Big Mutt*, John Reese, The Westminster Press.

1953   Picture Book: *Pet of the Met*, Lydia and Don Freeman. The Viking Press, Inc.

Eight to twelve: *Captain Ramsay's Daughter*, Elizabeth Fraser Torjesen. Lothrop, Lee & Shepard Co.

Older boys and girls: *The Ark*, Margot Benary-Isbert. Harcourt, Brace & World, Inc.

1954   Picture Book: *Alphonse: That Bearded One*, Natalie Savage Carlson. Harcourt, Brace & World, Inc.

Eight to twelve: *Winter Danger*, William O. Steele. Harcourt, Brace & World, Inc.

Older boys and girls: *Engineers' Dreams*, Willy Ley. The Viking Press, Inc.

1955   Picture Book: *Frog Went A-Courtin'*, Feodor Rojankovsky and John Langstaff. Harcourt, Brace & World, Inc.

Eight to twelve: *Crystal Mountain*, Belle Dorman Rugh. Houghton Mifflin Company.

Older boys and girls: *The Buffalo Trace*, Virginia S. Eifert. Dodd, Mead & Company, Inc.

1956   Picture Book: *Lion*, William Pene Du Bois. The Viking Press, Inc.

Eight to twelve: *Beaver Water*, Rutherford G. Montgomery. World Publishing Company.

Older boys and girls: *Cold Hazard*, Richard Armstrong. Houghton Mifflin Company.

1957   Picture Book: *Madeline and the Bad Hat*, Ludwig Bemelmans. The Viking Press, Inc.
Eight to twelve: *Gone-away Lake*, Elizabeth Enright. Harcourt, Brace & World, Inc.
Older boys and girls: *Because of Madeline*, Mary Stoltz, Harper & Row, Publishers.

1958   Picture Book: *Crictor*, Toni Ungerer, Harper & Row, Publishers.
Eight to twelve: *Chucaro, Wild Pony of the Pampa*, Francis Kalnay. Harcourt, Brace & World, Inc.
Older boys and girls: *Sons of the Steppe*, Hans Baumann. Henry Z. Walck, Inc.

1959   Picture Book: *Six Lives on Kilimanjaro*, Astrid Lindgren. The Macmillan Company.
Eight to twelve: *The Long-Nosed Princess*, Priscilla Hallowell. The Viking Press, Inc.
Older boys and girls: *An Edge of the Forest*, Agnes Smith. The Viking Press, Inc.

1960   Picture Book: *The Secret Hiding Place*, Rainey Bennett. World Publishing Company.
Eight to twelve: *The Trouble with Jenny's Ear*, Oliver Butterworth. Little, Brown & Company.
Older boys and girls: *The Walls of Windy Troy*, Marjorie Braymer. Harcourt, Brace & World, Inc.

1961   Picture Book: *Gwendolyn the Miracle Hen*, Nancy Sherman. Golden Press, Inc.
Eight to twelve: *Norwegian Folk Tales*, Peter C. Asbjernsen and Jorgen E. Moe. The Viking Press.
Older boys and girls: *Adventures in the Desert*, Herbert Kaufmann. Ivan Obolensky, Inc.

1962   Picture Book: *Adam's Book of Odd Pictures*, Joseph Low. Atheneum Publishers.
Eight to twelve: *The Orphans of Simitra*, Jacque Bonzon.
Older boys and girls: *Dawn Wind*, Rosemary Sutcliff. Henry Z. Walck, Inc.

1963   Picture Book: *The Seven Ravens*, the Brothers Grimm. Harcourt, Brace & World, Inc.
Eight to twelve: *A Dog So Small*, Philippa Pearce. J. B. Lippincott Company.
Older boys and girls: *The Cossacks*, B. Bartos-Hoppner. Henry Z. Walck, Inc.

1964   Picture Book: *The Coconut Thieves*, Catherine Fournier. Charles Scribner's Sons.
Eight to twelve: *The Family Conspiracy*, Joan Phipson. Harcourt, Brace & World, Inc.
Older boys and girls: *The Story of Design*, Marion Downer. Lothrop, Lee & Shepard Co.

1965 Picture Book: *Salt*, Margo Zemach. Follett Publishing Company.
Eight to twelve: *Drop Dead*, Julia Cunningham. Pantheon Books, Inc.
Older boys and girls: *Jazz Country*, Nat Hentoff. Harper & Row, Publishers.

1966 Picture Book: *Nothing Ever Happens on My Block*, Ellen Raskin. Atheneum Publishers.
Eight to twelve: *Boy Alone*, Reginald Otley. Harcourt, Brace & World, Inc.
Older boys and girls: *This Is Your Century*, Geoffrey Trease. Harcourt, Brace & World, Inc.

1967 Picture Book: *Moon Man*, Toni Ungerer. Harper & Row, Publishers.
Eight to twelve: *The Egypt Game*, Zylpha K. Snyder. Atheneum Publishers.
Older boys and girls: *The Little Fishes*, Erik C. Haugaard. Houghton Mifflin Company.

1968 Picture Book: *Why the Sun and the Moon Live in the Sky*, Elphinstone Dayrell. Illustrated by Blair Lent. Houghton Mifflin Company.
Eight to twelve: *A Race Course for Andy*, Patricia Wrightson. Harcourt, Brace & World, Inc.
Older boys and girls: *Young Mark*, E. M. Almedingen. Farrar, Straus & Giroux.

1969 Picture Book: *Thy Friend, Obadiah*, Brinton Turkle. The Viking Press, Inc.
Eight to twelve: *Whose Town?* Loreny Graham. Thomas Y. Crowell Company.
Older boys and girls: *My Enemy, My Brother*, James Forman. Meredith Publishing Company.

Jane Addams Children's Book Awards

1953 *People Are Important*, Eva Knox Evans. Capitol Publishing Company, Inc.
1954 *Stick-in-the-Mud*, Jean Ketchum. William R. Scott, Inc.
1955 *Rainbow Round the World*, Elizabeth Yates. The Bobbs-Merrill Company, Inc.
1956 *Story of the Negro*, Arna Bontemps. Alfred A. Knopf.
1957 *Blue Mystery*, Margot Benery Isbert. Harcourt, Brace & World, Inc.
1958 *The Perilous Road*, William O. Steele. Harcourt, Brace & World, Inc.
1959 (No Award)
1960 *Champions of Peace*, Editor Patterson Meyer. Little, Brown & Company.
1961 *What Then, Ramon?*, Shirley L. Arora. Follett Publishing Company.
1962 *The Road to Agra*, Aimee Somerfelt. Criterion Books, Inc.
1963 *The Monkey and the Wild Wild Wind*, Ryerson Johnson. Abelard-Schuman, Ltd.
1964 *Profiles in Courage*, John F. Kennedy. Harper & Row, Publishers.
1965 *Meeting with a Stranger*, Duane Bradley. J. B. Lippincott Company.

1966   *Berries Goodman.* Emily Cheney Neville. Harper & Row, Publishers.
1967   *Queenie Peavy,* Robert Burch. The Viking Press, Inc.
1968   *The Little Fishes,* Erik Christian Haugaard. Houghton Mifflin Company.
1969   *The Endless Steppe: Growing up in Siberia,* Esther Hautzig. Thomas Y. Crowell Company.

FOR FURTHER STUDY

Barbe, Walter B., *Teaching Reading.* New York: Oxford University Press, 1965. Chapter 31, "Studies of Children's Interests—A Brief Summary," pp. 359–374.

Burton, William E., *Reading in Child Development.* Indianapolis, Ind.: The Bobbs-Merrill Company, Inc., 1958. Chapter 11, "The Importance of Free Reading in the Instructional Program," pp. 360–412.

Gans, Roma, *Common Sense in Reading.* Indianapolis, Ind.: The Bobbs-Merrill Company, Inc., 1963. Chapter 12, "Motivation in Reading—And Conflicting Pressures," pp. 229–246; Chapter 13, "Satisfying Whetted Reading Appetites," pp. 247–265.

Harris, Albert J., *Readings on Reading Instruction.* New York: David McKay Company, Inc., 1963. Chapter 12, "Motivating Reading," pp. 330–357.

Huck, Charlotte, and Doris Young Kuhn, *Children's Literature in the Elementary School.* New York: Holt, Rinehart and Winston, Inc., 1968.

Jacobs, Leland, *Using Literature with Young Children.* New York: Teachers College Press, Columbia University, 1965. Pages 1–63.

Jennings, Frank G., *This Is Reading.* New York: Teachers College Press, 1965. Chapter 9, "Why Do We Read?" pp. 122–148; Chapter 10, "Youth Reads for What?" pp. 149–171.

Larrick, Nancy, *A Teacher's Guide to Children's Books.* Columbus, Ohio: Charles E. Merrill Books, Inc., 1964.

McKee, Paul, *Reading: A Program of Instruction for the Elementary School.* Boston: Houghton Mifflin Company, 1966. Chapter 12, "Instruction in Children's Literature," pp. 436–466.

Smith, Dora V., *Fifty Years of Children's Books.* Washington, D.C.: The National Council of Teachers of English, 1963.

Smith, Nila B., *Reading Instruction for Today's Children.* Englewood Cliffs, N.J.: Prentice-Hall, Inc., 1963. Chapter 12, "Literature in the Space Age: Status and Values," pp. 387–395; Chapter 13, "Guiding Children's Interest in Television, Comics, Newspapers and Magazines," pp. 396–407; Chapter 14, "Establishing Lifetime Interests and Tastes," pp. 408–441.

Stauffer, Russell G., *Directing Reading Maturity as a Cognitive Progress.* New York: Harper & Row, Publishers, 1969. Chapter 8, "Libraries and Reading Instruction."

Tinker, Miles A., and Constance M. McCullough, *Teaching Elementary Reading.* New York: Appleton-Century-Crofts, 1968. Chapter 15, "Interests and Tastes," pp. 301–317.

Veatch, Jeannette, *Reading in the Elementary School.* New York: The Ronald Press Company, 1966. Chapter 13, "Sharing," pp. 481–498; Chapter 14, "The Beautiful World of Books," pp. 499–524.

QUESTIONS FOR THOUGHT AND DISCUSSION

1. Although the term *developmental value* originated with the Center for Children's Books of the University of Chicago, it reflects an approach to children's reading that is almost as old as children's books themselves and that has been in the past, and still is, put to use under such synonymous terms as *reading guidance, character formation,* and the like. As used by the Center, the term implies those elements of a book that help a child to grow in understanding of himself as an individual and as a member of society. How can the classroom teacher go about assisting a child to develop in this respect?
2. There are children's book prizes which authors, artists, and publishers would like to win. The Newbery Medal is given to the most distinguished contribution to children's literature during a given year. The Caldecott Medal is awarded for the most distinguished American picture book in a given year. The range continues downward to the point where on the local level the system of awards continues, and it is not unusual to see children being singled out for having read many books over a given period such as the summer vacation. Is this a good thing at any level? Be able to comment on the practice at the local level.
3. Certain book publishers employ children to act as junior reviewers. Very frequently, armed with sets of questions and governed by certain rules, these youngsters can perform a type of service otherwise unavailable. Can you envision ways in which you could utilize junior reviewers in your classroom? What ground rules would you set up? What questions might be used as guides?
4. Some research seems to suggest that improved reading interests and habits result from a careful study of children's present interests and a varied school program for developing more desirable reading habits and tastes. Do you know of such a program? If so, what are some of its salient features?
5. In a well-known study of children's reading interests, it was noted that the interest scores of hundreds of stories and poems found by testing demonstrate that there exist frequent crucial differences. Some selections liked by boys are rejected by girls; very many enjoyed by girls are

scorned by boys; yet another group is rejected by both boys and girls. What do these findings imply for the teacher who is interested in developing children's reading interests?

6. What are the inplications for classroom practices of the following point of view?

> Picture reading consists of gazing at the pictures of a book or an over-illustrated text or supplementary reading book with a minimum of printed matter. Picture reading is not actually a form of reading, nor is it sensibly viewed as a pre-stage of real reading. It is an evasion of reading and almost its opposite. Habitual picture readers are severely handicapped in the task of becoming readers of books later, for the habit of picture reading interferes with the acquisition of well-developed reading habits.

7. What are the sources to which a teacher can turn to become acquainted with the realm of children's literature? Where can the teacher find lists of selected children's books? of poems for children? How can the teacher keep informed about children's books?

8. Why, in your estimation, is it preferable for an elementary school to have both a school library and a library in each classroom? What points do you think should be kept in mind about a classroom library?

9. During recent years the value of the book report has been questioned. What did the book report mean to you as you came up through school? What does it mean now? Has this concept really changed? Do you "hate" book reports now as then? Can book reports be effective means of interesting children in books?

PART THREE

THE READING PROGRAM
IN ACTION

CHAPTER 11

Reading in the Content Areas

In Part Two we focused our attention on the development of various skills and abilities important to all types of reading situations. Now we consider how application can be made of these learnings to the reading program in action. Our first consideration is reading in the content areas.

Careful studies have indicated that reading is not a general ability but a composite of specialized skills. These specialized skills are required in various curriculum areas. The correlations between general reading ability as measured by standardized tests and ability to read materials in specialized fields have usually been low. The necessity of paying particular attention to reading in the content areas is also emphasized by the fact that many teachers in the intermediate grades believe that a major reason for failure of boys and girls in the social studies, for example, is lack of skill in reading the material. Teachers of mathematics in the elementary school have long known that inability to read the "story problems" of arithmetic constitutes a real problem for many pupils. In science, in health, in literature—in whatever area reading is expected of the pupils—a low degree of reading skill constitutes a serious handicap.

Obviously one reason for the problems some boys and girls encounter when reading in the content areas is their failure to have acquired the skills essential to all reading. If a pupil has failed to develop skill in word recognition, in comprehension, in reading at appropriate rates, and in other essentials of reading of all types, he will, of course, be unable to read effectively in the content areas. However, some boys and girls who are efficient readers in their basal reading textbooks or who read many kinds of trade books with ease have decided problems when reading in the content areas. The problem may be that they read all materials as they would read that given in reading textbooks or in books for recreatory reading. Their difficulty may be that they cannot effectively meet the problems in word recognition, comprehension, and other aspects of reading that are somewhat peculiar to reading in the areas of history, geography, science, or mathematics.

SPECIAL PROBLEMS IN READING IN THE CONTENT AREAS

Although there are various possible problems in reading in the content areas, there is probably not a single one that is unique to any one of the areas. The problems are special only insofar as they occur often or are more crucial in a content field or that they require special attention for other reasons. These problems in word recognition, comprehension, reading at appropriate rates, reading orally, locating information, and doing independent reading in the content areas will now be considered.

Problems in Vocabulary

Often the problem in the content areas of a child who reads up to the norm for his grade in the basal reading textbook is one of vocabulary. In the social studies the pupil encounters such "new words" as *isthmus, environment, latitude, legislature, emancipation, adaptation, culture.* In elementary school science many words occur of which the child previously has had no knowledge, such as *planetarium, solar, convection.* In mathematics words such as *equation, dividend, quotient* and in books about music and art words such as *percussion, bas relief, perspective* frequently give difficulty. Words unfamiliar to the reader will be found in any reading material likely to help the child increase in knowledge and power with words. In fact, textbooks in reading beyond the beginning stages of reading instruction are designed to present some words that are new to the child. The special point of difficulty in vocabulary in reading in the content areas is that the child is often confronted with a large proportion of words unknown to him, a proportion larger than in the basal readers.

Frequently, too, in the content areas a word may have a different meaning from the one that the child has been accustomed to associate with it. Neither the word *range* as used in the phrase *mountain range* nor the word *mouth* in the expression *mouth of the river* has the meaning that some children have previously associated with it. The *page* of the Middle Ages, the *draft* of the Constitution, the *cradle* of civilization can be a source of difficulty for the child who has given other meanings to those words. Homonyms, particularly, are often a source of trouble. The steppes of some near-polar regions are not the steps with which the pupil has had contact.

Another vocabulary problem lies in the number and difficulty of the concepts presented. Expressions such as *no taxation without representation* or the *consent of the governed* need to be made meaningful to many pupils before they can comprehend the material they read in the social studies. The teacher, however, cannot expect the children to comprehend the full meaning of many of the concepts all at once. *Liberty* can acquire added meaning to the child as he reads about and discusses from year to year more and more situations in which liberty or lack of it is evident. It will mean more and more to him as again and again, with increasing insight, he notes the beneficial effects of environments characterized by a spirit of liberty and the deleterious results of regimentation. The boys and girls will grow in noting the difference between liberty and license. They will, hopefully, in time come to realize that liberty should be sought not only for self but also for others. The first time the children read or hear the term *scientific method,* the teacher may find it wise to explain and illustrate the meaning of the expression. Then, year after year, the children can be guided so that they will develop a more accurate understanding of its meaning and a deeper appreciation of its value when applied to situations to which it is applicable. At each stage of development the pupil will probably be benefited if he is helped to increase his understanding until he finally comprehends what a mature educated adult understands when he reads or hears a term symbolizing such a concept.

Problems in Comprehension

There are problems of understanding besides those pertaining to vocabulary that confront many pupils reading in the content areas and that, therefore, necessitate careful reading. To be sure, not all reading in the content areas should be of the study type. However, much of the material in these areas requires more meticulous reading

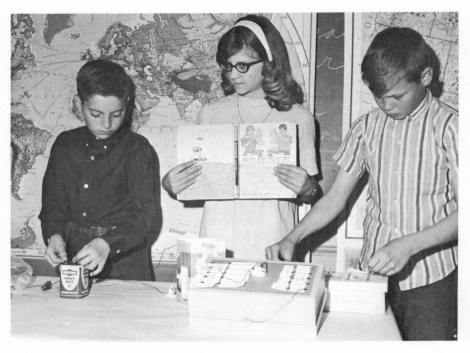

Learning science through reading. (Photo courtesy Boise, Idaho, Public Schools.)

than that which the pupils need in basal reading textbooks or books of fiction. This point is especially true of many of the problems presented in mathematics. Following directions for performing an experiment in science, too, requires attention to details that is often unessential—in fact, even undesirable—for reading many other types of materials. In the social studies, where material often shows a bias, critical evaluation is frequently needed. Reading with the intent to recall for a long time or possibly always is also often demanded of the reader who wishes to accomplish worthwhile objectives that he may set for himself when reading in the content areas. The many references to names and places often put a tax on the memory. Referrals to maps and pictures, helpful though they may be, may interfere with the sequential reading of the person unaccustomed to reading material in which many references of that type are made. Charts, graphs, maps, and diagrams often need to be studied in order to make the text meaningful.

The organization of the material in the social studies is often more complex than that to which the pupil is accustomed in much of his other reading. In the basal reader and in the story book, chronological order usually has been the simple determinant of the organization. In the social studies, cause-effect relationships, inverted sequence of time, and progression from incidents to generalizations or from generalizations to incidents many times form the basis of the organization. Center heads, side headings, and other organizational clues, although helpful when their use is understood, can be a stumbling block for the reader not skilled in their use.

For the reasons stated in the preceding paragraphs—and others—the pupil may have problems in comprehension as he reads in the content areas unless he is given help in meeting difficulties as they arise.

REMEMBERING WHAT IS READ The expectation that pupils should remember a good deal of what they read in the content areas—especially in textbooks—forms one of the chief problems in reading in those fields. When reading in the basal reading textbook, the child usually does not need to remember long after he has read the material what he read. When reading in the social studies, however, it is often important to remember many points. Some should be remembered for a long time; others should be remembered always. Frequently unless a pupil can remember what he has read one day, what he reads on subsequent days has little meaning for him.

In the social studies names of persons and events, which in the typical textbook occur in great numbers, are often a special cause of difficulty. The reader is frequently unable to determine which names are important enough to remember. Guidance in discerning that which is worth remembering is often essential.

In science, too, it is often imperative that the boys and girls be given help in determining what points should be retained. The pupil who one day reads and understands what convection is but does not remember what he learned will be at loss when at a subsequent time reference is made to it, possibly in the same textbook, with the assumption by the author that the pupil remembers what is meant by the term. His problem in remembering may be caused by the fact that he never really understood what he read. Or it may be that he tries to remember every fact without relation to the generalization that can at times be drawn from facts. Lack of purpose in reading, other than possibly to answer factual questions, too, may be the cause of much undesirable forgetting of what is read. Another cause of inability to remember what is read may be failure to do what is sometimes referred to as *associational reading*. Many boys and girls seem to make relatively few, if any, associations with past experiences, either firsthand or vicarious, as they read in the content areas.

In mathematics both immediate and long-time recall is often essential. Whenever there is a problem to be solved, the pupil must remember the conditions stated until he has solved it. Some children do not do so; they forget what they have read even before they have finished the sentence or group of sentences that give the terms of the problem. Long-time recall in solving problems in mathematics is often not necessary or desirable. As a rule, the reader does not need to remember the information presented in a problem after he has correctly solved it. However, there are many points learned in mathematics that should be remembered permanently and should be remembered with exactitude. The child who has noted that twelve inches equal one foot needs to learn that fact so that he remembers it all his life and so that he remembers exactly how many inches equal one foot.

ORGANIZING WHAT IS READ   Another problem that confronts many pupils when reading in the content areas is understanding the organization of a book and organizing in their own minds material they have read. Frequently in both the social studies and science the organization followed by the author is presented through center headings, side headings, and divisions subordinate to the second order of classification. (Sometimes the major divisions of the material are indicated by center headings, with side headings as the first order of division of the center headings; at other times the major divisions of the topic are shown by side headings, with center headings as the first subdivision of side headings.) Since such organizational clues are there to help the reader, failure to make adequate use of them can greatly increase the difficulty of reading the material with comprehension.

The ability to organize what is read by means of summarizing it is often needed in reading in the content areas—more often than in basal reading textbooks, in which boys and girls often have had most of their reading instruction. One way of summarizing information is through making an outline. Outlining is usually not needed for reading books of fiction or the basic reading books. To be able to outline, however, can be a decided aid when reading for certain purposes in the content areas.

CAUSE-EFFECT RELATIONS   Reading materials in the social studies and in science abound in important references to cause-effect relations. For example, in history the understanding of the relation between slavery and secession and the Civil War may be essential to intelligent reading of material dealing with this subject.

In geography the causes of erosion may constitute the theme of a selection. Understanding in science may be based on the effect of a law of motion in a situation described. Failure to recognize the relation may interfere with comprehension and later with recall.

Even though an author explicitly states that one event caused a second one, the pupil may not understand how the one caused the other. At times, too, the reader may erroneously attribute such a relation to two events that do not have a causal relation but are both the cause or the result of a third event. The wrong association is at times made because the two are discussed in proximity in an article or because they took place at the same time. Failure to comprehend a cause-effect relation or to assume one when there is none may seriously interfere with comprehending what is read in the content areas.

MAKING GENERALIZATIONS   The reading of materials in the social studies and in science present many occasions when the reader is in special need of the skills important in making generalizations. If he arrives at a wrong generalization or accepts one that is false, the reading can have disastrous results. In the social studies skill in reading depends to a large extent on the degree to which the reader can arrive at sound conclusions and on the extent to which he can detect errors in reasoning of which the writer may have been guilty.

There are several dangers in arriving at generalizations. The pupil may (1) make generalizations on insufficient data; (2) make over-generalizations on data presented; (3) make under-generalizations on data given; (4) fail to distinguish between generalizations and data given to support them, confusing a detail with a generalization and a generalization with a detail; (5) be unable to detect when a generalization made in a book is too broad for the data presented; (6) be unable to apply generalizations to situations with which he is later confronted.

JUDGING THE AUTHENTICITY OF STATEMENTS   Especially in the social studies there is much need to consider whether or not statements are authentic. A pupil needs to note, for example, when certain information was published. A statistic on the population of New York City in a book published in 1954 should indicate to the pupil that to learn how many people are presently living in New York City, he needs more recent information. When controversial issues are discussed, the reader needs to be able to take into consideration who made the claims, in order to detect on the part of the writer possible prejudice, lack of information, or a reputation for accuracy or inaccuracy. When reading some types of social studies materials, he needs to be able to judge whether a fact or an opinion is being expressed. For reading historical fiction the ability to determine which points are historical and which are embellishments on actual happenings is needed.

In science, too, it is important to have or to develop skill in judging the authenticity of what is read. Who makes the claim as to the achievements of the Americans or of the Russians in space ventures may make a difference in what is recorded. Whether the person writing an article is likely to have sufficient information to speak with the authority he assumes is another point that needs to be considered in reading science materials. Surely with the vast explosion of scientific knowledge during recent decades, the date on which a report was written is of great importance in some areas of science. However, along with developing skill in judging statements through examination of the date when they were made, the pupil needs also to be aware of the fact that some information in the area of science recorded several decades ago is as authentic now as then. An illustration is the statement that many animals have protective coloring. Another example is the fact that Benjamin Franklin invented the Franklin stove. Furthermore, a report on possible next steps in the exploration of space needs to be interpreted in terms of the background of the writer, not only his possible prejudices but also his knowledge.

ADDITIONAL WAYS OF READING CRITICALLY   Several of the skills of critical reading to be noted in particular when reading in some of the content areas have been discussed in preceding paragraphs on organizing what is read, on noting cause-effect relations, on making generalizations, and on judging the authenticity of statements. Still other skills in reading critically—some related to those already mentioned—are of special importance in content areas. At times there is greater need than when reading basal reading textbooks to be able to predict outcomes, to do associational reading, or, in literature, to judge the literary quality of material.

INTERPRETING GRAPHS, TABLES, CHARTS, AND MAPS Books on both the social studies and science, especially the former, contain many graphs, tables, charts, and maps. Frequently these are essential to full understanding of the text. However, many boys and girls are not aware of their value and consequently do not try to interpret them. Others, recognizing the value of these illustrative materials, lack skill in interpreting them and consequently do not take time to "read" them. Still others, because of lack of knowledge of the proper use of these aids to learning, make errors in interpreting them. Since very little "reading" of this type is required in basal reading series and in books of fiction, it is important that the teacher recognize the need for special instruction as pupils read in the content areas.

Problems in Reading at Appropriate Rates

Reading at inappropriate rates material in the content areas may be due to lack of comprehension skills. Or it may be due to other factors discussed in Chapter 7A, "Reading Rates." A special problem pertaining to the rate of reading in the content areas is that some pupils who have done most of their reading in material easy to comprehend and for purposes that could well be achieved through rapid reading try to read more difficult material for study purposes at the same rate at which they had previously been reading. The premium teachers often erroneously place on speed of reading at all times may cause the better readers to have a handicap when studying in the content areas. The problem in reading at appropriate rates in the content areas is essentially that of learning to read as rapidly as possible without tension or undue strain materials of all types in the content areas, in harmony with the difficulty of the material and the purpose of the reader.

It is wrong to assume that all reading in the content areas is study-type material. If that is the only kind of reading the pupil does, his range is too limited. For some of the materials in the content areas—such as reports in newspapers or magazines—the most desirable rate to accomplish the purpose of the reader might be skimming. At times, rapid reading but not skimming might be the rate at which the reader's purpose is best attained, for example, when he is reading an anecdote about Abraham Lincoln. Reading at a moderate rate might be desirable when the pupil is reading fairly easy material in his textbook in order to answer questions he has been given. At times, however, to find answers to questions, especially when the material is rather difficult, the slowness of careful study might be the most suitable rate. Thus the need for flexibility of rate should be recognized. Furthermore, a pupil may need to be warned against dawdling habits when reading at any of the rates indicated. It is possible to dawdle when skimming, that is, not skim as rapidly as one could for the purpose in mind. It is possible to dawdle when doing careful study-type reading. At each of the levels of reading rates the pupil should be encouraged to read as rapidly as he can commensurate with the fulfillment of his purpose in reading.

Problems in Locating Information and Using It

When the single textbook was the vogue in social studies classes and in science classes, the need for locating information when studying was not nearly as great as it is now when a variety of reading materials are utilized in those areas. To be sure, even when only one textbook is used, pupils can often benefit from guidance in using the table of contents, the index, the appendix, and other special features of the textbook. However, in classrooms in which one textbook does not constitute the curriculum of a content subject, it is imperative that boys and girls know how to locate information from various sources and how to make use of it. The teacher who merely tells a pupil, when making an assignment for outside reading, that he should look up information on a given topic is not giving the help that many children need. For greatest effectiveness there is need of guidance in locating information and utilizing it along all the lines indicated in Chapters 8A and 8B. These skills include, among others: (1) developing the basic skills of finding words arranged in alphabetical order, deciding on key words, and discovering what types of information are given in various kinds of books; (2) interpreting punctuation marks, diacritical markings, abbreviations, and symbols; (3) selecting points that have bearing on a given problem; (4) utilizing information gained; (5) developing skill in using nonreference books; (6) developing skill in using the dictionary; (7) developing skill in using reference books other than the dictionary; and (8) locating materials in a library.

As in the case of guidance in the use of other special skills needed for reading intelligently in the content areas, the content subjects afford excellent opportunity for teaching skill in locating information. They serve three purposes. They present situations that require knowledge of how to locate information, thereby furnishing an incentive for learning needed skills. They can also provide practice needed for perfecting a skill that is being learned. Furthermore, they help the child obtain information in the content areas.

Interesting Pupils in Independent Reading
in the Content Areas

Far too often in the past pupils' independent reading has been largely confined to books of fiction. With the excellent array of books for children in the areas of the social studies, science, art, and other content areas, it is, indeed, unfortunate if the pupils in an elementary school do not read them. Books on history, minority cultures, biography, far-away lands and people, health, music, and art can give boys and girls insight into themselves and the world around them. It is unfortunate if a child chooses to read none or only a few of the books of these types.

The chief problem in relation to independent reading in the content areas is getting the "right book to the right child." Another is helping boys and girls develop in skill in evaluating the authenticity of the material they are reading. Still another is helping the pupils to differentiate between fact and fiction—between what is historical background, for example, and that which is an embellishment of the facts of history.

GUIDING GROWTH IN READING IN THE CONTENT AREAS

In Part II of this book suggestions were given for solving each of the problems associated with reading in the content areas that are discussed in this chapter. The following guidelines are especially applicable for fostering growth in reading in the content areas.

Guidelines

1. *Every teacher of the content subjects should consider herself a teacher of reading.* In departmentalized set-ups teachers of content subjects often fear that the time they might spend on helping pupils to read better in their field is time lost to them for teaching the subject matter of their area. Their fears are groundless. Effective teaching of reading skills important to a content subject will improve the pupils' comprehension of the subject matter.
2. *The teacher of the content subjects, whether or not she is the room teacher who has the pupils for all subjects, should have clearly in mind reading objectives for her area of learning.* These goals should include primarily those skills particularly important for reading in the area. For example, one objective might deal with guiding the child in learning the specialized vocabulary that he encounters in her subject.
3. *The program for guiding boys and girls to read more effectively in the content areas should include various types of approaches.* Among these approaches are: (a) presentation lessons in which the pupil is helped to understand how he can improve in some skill needed for effectiveness in reading in a given area; (b) practice exercises in which special help is provided in the maintenance of a needed skill; and (c) incidental means of strengthening the skills needed which could be supplied by activities in the ongoing school program.
4. *The readiness principle applies with special force to reading in the content subjects.* Before a pupil is asked to read a chapter or a part of a chapter in a textbook, he should be mentally prepared for the task. The words he encounters on the printed page are abstract symbols to him unless he can bring a body of experience to the reading. Moreover, often he should have had prior experience with words that symbolize the images and concepts he is to learn.
5. *Pupils should learn to approach a reading assignment in the content areas*

with clearly conceived purposes. They should know what they are looking for, and why. Such purposes may arise out of previous class discussions, demonstrations, or experiments.

6. *Opportunity for pupil evaluation of growth in needed reading skills should be provided.* For such evaluation to be most beneficial it is, of course, important that the pupils, too, have in mind goals to be achieved.

7. *An effective program of reading in the content subjects should stimulate the boys and girls so that they will want to read in those areas during leisure time as part of their independent reading.* Unless the boys and girls are stimulated to read such materials outside of school and in later years, the program will not have been entirely successful.

Meeting the Problems

Below are given some suggestions for putting into practice guidelines such as those described in the preceding paragraphs.

PROBLEMS OF VOCABULARY   It is hoped that suggestions such as the following will stimulate the teacher to think of additional ones that will be peculiarly adapted to the needs of at least some of the boys and girls in her class.

1. Before the pupils begin reading a selection, the teacher might write on the chalkboard, frequently in context, the words with which she thinks her pupils will be unfamiliar. For example, she might have on the chalkboard the words *taxation without representation,* using the expression within the context of a sentence. The sentence might be, "The colonists were opposed to *taxation without representation,*" with the phrase to be studied underlined. She might then say to a fifth-grade class that she imagines everybody knows what taxes are and that consequently they will have no trouble with the word *taxation* (at which she points in the sentence on the chalkboard). Thereupon she might ask the class to read the sentence silently to see if anyone can figure out what the word *representation* means in the sentence. If no one can give an adequate explanation, she might explain the word or she might tell the boys and girls that as they read a certain part of the social studies work for that day she thinks they may be able to find out what is meant by the expression *taxation without representation.* After the class has read silently the selection in which the term occurs, discussion should follow. Pupils might make up meaningful sentences of their own from which it is evident that they know the meaning of the term.

2. The teacher might help the boys and girls with variants of a word they are studying. For example, if the phrase *taxation without representation* is taught as suggested in the preceding paragraph, the class might give the root of the word *taxation* and then name variants such as *taxed, taxes, taxing, taxable.* Similarly, they could proceed with the word *representation,* as they name the root word *represent* and suggest variations of the word, such as *represents, representing, represented.*

3. The boys and girls might make an illustrated chart highlighting some of the words in the specialized vocabulary that they are studying in connection with a unit of work or an area of learning. For example, having completed a unit on "Neighbors around the World," the pupils might make a chart illustrating words such as *igloo, pyramid, scroll, totem pole, fiord.*

4. The class could have a quiz program based at least in part on the vocabulary they had studied in connection with a unit of work.

5. Through a test with items such as the following the boys and girls could check their knowledge of vocabulary studied while concentrating on a unit of work or area of study.

> *Directions.* Draw a line under the group of words that best explains the meaning of the word *mouth* as it is used in the illustrative sentence.
>
> *Illustrative sentence:* The *mouth* of the Mississippi River is in the Gulf of Mexico.
>
> *Test item. Mouth* means (a) the beginning or origin of a river; (b) the part of a river that empties into another body of water; (c) the branch of a river; (d) a cavelike opening through which a river flows.

PROBLEMS OF COMPREHENSION   A few recommended procedures are listed below that may help boys and girls increase in power to read with comprehension in content areas. Suggestions are given relative to (1) remembering what is read, (2) organizing what is read, (3) cause-effect relations, (4) making generalizations, (5) judging the authenticity of statements, and (6) interpreting graphs, tables, charts, and maps.

Remembering what is read. In an attempt to help boys and girls improve in ability to remember what they read in the social studies or other content areas, the teacher might do the following:

1. Have the pupils list details stated in a paragraph that support the main idea of the paragraph.

2. Help the pupils construct a paragraph that includes various details supporting a stated topic sentence. For example, after reading about the hard winter at Valley Forge, the pupils could write a paragraph, either individually or as a class, that furnishes details to support this topic sentence: "The winter at Valley Forge was a discouraging period of our history."

3. Assist the pupils in determining which details are important to illustrate in a mural on a theme such as the history of transportation or life in the Far West.

4. Select the details that throw light on how a character should act in a

play the class is planning to give on a subject such as the first Thanks-giving in Plymouth or on the topic "Man Walks on the Moon."

5. After the pupils have read a problem in mathematics silently, have them answer questions on information given, without recourse to the problem, such as: (a) Was the house sold at a gain or a loss? (b) What are we *to find* in this problem?

6. For a social studies class make a chart listing all the people important enough for the pupils to remember always. Have the class decide upon an important sentence about each, one that summarizes the work of the person. Then, from time to time, have pupils give the important sentence to be remembered about each person. So that the boys and girls can review the statements by themselves, they might be given a duplicated list of the sentences decided upon or they might copy the sentences into a notebook. Illustrations of possible sentences to remember are:

> Columbus discovered America in 1492.
> De Soto discovered the Mississippi River.

Instead of important people, the chart might be made on important dates or on important events. Summarizing sentences such as these might be decided upon for the chart on dates:

> In 1492 Columbus discovered America.
> In 1607 the first permanent English settlement in America was made in Jamestown, Virginia.

For the chart on important events sentences such as this one might be remembered:

> The Treaty of Paris of 1676 stated that all land in North America east of the Mississippi River excepting New Orleans would belong to England and all land west of the Mississippi River and New Orleans would belong to Spain.

Organizing what is read. In order to develop skill in organizing what is read in a content subject, some pupils might do the following:

1. State which of two or more summaries of a paragraph is the better.
2. Note the use of center headings and side headings in books in the social studies or science.
3. Predict what will be reported under a side heading in a book, after having read the account given under the preceding side heading.
4. Group questions the boys and girls have set for study of a unit. For example, in answer to the inquiry by the teacher as to what questions they

would like answered in a study of the problem, "In what ways is Mexico a land of contrasts?" at first the questions could be listed on the chalkboard in whatever order pupils give them. Next the teacher could explain that it will be easier to find answers to the questions if the class organizes them around main topics. Thereupon the pupils could decide upon the groupings, with the guidance of the teacher.

5. Find the topic sentence in a paragraph and note the details supporting it.
6. Check the correspondence between (a) the center headings and the side heading of a given selection in a social studies or science book and (b) the parts of an outline the teacher has made.
7. Rewrite an incorrectly made outline of subject matter in the content areas.
8. Make an outline of a selection using the center headings and the side headings of a well-organized selection as determiners of the outline.
9. Give a talk according to an outline determined by the person giving the talk, with the help of the teacher.

For additional ideas on organizing what is read the reader is referred to the part under "Making Summaries and Organizing Material" given in Chapter 6B. (See page 201.)

Cause-effect relations. To help the boys and girls gain in proficiency in understanding cause-effect relations as they come across them in their reading in the content areas, they might engage in activities such as the following:

1. Explaining how a given event caused another.
2. Stating what they think might have happened had a given event not occurred in the manner that it did.
3. Making a list of cause-effect relations stated in material assigned.
4. Matching a cause with its effect as given in a two-column exercise, in which in column A are given the causes of events listed, and the effects in a different order, in column B. For example, one item in column A might be *secession,* to be matched with *Civil War* in column B.
5. Indicating what would be likely to happen if a certain direction in a science experiment were not followed.

Making generalizations. The teacher might help pupils acquire skill in making generalizations when reading in the content areas by:

1. Having the pupils test stated generalizations in terms of the details given to support them.
2. Asking the pupils to select among a list of details the one that does not contribute to the generalization reached.
3. Having the pupils write a generalization that can be made from a list of facts presented.

4. Giving the pupils an exercise such as the following.

> *Directions.* Decide which of the following sentences contain generalizations about Benjamin Franklin and which contain facts that might help support a generalization. If a sentence contains a generalization, write the letter G (for *generalization*) on the blank to the left of it; if it contains a detail that might support a generalization, write the letter D (for *detail*) on the blank.
>
> ——— He invented the Franklin stove.
> ——— He was ambassador to France.
> ——— He helped draft the Constitution.
> ——— He did much to help his fellowmen.
> ——— He helped frame the Declaration of Independence.

5. Asking the pupils to find details that support a given generalization.
6. Having the pupils compile a list of generalizations of questionable validity in a given content area that they have heard. The pupils could be asked to give reasons for their questioning of each generalization.

For additional ideas on making generalizations the reader is referred to "Developing Ability To Arrive at Generalizations and Come to Conclusions" in Chapter 6B, pages 203–205.

Judging the authenticity of statements. Through suggestions such as those given in the preceding list under "Making generalizations," the teacher can also help boys and girls judge the authenticity of some types of statements. Following are additional ways in which she can do so.

1. Having the pupils compare two somewhat contradictory reports in newspapers on a current event, as they note points of contradiction and as they try to explain them.
2. Asking the pupils to read a report on a political issue that is controversial and have them decide what sentences would probably be deleted or changed if a person on the other side of the controversy were to report on the issue.
3. Reading the qualifications of two people writing on the schools of Russia. The background of one, as described, should be such that it would be highly probable that he could write with authority on the subject, while the background of the other would be such that his report would not bear the weight of that by the other writer.
4. Rewriting an article about American or Russian successes in the space race appearing in an American paper so as to express the point of view that might be taken in a Russian newspaper.

Additional suggestions are given, on page 208 under "The Author" and on pages 208–209, under "Propaganda Techniques."

A warning is in order here. Critical reading of material in the social studies is not to be interpreted as calling for a "debunking" of characters in history. More harm than good is done, it would seem, by those who propose to show boys and girls that there were many flaws of character in some men who have made outstanding contributions. The opposite extreme, however, should also be avoided. For example, the biographer who pictures heroes of history as infallible persons is missing the mark. Furthermore, the author of a history book who assumes that the United States is and has always been right is a menace to clear thinking. The boys and girls should be taught to recognize writings of such an author by the style and content.

Interpreting graphs, tables, charts, and maps. For some ways in which the teacher can help boys and girls learn to interpret graphs, tables, charts, and maps the reader is referred to the section of Chapter 6B entitled "Learning To Read Graphical and Tabular Material." A few additional ones as they apply to the content subjects are here given.

1. Place on the bulletin board an exhibit of various types of graphs, including line graphs, bar graphs, circular graphs, and pictorial graphs. Post interesting questions of significance in the social studies or science that can be answered through a study of the graphs.
2. Encourage the boys and girls to use charts, graphs, tables, and maps when they give special reports which could be made clearer to the class by use of these aids.
3. Have a quiz program in which questions are asked about one or more content areas that can be answered through examination of a graphical or tabular aid recorded on transparencies and projected so all can see.
4. Assist the pupils in making charts that clarify some important learning that they have acquired while studying a topic in a content area, for example, (a) the proportion of persons on the earth belonging to each of the races, (b) the territorial expansion of the United States, (c) the work of parents of the boys and girls in the class, and (d) the increase or decrease in the cost of living.

PROBLEMS OF READING AT APPROPRIATE RATES   The following suggestions illustrate how pupils can get practice in reading at appropriate rates in the content areas when working on a unit or area of study.

Developing skill in rapid reading. Some of the ways in which the boys and girls can get helpful practice in skimming or other rapid reading when working on a unit on Mexico are:

1. Glancing at books such as the following to see which ones they would like to read: *The Watchdog* by Laura Bannon (Whitman Publishing Com-

pany); *My Pet Peepolo* by Ellis Credle (Oxford University Press); and *Let's Read about Mexico* by Stella Burke May (The Fideler Company).

2. Reading one or more books on Mexico rather rapidly, merely to get the story.
3. Skimming an article in an encyclopedia to see if it contains information about the observance of September 16.
4. Skimming a page in an index of a social studies book to find out if it contains an entry on Miguel Hidalgo.
5. Glancing at the table of contents in the book *The Real Book about Explorers* by Irvin Block (Garden City Books) to see if a chapter is devoted to Hernando Cortez.

Developing skill in reading when a moderately fast rate is required. The boys and girls can get practice in reading material at the optimum rate when moderately fast reading is desirable in the following ways:

1. Reading a selection in a social studies textbook on Mexico City in order to find the answer to a set of relatively easy questions that the reader has seen before he began to read.
2. In a book that is moderately easy to read, reading about Mexican art in order to be able to tell the rest of the class a few points of interest on the subject.
3. Reading the writing under a picture of a Mexican housewife grinding corn on a huge stone to find out what the woman is doing.

Developing skill in reading when a slow rate is required. Opportunity to help pupils read at the maximum efficiency when a rather slow rate is required may be provided in situations such as the following:

1. Reading preparatory to giving a talk on the Mexican and the American sides of issues leading up to the Mexican War.
2. Studying directions in order to make a Mexican dish, tortillas, for example.
3. Studying the history of Mexico in order to be able to make a frieze portraying important events in the history of the country. Events such as these might be pictured: the arrival of Cortez in Mexico; the conquest of the country by Cortez; the attitude of European settlers who came to Mexico; the work of the missionaries; the long struggle for freedom; the war with the United States; and, finally, the progress Mexico is making in the present century.

READING ORALLY   In connection with some of the content subjects there are many opportunities for oral reading.

Opportunities for oral reading. The pupils might do the following:

1. Listen to a selection that the teacher reads to the class.
2. Read one or more sentences in answer to a question asked or to prove a point that has been made.
3. Read a longer selection to give background information to the class.
4. Read the script of a dramatic episode of history.
5. Read the script for a puppet play depicting some phase of historical, geographical, anthropological, or sociological significance.
6. Do choral reading of parts of a famous document of history, such as the Declaration of Independence or the Emancipation Proclamation or the Gettysburg Address.
7. Read singly or in chorus poems with an historical setting such as "Paul Revere's Ride" or "Barbara Frietchie."
8. Read reports written by pupils for one of the content subjects.
9. Read questions the pupils have formulated for investigation and discussion.
10. Read directions for making something pertaining to a content subject. For example, someone could read the directions, step by step, for making papier-mâché for construction of puppets.

Guidelines for oral reading in the content areas. Some of the guidelines that should be followed in connection with oral reading in the content areas are the following:

1. *Oral reading should be done in the content subjects in order to enrich the learning in that area.* It should not be done only to provide practice in oral reading.
2. *Although the primary purpose of oral reading in the content subjects should lie in the contribution it makes to that area, standards for effective reading should be maintained.* In fact, the oral reading in the content subjects might be part of a program of "audience reading," described in Chapter 9B.
3. *Care should be taken that material suitable for oral reading to a given group is used.* The material needs to be such that it can be easily comprehended by the listeners. Anecdotes, stories, and sketches from biography often are suitable. Textbook material is usually not desirable for oral reading; it is planned for silent reading.
4. *As a rule, before either the teacher or a pupil reads a selection orally to the class, the listeners should be prepared so as to get the maximum benefit from the reading.* The teacher or the reader might do any of the following to prepare the class for the reading: (a) State that the selection to be read gives them additional information about the topic that has been discussed. (b) Tell the pupils what the report is about. (c) Tell them

what to look for as they listen to the reading. (d) Refer them to questions on the board for discussion following the reading. (e) Show them one or more illustrations that will make it easier for them to understand the selection. (f) Explain one or more terms used in the selection. (g) Ask questions of the class as to their own experiences that might serve as a background for better comprehension of the selection.

5. *There should be a follow-up after the oral reading unless, as in the case of some stories, nothing would be gained by it.* The method of follow-up will at times depend on the type of preparation given before the reading. For example, if questions were posed beforehand, they should be answered after the reading. Other possible follow-up activities are: (a) answering questions that the reader asks following the reading of the selection; (b) giving additions to what was read; (c) discussing what was read; (d) drawing an illustration of a scene or event described in the reading; (e) showing pictures to illustrate a point made; (f) taking a quiz, possibly with each of the items—maybe three or four in all—to be answered in one or a few words.

LOCATING INFORMATION AND USING IT   In unit work carried on in the social studies or science many situations arise in which the need for locational skills becomes evident and in which practice in improving these skills can be given. As the possibilities for the development of locational skills in connection with a unit are considered, it is important for the teacher to bear in mind that only those activities dealing with locational skills should be performed in connection with the unit work that really help toward the accomplishment of the objectives set for that work. If more work on any of the skills is needed than is provided by activities that help in the attainment of the objectives for the unit study, this practice should usually be given at other times through exercises and lessons specifically designed for the development of these skills. Otherwise it is probable that the work on the problem of study will lack the unity which the very name *unit* implies.

Developing locational skills in a unit on community workers. Even in a unit planned for the primary grades, many locational skills can be developed as problems that arise in connection with the unit are being solved. The following list suggests some ways in which a unit on community helpers can be instrumental in developing skill in locating information and using it.

1. The boys and girls could place in a file mounted pictures of community workers. The pictures could be arranged alphabetically by groups, with those of firemen preceding those of postmen, because the *f* of *firemen* precedes the *p* of *postmen*. Guide cards could be made similar to those used in a card catalog.

2. The pupils could look for books on the various community workers they are studying.

3. They could examine the table of contents of some of the books on community workers to find out on what page information is given on a worker.

4. The members of a committee or one individual could look for information in a book that will give them the answer to a specific question, for example, "What does a fireman do when he hears a fire alarm?"

5. They could compile a list, arranged in alphabetical order according to the last name of the author, of books on community workers. They could use three-by-five-inch cards to be filed or sheets of paper on which they could list a number of references.

6. Before drawing pictures for a "movie" or a frieze on community workers, they could look in books for pictures that would give them some needed background information.

7. As a group project they could make a picture dictionary containing words learned while working on the unit.

8. For a booklet that the group could make, the pupils could write a table of contents, a preface, and an appendix. In the appendix they might include: (a) a table showing the work of each of the workers studied; (b) a picture of each community worker, showing the type of uniform or clothes he wears; (c) a diagram showing where the workers work. This diagram could indicate, for example, the location of the post office, the fire station, bakeries, and police headquarters.

9. The more mature pupils could find information that deals with the topic in *Compton's Pictured Encyclopedia* or the *World Book Encyclopedia*. Younger ones could find information in *Childcraft*.

10. As the pupils notice that the teacher finds information in encyclopedias, they can learn some of the uses of these books.

11. Skill in learning to make use of information located can be provided as the boys and girls give talks to their classmates or others about what they have read.

12. The pupils could be helped to find in their picture dictionaries the spelling of words needed for writing.

13. They could look for poems useful for the unit and make an index of poems found.

14. They could collect songs about community workers and make a file showing in which books the songs are printed.

15. They could get help in interpreting charts and graphs that are of value in connection with the unit and they could show graphically such data as: (a) the number of milkmen, policemen, postmen, firemen, bakers, and doctors in the community; (b) the number in each of the categories of community workers who are fathers or mothers of the boys and girls in the room; (c) the increase in the number of firemen in the community during various intervals in the past few decades. Pictorial graphs could be made to show some of the suggested data.

Developing locational skills in a unit on the western states.
Skill in the location of information can be developed in a large variety
of situations in connection with a unit on the western states, work
typically taken up in the fifth grade. The following ways in which
locational skills can be learned in such a unit will, it is hoped, suggest
many others.

1. A committee of boys and girls could look up material in encyclopedias
    and in history books other than the textbook preparatory to putting on a
    skit on an interesting episode in the settlement of the West. Topics might
    be the work of Sacajawea; the building of the first transcontinental rail-
    road; traveling westward by covered wagon; the discovery of gold in
    California. An activity of this type could provide the boys and girls
    with practice in such locational skills as the following: (a) clarifying the
    problem that they wish to investigate; (b) deciding in what books to look
    for information; (c) learning to locate the books they wish to use; (d)

Relating a social studies unit on the westward movement to a study of plant
and animal life of the early West. (Photo courtesy Columbia, Missouri, Public
Schools.)

using the table of contents; (e) deciding on possible key words and looking for these words in an index or in an encyclopedia; (f) locating the information needed on a page; (g) making an outline of the information gathered from various sources; (h) using the outline to prepare the skit.

2. The pupils could make a collection of pictures dealing with the Far West and file them alphabetically, using guide cards to indicate their position in a filing drawer.

3. Individuals, committees, or an entire class could make a notebook on some phase of the western states and include in it a preface, an introduction, an appendix, and an index. Some topics that might be chosen are beauty spots of the West, the opening of the West, the coming of missionaries, and famous men and women in the settling of the West. A few suggestions for the content of the appendix are: (a) a list of important dates; (b) a page giving biographical data about the famous people connected with the Far West; (c) a sheet giving data in tabular form about the national parks of the West.

4. Many locational skills could be used in making a frieze showing the means of communication used in pioneer days of the West: wagon, clipper ship, stagecoach, pony express, overland stage, railroad, and telegraph. Some of the locational skills that could be used in a project of this type are: (a) finding pictures of the various means of communication; (b) using encyclopedias and history and geography books for wide reading; (c) selecting the points that have bearing on a given problem; (d) finding the dates when a given means of communication was used so that the correct sequence of events will be known; and (e) making use of the information found.

5. A large variety of locational skills could be used in giving a talk on topics on the western states, for example, any one of the states of this section of the country; famous pioneers like John C. Frèmont, Kit Carson, John McLoughlin, Marcus and Narcissa Whitman, Buffalo Bill; and important events, such as the discovery of gold in California.

6. The pupils could make a card file of books of value in connection with the study of the West. They could make subject cards, title cards, and author cards. Guide cards, similar to those used in the card catalog, could also be made.

7. When drawing pictures to show, for example, the life history of a salmon, they could consult various textbooks and reference books—encyclopedias, the *World Almanac,* an atlas, and history and geography books.

8. Making an illustrated dictionary of words and phrases learned while studying the unit could involve such locational skills as: (a) arranging words in alphabetical order; (b) looking words up in a dictionary or other reference books; (c) finding illustrations of the terms; (d) using a dictionary to find out the spelling of words.

9. If a pageant or play were given showing, as a culminating activity, the development of the western states, various skills named earlier in this

chapter could be used—namely: (a) finding words in alphabetical order as the pupils locate words in an index or encyclopedia; (b) finding quickly a given page in a book; (c) deciding on key words under which needed information might be expected to be found; (d) deciding on the type of book in which needed information could be likely to be found; (e) interpreting punctuation marks, diacritical markings, abbreviations, and symbols used in the various references; (f) selecting points that have bearing on a given problem; (g) utilizing information gained; (h) using the parts of the usual type of book (nonreference book), such as preface, introduction, table of contents, main part, index, appendix, and glossary; (i) using encyclopedias, dictionaries, and other reference books; and (j) locating material in the library.

INDEPENDENT READING IN THE CONTENT AREAS   As stated earlier in this chapter, as far as independent reading in the content area is concerned, one of the chief responsibilities of the teacher is to interest the pupils in reading in these areas and to try to get "the right book to the right child." Getting the right book to the right child involves knowing the child (his interests both in books and in non-reading situations) and knowing books.

Guidelines for deciding on the "right book" in the content areas. Books in the content areas should be equal in quality to those of other types. For example, in historical fiction, as in all fiction, there should be a worthwhile theme, a strong plot, and convincing characters. However, certain criteria pertain in particular to books in the content subjects designed for independent reading. Some of these are as follows:

1. If the book is historical fiction, it should be historically accurate. While many of the details of this type of book will understandingly not report actual happenings, the background on which the story is based should be in harmony with what history records.
2. The story elements should not be sacrificed in historical fiction. It should tell a good story.
3. Any book on history should give the pupil improved perspective of happenings in the past.
4. Fiction based primarily on a geographical background, such as *Heidi,* should give the pupil a clearer portrayal of life in a region than he had before reading the book. The differences among people should be emphasized less than the likenesses, in needs, in longings, and in hopes. Nor should generally outmoded customs, such as the wooden shoes of Holland, be presented as typical of a country.
5. Regarding supplementary books in science, there should be an affirmative answer to these questions: (a) Are the points presented as facts

scientifically accurate? (b) Unless the book deals primarily with the history of science, does it give up-to-date information?

6. Books dealing with minority groups should serve to help pupils from both the minority and the majority groups to better living without resorting to so-called moralizing.

7. Books dealing with minority groups should present the point of view that all problems faced by minority groups are common problems of both minority and majority groups and that they require concerted effort for best solution.

8. A biography for children should be about a person who is worthy of admiration, at least in some respects.

9. A biography for children should not deal with problems beyond the understanding of the reader.

10. All books for independent reading in the content area should be such that if the "right child" reads them, he will want to read additional worthwhile books in that area.

Ways of interesting children in independent reading in the content areas. Many of the suggestions given in Chapter 10B are applicable to independent reading in the content areas. A few additional ones are here listed.

1. To interest boys and girls in books on aviation a sign written in white letters on a blue background (to simulate sky writing) with the words *All About Aviation* could be placed near a number of books on that topic. The writing could be done in cursive writing, with a flourish to resemble that of sky writing. A small airplane could be drawn on the sign to attract further attention.

2. A pupil-made model of the home of one or more animals could be placed near books on animals. The home of the beaver might, for example, be made of papier mâché. One illustration could show the exterior of the home, with considerable emphasis on the unique surroundings of the beaver's habitat. A second model of the home might be a cross-section view of the home, showing the interior. A pupil or a group of pupils might explain their production to the rest of the class and refer them to additional books about beavers and other animals.

3. To interest boys and girls after a study of various people of the world in continuing reading on the subject, a series of dioramas might serve as a powerful stimulation. Homes of dwellers of Arctic, temperate, and tropical regions, of primitive and modern man, could be placed on exhibit and titles of books, with the authors' names and an indication of where the books can be obtained, listed near the dioramas.

4. As a pupil gives a report on a book of historical fiction in order to interest his classmates in reading it, he might add to the interest of his report by showing the class a time line which he has drawn to illustrate the events of history that occurred during the time when the story took place.

5. An imitation travel bureau in the room could display travel folders along with books that will help a child "travel" in imagination to a place or country of interest.

6. Dramatizing scenes from a book of biography by some of the pupils who have read the book might interest others in reading it. What child of fifth-grade reading ability could resist wanting to read Kate Seredy's *The Good Master* after seeing scenes dramatized such as these that are described vividly in the book: (a) Kate's arrival at the railroad station and Jancsi's disappointment when he met the girl who had wrongly been described to him as a "delicate" person; (b) Kate marooned on the rafters of the kitchen waiting for the stove below the rafters to become cool enough for her to use it as a ladder for her descent.

NONREADING EXPERIENCES AS ENRICHMENT FOR READING

Although this book deals primarily with means of helping boys and girls grow through reading, it is important to note that reading in various content areas can be greatly enriched through the use of nonreading procedures. The many types of audio-visual equipment can be a decided source of help in the teaching-learning situation in the content subjects. The reader is referred to several means of vitalizing the social studies that have of late received considerable publicity, namely, that of "games and simulations" as proposed and developed by Jerome Bruner and associates and that of the "process analog" advocated by William Fiedler. Both employ dramatization, including role playing.[1] The contention of the writers of this book is that "games and simulations" and the "process analog," if used, should be a supplement or complement to reading in the social studies, not a substitute for it.

Benefits that can be derived through nonreading experiences in the content areas are not limited to the social studies. With the rapid inventions in science, visual aids to learning are especially needed in that area. Arithmetic problems can be made more meaningful to the boys and girls through the use of transparencies, filmstrips, and other visual aids.

USE OF THE TEXTBOOK IN THE SOCIAL STUDIES

In the majority of the schools of this country a textbook is used in the area of the social studies. Nor with the many excellent text-

---

[1] For a brief description of both means of enriching the social studies, see William R. Fiedler, *"An Alternative to Reading for the Social Studies,* pp. 205–211. Thirty-first Yearbook, Claremont Reading Conference, Malcolm F. Douglass, (ed.). Claremont, Calif.: Claremont Graduate School Curriculum Laboratory, 1967.

books on the market is this practice to be criticized. Much of the criticism that has been hurled against textbooks in the social studies should be directed not against the use of textbooks but against the misuse of them.

Cautions in the Use of Textbooks in the Social Studies and Science

The following are some of the cautions to be observed when using a textbook in the social studies or in science, for which textbooks are becoming more and more common in the elementary school:

1. One textbook should not constitute the curriculum.
2. Many books other than the basic textbook should be made available. In some rooms boys and girls have ready access to a few copies of each of several textbooks. Well-selected trade books on varying levels of difficulty should also be available to the pupils, some in the home room and others in the school library or learning center.
3. Magazines and current events papers should be part of the classroom or school library.
4. An abundance of visual aids to learning should be utilized. Films, filmstrips, slides, transparencies, still pictures—these as well as many others can richly complement or supplement the reading.
5. Pupils should not, as a rule, be asked to read a textbook without help being provided in the comprehension of material presented. The material in a textbook is not to be "covered," but, as someone said, it is to be "uncovered" with the guidance of the teacher.
6. Use of the study-recitation type of procedure should be avoided, as a rule.
7. A child reading orally the material from the textbook while others in the class presumably follow in their books is undesirable procedure. It is to be criticized for various reasons, these among them: (a) the reader has little incentive for reading well orally when a true audience situation is lacking; (b) the persons not reading are likely to half listen and half read, thereby getting poor practice in both those facets of the language arts; (c) the subject matter of a textbook for a grade usually is not adapted to oral reading or to hearing it read orally.
8. Not all the material in a textbook needs necessarily to be read by the pupils, especially not if the large number of worthwhile activities other than studying the textbook make it impossible to do justice to them and to all the reading material in the textbook. It is important that some topics in the social studies be studied in much more detail than presented in the textbook. Consequently, the teacher, to save time for those additional types of activities, might present essentials related to other

topics in the textbook without requesting all to read everything given in the textbook on those topics.

Suggested Procedures for Using a Textbook in the Social Studies in the Intermediate Grades

Although the procedures suggested in the pages following are geared to teaching with the use of an intermediate-grade social studies textbook, many of the ideas the reader of this book might also, with adaptations, use with upper primary grade pupils. Many, too, can be utilized when reading textbooks in science.

One of the points emphasized in the preceding list of cautions to observe when using a textbook in the social studies or science is that the teacher should help the boys and girls with the study of the textbook. As a rule, parts of the textbook should not be assigned for study during a period preceding a "recitation period." Rather, during class time the boys and girls should be helped with the study of the textbook. Nor is it enough, as a rule, to give the pupils some help preliminary to their reading the selection for the day and then having them discuss what they read afterwards. To provide more help with textbook reading in the social studies, when most of the day's work is based on the textbook, the reading material for the day could be divided into several parts; help could then be given preceding and following each of these parts. An outline that might be followed with such a lesson, when the textbook material for the day is divided into three parts, could be something like this:

1. Introduction to the work for the day. This part might include any of the following:
   a. Connecting the work for the day with that which preceded and/or which is to follow
   b. Interesting the pupils in the work of the day
   c. Statement of the aim(s) for the day's work
2. Word study and/or location of places.
3. Initial study of the first part of the textbook to be studied that day.
   a. Activity or activities preceding the silent reading of the part
   b. Silent reading of the part, with a stated purpose
   c. Activity or activities following the silent reading of the part
4. Initial study of the second part of the textbook to be studied that day. (To be studied as indicated under 3)
5. Initial study of the third part of the textbook to be studied that day. (To be studied as indicated under 3)
6. Follow-up activity or activities. Possible activities here are giving a report, having a panel discussion, summarizing.

ACTIVITIES TO PRECEDE SILENT READING OF A PART
OF A DAY'S WORK WITH A TEXTBOOK   Item 3a on page 420 states,
"Activity or activities preceding the silent reading of the part." Below
are suggestions for activities, one or more of which might precede the
silent reading of one of the parts to be studied on a given day, with a part
possibly from one to three paragraphs in length.

1. The pupils read silently questions on the selection placed on the chalk-
    board or duplicated on sheets of paper.
2. The pupils comment on what they already know on the topic about to
    be read. Questions are so directed by the teacher that the pupils utilize
    their own experiences, both firsthand and vicarious.
3. The teacher asks a question of the pupils orally. For example, she
    states in question form the purpose for the reading of the part without
    giving time for discussion of the question before the reading. She might
    ask, "What is the difference between winter and spring wheat? Read
    the next two paragraphs to find the answer."
4. The teacher distributes to some pupils questions on one or more slips
    of paper, which are to be answered after the reading of the part in the
    textbook. No pupil is given more than one question.
5. The teacher indicates to the pupils a list of points to note in the selec-
    tion. These points may be written on the chalkboard before class.
6. The teacher helps the pupils with the pronunciation and/or meaning of
    difficult words used in the selection.
7. The teacher gives a brief resumé of the part the pupils are then to read
    in order to obtain more ideas or a clearer concept.
8. The teacher or a pupil reads a short story or part of a story bearing
    on the topic of the selection. A brief discussion of it might follow in
    order to give purpose or background for the reading of the selection in
    the textbook.
9. The teacher or a pupil tells a story or anecdote to serve as purpose or
    background for the reading of the selection. For example, an anecdote
    about Lincoln might precede reading about him.
10. The teacher or a pupil gives a report to serve as purpose or background
    for the part to be read silently.
11. The teacher points out the relation of a selection to the major purpose
    of the study of the unit on which the boys and girls are working. For
    example, if the pupils are working on a notebook of important cities, it
    might be made clear by the teacher that reading a given selection will
    provide them with data for the project.
12. The pupils look at pictures, either in the textbook or elsewhere, in
    order to gain background for the reading.
13. The class study maps in order to gain background for the reading.
14. The teacher or a pupil makes reference to an exhibit on a bulletin
    board that serves as background for the reading to follow.

15. The teacher or a pupil shows objects related to the topic of the part to be read. For example, if the pupils are to read about the invention of the cotton gin, a sample of raw cotton with seeds in it, with a little experimentation with the removal of a seed from the cotton, puts meaning into the statement in the textbook that it is difficult to separate the seeds from the cotton by hand.

16. Some pupils give a brief skit, sing a song, or play a game that serves as background for the reading. For example, before the boys and girls read about the discovery of gold in California, a few pupils might put on a skit dramatizing Sutton's discovery. Or before the pupils read about the play activities of boys and girls in some foreign country, a game popular in that country can be played, for demonstration, by a few pupils.

ACTIVITIES TO FOLLOW THE SILENT READING OF A PART OF A DAY'S WORK WITH A TEXTBOOK.   Item 3c in the outline on page 420 states, "Activity or activities following the silent reading of the part." Below are possible activities that could be used following the silent reading of one of the parts of the textbook to be studied on a given day. (The part often will be only one, two, or three paragraphs in length.) Such follow-up procedures are usually desirable to assure that learning has taken place and to serve as further stimulation. It will be noted that some of the procedures already suggested for possible use before a part is read are also included in the following list for use after a part has been read.

1. The pupils answer questions that have been written on the chalkboard or duplicated on sheets of paper.
2. The pupils answer questions that the teacher or a pupil asks orally.
3. A pupil summarizes important points of a selection.
4. The pupils answer questions on the content of a selection, written on numbered slips of paper on each of which is a different question.
5. The teacher or pupils state related facts not given in the textbook.
6. A pupil lists on the board important information given in a selection.
7. **The class outlines the selection, either individually or as a group, or completes an outline partially made by the teacher. This is an example of an incomplete outline, which the pupils could fill in.**

THE "STARVING TIME" IN VIRGINIA

   I.   Causes of the "starving time"
        A.
        B.
   II. Rules John Smith made to end the "starving time"
        A.
        B.

III. Effects of John Smith's regulations
    A.
    B.
    C.

8. The pupils decide on illustrative material that they can bring to expand the ideas given in the selection.

9. The pupils illustrate what is described in a selection. For example, if a paragraph describes the moat around a castle, the pupils draw a diagram of one.

10. The teacher helps the pupils with word study.

11. The pupils locate places mentioned in the selection.

12. The teacher or a pupil tells an anecdote to make clearer the meaning of a selection read.

13. The teacher or a pupil gives a report to enlarge upon learnings from the selection read.

14. The pupils study pictures or examine objects that make clearer the meaning of the selection.

15. The teacher or a pupil gives a demonstration pertinent to the material studied. For example, a cause of erosion might be demonstrated.

16. The teacher or a pupil makes reference to a display on a bulletin board explaining a phase or all of the part read.

Adapting a Textbook Lesson to Individual Differences

In a typical intermediate-grade class there are usually two or more pupils for whom the reading of the textbook is on the frustration level. These boys and girls deserve the serious attention of the teacher. There are various ways of coping with the situation, none of them perfect.

SUGGESTED PROCEDURES   It is hoped that some of the procedures suggested here will help the teacher in meeting the needs of the boys and girls for whom the reading of the textbook in the social studies or science is too difficult. With each of the suggestions, one difficulty with the procedure is stated, not to discourage the reader of this book from trying to do something about the problem but to fore-warn him of the shortcomings of the situation.

1. Finding parallel reading material for the retarded readers—some on their level. However, day-in and day-out it is difficult for the teacher to find such material.

2. Helping the poorer readers while the rest of the class reads silently. Care needs to be taken, if this procedure is followed, that the rest of the class is not deprived of some of the attention of the teacher to which they are entitled.

3. Having a better reader read the material to a retarded reader. While this

practice may be all right at times, it cannot be followed repeatedly without "short-changing" the able reader, whose time should be spent primarily in self-improvement, not chiefly in tutoring.

4. Gearing the activities preceding and following the silent reading so that the retarded readers can profit from them. A difficulty, however, lies in the fact that if the activities are geared to the child who is retarded in reading and not able to read effectively, there is danger that they are not geared to the better readers who are doing all the silent reading.

REWRITING TEXTBOOK MATERIAL ON THE LEVEL OF THE RETARDED READER   One fifth-grade teacher was pleased with the results she obtained when she rewrote for a time the material in the textbook on the level of some of her pupils who were several years retarded in reading. They would participate in the activities preceding and following the various times for silent reading, either actively or passively. Questions asked them or words with which they were helped would be of some value in reading the rewritten selection. Then while the rest of the pupils were reading a part of the textbook, the retarded readers would be reading their adapted versions. Sometimes the teacher had guiding questions listed on the retarded readers' rewritten material. Then these pupils were asked some of these questions during the activities following silent reading.

When reporting upon the venture, the teacher of the fifth-grade pupils reported that soon after the plan had been put into operation, she noticed that the children who had previously been sitting listless and bored had begun to participate in answering questions on their level and were taking an active interest in the work. What pleased the teacher particularly was the response she received after she had for a time rewritten the material for these slower pupils. On a certain day she explained to the group that she did not have material for them and suggested that that day they read out of the textbook with the rest of the class. She was greatly encouraged that, after the experience of success that the pupils had had with reading on their level, they not only read the assigned textbook material but also took an active part in questions and discussions that followed. The children had evidently, under the time-consuming plan the teacher had worked out in rewriting materials for them, broken their blocks of not trying to read because of frustrations in the past. Success in reading the simpler material was instrumental in giving the children confidence to take part in more difficult assignments.

A shortcoming of the type of procedure just described is that it takes a considerable amount of the teacher's time to rewrite the material that is given in a textbook.

FOR FURTHER STUDY

Binter, Alfred R., John J. Diabal, Jr., and Leonard K. Kise (eds.), *Readings on Reading.* Scranton, Pa.: International Textbook Company, 1969. Part VII, "Reading in the Content Areas," containing articles by Gertrude Whipple, E. Elona Sochor, Maurice L. Hartung, and George G. Mallinson, pp. 345–374.

Bond, Guy L., and Eva Bond Wagner, *Teaching the Child To Read,* New York: The Macmillan Company, 1966. Chapter 13, "Reading Content-Subject Materials," pp. 253–286.

Fay, Leo, Thomas D. Horn, and Constance McCullough, *Improving Reading in the Elementary Social Studies.* Washington, D.C.: The National Council for the Social Studies, 1961.

Harris, Albert J. (ed.), *Readings on Reading Instruction.* New York: David McKay Company, Inc., 1963. Part XI, "Reading in Content Areas," containing articles by Martha Dallmann, Edith F. Miller, Martha Gesling Weber, the Metropolitan School Study Council, and Mauree Applegate, pp. 304–329.

Huus, Helen, *Children's Books To Enrich the Social Studies.* Washington, D.C.: National Council for the Social Studies, 1961.

Mazurkiewicz, Albert J. (ed.), *New Perspectives in Reading Instruction.* New York: Pitman Publishing Corporation, 1964. Part Eleven, "Reading in the Content Areas," containing articles by Albert A. Gallen, Glenn O. Blough, Robert V. Duffy, John R. Clark, Leland B. Jacobs, Alvina Treut Burrows, and Miriam Wilt, pp. 443–486.

Spache, George D., and Evelyn B. Spache, *Reading in the Elementary School,* 2d ed. Boston: Allyn and Bacon, Inc., 1969. Chapter 9, "The Combined Program for the Intermediate Grades," pp. 274–320.

CHAPTER 12

Providing for Individual Differences

Throughout this book we have had frequent occasion to refer to the problem of individual differences among children and the need to adapt instruction to those differences. Much research has been done on the extent of human variability and upon the effect of various methods of dealing with it. Even without the research, experienced teachers are aware that a third-grade class will usually consist of some children reading at the first-grade level and of others at the fifth-grade level. Moreover, the children differ in their *rate* of learning, so that a second-grade child placed with a third-grade child of equal reading achievement will probably soon outstrip him. Table I serves as an illustration of the usual range of differences.

Children differ not only in their achievement levels and their rates of learning, but also in almost every identifiable human characteristic. They differ when they come into the world; they differ in their early home environments, in their physical, emotional, and temperamental characteristics, in their mental potential, in their social attitudes, in their interests and special talents. They differ also in their ways of "unlocking" words. No system of instruction could possibly do full justice to all these differences in all their aspects. The important principle to remember is that differences are normal, that in many respects they contribute to the appeal as well as the difficulty of teaching.

METHODS OF DEALING WITH INDIVIDUAL DIFFERENCES

The methods used in dealing with individual differences are concerned primarily with (1) grouping and classification and (2) teaching technique.

TABLE I

DISTRIBUTION OF READING GRADES FOR PUPILS IN THE SECOND THROUGH SIXTH GRADES OF A SMALL SUBURBAN SCHOOL SYSTEM

READING GRADE*	NUMBER OF PUPILS ACTUAL GRADE				
	2	3	4	5	6
10.6 – 11					1
10.1 – 10.5					2
9.6 – 10.0					2
9.1 – 9.5				2	2
8.6 – 9.0		1	1	5	11
8.1 – 8.5		1	0	6	7
7.6 – 8.0		1	3	9	6
7.1 – 7.5	1	0	2	11	8
6.6 – 7.0		1	5	8	6
6.1 – 6.5	1	3	7	4	6
5.6 – 6.0	5	6	18	7	7
5.1 – 5.5	8	8	7	9	2
4.6 – 5.0	8	10	14	9	4
4.1 – 4.5	12	10	10	4	1
3.6 – 4.0	20	11	10	2	
3.1 – 3.5	27	20	7		
2.6 – 3.0	11	16	2		
2.1 – 2.5	3	5	1		
1.6 – 2.0		1			
1.1 – 1.5					
Total Number†	96	94	87	76	65
Mean Reading Grade‡	3.9	4.2	5.1	6.5	7.4

* Scores based on end-of-the-year testing with the Iowa Test of Basic Skills, Reading Comprehension Section, in the third through sixth grades, and Gates Advanced Primary in the second grade.

† Larger numbers of pupils in the lower grades were due to an influx of families with young children into the district.

‡ Computed on ungrouped data. Small change in mean score from second grade to third grade may reflect differences in norms of tests used.

Source: Walter W. Cook and Theodore Clymer, "Acceleration and Retardation," *Individualizing Instruction,* p. 187. Sixty-first Yearbook of the National Society for the Study of Education, Part I. Chicago: University of Chicago Press, 1962.

Grouping

Various methods of grouping to lessen heterogeneity have been tried and are still in vogue.

GROUPING WITHIN A CLASSROOM   One of the widespread methods of dealing with individual differences within a single class is to subgroup children according to ability, often on three levels. The effort to reduce the range in instructional groups is justified by facts such as these supported by many studies:

At the first-grade level, the range of achievement can be expected to be two or more years.

At the fourth-grade level, the range of achievement in a class may be four years or more.

At the sixth-grade level, the range of achievement in a class may be six years or more.

Grouping within a room is, of course, not without its limitations. The three-group plan or any other plan for homogeneous grouping may make the children and their parents conscious of differences in achievement and create pressure on one child to measure up to others in reading. Individual differences remain within the groups, and there is some danger that the teacher will assume that the differences have been cared for by the mere fact that the three-level plan is in operation. Certainly the problem is not solved if the teacher uses the same material with all pupils, allowing only for a difference in the speed with which the groups are expected to read them. However, when she uses different material for the groups, her needed daily preparation of work is increased decidedly; and there is a limit to the amount of work that can be expected even of an excellent teacher.

Much of the effectiveness of subgrouping within the class will depend on the teacher's understanding of the purpose for which the children are assigned to the groups. Great importance should be attached to how the teacher and the children feel about the group. All writers emphasize the need to keep the groups flexible. Classification of children in groups should frequently be determined by specific purposes. For example, groups may be organized for the express purpose of providing instruction in developmental reading, and individual children should be regrouped as their performance requires. In other cases, a group may be devoted to the study of specific skills, regardless of the general proficiency of the members. Research groups may be formed for pupils who wish to investigate a similar problem. Other groups, interested in the same theme, such as pets, airplanes, plants, farm life, railroads, and the like, may plan presentations to the whole class. In some instances, a group may be formed in which the better readers help the slower ones—all, of course, under the supervision of the teacher.

Especially in the case of the beginning teacher, there is the problem of what to do with groups not under the immediate direction of the teacher. No group should be left to itself without some specific task. If a group is asked to spend a period in silent reading, the teacher should make sure that each child has found a suitable book to read or is in the process of finding one at the book table. If a group is planning a display or a report to the class, the nature of the task should be clear to everyone, and the questions to be asked and answered should be well formulated in advance. In no case should a group be left with mere busywork. Games and seatwork should be carefully planned to provide needed practice in skills previously taught.

Teachers who follow the practice of subgrouping within the class should be keenly aware of the limitations and dangers of the method. First, it has been estimated that dividing pupils into three groups reduces variability in achievement only to about 83 percent of that in normally organized groups. Second, the tests commonly employed in the classification of pupils measure only a small, although significant, number of the desired competencies. Third, the relative performance of individuals within the groups will change as the instruction proceeds. Fourth, studies have shown that academic progress under a system of ability grouping is only slightly greater than under a system of heterogeneous groupings.

More important, perhaps, than any of the foregoing caveats is a concern for the over-all psychological effect of grouping on the child. If the grouping is flexible and if the child understands why he is a member of a certain group at any specified time, grouping may be quite harmless, even helpful. If the grouping stigmatizes a child with himself or others, the effect may be more serious than any loss in reading progress. Speed in learning to read is certainly no more important than growth in social maturity. Reading ability is valuable only insofar as it contributes to the general happiness and well-being of the individual and his functioning in society. We must not sacrifice the child to our desire to exhibit favorable reports of reading scores.

HOMOGENEOUS GROUPING FOR SCHOOL ACTIVITIES In many schools in which there are more children in a grade than can be taught in one classroom, it is not uncommon to organize for greater homogeneity through division of the pupils into rooms of relatively equal ability. The pupils who are considered better equipped intellectually or academically are placed in one classroom and, if there are only two rooms to the grade, the others are placed in another room. In larger schools there may be one or more rooms with intermediate groups. In this plan of organization the 4A class (the better group), for example, would be assigned to one teacher and the 4B to another teacher throughout all or most of the school day.

Fortunately often the rooms are not designated as the A and B rooms. However, even though the rooms may not be labeled so as to indicate the superiority of one group over others, even the children in the slower group are quick enough to discover before long what their classification is. And should they not by themselves rapidly make the discovery, associates from the brighter group are quite certain to let them know. Herein lies one of the serious objections raised to homogeneous grouping, as explained earlier in this chapter. In fact, when the division is into rooms rather than into homogeneous subgroups within a room, the effect on a child in a lower group may be more disastrous. After all, a child in a low group in reading only may find the stigma less humiliating than if he were in a low classification in all activities he performs. To be sure, it can be argued that a teacher can tactfully explain to her class that grouping should not cause anyone in a lower group to feel unhappy. Cases of lack of success in such an effort on the part of even very understanding teachers are too numerous for school personnel to overlook this very serious problem.

As in the case of grouping within a room through use of sub-groups, even the best efforts at homogeneity when grouping is among rooms still leaves a group hetereogeneous, though, to be sure, homogeneity can be increased through grouping. No criterion used for grouping—whether intelligence quotient, mental age, general school achievement, reading achievement—will equally affect the range according to other bases of classification that could well be used. For example, if intelligence of boys and girls in a fourth grade is the criterion for assignment to different rooms, the diversity in intelligence will show considerable range; maybe even greater will be the difference of the group in, let us say, reading achievement. If reading achievement forms the basis for assignment to a given room, while there will be great differences even then in the room in reading achievement, there may be even a more marked variation in average of school marks, in intelligence quotients, in mental age, and in various other significant characteristics of the boys and girls in the room.

When subgrouping within a room is the means through which greater homogeneity is sought, it is relatively easy to keep the grouping flexible. When the grouping is achieved through division of the children into different rooms, much greater rigidity in classification is likely to result. Administratively schools seem to find it inadvisable to make changes between rooms frequently. Consequently, a person beginning in a slow group, because of unevenness in rates of learning among pupils, may before long read so well that he equals in achievement those in a room of superior rating. Yet usually such progress is not cause for change in assignment to a room. Thus homogeneity within a room is likely to decrease as the year progresses.

HOMOGENEOUS GROUPING FOR READING ON A MULTIAGE OR MULTIGRADE BASIS   Some schools are organized so that boys and girls are assigned to reading groups without regard to their exact grade. Frequently this type of organization in the elementary school is limited to the intermediate grades. The plan can be followed even if there is only one fourth-grade, one fifth-grade, and one sixth-grade room within a building. During most of the school day the boys and girls are in their own grade room, but for reading class they are assigned to a room of their approximate reading level. For reading instruction pupils lowest in achievement in reading among the intermediate-grade pupils will be with one teacher, regardless of their regular grade placement. Thus a sixth-grade pupil might be reading in the lowest of the three groups. Similarly, the pupils among the highest in reading achievement will be taught by another teacher regardless of

Adapting reading instruction to the needs of individuals. (Photo courtesy Oak Park, Illinois, Public Schools, District No. 97.)

whether regularly they are in the fourth grade, fifth grade, or sixth grade. Obviously, if there are more than three intermediate-grade teachers within a building, the children can be divided into four or more ability groups for reading instruction.

It is not difficult to recognize some advantages of homogeneous grouping on a multiage or multigrade basis. The superiority of this system over that of grouping for all activities by rooms is that the stigma of assignment to a lower-level group is likely to be less if a child is in a lower section for reading only but is with classmates of a variety of abilities in all other areas of the curriculum. There are, however, significant shortcomings to this system of classification, some of which are listed for other types of homogeneous grouping earlier in this chapter. Even when ability in reading is the basis of classification, there will be considerable variation within a group. The children may be fairly alike in ability to read at appropriate rates but greatly different in ability to comprehend what they read or in doing critical reading. Furthermore, when boys and girls are assigned to different teachers for reading, there is danger of divorcing reading instruction from reading activities other than those in reading classes, as, for example, from reading in the social studies. Lack of correlation of activities during the reading class with nonreading activities during other times of the school day constitutes another shortcoming. Other arguments frequently advanced against departmentalization in the elementary school also hold for multiage or multigrade grouping. The danger is there that the teacher who teaches only reading to a child, and therefore does not know him as well as she could if she were his regular classroom teacher, may be more interested in the learning acquired than in the learner.

The debate concerning the superiority of homogeneous or hetereogeneous grouping has not been settled. Undoubtedly there is no one quick answer to the question, "Shall we group homogeneously in our school?" Many factors need to be taken into consideration, among them the size of the enrollment, the extent of variation among the pupils, and the attitude of parents and teachers. While the writers of this book believe that in general the arguments against homogeneous grouping by rooms outweigh those for it, it is probably safe to make this observation: Homogeneous grouping is not as desirable as its strong proponents claim it is, nor as undesirable as its equally strong opponents argue that it is. Surely, however, no school system should adopt it as a plan of organization without careful study of the shortcomings likely to manifest themselves.

To summarize, some kind of grouping or system of individualization is often necessary in view of the large number of children with whom the average teacher must deal. But whatever the system, priority should be given to the general developmental and social needs of individual children.

Individualizing Instruction without Grouping

Silent reading is essentially an individual activity. The communication is not between one pupil and another but between author and reader. The development of silent reading skills, although possibly accompanied by oral reading activities, is necessarily individual in nature; no two children have exactly the same needs, no two children progress at exactly the same rate. For this reason efforts have long been made to devise means by which reading and other skills could be taught by individualized means.

Among the more famous plans of individualization of past years are those of William T. Harris of St. Louis, Preston W. Search of Pueblo, Colorado, Frederic Burk of Santa Barbara, William Wirt of Gary, Indiana (the platoon school), Helen Parkhurst of Dalton, Massachusetts (the contract plan), Carleton W. Washburne of Winnetka, Illinois, and James E. McDade of Chicago. Although such research as we have has favored the individualized plans, most of these plans were discontinued after a time, and none has enjoyed widespread acceptance in American schools. Distinguishing features of all of these plans have been the use of the classroom as a laboratory instead of a lecture and recitation room; the use of diagnostic and achievement tests, practice materials, and record forms; the adaptation of learning tasks to the achievement levels of the pupils; and pupil participation in the management of the system. All of them, while making effective use of the teacher, stressed the idea of self-teaching, suggestive of the modern vogue of programed instruction. All of them provided, in addition to the individualized work, for a rich program of socializing activities.

The vigor and diversity of the plans enumerated in the preceding paragraph probably explain why the idea underlying them has not died. We are witnessing today a widespread resurgence of interest in programs of individualized instruction in reading. Scores of articles describing such programs have appeared in recent years. Hardly a single reading conference is without one or more papers dealing with the subject.

One example of the current interest in individualized instruction in reading is the popularity of "reading laboratories," an example of which is the Science Research Associates Reading Laboratories. The

Science Research Associates "laboratories" consist of cases of practice materials for each of the elementary school levels. They contain, in addition to the reading selections, answer keys, check test pads, student record books, and a teacher's handbook. Materials in each grade vary in difficulty from easy to hard. Phonics surveys, word games, and colored pencils corresponding to the colors of the reading selections are included. Pupils are expected to move ahead as far and as fast as their learning rates and capacities will permit. The plan is essentially a variation and refinement of those used in Washburne's and McDade's systems. Emphasis is placed upon the successful response and on the use of intrinsically interesting materials.

PROGRAMED READING INSTRUCTION   Programed instruction, while not a new idea in education, has been receiving extraordinary attention in recent years. Often erroneously referred to by the term *teaching machines*, it is considered by many to be the application of the industrial use of automation to the teaching-learning process. Actually the idea, so far as reading instruction is concerned, does not differ fundamentally from the plans of individualization described in foregoing paragraphs. The machines that are being perfected are by no means essential or, at the present stage, always appropriate to the plan. For many programed materials no teaching machines are used; many programs are written in workbook-type booklets.

In programed instruction, the pupil is presented with instructional materials that enable him to learn on his own. The exercises, prepared after careful editing and experimentation, are graduated in very small steps, so that even the slowest learner can, at his own rate, arrive at the desired generalization. An exercise, or "frame," usually presents an explanation followed by a sentence containing a blank to be filled in, or, if a machine is used, by a button to be punched or a lever to be moved. The correct answer, given immediately below or on a page to which the pupil is referred, enables the pupil to compare his own answer with the correct answer, so that he is "reinforced" if the answer is right or corrected if the answer is wrong. A program, or sequence of frames, is selected for the individual in terms of his specific stage of learning. The method is one of self-teaching. In the case of reading, the programs may deal with the basic skills of word recognition, such as phonetic analysis, context clues, and structural analysis, or with comprehension and critical reading.

Following is one example of a "frame":

Q46.   The bird's nest fell from the tree.
We see the ending 's on the word *bird*.

The nest *belongs to* the _____.
A46.   bird.[1]

Since programed material is self-teaching, the work of the teacher differs from that required in the conventional classroom. Her task is primarily that of a counselor, guide, and motivator, once she has provided each pupil with the materials appropriate for him.

Programed reading instruction is still in the experimental stage. However, studies like those of W. G. Ellson and associates and of John McNeil seem to indicate that phases of reading can well be taught through the use of programed materials.[2]

Without doubt, the plan will continue to be the subject of spirited debate among educators. It will be examined not only from the point of view of its efficiency in achieving academic objectives, but especially from the point of view of its total effect upon the pupil. Certainly in theory it has much to commend it, particularly in its stress upon the principle of success in learning and upon self-activity. In any case, teachers and administrators should acquaint themselves with programed materials as they appear and with the growing body of research on this subject. (For a more detailed discussion of programed reading instruction see page 569.)

INDIVIDUALIZED READING: SEEKING, SELF-SELECTION, AND PACING   The term *individualized reading* has many possible meanings. The method described in the following paragraphs is capitalized—Individualized Reading—to indicate that reference is being made to a program of reading in which the total program is on an individualized basis.

The common elements that underlie Individualized Reading as practiced in numerous schools and school systems are: (1) the use of many books, diversified as to interest appeal and ability level; (2) little or no reliance upon basal readers as instructional tools; (3) major emphasis on children's preferences in the selection of reading materials. In general, the skills of reading are taught in connection with problems the child actually encounters in his reading. Isolated exercises

---

[1] P. Kenneth Komoski, "Teaching Machines and Programed Reading Instruction," *Controversial Issues in Reading and Promising Solutions*, pp. 109–120. Compiled and edited by Helen M. Robinson. Supplementary Educational Monographs, No. 91. Chicago: University of Chicago Press, 1961.

[2] W. G. Ellson and associates, "Programed Tutoring: A Teaching Aid and a Research Tool," *"Reading Research Quarterly,* I (Fall 1965), pp. 77–127. John D. McNeil, "Programed Instruction vs. Usual Classroom Procedures in Teaching Boys to Read," *American Educational Research Journal,* I (March 1964), pp. 113–120.

and drills for a whole group, and even for individual pupils, are rarely, if ever, used. It should be made clear, however, that Individualized Reading follows no rigid formula. The procedure is varied and supplemented in numerous ways according to the needs of the children and the creativity of the teacher.

In commenting on programs of Individualized Reading, Leland Jacobs makes the following significant observation:

> Individualized reading is no panacea for all the ills of teaching reading. It can never be effectual in improving children's abilities to read if it becomes a patent procedure, a sentimental devotion, a rite or ceremony, an exclusive ideology, a vacuous symbol, a standardization, a slogan, a dogma. Its usefulness is dependent upon well-defined purposes and values in operation and action, upon creative uses of time, materials, and procedures suitable to

Self-Selection, an aspect of Individualized Reading. (Zimbel–Monkmeyer Press Photo Service.)

the content for consideration, upon critical appraisal and assessment. . . .[3]

Jacobs goes on to offer practical suggestions for the organization and administration of the program:

1. The teacher provides ample time for individual reading and for various kinds of group reading.
2. He arranges for individual skills reading and for independent recreational reading.
3. He provides time for children to share their reading accomplishments.
4. The teacher provides a varied, extensive collection of reading matter from which a child can make his choices.
5. He provides a variety of practice materials.
6. He encourages the child to select reading matter that extends the learner's growing edges.
7. The teacher develops an adequate system of record-keeping.
8. He utilizes appropriate evaluation procedures.
9. He makes appropriate arrangements for independent work for others while an individual is working with the teacher.

One of the early proponents of the method under discussion was Willard C. Olson, who used the expressions *seeking, self-selection,* and *pacing* to describe the process. By pacing he meant the adjustment of teaching materials and experiences to the child's own rate of growth.[4] It should be noted that many teachers doubt seriously the young child's ability to select reading material best suited to his needs. However, extensive experimentation with the plan has been carried on in the New York City public schools under the leadership of May Lazar[5] and by teachers in many other parts of the United States. From the voluminous literature that has grown up about Individualized

[3] Reprinted with the permission of the publisher, from Leland B. Jacobs and others, *Individualizing Reading Practices,* Alice Miel, (ed.). New York: Teachers College Press, Columbia University, © 1958.

[4] Willard C. Olson, *Child Development.* Boston: D. C. Heath and Company, 1949, and *The Packet,* Vol. 7, No. 1 (Spring 1952).

[5] Described in the brochure, *A Practical Guide to Individualized Reading.* Prepared by Marcella K. Draper and Louise H. Schwietert; revised and edited by May Lazar. Publication No. 40, Board of Education, City of New York, Bureau of Educational Research, October 1960. Dr. Lazar has also described the program in *Reading in Action,* pp. 141–144. Conference Proceedings of the International Reading Association, Vol. II. New York: Scholastic Magazines, 1957.

Reading, one gathers that both the teachers and the pupils involved are enthusiastic about the plan. Readers of this book are urged to examine thoughtfully many of the references listed at the end of this chapter.

What do we know about the results of the Individualized Reading program? Hard evidence on this question is still lacking. Such studies of the program as have been made do not reveal dramatic gains nor significant losses in the pupil's performance on standardized tests of reading.[6] It is possible that, with teachers of comparable ability and creativity and with suitable instructional materials, no great differences will be found.

There are, however, other values that must be considered in evaluating the desirability of an Individualized Reading program. If, as its proponents claim, the method causes more children to like reading and to develop habits of extensive independent reading, the program will have more than justified itself. If it contributes to a happy, carefree climate in the classroom, and if it builds self-confidence in children, it must be given serious consideration by teachers and administrators. If it removes invidious distinctions between "slow" and "fast" readers, it can overcome one of the most serious dangers of individualization through ability grouping.

The inexperienced teacher not trained in the techniques of Individualized Reading and lacking the advantage of a sympathetic, able supervisor is well advised not to plunge into the program. It is best to study the plan first, examine carefully the books, articles, and manuals on the subject, and then to make tentative beginnings. Of supreme importance, also, is a wide knowledge of and love for children's books. The young teacher who has not had a good course in children's literature should probably spend at least a year in reading children's books and consulting the numerous guides, commentaries, and lists now available.

The place of the basal reader in Individualized Reading is a subject of great importance at a time when, as at present, it dominates

---

[6] Research summaries and evaluations relating to the effectiveness of Individualized Reading programs may be found in the following sources:

Paul Witty, with the assistance of Ann Coomer and Robert Sizemore, "Individualized Reading: A Summary and Evaluation," *Elementary English,* 36 (October 1959), pp. 401–412, 450.

George D. Spache, *Toward Better Reading,* pp. 155–157. Champaign, Ill.: Garrard Publishing Company, 1963. (Spache's entire chapter on individualized reading may be read with profit.)

David H. Russell and Henry R. Fea, "Research on Teaching Reading," *Handbook of Research on Teaching,* N. L. Gage, (ed.), p. 914. A Project of the American Educational Research Association. Chicago: Rand McNally Company, 1963.

instructional practice in reading throughout the country. Clearly its use as a primary resource would violate the essential principles of the Individualized Reading plan. On the other hand, the leading basal reader series are physically attractive. They represent vast investments in research and planning. They should certainly be prominently displayed on reading tables, and children should be encouraged to make much use of them.

RELATED POLICIES AND PRACTICES

In addition to the means of adapting instruction to individual differences discussed on preceding pages of this chapter, there are a few other school policies and practices designed either in part or in entirety to adapt school practices to the individual rather than the individual to the school.

The Nongraded Primary School

The introduction of the graded system about the middle of the nineteenth century was an early effort to achieve a degree of homogeneity in elementary school classes. The aim was to group children together according to chronological age, on the apparent assumption that children of the same age would be able to deal successfully with subject matter of approximately equal difficulty. Thus by graduating the difficulty of school work from one grade to the next, it was thought possible to set standards of achievement, so that those who successfully completed all the grades would have mastered all the basic requirements of the elementary school.

Of course, the effort to achieve homogeneity by this means did not succeed. The range of height and weight of children of the same age remained very great. Under a system of promotion and nonpromotion, even chronological age varied considerably in the same grade. As for scholastic achievement, all one could say about a sixth-grader was that he was in the sixth grade. He might be at the second-grade or the tenth-grade level in reading or arithmetic ability. Indeed, the number of children in the sixth grade who performed at a sixth-grade scholastic level was generally below 50 percent. And this is essentially so at the present time.

The overlapping of children's abilities from grade to grade has led some school systems to abandon grade distinctions at the primary level, some also on the intermediate-grade level. Under this plan, the idea of failure and promotion is eliminated. Emphasis is placed on early and continuous success. Most children remain in the primary division for six semesters. At the end of the primary period, typically each child's growth is evaluated to determine whether he is ready for fourth grade work. If a child spends seven or eight semesters in the primary division, his program is stretched out to accommodate his slower rate of learning, but he is not marked a failure. A few children may be passed to the fourth grade before the expiration of six semesters.

When grade levels are abolished, a primary administrative problem becomes one of grouping. Usually the classroom teacher's judgment is crucial in the selection of children for instructional groups. Account is taken not only of the child's performance on tests and classroom work but also of work habits, social adjustment, attitudes, interests, and special personal problems. Any one group may include children who have been in school for one or more semesters and who represent different learning levels. The identifying card on the door simply says, "Primary."

Careful records are kept on the progress of each child. The record includes a child's progress from one level to another and specific indications of growth in the various reading skills and attitudes. Competition is kept at a minimum, except with the child's own past performance. Great stress is therefore laid upon the individualization of instruction.

Promotion and Nonpromotion

Teachers of reading, particularly those in the primary grades, are vitally concerned with the question of promotion and nonpromotion. It has been found that in schools where the practice of promotion is followed, the highest rate of failure is in the first grade. Since reading ability is so important in all school work, it is often felt that a child should not be passed on to the next grade unless he meets certain standards of proficiency in reading.

We can dispense here with the philosophical argument against nonpromotion, except to point out that to a child the failure to be promoted is usually regarded as punishment and that there is an injustice in punishing a child who has done what he could with the capacity he has. In some instances, in fact, his plight may be the result of poor teaching. The practice of nonpromotion for inadequate learning is somehow reminiscent of the colonial practice of flogging a child for giving a wrong answer.

But we are here concerned with teaching efficiency, with the welfare of the child. The question is solely whether nonpromotion is conducive to greater learning. Fortunately, on this point there is research evidence. After referring to the studies summarized in the *Encyclopedia of Educational Research* (3d edition, pp. 4–10, The Macmillan Company, 1960), John I. Goodlad declares that "slow-learning children profit significantly more from promotion than from nonpromotion." He goes on to point out the following facts:

> Neither promotion nor nonpromotion, in and of itself, can change a child's basic learning rate.
>
> Very few children in a given grade approximate the grade norms for that grade in their achievement. For example, only three or four children out of a class of thirty are found to be at grade norm in all subjects at the middle of the year. And this is true even when "grade norm" is defined generously to include a one-year spread in achievement from subject to subject.
>
> A child seldom approximates arbitrary grade norms in all areas of endeavor. He may be significantly above in one and below in another and only slightly above or below in still others.
>
> The spread in mental age among a group of children, already as much as four years in the first grade, becomes greater as these children progress through the elementary school. The spread in academic attainment, in turn, will tend to keep pace with the broadening spread in mental age, especially under conditions of good teaching.[7]

The facts, therefore, do not support those critics of American education who blame all its failings on the practice of "social promotion." Actually, the concept adopted by modern schools can better be described as "continuous progress." Nor does all this mean that a child should never be "retained." There may be compelling reasons why an individual child should not pass on to a group of older children in the next grade. But the reasons should be truly compelling. The threat of nonpromotion does not result in increased learning. And in most cases the cost in terms of emotional stress is greater than any theoretical academic advantage would warrant.

Team Teaching

In recent years team teaching has grown in popularity. The term *team teaching* is difficult to define, since a variety of types of

[7] Reprinted by permission of the Association for Childhood Education International, 3615 Wisconsin Avenue, N.W., Washington 16, D.C. From bulletin No. 5–A, *Toward Effective Grouping,* Copyright 1962; "To Promote or Not To Promote" by John I. Goodlad, p. 34.

teaching situations have been so designated. A common element in team teaching is that more than one teacher, professional or paraprofessional, work together to instruct a given group or groups of pupils, either homogeneously or heterogeneously divided. One of the frequently used plans of organization is that in which two or more teachers together work with a group of elementary or secondary schools pupils in a program structured by the participating teachers. At times, as for example in a presentation lesson, one teacher alone may lead the class; at other times, while one instructor works with some of the pupils, another instructor may be helping others, individually or in a group. In some set-ups for team teaching two or more teachers with different specialties—such as the social studies, mathematics, or science—teach the same group of pupils, each in the field of her special skill. It should be noted, however, that if the line of cleavage between the teaching of the different subjects is pronounced, there may be but little advantage in this type of teaching over departmentalization. At its best team teaching may maximize the strengths and minimize the weaknesses of departmentalization without team teaching. Excellent results have been reported for team teaching. When teachers work closely together in team teaching and when the program is well organized under competent adults, benefits to the pupils may understandingly accrue.

The purpose of team teaching in many schools is not restricted to adapting instruction to individual differences even though that frequently is one of the major goals sought and often accomplished to some extent. Primary objectives often are to improve instruction in general through greater cooperation among teachers, through increased opportunity for the instructors to make contributions in the area of their strengths, and through provision for utilizing the abilities of adults other than teachers who may be highly successful in the educational program in a team teaching situation where they work closely with professional teachers. At a time when there is a scarcity of teachers, help from those interested adults without professional preparation may be greatly needed.

In Chapter 13 special attention is paid to types of individuals who vary greatly from the average, namely, the retarded readers and the unusually gifted boys and girls.

FOR FURTHER STUDY

Barbe, Walter B., *Teaching Reading*. New York: Oxford University Press, 1965. Chapter 12, "Individualized Reading," pp. 374–386.

Bond, Guy A., and Eva Bond Wagner, *Teaching the Child To Read*. New

York: The Macmillan Company, 1966. Chapter 16, "Adjusting to Individual Needs." pp. 347–378.

Deterline, William A., *An Introduction to Programmed Instruction.* Englewood Cliffs, N.J.: Prentice-Hall, Inc., 1962.

Gans, Roma, *Common Sense in Reading.* Indianapolis, Ind.: The Bobbs-Merrill Company, Inc., 1963. Chapter 17, "The Struggle To Meet Individual Differences," pp. 301–318.

Goodlad, John L., and Robert H. Anderson, *The Nongraded Elementary School.* New York: Harcourt, Brace & World, Inc., 1963.

Harris, Albert J., *Readings on Reading Instruction.* New York: David McKay Company, Inc., 1963. Chapter 6, "Grouping for Effective Reading Instruction," pp. 134–169; Chapter 7, "Individualized Reading," pp. 170–200.

Hester, Kathleen B., *Teaching Every Child To Read.* New York: Harper & Row, Publishers, 1964. Part 6, "A Teacher Plans an Effective Reading Program," pp. 273–316.

Morgenstern, Anne (ed.), *Grouping in the Elementary School.* New York: Pitman Publishing Corporation, 1966. Pages x–118.

Smith, Nila B., *Reading Instruction for Today's Children.* Englewood Cliffs, N.J.: Prentice-Hall, Inc., 1963. Chapter 6, "Grouping Takes on New Forms," pp. 108–128; Chapter 7, "Individualized Instruction Receives Attention," pp. 129–161.

Smith, Wendell I., and J. William Moore, *Programed Learning.* Princeton, New Jersey: D. Van Nostrand Co., Inc., 1962.

Stauffer, Russell G., *Teaching Reading as a Cognitive Process.* New York: Harper & Row, Publishers, 1969. Chapter 5.

Tinker, Miles A., and Constance M. McCullough, *Teaching Elementary Reading.* New York: Appleton-Century-Crofts, 1968. Chapter 14, "Individual Differences," pp. 285–300.

Tyler, Fred T., and others, *Individualizing Instruction.* Sixty-first Yearbook of The National Society for the Study of Education, Part I. Nelson B. Henry, (ed.) Chicago: University of Chicago Press, 1962. Pages 42–92, 177–284.

Veatch, Jeannette, *Reading in the Elementary School.* New York: The Ronald Press Company, 1966. Chapter 5, "The Independent Work Period," pp. 61–119; Chapter 6, "The Individual Conference," pp. 120–165; Chapter 7, "Grouping," pp. 166–204.

Yates, Alfred (ed.), *Grouping in Education.* New York: John Wiley & Sons, Inc., 1966. Pages xvi–314.

CHAPTER 13

Helping the Retarded
and the Unusually Gifted
Child in Reading

The importance of adapting instruction to all individuals was discussed in some detail in the preceding chapter. In this chapter special attention is given to the atypical child—to the retarded and to the unusually gifted.

THE RETARDED READER

School and public alike are justifiably concerned about pupils in elementary and high schools who are retarded in reading. Reading ability is essential to success in all school work and in life outside of school. In addition, therefore, to providing the developmental reading instruction that all pupils need, the school has the task of giving special attention to those who have serious difficulties in learning to read.

It is not possible to state what percentage of pupils are retarded in reading. Obviously 50 percent of children fall at or below the average for their age or grade. Averages are computed from the full range of abilities found at any given age or grade level, and the range tends to be greatest when the instruction is the most efficient. We do know that many readers—good, average, and poor—are "underachievers," that is, readers who are not performing up to their capacity. When a reader is both a slow learner and an underachiever, we may be sure that he needs special help.

Who Is the Retarded Reader?

Some writers consider a pupil retarded if his reading score is considerably below the average for his chronological age or for his grade in school. Others hold that he is retarded if he falls below the norms for his mental age. Still others believe that a child, regardless of mental age, cannot be called a retarded reader if he achieves the average for his grade, even if his mental age is above average for his grade. Such a child should be spurred on to better performance, but he cannot be classified as retarded. In this view, a child is retarded if he reads well below grade level but has the capacity to perform at a higher level.

For practical purposes, the term *reading retardation* as employed in this book refers to backwardness in reading that can be corrected by special instruction. The above-average reader is not considered backward—even if he fails to realize his full potentialities. All children need the kind of guidance that will lead them to full development of their powers. Moreover, the distinction between remedial and developmental reading is at best ambiguous. This chapter will, therefore, deal with children who fall below the average for their age group but who have the capacity to grow more rapidly in reading ability than they presently do.

Capacity for learning to read is commonly measured by group intelligence tests. These are very useful in providing estimates of children's ability to learn. They are, however, by no means infallible. For example, group intelligence tests generally require a certain amount of reading ability. Children who are handicapped in reading may not be able to show their real mental abilities in these tests. For this reason teachers should weigh the mental age records of children with great caution.

The child who reads at or above his grade level but who could do better needs particular attention. The teacher should not be satisfied with the reading of a boy with an intelligence quotient of 120 who reads only as well at the age of ten as the average ten-year-old. However, the help he needs to learn to read up to his capacity is not usually the kind needed by the child who reads below both his grade level and his intellectual capacity. He is not, in our sense of the term, a retarded reader.

The strong interest in reading retardation now evident in elementary schools had its inception in the decade of the twenties and reached great heights in the thirties. When the problem of reading deficiency first attracted the attention of school people, the tendency was to organize many classes in remedial reading. Children who were one year or more below grade level were often placed in special classes or singled out for tutorial instruction. The idea of providing for individual differences in normal classes gained acceptance only slowly.

Today we recognize at least three types of retarded readers. One is the youngster who is not reading as well as he can but who is able to improve his performance under the guidance of his regular classroom teacher. Another has difficulties that are serious enough to require the assistance of a remedial teacher, usually in a special remedial reading class. A third type, fortunately an exception, has problems which call for intensive study by the staff of a reading clinic. When a child fails to make progress in reading, in spite of persistent efforts by the school to help him, he needs the attention of specialists who are skilled in the investigation of causes that interfere with progress in reading. For most children, however, a flexible program that takes account of the wide differences in reading ability will be sufficient to meet their varying needs.

Causes of Reading Retardation

Knowledge of the causes of unsatisfactory progress in reading is valuable from two standpoints. Such understanding can help the teacher (1) to prevent retardation and (2) to deal intelligently with difficulties as they arise. The task is to look behind the symptoms and to find the causes. These will usually be a combination of several elements; indeed, multiple causation is a basic principle of remedial reading. The causes of reading difficulty are usually numerous, complex, and interrelated.

The principle of multiple causation does not, however, mean that the classroom teacher cannot cope with the reading problems of most retarded pupils. Although a few children will require study by experts, the thoughtful and sympathetic efforts of the classroom teacher are usually sufficient to help meet children's needs. What is necessary is a careful study of each child's background and an analysis of the skills in which he is deficient.

Because of their interrelatedness, the search for causes should not end when one apparent cause has been found. Frequently a primary cause of retardation in reading, especially if the difficulty is one of long duration, results in one or more secondary causes, which may in turn greatly influence the effectiveness of the reading. Thus, for example, illness, with consequent irregularity of school attendance, may be at the root of a child's reading difficulty. It may result in lack of interest in learning, which by itself is significant enough to bring about serious problems in learning to read.

READING DEFICIENCY AND PERSONALITY   Reading problems are often associated with personality problems. Since reading is so important in the life of every child, failure in this activity may be expected to cause anxieties, feelings of insecurity, and even aggressive behavior. On the other hand, children who come to school with a sense of inadequacy, a feeling of being unloved, or an unconscious hostility against the adult world may lack the necessary incentive to learn to read or may be prepared to resist efforts on the part of the teacher to teach them. The factors of personality problems and reading problems are no doubt usually reciprocal. For this reason, it is commonly necessary to provide personal guidance along with the corrective instruction in reading. Certainly the teacher needs at all times to consider the total development of the child, not merely his reading needs.

The evidence to date on the relation between language and personality development has been ably summarized by Russell. In his conclusion, he states:

> Although results are still meager, there exists some evidence that amount and type of language behavior is often closely related to other phases of personality. At present the most detailed analysis seems to be in the area of social-emotional disturbances as related to reading difficulties. A promising lead has been opened up in the influences of reading, discussion, sociodrama, etc., on personality not only as catharsis and therapy in difficult cases but as procedures with normal children. Language activities are causes, concomitants, or results of personality factors, but many detailed relationships must be explored if teachers and parents are to have the help they sometimes need in guiding growth in both language and personality.[1]

READING DEFICIENCY AND THE HOME SITUATION
Helen M. Robinson has reported on an intensive study of the causes of reading failure.[2] She found that social, visual, and emotional difficulties appeared most frequently as causes of poor progress or failure in learning to read. Maladjusted homes or poor family relations were found to be contributing causes in more than 54 percent of the cases studied. Her findings, based upon data from the field of social work,

[1] David H. Russell, "Interrelationships of the Language Arts and Personality," *Elementary English,* 30 (March 1953), pp. 167–180.

[2] Helen M. Robinson, *Why Pupils Fail in Reading.* Chicago: University of Chicago Press, 1946.

psychiatry, pediatrics, neurology, ophthalmology, speech correction, otolaryngology, endocrinology, and psychology, confirm conclusions by other investigators. It seems clear that home conditions may have much to do with children's reading progress in school.

The emotional stresses resulting from conflict or deprivation in the home are only one source of reading retardation in school. Indifference on the part of parents toward a child's reading may be responsible for a lack of incentive to learn to read. Paradoxically, over-solicitude on the part of parents may also create tensions that impede reading progress. If there is hostility between child and parent, the very eagerness of the mother and father to note reading progress may serve as motive for holding back. More typically, the desire of the child to gain parental approval results in fears that inhibit normal and felicitous growth in reading.

The reading background provided by the home is a potent factor in determining how well the child will succeed in school. When parents show an enthusiastic interest in their children's reading, when they read stories to them and show them the pictures, when they discuss the contents of the books with them, they are laying strong foundations for pleasurable, independent reading. Especially important is the presence in the home of a variety of attractive, appealing books for children. Time for quiet reading provided at home and a reasonably comfortable place for reading, too, help to start the child on the road to the enjoyment of books.

Fortunately, many children who come from impoverished or otherwise unpromising home environments nevertheless become excellent readers. Perhaps in a few instances the very lack of favorable home surroundings may serve as an incentive for greater effort in learning to read. The example of Abraham Lincoln comes to mind. Such cases, however, are exceptional. As a rule, when children from unfavorable home environments become good readers, as they often do, it is in spite of, not because of, their early deprivation.

READING DEFICIENCY AND EARLY EXPERIENCES WITH READING   Children's first experiences with reading will in great measure determine their later progress. If they are faced with reading tasks for which they are not ready, they may build antagonistic attitudes toward reading which interfere with normal growth. Moreover, they may develop inappropriate habits of word attack or sentence reading which will cause trouble throughout the formative years.

Examples of such habits are many. The child may develop the habit of sounding the words without giving attention to the meaning. Or he may feel that partial recognition of words is satisfactory. Word pointing and its companion, line pointing, may serve too long as a crutch in silent or oral reading. These devices may be harmless or even helpful at the very beginning, but children should soon learn to do without them if they are to read for meaning and develop appropriate speed. The same may be said about the use of markers (strips of paper moved from line to line during reading). The child should be encouraged as early as possible to develop independence in making accurate return sweeps from line to line. Extremely slow rate of reading, word-by-word reading, and overanalytical methods of word attack may also be responsible for unsatisfactory growth in reading.

READING DEFICIENCY AND THE SCHOOL CLIMATE The general atmosphere of the school can be an important factor in children's success in reading. If there is a feeling of tension or pressure, if the child senses that the school authorities are anxious about his reading, he may develop harmful attitudes toward the reading progress. On the other hand, if there is a bright, relaxed atmosphere, reading tends to take on the aspect of a delightful challenge. Such an atmosphere is created primarily by the ways in which teachers talk about reading, by their reactions to children's successes and failures, and by the variety of stimulating activities going on in the school. Physical surroundings, too, play a part in forming children's attitudes toward reading. Dreary, unstimulating classrooms lacking in suitable reading materials may inhibit the reading growth of pupils who might burgeon in a more evocative environment. Overcrowded classrooms, regimented instruction, antiquated textbooks, and lack of good school libraries may be responsible to a degree for much of the reading retardation found in our schools.

READING DEFICIENCY AND OTHER FACTORS Basically, the causes of reading deficiency must be sought in the presence or absence of the elements requisite to growth in reading, discussed in Chapter 3. Physical well-being, visual and auditory acuity, intelligence, experience background, mental health, and interest and purpose in reading are essential factors to be investigated when the child fails to make expected progress in reading. The process of exploring causes of reading retardation is essentially one of finding out which of these essential elements are lacking in significant degree.

Diagnosing Reading Difficulties

"Diagnosis" of reading difficulty usually involves three tasks: (1) determining whether true retardation exists; (2) determining the nature of the difficulty; and (3) determining the causes that have brought about the difficulty. Very often these purposes can be accomplished in a single step. In undertaking to determine who is the retarded reader, the teacher frequently learns much of the nature of the difficulties and sometimes something of the causes. Various procedures may be employed to secure these types of information. The reader should bear in mind that, in general, the procedures recommended for use in the diagnosis of difficulties of the retarded reader are similar to those that can be employed in the evaluation both of problems and of strengths of all readers—the retarded, the average, the superior.

INFORMAL OBSERVATION OF THE PUPIL   The first method in diagnosis is one that alert, sympathetic teachers have always used: a careful observation of the child's over-all performance, his attitudes toward books and reading, his play interests, his hobbies, and his reading interests. The observation may take place in nonreading as well as in reading situations. For example, a child may unintentionally reveal a dislike for reading while working with classmates on a model airplane or while discussing what he would like for Christmas. The teacher may note the kinds of book choices a child makes during the free reading period. She may observe the child's behavior as he reads a book— whether he squints, whether he stops often in his reading, whether he assumes good or poor posture as he reads.

USE OF ANECDOTAL RECORDS   Since few teachers are able to keep in mind the developing characteristics of many children over a period of time, it is helpful to keep an informal record of the day-by-day observations. A file folder should be kept for each pupil suspected of having difficulty in reading; in fact, teachers will find it helpful to keep such a folder for every pupil in the class. In this folder the teacher should insert, from time to time, any material that may throw light on the child's reading problems. The folder should include samples of the child's writing and drawing as well as reading exercises he may have performed. But perhaps the most important material is the teacher's report of the child's observed behavior. This may be in the form of a sentence or two for a given day (the date should be noted), such as: "Today Axel spent 15 minutes in uninterrupted reading of *The Little House in the Big Woods*. He has never concentrated before for so long on his reading, as far as I know." The notations should usually not be of a general nature, as, "I think Axel is improving." The anecdotal record should essentially be a behavioral record. In the course of six months it should be possible to discover from the record in what direction the child is moving with respect to significant aspects of reading growth. The type of information described in this paragraph cannot be secured from even the best of the standardized tests of silent reading.

STUDY OF PUPIL RECORDS   Many schools keep detailed records of the history of individual children. These usually include reports on health examinations, past school attendance, achievement and intelligence tests, home visits that may have been made, and other information. An examination of such records may often give the teacher important clues as to the reasons why a child is not succeeding in reading. For example, a child from a migratory family may have had to make numerous adjustments to new school situations and may have had special difficulties in following different systems of reading instruction. (Incidentally, the problem of mobility in American families poses an increasingly critical problem to American schools.) Absence from school because of illness or other causes may also be responsible for backwardness in reading among pupils who would otherwise make normal progress. The more information the teacher has about a pupil's past experiences, the more she will be able to deal intelligently with his reading problems. School records should, of course, be kept confidential and be strictly reserved for professional use.

USE OF INFORMAL TESTS   The late E. W. Dolch once suggested a simple, common sense method of testing a child's reading ability with the aid of a textbook.[3] In an interview with a pupil, the teacher selects a book from the shelf and says, "Let's see how the reading goes." The book is one that is probably not too difficult for the pupil, but it is one he has not read before. First, the teacher asks the pupil to read a passage aloud. He supplies the words the pupil does not recognize. By this means he determines whether the pupil is lacking in knowledge of common words he should know. Second, he asks the pupil to close the book and tell in brief as much as he can of what he has read. He praises the pupil for correct answers and encourages him to go on. This step is intended to reveal whether the pupil reads with any comprehension. Third, the teacher selects another passage and asks the pupil to read it, but he does not supply any words missed. He asks, "What do you *think* the word is?" Thus the teacher learns something of the pupil's ability to use context in word recognition. Fourth, in another selection the pupil is called on to tell the first letter of a word he does not recognize—then the next, and the next, until the pupil can supply the whole word. In these four steps the teacher has discovered, in a

[3] E. W. Dolch, "Testing Reading with a Book," *Elementary English,* 28 (March 1951), pp. 124–125, 165.

very short time, many of the kinds of difficulty the pupil encounters in his reading.

Many periodicals and books designed for elementary school instruction in reading contain informal, nonstandardized, but more or less objective tests based upon specific reading selections. These enable the teacher to make a quick check of pupils' comprehension and vocabulary knowledge. Some of these are timed tests and thus provide the teacher with a rough measure of a pupil's reading rate for a given type of material.

Informal tests to determine a pupil's success in reading can also be constructed by the teacher herself. From time to time, the teacher may wish to discover the extent to which pupils have comprehended the meaning of an assigned passage.

Informal tests may be of many kinds: checklists—including teacher-constructed reading inventories—oral reading tests, anecdotal records based on points observed. Objective tests may include items to be matched, true-false statements, best-answer or other multiple choices, matching items, and many others.[4] Among these, perhaps one of the most useful and reliable is the multiple-choice item. A multiple-choice item consists of (1) a "stem," which is an incomplete statement and (2) a series of three or preferably four or more alternatives, or options, from which the pupil is asked to select the expression that best completes the statement. Examples of such items are the following:

1. In this story Leonardo appears as
   a) a fairy
   b) an angel
   c) a dwarf
   d) Santa Claus.
2. The children were not frightened by Leonardo because
   a) They were accustomed to seeing strange creatures
   b) They recognized him
   c) Their mother had told them who he was
   d) Leonardo revealed himself to them.

The correct expression in the item is called the key. The other alternatives should, if possible, be such that a person who had not read

---

[4] For a fuller description of such tests, the student is referred to one of the many good books on educational measurement. One of these is *Test Construction: Development and Interpretation of Achievement Tests* by Dorothy A. Wood. Columbus, O.: Charles E. Merrill Books, Inc., 1960.

the passage would be unable to make an obvious choice. At the same time, they should be unambiguously incorrect responses.

USE OF STANDARDIZED TESTS   A common instrument in the diagnosis of reading problems and strengths is the published standardized test. It, like other evaluative means described here, is of great value not only in the appraisal of retarded readers but of all readers in the elementary school. The standardized test has the advantage of being based upon the responses of a large number of pupils of specified ages and grade levels. Thus it is possible to compare the performance of an individual or a group with that of a representative sample of pupils in the same age or grade classification. Standardized tests serve two important purposes. One is to relate the average reading performance of a pupil to that of other pupils over the country who are of the same age or in the same grade in school. The pupil's achievement may be compared to that of typical pupils at various levels—the median, the first quartile, the third quartile, the first percentile, or the 99th percentile. While norms for these various levels are usually supplied, they should not be regarded as infallible standards. Their value depends upon the size and representativeness of the sample. The second purpose of the standardized test is to help the teacher make an analysis of the specific skills in which the pupil is strong or weak.

Standardized tests are often classified as survey tests and diagnostic tests. The former provide an average score; the latter undertake to break down the average into specific strengths and weaknesses. The scores on a survey test tell the teacher how well a pupil can read a given collection of words, sentences, and paragraphs in comparison with other pupils of the same age and grade. The scores on a diagnostic test tell how skillful the reader is in specific aspects of reading, in comparison with other pupils of the same age and grade in school. Both types of tests, if wisely used, are valuable in dealing with the reading problems of children. In the study of children's reading ability, we, therefore, make use of both the survey test and the diagnostic test.

In making a selection of standardized reading tests, the teacher should study carefully the teachers' manuals supplied with them. Manuals will tell of the *validity* of a test, which indicates the degree of accuracy with which the test measures what it is intended to measure, and of the *reliability* of a test, which indicates the degree to which a test yields consistent results. The teacher should keep in mind also the purpose for which she intends to use the test. For example, tests that consist chiefly of vocabulary items may not adequately measure the degree to which a pupil is able to deal with words in context. The length of the test and the time available to teachers and pupils may also be important factors. Finally, the relative recency of the test may have a bearing on the selection.

Various sources may be consulted for the names and publishers of standardized tests in reading. Catalogs of such publishers as Harcourt, Brace & World (New York), The Public School Publishing Company (Bloomington, Illinois), Educational Testing Service (Princeton, New Jersey), California Test Bureau (Los Angeles), Educational Test Bureau (Minneapolis), Bureau of Publications, Teachers College, Columbia University (New York), and Science Research Associates (Chicago) may be secured on request. Oscar Buros' *Mental Measurements Yearbooks* present, in their various editions, the necessary publication facts about standardized reading tests, along with critical reviews by experts of their general value, utility, reliability, and validity. They are published by Gryphon Press, Highland Park, New Jersey. A very comprehensive listing, with descriptions, is found in Anthony P. Witham's article, "The Index to Reading Material," in *Elementary English* for March 1963, pages 318–327 (available separately from the National Council of Teachers of English, 506 S. Sixth St., Champaign, Illinois).

Following is a list of the more widely used standardized tests in reading:

Basic Sight Word Test, by E. W. Dolch, Survey. Grades 1–2. Garrard Publishing Company, Champaign, Ill.

The Botel Reading Inventory, by M. Botel and others. Survey. Grades 1–12. Follett Publishing Company, Chicago.

California Reading Test, by E. W. Tiegs and W. W. Clark. Survey. Grades 1–14. California Test Bureau, Monterey, Calif.

Chapman-Cook Speed of Reading Test, by J. C. Chapman and S. Cook. Survey. Grades 4–8. Educational Test Bureau, Minneapolis.

Detroit Reading Test, by C. M. Parker and E. A. Waterbury. Survey. Grades 2–9. Harcourt, Brace & World, Inc., New York.

Detroit Word Recognition Test, by E. F. Oglesby. Survey. Grades 1–3. Harcourt, Brace & World, Inc., New York.

Developmental Reading Tests, by Guy L. Bond, Theodore Clymer, and Cyril Hoyt. Lyons and Carnahan, Chicago.

Diagnostic Reading Tests, by Committee on Diagnostic Reading Tests. Diagnostic. Grades K–13. The Committee, Mountain Home, N.C.

Durrell Analysis of Reading Difficulties, by D. D. Durrell. Diagnostic. Grades 1–6. Harcourt, Brace & World, Inc., New York.

Flash-X Sight Vocabulary Test, by George D. Spache and Stanford E. Taylor. Educational Developmental Laboratories, Huntington, N.Y.

Gates Reading Diagnostic Tests, by A. I. Gates. Diagnostic. Grades 1–8. Bureau of Publications, Teachers College, Columbia University, New York.

Gates Reading Readiness Tests, by A. I. Gates, Readiness. Grade 1. Bureau of Publications, Teachers College, Columbia University, New York.

Gates Reading Survey Tests, by A. I. Gates. Survey. Grades 4–10. Bureau of Publications, Teachers College, Columbia University, New York.

Gates Reading Tests: Primary-Advanced Primary, by A. I. Gates, Survey. Grades 1–3. Bureau of Publications, Teachers College, Columbia University, New York.

Gray Oral Reading Tests, by William S. Gray. Edited by Helen M. Robinson. Diagnostic. Grades 1–12. The Bobbs-Merrill Company, Inc., Indianapolis.

Iowa Every-Pupil Tests of Basic Skills: Silent Reading, by H. F. Spitzer and others. Survey. Grades 3–9. Houghton Mifflin Company, Boston.

Metropolitan Achievement Tests: Reading, by W. N. Durost and others. Survey. Grades 3–9. Harcourt, Brace & World, Inc., New York.

Murphy-Durrell Diagnostic Reading Readiness Test, by H. A. Murphy and D. D. Durrell. Diagnostic. Grade 1. Harcourt, Brace & World, Inc., New York.

The Nelson Silent Reading Test, by M. J. Nelson. Survey. Grades 3–9. Houghton Mifflin Company, Boston.

Peabody Library Information Test, by Louis Shores and Joseph E. Moore. Educational Test Bureau, Minneapolis.

Pressey Diagnostic Reading Tests, by S. L. and L. C. Pressey. Diagnostic. Grades 3–9. Public School Publishing Company, Bloomington, Ill.

Sequential Tests of Education Progress: Reading, by the staff of the Educational Testing Service. Survey. Grades 4–14. Cooperative Test Division of the Educational Testing Service, Princeton, N.J.

Standardized Oral Reading Check Tests, by W. S. Gray. Oral, diagnostic. Grades 1–8. Public School Publishing Company, Bloomington, Ill.

Stanford Achievement Test: Reading, by T. L. Kelley and others. Survey. Grades 3–9. Harcourt, Brace & World, Inc., New York.

It must be kept in mind that standardized test scores are reliable only if those who take the tests understand what is expected of them and if their attitude toward the test situation is favorable. As in the case of all standardized testing, the instructions in the teacher's manual as to procedure and timing must be followed exactly.

Unfortunately, in many school situations the scores made by children on standardized tests are merely tabulated and filed for possible use when a special problem arises in connection with individual children or when questions are raised about the general performance of the class. Such use of tests hardly justifies the expense, time, and effort involved. Tests scores can reveal the approximate performance of a class with norms for the general population in the respective age groups. They can help identify the pupils who need special instructional assistance in reading. They can reveal specific weaknesses on the part of individuals or whole groups. They are only a part, but a very important part, of the total program of evaluation and diagnosis.

Just as the child needs practice in taking tests, so the teacher needs experience in the interpretation of the results. With practice, the teacher soon learns to recognize characteristic patterns in the curves yielded by test scores. Some children are weak in all phases of silent reading; others are particularly in need of help in specific aspects. So also the teacher knows that the test usually measures reading at the "instructional" level and that a child's independent reading may not measure up in all respects to the level of test performance.

USE OF CHECKLISTS   Interest inventories and lists of specific reading skills are often helpful in identifying points of difficulty in children's reading. An illustrative checklist of reading skills is suggested by Wheeler and Smith:

SUGGESTIONS ON HOW TO FIND A CHILD'S READING LEVEL

1. Select a series of good basic readers which will, in your opinion, best suit the child.
2. Estimate roughly, from a standardized reading test, the child's instructional reading level and select a reader about one grade under the standardized test level or grade placement.
3. Have the child read the first complete sentence at the beginning of the pages sampled and keep a record of his errors. A suggested form for recording errors is given below.
4. As the child reads, count as errors mispronunciations, omissions, substitutions, hesitancies over three seconds, distortions, and word assists by the teacher. Do not count as errors mistakes on proper names.
5. If the percentage of errors per hundred words is more than 3 to 5 percent, drop down to the next grade level in the series. If the percentage of errors is less than 2 percent move up to the next grade level in the series.

6. When you have found the level at which the child's errors constitute approximately 3 to 5 percent of the running words, test his paragraph reading. Select four or five paragraphs and have the child read these, both silently and orally, noting the difficulties.

7. Remember that series differ in difficulty; therefore, teach the child in the series used to evaluate him, or retest him in the series to be used for instruction.

8. If the child passes the sentence test but not the paragraph test, teach him on the level indicated by the sentence test. This holds true *only* on the primary level because at this level few children have difficulty with the concepts offered, and the vocabulary problem is not so much one of meaning as of recognition.

9. Children who show difficulties of organization, retention, and understanding can be taught in material where they know at least 95 percent of the running words.

10. We might summarize the following practical underlying assumptions from clinical and teaching experience:

   a. A child can read materials without any assistance when he knows and understands 98–99 percent of vocabulary and comprehends 75–90 percent of main ideas. This is his independent, library, or free reading level.

   b. The child's instructional or teaching level is the point at which he knows and understands the meaning of 95–98 percent of vocabulary and comprehends about 75–90 percent of main ideas. "Instructional level" implies that the child needs word analysis of unknown words and comprehension direction.

   c. The child's frustration level is the point at which he recognizes or knows less than 95 percent of vocabulary and comprehends less than 75 percent of the main ideas. Frustration is reading generally increases with a decrease in recognition, meaning vocabulary, and general comprehension of materials the child is reading.

11. One of the main purposes of the diagnosis is to determine the free reading, instructional levels for teaching purposes, and also to learn the frustration level where the material is too difficult for the child to read.[5]

---

[5] Adapted by L. R. Wheeler from the article by Lester Wheeler and Edwin A. Smith, "A Modification of the Informal Reading Inventory," *Elementary English*, 34 (April 1957), pp. 224–226. Used by permission of the National Council of Teachers of English.

CONDENSATION OF THE INFORMAL READING INVENTORY CHECK SHEET USED AT UNIVERSITY OF MIAMI READING CLINIC

Name_____Date_____Age_____Grade_____
Series used_____Frustration level_____
Instructional level_____Probable mental level_____
Independent level_____

Vocabulary Difficulties

Phonics poor_____
Syllabication poor_____
Use of configuration poor_____
Use of picture clue poor_____
Sight vocabulary poor_____
Use of context poor_____

Comprehension Difficulties

Sentence reading poor_____
Paragraph reading poor_____

Perception Difficulties

Memory poor_____
Organization poor_____
Reverses words_____
Reverse letters_____Detail reading poor_____
Omits beginnings_____Critical reading_____
Omits endings_____Inference reading_____
Omits words_____Diagrammatic reading_____
Sounds confused_____Reading for ideas_____
Sounds added_____Reading to visualize_____
Omits sounds_____Ability to visualize_____
Other factors_____Ability to anticipate_____
_____Ability to follow directions_____

Rate Difficulties

Directional problem_____Scanning_____
Word-by-word reader_____Reading for ideas_____
Regression movements_____Reading to anticipate meaning_____
Points at words_____Reading materials at different rates___
Loses place easily_____
Quick recognition of vocabulary_____Reading to visualize_____
Reading key words in sentences_____Pictorial reading_____
Reading key sentences in paragraphs__Ability to read rapidly different
_____ materials_____
Skimming_____Ability to read under time limits_____

USE OF THE READING CLINIC   The reading difficulties of some children are so complex and deep seated as to require the study of specialists. Their problems may often be identified by means of the combined efforts of physicians, psychologists, psychiatrists, and specially trained teachers of remedial reading. A number of reading clinics have access to the services of these and other specialists. Unfortunately, however, clinical facilities available to teachers in most parts of the country are inadequate, and where they do exist, they are often expensive and beyond the means of many parents. Most large city school systems offer clinical services. Many states support excellent clinics, which usually have long waiting lists. The principal and the teacher should be informed about the services that are available and should make use of them when they are needed.

Teaching the Retarded Reader

Perhaps the first thing a teacher should keep in mind in teaching the retarded reader is the need to enlist his enthusiastic effort in the process of improvement. Most pupils who have had severe and persistent difficulty in learning to read have developed negative attitudes toward reading. They have, for one reason or another, experienced repeated frustration in a task that they recognize as the most important challenge facing them day after day. The result may be fear or hostility or indifference. Sometimes the awareness of parents' concern or annoyance pursues them to the school door. They may feel that the good opinion of teacher or classmates depends on their performance.

Such children are in great need of "success experiences." The school day must be a day of achievement. The teacher should patiently seek out opportunities to enable the retarded reader to excel in some activity, whether in singing or dancing, in making something, or reporting an everyday experience. Sometimes a retarded reader may do very well in taking part in a dramatic activity. The child must feel that he belongs, that he is respected. He should have something good to report when he returns home.

The experience of success is, of course, of greatest consequence in his work in reading. If the materials he is called upon to read, or the phonics and other reading exercises, are chosen with a view to his abilities, he will be emotionally prepared to take the next step. He need not be praised for every correct response, but he must know when he has done well.

Related to the principle that a child's reading tasks should be adjusted to his present capacity is the often forgotten fact that a slow reader is not necessarily an inferior reader. When we use the term *retarded*, we mean that the child has been slowed up by some inhibiting factor that can be removed with good instruction. It does not follow, however, that a learner whose progress in reading is slow is a poor reader. Some children with quite adequate or even superior potential simply arrive at their goals later than others. The teacher should feel at ease about them, provided they are making progress.

Every effort should be made to stimulate the child's desire to read independently in books of his own choosing. It is quite possible to cultivate in retarded readers an interest that will lead to lifetime habits of reading. The use of pictures, dramatizations, conversations about books, and other devices for arousing interest are doubly important in the case of the retarded reader. Easy, well-illustrated books and magazines should be attractively displayed on the book table and the magazine rack.

Too often the physical environment and the program for the special class in remedial reading are barren and forbidding. The over-conscientious teacher feels that every moment must be spent with reading workbooks, objective tests, and laborious oral reading. The remedial reading room should be one of the most inviting rooms in the school. The program should include the showing of films, group discussions, "creative writing," the exchange of jokes and riddles, and oral reports of personal experiences. Reading then becomes what it ought to be—a part of the communication process and the outgrowth of real-life experiences. Under circumstances such as these, teachers who dreaded that "period with the slowpokes" may find teaching the retarded the most rewarding experience of the school day. If remedial reading instruction is to be successful, both pupil and teacher must find pleasure in it.

A word should be said at this point about the relation between pleasure and learning. The commonly used expression, "reading for fun," refers not to a marginal or frivolous use of reading ability but to an essential condition for learning to read. Only when the learner finds satisfaction in the activity may we look for the free and unrestrained flow of childhood energies into the task of converting visual symbols into sound and meaning. Even very difficult reading material affords satisfaction when the reader feels that he is achieving a clearly understood purpose. For the young child the appearance of too many unfamiliar words or concepts in the reading material is a distraction and a hindrance to enjoyment. For the retarded reader, especially, the prescription must be easy, abundant, interest-charged reading material.

Another consideration in the planning of work with the retarded reader is the role of the parent. Teachers who have responsibility for large numbers of children cannot be in frequent communication with all the parents, but in the case of the severely retarded reader such communication is essential. The personal interview is the most effective form, but in the absence of opportunity for face-to-face discussions the letter-report can be most useful. Parent and teacher have much to learn from each other about the child. The teacher needs to know as much as possible about the child's home situation and his behavior with respect to play, TV habits, sleeping habits, and especially his reading at home. On the other hand, the parent needs to have advice as to methods of reinforcing the efforts of the teacher in providing appropriate reading guidance.

In some instances the parents are indifferent to the child's school problems. In others, they are overconcerned and competitive and place undue pressure on the child. Sometimes the parent adopts a punitive attitude toward the child who is not doing well in reading. The parent should be informed early about any important difficulty a child is having, so that he or she will not be shocked or agitated to discover that the child needs special help. As a rule, parents should be discouraged from attempting to give reading instruction at home; they should be encouraged to provide the environment, the stimulation, and the good example that will strengthen the teacher's efforts to build constructive attitudes toward reading on the part of the child.

Finally, appropriate guidance for the retarded reader should extend to the work in the content subjects. Gains achieved in the reading period can be quickly canceled out if the child is confronted in science, social studies, hygiene, and other subjects with regimented textbook materials that yield little meaning for him. Habits of partial comprehension acquired in the course of the school day may nullify whatever has been learned in remedial reading sessions. Careful preparation in the way of concept formation, explanation of new terms and old terms with specialized meanings, and the use of diversified reading materials at many different levels of difficulty are some of the procedures required by all pupils but particularly by those who are seriously deficient in reading ability.

GUIDELINES FOR HELPING THE RETARDED READER
The following are some suggestions that should govern the work in remedial reading:

1. *Be encouraging, but, of course, not beyond the point of truthfulness.* While every good teacher tries to encourage all children, optimism is especially important in the case of the backward reader. Frequently the retarded reader is a discouraged person. Again and again, without success, he has tried to learn to read. Often he has come to think of himself as a failure not only in reading but in almost every-

thing. Consequently, primary emphasis sometimes needs to be placed upon providing an activity in which the child can perform with superior results.

The teacher must, however, guard against encouragement that belies facts. A child should not be given the impression that it is going to be easy for him to become a good reader, for, unfortunately, such is usually not the case. As a rule, learning to overcome ineffective habits of reading is a slow and laborious task. The child who has been promised an easy path to learning to read will be discouraged when he later discovers that it is difficult.

The extent to which the teacher can be encouraging as she begins to give help in remedial reading will vary greatly with the situation. In some instances it is fairly easy to predict that the task will not be an unduly arduous one. In other instances it may be a long time before the child acquires the basic skills of reading. The teacher's remarks and her attitude toward teaching a retarded reader must be greatly influenced by a large variety of facts. The more background data the teacher has, the more readily she will be able to make accurate predictions of success.

In most instances there are some points that the teacher should make clear to a pupil at or near the beginning of the work on remedial reading. She can tell the child that there is reason for believing that he can learn to read. She may wish to tell him, too, that many boys and girls who have problems like his have learned to read when taught by methods that will be followed in his case. Early in the period of giving special help it is sometimes desirable to point out to the child that much depends upon his own willingness to work hard to learn to read. Many of the children are old enough to profit from being told that they themselves need to put forth real effort if they want to become better readers.

2. *Interest the pupil in reading.* Frequently the retarded reader lacks interest in reading; repeated failure or inability to read as well as his peers is not conducive to the development of such interest. Consequently, one of the first problems, and one of the most difficult, is to inspire the reader to want to read. Sometimes an interest in reading is stimulated through assurance to the child that he can most likely learn to read. Another means is surrounding him with books that contain many pictures on topics in which he is interested. Since often he cannot read these books, the teacher should devote some time daily in telling him points of significance about one or more of them. Another device often used is having some of the pupils tell about points of

special interest they have learned from books as they are showing them to their classmates.

Everything that has been recommended earlier in this book as a means of interesting boys and girls in reading also holds, at least to some extent, in the case of the retarded reader. It should be remembered, however, that it is usually much harder to develop reading interest in the retarded reader than in the average or superior reader.

3. *Select carefully the time of day when the special help is given.* It is unwise to ask the child to do special work in reading at a time of day when he is tired. It is usually undesirable to schedule remedial work for a recess period, for the retarded reader is even more likely than the others to require the relaxation of the play period. Moreover, a child who is deprived of the activities of the recess period may become resentful toward the remedial-reading program. The same principle applies to other parts of the school day in which he would be deprived of the opportunity to take part in some activity that he likes particularly well. Usually it is not conducive to maximum achievement to keep the child, because of the special help, from participating in music, art, or other activities that particularly attract him. Special help in reading should, if possible, be given during a period regularly set aside for reading instruction.

4. *Use appropriate materials of instruction.* Teachers of retarded readers often point out that not enough suitable material is available on the child's level of development and at the same time on his reading level. The complaint is justified. A fourteen-year-old boy with a reading ability of a typical second-grade child is not going to care much about reading a second-grade reader. However, the problem is no longer quite as acute as it used to be. A large number of trade books, on subjects of great interest to children throughout the intermediate grades, are written so simply that even a retarded reader can enjoy them, especially with a little help. Some sets of readers, too, are especially designed for the retarded reader.

A number of reading lists have been prepared to aid the teacher in locating suitable books for slow readers in the elementary school. Among these are:

Dunn, Anita E., *Fare for the Reluctant Reader.* Albany, N.Y.: Teachers College, State University of New York, 1952.

Durrell, Donald D., and Helen B. Sullivan, *High Interest Low Vocabulary Booklist.* Boston: Educational Clinic, Boston University School of Education, 1952.

Groff, Patrick, "Recent Easy Books for First-Grade Readers," *Elementary English*, 13 (December 1960), pp. 521–527.

Guilfoile, Elizabeth, *Books for Beginning Readers,* rev. ed. Champaign, Ill.: National Council of Teachers of English, 1963.

Hill, Margaret Keyser, "A Bibliography of Reading Lists for Retarded Readers." *State University of Iowa Extension Bulletin,* No. 37, April 1, 1953. Iowa City: State University of Iowa.

Hunt, J. T., "Easy Non-Fictional Materials for the Handicapped Reader," *High School Journal,* 39 (March 1956), pp. 322–332.

———, "Easy and Interesting Fiction for the Handicapped Reader," *High School Journal,* 39 (April 1956), 378–385.

Kircher, Clara J., *Recreational Books for Retarded Readers.* Newark, N.J.: School Libraries Division, Public Library, 1951.

Matson, Charlotte, *Books for Tired Eyes.* Chicago: American Library Association, 1951.

Ramsey, Eloise (comp.), *Folklore for Children and Young People.* Philadelphia: American Folklore Society, University of Pennsylvania, 1952.

Robinson, Helen M. (ed.), "Trade Books for Poor Readers," *Clinical Studies in Reading II,* pp. 177–181. Supplementary Educational Monographs No. 77. Chicago: University of Chicago Press, 1953.

Spache, George, *Good Books for Poor Readers.* Champaign, Ill.: The Garrard Publishing Company, 1964.

Strang, Ruth, *Gateways to Readable Books.* New York: The H. W. Wilson Company, 1952.

Wurtz, Conrad, *A Bibliography of Reading Lists for Retarded Readers.* Bulletin, 640. Iowa City: State University of Iowa, 1949.

The problem of finding appropriate materials is more serious with the child who has so small a reading vocabulary that he cannot even recognize the words in a preprimer. Books that are challenging in thought to a nine-year-old child who cannot read on the preprimer level are not available. Sometimes with the intelligent child who cannot read, the teacher can explain that at first he will find the books decidedly below his level of interest. He should also then be made to feel that his chief interest should be in the results he accomplishes on his road to becoming a good reader, rather than in the subject matter. One teacher showed a child some books in a series that she had selected for his reading, explaining that while the earlier books lacked subject matter that would be challenging to him, the later ones contained many selections of real interest. The teacher might also tell the child that he may find, too, as many adults do, that sometimes it is fun to read subject matter that is chiefly designed for younger readers.

Many teachers inquire as to the place of workbooks and other published exercises in teaching the retarded reader. No one authoritative answer can be given that will be specific in its application. Some workbooks and other exercise material furnish economically the additional practice that a pupil who has difficulty in reading often needs. The same principles in general apply to the use of workbooks with the retarded reader that have already been stated earlier in this book in connection with teaching other children. Special caution, however, should be taken to use the workbooks in such a way that they will not cause the child to lose interest in reading.

Teacher-made materials sometimes contribute to the solution of the problem of what to have the retarded child read, particularly in the early stages of learning to read. The teacher can often write material, either dictated by the pupil or written by the teacher without contributions from the child. It is too time-consuming, however, for the teacher to continue to write all the material that a child will be reading.

5. *Decide on the methods to be used on the basis of a careful diagnosis.* The teacher who uses the same methods of procedure with all retarded readers will usually not get satisfactory results. Considerable time spent on diagnosis can be very valuable if the results are utilized in planning the program.

Correct diagnosis of reading difficulties is merely a first step in helping the retarded reader. A frequently quoted story is that of the teacher who, after she had given standardized tests year after year to her pupils, complained, "I no longer believe in standardized tests. I have given them to my pupils year after year and they are no better than they were before I started giving the tests." Diagnosis without the intent to profit by the discoveries made is of little, if any, value.

Certain common failings will usually be revealed by observation of the pupil's reading habits and the various tests that may be employed. These include word-by-word reading, vocalization or sub-vocal sounding, finger pointing, head-swinging, lip reading, backtracking, daydreaming, and limited vocabulary. Habits such as these should be noted for later work with individual children.

6. *If a method does not seem to work with a given pupil, change your procedure after you have given your method a fair trial.* No one method is so much superior to all others that the teacher should persist, in spite of lack of results, in using it with any child. Even if the teacher has used a given procedure effectively with many other children whose needs seem to be similar, she should change her plans with a specific pupil if they are not productive of results with him. However, she should not shift from one method to another without persisting long enough with the first to be sure that it will not be successful. Some children take a long time to learn by any method at all. Too much

change in method, here as in other learning situations, is likely to result in confusion.

7. *Make appraisal of the pupil's progress and encourage him to do likewise.* Charts or graphs, kept by either the teacher or pupil, can serve as an incentive to learning. However, because of the complexity of the reading act, these records often can show but one segment of the total activity. The pupil should be aware of this fact. The records should deal with some aspect of reading on which fairly objective data can be obtained. A record may be kept of the number of words a child has learned during intervals of time—a week or ten days, for example. A chart may be kept showing the number of pages in trade books that a pupil has read. Other accomplishments that may be recorded are: the number of questions a pupil answers correctly on teacher-made tests; the rate of reading for stated purposes; the number of words missed when reading orally from a designated book; the number of words recognized from a standardized word list.

The child should be helped to realize that if he fails at times to show progress on a record, it may not necessarily indicate that he is not learning. The nature of learning curves, including plateaus, may need to be explained to the child, in language, of course, that he can comprehend.

8. *Use a variety of methods.* The use of one method, no matter how good, to the exclusion of others usually does not produce the best results. No one method alone is likely to be best fitted to the needs of any individual, for reading is so complex a process and retardation in reading is ordinarily caused by such a multiplicity of factors that various types of approaches are needed. It is especially important that a variety of methods be used when several persons are being taught as a group. Frequently one method, although helpful for all, is not the most felicitous one for every individual in the group.

There is, however, also danger in too much variety of method. The number should be limited somewhat so that it will not be necessary for the child to expend an unwarranted amount of time and energy in becoming accustomed to various ways of learning to read. Best results are usually attained only after a person has had considerable experience with a particular method.

9. *If instruction is given in group situations, make certain that it is provided under the best circumstances possible.* Some work with retarded readers can be done satisfactorily only if help is given on an individual basis. At other times, however, work in small-group situations seems advisable. Further, there are instances when sheer lack of

time on the part of the teacher makes it necessary to give help to two or more persons at one time.

If instruction in learning to read is given to retarded readers in a group situation, the following suggestions may prove helpful: (a) *Group the pupils in terms of their needs.* Sometimes it is advisable to group them according to level of reading ability. At other times, it is best to group the children in terms of the type of skill in which they need most help. All those of approximately the same level of reading ability who need help in word recognition may be taught in one group, while those whose major difficulty is one specific phase of comprehension may be grouped together. (b) *Keep the groups flexible so that changes can quite readily be made as needs change.* The administration of any program of helping the retarded reader should allow for the maximum of change from one group to another, whenever such a shift would be to the best advantage of the learner. (c) *In group work, pay special attention to the needs of each person.* Even when the teacher is helping several children at the same time, much can be done to individualize the work. A child who has more skill than the others in his group in oral reading could be asked to read orally the more difficult parts of a selection. A child who has particular trouble with a certain word should be given the appropriate help in deciphering it. (d) *Help each individual to realize that he is an important member of the group.* The attitude of the teacher has much to do with whether a child feels important. The teacher can find many ways to show each child that she considers him of real value as a contributing member of the group. Even the boy or girl who cannot read can be helped to feel his worth if he can show pictures of interest to others or tell of experiences that his age-mates recognize as valuable contributions.

SPECIAL METHODS FOR REMEDIAL READING   In general, the procedures that are most effective for the retarded reader are the same as those that can be recommended for other boys and girls. Remedial reading at its best is essentially an adaptation of the same procedures effectively used with normal readers to the individual needs of retarded persons. A child with difficulty in word recognition can, as a rule, be helped most to acquire power in this respect by the same means used with other readers. Similarly, a child retarded in skill in selecting significant details can usually progress to the best advantage if he is helped to develop this comprehension skill by means of the same general procedures used with other children, if special attention is paid to his level and his responses in learning situations.

There is no bag of tricks nor list of teaching devices that can be presented with the guarantee that these will change retarded readers to average or above average. There are, however, several methods of teaching reading that are often associated primarily with remedial reading. These are briefly described here.

1. *The Fernald Kinesthetic Method.*[6] Although Dr. Fernald recommends her method for use with any children, it is more often used with seriously retarded readers who do not respond to other methods. Important aspects of the method are these: (1) In the earliest stage of instruction the teacher writes the word to be learned in large letters as the child watches her. Then the child traces the word with his finger as he says it part by part. Thereupon he tries to write it from memory. As he writes the word, he again says it. He then compares his copy with the original and, if he finds an error, tries again to learn the word by the same method he has employed so far. Emphasis is placed upon reading words that the pupils use as they describe experiences they have. Consequently, experience charts are often used with this method. (2) When the child has learned quite a number of words, he is no longer asked to trace each new word. He is instructed to write words that he learns on cards and to file them in an individual word box. When he writes stories he is encouraged to use this file if necessary. (3) When the pupil has made considerable progress in learning a word by this method without tracing it, new words are presented to him in print, not in writing. It is then that the pupil advances to the stage at which he is able to recognize a new word through its resemblance to a known word and through the aid of context clues.

Many teachers consider this method too slow and laborious and mechanical to use in a developmental reading program. Some object to emphasis upon this method even in remedial reading. There are, however, pupils who have learned to read by the Fernald method who have encountered only failure in the use of others. It is for this reason that some teachers, who do not favor its use even with all retarded readers, try it with some of them when little, if any, progress has been made with other methods. Many adaptations of the Fernald method have been made. Use of the typewriter by the pupil is part of one of the modifications.

2. *Use of Experience Charts.* Some teachers rely heavily in work with retarded readers on experience charts, of which a detailed description and evaluation are given in Chapter 4B. Modifications of the typical procedures followed in group situations are, of course, required. As in the experience charts for groups of children, the teacher

[6] Grace M. Fernald, *Remedial Techniques in Basic School Subjects.* New York: McGraw-Hill Book Company, Inc., 1943.

records in writing the sentences that are dictated to her. Then the child "reads" the sentences, often in part from memory. Sometimes these reports are in the form of book reports on picture books, on simple stories that the child has read, or on books the teacher or others have read to him. Autobiographical sketches are frequently dictated and also illustrated by the child. Since these materials are ordinarily for individual use, they are usually recorded on sheets of paper rather than on tagboard.

3. *Use of games and other drills.* Special mention is made of games and drills in connection with teaching the retarded reader because with such readers it is often more necessary than with others to use these activities to a considerable degree. This is true because frequently these children need more repetitive practice than the nonretarded reader. The same criteria for drill should be observed in connection with work in remedial reading as are valid at other times. Some important points to note are: (1) The game or drill should be of value. (2) The results obtained should be commensurate with the time spent on the drill. (3) The purpose of the activity should, as a rule, be recognized by the pupil and be accepted by him as worthwhile if the maximum benefit is to be gained from it. (4) There should be variety in type of drill used. (5) The spacing in practice should be in harmony with the findings of educational psychology.

Organization for Helping Retarded Readers

Help can be given to the retarded reader under a variety of plans. Most of it can undoubtedly be provided most effectively by the teacher from day to day as she adapts all her instruction to the needs of her class. Individual help given by the teacher during or just after a class period will frequently clear up the difficulties of a child who is falling behind in acquiring a reading skill. Prevention of further retardation through early attention to problems is the keynote of this informal plan. Those boys and girls who have some special difficulty in reading can sometimes be put, for a day or a week or longer, in a group by themselves for special help. Such instruction at times may be a substitute for work with the child's usual group; in other instances it may be in addition to the regular classwork in reading. Groups can be formed for longer duration, possibly for the whole year. Thus much of the problem of remedial reading can be dealt with informally in the regular classroom.

There are instances, however, when a more formal plan for remedial reading may be warranted. In some schools children seriously

retarded in reading are assigned to a classroom by themselves, preferably with a teacher qualified to deal with problems in this area. Ideally
such a class is kept considerably smaller in enrollment than the average.
If more than fifteen pupils are placed in it, the effectiveness of the
program of instruction is likely to be greatly reduced. A criticism of this
organization is that all the school associations of a pupil in a class for
retarded readers are with boys and girls with the same limitations. The
stigma that is likely to become attached to such a class is another factor
frequently raised as objection to this plan. Further objection lies in the
expense of any program where classroom size is necessarily limited to
the extent that it ideally ought to be in a room reserved for retarded
readers. Furthermore, unless the special class serves a large district,
there are not likely to be enough retarded readers of similar age and
intelligence to constitute even the small number of pupils desirable for
it.

Often the plan followed is that of having a specialist in reading meet with pupils from various rooms for limited parts of the school
day. Under such a plan, the reading teacher ordinarily has a room of
her own, often designated as the reading room. During the first half of
the forenoon she may help one group of children who have been
excused from their homeroom for that length of time. At the middle of
the forenoon these boys and girls go back to their own rooms where
they resume work with their classmates. At that time another group
begins its half-forenoon session with the reading teacher. The afternoon
can be divided similarly. The school day can be divided into more than
four parts, possibly periods of sixty minutes' duration, to allow for
more shifts of pupils during the day.

One of two plans is typically used to determine which pupils
needing extra help in reading should be in the reading room at the same
time. For purposes of administration, it is usually easier to assemble at
one time in the reading room all the children from a given classroom
who need extra help in reading work. To facilitate matters of programing, many of the homeroom teachers concurrently conduct reading
classes for those of their children who are not in the reading room; thus
the retarded readers do not miss work in social studies or other areas
of study. Such a plan usually interferes less with the other activities of
the boys and girls than one in which the reading teacher has, at the
same time, those pupils from all rooms who have the same or similar
reading problems. According to this latter plan children reading on preprimer level, for example, regardless of their homeroom or grade, would
meet with the reading teacher at the same time. Not only does such a

plan often create many disrupting influences in the other learning activities of the children, but frequently, too, the resulting grouping is undesirable from the point of view of the socialization of the child. Under such a plan a sixth-grade pupil may be grouped for reading with a second-grade child.

HELPING THE BRIGHT CHILD IN READING

Since the school in a democratic society regards all children as of equal moral worth, it does not, in its distribution of effort, deliberately discriminate against any group because of low, average, or high academic aptitude and achievement. There are compelling reasons why all should learn to read as well as their capacities permit. Nevertheless, because teachers are human and fallible and because time and resources are not unlimited, they cannot always do complete justice to all the children in their classes. Many teachers find that work with retarded and average pupils is so time-consuming and the needs of these children so apparent that they tend to neglect those who obviously are superior in academic ability. The growing concern about the gifted child is therefore justified.

The type of instruction required by the bright child does not differ in kind from that given to other children. The physical, sensory, emotional, and other factors essential to good reading, as well as the specific skills of reading, are important to all. The difference is to be found in the range and level of difficulty of the materials and in special problems peculiar to the very bright child.

One difference, for example, is the fact that bright children often acquire many of the reading skills independently and almost unconsciously in the course of their extensive, highly motivated reading. Special lessons and drills in these reading skills can and should be bypassed for them. All that the teacher needs to do in such situations is to be sure that these skills have been mastered.

Specialists in the education of the gifted child recognize that social maturity does not necessarily go hand in hand with academic achievement. There is no evidence that bright children as a group are less mature socially than other children. In fact, intellectual maturity is commonly accompanied by social maturity. It would not be surprising, however, if we found that some very bright children were less conforming, that they demanded reasons for rules of behavior and exhibited some impatience with other pupils less well endowed.

A degree of nonconformity is a desirable personality trait.

Independence of mind is essential to social and scientific progress and to artistic creation. But it is of the greatest importance that our ablest individuals learn early in life to act responsibly and to be concerned about the well-being and happiness of others. The codes of the physician, who places the well-being of his patient first, and the scientist, who weighs the effect of his discoveries on society, has its origin in the early face-to-face experiences of childhood. In our fascination with a child's brilliance we cannot afford to forget the great influence for good or evil that he will have upon society. Reading is one of the potent means at our disposal to lead the child on the road to responsible and constructive effort.

The present-day drive toward "academic excellence" is overdue, but it must not be permitted to distort the humanistic goals of education. The child who reads about people in other cultures and other lands should be doing more than adding to his knowledge and understanding. He should be cultivating the art of unlimited kinship with people.

Discussions of the problems of educating the gifted child rarely concern themselves with questions relating to emotional growth and attitude formation. They are concerned chiefly with the conservation of intellectual talent now so often going to waste because of unfavorable home and community environments and school programs not sufficiently adapted to the needs of the gifted child. One difficulty is that emotions are hard to discover and to measure; it is almost impossible to formulate defensible educational objectives with regard to them, except as they result in serious and persistent antisocial behavior. Nevertheless, any consideration of the teaching of reading and literature which does not embrace the emotional dimension is necessarily incomplete and distorts any valid conception of the teacher's task.

The bright child usually has little difficulty in learning to interpret the literal and figurative meaning of a selection appropriate to his general maturity. What we cannot be so sure of is that the child will know how to identify with situations he reads about or utilize what he reads in building a mental image of the social and human consequences of conditions and events. Speed and comprehension in the reading of a poem, for example, are not enough. There must be moments of contemplation in which the reader visualizes a scene, laughs or weeps with a character in a story, and thinks with wonder about a deed of heroism. Speed tests in reading do not measure these capacities for feeling. Social sensitivity and human understanding should occupy a high place among our objectives in reading instruction.

Identifying the Unusually Gifted Child

All children are gifted. Without gifts, a child would be un-educable. The gifts may be few and very small, or they may be many and very great.

What shall we call those whose gifts are many and great? Many terms have been used. These children have been called "able," "bright," "talented," "academically superior," "children of high academic aptitude," "intellectually gifted," "academically talented," among other expressions. These terms sometimes have special meanings; in some cases they are applied to children with special aptitudes in art, music, or mechanical activity and in other cases to children whose intellectual potential amounts to genius. In Terman's famous study of gifted children, those with IQ's of 130 and higher were included. Havighurst speaks of children gifted with qualities of social leadership and of children who possess "creative intelligence." Gallagher divides the gifted into three categories: those with IQ's of 116 and over (15–20 percent of the school population); those with IQ's of 132 and over (2–4 percent of the school population); and those with IQ's of 148 and over (0.1 percent of the school population). These are the academically talented, the gifted, and the highly gifted.

There are in fact no sharply defined boundaries among these groups, although the problems of instruction may differ as we go up on the scale. Any dividing lines must be arbitrary. In our discussion we shall deal with the largest group of superior learners, and for convenience draw the line at approximately 120 IQ. We shall use most of the terms mentioned above interchangeably.

The usual methods of identifying bright children involve the use of individual and group tests of intelligence, achievement tests, and teacher observation. Individual intelligence tests are probably the most accurate of the methods, but they are time-consuming and require trained examiners. Group intelligence tests and achievement tests are useful as screening devices, but they may be quite inaccurate in assessing an individual's true capabilities. Errors in these tests more often result in underestimation than in overestimation of a child's potential. Teacher observation is an essential part of the evaluation process because it may reveal aspects of a child's mental powers not reflected in any test. It is not unusual for a group test to rate as many as 25 percent of the gifted children below their true intelligence level. Nevertheless, for the average classroom teacher the best available method for identifying the gifted child is a combination of one or more group intelligence tests and careful observation of the pupil's behavior and performance.

The teacher will find it helpful to look for specific characteristics that distinguish the bright child from the average or below-average child. Numerous lists of such characteristics have been published. According to one such list, compiled by Kough and DeHaan,[7] the teacher can recognize the superior learner in her class by observing to see which of the students:

1.   Learns rapidly and easily.
2.   Uses a lot of common sense and practical knowledge.
3.   Reasons things out, thinks clearly, recognizes relationships, comprehends meanings.
4.   Retains what he has heard or read without much rote drill.
5.   Knows about many things of which other children are unaware.
6.   Uses a large number of words easily and accurately.
7.   Can read books that are one to two years in advance of the rest of the class.
8.   Performs difficult mental tasks.
9.   Asks many questions. Is interested in a wide range of things.
10. Does some academic work one to two years in advance of his class.
11. Is alert, keenly observant, responds quickly.

Teachers' judgments of pupils are often clouded by the fact that a gifted pupil may be restless, complete his work quickly, and turn to "mischief" to amuse himself, and thus appear to the teacher as a behavior problem rather than simply a child lacking in challenge or interest. Sometimes, too, a child's exceptional ability may be hidden by emotional problems which interfere with adequate performance in school work. Only through conscious effort and much experience can the teacher become expert in discovering superior academic ability in those children whose giftedness is not obvious to the casual observer.

Creating the Conditions for Maximum Learning

The key to good teaching is the teacher herself. Materials and methods are important, but no amount of pedagogical theory, library resources, audio-visual aids, laboratories, auditoriums, or testing programs can compensate for the lack of the competent, resourceful teacher. This fact is doubly significant in the case of the academically superior pupil.

---

[7] Jack Kough and Robert DeHaan, "Identifying Children Who Need Help," *Teacher's Guidance Handbook*. Chicago: Science Research Associates, 1955.

The bright child needs a bright teacher. All children need teachers who are above average in intelligence, devoted to teaching, and sympathetic to children's educational needs. But the bright child needs a teacher who is distinctly superior in mental ability. Her IQ need not be as high as that of the brightest child in her class, but she should be bright enough to feel secure in her relations with him and to command his respect. She should be willing to learn from the bright child, and sometimes to let him teach the things she does not know as well as he.

Statements by gifted children describing teachers they like reveal that they want teachers who know their subject, related fields, and current events, who use humor and illustrative material to add interest to the subject, and who are skillful in relating the subject to other fields and to the pupils' lives. They want teachers who require them to learn, to work together on class projects, to discuss problems together, and to assume initiative and responsibility. They like teachers who are versatile, fair, even-tempered, and patient.

The teacher of the gifted can and should be more permissive in her assignments to gifted children than to those of more limited abilities, who usually desire and need definite and detailed instructions for a task. Gifted children are more likely to ask questions about the *why* of the methods employed by the teacher, and the teacher should freely discuss her reasons and objectives with them. If the pupil is egotistic or immature because of coddling at home, the teacher should set challenges and require performance that will result in the development of a more accurate self-image on the part of the child. In short, the teacher of the academically superior child should have all the qualities of any good teacher, but she should have them in high degree.

Next to a good teacher in importance is the provision of abundant reading materials difficult enough and diversified enough to provide a genuine challenge and to appeal to the wide range of interests so characteristic of the bright child. For truly gifted children the book and magazine resources of most elementary schools are inadequate. Public libraries, state traveling book collections, and even the paperback selection in supermarkets and elsewhere need to be utilized to meet the need. Academically superior students tend to be omnivorous readers, particularly when suitable reading materials are readily accessible. They are attracted, also, to encyclopedias, atlases, dictionaries, and all types of reference materials. As a consequence, the school library assumes great importance in the reading guidance of gifted children. Failure to provide proper library facilities in elementary schools must necessarily result in great waste of the precious resources represented by the learning potential of these children.

The need for more and better reading materials implies also the necessity of a wide knowledge of children's literature on the part of the teacher. No teacher can possibly have read all the books that gifted children are likely to read or should read, but fortunately there are excellent guides and booklists which should be available to the teacher in the school library. Aids of this type are discussed and listed in detail in the chapters on children's interests in this book.

In providing books for individual reading, teachers should make certain that they include titles that will challenge the able reader. Many superior readers in the upper elementary grades enjoy reading books generally considered adult fare. They should be encouraged to read suitable books on that level.

Reading can be fun. (Shackman—Monkmeyer Press Photo Service.)

Planning Reading Programs for Bright Children

Studies of the reading habits of gifted children reveal that they tend to be omnivorous readers, that they spend about six hours a week in reading at age seven and up to twelve hours at age thirteen, that they have wider interests and do more voluntary reading than the average child, and that about half of the highly gifted read before they enter school. Significantly, they learn to read by a great variety of methods, and it may be assumed that in their case the method employed is far less important than the versatility and skill of the teacher and the availability of suitable reading materials.

Plans employed for meeting the needs of gifted children in general fall into three main categories: (1) enrichment, (2) acceleration, and (3) special grouping. Of these, perhaps the most popular plan is that of enrichment. In an enrichment program provision is made for individual differences in ability within the setting of the regular classroom. The gifted child remains with his age-mates, but is encouraged to take on more complex tasks. More emphasis is placed on original thinking and problem solving. In the case of reading, the academically superior child is expected to choose books calling for higher levels of comprehension than those possessed by others members of the class.

A promising form of enrichment is the unit organization of instruction, especially in the middle grades. In this plan the teacher may propose a number of topics for study from which all the pupils make a choice. With the aid of the teacher, the class assembles a bibliography for the chosen topic, using the various reference aids in classroom and library. The teacher then assists the pupils in developing the topic. Some of the reading selections may be read and enjoyed by all the pupils, but the abler members of the class will also select reading materials commensurate with their abilities. The task of the teacher is to assist all pupils, regardless of reading ability, with the particular reading problems that may cause difficulty.

The policy of acceleration may take different forms. One of these is early admittance to school of the bright child. Certainly there is nothing sacred about age six as the earliest entering age, particularly since the differences among children of the same chronological age are so wide. In schools with an ungraded primary division it is possible to permit bright children to complete the three-year period in less time, especially if they are socially and emotionally well adjusted. Double promotion is another plan of acceleration, but one to be used with great caution to avoid the danger that the child will miss basic steps in skill development or the building of background information.

Many parents and school officials are reluctant to adopt a policy of acceleration because of the fear that the accelerated child will have difficulty in making a good adjustment in a group of children of higher chronological age. Research studies have indicated that, in general, pupils have benefited from programs of acceleration and that the fear of social maladjustment because of acceleration is usually unfounded. Nevertheless, the needs and social maturity of each child should be carefully studied before he is advanced to a group of older children.

Special classes for gifted children have been organized in a number of elementary schools. These have the advantage of enabling pupils to enjoy the opportunity of working with their intellectual peers and to benefit from the give and take of planning and discussion with other children equally alert and eager to think and to explore. The plan does not eliminate the need for attention to individual differences, but it does avoid the neglect of gifted children, which is almost inevitable in heterogeneously grouped classes. In most systems employing special classes for the gifted, the children are kept with their age-mates for part of the day, usually in such classes as music, art, and physical education.

Helping the Bright Underachiever

In a sense, almost everyone is an underachiever. We tend to perform up to full capacity only under pressure. The pressure may consist of a drive or ambition, a keen but perhaps transitory interest, circumstances that demand the full exercise of our powers, or a strong desire to win the approval of others in certain situations. Some children are driven to high achievement in school subjects by a desire to compensate for a real or fancied deficiency in physical skill or in general social adjustment.

What concerns the teacher of reading, however, is persistent failure of the bright child to perform up to his full potential in reading and to achieve the kind of growth that may reasonably be expected of him. It is of great importance that the causes of his inadequate performance be discovered as early as possible.

The possible causes of underachievement in bright children are numerous, and for the most part they do not differ in kind from the causes of underachievement among average and below-average children. Among these causes is the familiar one of a lack of a strong foundation of reading skills, such as methods of attack on unfamiliar words, getting the main idea of a passage, and reading at appropriate rates. Although many able learners acquire these skills on their own, others do not. Like most children who fail to learn the basic skills early, the bright child may develop negative attitudes toward reading which persist throughout the elementary grades and beyond. Indeed, the bright child tends to be more sensitive than others to his unsuccessful efforts in reading during the initial stages.

In some instances conditions in a bright child's home may be responsible for underachievement in reading. If parents do not place a high value on academic excellence, if the home has few books or magazines of quality, if the child is not given encouragement or opportunity to read at home, he may never realize his own potential or set himself goals commensurate with his abilities. It then becomes necessary for the school to compensate for the impoverished cultural environment at home by providing intellectual and cultural stimulation through an abundance of direct and vicarious experiences.

Some bright children, perhaps *because* they are bright, enter school before they are matured sufficiently to cope with the adjustments and the tasks required by the school situation. Others are handicapped by being transported from one school situation in which they felt secure to another in which the surroundings are strange, the methods different, and the teacher's personality contrasting with that of the one they had before. Frequent absence from school because of illness or others factors is detrimental to the educational progress of most able pupils, as it is to that of average or slow learners.

Emotional problems, often stemming from discordant family relations, may interfere with satisfactory growth in reading. Children who experience continued anxiety, feel rejected, or show hostility toward the adult world frequently suffer a lack of self-confidence that is necessary for learning; they are emotionally distracted when they should be concentrating on their reading. This is not to say that all bright underachievers are emotionally disturbed or that emotional difficulties always results in underachievement. The teacher should, however, be alert to the possible presence of emotional factors as a possible block to the full realization of the bright child's reading potential.

It has been estimated that as many as 25 percent of the gifted children in a typical class are underachievers. Whatever the true proportion may be, we cannot afford the waste of talent arising from any child's failure to reach attainable goals in reading. We must do all we can to discover the obstacles to maximum growth and, so far as possible, to remove them.

FOR FURTHER STUDY

On Problems of the Retarded Reader

Barbe, Walter B., *Teaching Reading.* New York: Oxford University Press, 1965. Chapter 40, "Machines and Reading," pp. 335–339; Chapter 41, "A Reading Program That Did Not Work," pp. 339–342.

Burton, William E., *Reading in Child Development.* Indianapolis, Ind.: The Bobbs-Merrill Company, Inc., 1958. Chapter 12, "Vision Education: The Development of Efficient Seeing," pp. 412–428; Chapter 13, "Hearing, or Listening to, or Interpreting Spoken Words," pp. 428–444.

Dechant, Emerald V., *Improving the Teaching of Reading.* Englewood Cliffs, N.J.: Prentice-Hall, Inc., 1964. Chapter 14, "Materials for Teaching," pp. 403–475.

Della-Piana, Gabriel M., *Reading Diagnosis and Prescription: An Introduction.* New York: Holt, Rinehart and Winston, Inc., 1968.

Gans, Roma, *Common Sense in Reading.* Indianapolis, Ind.: The Bobbs-Merrill Company, Inc., 1963. Chapter 19, "Readers in Slow Gear," pp. 335–351; Chapter 20, "Providing Help through Remedial Methods," pp. 352–371.

Harris, Albert J., *Readings on Reading Instruction.* New York: David McKay Company, Inc., 1963. Chapter XIII, "Materials for the Reading Program," pp. 358–386; Chapter XVI, "Help for the Retarded Reader," pp. 424–461.

McKee, Paul, *Reading: A Program of Instruction for the Elementary School.* Boston: Houghton Mifflin Company, 1966. Chapter 9, "Studying Informative Material," pp. 316–376.

Monroe, Marion, and Bernice Rogers, *Foundations of Reading: Informal Pre-Reading Procedures.* Chicago: Scott, Foresman and Company, 1964. Chapter 7, "The Causes of Difficulties in Learning To Read," pp. 142–179.

Spache, George D., *Reading in the Elementary School.* Boston: Allyn and Bacon, Inc., 1964. Chapter IV, "Estimating Readability," pp. 21–28; Chapter V, "Trade Books Useful for Poor Readers," pp. 29–57; Chapter VI, "Adapted and Simplified Materials," pp. 58–67; Chapter VII, "Textbooks, Workbooks, and Games," pp. 68–96; Chapter VIII, "Magazines and Newspapers," pp. 97–102.

Tinker, Miles A., and Constance M. McCullough, *Teaching Elementary Reading.* New York: Appleton-Century-Crofts, 1968. Chapter 16, "Materials," pp. 318–338; Chapter 26, "Remedial Reading in the Classroom," pp. 594–611.

On Reading Problems of the Gifted Child

Barbe, Walter B., *Teaching Reading.* New York: Oxford University Press, 1965. Chapter 34, "Reading Accomplishment of Gifted and Average," pp. 281–284.

De Boer, John J., "Creative Reading and the Gifted Student," *The Reading Teacher,* 16 (May 1963), pp. 435–441.

Durr, William K., *The Gifted.* New York: Oxford University Press, 1964.

Durr, William K., *Reading Instruction: Dimensions and Issues.* Boston: Houghton Mifflin Company, 1967. "The Able Reader," pp. 191–193; "Creative Reading and the Gifted Student," pp. 194–199; "Do Parents Help Gifted Children Read?" pp. 200–204.

Frost, Joe L., *Issues and Innovations in the Teaching of Reading.* Chicago: Scott, Foresman and Company, 1967. "The Reading of Gifted Children," pp. 252–255; "The Able Reader," pp. 255–258; "Organizational Modification for Gifted Children," pp. 259–262.

King, Martha L., Bernice D. Ellinger, and Willavene Wolf (eds.), *Critical Reading.* Philadelphia: J. B. Lippincott Company, 1967. "Critical and Creative Reading," pp. 84–89; "Creative Reading: A Neglected Area," pp. 89–95; "Creative Reading at All Grade Levels," pp. 95–99; "Developing Creative Readers," pp. 100–111; "Language and the Habit of Credulity," pp. 243–252; "Reading Skills in Teaching Literature in the Elementary School," pp. 294–301; "Teaching a Picture Book as Literature," pp. 312–319; "Critical Thinking through Children's Literature," pp. 319–325.

Schubert, Delwyn G., and Theodore L. Torgerson (eds.), *Readings in Reading.* New York: Thomas Y. Crowell Company, 1968. Chapter 37, "Reading Instruction for Children of Superior Ability," pp. 256–263.

CHAPTER 14

The Reading Program
at Various Grade Levels

This chapter undertakes to indicate how reading instruction in the elementary school is integrated with the total educational program. The description is presented in three parts: (1) the primary-grade reading program, (2) the intermediate-grade reading program, and (3) the school-wide program.

READING PROGRAM IN THE PRIMARY GRADES

The primary grade reading program can be divided into (1) the prereading stage, (2) the beginning reading stage, and (3) the program in grades two and three.

The Prereading Stage

Many first-grade teachers, especially beginners, are uncertain as to how to proceed when school opens in September. They usually have some knowledge of the factors related to reading readiness and of procedures for developing readiness. Nevertheless, they have difficulty in visualizing the techniques in operation and in making the all-important decisions required on the opening day.

PREPARATION FOR THE FIRST DAY OF SCHOOL   Probably the most significant day in the pupil's entire school life is his first day of school. His attitude toward school and toward reading for months and perhaps years to come may be influenced by the initial impressions of school life. First-grade teachers are therefore quite properly concerned with the question, "How can I prepare for that crucial first day?"

It will greatly help the new teacher's self-confidence, and at the same time improve her efficiency, if she gathers a goodly amount of information about the school in advance. For example, if the school makes available a course of study, a careful examination of this document may provide the teacher with clues to the expectations of the school concerning the work of the first grade and with valuable suggestions regarding instructional procedures in the early days of the school term. Examination of the basal readers and other textbooks used in the school should likewise be a part of the preparatory process. Existing routines and materials should not be discarded until well-considered substitutes have been devised or secured. A visit by the new teacher to the classroom to which she will be assigned may reveal to her the nature of the available equipment—charts, supplies, and supplementary reading material. Certainly if it is possible she should visit the school library, the gymnasium, the playground, and other physical facilities the school may have. In her interview with the principal or supervisor before the opening of the school term, she should have numerous questions in readiness with regard to routines, facilities, procedures, responsibilities of teachers, and the relative freedom allowed teachers for the organization of instruction. She should especially make the acquaintance of those colleagues and members of the supervisory staff who can be of assistance to her.

Knowledge about the number and kinds of children in her class may be difficult to gather. The administration office of the school usually has a fair, but not infallible, estimate of the size of the fall enrollment. Unless the children have been previously enrolled in the kindergarten, the school may not know even the names of the children who enter the first grade. Often only general knowledge, based on earlier experiences, can serve as a guide.

Planning in advance of the opening of school is so essential to the development of a successful instructional program that many schools and school systems now hold preschool conferences or institutes for periods extending from one or two days to several weeks. The activities of such conferences are varied. Visiting speakers are often invited. Committees of teachers, grouped by grade levels or subject interests, discuss procedures and questions of concern to them. Usually the more experienced teachers provide information and help to the newcomers in these committee meetings. In addition, time is frequently set aside for individual preparation on the part of the teacher. She can, during this period, arrange her classroom attractively by placing interesting picture books on tables and shelves, mounting attractive pictures on the bulletin boards, perhaps bringing a few flowers and a plant or two, and seeing that the furniture is in place. If the names of the children are known in advance, the teacher can prepare identification cards to be worn the first few days and other cards to label the children's desks or places at the table.

ACTIVITIES ON THE FIRST DAY OF SCHOOL   As has been pointed out, success on the first day of school depends in large measure upon previous planning. It should be remembered that many of the children have not hitherto been members of so large a group and may feel somewhat insecure. Provision should therefore be made to make them feel at home at once, to make them acquainted with their classmates, and to keep them occupied with interesting activities. Pinning name cards to their clothes (the teacher should wear one, too) is a good "ice-breaking" activity and at the same time a good introduction to the concept of reading as meaningful communication. Other first-day activities might include telling or reading a story to the children, playing a simple game, drawing pictures, or learning a song. Discussion, too, is an important aid to children in making that first significant orientation to the larger group. Boys and girls may be asked, for example, to tell in turn how many brothers and sisters they have, what their father's occupation is, and where they live.

Meanwhile there is much to explain to the children about procedures. They need to learn how to take care of drawing and other supplies, where to place their wraps, what routine is followed when going to the toilet, and how to take turns when talking. These explanations should, of course, not be made in rapid succession. On the first day, only the briefest and most essential directions should be given. The routines are learned gradually over a period of many days.

At the end of the day each child should feel that he has learned something. Since many boys and girls come to school believing that they will immediately learn to read and write, the teacher should not disappoint them. She may have them "read" their names and a few words, in a functional setting, that she writes on the board, like "Good Morning," or "There are 26 children in our room." The children can be satisfied that they have been writing, if, for example, the teacher asks them to copy their names from the name cards on the pictures they draw.

TESTING   It is generally unwise to give intelligence or reading readiness tests during the first week or two in a first grade.

Many children, finding themselves in a completely new kind of environment, are not totally at ease in school during the first days and weeks. Their real abilities may therefore not be reflected in the standardized tests. Moreover, the tasks that are set in the standardized tests may leave the initial impression with some children that life in school can be quite difficult.

When tests are given, they should be administered in the spirit of play. The number of pupils who take them at one time should be limited—perhaps to ten or twelve—so that the teacher will have no difficulty in making the directions clear and in supervising each child's responses to the directions. Under some conditions the number should perhaps be even smaller. In order that the necessary condition of reasonable quiet prevail during the testing, it is desirable to conduct it away from the presence of other children. If possible, the other children should be cared for at this time by some other teacher. If this is not possible, independent work or play activities should be arranged for the other children.

Tests are often given to children individually at various times of the school day. Since the tests are relatively short, it is often possible to give them to two or three pupils a day. The testing can thereby be completed within a few weeks. In schools that do not use standardized tests, teachers are encouraged to keep particularly detailed records of their observations of pupil performance. During the pretesting and testing periods especially, all teachers should be alert to information with respect to the readiness factors discussed in Chapter 4B, such as physical health and maturity, sensory acuity and discrimination, experience background, interest in reading, language development, and ability to follow directions. Such information should whenever possible be included in anecdotal form in the pupils' folders.

ORGANIZATION OF THE PREREADING PROGRAM   Different approaches may be made to the organization of instruction during the prereading period. Those who believe in complete individualization of instruction in silent reading in the primary grades hold that the organization should be very informal. They advocate a wide and rich variety of nonreading activities for all children. They stress the need for a great variety of attractive reading materials and much story reading and storytelling. They assert that children who are ready will soon begin to want to read by themselves and will call on the teacher for help and that others will soon want to follow their example. If the teacher has carefully observed the children, she will have ideas as to which ones to encourage to read and with what reading materials to supply them. Other pupils will try, find it too hard and therefore uninteresting, and will give up for a time. With the teacher's encouragement they will return to the books when they are ready. Advocates of this plan insist that it is not a haphazard one. They believe it is the natural way to learn to read and that it will lead to the growth of sturdy habits in reading. Certainly such a plan calls for teachers of ability, but it is argued that many, if not most, teachers could learn to use it with success and satisfaction.

More formal plans are in use in most schools, especially those with large classes. In the larger elementary schools the first-grade pupils are often sectioned into more or less "homogeneous" classes. In certain of these classes, most or all of the first year is spent in "readiness" activities. In others, the formal reading instruction does not begin until after one or even several months of school. Still other classes begin reading instruction at once, if the children appear to be ready.

Since in a large number of elementary schools there is but one class for each grade level, grouping within the class is common. As the teacher studies the results of her appraisals, she will usually find great variation among the boys and girls. Typically she will have a small number who are already reading or who are ready or almost ready for beginning reading. She is likely also to have another group, frequently a larger one, for whom it is perhaps wise to postpone beginning reading instruction for a few weeks or longer. Almost always there will be a few pupils for whom it will be best to wait with book reading for a rather long time, possibly for several months. In addition, there may be one or more pupils who may not be ready for systematic reading instruction throughout most of the school year. The division into reading and reading readiness groups should be made after appraisal of all known factors related to beginning reading has been made. The groupings should be flexible so that no rigid barriers of administration will hinder a child from transferring easily from one group to another if his best interests are served by a change. The teacher also needs to give consideration to the size of the group. Many teachers have found groups of more than ten or twelve rather unwieldy when planning first-grade reading or prereading groups.

After the teacher has decided on desirable means of grouping, she is ready to make preliminary plans for the work both for small groups and for individuals. When making plans for those not ready to read, she will probably want to follow many of the suggestions given in Chapter 4B, "Developing Readiness for Reading."

INDEPENDENT WORK ACTIVITIES   Many primary-grade teachers ask, "While I am working with one reading group, how can I keep the other boys and girls engaged in worthwhile activities?"

Independent work activities can be valuable if the teacher is guided by the following principles:

1. *Independent work activities should help accomplish educationally sound objectives.* Mere busy work, intended to give the boys and girls something to do, cannot be justified. School time is too valuable to squander.

2. *The learning acquired through independent work activities should be commensurate with the time and energy expended.* For example, it is questionable to have boys and girls engage in a page of work that requires them to spend most of the time cutting and pasting in order to align given printed material with corresponding pictures. The same educational objective, accomplished through practice in reading, can usually be achieved more economically if, instead of cutting and pasting, they draw lines connecting words or sentences with the appropriate pictures.

3. *The activity should be free of undesirable features.* Much of the coloring of outlines on duplicated sheets or in workbooks is not only questionable as far as the accomplishment of educational objectives is concerned; it can actually be harmful if through the coloring the pupil becomes less creative in his subsequent expression of art. That such a danger exists many specialists in art as well as large numbers of classroom teachers attest.

Another undesirable feature of some independent activities is that through them the pupil loses interest in accomplishing the objective for which the work was assigned. If, for example, the purpose is to provide further practice on the vocabulary of reading selections, tedious drill on vocabulary exercises can be an interfering factor.

4. *Independent work activities should be adapted to individual differences.* To require all pupils at all times to do the same work is in flagrant violation of the findings of the psychology of learning. It is a waste of time to assign to a child work designed to give further practice on a skill he has already perfected. Furthermore, such practice may lead to boredom on the part of the child. Although it is often difficult to recognize what work a child needs, the teacher should try to adhere to the principle of assigning to an individual only those activities that would seem to be of value to him.

What has been said about the need of differentiated workbook activities also applies to sheets for independent activities produced by the teacher.

5. *The teacher should make certain that the boys and girls understand what is required of them.* Careful explanation and demonstration are often essential, especially if it is the first time that the boys

and girls perform that type of activity. With children who can read directions, silent reading of the directions is usually desirable. Sometimes it is helpful to have one or two examples of the type or types of activities to be performed worked out by the pupils beforehand as the teacher or a pupil does the necessary work on the chalkboard. Or all might do the first item or two in an exercise together and report what they did before the group starts independent work on the activity.

The Program for Beginning Reading

Each succeeding stage in the process of learning to read has problems peculiar to itself. The period of beginning reading, which usually starts for the child some time quite early in the first grade, if not before, and continues throughout that school year and often into the next, is no exception to this rule. In fact, in some respects the problems in this stage seem more crucial than those arising at any later period.

Some of the questions pertaining to instruction in beginning reading that are often asked by teachers are: What should be the role of the textbook in beginning reading? How can the textbook be used effectively? What provisions for directed reading beyond the use of the basal textbook can be made? How can reading be encouraged through group projects?

With these questions in mind, let us see what happens in the typical modern elementary classroom.

CLASSROOM PROCEDURE   The following description of activities pertaining to reading in which first-grade children engage is not based on any one classroom, but it is characteristic of an increasing number throughout the country.

Before school in the morning the boys and girls in the classroom are engaged in a variety of activities. Some are playing in the corner of the room in a playhouse made out of crates and furnished with equally rough furniture. Three boys are looking at the bulletin board on which the teacher has posted a picture of a calf, a sheep, and a dog above the question written in manuscript, "Do you have a pet?" One boy, who had previously asked the teacher what the question is, triumphantly reads it to his two classmates. Three boys and two girls are looking at picture books as they sit at the nicely arranged table in the library corner. At the same table several children are reading easy picture books with very simple text. Two other girls are asking the teacher what the text says under a picture in a book that intrigued them, which they found on the bookshelf near the library table. Two boys are feeding the rabbit according to simple directions posted on the chart. Still others are talking with one another about happenings of interest to them that took place since they had last seen each other. In this relaxed atmosphere the boys and girls begin their school day. Much of significance even for the reading program of the grade takes place during this period.

During the brief sharing time that marks the opening of school, incidental use is made of reading. As one of the boys shows small branches of two evergreen trees that his father has just planted in the yard of their new home, the teacher writes the words *pine* and *spruce* on the chalkboard and suggests that the boy attach the evergreens with binding tape at the appropriate place to the chalkboard so that all can see them. Another child, a girl, shows her new picture book and reads to the class what it says under an especially exciting-looking picture.

While plans are being made for the day's activities, opportunity for reading is again afforded incidentally. The teacher writes on the board the brief listing of events for the day as she and the children determine them. The question, "What do we do next?" as the teacher points to the words "Bob's group," attracts additional attention to the use that can be made of reading.

This is an exciting day for Bob's group. They can hardly wait for the teacher to come to their semicircle in the front of the room. The teacher had told the group yesterday that today would be a red-letter day for them, the day when they could begin reading out of books. Until this time they have confined their reading to experience charts of a variety of kinds, to labels in the room that have served a significant purpose, to notes the teacher has written on the bulletin boards or chalkboards, and to picture books that have had only little text, which from time to time the teacher read to them individually as they "followed" in the book. But now they are to have books all their own to read.

After the teacher has distributed the preprimers, the boys and girls are given time to examine the books and to make comments on pictures about which they think they will enjoy reading. After that the teacher, to use the terminology of the manuals published with this preprimer, makes the "approach" to the first lesson. Since this first story is about a boy and a girl who have a pet dog, the teacher gives the children an opportunity to tell briefly about their own pets. Reference is also made to the bulletin board on which pictures of pets are posted. Then the teacher says, "The boy and girl in our story also have a pet. It is a dog named...." As she gives the name of the dog, she refers to it on the chalkboard. She then has several of the boys and girls say the name. Similarly she introduces the pupils to the names of the boy and girl. She provides for practice on words in the story that the pupils have learned through experience charts or other incidental means. Then she presents the new words in the story. The boys and girls pronounce them and find some of them in their books. The teacher asks a leading question on the story before the pupils begin reading the selection sentence by sentence, first silently and then orally. Discussion, centered on content read, on the pictures, and on some of the words, takes place as the pupils read the few simple pages of the preprimer. The reading is followed by a short period during which the pupils discuss possibilities of what may happen next. As the teacher tells them that tomorrow they will find out what does happen, she notes the reluctance with which the pupils pass in their books. The main objective of the period has been accomplished: the boys and girls are eager to continue reading their new books. The teacher hopes always to plan her reading program so that the boys and girls will leave her reading group looking forward with anticipation to the next reading period.

Before the boys and girls go to their seats the teacher explains to them a "surprise" that she has for them. She has written in manuscript the new words that can be illustrated, one each at the bottom of a sheet of paper. Each child is given four pieces of paper, with the names of the boy and girl and the dog in the story and the word *pets*. The teacher explains to the children that they can make a booklet that will help them remember the new words they will meet in their first book. Brief practice in reading the words on the papers follows and plans are laid for drawing the pictures while the teacher works with one of the other groups.

In the meantime the rest of the boys and girls have been busy. One group, which has already finished the two levels of preprimers and of primers in the basal textbook series and has just been introduced to the first readers, has spent twenty minutes reading and illustrating a simple story about children playing that the teacher has written and duplicated. In planning the story, the teacher has taken care to use no words new to the pupils, for the children are still unable to attack words independently, unless the new word presents only a minor structural difference from one they already know. For example, they may be able to figure out the word *dogs* independently since they know the word *dog*. Similarly they probably can tell in context what the new word *playing* is because they have learned *play* as a sight word.

The boys and girls in Christine's group have been spending the same twenty minutes making new name cards for their desks. The children in the group have had no previous formal reading instruction.

The teacher has suggested that they might want to practice writing first on other paper. During the next twenty minutes, while the children in Maria's group are reading with the teacher, the pupils in Christine's group who have finished making their name cards are engaged in a variety of activities. Some are looking at picture books. Others are drawing pictures needed for the unit on which they are working, entitled, "Our First Grade." Still others are doing some housecleaning in the playhouse. All are participating in activities filled with possibilities for growth and development.

After the boys and girls in Maria's group assemble, a few minutes are taken to discuss progress in their illustration of the storybooks on which they had been working while Bob's group was reading. The reading lesson for the period, based on a story of activities of children at school, is divided into three parts: the approach to the lesson, the silent and oral reading of the story, and more intensive study of words than was made during the approach. The approach consists of the teacher's orienting the pupils to the story, through providing opportunity for them to discuss what they think the children in the story would play during their story hour. The teacher then tells them that in the story they will meet new words. She tells them she will help them beforehand with those words that she thinks they probably will not be able to figure out by themselves, but that she will not assist them with two that she is quite certain they will be able to decipher alone.

As the teacher helps the boys and girls with some of the new words, she makes use of various ways of presenting words, teaching some as sight words and others by means of context clues, and possibly some through phonetic or structural analysis. Then follows the period of actual reading. This time the selection is not broken up into parts only a sentence in length, as it had been for Bob's group. These boys and girls are able to read the story in their first reader paragraph by paragraph and occasionally even more than one paragraph at a time without help from the teacher. Before each of these parts is taken up, the teacher prepares the children for reading the paragraph or group of paragraphs by asking stimulating questions, by giving the pupils purpose for reading, by directing their attention to questions on the chalkboard which they will answer later, or by having them point to a designated new word that occurs in that part.

The membership of Christine's group is made up of three boys and girls for whom, on the basis of a variety of criteria, it was deemed inadvisable, as indicated earlier, at this time to begin reading in books. During their so-called reading period they are engaged in work on an experience chart for which, in connection with their unit on "Our

First Grade," they dictate to the teacher simple sentences describing their library corner. So that they can read the chart to the other groups, they then learn to "read" the sentences, as described in Chapter 4B, "Developing Readiness for Reading." At the same time they learn to identify a few of the new words of the chart. The words selected by the teacher are chiefly those that they are likely to need later in beginning reading.

GROUP PROJECTS   Participation in group projects in connection with the classroom reading experiences can serve a twofold purpose. It can make the children's reading more significant to them and it can help them derive the benefits inherent in activities other than reading. For example, oral reading can not only help the child become a better reader but also enable him to gain more self-confidence in other activities.

Here are some group activities that the teacher might encourage in order to accomplish the types of objectives suggested in the preceding paragraph. Brief mention of some of them has been made earlier.

1. Dramatizations can be used to provide interesting variety in teaching methods. In the early stages of so-called dramatization in the primary grades, the children can read by parts the direct quotations given in the book. This reading can in many cases profitably be preceded by preparation like the following: (a) children indicating the exact words of each speaker; (b) several pupils reading a given quotation as each child thinks it should be read; (c) members of the group commenting on the effectiveness of the reading; and (d) the class discussing the help of quotation marks in reading a selection by parts. Later on in dramatizations the children might supplement the reading by parts with simple actions suggested by the words. A discussion of appropriate actions might either precede or follow the initial dramatization. As children become more adept at dramatization, they might get along without their books and give the content of the story in their own words. Some groups have written their own plays based on a story that they have read. How perfect a production should be before work on it is abandoned must be determined in the light of the objectives to be accomplished. Some teachers spend altogether too much time on a given dramatization; others err in that they move on to another activity before the boys and girls have received the joy and other values of desirable perfection in the undertaking.

2. One form of dramatization that deserves special explanation is the puppet play. Even in the primary grades puppet plays can serve a useful purpose. While it is impossible to state the relative values

to be gained through puppetry as compared with other means of dramatization, there are doubtless advantages as well as shortcomings in puppet dramatizations. Some teachers find that through puppetry the shy youngster who feels self-conscious when he is seen by his audience can be helped in overcoming his reticence, since in puppet plays he can put dramatic quality into his voice while he himself is hidden from view. As in the case of other dramatizations, the presence of an audience lends purpose to the performance.

To use intricate puppets in the primary grades is, of course, undesirable. Some first-grade children will like to make simple paper dolls mounted on sticks as their puppets. Puppets made from paper bags admirably serve the purposes of some first-grade children. Suggestions on puppetry are given on pages 325–327.

3. The home-made "movie" is a project that has been used by many primary teachers with great success in connection with reading activities. In one first grade this procedure was followed in illustrating the story "The Circus" in the book *I Know a Secret*.[1] After the children in one reading group had read the story, they decided to make a "movie" to show to the other children in their first grade. First the teacher listed on the board the children's suggestions for pictures to be included in the "movie," along with her own. Then the group, under the direction of the teacher, worked out the sequence in which the pictures were to appear. Next, as they discussed what was to be written under each picture, the teacher jotted down the recommended comments. Thereupon each child agreed to draw one or more pictures on paper of the size to fit into the home-made stage. After the boys and girls had altered some of their pictures to incorporate suggestions that seemed helpful, the pictures, followed in each case by the appropriate sentences written in manuscript by the teacher, were fastened together with pressure-sensitive tape to form the roll to be shown on the "stage." The children next practiced reading the words of the "movie." Thereupon the "movie" was shown to the guests. The following three sentences, suggestive of the others, were used with the first three pictures:

Father is taking Bob and Nancy to the circus.
Bob is mailing a letter to Jack and Jean.
Jack and Jean are showing Mother the letter.

4. Various methods can be employed to enrich the children's background for reading. Field trips, when well conducted, can make

[1] Gertrude Hildreth and others, *I Know a Secret*, pp. 106–131. New York: Holt, Rinehart and Winston, Inc.

significant contributions to the reading program. For example, comprehension of a reading unit on the farm and interest in it can be increased through a visit to a farm. A few of the many other field trips that might be of profit in connection with reading in the primary grades are trips to the post office, the fire station, the airport, the zoo, and the grocery store. To get the most value from a field trip it is necessary to make careful preparation for the trip and, after the trip is completed, to make effective use of what was observed.

5. To give children a better background for reading, there are times when exhibits prove more profitable than field trips. Collecting and then exhibiting interesting and significant objects constitute one means of extending the children's horizons. Sometimes reproductions of objects like airplanes or silos can be made and put on exhibit. In one grade that was reading about the Arabs, objects similar to those used by those people were made and shown to the rest of the boys and girls.

In these and in many other ways, activities for reading or for encouraging reading can be provided throughout the school day as the boys and girls participate in a primary grade program rich in opportunities for growth. As they experiment with the effect of water on plants, for example, they can read the labels *water* and *no water* that are placed near the appropriate flower pots. A record that indicates on what days the one plant is to be watered also furnishes meaningful material for reading even for the child in the prereading period. Some children in that stage read the captions which, at their dictation, the teacher has written under their pictures illustrating the need plants have for water. In connection with a unit on "Our First Grade," the children could read an experience chart about their library corner which they had dictated to the teacher. Thus reading is also taught during periods not set aside for that purpose alone; in fact, some of the best opportunities for reading are afforded during parts of the school day not designated as reading periods.

Reading in Grades Two and Three

It is in grades two and three that there usually is rapid growth in developing independence in the identification and recognition of words, in comprehending relatively difficult material, in learning to read at appropriate rates, in reading a large variety of materials, and in using reference materials suited to the level.

In order to help boys and girls attain the objectives implied in the preceding paragraph, many teachers find it desirable to include within their program of reading instruction three phases—namely:

(1) reading as carried on in connection with a basal reading textbook; (2) reading in connection with other areas of the curriculum; (3) independent reading. On the next few pages are given suggestions as to how the teacher of the second or third grade can guide the learning in the first two phases of the reading program named here. How she can help pupils with reading in connection with the content areas is discussed in Chapters 11A and 11B so that, as a result of harmonious development in all of these aspects, the child will leave this stage of learning to read possessing the ability to read books on his level independently and with enjoyment.

USE OF BASAL READING TEXTBOOKS   The procedures best fitted to the use of reading textbooks in grades two and three are different in some respects from those that can be used most advantageously during the period of beginning reading. These differences result in part from the characteristics of the average boy and girl at that stage of development and in part from the fact that boys and girls have already acquired—to only a small extent, to be sure—some of the skills of reading that were previously lacking.

Since the need for grouping and individualization of work in reading persists, the problem of providing activities for children working independently at their seats is still present. However, it no longer taxes the ingenuity of the teacher quite as much as in the preceding stage of reading, for, once the child has acquired enough independence to read without help for a twenty-minute period or longer, the independent activities can be closely related to the reading he is doing in the basal reader. The following recommendations suggest some of the ways in which the teacher can help the pupils utilize to good advantage the time during which the teacher is busy helping other boys and girls.

1. In the independent work period set aside time for reading silently a part of the reading textbook, for which the preparation has been given during the reading period. In order to use this procedure to best advantage it is usually desirable to have the study period follow, rather than precede, the class period. In this way, the children first get the needed help on a selection as their reading group meets and then do part of the reading on that selection independently when the teacher no longer is free to help them. It is especially important that this be the case with the poorer groups. When it is not possible to have the independent work period immediately follow the class period, it is often necessary for the teacher to spend a few minutes with each group immediately before they begin their independent work. The teacher will need to use these minutes to remind

the group of the assignment made earlier and sometimes to review briefly the new words or in other ways prepare the boys and girls for the silent-reading work. It is usually best to avoid using such a period as preparation for the next class.

2. If during the period of independent work the pupils read some pages of the reading textbook for the first time, the last part of that period should frequently be used for testing their comprehension. For example, if the boys and girls have read a selection during this study period, the teacher may wish to tell them that when they have finished the reading they should answer questions, copies of which have already been distributed to the children. If the aim is to test recall without the use of the book to facilitate recall, the teacher should make certain that the boys and girls do not look at the questions before or while they are reading the book. The questions may be simple fact questions which require underlining, writing *yes* or *no*, or writing on a blank the correct word of a list that has been provided. (In such a method the child's concern is not with spelling the word correctly.) Some of these and other directions, which the pupils might follow to show their comprehension and retention of what they read silently, can well be modeled after some that are found in the better workbooks.

3. Make use of the workbooks that accompany the readers. Frequently the exercises in a workbook can be of value to many of the boys and girls. They should not be used, however, unless they serve a worthwhile purpose. Nor should all pupils be required to do an exercise if in the best judgment of the teacher not all would profit from doing it. Two types of purposes can be accomplished by means of the workbooks. They can be used to test the pupil's comprehension as well as to provide more practice in reading, especially in reading to follow directions.

At times it is desirable, either during the preceding class period or else for a few minutes at the beginning of the independent work period, for the teacher to help the boys and girls in getting started on the workbook exercise. As a rule, if they can read the directions silently, neither the teacher nor one of the pupils should read them orally to the group; the silent reading of the directions affords such good practice in reading directions that usually the children should not be deprived of this opportunity. To make certain that everyone knows what to do after he has read the directions silently, the teacher may at times wish to ask the pupils to tell in their own words what they are to do. Sometimes, however, mere reading of the directions and stating of them are not enough. At such times the boys and girls could be helped, as a group, to do an item written on the board that is similar to those in the exercise. It may also be helpful to have the group as a whole, under the guidance of the teacher, do the first one or two parts of the workbook exercise so that there will be no question as to procedure.

Boys and girls able to read second- and third-grade readers can often profit greatly by correcting their workbooks during the class period. The teacher, however, will usually find it desirable to check the work herself, for through her examination of the work she can determine not only whether the boys and girls are finding their errors but also what their mistakes are. The latter type of information should be utilized in planning further learning activities.

4. Have the boys and girls read orally in small groups. While the teacher is engaged with one reading group, the other boys and girls can be reading to each other quietly in other sections of the room. It is usually advisable that in the second and third grades the size of the groups reading orally without the teacher's help should be limited to three or four. Provision should be made for a pupil in each group to serve as leader. The material read at this time can be either from the textbook material that has already been read in class or from some related reading material the pupils have had an opportunity to read silently or orally beforehand. Unless the teacher has established in the room a spirit of work, however, she should not attempt small-group work at times when she is busy with one reading group. On the other hand, in a well-organized room where orderliness conducive to work is the accepted standard, with proper guidance the boys and girls can, in this manner, be taught to get part of the needed practice in oral reading. One precaution that should be observed is that after the boys and girls have once learned to read more rapidly silently than orally, the listeners should not follow in their books while someone is reading to them.

5. Provide opportunity for the pupils to read references other than their basal textbook in order to gain information that they will need in connection with selections studied in their reader. If, for example, while reading a section on "Animal Friends" in their textbook the group has decided to make a booklet on some of the "animal friends" in their section of the country, one animal may be assigned to each child for further study. If the work that the boys and girls are to do during the study period is well planned beforehand, many of the skills required for locating and utilizing reference material can be developed. The pupils could prepare as talks the important information that they have gathered, and later, with further help from the teacher,

record it either in paragraph form or as separate sentences containing facts about the animals studied. If the boys and girls use the study period in this manner, the tasks should be on their level of development. When the children are in the earlier stages of learning to make use of such materials, the teacher will often find it advisable to select for each pupil a book in which he will find information on his topic. After the pupils have developed more skill, they can be helped to make use of more than one reference book and to find books without the teacher's help. Many suggestions for using reference materials during study periods are found in Chapters 8A and 8B.

6. Set aside some periods for illustrative work on the materials taken up in the basal textbook. Sometimes this can be in the form of making a picture dictionary on words and concepts learned while reading a section of the textbook. At other times it may be work on a mural suggested by the story. Whatever the type of illustration, it is important that the work should not be done just as "busywork." If it is to be justified as an activity that extends the reading in the textbook, it must serve such purposes as the following: to interest the boys and girls further in the book; to whet their appetites for more reading on the subject discussed in the book; to stimulate the pupils to read the selections in the book more carefully; to serve as a means by which the teacher can evaluate how adequately the pupils have comprehended and retained the information given in the book.

7. Let the pupils plan dramatizations of stories in the textbook. If during the reading period the boys and girls have worked out carefully with the teacher plans for dramatizing a story given in the book, during the independent work period they can meet without the teacher in small groups to work out the scenes, settings, and costuming. Again, a caution should be noted: a teacher who has difficulty in maintaining a good spirit of work and cooperation in her room should not attempt to have the pupils work in groups when she is busy with a reading group, for chaos may result.

The suggestions that have been made for utilizing the independent work period effectively can be adapted with slight modifications for use during the reading class. The following are additional suggestions for the period when the teacher is helping one of the two or three "homogeneous" reading groups.

1. During the approach to a lesson, if it seems advisable to present some of the new words before the pupils meet them in their reading, one of the aims of the teacher should be to help the boys and girls grow toward independence in word recognition as rapidly as possible, but without haste or tension. To accomplish this purpose

the teacher can make use of many suggestions listed in Chapters 5A and 5B.

Other aims of the teacher during the approach should be to provide the informational background for the selection and to stimulate interest in it. In the case of a selection about Indian children, for example, the boys and girls might first discuss some of the ways in which life of Indian children differs from theirs or they might discuss a picture showing how an Indian woman taught her little daughter to weave a basket. After this discussion leading up to the selection to be read, the teacher might state the objective—in this case, "Let's read the story to find out in what ways the Indian children's education differs from ours."

2. During the reading of the selection it is not, as a rule, necessary, or even desirable, to break up the material for reading into the short parts suggested for the beginning reading period. In grades two and three the pupils can often read one or two or even three pages without a break in the silent reading. For example, in a seven-page selection for reading during a class period, the teacher may decide to divide the material into only three parts, after the approach to the entire selection has been made. Preceding the reading of each of the three parts, she can help the pupils to increase their awareness in reading by having them read silently, before they begin reading the part in the book, questions on the board to which they will find the answer in the part to be read; by giving orally an objective they should have in mind while reading that part; or by asking questions as to what they think will happen, followed by comments such as, "Let's read to find out what really happens." After the pupils have read the part silently, comprehension can be increased and checked by having them answer questions on the board, discuss questions asked orally, read orally sentences that prove a point, or locate some of the new words. The part may then be read orally by one or more pupils. In these grades it is usually wise to divide the story for the period into several parts in the manner indicated rather than to have the pupils read the whole selection for the day without any break through comments or questions or directions. The latter type of reading, which is very valuable, can as a rule be done by the pupils during periods when the teacher is not available to guide their reading more carefully.

3. The follow-up to the reading in parts in grades two and three can be in the form of word study, which not only should emphasize the new words found in the selection but also assist the children to improve in ability to arrive at independence in word recognition.

Help should be given in making use of context clues, in recognizing words by means of structural analysis, and in making use of phonics. How this can be done is suggested in Chapters 5A and 5B dealing with word recognition.

READING IN VARIOUS CURRICULUM AREAS   Reading in the social studies and science in the primary grades is primarily a means of acquiring much interesting and significant information. Furthermore, when wise guidance is given as the boys and girls read both textbook material and supplementary books, they will improve in ability to read a number of types of material. Chapter 11 is devoted to a discussion of reading in the content areas for both primary and intermediate grades.

INDEPENDENT READING   No program of reading instruction in grades two and three can be considered complete if it does not make provision for extensive free, independent reading.

One of the chief problems in respect to independent reading in these grades is helping boys and girls find material on their level. If they cannot find books that they will enjoy reading, they are not likely to continue reading during their leisure time. It is for this reason that many primary-grade teachers are constantly looking for suitable books. The teacher equipped with information about new and old books of high quality for children is then able to make specific recommendations for books to be added to the room library or to the school library. She can also be of help in guiding boys and girls to find suitable books in the public library. Furthermore, many librarians in public libraries welcome suggestions for ordering books when the recommendations are given by teachers who show that they know the field of literature for children.

An attractive library table in the classroom can be an important factor in encouraging children to do independent reading. Even in the lower grades the pupils can be given the opportunity to read at the library table not only before school and during part of the noon intermission but also at times during the school day while another part of the class is engaged in other activities. A stimulus for independent reading is often provided when the teacher sets aside, from time to time, a period of the school day during which the boys and girls can read their so-called "library books."

Thus a rich program of reading instruction can be set up for boys and girls in grades two and three if the teacher makes adequate provision for a basal reading program, for free reading, and for reading in connection with units of work and with other activities in the various subject areas. (See Chapters 10A, 10B, and 11.)

THE READING PROGRAM IN THE INTERMEDIATE GRADES

The first part of this chapter shows how some of the suggestions for developing reading growth given earlier in the book can be incorporated into the primary-grade reading program. This part similarly gives recommendations for putting into operation a well-rounded program in the intermediate grades.

Problems Confronting the Teacher

A few of the problems that appear quite persistently with intermediate-grade teachers and their supervisors will be considered in this section of the chapter.

WHAT SHOULD BE ACCOMPLISHED? One reason why teaching reading in the intermediate grades presents problems is that teachers often do not have clearly in mind what should be accomplished in those grades. Many have only a general objective in mind—for example, "helping the child to become a better reader"—and consequently they often proceed to teach reading rather haphazardly without having valid criteria for determining methods of teaching or means of evaluation to be used.

Some of the chief reading tasks of the average reader in grades four, five, and six are: (1) to become skillful enough in reading so that through reading he can greatly extend and enrich his experiences and can thereby acquire much information and knowledge; (2) to continue in the development of speed in silent reading so that he will be able to read easy material on his level much more rapidly silently than orally and to learn to read at appropriate rates for various purposes using materials of varying difficulty; (3) to learn to read so well orally that it is interesting to listen to him; (4) to acquire complete independence in the ability to identify new words; (5) to develop skill in the use of the dictionary; (6) to acquire so much ability in comprehending what he reads that he can understand fairly difficult materials; (7) to achieve power in reading with discrimination; and (8) to acquire interest and skill in reading in various fields of learning.

Chapters 10A and 10B give many additional suggestions for interesting children in doing independent reading.

SHOULD A PERIOD BE SET ASIDE FOR READING INSTRUCTION? No simple *yes* or *no* answer can be given to this question. Undoubtedly some teachers have attained excellent results without providing for a special period in the daily program for instruction in reading. The objectives of reading in the intermediate grades can be accomplished with or without such a period.

It is probably safe to say that generally most teachers should be advised to plan their intermediate-grade program to include a separate period for teaching reading. This recommendation is made because many teachers do not have the time to devise an adequate program of reading instruction in which all the work on reading needed to accomplish the objectives can be done in connection with the various content areas. Furthermore, some teachers do not possess the skill needed for this type of well-planned, yet incidental, teaching. For these reasons and others, many teachers find they can more readily achieve the objectives of reading instruction in the intermediate grades if they have a daily reading period. Even in programs that include such a period, however, it is still very important that emphasis be placed on reading at other times of the school day, for not all the objectives can be accomplished adequately if the instruction is confined to the reading period.

WHAT SHOULD BE TAUGHT DURING THE READING PERIOD?   Teachers who have decided to set apart a period in the school day for teaching reading often wonder what should be taught during that period and what work in reading should be reserved for other times in the day. Again, no short authoritative answer can be given. It probably makes little difference as to what part of the school day is devoted to procedures that will help accomplish the objectives of reading instruction. The important thing is that learning-to-read activities should be done under those circumstances that are likely to be most productive of results. For example, dictionary work can be carried on effectively either during a reading period or in connection with reading in the social studies.

Even though no definite allocation of work to the reading period and to other times of the school days can be made, there are a few guidelines that the teacher may find helpful to follow. One is that it is often desirable to use the reading period when a new phase of a reading skill is to be developed or when more practice than that afforded by the incidental reading during other times in the school days seems necessary. Another guideline is that the incentive for learning a new skill can often originate in connection with work other than that taken up during the reading period. For example, real motivation to learn to use an encyclopedia can develop for a child if in science he finds he needs more information than that given in books other than encyclopedias. On the other hand, application of learnings acquired during reading class can be made when pupils are working on a unit, solving some problems in arithmetic, or studying in some other area.

SHOULD THE CLASS BE DIVIDED INTO READING GROUPS? The intermediate-grade teacher who has decided on having a separate period in the school day for reading instruction needs to make the further decision as to whether she will teach all the boys and girls in the room at the same time or whether she will divide them into groups during the reading class. Although much can be done to adapt instruction to the needs of the boys and girls in a nongrouped situation if proper attention is paid to individual differences, nevertheless many teachers find they can work more advantageously if they have at least two groups for reading. Their decision is often based to a considerable extent on the wide variations in reading skills in the typical fourth or fifth or sixth grade. It is not at all uncommon, for example, to find in a fifth grade a pupil who reads no better than the average second-grade child and at the same time to find one or more who read on the level of the average pupil in the sixth or seventh grades.

One argument frequently advanced against grouping in these grades is that with the many other studies in the intermediate grades not enough time is available for reading to make grouping advisable. If, for example, only forty minutes can be devoted to the reading class, and the class is divided into two groups, the teacher may be able to spend only about half of that time with each. Through skillful planning, however, the teacher can provide valuable reading activities for one group during the time when she is helping another section of the class.

Description of Classroom Procedure

In order to see how the suggestions for teaching reading in the intermediate grades can be put into practice, let us take note of what can be observed in a modern elementary classroom in which reading is taught effectively. Descriptions will be given of several types of hypothetical classroom situations that are typical of many.

A CLASSROOM WITH A GROUPED READING CLASS In Miss Westlund's fifth grade the thirty-five pupils have been divided into two sections. In the lower group there are nine pupils who are a year or more below grade level in reading, one as much as two years below. The grouping was determined through the use of standardized tests as well as by means of teacher-made tests, observations by the teacher, and study of records of past progress. More pupils were placed in the upper group, in this case, because the teacher wished to have in a separate group those boys and girls whose ability was decidedly below that of their grade level. The teacher, however, recognized that the division need not necessarily have been made at that point. She was also aware of the fact that it is not necessary in all cases to place more pupils in the brighter group. She knew that there are many possible justifiable points of division if a teacher will teach each group according to the characteristics of the boys and girls as they are sectioned.

Miss Westlund did not try to hide from the boys and girls the fact that the grouping was done on the basis of ability. She realized that if she tried to make a secret of the method of grouping, the children would soon find out for themselves why they were so divided. Rather, she discussed the situation with them frankly and thereby did much to help avoid the feeling of disgrace often experienced by a child who is placed in a lower group and learns of his placement without the understanding, yet factual, explanation of the teacher. The teacher tried to explain the division by telling the pupils that she had attempted to place each child in the group in which she thought he could most advantageously learn to read. A similar explanation was made to the parents. Although it would be an exaggeration to state that each child in the lower group was happy to be in that section, nevertheless most of the children did not feel the stigma of the placement as they might easily have done had they learned of it through unkind remarks from classmates.

Miss Westlund set aside, as a rule, 50 minutes daily for reading instruction. She did not designate 25 minutes for each group, but rather kept the division of the total 50 minutes elastic so that according to the work planned for each group for the day she could decide how best to use the time. Occasionally the children in one of the groups spent the entire period reading without the teacher's help, while Miss Westlund devoted her time to the other group. At times she spent the 50 minutes helping individuals in both groups while the rest of the pupils were engaged in well-planned work on reading. At still other times she taught the entire class as a whole, either during part of the period or during all of it. She used the latter method, for example, in presenting work on how to use an encyclopedia, a set of which belonged to the room. At the same time, however, she recognized the differences in ability of the boys and girls and adapted the instruction to those individual differences. At one point a child in the lower group gave his interpretation of a picture, while another child from the higher group read to the class the short paragraph that answered a question the teacher had asked.

When the class was divided into two groups throughout the period, the teacher would sometimes help those in the lower group first and at other times she would first work with those in the higher section. The order was determined by the type of assignment. The following are two examples of how the 50 minutes might be divided. (Group One designates the higher group.)

9:00–9:10   *Group One:* Presentation of new work, under teacher direction
            Group Two: Silent reading of a brief selection presented the preceding day

9:10–9:40   *Group One:* Silent reading of the part presented from 9:00 to 9:10, followed by pupil answering of questions in writing, to serve as a check on comprehension of what was read
            Group Two:
            a. Oral check on interpretation of material pupils read silently during the preceding ten minutes, with oral reading of parts to prove a point
            b. Timed silent reading

9:40–9:50   *Group One:*
            a. Checking written work that pupils did during part of the preceding half hour
            b. Explanation of assignment of work pupils are to do independently at the beginning of the reading period on the following day
            Group Two: Pupil writing of answers to questions on the material they read silently at the end of the preceding half-hour period

9:00–9:30   *Group One:* Planning, under the teacher's guidance, the dramatization of a story the pupils had finished reading during the preceding day
            Group Two: Reading silently material on their level on topics assigned individually, on which they will report to the class; beginning work on planning the reports

9:30–9:50   *Group One:* Independent planning by each pupil of work for his part of the dramatization
            Group Two: Further work, under teacher guidance, on reports to be given to the class

A CLASSROOM WITH A NONGROUPED READING CLASS

In contrast to the plan adopted by Miss Westlund for her fifth-grade class, Mrs. Henricks did not divide her class into two groups, although she was aware of the fact that the range in reading ability in her class was approximately the same as that in Miss Westlund's. She realized, of course, that she would need to pay special attention to the needs of the individuals in her class if she was to make the reading class profitable for everyone.

Like Miss Westlund, Mrs. Henricks tried to discover the ability of each child through standardized tests, teacher-made tests, study of records, informal observation, and conferences. She then set varying objectives that she hoped to be able to have each child, individually, reach. She also planned how she might help each pupil most effectively. As she did so, she found that certain boys and girls had some problems in common. Six of them were markedly deficient in the ability to use phonics as a means of unlocking new words. Their problems were similar enough so that the teacher knew that at times she could meet with them in a small group to give them special help. Two of these six pupils, as well as two others, were unable to find words rapidly in the dictionary because they were not certain of the alphabetical order of letters. In the case of these four the teacher also made plans for helping them in a small group from time to time, even though she also knew that within this small group she would have to individualize the work because the problems of these pupils, though similar, were not identical.

The small-group work was often done during part of the 50-minute period that Mrs. Henricks set aside daily for reading class. While she helped either individuals or small groups, the other boys and girls were engaged in reading activities which they could do without her immediate attention. She also, at times other than reading class period, met with either the small groups or individuals needing special attention; occasionally these meetings were held before or after school. While the rest of the pupils were doing independent work in the social studies or science or arithmetic, Mrs. Henricks was alert to possibilities for helping those boys and girls who needed special attention in any field, reading included.

In addition to helping pupils individually or in small groups on their special problems, Mrs. Henricks from time to time, in a carefully planned program, tried to adapt instruction to individual differences by means such as the following:

1. When she assigned oral reading for an audience-type situation, she gave the easier selections to the children whose skill in reading was below average.

2. She often asked the easier questions of the pupils who were having some difficulty in answering harder ones. She also tried to ask questions of the better readers that would challenge them.

3. Often when she introduced new work during a reading class, she would have the entire group together at the beginning of the period. After part of the class was ready to work independently on the problem, she would assign work to them that they could do without

her help. Then she would continue working with the pupils who needed more attention before they could go ahead with the new work independently.

4. While some pupils who did not need teacher help at a given time were doing independent reading, often in books of their own choice, the teacher gave additional help to those who seemed to require more guidance on the phase of learning to read on which the class was working.

A CLASSROOM WITH NO READING CLASS Miss Leamington's fifth grade is an example of a modern elementary classroom in which no time on the daily schedule of work is devoted to a reading class. The work is not haphazard, for Miss Leamington plans her work carefully and systematically so that it will fit the needs of the various individuals in her classroom.

Like Miss Westlund and Mrs. Henricks, Miss Leamington set out at the beginning of the school year to ascertain the abilities of each of her pupils. She, too, did this through standardized and teacher-made tests, through examination of records, through informal observation, and through conferences. Next she set up the objectives that she wanted to accomplish with each child. Roughly, too, she tried to determine what activities connected with the work in the various curricular areas each child might profitably engage in in order to acquire the skill that she hoped he would be able to achieve. She also was confronted with the problem of sequence—that is, deciding at what times the pupils could most profitably engage in each type of activity. Thus, in her plans for the year, she tried to take into account the individual needs of the children.

Miss Leamington gave some of the help in reading as the pupils did leisure-time reading. Most of it she gave in connection with the content subjects as she used procedures such as those discussed in Chapter 11, "Reading in the Content Areas." Often she used such procedures as a springboard, for teaching needed generalizations. The following one will serve as an example.

Sometimes after the pupils had read a selection in the content areas, she would ask the pupils to name words that they could not identify. She would then help them with these words, trying to give the help in such a way that the pupils would grow in power to learn new words independently. At times she would stop to give them aid in developing some rule of phonetic or structural analysis that they needed; at other times she would give them additional practice on the application of some generalization that they had been helped earlier to make.

THE SCHOOL-WIDE PROGRAM IN READING

An effective program of reading instruction in the school calls for aggressive leadership and careful overall planning. In this section we shall consider: (1) what conditions are essential to a strong reading program; (2) what steps are needed for the development of the school-wide program; and (3) in what ways the program can be interpreted to parents. Part of what we consider here is a summary or an application of principles discussed earlier in this book.

Conditions Needed for an Effective Program

The teaching of reading is not carried on in a vacuum. Effective reading instruction calls for a school environment favorable to learning, to growth, to solid achievement. Teachers can do much to create the conditions that are needed for helping children to read. The following are some of these conditions:

1. *The physical surroundings should be suitable.* While it is true that some children learn to read under the most unfavorable physical conditions, if we are to get the best results with the huge numbers of children who come to us for reading instruction, we must provide schoolrooms that are light, comfortable, and colorful. The furniture should include comfortable seats, movable desks adjustable to the physical requirements of the children, a display table for books, many open shelves along the walls, and a reading corner with a table, a lamp, and an easy chair or two. Colors in the room should be bright and cheerful. Plants in the windows; bulletin boards with constantly changing exhibits of pictures, announcements, information about the date, recent incidents affecting children in the room, and other subjects of interest to pupils; objects brought by teacher or pupils for reading and discussion—all these, and many other "conversation pieces" that may stimulate reading and discussion, should be a part of the elementary school classroom. Records, films, filmstrips, and other audio-visual aids should be readily available when the occasion calls for them.

2. *The children should be surrounded by an abundance of attractive reading materials.* Children's books, tastefully arranged, representing a wide range of reading difficulty and a great diversity of interests should be found on the shelves and on the tables in all classrooms. Suitable magazines, pamphlets, and pictorial matter should be displayed on racks or deposited in files to which teacher and pupils have easy access.

3. *A well-equipped and well-managed central library is essential to the school-wide reading program.* The library should have the latest reference books, an up-to-date card index, vertical files, a wide variety of children's magazines, and an abundance of books, including the great children's classics and books on hobbies, adventure, humor, science, history, biography, and fiction. The library should be the center of the "cultural" activities of the school. It should display paintings, sculpture, and other art objects that may be acquired by the school through loan or purchase. Science materials of various kinds may be exhibited here. It should, if possible, have two or more small conference rooms for pupils' committee work. It should have a librarian's office and workroom, and a storage room for back issues of magazines and other materials. It should be the repository for the visual aids to be made available to all classes in the school. Moreover, the library should be large enough to accommodate not only a whole class which may come for one or more periods during the week for browsing or for special assignments but also small groups and individual pupils who are doing research in connection with classroom projects. Arrangements should be made for systematic use of library facilities by whole classes, and individual pupils should be encouraged to make frequent use of the library. Its use should not be reserved as a "privilege" for the bright or the "best-behaved" pupils.

4. *Reading problems should receive attention in all of the content subjects.* The teaching of reading should not be confined to a single period in the school day. Chapter 11 deals with reading in the content areas.

5. *The morale of the teaching staff should be high.* No school-wide program or reading improvement can be really successful if it does not enjoy the enthusiastic support of the entire teaching staff. For this reason every effort should be made to provide the conditions under which high morale may flourish. This book is not the place to discuss in minute detail the factors contributing to staff morale. These factors are complex and often elusive. Good salary levels, job security, pension funds, reasonable teacher load—all of these are essential, but by themselves they will not guarantee good morale. Strong administrative leadership coupled with sincere adherence to the democratic process on the part of everyone, respect for each other's opinions, and sympathetic concern for each other's problems are likewise important elements in the building of morale. Good communication, too, is necessary. Facts regarding the general reading situation in the school should be disseminated among the staff. In-service training of teachers by providing time, opportunity, and encouragement to study the reading

problem is not the least of the factors needed to mobilize the professional resources of the school for the improvement of reading.

6. *The classroom climate should be conductive to pleasant learning experiences.* Many of the factors that contribute to good school morale are also needed in the creation of a classroom climate favorable to efficient learning. Strong teacher leadership combined with a high degree of pupil participation in decision-making, a sympathetic interest in the individual needs of pupils, and an atmosphere of encouragement to explore, to question, and to discuss are needed to stimulate maximum effort on the part of pupils. In such a climate, children feel accepted. Rivalry and competition are kept on a friendly basis. Humor and spontaneous laughter are familiar experiences in each day's activities.

The nature and organization of the curriculum, too, may vitally affect the learning climate of the classroom. If there is an abundance of purposeful activities related to problems of genuine interest to children, reading also is likely to be zestful and purposeful.

The way in which the children are grouped in the classroom has much to do with classroom climate. A plan of flexible grouping, described earlier in this book, is less likely to lead to hostilities and frustrations than a rigid one. It has been suggested that groups should be known by the names of their leaders rather than by such designations as the Bluebirds or the Bunnies and that leaders should be changed often. Every child has the right to feel wanted and needed in the group in which he works.

Basically, however, the classroom climate depends upon the relations between the teacher and the class, and among the children themselves. The moods and attitudes of the teacher are quickly communicated to the children. If the teacher seems to regard her job chiefly as one of discovering the children's failures and shortcomings, the children soon come to see their own role as one of outwitting her and of doing as little work as possible. If the teacher thinks of her responsibility as one of stimulating and challenging the children, they are likely to take a positive attitude toward the work. They will find pleasure in it, and they will learn more because they enjoy what they are doing. Thus a teacher who calls on a pupil to read a paragraph aloud and then asks the class to point out the mistakes he made is likely to produce little else than embarrassment in both the pupil and the rest of the class. A teacher who says to the class, "Let's find as many colorful words in this passage as we can" and asks a child to write them on the board as the words are called is inviting her pupils to an exciting hunt.

The children should have the feeling that the teacher likes them, often in spite of their eccentricities and their deviation from the cultural norm.

Steps in Planning a School-wide Program

The initiative in undertaking a school-wide program of reading instruction may come from any one or more of many sources. Sometimes a series of newspaper articles or a critical book may focus attention on the problem and hence lead to thoughtful re-examination of current practices in reading instruction. Sometimes an enthusiastic administrator, or a teacher freshly returned from a semester of professional study, sparks the program. Frequently a study will emerge from faculty discussions of a commonly felt need. Whatever its impetus, the program can be successfully undertaken only if a large proportion of the teaching staff sees the need for it and volunteers to participate in it.

DETERMINING THE READING STATUS OF PUPILS "How are we doing?" is the first question to ask when we plan the school-wide program. We need to know whether our present program is getting results, whether our achievements are above or below national norms, and, especially, what our special strengths and weaknesses are. Teachers know that many of their pupils do not read as well as they should, but they will find it helpful to have specific information as to the range of pupils' reading abilities and the degree of reading retardation that exists in their schools. The first step in a general reading program, therefore, is a careful study of the existing situation with respect to pupils' reading.

Although standardized reading tests have definite limitations and should never be regarded as infallible barometers of reading ability, they are useful indicators of the presence or absence of important reading skills. They are especially valuable as general screening and classification devices and as measures of the over-all effectiveness of the reading program. They are one important means of determining the reading status of large groups of pupils.

When the testing program is designed to reveal whether a school or school system rates high or low in comparison with national averages, it is not necessary to test every pupil. It is sufficient to administer standardized reading tests to a carefully selected sample of the pupils. Thus a relatively small sample, including an equal number of boys and girls and embracing a typical range of both chronological age and mental age, is likely to reflect the situation with respect to the group as a whole. Of course, a large sample is likely to inspire more confidence among teachers and the general public; if any number less than the entire group is tested, it is of the greatest importance that the sample be truly representative.

When the data yielded by the testing program have been compiled, they should be presented to all teachers and their significance interpreted. Graphs and charts may be used to excellent advantage in this process.

The standardized tests reveal what pupils can do in a test situation. Of equal importance are the extent and quality of the voluntary reading activities of the pupils. Reading ability is of no value unless it is used. For this reason, a survey of reading attainments in a school or school system should include a study of the cumulative reading records kept by pupils of their personal, voluntary reading. Such a study does not lend itself so readily to statistical summary and analysis as data from standardized tests do, but it is no less important. In the interpretation of the records, the *nature* of pupils' choices should be given as much consideration as the number of books read.

Since so much of contemporary reading is done in the mass media, the preliminary survey should include an inquiry into the newspaper and magazine reading habits of children; indeed, perhaps the best index of the success of the reading program is the extent and quality of young people's reading in these two sources. The inquiry should deal not only with the amount of time spent in a day or week in the reading of newspapers and magazines but especially with the pupils' preferences among the various features and the range of their interests.

For a somewhat detailed discussion on evaluation the reader is referred to the section, "Diagnosing Reading Difficulties" in the preceding chapter. The section, "Is This Child Ready To Read?" in Chapter 4A also gives information on evaluation.

PROVIDING BASAL READING INSTRUCTION   Having obtained the necessary background information, the staff is now ready to plan its over-all strategy. First, it must decide whether special classes in basal reading instruction will be needed. While some teachers believe that reading instruction can best be carried on in connection with other learning experiences, chiefly on an incidental basis, the great majority of American schools provide for systematic reading instruction, in scheduled periods, employing basal readers designed for such instruction. Systematic instruction in basal reading skills does not, of course, preclude incidental instruction during a school day.

While it is true that some children learn to read well without any systematic instruction, acquiring all needed skills through abundant and highly motivated reading, the vast majority of children need instructional assistance if they are to learn to read at their best. The regularly scheduled reading period and the basal reader will continue to be indispensable for most teachers and with most children if essential skills are to be developed. Extensive reading may be sufficient for bright children under the guidance of skillful teachers, and it is likely to produce rapid readers, readers who readily grasp the total meaning of a passage. For most pupils, however, it should be supplemented with intensive instruction for the continuous development of increasingly difficult skills such as word recognition, comprehension, and locating information in printed sources.

Certain general cautions should be observed in the planning of the basal reading program. These cautions grow out of facts and principles developed earlier in this book. For example, reliance should not be placed upon a single basal reader for the whole class; indeed, it should not be placed upon an entire single series. In any given class, basal readers designed for many levels of reading ability and containing many different kinds of material should be provided. Basal readers should not be labeled according to grade level of difficulty, although the publisher's estimate of difficulty level may be indicated by some code device. All basal readers should be amply supplemented with general reading materials on many subjects and representing many levels of reading difficulty. In the primary grades every effort should be put forth to make the initial experiences with books pleasurable and rewarding. In the intermediate grades the teacher should try to relate specific reading skills to the reading situations arising in the various curricular areas. The reading in basal readers should be accompanied by reading activities in other textbooks calling for similar skills, such as locating information, summarizing a paragraph, or using the dictionary. Basal readers should not be used for mere oral drill, in smaller or larger groups, in which everyone marks time while one pupil struggles through a passage. Pupils who are able to complete the material in the basal readers rapidly and without instructional assistance should be permitted to go on to more difficult materials. Basal readers, while building skills in word recognition, finding information, organizing ideas, applying what is learned to problems and questions discussed by the group, and similar abilities, should offer satisfaction and pleasure to the boys and girls using them.

SETTING DEVELOPMENTAL GOALS IN THE CONTENT SUBJECTS   While the foundation of reading ability for most children is laid in the "reading class," the progressive development of this ability must take place chiefly in the study of the special subjects and in free, personal reading. Teachers can give guidance and encouragement to pupils who encounter reading difficulties in the specialized materials in the subject areas. They can and they should set up clear-cut goals for the development of specific skills called for in the content areas. Dealing with specialized vocabularies, reading charts and graphs, analyzing verbal problems in arithmetic and science, looking for crucial details in technical explanations, noting the organization of paragraphs, slowing down to read the more difficult passages, carrying on supplementary research in the library, building background through extensive easy reading in such magazines as *Popular Science* and *Popular Mechanics*—these and other special skills can be cultivated by the teacher who is alert to reading problems in the content fields.

Teachers of the content subjects, especially those working in a departmental organization, often hesitate to give attention to reading problems because they feel unprepared to deal with them. Sometimes they will rationalize their neglect of the reading needs of children by pleading that they lack time to do more than communicate the necessary subject matter. It is, of course, quite true that specific training in the teaching of reading is highly desirable. However, any competent teacher who is thoroughly familiar with her subject can, if she wishes, learn a great deal about the reading problems children encounter in the content areas and about ways of helping them. As to the additional time required, no more effective way of communicating subject matter could be conceived than to promote in the learner the habits and skills needed for efficient reading in the special subject areas. (For further suggestions on reading in the content areas the reader is referred to Chapter 11.)

ESTABLISHING RELATIONS WITH THE SCHOOL AND PUBLIC LIBRARIES Essential to any well-planned school-wide reading program is a well-functioning, well-coordinated central library. Good room collections are useful in supplementing the basal reading program, but they cannot fully meet the demands created by the endlessly varying interests of young people. School administrators should so far as possible resist the temptation, in times of rapidly increasing enrollments and shortage of space, of converting library rooms into classrooms. The library is an educational essential, not a luxury.

Helpful also is a friendly working relation with the local public library. Representatives of the public library may be invited to visit classes, to explain the workings of the public library, and to encourage children to take out library cards. Teachers may take their classes on excursions to the public library. In some communities teachers inform public librarians about the reading abilities of their pupils. On the basis of this information the librarian often is able to annotate the children's library cards and can thus provide intelligent guidance for each child in the selection of books.

ORGANIZING READINESS CLASSES   Not all children who enter first grade are, as we have seen, "ready to read." When the initial testing program reveals that a considerable number of boys and girls are not as yet likely to succeed in a program of formal reading instruction, it may be desirable to organize one or more readiness classes, or, as they are sometimes called, transition units. In such classes many nonreading experiences such as construction activities, rhythm games, art work, listening to records, and especially oral language communication are provided.

ORGANIZING A NONGRADED PRIMARY UNIT   In many schools the primary school unit is left ungraded. While normally the primary school period extends over three years, in the nongraded unit the child progresses at his own rate and remains in the primary school for as long as he requires to master the initial skills of reading or for as long as he seems to benefit socially from association with primary school children. There are no "promotions" or "failures." Tasks set for children will be commensurate with their abilities, not dictated by arbitrary grade standards. In large schools or school systems it is possible to follow a dual plan, in which some children are assigned to nongraded units, while others enter conventional graded classes. (The nongraded primary school is also discussed in Chapter 12.)

ORGANIZING REMEDIAL CLASSES   Even under ideal conditions, in which differentiated instruction in reading is given in regular classes, some pupils will be so severely retarded that they will require special help in separate classes. The classrooms in which remedial instruction is carried on should be attractive, well lighted, and colorful and equipped with tables, bookshelves, magazine and newspaper racks, a motion picture screen and opaque curtains, a reading corner, radio or television or both, a phonograph, files, and storage cases. The walls and chalkboard should be done in bright colors. There should be ample bulletin board space. Newly constructed buildings should generally include rooms especially equipped for remedial reading instruction. Rooms in old school buildings have frequently been remodeled and redecorated at moderate cost.

Assignment of pupils to remedial classes will present problems. At what point on the scale should pupils be classified as remedial? Should superior pupils who are not reading up to their potential capacity be assigned to remedial classes? What types of tests should be used for screening pupils? What adjustments need to be made in the time schedule of the regular classes to allow for the work of the remedial classes? How long should the remedial class periods be? Who should determine what pupils are to be assigned to the special classes and when they are to be returned to regular instruction? How large should remedial classes be?

These and many other questions will occur to the administrator and the teacher who are concerned with the reading problem. The solution of most of them will depend upon local conditions. Generally speaking, the superior pupil who is not reading up to his capacity should not be assigned to a remedial class. He should be given individual attention in regular instruction and provided with new challenges in the form of more difficult reading materials and more demanding classroom tasks. The point on the table of reading scores at which pupils should be assigned to special classes will usually be determined by the number of teachers and classrooms available for remedial work. Quite probably the pupils who fall in the lowest 10th percentile will require the skilled help of the special teacher, regardless of their general learning capacity. When the general achievement of the school population is low, the number may be greater. Screening tests should be of the survey type because the diagnostic test is expensive and time-consuming. However, diagnostic tests, including one such as the Gray Oral Reading Paragraphs, should be given in the remedial classes to determine specific instructional needs and in regular classes when reading instruction is planned. Most survey tests include some diagnostic features which will be useful in any reading instruction. In general, remedial class periods should not extend much beyond forty-five minutes in length, and the class size should not exceed fifteen; ten pupils is probably an ideal number. Assignment to remedial sections should be based on consultation between the classroom teacher and the remedial teacher or principal. (For further suggestions related to remedial reading the reader is referred to Chapter 13.)

ESTABLISHING A READING CENTER   In every school system there will be some pupils who do not respond to instructional guidance, either in regular or special classes. In a few cases such lack of progress may be due to extremely low mental ability, but pupils so deficient are rare and will normally be entered in special schools. More commonly the difficulty will stem from some physical, emotional, or other handicap which can be at least partially overcome through expert diagnosis and guidance. The problem is chiefly one of intensive and patient study.

Because most teachers have neither the time nor the specialized training to make such diagnoses or to plan such guidance, expert help is needed. Unfortunately, however, the supply of highly trained personnel is as yet severely limited. Many universities and some hospitals conduct psychoeducational clinics in which help in reading is given. Some governmental agencies, such as the Institute for Juvenile Research in Illinois, provide diagnostic service, but they usually have long waiting lists and are seriously understaffed. Most clinics are obliged to charge a fee. Large school systems generally operate reading centers, but small town and rural schools are lacking in clinical facilities. There is great need for county units to provide the service that the small school cannot give.

The staff of the reading clinic should include, if possible, psychologists, physicians, family visiting teachers, remedial reading teachers, and secretaries, the number of each of these depending on the enrollment in the clinic. The clinic should be equipped with bookshelves, files, audio-visual materials, and such mechanical devices as the staff may require for diagnostic or remedial purposes.

One of the values of the reading center is the opportunity it provides for in-service education of teachers. Although the nucleus of the center must necessarily be the technically trained clinic staff, the great amount of individual instruction required by children referred to the clinic will call for the aid of a number of qualified teachers. In some cities, teachers are relieved of regular teaching duties in the classroom for a year or two to serve as teaching assistants in the reading center. After their work with severely retarded readers in the center, they return to their classrooms with a better understanding of the problems of retarded readers and with more skill in dealing with reading problems in the classroom. Teachers who have served in reading centers are often qualified to act as reading supervisors and to aid in developing remedial programs in elementary schools.

Interpreting the Reading Program to Parents

In any school-wide reading program, careful consideration needs to be given to the role of the parent. In the first place, parents have a right to know what the school's objectives in reading are and why it is using the particular procedures it has adopted in reading instruction. The intelligence and good judgment of parents should be respected. Most parents who are interested in their children's schooling are perfectly able to understand the principles upon which the school's policies are based when these are clearly explained to them. The school should make clear that it regards the education of children as a team project in which the home and the school have a common interest. It is no accident that in those communities where there has been friendly cooperation and good communication between home and school, the recent unreasonable criticisms of modern reading practices have had least effect.

Moreover, the school very much needs the help of the home in teaching the child to read. Parents can do much in creating a home atmosphere favorable to the development of reading ability. They are often in a better position than teachers to discover children's interests and to perceive the emotional reactions that children have toward the reading situation. By surrounding the young child with good books adapted to his level of ability, by setting the example of silent reading, by reading aloud to him and talking with him about stories and pictures, and in general by making reading an enjoyable experience for him from the earliest years, parents can lay the indispensable foundation for later success in reading.

Most parents, however, do not have the needed training for developing specific reading skills. While they should be kept informed about the changing trends in reading instruction, they should normally leave the formal instruction to the classroom teacher. When children ask questions about words or ideas encountered in the reading, they should, of course, not hesitate to give needed help. Reading drills, except perhaps occasionally at the request of the teacher, have no place in the home. Reading "games," yes; easy, attractive books for pleasurable reading, yes; but word drills and phonics (except in play) at home, no. The best contribution parents can make to the reading progress of their children is to provide them with a secure and happy home, an abundance of love and encouragement, a great variety of play, creative and constructive experiences, and unlimited opportunity for free reading in good books and magazines. Time to read, encouragement to read, and materials to read are necessary; pressure and a sense of urgency may be dangerous.

CONCEPTS OF SPECIAL INTEREST TO PARENTS   Parents can be helped to understand a number of important concepts of modern reading instruction. One of these is the concept of readiness, which has been discussed earlier in this book. We know that not all children are ready to begin learning to read at the same chronological age. Since most parents assume that first grade is the time for all children to learn to read, it becomes necessary to explain to them that children vary in their readiness for initial reading instruction. Delay in any of these processes is by no means evidence of backwardness. The important thing to remember is that the first experiences with reading should be happy, successful ones. If for any reason a child is not ready to read with fluency and satisfaction, he should be given the opportunity to develop the needed maturity.

A second concept that frequently needs to be explained to parents is the importance of meaningful reading from the very outset of instruction. Parents are frequently puzzled by the practice of confronting the beginning reader with large units which may even include whole sentences, for they may remember their own instruction, which possibly began with the alphabet or with phonograms. Modern schools vary in the type of initial experiences in reading provided for young children; many stress the thought approach from the beginning. This principle can usually be understood and appreciated by parents of children who are impatient to begin "reading." To some parents the debate about the code approach versus the meaning approach (see Chapter 5A) in beginning reading instruction may profitably be explained.

A third concept concerns the role of oral reading. Modern schools teach children to read orally, and most of them use a certain amount of oral reading in the initial stages of reading instruction. However, they recognize that most reading outside of school is silent, that adult silent reading should usually be at least twice as rapid as oral reading, and that the skills of silent reading differ in important respects from those of oral reading. Schools therefore stress silent reading throughout the grades, giving attention to oral reading as a significant separate skill or using it as an aid in the improvement of silent reading. Parents in whose own recollections school reading is associated with oral communication or sounding of words may be interested in the reasons for the new emphasis. Most of them will be pleased to note the increased use of purposeful oral reading and the decline of oral reading exercises which required the class to mark time while one pupil recited.

Finally, parents should be informed about the more recent techniques of teaching word recognition. A great many parents believe, or have recently been convinced by popular publications, that the chief weakness of modern reading instruction is the neglect of phonics. Such complaints have been heard for a long time. They were especially vigorous in the decade of the twenties, when the importance of silent reading began to be stressed in many quarters. Parents should be assured that phonics instruction is still given in school; that in many schools it relies less upon mechanical and memorization methods and more on natural analytic methods; that in these schools it is given at strategic times and to pupils who need it; and that it occupies an important place in the total reading program, in the basal readers, and in the teachers' manuals. They should also be helped to realize, however, that phonics is only one of many helps to the recognition of words. The use of additional methods, involving context clues, general configuration, and syllabication, has strengthened pupils' ability to recognize new words. If reading programs involving i/t/a, words-in-color, a linguistic approach, or other innovations are in operation or are being planned, they should be discussed with the parents. Parents will be pleased to know that the schools are not standing still in their efforts to teach children the diverse skills of word recognition.

METHODS OF COMMUNICATING WITH PARENTS   The best of all the methods of promoting home-school cooperation is the personal interview. In one elementary school, for example, the principal systematically interviews one or both parents of every child entering school for the first time. In the course of his conferences, he tries to discover the viewpoints of the parents and their assessments of their children's needs and capacities, for he believes he has much to learn from parents. At the same time, he explains to the parents the plan of reading instruction followed in the school and the major considerations that led to the adoption of the plan. Since he is able to show that the plan is getting good results in terms of national averages, the great majority of parents are enthusiastic, in spite of the fact that the reading program in the particular school is unconventional.

In other schools, certain days are set aside each year for teacher-parent conferences. On these days all teachers meet individually with parents of pupils in their classes. In these conferences teachers report the progress that the children are making in school and answer parents' questions about the instructional procedures employed. While the method is time-consuming, it recognizes the important fact that parents are most intimately concerned with the progress of their children and hence should be both consulted and informed.

Some school systems, such as that in Seattle, Washington, publish attractively illustrated leaflets, addressed to parents, setting forth in some of them the rationale of the reading program in the schools. Parents in many communities are invited, even urged, to visit the schools and to observe the reading program in action. In some schools colored slides illustrating the use of modern reading techniques are shown at PTA meetings and to civic groups. Tape recordings made in the classroom are played at such meetings to demonstrate progress that has been achieved in certain aspects of reading.

Another valuable device for involving parents in the work of the school is the occasional chatty newsletter, written by the teacher especially for the parents of her children. Such a newsletter can include the names of the children, some information about the teacher herself, references to the principal, clerk, nurse, custodians, and their duties, notes of appreciation for things parents have done for the school, and announcements of PTA meetings. Succeeding newsletters can report plans for various class activities, invite parents to visit the class, request materials for baking, construction, nature study, and the like, and, particularly, explain the educational significance and purpose of the activities.

FOR FURTHER STUDY

Barbe, Walter B., *Teaching Reading*. New York: Oxford University Press, 1965. Chapter XIV, article 52, "The Teaching of Reading—Objective Evidence vs. Opinion," pp. 405–416.

Bond, Guy L., and Miles A. Tinker, *Reading Difficulties: Their Diagnosis and Correction*. New York: Appleton-Century-Crofts, 1967. Chapter 2, "The Nature of Reading Growth," pp. 20–41.

Burton, Wiliam E., *Reading in Child Development*. Indianapolis, Ind.: The Bobbs-Merrill Company, Inc., 1958. Chapter 4, "Reading in the Total Program of Instruction," pp. 112–135.

De Boer, John J., and Gertrude Whipple, "Reading Development in Other Curriculum Areas," *Development through Reading*, pp. 54–76. Sixtieth Yearbook of the National Society for the Study of Education. Chicago: University of Chicago Press, 1961.

Durr, William (ed.), *Reading Instruction: Dimensions and Issues*. Boston: Houghton Mifflin Company, 1967. "Developing Reading Independence in the Primary Grades," pp. 101–104; "A Phonetic-Linguistic View of the Reading Controversy," pp. 112–125; "Critical Reading in the Primary Grades," pp. 160–164; Section 12, "Linguistics," pp. 272–310.

Fay, Leo, Thomas D. Horn, and Constance McCullough, *Improving Reading in the Elementary School*. Washington D.C.: The National Council for the Social Studies, 1961.

Frost, Joe L., *Issues and Innovations in the Teaching of Reading*. Chicago: Scott, Foresman Company, 1967. Part V, "Linguistics and the Teaching of Reading," pp. 199–222; Part VI, "What Content for Today's Children?" pp.

223–250; "Assessing the Experimental Evidence for Various Beginning Reading Plans," pp. 327–334; "First-Grade Reading Studies: An Overview," pp. 335–343; "A Longitudinal First-Grade Reading Readiness Program," pp. 345–350.

Gans, Roma, *Common Sense in Reading*. Indianapolis, Ind.: The Bobbs-Merrill Company, Inc., 1963. Chapter 14, "Parent Responsibility and the Child's Reading," pp. 266–282.

Hechinger, Fred M. (ed.), *Pre-School Education Today*. New York: Doubleday & Company, Inc., 1966. Chapter 7, "A Saturday School for Mothers and Pre-Schoolers," pp. 137–143.

Hester, Kathleen B., *Teaching Every Child To Read*. New York: Harper & Row, Publishers, 1964. Chapter 23, "Building Better Parental Relations," pp. 332–340; Chapter 24, "Participating in In-Service Education Programs," pp. 341–351.

Huus, Helen, *Children's Books To Enrich the Social Studies*. Washington, D.C.: The National Council for the Social Studies, 1961.

King, Martha L., Bernice D. Ellinger, and Willavene Wolf (eds.), *Critical Reading*. Philadelphia: J. B. Lippincott Company, 1967. Chapter 3, "The Critical Reader," pp. 25–29; Chapter 5, "Developing Critical Readers," pp. 35–44; Chapter 8, "Attitudes and Critical Reading," pp. 70–80; Chapter 11, "Creative Reading at All Grade Levels," pp. 95–99; Chapter 19, "Classroom Activities in Critical Reading," pp. 167–175; Chapter 22, "Critical Reading in the First Grade," pp. 190–196; Chapter 23, "Productive Reading-Thinking at the First Grade Level," pp. 197–201; Chapter 24, "Critical Reading in the Primary Grades," pp. 202–206; Chapter 25, "Readiness for Critical Reading," pp. 207–213.

Mazurkiewicz, Albert J., *New Perspectives in Reading Instruction*. New York: Pitman Publishing Corporation, 1964. Chapter 7, "Reading and the Curriculum," pp. 73–76; Chapter 10, "Instructional Practices in Reading: An Assessment for the Future," pp. 96–111.

Sleisinger, Lenore, *Guidebook for the Volunteer Reading Teacher*. New York: Teachers College Press, 1965. Pages ix–51.

Smith, Nila B., *Reading Instruction for Today's Children*. Englewood Cliffs, N.J.: Prentice-Hall, Inc., 1963. Chapter 19, "Working with Parents," pp. 509–521; Chapter 20, "Giving Advice to Parents," pp. 522–537.

Spache, George D. and Evelyn B., *Reading in the Elementary School*. Boston: Allyn and Bacon, Inc., 1969. Chapter 3, "Using the Basal Reader Approach."

Tinker, Miles A., and Constance M. McCullough, *Teaching Elementary Reading*. New York: Appleton-Century-Crofts, 1968. Chapter 2, "The Reading Teacher as A Reader," pp. 23–51; Chapter 19, "Parents as Partners in the Reading Program," pp. 401–417.

PART FOUR

A SUMMARY
OF RECENT EMPHASES

CHAPTER 15

---

*Teaching Reading to Children
from Culturally Disadvantaged
and Non-English-Speaking Homes*[1]

We noted in earlier chapters of this book that the home background and the general experience background of a child can greatly affect his ability to profit from instruction in reading. Because of this fact, much of this chapter is devoted to problems of teaching reading to children from culturally disadvantaged homes. We have also noted the close interrelation between oral language and reading. Consequently, this chapter also deals with special problems in learning to read English for children from homes in which English is not spoken.

BASIC CONSIDERATIONS

Before we discuss some of the problems in learning to read faced by children from culturally disadvantaged homes, let us clarify the use of some terms.

Terminology

Terms such as *culturally deprived* and *culturally disadvantaged* have been criticized as being insulting to those described. Reasons for such objection are not difficult to understand. Various terms are used—for example, Josephine Benson used the expression *culturally*

---

[1] Contributed by Walter J. Moore.

different as she referred to these children in the following paragraph.

> The culturally different child may be the product of many different environments. There are: (1) the transient child who moves often from one school to another within the city; (2) the child of migrant workers; (3) the child who moves from a rural community to the city where life is much more complicated; and (4) the bilingual child to whom English is a second language, little used and poorly spoken.[2]

It is not uncommon to encounter the term *undereducated* or, more frequently, the *undereducated adult* or the *undereducated worker*. These expressions seem to be somewhat more acceptable or less offensive to those individuals who are so designated. However, the expressions are not synonymous with *culturally deprived* or *culturally disadvantaged*. Many undereducated persons are not "culturally deprived" if we accept Francis Gregory's definition of the term *undereducated*. Gregory points out that persons in most lines of work cannot compete in today's labor market. He adds, "In terms of the labor market, then, we are probably safe in describing all persons who have an elementary but not a high school education as undereducated."[3] If that is the case, it can be expected that the dependents of the undereducated worker (the one without a high school diploma) may be or become "culturally underprivileged."

While there is need for more desirable nomenclature, we cannot bypass the acute problem that exists while we search for the words that satisfactorily designate the persons whom we are attempting to assist. We cannot postpone providing an improved program of learning experiences for the boys and girls in the groups to which we refer while we attempt to find appropriate terms. The pupils that we refer to as the culturally deprived or the culturally disadvantaged are those who come from homes in which there is a decided lack of an adequate self-concept, of loving parental concern, of idealism, of positive attitudes toward education and schooling, and of conversational or intellectual

[2] Josephine Benson, "Teaching Reading to the Culturally Different Child," in *Progress and Promise in Reading Instruction*, pp. 140–151. Twenty-second Annual Conference and Course on Reading, Pittsburgh, 1966. Quoted from the reprint of the article in Alfred R. Binter, John J. Diabal, Jr., and Leonard K. Kise (eds.), *Readings on Reading*, p. 259. Scranton, Pa.: International Textbook Company, 1969.

[3] Francis A. Gregory, "The Undereducated Man," *Education Digest*, 30, p. 19 (December 1964). (Reported from *Focus*, the Yearbook of the National Association for Public School Adult Education, Washington, D.C., 1965, p. 41.)

communication that would aid children in the present reading programs in our schools. Poverty, to be sure, is often but not necessarily associated with cultural deprivation; but not all culturally deprived pupils are poor. *Economically deprived* and *culturally deprived* are not synonymous terms.

We are also in need of a term that will adequately name an educational program for the culturally deprived. *Compensatory education* is frequently used to refer to educational programs, techniques, and projects designed to overcome the deficiencies of children from culturally disadvantaged homes. However, that term, too, is the subject of criticism. It is rejected by some on the basis that it implies special "catch-up programs" as opposed to strong, continuing educational policies and practices.

Differentiation between Children from Culturally Disadvantaged and Non-English–Speaking Homes

The reader is warned against assuming that because the reading problems of children from culturally disadvantaged homes and those from non-English–speaking homes are discussed in the same chapter the authors are wrongly equating these two kinds of homes. Some of the least culturally deprived homes in this country are those in which English is not spoken. Undoubtedly, too, for a child raised in such a home many advantages can accrue from the fact that he is familiar with another culture, including the language. The zeal with which in many elementary schools foreign languages are taught attests to the fact that many educators think it highly worthwhile for the young child to learn a language in addition to English. However, we are here not concerned primarily with the advantages resulting from a home in which from early childhood a boy or girl learns what will later serve for him as a second language, even though we must not overlook the benefits that result from being bilingual. We are here concerned with the fact that special problems in learning to read English confront the child to whom on entering school English is an unknown or almost unknown language. When learning to read English such a pupil is confronted with a difficult situation. The problem is especially complex when the teacher unknowingly assumes that the same practices can effectively be used with children from non-English–speaking homes as with those who are familiar with English.

Even though unfamiliarity with the English language is not a sign of being culturally deprived, at the present time in our country a large number of homes in which English is not spoken fall into that category. One needs only to consider the situation of the Puerto Rican in our big cities to understand this fact.

When considering the problems in teaching reading to the child from non-English–speaking homes we must be clear whether we are referring to children from such homes who are culturally deprived or to those who are not. Both groups will have special problems in beginning reading, but many of the difficulties and their solutions will differ vastly for children from these two kinds of non-English–speaking homes.

PROBLEMS FACED IN TEACHING READING

The problems faced in devising reading programs for disadvantaged children are multidimensional but not insurmountable.

Nature of the Problems

In considering the problems of teaching reading to children from culturally disadvantaged homes or from non-English–speaking homes, one cannot escape the more general questions relating to the physical and psychological needs of these pupils. Many of the boys and girls from deprived areas come to school hungry. Often, because of home conditions, they are also sleepy. Disease and malnutrition may interfere with academic learning of any kind. Unless the school takes into consideration the handicaps under which these boys and girls may be living, and unless it makes a strong effort to reduce or eliminate these factors, other strategies to improve the reading program for these children are doomed to fall short of the success desired. The first prerequisite to effective teaching of reading to underprivileged children, therefore, is to know these pupils as human beings.

INADEQUATE EXPERIENCE BACKGROUND   It would be presumptious to claim that the child coming from a disadvantaged home lacks in experience background. He may have a background quite sufficient for what is required of him in the type of home from which he comes. He may be in possession of much information essential to him for survival in his culture, information often quite remote from the teacher's stock of knowledge. However, his background is often one radically different from the one on which the usual school program is seemingly based. The seriousness of this problem is enhanced by the fact that many middle class teachers seem to assume that such a child has certain types of information that children from the inner city or from a disadvantaged section of a rural area do not have. If she talks of a violin, she may discover that some of the children in her room have neither seen nor heard one. Some of the youngsters may not know the difference between a knife and a fork.

At times the teacher assumes that a culturally disadvantaged child with a broad background, for example, of travel, if he is the child of a migrant worker, would have much to build on that would be of value to him in school. Frequently, however, the disadvantaged child has not adequately experienced what he has seen and heard. With no one in his family interested in drawing his attention to much of what he sees on an extensive journey from one part of the country to another, he may lose much of the benefit that might accrue to a child whose parents are helpful in pointing out to him, through question or comment, points of significance and interest. Consequently, lack of an experience background is not the only problem; failure to utilize the background experienced constitutes an additional problem.

LACK OF MOTIVATION   Teachers too often assume that almost all children want to learn to read. They are frequently wrong in this assumption when teaching the disadvantaged child. Lack of parental interest in reading—possibly because of lack of skill in reading —brings the culturally deprived child to school without motivation to learn to read.

Some boys and girls may even have a decided antipathy toward learning to read. They may have seen a child in their neighborhood ridiculed because he enjoyed reading or because he received good grades. They may have as hero the member of a gang who scoffs at reading and at anything associated with school. They may have heard brothers and sisters and other children tell tales about school—some of which may be true—that have prejudiced them against all school learning before they even step inside a school building. To such children no teacher needs try to make advances by telling them that they are about to start on a wonderful adventure, that of learning to read. They know more exciting adventures.

THE LANGUAGE PROBLEM   That there is a language problem in learning to read English for the child from a non-English–speaking home, even when the home is not culturally deprived, is easily recognized. The problem may be equally acute and frequently much more persistent in the case of the child from an English-speaking culturally deprived home. It is important that the school be cognizant of the extent of the problem faced by the child whose language differs greatly from standard English. The "language of the book" may be almost like a foreign language to the child who speaks a dialect or uses poor English or who has a limited vocabulary of the kind used in school books.

Most authorities would agree that there is a close relation between language and thought, and consequently also between language and thought and reading. For example, it is believed that the acquisition of a language system involves the reorganization of all the child's mental processes, because the word becomes a factor that forms mental activity, perfects the reflection of reality, and creates new forms of attention or memory. The word has a basic function not only because it indicates a corresponding object in the external world but also because it abstracts and isolates the necessary signal. At the same time, the word generalizes perceived signals and relates them to certain categories. It is this systematization of direct experience that makes the role of the word in the formation of mental processes so important. Language is the essential ingredient in concept formation, in problem-solving, and in relating to and interpreting the environment. All these abilities are closely related to reading—in fact, they are part of reading.

While we are told that the language of the child from a culturally deprived area may be as adequate for his needs at home and in his social setting as is that of the middle class child for his environment, it is less helpful to him at school because basal readers generally portray life of middle class boys and girls. The textbooks use words and present concepts frequently foreign to the child from a deprived neighborhood. With the emphasis in many systems of teaching beginning reading on keeping the reading vocabulary within the realm of the understanding and speaking vocabulary of the learner, it is little wonder that the child unfamiliar with the vocabulary of the reading book has a double burden—that of learning the meaning vocabulary and the reading vocabulary. The burden becomes great when such a child is taught by a teacher who does not realize the difficulty or ignores it or does not know how to deal with it.

Figuerel reported on a study of the vocabulary of under-privileged children and concluded, on the basis of a comparison of the words in the vocabulary of underprivileged children with the words in controlled vocabularies for grades two through six, that very little effective reading can be expected to be done in the textbooks in use in these grades. He found almost all of the words in the controlled vocabularies unknown to underprivileged children in the various grades. He observed:

> The vocabularies of underprivileged children reveal a limited experiential background. Although the number of words known in

such areas of experience as clothing, eating, housekeeping, and recreation seems large, their number is still small and very limited when compared with terms privileged children know. Only in the area of school experience are privileged and underprivileged children comparable. If reading competency is commensurate with one's experience, and much evidence seems to prove that this is true, underprivileged children, with their limited experiences, can be expected to do very little effective reading in textbooks they now use.[4]

Figuerel reported his conclusion in 1949. Some fifteen years later he was still reiterating the observations he made and the conclusions he drew from his earlier study. In his 1964 report he pointed out, too, that despite our knowledge of the limited vocabularies of underprivileged children, very little progress had been made with the passage of the years.[5]

Nor is the problem of vocabulary due only to the fact that the deprived child does not know the meaning of some of the words in his reading book—words that often the teacher assumes he knows. There is a less tangible but more pervasive problem. The language a person hears in his preschool years and that which in turn he then speaks becomes an integral part of him. As inadequate as that language may be, it cannot be taken away from a person, intentionally or unintentionally, without something resembling a shock to the system. (Most of us have experienced nostalgia when we hear an expression somewhat restricted to our family circle when we were youngsters; we can, therefore, have an idea of the emotional involvement with the language of one's home.) Furthermore, the language of the basal reader may seem so lacking in emotional content and so stilted to the child from the home in which substandard English is spoken that to him the reading material is cold, uninteresting, and boring. The dilemma in which the child thus finds himself is difficult to solve. However, teachers interested in all the pupils whom they are privileged to teach will not refuse to do something about the situation merely because no final solution is readily apparent.

[4] J. Allen Figuerel, "The Vocabulary of Underprivileged Children," *University of Pittsburgh Bulletin*, 45, p. 389 (June 1949).

[5] J. Allen Figuerel, "Limitations in the Vocabulary of Disadvantaged Children: A Cause of Poor Reading," *Improvement of Reading through Classroom Practice*, Vol. 9, 1964, p. 164. Proceedings of the Annual Convention, Newark, Del.: International Reading Association.

Extent of the Difficulties Faced

The extent of the problems facing the culturally deprived pupils is evidenced in the rioting that has swept the country. It is a matter of conjecture how much of the unrest and revolution might have been avoided had we known how to teach reading more effectively to those who are violently objecting to current-day practices. It may be, had the schools been able to make not only efficient readers out of these young people but also readers who want to read worthwhile materials, that they would be using more peaceful means of making equality among men more than a slogan or a dream.

DATA ON THE UNDEREDUCATED ADULT   Some indication of the extent of the problems faced is given by Gregory, who points out:

> In 1960 there were 20 million such workers [without a high school diploma, who had, however, completed at least an elementary education] in the United States labor force. The 10 million workers without an elementary education would require one-third of the desks we now have in our elementary schools across the nation. The 20 million without a high school diploma [who, however, had at least an elementary education] would require that we double the number of desks in our high schools.[6]

No one claims that the elimination of illiteracy will cure all the evils of unemployment, discrimination, low standards of living, or problems of child rearing. But there is no question that educational requirements are mounting. It has been found that the unemployed cannot even qualify for training or retraining because of their lack of education. An elementary education is not enough to qualify one for a job; today high school dropouts are having great difficulty in securing employment. Despite the fact that the attainment of functional literacy for adults is not a cure-all, as well as the fact that illiteracy is diminishing, low educational attainment is a cause for serious concern.

READING RETARDATION AMONG UNDERPRIVILEGED CHILDREN   While many a child who is not underprivileged is retarded in reading, the incidence of retardation among culturally deprived children is much greater than it is among children with greater cultural advantages. Josephine T. Benson claims: "In middle class communities, the number of children retarded in reading averages between ten and twenty per cent while in low socio-economic areas it may range as high as eighty per cent."[7]

A survey of the New York public schools is summarized in

[6] Gregory, p. 41.

[7] Benson, in Binter, Diabal, and Kise, p. 266.

part by Figure I (page 538), which shows the results of testing in the spring of 1967. The relation of the figures on reading retardation have bearing on the dilemma of the underprivileged when we realize that it was reported that in predominantly Negro and Puerto Rican neighborhoods by the time pupils were in the seventh and eighth grades they were generally one or more years farther behind than the average of the years of retardation for all the pupils within a given grade in the public schools of New York City.

REPORT ON PRE-FIRST–GRADE ATTENDANCE   The U.S. Department of Health, Education and Welfare surveyed children attending nursery school or kindergarten and found that in October 1964, 3.2 million children aged three through five, or about one-fourth of all American youngsters, were enrolled. Nursery schools, the survey noted, are predominantly private and generally beyond the reach of low-income families. And kindergartens, more predominantly public, have not been established in many areas. These findings make it clear that large numbers of American boys and girls who most need assistance in the early stages of the educational process are not getting it.

The reference to the report in the preceding paragraph is of special significance to the problem of reaching the underprivileged early if we are in agreement with the point of view stated in the report of the Educational Policies Commission:

> Yet these qualities [intellectual ability and intellectual interest] are greatly affected by what happens to children before they reach school. A growing body of research and experience demonstrates that by the age of six most children have already developed a considerable part of the intellectual ability they will possess as adults. Six is now generally accepted as the normal age of entrance to school. We believe that this practice is obsolete. All children should have the opportunity to go to school at public expense at the age of four.[8]

PROBLEMS OF PERSONS FROM NON-ENGLISH–SPEAKING HOMES   A report by Harold Allen gives some indication of the extent of problems of children unfamiliar with English:

> Except for foreign students temporarily in the United States, the chief problem in all educational categories [of "non-English speakers" in the United States] is presented by the culturally disadvantaged environment of the students. In the elementary schools three-fourths of the children of non-English–speaking homes are

[8] Educational Policies Commission, *Universal Opportunity for Early Childhood Education*, p. 1. Washington, D.C.: National Education Association, 1966.

considered by both administrators and teachers as handicapped by conditions primarily due to poverty. Two-thirds of the high school students are similarly classed, and one-third in adult classes. This circumstance points to the discrepancy between textbook descriptions of American life and the life which they know, as well as to the lack of family means to obtain the material things described in the books.[9]

Tables I–III from the TENES survey present significant data.

TABLE I
PROBLEM AREAS RELATED TO TENES: INSTITUTIONAL SURVEY

	Elementary (N = 163) No. Pct.	Secondary (N = 89) No. Pct.	Adult (N = 132) No. Pct.	College (N = 229) No. Pct.	All Respondents (N = 510) No. Pct.
Culturally deprived environment of students	123 75.5	57 64.0	42 31.8	19 8.3	173 33.9
Disruptive family environment of students	85 52.1	39 43.8	28 21.2	7 3.1	114 22.4
Negative parental attitudes toward education	78 47.9	32 36.0	15 11.4	5 2.2	89 17.4
Lack of student motivation (conflict with other educ. goals, etc.)	67 41.1	29 32.6	23 17.4	41 17.9	123 24.1
Negative community attitudes toward non-English speakers	26 16.0	19 21.3	20 15.2	11 4.8	53 10.4
No Response	29 17.8	29 32.6	74 56.1	175 76.4	278 54.5

Source: Harold B. Allen, *TENES: A Survey of the Teaching of English to Non-English Speakers in the United States,* p. 80. Champaign, Ill.: The National Council of Teachers of English, 1966. Used with the permission of the Council.

[9] Harold B. Allen, *TENES: A Survey of the Teaching of English to Non-English Speakers in the United States,* p. 79. Champaign, Ill.: The National Council of Teachers of English, 1966. Used with the permission of the Council. On page 8 of the TENES report, this explanation of Table I and Table III is given: "Copies of this questionnaire were distributed in person or by mail to 3726 teachers early in 1965. Of these only 1410 were returned, and 1242 of which proved to be usable. *The cumulative total by level was greater than the actual number of responses because some teachers reported responsibility for teaching in more than one system or on more than one level and hence were included in two or more categories.*"

Partly but not wholly related to this first problem are two others listed as serious by both administrators and teachers, according to the TENES findings. One problem is that of the disruptive family environment of the boys and girls. About one-half of the responses report some pupils suffering from improper home conditions. The other is the presence of negative parental attitudes toward education.

LARGE-SCALE ATTEMPTS TO DEAL WITH THE PROBLEMS

Many people and many agencies are deeply concerned with the problems faced by boys and girls from underprivileged and from non-English–speaking homes. Individuals, private organizations, foundations, and city and federal agencies have studied or are studying the

TABLE II
OTHER PROBLEMS AND PROBLEM AREAS LISTED AS
WRITE-IN COMMENTS BY RESPONDENTS

	Elementary	Secondary	Adult	College	Total
Inadequate grouping	1	1	2	15	19
Inadequate testing (diag. & achiev.)	1	–	1	17	19
Lack of personnel:					
Trained teachers	9	6	1	3	19
Other	2	–	9	2	13
Lack of adequate materials	9	6	13	12	40
Inadequate program	6	2	1	10	19
Not enough class time	3	1	1	6	11
Too large classes	2	–	–	1	3
Too heavy teacher loads	–	–	1	1	2
Lack of training facilities	1	–	8	2	11
Lack of rooms	2	–	3	1	6
Negative attitude (administration, other teachers)	3	2	1	6	12
Irregular attendance	2	3	4	–	9
Too heavy course loads for students	–	–	–	6	6
Too few students	–	1	14	5	20
Lack of transportation	–	–	5	–	5
Poor health of students	3	–	–	–	3
Inadequate budget	1	1	–	1	3
Insufficient lab space	–	–	2	1	3
Poor pay for teachers	–	–	2	–	2

Source: Harold B. Allen, *TENES: A Survey of the Teaching of English to Non-English Speakers in the United States,* p. 80. Champaign, Ill.: The National Council of English, 1966. Used with the permission of the Council.

problems in the hope of coming up with recommendations for improvement. Some have devised means by which they are attempting to eradicate some of the present ills. The work of a few of these groups is here summarized.

Focus on Fundamentals

In 1967 it was found that in the school system of New York City pupils were continuing to lose ground in reading in spite of efforts to remedy the situation (see Figure I, p. 538). One in every three pupils in the city schools was a year or more behind in reading. The gap between the achievement of city pupils and the national norms showed up in the second grade, the first level tested, and became more pronounced, as would be expected, in the upper grades. As stated earlier,

TABLE III
PROBLEM AREAS RELATED TO TENES:
TEACHER SURVEY

	Elementary (N = 618) No. Pct.	Secondary (N = 220) No. Pct.	Adult (N = 230) No. Pct.	College (N = 276) No. Pct.	All Respondents (N = 1242) No. Pct.
Culturally deprived environments of students	460 74.4	149 67.7	66 28.7	23 8.3	647 52.1
Disruptive family environment of students	380 61.5	113 51.4	45 19.6	14 5.1	515 41.5
Negative parental attitudes toward education	309 50.0	87 39.5	9 3.9	4 1.4	392 31.6
Lack of student motivation (conflict with other educational goals, etc.)	207 33.5	100 45.5	28 12.2	78 28.3	380 30.6
Negative community attitudes toward non-English speakers	105 17.0	40 18.2	22 9.6	23 8.3	173 13.9
Special problems other than those comomn to TENES	171 27.7	84 38.2	107 46.5	118 42.8	431 34.7
No Response	95 15.4	42 19.1	80 34.8	107 38.8	295 23.8

Source: Harold B. Allen, TENES: A Survey of the Teaching of English to Non-English Speakers in the United States, p. 81. Champaign, Ill.: The National Council of Teachers of English, 1966. Used with the permission of the Council.

by the time the boys and girls were in the seventh or eighth grades, those in predominantly Negro and Puerto Rican neighborhoods were generally one or more years behind the average for the city school system.

In the fall of 1967, the New York City schools launched a massive program called *Focus on Fundamentals*. It was begun in early childhood classes in 267 poverty areas. The program from the outset provided for smaller classes, more books and other supplies, parental involvement, and a diagnostic program for second graders in many districts. The graph presented in Figure II appeared in the December 2, 1968, issue of the *New York Times*. If this graph is compared with that in Figure I, which was reported in the November 3, 1967 issue of the *New York Times*, it will be noted that although in all grades of the elementary school the averages for reading were still below national norms, progress had been made. However, in 1968, as before the launching of the *Focus on Fundamentals* program, areas populated primarily by Negroes and Puerto Ricans continued to show the most serious deficiencies.

Operation Headstart, Project Follow Through, and Project Upward Bound

Operation Headstart, the most popular of the antipoverty educational programs, was designed to give children, before entering first grade, a "head start" in schooling planned for their needs. It was begun in 1965. In late 1967 it was followed by a pilot program, *Project Follow Through*. *Follow Through* came into existence because many studies convinced educational and government experts that *Headstart* "graduates" seemed to benefit from early education. It was found that these pupils begin regular school only slightly behind their middle class schoolmates and well ahead of other impoverished children who have not had preschool experience. Unfortunately, however, it seems that the educational advantage of *Headstart* youngsters fades after six or eight months in the public schools. A somewhat related type of endeavor, *Project Upward Bound*, provides special services for economically deprived high school students. From its inception in 1965 through 1968, some 25,000 pupils had been enrolled, and of these 80 percent had gone on to further study at higher levels.

The recent experience with *Operation Headstart* and *Project Follow Through* seems to endorse earlier findings that a special feature of the learning difficulty of the educationally deprived child is his language deficiency. Since verbal ability or disability unquestionably

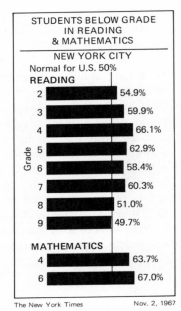

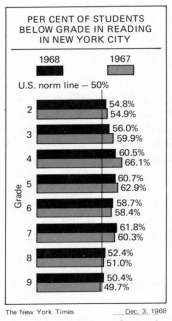

Figure I (left): Students below grade in reading and mathematics, New York City. The *New York Times,* November 2, 1967. © 1967-1968 by The New York Times Company. Figure II (right): Percent of students below grade in reading in New York City. The *New York Times,* December 3, 1968. © 1967-1968 by The New York Times Company. Reprinted by permission.

permeates all areas of academic learning, a closer examination of this condition is imperative. It is not enough simply to assume that a child is "nonverbal" or "less verbal."

The Task Force

Yet another large-scale attempt to seek solutions to the problems of culturally deprived and non-English–speaking students was undertaken by the National Council of Teachers of English, which established *Task Force* in order to survey and report upon individual programs in language and reading for disadvantaged students throughout the country.[10] The program was concerned with the teaching of

---

[10] Richard Corbin and Muriel Crosby, *Language Programs for the Disadvantaged: Report of the NCTE Task Force on Teaching English to the Disadvantaged,* pp. 65–69. Champaign, Ill.: The National Council of Teachers of English, 1965.

language in all aspects—reading, literature, spelling, writing, and speaking—from preschool language programs through those that provide postschool opportunities for adults.

The *Task Force* consisted of twenty-two members and three consultants enlisted from schools, universities, and educational agencies who represented the various segments of the profession concerned with teaching English to the disadvantaged. For three months this group visited and reported in detail on 190 programs located in 64 cities. The programs selected were those that had been recommended by members of the *Task Force*, by specialists in the U.S. Office of Education and in state departments of education, and by directors of major projects in urban centers as well as those known to leaders of the National Council of Teachers of English to be of national significance.

Of all the programs reviewed by the *Task Force*, the preschool programs gained the most favorable attention. Several observers felt that programs at this level were less hampered by tradition. Others noted that parents of preschool children seem to be more interested than parents of children in higher grades. Whatever the reasons, it appeared that, beginning at the intermediate-grade level and extending upward, the programs were more structured and formal and more related to traditional school practices.

The *Task Force* and other agencies that have directed their attention to the problems of the disadvantaged child are in general agreement in respect to the so-called deficits that have accrued by the time such a pupil enters school. The *Task Force* sees the deficiencies as falling into three general areas: (1) conceptual development, (2) language facility, and (3) self-concept. In confronting these deficiencies, the school can take two possible approaches. The school can either change the child before he enters school (through the preschool program) or it can change the school to meet the needs of the child. A combination of these two approaches seems to be the most effective. An attempt should be made to prepare a child and to overcome his areas of deprivation as much as possible before he enters school; yet, once he is in school, the school must adapt itself to the child's needs and provide help in areas in which he requires attention. (See page 549 for other recommendations of the *Task Force*.)

Volunteer Workers for Staffing the Programs

The key person in an educational program for helping the underprivileged child and the child from a non-English–speaking home undoubtedly is the classroom teacher. Suggestions as to ways in which the teacher can help are given in the last part of this chapter.

With the shortage of teachers and of funds it has been necessary for many school systems to look beyond the classroom to find people to work with underprivileged pupils. In large urban centers it has frequently been customary to depend upon volunteers for the full implementation of a program. It is to volunteers, too, that many agencies have turned in order to give help to underprivileged boys and girls. In partial explanation of the role of the volunteer, Eunice Newton observes:

> In some instances, volunteers are sought who have exceptional skills needed for special services in recreatory or rehabilitative programs—arts and crafts, dancing, music, sports, and the like. To assist in the basic literacy programs, however, volunteers are recruited who have frequently just three things: time, zeal, and reading ability.[11]

It is readily recognized that there is more to a program for the underprivileged than mere possession of these three assets, however important they may be. And they are important, for the zeal and empathy of the volunteer reading teacher are tremendous forces for effective learning which may outweigh or, as Newton believes, even transcend the naiveté of the teacher's methods. Newton's *Syllabus for Training the Volunteer Reading Tutor*, contained in the article cited, ought to be read by all who are involved in the teaching of reading to the educable illiterate in our population.

Charlotte Mergentime has described one of many community projects with lay volunteers, the School Volunteer Program, which was organized about a decade ago by the Public Education Association, which is now a service of the New York City Board of Education:

> The project is based primarily on the use of dependable, intelligent volunteers, men and women, who are trained to work with children in the schools. The volunteers report one or two days a week for a minimum of three hours a day and assist pupils in content subjects, but since reading retardation is such a widespread problem, the school volunteers concentrate much of their effort on special reading programs. The emphasis in these programs is

[11] Eunice S. Newton, "Training the Volunteer Reading Tutor," *Journal of Reading*, 7, p. 169. (January 1965). Reprinted with the permission of the author and the International Reading Association.

heavily weighted in the direction of providing experiences and skills that make for interested readers.[12]

The goals of tutoring programs and after-school study centers are many. Volunteer workers seek to uncover new interests in underachieving youngsters, to establish meaningful relations with them out of which new attitudes and stronger motives for learning can emerge, and to help them master basic academic skills. Gayle Janowitz believes that the reason that study centers and tutoring projects have become part of the war on poverty is that they represent a genuine grass roots movement of interested citizens.

> The fact that high school and college students, housewives, professionals, and retired men and women are volunteering by the thousands means that there is an enormous reserve of good will and labor available. It also means that academic help for children is a cause which has wide appeal. It is impressive that women who cannot afford to hire a sitter exchange babysitting in order to give an afternoon a week to a center. Many volunteers have been working in projects for as long as three years and expect to continue.
>
> Volunteer work has always been a tradition in America. The new aspect of this work is that volunteers have become interested in education because of increased awareness of the inequalities in educational opportunity. The job to be done is so great that the need for these people will continue for years.[13]

Schools, too, with the pupils attending them, could perhaps make greater use of volunteer workers, according to Peggy Lippitt and John Lohman.[14] They argue that it can be shown that children, with proper training and support from adults, are able to function effectively in the roles of helpers and teachers of young children. Furthermore, they claim that older children find this type of experience meaningful, productive, and valuable for learning for themselves. This provocative

[12] Charlotte Mergentime, "Tailoring the Reading Program to the Needs of Disadvantaged Pupils: The Role of the School Volunteer," *Improvement of Reading through Classroom Practice*, Volume IX (1964), p. 162. Proceedings of the Annual Convention. Newark, Del.: International Reading Association. Reprinted with the permission of the author and the International Reading Association.

[13] Gayle Janowitz, *Helping Hands: Volunteer Work in Education*, p. 7. Chicago: University of Chicago Press, 1965.

[14] Peggy Lippitt and John Lohman, "Cross-Age Relationships: An Educational Resource," *Children*, XII, p. 113 (May–June 1965).

article describes a series of pilot projects of three years' duration carried on first in the University of Michigan laboratory school and later in several biracial classes in a public school in a neighborhood of blue collar workers and in a summer day camp for boys and girls from four to fourteen years of age.

In the school pilot projects described by Lippitt and Lohman, sixth-grade pupils were involved as academic assistants in the first, second, third, and fourth grades. They helped the younger children with reading, writing, arithmetic, spelling, and physical education. In addition, they were used as laboratory assistants in social science laboratory periods, working as group discussion leaders and producing "behavior specimens" presented for observation and study. Their success was the result of several carefully planned steps in the development of collaborative cross-age interaction. These included: (1) providing opportunities for cross-age interaction through collaboration between adults; (2) teacher-student collaboration; (3) building a peer group attitude that supported the value of helping youngsters and being helped by elders; (4) training for the helper role (training in academic procedures, feedback sessions, seminars); (5) "at-the-elbow" help.

EVALUATION OF PROGRAMS

Unfortunately, it cannot be said that all the programs for helping children from underprivileged backgrounds have been successful. They have not. But even in their failure valuable insights have been obtained. A case in point is the highly publicized New York City *Higher Horizons* program. According to the *New York Times* of September 1, 1965, the effort to raise the educational, vocational, and cultural aspirations of disadvantaged children had had virtually no measurable effect on the achievement of the pupils enrolled. The Bureau of Educational Research of the Board of Education of the City of New York, through its director, J. Wayne Wrightstone, had to concede that there were little differences in many of the areas evaluated between pupils in *Higher Horizons* schools and those in similar schools without the program. The research team, in an introductory statement to the bureau report, emphasized that the study conducted from 1959 to 1962 had a marked influence on the future educational program of both the city and the nation. The report stated, "The growing awareness of the need for special efforts and imaginative innovations in the education of the socially disadvantaged is at least a partial consequence of the leadership of New York City and its early concern with these problems."[15] That was in 1965.

After several years of federal subsidy to upgrade educational achievement of disadvantaged pupils, there is still little evidence that the problem is being overcome. In fact, pupils in the inner cities are falling farther below the national averages. Joseph Froomkin, assistant commissioner for program planning and evaluation, U.S. Office of Education, has stated that most of the programs are not yet strong enough to insulate the child from the failure and detrimental effects of his home environment. He has observed:

> Our approach to the poor has been irrational: We have classified children according to their ability level and have provided each group with the same resources and services, and then we act puzzled—if not indignant—when we continue to get unequal results. A child who has not learned to read by the fourth grade requires massive effort to help him catch up. We need to apply the best of the newest methods we know to make him learn, yet we don't know too much about what those methods are. In the few instances when we do know, very often nothing is done to apply them. For instance, 50 per cent of the local educational authorities still use basal readers in their remedial reading programs. I do not share the optimism of teachers who failed to teach deprived children how to read English—yet believe that they can succeed with the same method simply by putting the children into smaller groups and drilling them just a share harder. Different approaches —be they phonic or linguistic—are probably more appropriate for remediation than the basal reading approach. Yet we use them far too seldom.[16]

What has been learned from the programs to date? Froomkin said an analysis of the results of Title I, Elementary and Secondary Education Act programs, in sixteen cities "gives modest grounds for optimism." About 20 percent showed some improvement, 11 percent some decline, and the others showed no change. The results would be better, Froomkin predicted, if the schools intervened earlier in the child's life—at age three or four—and stressed task and cognitive programs. "I would also bet on individually prescribed instruction (IPI) and

[15] Robert H. Terte, "*Higher Horizons* Is Found Wanting," *New York Times*, September 1, 1965, p. 33.

[16] Joseph Froomkin, *Washington Monitor*, Supplement to *Education U.S.A.*, March 18, 1968.

other careful curriculum structures." Froomkin recommended vigorous efforts to build up the ego of children and to develop after-school instructional programs. He also stated:

> I would not be candid if I did not voice my disappointment with the orientation of most remedial programs. For instance, we know how important family behavior and family attitudes are in determining the success of a child in school. But the majority of programs I have observed are guilty of class snobbism. We hope to change the fabric of the culture of the poor through the most casual contacts with them: a lecture, a PTA meeting, at most a weekly visit to the home of a student is believed sufficient to change the life patterns of the poor. New methods of working with families must be developed.[17]

With the mingled failure and success of various programs for helping the underprivileged in learning to read and in other areas, the challenge remains, greater than ever.

THE ROLE OF THE SCHOOL

No matter how many agencies assist in the program of providing for equalizing opportunities for the underprivileged or the handicapped, the final responsibility for teaching reading lies with the school. It is a responsibility that the school cannot escape, though it welcomes help from the outside. In this final section of the chapter these topics relevant to the role of the school are discussed: (1) teacher expectations, (2) guidelines for the teacher, (3) materials of instruction, and (4) recommendations for a school-wide approach.

Teacher Expectations

Probably one reason why results in reading with the culturally handicapped have not been better in spite of tremendous efforts to overcome shortcomings of earlier programs is the attitude of many teachers. A large number of teachers do not expect much of their pupils. In some partly inexplicable way, low expectations by the teacher seem to encourage poor achievement, while high expectations seem to discourage it. A fine resource on this general problem is available in the form of *Pygmalion in the Classroom* by Robert Rosenthal and Lenore Jacobson.[18]

---

[17] Froomkin, p. 4.

[18] Robert Rosenthal and Lenore Jacobson, *Pygmalion in the Classroom*. New York: Holt, Rinehart and Winston, Inc., 1968.

Robert Rosenthal discovered some time ago that rats perform more intelligently if their human mentors, the researchers, are made to believe that the rats have been bred for special intelligence. When he put the theory to the human test in classrooms, he found the effects to be the same. Teachers were told that certain children were likely, according to fictitious pretesting, to "spurt ahead." The children *did* spurt ahead.

What makes the experimentally documented findings valuable is not that they tell something radically new but rather that they offer documented evidence of the shortcomings of the present attitudes of some teachers. Thus they may focus on unnecessary failures which result from low expectations.

In the "Pygmalion" experiment, children falsely labeled as potential "bloomers" tended to bloom with extraordinary frequency—without any special tutoring or crash programs. The tests on which the findings were based were externally administered to avoid the risk of bias. But it turned out that the teachers tended to grade their "special" children more severely than the others and to spend less time babying them. In other words, they respected them more and spoonfed them less. Incidentally, the performance of the "ordinary" pupils in the same classroom tended to improve, too, although not as dramatically. The infusion of confidence seemed contagious. "What was done in our program of educational change was done directly for the teacher," Rosenthal writes. "Perhaps, then, it is the teacher to whom we should direct more of our research attention."

Guidelines for the Teacher

One guideline for the teacher is elaborated upon in the preceding paragraphs. It might be summarized by this statement: "The teacher should have and reveal an attitude of expectancy." Below are additional points the teacher should bear in mind when planning and putting into practice a program for work with the culturally deprived or the language handicapped.

1. She should seek to understand the child who is culturally different.
2. She should consider the child's assets, not only his handicaps.
3. She should learn from both success and failure.
4. She should zealously guard the right of the child to love his home, no matter how culturally deprived or how different it may be.
5. She should help the child to see that to be different does not mean to be inferior.

6.   She should help the child to develop or maintain self-respect, a self-respect that recognizes the rights of an individual and the contributions that he makes or can make to others.

7.   She should be more interested in the learner than in what he is learning; that is, she should be more interested in the whole child than in his reading ability.

8.   She should make living in her classroom a happy experience and, at the same time, a beneficial one.

9.   She should teach all the boys and girls in her charge that one human being is as important as another.

10.   She should start where the child is and build on what he knows.

11.   She should read widely about work with underprivileged children—about problems that they face as well as about resulting successes and failures.

These guidelines are important to all teaching; when teaching children with handicaps, however, they are a *must*.

Materials of Instruction

As discussed earlier in this chapter, one problem connected with teaching the underprivileged child to read is that the vocabulary of the textbook may be quite unlike his own. Often it is not the vocabulary alone that is the source of trouble. The fact that frequently the life style portrayed is not that with which the child is familiar constitutes another difficulty. The difference may make him resentful that he is shut out of the happy world frequently pictured as representative of the family life of the boys and girls filling the pages of the books. At best the underprivileged child may feel he is reading about a life alien to him, possibly one about which he does not even care to read because of its remoteness, as far as he is concerned, from reality.

Writers of textbooks—chiefly teachers on one or another rung of the educational ladder—have of recent years been greatly concerned about the lack of adequate textbooks for the underprivileged. They have recognized that from the point of view of material for learning to read, most textbooks are inadequate for these pupils. They have also been deeply concerned about the undesirable sociological impact that certain textbooks may have on these boys and girls. An encouraging beginning has been made in the production of suitable materials, but only a small beginning.

The Detroit Public Schools in their City Schools Reading Series are paving the way for other schools. Josephine Benson describes the books on the preprimer level:

The books show children of multi-racial groups in urban settings to give the children an opportunity to identify themselves with characters that are familiar. The environment shown in these books is not that of the tenement or housing development type, but is one to which culturally different children might reasonably aspire. . . . The vocabulary was carefully chosen to meet the needs of these children and much repetition of words has been provided. An evaluation of the first three pre-primers showed the City Schools Series to be signifiicantly more effective in stimulating interest in reading and word recognition than the regular basal series.[19]

The Bank Street Readers, produced by staff members of the Bank Street College and published by the Macmillan Company, were also developed to give underprivileged boys and girls an easier chance to learn to read than by using the regular school readers as basal readers.[20] These books emphasize life in the big cities, on various economic levels. They are, however, recommended not only for the underprivileged. The publishers suggest that they would also be valuable as readers for all children, probably to supplement other readers, so that those who are privileged can better understand those who are not. Similarly, it has also been recommended that underprivileged children, read the regular readers as supplementary to the Bank Street Readers. These recommendations seem to be in the right direction.

Another venture into the realm of materials designed for use with pupils whose background is deemed deficient was that by the Reading Improvement Project of the Center for Programmed Instruction in 1962.[21] The particular interest of this organization was to explore the potential of programed materials for use with problem readers at the junior high school level. However, an examination of these books may suggest a similar procedure for use with boys and girls in the intermediate grades. The center stated at the outset that it believed that vocabulary is the most significant measure of reading speed and comprehension. Thus the primary direction of the project has been toward the development of programed units to teach vocabulary that is basic to seventh- and eighth-grade subject matter. This

[19] Benson, in Binter, Diabal, and Kise, p. 267.

[20] Irma Black (ed.), *The Bank Street Readers.* New York: The Macmillan Company, 1965.

[21] "Reading Improvement Project of the Center for Programmed Instruction: Progress Report, July 1, 1963." New York: Center for Programmed Instruction, 1964. Distributed by Teachers College, Columbia University, New York.

particular vocabulary was selected for two reasons. First, programing seventh-grade vocabulary for children who read at the fourth-grade level provides an opportunity to uncover and solve problems of teaching higher-order concepts with lower-order language. Second, the vocabulary and concepts that are taught are those encountered by the students in their textbooks. Much of the work done at the Center for Programmed Instruction seems to derive from the theories of speed, comprehension, and power as described by Jack Holmes, who has maintained that this "power of reading" is greatly dependent upon a knowledge of words and the concepts they symbolize. Holmes advocates "introducing into our programs of reading textbooks that have not only a graded list of words, but a graded list of concepts and that these concepts must become deeper, more difficult, and more complex than we have previously thought possible for children to learn." [22]

One source of suitable reading materials for the underprivileged child must not be overlooked. That is the materials produced as experience charts, in which the teacher, at the dictation of the pupils, records experiences of the boys and girls. When culturally disadvantaged children do the dictating, the reports have a good chance of dealing with the lives of those boys and girls. The problem of suitable vocabulary for the culturally deprived or the language handicapped can diminish in the experience chart. In many respects the language-experience approach to beginning reading seems most ideally suited to children in deprived areas as well as to children from non-English–speaking homes. Sometimes these charts may be the record of class experiences; at other times they can be records of those of one individual. (The reader is referred to page 85 for a discussion of experience charts and to page 564 for further information on the language-experience approach.)

It may well be that some of the readers of this book will be interested in making a contribution to education by helping in the preparation of materials especially designed for the culturally underprivileged child. It is an area of many possibilities. There are various aids for anyone wanting to set forth on such a venture. One very valuable resource is the *Writers' Handbook for the Development of Instructional Materials,* especially the section devoted to "Developing

---

[22] Jack A. Holmes, "Speed, Comprehension and Power in Reading," *Problems, Programs and Projects in College-Adult Reading,* p. 14. Eleventh Yearbook of the National Reading Conference, 1961. Milwaukee: National Reading Conference, 1962. Reprinted with the permission of Mrs. Jack A. Holmes and the National Reading Conference, Inc.

Materials for Language Arts." [23] Constance McCullough's book *Preparation of Textbooks in the Mother Tongue* is a recent relevant contribution. Another helpful resource for those interested in writing materials suited to particular groups is Howard Ozmon's article, "A Realistic Approach to the Writing of Children's Textbooks for Deprived Areas." [24] A series of articles appearing in *Improving English Skills of Culturally Different Youth* is also recommended.[25] These include "A Realistic Writing Program for Culturally Diverse Youth" by Don M. Wolfe; "Give Him a Book That Hits Him Where He Lives" by Charles G. Spiegler; "Ways To Improve Oral Communication of Culturally Different Youth" by Ruth I. Golden; and "Subcultural Patterns Which Affect Language and Reading Development" by Donald Lloyd.

Recommendations for a School-wide Approach

Many of the suggestions given in various parts of this chapter could be incorporated into a school-wide approach to the problems of teaching reading to the culturally disadvantaged child and to the child from a non-English–speaking home. They will not be repeated here.

Two helpful summaries of recommendations are those by the *Task Force* of the National Council of Teachers of English. (See page 538 for an account of the work of the *Task Force*.) Although the first list was written for guidance for the preschool program, it is here quoted because it also contains valuable suggestions for administrators and first-grade teachers whose pupils have not had the opportunity to attend preschool programs.

> (1) The development of language skills and concept formation should be the major concern of preschools for disadvantaged children. Preschools have a limited time to prepare these children for future learning; therefore, they must be selective in their

[23] Barbara Nolen and Delia Goetz, *Writers' Handbook for the Development of Instructional Materials*. Bulletin 1959, No. 19. Washington, D.C.: U.S. Department of Health, Education and Welfare, 1959.

[24] Howard A. Ozmon, Jr., "A Realistic Approach to the Writing of Children's Textbooks for Deprived Areas," *Elementary English*, 38, pp. 534–535 (December 1960).

[25] Arno Jewett and associates, *Improving English Skills of Culturally Different Youth in Large Cities*. OC-30012. Bulletin 1964, No. 5. Washington, D.C.: U.S. Department of Health, Education and Welfare, 1964.

objectives. By trying to accomplish everything, often nothing is accomplished.

(2) Every preschool classroom for disadvantaged children should contain a library with a wide selection of children's books. These children have little, if any, reading material in their homes, and need these books to develop reading and to provide content for oral expression.

(3) Preschool curricula for disadvantaged children should include small-group instruction in basic vocabulary and concept patterns. These children lack the experiences which develop many concepts and do not live in homes where vocabulary is stressed or used properly.

(4) Non-standard English dialect should be a concern at the preschool level only to the extent that it interferes with fundamental language learnings. The main purpose is the relation of language to thinking. "Proper" English pronunciation is not as important as the ability to express oneself and to develop conceptual language.[26]

The second list of *Task Force* recommendations, for elementary school programs for the disadvantaged, is as follows:

(1) The school should reflect the particular educational needs of the disadvantaged student. These children are not prepared to enter a normal program planed for middle class students.

(2) First grade disadvantaged children not ready to enter a formal reading program should be enrolled in a language-oriented program. These need to broaden a child's background in language and concepts.

(3) Children with serious reading deficiencies should be placed in a special curriculum taught by a teacher specially trained to teach reading in relation to language development.

(4) Teachers and administrators should question the traditional graded organization. Often, children become obsessed with the notion of failure, and become convinced of their inability to succeed. A non-graded program may overcome this problem.

(5) Schools should involve parents in assisting with its academic program. This involvement is necessary to extend the school's influence into the child's home environment.

(6) Schools should have good classroom and school libraries.

(7) All elementary schools, but especially those teaching disadvantaged children, should re-evaluate their programs in oral language development. Children lacking oral language facility will be handicapped in their reading and writing.[27]

[26] Corbin and Crosby, pp. 65–69.

[27] Corbin and Crosby, pp. 96–98.

Item 5 above indicates the need for parent cooperation. Any consideration of a school-wide plan to help culturally deprived or language-handicapped children learn to read would be incomplete without reference to the importance of gaining the cooperation of parents. Sometimes it is erroneously assumed that culturally deprived parents are not interested in their children. Many of them are deeply concerned about their children's welfare. If the school can convince them that it is really trying to help the boys and girls, many parents will cooperate even at considerable sacrifice to themselves.

The first step in getting the assistance of parents, then, is to convince them that the teachers' interest in their children is sincere. Another step is to explain in understandable terms what the school is trying to do. Along with this explanation should come, from time to time, suggestions as to how parents can help—through providing needed quiet (if possible) in the home for reading, through giving the child time to read, through listening to a child read or tell about what he has read, through encouraging him to go to the library. It will take resourcefulness, ingenuity, and hard work to enlist the cooperation of the home to the fullest extent possible, but the results may well be worth the cost.

FOR FURTHER STUDY

Allen, Harold B., *TENES: A Survey of the Teaching of English to Non-English Speakers in the United States.* Champaign, Ill.: National Council of Teachers of English, 1966.

Black, Irma (ed.), *The Bank Street Readers.* New York: The Macmillan Company, 1965.

Black, Millard H., "Reading in a Compensatory Education Program," *Improvement of Reading through Classroom Practice.* Vol. 9, 1964, pp. 160–161. Proceedings of the Annual Convention. Newark, Del.: International Reading Association.

Corbin, Richard, and Muriel Crosby, *Language Programs for the Disadvantaged.* Report of the NCTE Task Force on Teaching English to the Disadvantaged. Champaign, Ill.: National Council of Teachers of English, 1965.

Educational Policies Commission, *Universal Oportunity for Early Childhood Education.* Washington, D.C.: National Education Association, 1966.

Fader, Daniel N., and Elton B. McNeil, *Hooked on Books: Program and Proof.* New York: G. P. Putnam's Sons, 1968.

Fantini, Mario, and Gerald Weinstein, *Making Urban Schools Work: Social Realities and the Urban School.* New York: Holt, Rinehart and Winston, Inc., 1968.

Figuerel, J. Allen, "Limitations in the Vocabulary of Disadvantaged Children: A Cause of Poor Reading," *Improvement of Reading through Classroom Practice*, Vol. 9, 1964. Proceedings of the Annual Convention. Newark, Del.: International Reading Association.

Figuerel, J. Allen, "The Vocabulary of Underprivileged Children," *University of Pittsburgh Bulletin*, 45 (June 1949).

Fusco, G. C., *School-Home Partnership in Depressed Urban Neighborhoods*. OE-31008. Bulletin 1964, No. 20. Washington, D.C.: U.S. Department of Health, Education and Welfare, 1964.

Gray, William S., *The Teaching of Reading and Writing*. Chicago: UNESCO-Scott, Foresman Company, 1956.

Gregory, Francis A., "The Undereducated Man," *Education Digest*, 36 (December 1964).

Hickcox, Zane, (ed.), *Call Them Heroes*. Morristown, N.J.: Silver Burdett Company, 1965.

Holmes, Jack A., "Speed, Comprehension and Power in Reading," *Problems, Programs and Projects in College-Adult Reading*, p. 6–14. Eleventh Yearbook of the National Reading Conference, 1961. Milwaukee: National Reading Conference, 1962.

Janowitz, Gayle, *Helping Hands: Volunteer Work in Education*. Chicago: University of Chicago Press, 1965.

Jewett, Arno, Joseph Mersand, and Doris V. Gunderson, *Improving English Skills of Culturally Different Youth in Large Cities*. OE-30012. Bulletin 1964, No. 5. Washington, D.C.: U.S. Department of Health, Education and Welfare, 1964.

Koblitz, Minnie, *The Negro in School Literature: Resource Materials for the Teacher of Kindergarten through the Sixth Grade. A Bibliography*. New York: Center for Urban Education, 1968.

Lippitt, Peggy, and John E. Lohman, "Cross-Age Relationships: An Educational Resource," *Children*, 12, pp. 110–115 (May-June 1965).

McCullough, Constance M., *Preparation of Textbooks in the Mother Tongue*. Newark, Del.: International Reading Association, 1968.

Marcum, Dixie E., "Experiences, Concepts, and Reading," *Elementary School Journal*, XLIV, pp. 410–415 (March 1944).

Mergentime, Charlotte, "Tailoring the Reading Program to the Needs of Disadvantaged Pupils: The Role of the School Volunteer," pp. 163–164. *Improvement of Reading through Classroom Practice*. Vol. 9, 1964. Proceedings of the Annual Convention. Newark, Del.: International Reading Association.

Newton, Eunice S., "Training the Volunteer Reading Tutor," *Journal of Reading,* 7, pp. 169–174 (January 1965).

Noar, Gertrude, *Teaching the Disadvantaged. What Research Says to the Teachers,* National Education Asociation, 1967.

Nolen, Barbara, and Delia Goetz, *Writers' Handbook for the Development of Instructional Materials.* Bulletin 1959, No. 19. Washington, D.C.. U.S. Department of Health, Education and Welfare, 1959.

Ozmon, Howard A., Jr., "A Realistic Approach to the Writing of Children's Textbooks for Deprived Areas," *Elementary English,* 38 (December 1960).

"Reading Improvement Project of the Center for Programmed Instruction: Progress Report, July 1, 1963." New York: Center for Programmed Instruction, 1964. (Distributed by Teachers College Press, Columbia University.)

Rosenthal, Robert, and Lenore Jacobson, *Pygmalion in the Classroom.* New York: Holt, Rinehart and Winston, Inc., 1968.

Sanchez, George I., "Significance of Language Handicap," *Learning a New Language.* Bulletin 101, pp. 25–32. Washington, D.C.: Association for Childhood Education International, 1958.

Sapir, Edward, *Language: An Introduction to the Study of Speech.* New York: Harcourt, Brace & World, Inc., 1927.

Serra, Mary C., "The Concept Burden of Instructional Materials," *Elementary School Journal,* 53, pp. 508–512 (May 1953).

Watt, Lois B. (comp.), *Literature for Disadvantaged Children: A Bibliography.* OE-37019. Washington, D.C.: U.S. Department of Health, Education and Welfare, 1968.

The reader is also referred to the many articles appearing during recent years in *Elementary English* on the topic of this chapter.

CHAPTER 16

Current Approaches
to the Teaching of Reading:
A Review[1]

As the gravity of the problems associated with reading instruction has come to be recognized by teachers and laymen, it has become inevitable that much thought would be given to means for improving the learning-to-read process. Throughout this book reference is made to many of the approaches to reading advocated in recent years, and suggestions for implementation of some of them are given. The present chapter supplements earlier discussions of various approaches to the teaching of reading.

DESCRIPTION OF APPROACHES

What, then, are the approaches to the teaching of reading that have come to the forefront during the past two decades?

The Flesch Approach

The book by Rudolf Flesch, *Why Johnny Can't Read,* which appeared in 1955, provoked a number of people, but it may be surmised that it also provoked some thought.[2] At the time the writers of various rebuttals or replies took Flesch to task for his alleged mis-

---

[1] Contributed by Walter J. Moore.

[2] Rudolf Flesch, *Why Johnny Can't Read—And What You Can Do about It.* New York: Harper and Row, Publishers, 1955.

representations of facts. Flesch outlined a system for *all* children as the means of learning to read and spell. He proposed that *all* children learn an extensive and difficult phonetic system *before* they did any reading whatsoever. His method required children to learn to recognize words by a complex procedure of building up word parts.

Children were to be taught to recognize and name the letters, both in print and in script. They were next to be taught to recognize the short sounds of the vowels, then most of the consonant sounds, and finally the long sounds of the vowels and the remaining consonants. They were to be taught also how to recognize and sound out each of a large number of phonograms. During this program they were expected to translate each of several hundred words into their sounds and then to recite or write them as wholes. Some eighty-eight pages of exercises make up the system. This elaborate program was to be taught *before* the child did any reading. Lessons should be taught, Flesch recommended, by the parents of the child about the time he reached five years of age.

The program advocated by Flesch was viewed by many authorities at the time as elaborate and extremely difficult. There are several hundred words in the exercises that children were expected to learn and to write and spell correctly. The exercises begin with words illustrating the sound of *a*. There are ninety words for the letter, such as *mat, wag, tan,* and *van*. Difficulties increase in the later exercises as such words as *independence, mysterious, banisters, asparagus, quizzical,* and *peevishly* are encountered. Flesch belived that this program of phonic synthetic work was all that was necessary for learning to read and to spell well.

Reading authorities disagreed with Flesch, who continued to maintain that the system could be learned by any child at the age of five. He insisted that phonics "is something that a child can master completely, once and for all, with the assurance that he has covered everything there is." [3] Flesch severely criticized studies that indicated that some phases of phonics are difficult to learn until children have acquired greater mental maturity than the beginning reader has.

Flesch brought criticism down on his head when he stated: "Anyone who has started with phonics in first grade goes through life reading every single word he reads letter by letter. He does this fantastically fast, and unconsciously, but nevertheless, he does it." [4]

[3] Flesch, p. 122.

[4] Flesch, p. 42.

The fact of the matter, which is apparent from many observations and careful experiments with children, is that all do not go through this process fantastically fast. The tendency, rather, is to labor through each word, sounding letters and phonograms, making many stops, and then struggling to blend these elements together in a slow, labored procedure. Unfortunately, some children often cannot see the forest for the trees. Even after a labored, piecemeal attack, some pupils are unable quickly and correctly to recognize the word as a whole. This inability tends to interfere with the quick perception of words which is necessary for rapid, intelligent reading.

Critics of Flesch argued that children taught by the method advocated by him would be lacking in other techniques which make for efficient, quick, and accurate word recognition. They claimed that his procedure provides instruction in only *some* of the skills that are essential for the development of the effective reader. They contended that modern basic programs and modern books on reading instruction provide the means for securing the whole array of techniques and the whole range of clues that have been found to be useful in quick and accurate recognition of words. They criticized Flesch for over-simplifying the learning-to-read process by claiming that reading is word recognition, and for further compounding this error by giving the definite impression that his brand of word recognition is reading.

As one examines Flesch's program, one can look in vain for a basic framework to see if the method has a grounding in an interrelated set of assumptions in philosophy, psychology, and education—an interrelation that is recommended for consideration by Lowry Harding in an article discussed later in this chapter.[5]

While it may well be true that some, even many, children have learned to read by Flesch's method, it is questionable if reading skills are fully attained when attention is not directed to the end that more than one kind of word recognition skill should be developed.

The Montessori Revival

Shortly after the book by Flesch appeared, educators became aware of a resurgence of interest in the teachings of Maria Montessori. Reading, according to Montessori, does not come as readily as writing, and thus it requires a longer course of instruction. Likewise, she claimed, it calls for superior prowess, since it treats of the "interpre-

[5] Lowry W. Harding, "Assumptions Underlying Methods of Beginning Reading," *Educational Administration and Supervision*, 37, pp. 25–37 (January 1951).

tation of signs" and of the "modulation of accents of the voice" in order that the word may be understood.[6]

The original development of the Montessori reading method began with the impression of letters, through the novel use of touch, enabling the child to learn the whole alphabet before his interest diminished. Fundamentally the original approach was a phonetic one. Because the Italian language was phonetically oriented, the teaching of reading proceeded without undue difficulties. It was the unphonetic character of English (American) spelling that largely influenced educators—not Montessori—to give up the alphabet method of teaching reading to children, for it was here that teachers were confronted by a serious obstacle.

American educators found it more effective to teach children whole words, sentences, or rhymes by sight, adding to sense impressions the interest aroused by a wide range of associations, and then analyzing the words thus acquired into their phonetic elements to give the child independent power in grasping new words. It occurred to some that a proper approach to teaching reading could systematically employ both phonetic analysis and the Montessori method for teaching the letters, with the exact adjustment depending to a large extent upon the individual system.

What Montessori understood as reading is given in the following statement. Her position in her own day was not always clearly understood, as it was not in the middle of the twentieth century when there was a revival of interest in her methods.

> What I understand by reading is the *interpretation* of an idea from the written signs. The child who has not heard the word pronounced, and who recognizes it when he sees it composed upon the table with the cardboard letters and who can tell what it means, this child *reads*. The word which he reads has the same relation to written language that the word which he hears bears to articulate language. Both serve *to receive the language* transmitted to us *by others*. So, until the child reads a transmission of ideas from the written word, *he does not read*.[7]

The didactic materials that Montessori used as aids in the teaching of reading were a collection of cards upon which the single letters of the alphabet were mounted on sandpaper and a set of larger

[6] Maria Montessori, *The Montessori Method,* pp. 266, 267. New York: Frederick A. Stokes, 1912.

[7] Montessori, p. 296.

cards containing groups of the same letters. The cards upon which the sandpaper letters were mounted were adapted in size and shape to each letter. The vowels were cut in light-colored sandpaper and mounted upon dark cards; the consonants and the groups of letters were in black sandpaper mounted upon white cards. The grouping was so arranged as to call attention to contrasted or analagous forms. The letters were cut in clear script form, with the shaded parts made broader. Montessori chose to reproduce the vertical script in use in the elementary schools during her time.

> In teaching the letters the directress began with the vowels and proceeded to the consonants, pronouncing the sound, not the name. In the case of the consonants, the sound was immediately united with one of the vowel sounds, and the syllables were repeated according to the usual phonetic method.[8]

Once the child had an essential mastery of the alphabet, he could proceed with the following steps.

First, a number of little cards were made from writing paper. On each card was written in large script some well-known word, one that had already been pronounced many times by the children and that represented an object actually present or well known to them, for example, dolls, balls, doll furnishing, and simple figures. If the word referred to an object that was before them, the object was placed before their eyes, in order to facilitate their interpretation of the word.

Montessori believed that there was no question of beginning with a word that was too easy or too difficult, since the child already knew how to read the sounds that composed the word. As part of this step the child would try to translate the written word slowly into sounds. With each vocal response he would speed up the sounds, until the word would finally burst upon his consciousness. He would assume an air of self-satisfaction upon reading the word and then place the explanatory card under the correct object. Thus the exercise progressed until completed.

A second step consisted of a "game" in which there were a basket of words and a large variety of toys on a table. The child (who could read) took a folded paper to his desk and later read it to the directress. If he could pronounce the word clearly and indicated the correct object, the directress allowed him to take the toy and play with it as long as he wished. After all the children had a turn,

[8] Montessori, p. 275.

the first drew from another basket which contained the names of children in the class who could not read. The child who could read the name correctly offered the person named his toy to play with until he tired of it. It was hoped that this would eliminate class distinction and make for a congenial atmosphere. (Later the children refused to play with the games and wanted only to draw out the cards and read, word after word. Montessori interpreted this preference as meaning that it was knowledge the children were seeking and not the game.)

The third step resorted to cards naming hundreds of objects—names of children, colors, cities, and qualities known through the senses. Again each child finished a box before passing it to another, being virtually insatiable in the desire to read, according to Montessori.

Changing the written word to print was part of the fourth step. This was not a very difficult task. Now remained only the presentation of a book. Yet Montessori thought that those available were not suited to her method, which emphasized meaning rather than mechanical skill. Consequently, children were not allowed to use books at this time.

Step five was the presentation of phrases and sentences until the children were ready for composing. It was at this time that Montessori actually came upon her "discovery of reading," for the children were able to interpret the meaning of whole sentences as she wrote them on the board.

Finally came the "game" wherein the child would select one card from a basket of cards that were covered with long sentences describing certain actions, for example, "Close the window blinds," or "Open the door." Silence prevailed as the children read the words and proceeded to act them out.

In summarizing the original development of the Montessori approach to reading, it can be said that Montessori believed that composition precedes logical reading. Her approach, she believed, if it is to teach the child to receive an idea, should be on the mental and not the vocal level. Such a system seemed to call for an individualized reading program so that the children could be free to work at their own pace. The entire process described could be given, under proper direction, to a child over a period of a fortnight, excluding the time necessary for teaching the letters, which was probably rather long. However, it was not expected that in this time the child would gain mastery of the skill. The materials were present for those who showed an interest; others were left to do the tasks that attracted them. Montessori believed that "the idea that *through the reading of a series of words the complex thoughts of others might be communicated to us,* was to be for my children one of the beautiful conquests of the future, a new source of surprise and joy." [9]

Present-day advocates of the Montessori method have employed, along with the foregoing steps, additional "reading games," more individualized work, and the teaching of reading skills in relation to history, science, and other content areas. It is interesting to note that originally Montessori did not intend to teach reading and the other skills to preschool children. Originally she was of the opinion that formal teaching of the skills should not begin until the child was six. But this view changed.

The hours that many of the children in a Montessori classroom spend in fingering sandpaper letters may result in learning the shape and direction of line through the sense of touch. And when there is visual and auditory imagery with this learning, there is the resulting impression that a given letter is, indeed, that letter. However, it cannot be agreed that this process of teaching reading will necessarily work for all children exposed to the system. Perhaps a better approach to teaching reading would be a system that would incorporate Montessori techniques with some of the old and new ideas that already exist in present systems.

The Individualized Reading Program[10]

GROUPING AS AN ATTEMPT TO ADAPT INSTRUCTION TO INDIVIDUAL DIFFERENCES   For a time during the history of American education grouping was looked upon by many educators as the solution to the problem resulting from the fact that, because of individual differences among boys and girls in the typical classroom, they could not advisedly be taught as if they were alike. Russell Stauffer has summarized the attempts that have been made to adapt instruction to individual differences by means of grouping:

> Much of the effort toward grouping resulted from the advent of standardized tests, increased knowledge of individual differences, and the expanding supply of materials. Accordingly, practices were modified so that the good readers could move ahead in a

[9] Montessori, p. 304.

[10] As background for the following discussion, the reader is asked to bear in mind the Contents of Chapter 12, "Providing for Individual Differences," especially the part on "Individualized Reading: Seeking, Self-Selection, and Pacing," pp. 435–439.

book while the slow ones were allowed to drop behind and move slowly in the same book.[11]

Grouping within the bounds of a basic reader was soon found to be inadequate. Thus some publishers of basic readers provided two books for each grade level beyond first grade and more books for first grade. This practice in turn led to that of bringing into a classroom a supplementary basic reader to be used by the third, or slow group. Now the three groups were provided with materials. The teachers, however, rigorously following the plans outlined in teachers' manuals, found themselves trapped even more completely than before.

For a while teachers tried to get around this time-material barrier by having groups II and III do workbook activities. The end result was that workbooks often were used as busy-work, since the teacher did not have time to guide or check this work. This misuse of workbooks was so common that many school administrators forbade their purchase.

Independent reading of other basic readers was tried next, but pupils soon discovered that basic readers were not trade books. Bringing other basic readers into a classroom immediately raised questions about the use of basic books that were not on the same grade level as the grade in which they were being used. The supplementary readers had to be at or below the grade level of the class. The administrators again protested as they found their book closets filled with six or seven different sets of basic readers.

To pick up the no-workbook slack, publishers flooded the market with special phonetic skill books. And strangely enough, many administrators approved the purchase of these materials even though they refused to buy study books planned to parallel a basic reading program.

Is it any wonder that out of all this came two movements— on the one hand, homogeneous grouping on an interclass basis using one book and, on the other hand, individualized reading instruction. The shortcomings of the whole-class lock-step method, with its meager diet and insufficient daily portion, do not need to be reviewed again, but the dimensions of group instruction and individualized instruction warrant being defined.[12]

---

[11] Russell G. Stauffer, "Individualized and Group-type Directed Reading Instruction," in *Winston Communication Program, Consultant Bulletin*, C², p. 4. New York: Holt, Rinehart and Winston, Inc., undated.

[12] Stauffer, p. 4.

OPERATION OF INDIVIDUALIZED READING PROGRAMS

Good teachers have always experimented with programs for teaching reading skills that give the individual child the time and attention he may require if he is to attain the effectiveness and efficiency of the mature reader. These teachers have tried to assess the strengths and weaknesses of pupils so that they—and the child—will know more precisely in what areas he is succeeding and those in which he needs to improve. They have tried to encourage children to make their own choices of reading material, and both teachers and children have concentrated their efforts on adequate record keeping in order to indicate the quality of the materials read, the specific skills and abilities worked on, and developing interests as these unfold. Teachers who have experimented with individualized reading techniques believe that such approaches allow the child to *seek* that which stimulates him, *choose* that which helps him develop most, and *work at his own rate* with what he has chosen. These are, indeed, the factors deemed important by Willard Olson, who identified the *seeking, self-selection,* and *pacing* patterns of children in their use of books.[13]

The administrative climate in which an individualized program operates must be a permissive one. Administrators, supervisors, teachers, and parents must be thoroughly convinced of the general utility of the approach, and careful planning must be the watchword. Programs geared to today's needs cannot be permitted to assume one-sided emphases which distort their true character.

The early 1950s marked the appearance of some definitive works in the area of individualization, but the whole venture into making programs more appropriate for pupils was fraught with many pitfalls. In far too many instances, teachers, eager but ill-informed, ventured into what they viewed as individualization. This tendency brought about the inevitable criticisms stemming from both their fellow-teachers and from parents, who feared that in embarking into the unknown realms of book reading some children, indeed, many, might fall behind in skills development. They believed that children would show this deficiency as they moved more freely on their own in book reading without adequate supervision and guidance by their teachers.

A question that frequently arose was, "How does one go about installing an individualized program in a classroom?" A growing

[13] Willard C. Olson, "Seeking, Self-Selection, and Pacing in the Use, of Books by Children," *The Packet,* VII, No. 1 (Spring 1952). Boston: D. C. Heath and Company, 1952.

literature described intermediate steps between basal programs with ability grouping and complete individualization. Leland Jacobs stated:

> While success in individualizing the teaching of skills and fostering independent reading does call for appropriate procedures and arrangements, these are not enough. Individualizing reading starts not with procedures but with a creative, perceptive teacher—one who believes that children want to learn; who thinks with children rather than for them; who basically respects the individual behavior of every youngster; who works with children in orderly but not rigid ways. Such a teacher sees the individualizing of reading as consistent with the total designing of living with children in the classroom. Individualization of reading, thereby, gears into the larger context for learning, in which, throughout the school day, children are using their reading for functional ends:
>
> > To understanding and using ideas
> > To acquiring important information
> > To solving problems
> > To participating in creative activities
> > To thinking critically
> > To developing viewpoints and ideals
> > To evaluating learnings, ways of behaving
> > To comprehending culture
> > To understanding self and others
> > To knowing, being, and becoming.[14]

INDIVIDUALLY PRESCRIBED INSTRUCTION (IPI)   While IPI, as the term indicates, is a program in which reading instruction is individualized, it differs in various respects from procedures of Individualized Reading so far here described—namely, the program that Jeannette Veatch in her book *Individualizing Your Reading* advocates.[15]

IPI was introduced by Robert Glaser and John O. Bolvin of the School of Education of the University of Pittsburgh in collaboration with the Learning Research and Development Center of the Baldwin-Whitehall school district in the Oak Leaf School in Pittsburgh. In the middle 1960s administrators and teachers from various parts of the United States began visiting the school for observation and

[14] Reprinted with the permission of the publisher, from Leland B. Jacobs and others, *Individualizing Reading Practices*, p. 17. Alice Miel, ed. New York: Teachers College Press. © 1958, Teachers College, Columbia University.

[15] Jeannette Veatch, *Individualizing Your Reading*. New York: G. P. Putnam's Sons, 1959.

participation in the IPI program of instruction. The program appeared to work well, particularly in those schools that had installed nongraded primary programs.

Beginning in kindergarten, children receive a complex battery of general aptitude and intelligence tests and a series of reading readiness tests, which determine ability and competence in particular areas of the curriculum. Children who are mature enough to begin reading instruction undertake this task at the kindergarten level. Some are moved immediately into a primary reading program because they have achieved a certain degree of competence in basic skills.

When pupils have successfully accomplished a designated set of skills at a particular level, they progress to a more difficult level for reading instruction. Currently, many school systems are moving their pupils through the ten levels of learning that were identified by the Oak Leaf School in Pittsburgh. Emphasis has been placed on the use of comprehensive diagnostic tests to assess the learning abilities of each child at every level of instruction. As soon as the child demonstrates that he has a high degree of competency in a particular skill, such as reading, spelling, listening, speaking, writing, or grammar, he is moved into a more difficult instructional program which is designed to challenge his innate abilities.

Using materials collected from commercially prepared sources, teachers' files, and newly innovated materials, master files are set up which are the core material for the entire program. "Prescriptions" are written for each child and IPI clerks fill these prescriptions, which may entail transparencies, filmstrips, records, supplementary readers, and the like. Many school systems have been most successful in developing their own variations of the Oak Leaf model.

The Language Experience Approach

Many educators have taken the position in recent years that far greater emphasis ought to be placed upon oral language. (See page 85, "Using the Experience Chart in the Prereading Period.") They believe that if this emphasis were present from the very earliest stages onward through the grades, many of the problems that arise could and would be circumvented. One such thrust has been the so-called language experience approach, which recognizes that the oral language background of each child is a basic ingredient in word recognition throughout the grades. Already in 1943 it was discussed by Lillian Lamoreaux and Dorris Lee in their book *Learning To Read*

Through Experience, a second edition of which was written by Dorris M. Lee and R. V. Allen in 1963.[16]

In the introduction to the second edition of *Learning To Read through Experience,* the authors observe that they have described a plan for developing reading ability as an integral part of all communication skills, for they see four principal aspects of the language arts— listening, speaking, reading, and writing—as being but different faces of the same understandings and skills. Allen, writing elsewhere, has stated that in a language experience program

> the thinking of each child is valued → which leads to expressing his thinking in oral language → which can be reconstructed (read) by the author → which leads to reconstruction of written language of others → which should influence thinking and oral language of the reader so that his spelling, writing, and reading improve.[17]

THE SAN DIEGO COUNTY READING RESEARCH PROJ-ECT   In the San Diego County Reading Research Project with which Allen was identified, the framework for the language experience program was erected on some 20 language experiences. They include three major emphases:

> (a) Extending experiences to include words that express them— through oral and written sharing of personal experiences, discussing selected topics, listening to and telling stories, writing independently, and making and reading individual books;
> (b) Studying the English language—through developing an understanding of speaking, reading, and writing relationships, expanding vocabularies, reading a variety of symbols in the environment, improving style and form of personal expression, studying words, and gaining some awareness of the nature of the English language (use of high frequency words and English sentence paterns); and
> (c) Relating ideas of authors to personal experiences—through reading whole stories and books, learning to use a variety of printed resources, summarizing, outlining, reading for specific purposes, and determining the validity and reliability of statements.[18]

[16] Dorris M. Lee and R. V. Allen. *Learning To Read through Experience.* New York: Appleton-Century-Crofts, 1963.

[17] R. V. Allen, "Language Experience Approach," in Helen K. Mackintosh, ed., *Current Approaches to Teaching Reading,* p. 2. Elementary Instructional Service Leaflet, Washington, D.C.: National Education Association, 1965.

[18] Mackintosh, p. 2.

THE LANGUAGE FOR LEARNING PROGRAM: A VARIA-
TION   According to Language Research, Inc., of Harvard University,
the Richards-Gibson approach to reading, using the Language for
Learning materials, constitutes far more than a reading program.[19]
These materials comprise an integrated language arts curriculum for
the primary grades, and through language they provide an introduction
to elementary mathematics, social science, general science, and literature. Through the language that was taught, children are able to understand and express verbally and in writing concepts and relations
that were beyond the purview of the conventional primary curriculum.
This acceleration is made possible, according to the publishers, through
the intensive use of a "high-utility vocabulary." The total vocabulary
for the first three grades consists of 1,000 words. This basic list is
called a "defining vocabulary"—a set of highly resourceful words
that could be used to explain other words and to express concepts
in many more areas of human endeavor than is possible with a "frequency vocabulary" list of the same length. This functional quality
has made it possible for children to master the spelling and syntax
of a segment of the English language which they can use to express
clearly and simply some very significant ideas and relations in mathematics, science, and literature.

Five characteristics distinguish the Language for Learning
program from conventional language arts programs:

1. Simplification of the perceptual and cognitive tasks involved in learning
   to read and write.
2. The development of a high-utility, rather than a high-frequency, vocabulary.
3. Avoidance of extrinsic motivational devices.
4. Emphasis upon reality rather than fantasy as the more important realm
   for formal language instruction.
5. Depth and range.

Let us for a moment take a look at the perceptual and
cognitive tasks referred to above. The perceptual task involved in
reading is simplified by limiting the number of alphabet characters
that comprise the words in the first sentences. One starts with seven
letters, but these seven (*a, h, i, m, n, s,* and *t*) permit the use of declara-
tive sentences from the very first page. Then the letters *e, d,* and *r* are

[19] Richard M. Everett, Jr., *Comparison between Conventional Basic Reading Programs and the Language for Learning Program*, p. 4. New York: Washington
Square Press, Inc., 1960.

introduced at wide-spaced intervals. Opportunities for incorrectly discriminating letters are held to a minimum by separating the characters with similar configurations (*b, d, p, q; o, c, e; u, n;* and *m, w*) and introducing these one at a time.

Another way in which the materials are said to differ is that they are used to teach letters rather than sounds. In the Richards-Gibson method, the learner concentrates on how marks on paper make words and sentences. The cognitive task is simplified through the presentation of sequences of sentence situations. These sequences are so devised that each situation prepares for those to come and is confirmed by those that follow. Thus each text is carefully graded in terms of the relations between the elements in the sequences. Because each element reinforces and is in turn reinforced by its companions in the sequence, the opportunities for misinterpretation are claimed to be minimal.

The publishers have this to say regarding their materials:

> Discourse of this kind is said to be *continuous* when the sentence situations are sufficiently clear to prevent misconception or misinterpretation. Continuous discourse is, of course, a state of perfection that can only be approached. It is because of this that learners need teachers or even teaching machines to confirm their responses. However, in the *Language for Learning* materials for teaching reading, the sequences have been so well programmed, or graded, that discourse is nearly continuous. As a result, learning is self-motivating. No elaborate or fanciful illustrations, no contrived plots or vacuous stories are needed to seduce the child into the act of reading. Rather, the assurance that is born of success encourages children to read in order to discover the nature of reality.[20]

In the Richards-Gibson or Language for Learning materials, the following appears: "This is a man. This is a hat. This hat is his hat. It is his hat."

It will be noted that in the Language for Learning approach parts of the materials are programed. (Programing is discussed later in this chapter.)

USE BY MACKINNON OF THE LANGUAGE FOR LEARNING MATERIALS Through the use of the Language for Learning materials A. R. MacKinnon did research in relation to an instructional

[20] Everett, pp. 4–5.

design for first steps in reading. Since the experiment was conducted in Scotland and since the report given at the Annual Convention of the International Reading Association was subsequently published in Canada, not much attention has been given to the study in the United States.[21] It is, however, worthy of attention in this country.

With small groups of children working under varying conditions and utilizing conventional materials and Richards-Gibson materials, MacKinnon sought to provide maximum opportunities for the pupils to reveal their *thinking* as they attempted to comprehend the meanings of the printed symbols on the presentation sheets. In addition, he was particularly interested in assessing pupils' growth in comprehension and perceptual discrimination after they had worked for several weeks with the Richards-Gibson materials. In summary, MacKinnon had this to say:

> The children's thinking as revealed on the Richards-Gibson material can best be described as a development of strategies for handling the tasks of written language. In the early stages, familiar patterns were fixed on in an effort to reduce the possibilities of error. As these patterns shifted, there was an increased awareness that the patterns had to be transformed in some way. The children reacted by reaching the illustrations for cues, by substituting known words for unknown words, by omitting parts of sentences, by inserting familiar patterns, and by even separating sentences into parts. These early modes were soon recognized as inadequate because of the incongruity between what was written and what was said. The children then tackled one problem at a time and once they had achieved some measure of success, an increasing transformation was made of the previous knowledge in order to accommodate the new tasks. Each step was evaluated by the learners within increasingly widening contexts of comparison. This often took the form of rereading spontaneously and of pointing to particular parts of the sentences.[22]

During the early meetings of children in the group, irrelevant suggestions from listeners waiting their turn encumbered the child in his efforts to read aloud. During the following meetings, there was increasing evidence that children could learn from one another and

[21] A. R. MacKinnon, "Research on Instructional Design for First Steps in Reading," *Changing Conceptions of Reading Instruction.* Vol. VI, 1961, pp. 164–167. Proceedings of the Annual Convention. Newark, Del.: International Reading Association.

[22] A. R. MacKinnon, *How Do Children Learn To Read?* p. 10. Toronto, Ontario: Copp Clark, 1959.

aid each other in their learning. The emergence of groups that could function in this way was intrinsically related to the nature of a task that required the children to make a study of language together.

Once the pupils knew, in a measure, what they were doing in reading, comments from the group forced the readers to examine the modes they used in dealing with printed symbols. The majority of time spent by any child in the group was taken up with silent reading. The children who worked with the Richards-Gibson material showed a general superiority, not so much in scores obtained but in the modes of thinking they developed to handle the complex tasks of language learning. They showed an increasing expertness in perceiving how the language they had learned could be utilized to handle new problems. They also indicated a superiority in perceptual discrimination of parts of words and a superiority in perceiving how words work together in sentences.[23]

MacKinnon took the position that an intensive study of an essential core of letters of the alphabet helped the children to develop effective modes of tackling perceptual problems, while "scientific design of material for learning to read does succeed in helping children to a greater language power, not only in reading but also in speaking and writing." [24]

AN EVALUATION Language experience approaches of various types have a good deal to commend them for they recognize more clearly than many other attacks on the problems of teaching reading that being responsible for teaching the language arts in the elementary school means that a teacher recognizes the fact that she is expected to advance pupils' skills in reading, oral and written expression, grammar, spelling, writing, listening, and literature. Although there is by no means universal agreement regarding the wisdom of combining so many and such diverse skills as those enumerated, there is agreement that the ties which bind these skills together are stronger than the forces which would have them taught entirely as separate subjects.

Programed Instruction in Reading

Reference was made in Chapter 12 (see page 434) to programed learning as one means of individualizing instruction, and in Chapter 15 (see page 547) it was discussed as a procedure for use with

[23] MacKinnon, *How Do Children Learn to Read?* p. 10.

[24] MacKinnon, *How Do Children Learn to Read?* p. 11.

pupils with a deficient background. Further discussion of the topic follows.

It was in the early 1960s that mechanical devices purported to "teach" everything from simple spelling to complex mathematics were being produced and sold throughout the country. But this was scarcely the beginning, for much earlier a good deal of concern had been and continued to be expressed about the place and use of "gimmicks" in reading. Arthur Gates had observed that mechanical devices of many sorts had been proposed and, indeed, used in American schools for more than a half century.

Gates observed that "projection lanterns, tachistoscopes, and other quick-exposure apparatus, phonics wheels and word ladders, flash cards and display racks had been in use for a long time when the motion picture, the flash meter, and a variety of other mechanical devices appeared. Various types of practice exercises and workbooks that were introduced twenty-five and more years ago embodied the principles found in some of the new teaching machines and in programed learning." [25]

One company, in marketing its product, provided an extensive explanation of the program it was selling by defining what programed instruction is; by demonstrating that it does not replace the teacher; by explaining how the program would work in the classroom; and by pointing out the advantages for the teacher in the use of programed instruction.

> The program may be offered to the learner through a teaching machine, on a deck of printed cards, in a book, through a motion picture or a series of still pictures, or in a variety of ways. The information which the learner sees or reads is generally broken down into fairly short units, referred to as "frames." Each frame may be a picture, a paragraph or two of information, a mathematical equation, or some similar unit which illustrates a single idea. After the student has observed each frame in turn, the program requires that he respond by answering a question, filling in a blank, solving a problem, or some similar action which indicates that he understands what he has seen and read.
>
> The answers to the question asked in each frame are readily available to the student. In BRL's (Behavioral Research Laboratories) programmed textbooks, they are printed on the same page. The student covers them with a narrow cardboard "slider" and moves this slider down the page as he proceeds through the

[25] Arthur I. Gates, "Teaching Machines in Perspective," *Elementary School Journal,* LXII, p. 1 (October 1961).

frames, thus revealing the correct answers. He may then review his work if he has answered incorrectly and will have knowledge of the correct answer before he proceeds further into the material. This assures his success. This feeling of success can completely change the classroom attitude of a student who has known only failure in his school work.

The early frames of the program offer simple, basic ideas in the subject. As the student proceeds, each frame introduces some new idea based on the previous information, or reviews previous information from a different point of view to reinforce the ideas that have been presented. Thus the student gains an ever-expanding understanding of the subject based on a gradual, orderly development of the content of the frames.

Through his regular responses, the learner is *involved* in the program and actively participates in the learning process. He is not a passive learner or reader, but must act upon the program. Because of the format and presentation of most programs, especially programmed texts, the learner may involve himself in a new material at his own pace. He may move more quickly through material that he understands easily and work more thoroughly and precisely through material of which he is unsure (all the while reinforced by immediate knowledge of the correctness of his response).

In order for a program to be successful, its developer must first decide what the student is to learn. What knowledge and concepts, skills and attitudes should the learner comprehend and understand as he proceeds through the program and how should he be able to demonstrate these effectively when he has completed the study? In other words, *what* is to be taught and how will the teacher determine, at the completion of the program by the learner, that it has been taught successfully?

So, before the program is written, the programmer might develop the tests that will be used upon completion of the program. This is a good place to start in the development of any instructional materials.

The programmer will then undertake the not-so-easy task of starting with very basic and simple ideas and information, building step by step and response by response upon these, and proceeding through a logical and ordered sequence to introduce the new ideas, concepts and skills to the learner. This entire procedure will lead up to the desired behavior of the student upon his completion of the program.

As mentioned above, many devices may be used to communicate the program to the learner. However, research substantially supports the fact that the device will teach no better than the program provided through it, and the quantity and quality of the learning are rarely affected by the format of presentation. Since books can be more easily and economically developed and produced than most of the alternatives, Behavioral Research Laboratories produces its programs in book form.[26]

Joseph Roucek has observed that the teaching machine has become an extension of the teacher, and programed learning consists in teaching without the direct mediation of a human teacher. In his book *Programmed Teaching* he attempts to impart an idea of the relative success-failure ratio derived from the use of machines in education, and to indicate how machines can best be employed in the future.[27]

Automated Reading

In 1959 attention was directed to research conducted at Yale University by Moore and Anderson, in which four young children ranging in age from two to four were taught to "read." [28] Moore later reported on progress made in the study, which then used thirty-five children, only two of whom would be ranked as gifted, with the remainder being within so-called normal ranges. All the children learned to type, to read, and to write. By May 1961, over 100 children had developed skills in these areas, and large-scale application of the method was made that year at Hamden Hall Country Day School in Hamden, Connecticut. Called somewhat facetiously "supervised play with a typewriter," because the basic instructional tool was the electric portable typewriter, children were permitted to "play" as they wished with the machine, which in time came to involve the striking of the keys. As the child struck a key, the teacher repeated the name of the letter or numeral. Thus the child rapidly learned that his striking of a key triggered a response from his teacher, that different characters appeared on the sheet of paper in the machine, and that he ought to reinforce his own activity by naming the symbol before his teacher had to do this for him.

[26] *The How and Why of Effective Teaching through Programmed Instruction: A Practical Guide for Teachers and Administrators*, pp. 2–3. Palo Alto, Calif.: Behavioral Research Laboratories, undated.

[27] Joseph Roucek, ed., *Programmed Teaching: A Symposium on Automation in Teaching*. New York: Philosophical Library, 1965.

[28] O. K. Moore, "Orthographic Symbols and the Pre-School Child—A New Approach," paper presented at the Third Minnesota Conference on Gifted Children, Minneapolis, October 1960.

A chalkboard and chalk were likewise utilized, and the child was encouraged to "draw" the letters and symbols on the board which he had seen in typewritten form.

> Once the child knows the letters, a simple projector is fastened to the typewriter, and the child reads and types out simple sentences. Finally he reaches the stage where he reads the projected sentences into a recording machine and types out stories from his own dictation, complete with punctuation.[29]

Moore has made various changes from the early procedures advocated. The following description by Mildred Wittick indicates some of the points of variation.

> The "talking typewriters" . . . can flash a picture on a screen, identify it by saying the word aloud, and guide the child into spelling the word on a typewriter keyboard. A transparent partition separates the picture, the typing mechanism, and the typed copy from the curious hands of the child who has produced it. When the machine shows the picture of a dog and spells D-O-G, all the letters on the keyboard lock except the D. When the child hits the D, the letter appears on the paper in the typewriter. The keyboard continues to lock in proper sequences until the child has spelled out the word *dog*.[30]

Moore believes that the activity has to be "autotelic," performed solely for its own sake and not because of extrinsic rewards or punishments. He believes that the curiosity or "competence" drive is all-important and that the sooner the child is put in a position to fulfill this drive the greater, wider, and more lasting the effects will be upon him as an individual.

Other Current Approaches

Several other current approaches to helping boys and girls learn to read are described in Chapter 5A. They are the linguistic approach, the use of i/t/a, the words-in-color approach, and the use

---

[29] *Carnegie Corporation of New York Quarterly*, IX (April 1961), p. 2.

[30] Mildred Wittick, "Innovations in Reading Instruction: For Beginners," *Innovation and Change in Reading Instruction*, pp. 95–96. Sixty-seventh Yearbook of the National Society for the Study of Education, Part II. Chicago: University of Chicago Press, 1968.

of the Diacritical Marking System. The last three, it should be noted, are recommended only for initial reading instruction. Furthermore, it should not be overlooked that phonics has been used more extensively as an aid to initial work in word recognition during the last decade and a half than it was during several decades preceding.

Thus during the 1950s and 1960s many attempts were made to solve various reading problems. The period had witnessed the appearance of the Flesch approach, the revival of interest in the Montessori method, the development of the individualized reading approach, the extension of the Language Experience approach, and the beginning of programed instructional techniques as applied to reading instruction. During this period the Hay-Wingo system was explained in *Reading With Phonics* (Lippincott); the Cordts system in *Readiness for Power in Reading* and *I Can Read* (Beckly-Cardy); the Fillmore system in *Steps to Mastery of Words* (Education Service, Inc.); the *Phonovisual Method* of Schoolfield and Timberlake (Phonovisual Products, Inc.); the Herr System in *Improve Your Reading through Phonics* (Smith and Hoist); the *Phonetic Keys to Reading* system (Economy Publishing Company); the Daniels-Diack approach in the *Royal Road Readers* (Chatto and Windus); the Barnhart and Bloomfield technique in *Let's Read* (Wayne University Press); and many others.

RECENT INVESTIGATIONS

When considering current approaches to the teaching of reading, one cannot escape the conclusion that an almost overwhelming concern has been with beginning reading instruction. Not only have many methods that were advocated during the fifties and sixties been focused on the initial learning-to-read process, but, as would be expected, among the most significant research in the field of reading during that period was that which dealt with "first steps" in reading.

The Search for the "Right" Start

The question as to when reading instruction should begin is considered at various places in this book. The first part of Chapter 4A is devoted to a discussion of the controversy concerning the optimum time for beginning reading instruction. An earlier section of the present chapter discusses the research of O. K. Moore on automated instruction for children from two to four. Summaries of other studies dealing with the question follows.

RESEARCH IN NEW YORK CITY News items in the press have for years drawn attention to full-scale efforts to cope with the critical deficiencies in the reading programs of the public schools in big cities. Consequently, beginning in about 1961, increased emphasis was placed on getting boys and girls ready for reading so that some children would be able to start learning to read before first grade. To accomplish this objective, an increasing number of kindergarten programs placed greater emphasis on preparing youngsters for the formal learning that usually comes in the first grade. In that year, in New York City, twenty-five selected kindergarten classes, meeting in afternoon sessions for an hour longer than was customary, experimented with ways of advancing reading readiness. In a second move involving reading experts at twenty-one colleges and universities in the metropolitan area, some forty faculty members served in what was formally called an academy of reading.

The members of the academy of reading met four or five times that year to report on experimentation in progress or contemplated. In addition, members of the academy worked directly in seminars organized for the training, retraining, and supervision of reading teachers in the school system. Other plans for the improvement of reading instruction included forty-seven in-service training courses for teachers given by the New York Board of Education in 1961–1962; a state-wide television course on the teaching of reading; special closed-circuit television courses at selected public schools; and on-the-job retraining of teachers through the use of special teachers of reading. The decision to take these steps came as the result of a report that expressed the belief that the city's elementary school children were losing ground in reading in comparison with children all over the nation.

Among the possible reasons for the critical situation suggested by reading specialists and teachers were the following:

1. A continuing influx of families from low economic backgrounds.
2. Increased home tensions that are carried over into the school.
3. Foreign language problems.
4. Overcrowding and short sessions in some parts of the city.
5. Lack of remedial and guidance teachers to help overcome these problems.

It was believed that in time, with the attack being made on many fronts, fewer New York City elementary school pupils would show up in the annual testings to be below so-called grade levels. Significantly, the emphasis upon additional, direct work at the kindergarten level was deemed vital to the effectiveness of the reading program in the middle and upper grades.

THE DENVER STUDY   Another concern—the claim that parents should not teach preschool boys and girls to read—was investigated in the public schools of Denver under a grant by the Carnegie Corporation (see page 38). The grant enabled the school system to revise and improve its parental instruction program. Much was accomplished through the use of television programs and the guidebook *Preparing Your Child for Reading*. It was claimed that this approach, based on a phonics emphasis, helped the child to associate words he knew orally with the way the words look on a page.

DURKIN'S RESEARCH   Dolores Durkin has reported on research on children who read before grade one. She had in progress, in the early 1960s, a longitudinal study of forty-nine California children who learned to read outside of school. These children were reading at grade levels ranging from 1.5 to 4.6 when they entered first grade. The design of the study was guided by certain general questions, one of which had to do with the frequency of occurrence of evidence of early reading ability. Durkin reported as follows:

As a way of selecting subjects, a word identification test was individually administered to the beginning first graders ($N = 5,103$) in one city. Children repeating first grade, as well as a small number of children who had been given some instruction in reading the latter part of kindergarten, were not tested.

Following this procedure, 49 first graders (29 girls and 20 boys) were identified as having some ability in reading prior to school instruction. Of these 49 children, 26 (53%) were Caucasian, 12 (24%) were Negro, and 11 (22%) were Oriental. The Oriental background accounted for seven of the ten bilingual children.

Family interview data concerned with socio-economic status indicated that seven of the children in the total group of 49 could be classified as upper-middle class, 15 as lower-middle class, 26 as upper-lower class, and one as lower-lower class. Intelligence test data, obtained from the Stanford-Binet in the second month of first grade, indicated IQ's that varied from 91 to 161, and MA's that varied from 5.1 to 10.7 years. The median IQ for the group was 121, and the median MA was 7.1 years.

Closely following the identification of subjects, and still within the first two weeks of first grade, standardized reading tests were administered. The scores ranged, according to grade norms, from 1.5 to 4.6, with a mean of 2.3. Reading tests administered at the end of the semester and again at the beginning and end of the summer vacation period showed encouraging gains in achievement. By this latter date, for example, the children's grade scores varied from 2.3 to 7.1, while the mean score was 4.0.[31]

Later, Durkin made additional observations.

> Some of these children initially learned when they were three years of age; some when they were four; and others, not until five. When the total group started first grade the average reading achievement for those who learned at three was, according to grade-level norms, 2.6. For those who did not learn until they were five, the average achievement was 1.7. Two years later, when the children were finishing second grade, the average reading achievement of those who learned first at three continued to be greater. Now, however, the difference between their achievement and that of the children who began at five was reduced by four months. Only time can tell in what direction the ultimate achievement of these two groups of children will go.[32]

To a certain extent time did tell, and Durkin was able much later to report findings of the longitudinal studies that had consumed her attention for a decade. Her book *Children Who Read Early* is a definitive work in the area.[33]

One of the things that stands out in the research by Durkin is that the children were very commonly described by parents, and later by teachers, as persistent, perfectionistic, and competitive children. A majority of them had, their parents and teachers agreed, extraordinary memories and possessed high ability to concentrate. In addition, they were described as curious, conscientious, serious-minded, persistent, and self-reliant. In all instances there were parents who took the time to answer children's questions; and there were older siblings who were both willing and able to teach interested brothers and sisters to read.

[31] Dolores Durkin, "Children Who Read before Grade One," *The Reading Teacher*, pp. 163–164, (January 1961). Reprinted with the permission of the author and the International Reading Association.

[32] Dolores Durkin, "Some Unanswered Questions about Five-Year-Olds and Reading," *Changing Concepts of Reading Instruction*, Vol. VI, 1961, pp. 167–170. Proceedings of the Annual Convention. Newark, Del.: International Reading Asociation. Reprinted with the permission of the author and the International Reading Association.

[33] Dolores Durkin, *Children Who Read Early*. New York: Teachers College Press, Columbia University, 1966.

Research on Reading in the Primary Grades

Although researchers have devoted much attention in recent years to the possibility of beginning reading instruction before a child enters first grade, comprehensive investigations have also been made dealing with the methods of teaching reading in the primary grades. Part of Chapter 5A deals with studies and reports on the code versus meaning approach to reading.

DURRELL'S STUDIES OF FIRST-GRADE READING SUCCESS   One series of significant investigations of reading on the first-grade level was made by Donald Durrell and associates. The instructional program for the more than 2,000 first-grade children involved in the studies under Durrell's direction was aimed at three objectives: to assure reading success among first-grade children; to evaluate reading readiness practices and concepts; and to study relations among the various aspects of growth in reading. Durrell stated:

> Clinical services have indicated that reading failures at first-grade level were usually overcome when the following abilities were established through effective teaching: knowledge of letter names, ability to identify sounds in spoken words, knowledge of applied phonics. Additional services commonly needed were meaningful word recognition practice and special help in beginning silent reading. It appeared that if these needs were identified and served in initial classroom instruction, much reading difficulty might be prevented. In addition, it was hoped that rapid learners might make higher achievement if unnecessary instruction were eliminated from the reading program.[34]

Ninety-one teachers in four communities and 2,300 first-grade pupils were involved in the study. Tests measured several levels of letter knowledge, the ability to identify separate sounds in spoken words, visual discrimination of words, learning rate in word recognition, and a group measure of intelligence. The following program, with testing in September, November, February, and June, is described by Durrell thus:

1. Children high in learning rate, in letter names, and in hearing sounds in words were grouped together. For them, reading instruction was started at once; both word recognition and applied phonics were presented immediately. The reading

[34] Donald D. Durrell, "First-Grade Reading Success Study: A Summary," *Journal of Education,* 140, p. 2 (February 1958).

readiness program of the basal reading system was skipped.

2. Children lower in learning rate and with gaps in letter and sounds-in-words knowledge were grouped together. Although some sight vocabulary was taught, the main emphasis was upon systematic instruction in letter names and on the ability to identify sounds in words. This was followed later by instruction in applied phonics.

3. Children who were low in learning rate and in letter and sounds-in-words knowledge were grouped together. These, too, started some sight vocabulary learning, but the major emphasis was on letter names and identifying separate sounds in spoken words.[35]

Help with word recognition in the stories in the basal readers was provided from the beginning, but at a slower pace for the slower learners. Systematic review of sight vocabulary emphasized response to word meaning rather than to the name of the word; special practice in silent reading was given through the use of sentence cards.

Some of the major findings and their implications, according to Durrell, follow.

1. Most reading difficulties can be prevented by an instructional program which provides early instruction in letter names and sounds, followed by applied phonics and accompanied by suitable practice in meaningful sight vocabulary and aids to attentive silent reading. Among the 1,500 children measured in June, only 18 had a sight vocabulary of less than 50 words; this is slightly more than one percent of the population. Four percent, or 62 children, had a sight vocabulary of less than 100 words.

2. Early instruction in letter names and sounds produces a higher June reading achievement level than does such instruction given incidentally during the year.

3. Children with high learning rates and superior background skills make greater progress when conventional reading readiness materials are omitted from their reading programs.

4. Children entering first grade present wide differences in levels of letter knowledge:

   a. All children were able to match capital letters as well as lower case letters. Exercises in this ability should be omitted from reading readiness materials. It appears to follow that matching of nonword forms and pictures as preliminary instruction for letter and word perception is relatively useless.

[35] Durrell, pp. 5–6.

b.   The average child in this population could, in September: give the names of 12 capital letters and 9 lower case letters; identify 17 capitals named and 12 lower case letters named; write 10 letters from dictation.

5.   Tests of knowledge of letter names at school entrance are the best predictors of February and June reading achievement.

6.   Chronological age shows little relationship to any of the factors measured at any testing period. It correlates negatively with reading achievement. Apparently no solution to reading difficulties is to be found by raising the entrance age to first grade.

7.   Mental age, as measured by the Otis Quick-Scoring Tests of Mental Ability, has a low relationship to reading achievement and to letter and word perception skills.

8.   There appears to be no basis for the assumption that a sight vocabulary of 75 words should be taught before word analysis skills are presented. Of the 1,170 children tested in February, only nine achieved a sight vocabulary of more than 70 words when they knew fewer than 20 letters. Of the children who knew more than 20 letters, 675 had a sight vocabulary of more than 70 words. While a knowledge of letter names and sounds does not assure success in acquiring a sight vocabulary, lack of that knowledge procedures failure.[36]

STUDIES SPONSORED BY THE U.S. OFFICE OF EDUCA-TION   The various endeavors in the search for the right start in beginning reading instruction were the forerunners of interesting developments at the national level. By the year 1961, the U.S. Office of Education had established *Project English,* which in its three-year life was to have widespread influence. It funded projects in basic and applied research, established a score of demonstration centers and curriculum centers, and launched dozens of allied endeavors involving workshops and institutes centering on research in English, including, in time, reading.

The following summary of the primary grade studies sponsored by the U.S. Office of Education is supplementary to the account given in Chapter 5A, "Word Recognition."

In the school year 1964–1965, twenty-seven first-grade reading studies were sponsored by the U.S. Office of Education. These studies were made in different localities and represented a good geographic distribution. They were concerned with different problems

[36] Durrell, pp. 5–6.

in each instance and were designed to avoid duplication of effort. Reports of these reading studies appeared in *The Reading Teacher.*[37] Later the International Reading Association published *First Grade Reading Programs.*[38] There were, in effect, twenty-seven independent studies so well coordinated in research design, instruments of measurement, information gathered, and comparability of data collected that comparisons among the studies were possible in ways that had not previously existed. The project involved nearly 30,000 children and 1,000 teachers. A wide variety of teaching approaches was involved in the studies. Included among these were basal reader, language experience, phonic emphasis, linguistic emphasis, new alphabet, early letter, individualized reading, reading readiness, audio-visual, teacher supervisor, and approaches that for want of a better term were grouped under the heading of approaches for culturally different pupils.

The U.S. Office of Education extended fourteen of the studies through the second and third grades thus permitting for inter- and intracomparisons of studies. In the January, 1969, issue of *The Reading Teacher* various investigators reported on their studies extended into third grade. The titles and main direction of a few of these included "Reading Achievement of First Grade Children Taught by a Linguistic Approach and a Basal Reader Approach—Extended into Third Grade" by J. Wesley Schneyer; "The CRAFT Project: A Final Report" (Comparing Reading Approaches in First-Grade Teaching with Disadvantaged Children) by Albert J. Harris and Coleman Morrison; "Comparison of Beginning Reading with i.t.a., DMS, and t.o. after Three Years," (initial teaching alphabet, Diacritical Marking System, and traditional orthography) by Edward Fry; and "A Three Year Look at i.t.a., Lippincott, Phonics and Word Power, and Scott, Foresman" by Robert B. Hayes and Richard C. Wuest.[39]

Speaking editorially, Russell Stauffer observed that "any attempt to compare method with method or study with study could easily produce misunderstandings and false conclusions. Each study must be examined on its own premises and results, and the reader

---

[37] *The Reading Teacher,* Vol. 19, No. 8 (May 1966); Vol. 20, No. 1 (October 1966).

[38] James F. Kerfoot, ed., *First Grade Reading Programs.* Perspectives in Reading Series, No. 5. Newark, Del.: International Reading Association, 1965.

[39] *The Reading Teacher,* Vol. 22, No. 4 (January 1969), pp. 315–319; 335–340; 357–362; 363–370, respectively.

must be careful that the conclusions he draws do not trespass on the premises and results."[40]

Later, commenting on the first-grade reading studies of the U.S. Office of Education, Stauffer pointed out:

> Regardless of the criterion used there is no one method and this is so in spite of the tragic consequences of the internal dynamism that some so-called methods have sought to advance—tragically, eccentrically, and captivatingly. Every method described used words, and phonics, and pictures, and comprehension, and teachers. True, they frequently use them differently, but they used them. There was no one phonics method that was pure or uncontaminated, if you wish, by other methods. There was no one linguistic method. ITA is not a method but a medium. Basic readers claim everything.
>
> And where does all this leave us? All the malingering that reading instruction has endured for the past decade has not led to the golden era. No approach has overcome individual differences or eliminated reading disability. As I have said before, now that we have slashed around wildly in the mire of accusations let us remember that reading without comprehension is not reading. Let us focus our efforts on the eleven other years in school and make critical and creative reading our goal. Maturity in reading—that is the objective each child must seek and every teacher must help each child to attain. The thin crust we have punctured was just that and no more![41]

JEANNE CHALL'S INVESTIGATION   One of the most referred to studies during the 1960s was the investigation made by Jeanne Chall, an investigation reporting results quite contradictory to generally pronounced claims of experts in the field of reading. Since her studies, as reported in her book *Learning To Read: The Great Debate* are summarized in Chapter 5A, space is not devoted in this chapter to her purpose, methods of procedure, and findings.[42]

[40] Russell G. Stauffer, "The Verdict: Speculative Controversy" (editorial), *The Reading Teacher,* Vol. 19, No. 8 (May 1966), p. 564. Reprinted with the permission of the author and the International Reading Association.

[41] Russell G. Stauffer, "Some Tidy Generalizations" (editorial), *The Reading Teacher,* Vol. 20, No. 1 (October 1966), p. 4. Reprinted with the permission of the author and the International Reading Association.

[42] Jeanne Chall, *Learning To Read: The Great Debate.* New York: McGraw-Hill Book Company, Inc., 1967.

MEANS OF EVALUATION

During the past decades many attempts have been made to solve a variety of reading problems. Many studies of moment were made, a considerable number of which dealt with the questions of when to begin reading instruction and what methods to use in this instruction. Among these were research studies in New York City, the Denver study, Durkin's research on preschool reading, Durrell's studies on first-grade reading success, primary grade studies sponsored by the U.S. Office of Education, and the investigation by Jeanne Chall.

As one surveys the accounts of approaches to reading instruction and the investigations in that area, one may well feel puzzled. There is no one clear answer to the questions of great import to those who would teach boys and girls to read as effectively as possible. Enthusiasts for specific methods of procedure in teaching reading make contradictory claims. Interpreters of the same research present different, often contradictory, conclusions. The teacher and the prospective teacher of reading as well as the parent may ask, "What is the truth about the teaching of reading?"

Still, a few suggestions for making progress toward the goal of finding the solution to some of the problems of teaching reading can be given. One such help is provided by Lowry Harding.[43] While in his article Harding focuses on beginning reading, many of his suggestions are applicable to the evaluation of programs throughout the elementary school.

Study of Relations among Assumptions in Philosophy, Psychology, and Education

Harding states his fundamental premise thus: "Much of the inconsistent practice in teaching beginning reading should be eliminated by examination of the relationships between assumptions in philosophy, psychology, and education."[44] Thus he suggests an analysis that provides aid in considering the fundamental assumptions affecting the teaching of reading. Harding classifies philosophical theory under the headings of *idealism, realism,* and *pragmatism.* Thereupon he indicates how a teacher accepting each of these fundamental assumptions in

[43] Lowry W. Harding, "Assumptions Underlying Methods of Beginning Reading," *Educational Administration and Supervision,* XXXVII, p. 25 (January 1951).

[44] Harding, p. 25.

philosophy would in the light of the accepted one be influenced in her teaching of beginning reading.

When discussing the psychological assumptions that have bearing on the teaching of reading, Harding states: "The psychological assumptions relating to methods in reading are based upon theories of learning." [45] Thereupon Harding writes: "Beyond acceptance of some theory of knowledge and of the learning process, there are a number of educational questions on which some position must be assumed if teaching is done." Among the questions he recommends for consideration are the purpose or the philosophy of education possessed by the staff, the nature and type of curriculum, how the school is organized, what materials are available for instruction, methods of appraisal, and the like.[46]

In the evaluation of some of the current approaches described in previous chapters and in this one, it will be found that some are lacking in that the assumptions, though possibly based either on philosophy, psychology, or education, are not founded on interrelations among these three fields of learning. The reader interested in testing an approach to the teaching of reading in the light of these relations is advised to study the article by Harding.

Use of Checklists

One device for evaluating reading programs is the checklist. Such a list, worked out by Sidney J. Rauch, contains these five parts:

The reading program
The administrative and supervisory staff
The teaching staff
The pupils
The parents.[47]

Each of these five parts is divided into questions to be answered by yes or no. A yes response constitutes a plus for a program.

Below are listed the questions in only two of the five parts named in the preceding paragraph. However, the other three categories also contain some points pertinent to the evaluation of an approach used in teaching reading.

[45] Harding, p. 28.

[46] Harding, p. 33.

[47] Sidney J. Rauch, "A Checklist for the Evaluation of Reading Programs," *The Reading Teacher,* Vol. 21, No. 6 (March 1968), pp. 519–522. Reprinted with permission of the author and the International Reading Association.

THE READING PROGRAM   The following questions fall under the first item of the checklist developed by Rauch.

1. Is it a K–12 sequential program where the skills of one level are built upon the skills of previous levels?
2. Are the following components of a good reading program emphasized?
    Word recognition skills
    Comprehension skills
    Study skills
    Planned literature program
    Recreational reading
3. What materials are being used to supplement basic instructional texts?
    Workbooks
    Programmed materials
    Instructional kits
    Trade books
    Audio-visual materials
    Others
4. Is a love for reading being instilled?
    emphasized?
5. Are the following three types of reading programs being
    Developmental (i.e., basically the type of program for "able" readers doing grade level reading and above).
    Corrective (i.e., basically the type of program for those pupils who are slightly below grade level and whose instructional needs can be met in the regular classroom).
    Remedial (i.e., basically the type of program for those pupils who are seriously below grade level, and who require specialized instruction in an individual or small-group situation).
6. Is the program being continually evaluated?
7. Is reading regarded as a process rather than a subject?[48]

THE PUPILS   Under this item are listed the questions that follow.

1. Are they reading on their own?
2. Is application of reading skills made to the content areas?
3. Do they recognize reading as a four-step process (William S. Gray's definition in *On Their Own in Reading*)?
    Word perception
    Comprehension

[48] Rauch, p. 520.

Reaction or evaluation
Integration of ideas
4. Is evaluation of reading skills an on-going process?
   Teacher observation
   Standardized reading tests
   Informal reading tests
5. Are they given opportunities to report on books?
   Written reports
   Oral reports
   Dramatization
6. Do pupils have a positive attitude towards the reading teacher or specialist?
7. Do they handle books and supplementary materials with respect?[49]

Other Means of Evaluation

Just as there is no one known method of teaching reading that is accepted as *the* method, so there is no perfect device for determining what is the best currently used approach. However, there are various ways of helping the teacher with this question in addition to those already described. The thoughtful reading of reports on experimental set-ups and of research on innovative programs can be of aid in determining which approaches to the teaching of reading should be followed. Study of the literature on the teaching of reading, as found in books on methods of teaching, in periodicals, and in other publications, can form a background against which to make appraisals. In this book, chapter after chapter, there are suggested, directly or indirectly, those theories and practices for teaching reading that the authors consider valid.

Engaging in what used to be commonly called action research, too, can be of value to the teacher who desires to follow a program in the teaching of reading that will bring the best possible results. In other words, the teacher can try out in her own classroom some of the methods and techniques that seem to her to be of promise.

Finally, even after the teacher has attempted to the best of her ability to evaluate various approaches to teaching reading, she will still find that her appraisal is lacking in objectivity. But she cannot wait idly for a better day to come when evaluation techniques will give her more specific directions. The teacher in the classroom cannot postpone teaching reading until research has discovered without

---

[49] Rauch, pp. 521–522.

a doubt the most successful approach. As day after day she attempts to do her work as effectively as she can, she must ever make use of the means of evaluation at her disposal, imperfect though they are. If she follows this suggestion, she will not be without a guide. If with such a spirit teachers face the reading problems of the 1970s and the 1980s, the trend in the teaching of reading in those two decades will continue to be upward.

FOR FURTHER STUDY

Chall, Jeanne, *Learning To Read: The Great Debate.* New York: McGraw-Hill Book Company, Inc., 1967.

Durkin, Dolores, "Children Who Read before Grade One," *The Reading Teacher,* 14, pp. 163–164 (January 1961).

Durkin, Dolores, "Some Unanswered Questions about Five-Year Olds and Reading," *Changing Concepts of Reading Instruction,* Vol. 6, 1961. Proceedings of the Annual Convention. Newark, Del.: International Reading Association. Pages 167–170.

Durrell, Donald D., "First Grade Reading Success Study: A Summary," *Journal of Education,* 140, pp. 2–6 (February 1958).

Everett, Richard M., Jr., *Comparison between Conventional Basic Reading Programs and the Language for Learning Program.* New York: Washington Square Press, Inc., 1960. Pages 1–4.

Flesch, Rudolph, *Why Johnny Can't Read—And What You Can Do About It.* New York: Harper & Row, Publishers, 1955.

Gates, Arthur I., "Teaching Machines in Perspective," *Elementary School Journal,* 52, pp. 1–13 (October 1961).

Harding, Lowry W., "Assumptions Underlying Methods of Beginning Reading," *Educational Administration and Supervision,* 37, pp. 25–37 (January 1951).

The How and Why of Effective Teaching through Programmed Instruction: A Practical Guide for Teachers and Administrators. Palo Alto, Calif.: Behavioral Research Laboratories, undated.

Jacobs, Leland B., *Individualizing Reading Practices.* Practical Suggestions to Teachers Series, No. 14. New York: Teachers College, Columbia University, 1958. Pages 1–17.

Jenkins, William A., "The Future of Children's Books," *Elementary English,* 42, pp. 502–513 (May 1965).

Kerfoot, James F., (ed.), *First Grade Reading Programs.* Perspectives in Reading Series, No. 5. Newark, Del.: International Reading Association, 1965.

Lee, Dorris M., and R. V. Allen, *Learning to Read through Experience.* New York: Appleton-Century-Crofts, 1963.

Mackintosh, Helen K., ed., *Current Approaches to Teaching Reading.* "Language Experience Approach," R. V. Allen. Elementary Instructional Service Leaflet, NEA. Washington, D.C.: National Education Association, 1965. Pages 1–6.

MacKinnon, A. R., *How Do Children Learn To Read?* Toronto, Ontario: Copp Clark, 1959.

MacKinnon, A. R., "Research on Instructional Design for First Steps in Reading," *Changing Conceptions of Reading Instruction,* Vol. 6, 1961. Proceedings of the Annual Convention. Newark, Del.: International Reading Association. Pages 164–167.

Montessori, Maria, *The Montessori Method.* New York: Frederick A. Stokes, 1912.

Moore, O. K., *Orthographic Symbols and the Pre-School Child—A New Approach.* Paper presented at the Third Minnesota Conference on Gifted Children, Minneapolis, October 1960.

National Society for the Study of Education, *Innovation and Change in Reading Instruction.* Sixty-seventh Yearbook of the National Society for the Study of Education, Part II. Chicago: University of Chicago Press, 1968.

Olson, Willard C., "Seeking, Self-Selection, and Pacing in the Use of Books by Children, *The Packet,* Vol. 7, No. 1 (Spring 1952). Boston: D. C. Heath and Company, 1952.

Rauch, Sidney J., "A Checklist for the Evaluation of Reading Programs," *The Reading Teacher,* Vol. 21, No. 6 (March 1968), pp. 519–522.

The Reading Teacher, Vol. 22, No. 4 (January 1969), pp. 315–319, 335–340, 357–362, 363–370.

Roucek, Joseph, ed., *Programmed Teaching: A Symposium on Automation in Teaching.* New York: Philosophical Library, 1965.

Stauffer, Russell G., "Individualized and Group-type Directed Reading Instruction," *Winston Communication Program, Consultation Bulletin C²*. New York: Holt, Rinehart and Winston, Inc., undated. Pages 1–9.

Stauffer, Russell G., "Some Tidy Generalizations" (editorial), *The Reading Teacher,* Vol. 20, No. 1 (October 1966), p. 4.

Stauffer, Russell G., "The Verdict: Speculative Controversy" (editorial), *The Reading Teacher,* Vol. 19, No. 8 (May 1966), pp. 563–564.

Veatch, Jeannette, *Individualizing Your Reading.* New York: G. P. Putnam's Sons, 1959.

Index